Good Reasons with Contemporary Arguments

SIXTH EDITION

Lester Faigley

University of Texas at Austin

Jack Selzer

The Pennsylvania State University

PEARSON

Boston   Columbus   Indianapolis   New York   San Francisco   Upper Saddle River
Amsterdam   Cape Town   Dubai   London   Madrid   Milan   Munich   Paris   Montréal   Toronto
Delhi   Mexico City   São Paulo   Sydney   Hong Kong   Seoul   Singapore   Taipei   Tokyo

In memory of our teacher and friend, James L. Kinneavy (1920–1999)

Editorial Director: Joseph Opiela
Senior Acquisitions Editor: Brad Potthoff
Director of Development: Mary Ellen Curley
Senior Development Editor: Linda Stern
Executive Marketing Manager: Roxanne McCarly
Senior Supplements Editor: Donna Campion
Senior Media Producer: Stefanie Snajder
Media Project Manager: Sara Gordus
Production/Project Manager: Eric Jorgensen
Project Coordination, Text Design, and Electronic Page Makeup: PreMediaGlobal
Senior Cover Design Manager: John Callahan
Cover Designer: John Callahan
Cover Images (clockwise from left): Courtesy of Lester Faigley, © Pixelbliss/Fotolia, © Igor S./FotoliaSenior
Manufacturing Buyer: Dennis Para
Printer/Binder: RR Donnelley/Crawfordsville
Cover Printer: Lehigh-Phoenix Color/Hagerstown

Credits and acknowledgments borrowed from other sources and reproduced, with permission, in this textbook appear on pages 580–583.

Library of Congress Cataloging-in-Publication Data
Faigley, Lester, [date].
   Good reasons with contemporary arguments / Lester Faigley, University of Texas at Austin, Jack Selzer, The Pennsylvania State University. — Sixth edition.
        pages cm
   Includes bibliographical references and index.
   ISBN-13: 978-0-321-90021-0
   ISBN-10: 0-321-90021-9
   1. English language—Rhetoric.   2. Persuasion (Rhetoric)   3. Report writing.
I. Selzer, Jack, author.   II. Title.
   PE1431.F35 2015
   808'.042—dc23
                                                    2013034099

10 9 8 7 6 5 4 3 2 1—DOC—16 15 14 13

www.pearsonhighered.com

Student ISBN 10: 0-321-90021-9
Student ISBN 13: 978-0-321-90021-0
ALaCarte ISBN 10: 0-321-95461-0
ALaCarte ISBN 13: 978-0-321-95461-9

Detailed Contents

Analyzing Arguments 57

Writing Arguments   95

PART 4
Designing and Presenting Arguments 207

PART 5
Researching Arguments 221

PART 6

Contemporary Arguments 295

Selections by Types of Arguments

Preface

Nothing you learn in college will prove to be more important to you than the ability to create an effective argument.

As a student you are already aware that campus life is itself filled with arguments. There are hot-button public issues that engage the academic community—how to deal with binge drinking, for example, or make the university more environmentally sustainable, or improve campus housing or study-abroad opportunities. Meanwhile, in the classroom and in research programs, you and your peers will present arguments on current controversies such as climate change and economic policy as well as on scholarly topics such as the structure of the human brain, the cultural achievements of ancient Egypt, or the means of determining the material composition of the planet Mercury.

After college, you will continue to need to communicate effectively your ideas and points of view. Your livelihood and your successful engagement in the life of your community will depend on it. Sometimes, as a citizen, you will be moved to register your views on how to improve your local school system or enhance local development; or as a member of a neighborhood group or a civic organization, you will be suggesting ways of making a positive difference. And certainly in the workplace you will often be making arguments to support your recommendations and to refute the flawed recommendations of others.

What This Book Offers You

For a number of years, we have studied arguments, taught students how to argue, and listened to others talk and write about the art of persuasion. Although there is no simple recipe for cooking up effective arguments, we've discovered there are definite strategies and tactics that writers can rely on in any situation to ensure that their ideas are considered seriously. However, we also know that regardless of the value of its content, a text will be ineffective if it cannot present its ideas in a way that is engaging, easy to use, and comprehensive. It has been our aim to create such a text in *Good Reasons with Contemporary Arguments*.

Lively, nontechnical language. We've pointedly avoided technical jargon in order to explain concepts and techniques as clearly as possible. Explanations, examples, captions, and exercises are all written with the goal of keeping language straightforward and accessible.

Emphasis on attractive design and visual arguments. *Good Reasons with Contemporary Arguments* is notable for its attention to visual as well as verbal arguments. In addition, the book itself demonstrates the value of visual argument in its attractive design that is liberally illustrated with graphics, photos, and other visuals.

Annotated student writing samples and numerous other examples. In line with our philosophy of showing rather than telling, chapters covering types of arguments include annotated student essays as well as annotated professional essays illustrating six basic types of arguments: definition, causal, evaluation, narrative, rebuttal, and proposal arguments.

Fresh, timely readings—including academic readings—on current issues. These readings demonstrate how complex conversations develop around important issues of interest to students today. Readings span a wide range of material from canonical essays to contemporary journal articles. We've also taken care to select readings that give different points of view on an issue.

New to This Edition

- **Seventeen new professional readings in Part 6,** including essays by Malcolm Gladwell, Elizabeth Royte, Salman Khan, and others

- **Deeply revised Chapter 22, now titled "Sustainability,"** with essays offering various perspectives on this vital public question and with a new Issue in Focus on sustainable urban growth

- **New Chapter 23 on education** with readings that engage college students in particular, including the economic value of a college education and the role of online education

- **Revised Chapter 24,** with a sharper focus on exporting American culture

- **New Chapter 4 on drafting arguments,** offering advice on how to focus your thesis, organize your argument, and connect with readers

- **New Chapter 5 on revising and editing arguments** that provides a checklist for evaluating your draft, advice on revising your draft, and tips on how to edit and proofread effectively

- **Deeply revised Chapter 6 on analyzing written arguments** with a detailed example of how to analyze the text and context of an argument

- **Revised Chapter 7 on analyzing visual and multimedia arguments,** with an increased focus on using graphs

- **Additional examples of fallacies** and how to spot them in Chapter 2

- New professional reading and annotated sample student essay in Chapter 10, "Evaluation Arguments"
- New professional reading in Chapter 11, "Narrative Arguments"
- Newly annotated professional readings in Chapter 12, "Rebuttal Arguments"
- New professional readings in Chapter 13, "Proposal Arguments"
- Updated mini-arguments in Parts 1 and 3, including many visual and multimodal examples
- Updated guidance in Part 5 on how to gather information from database, Web, and library sources and how to evaluate and cite that information
- Updated MLA and APA coverage in Chapters 20 and 21, including how to cite social media and *Twitter*.

Resources for Teachers and Students

Instructor's Manual

The **Instructor's Manual** that accompanies this text was revised by Brian Neff, of Colorado State University–Global Campus, and is designed to be useful for new and experienced instructors alike. The Instructor's Manual briefly discusses the ins and outs of teaching the material in each text chapter. Also provided are in-class exercises, homework assignments, discussion questions for each reading selection, and model paper assignments and syllabi.

Pearson MyLabs

MyWritingLab is an online homework, tutorial, and assessment program that provides engaging experiences to today's instructors and students. By incorporating rubrics into the writing assignments, faculty can create meaningful assignments, grade them based on their desired criteria, and analyze class performance through advanced reporting. For students who enter the course under-prepared, MyWritingLab offers a diagnostic test and personalized remediation so that students see improved results and instructors spend less time in class reviewing the basics. Rich multimedia resources, including a Pearson eText, are built in to engage students and support faculty throughout the course. Visit www.mywritinglab.com for more information.

CourseSmart eTextbook

Good Reasons with Contemporary Arguments is also available as a CourseSmart eTextbook. This is an exciting new choice for students, who can subscribe to the same content online and search the text, make notes online, print out reading assignments that incorporate lecture notes, and bookmark important passages for later review. For more information, or to subscribe to the CourseSmart eTextbook, visit www.coursesmart.com.

Acknowledgments

We are much indebted to the work of many outstanding scholars of argument and to our colleagues who teach argument at Texas and at Penn State. In particular, we thank the following reviewers for sharing their expertise: Jessie Carty, Rowan-Cabarrus Community College; Anne Corbitt, Kennesaw State University; LaToya Faulk, Wayne State University; John R. Hart, Motlow State Community College; Kimberli Swainston Holmquist, Arizona Western College; Elizabeth Meredith, University of Tennessee, Knoxville; Erin Stephens, Somerset Community College; and Marlea Trevino, Grayson College. We are also grateful to the many students we've taught in our own classes, who have given us opportunities to test these materials in class and who have taught us a great deal about the nature of argument. Special thanks go the students whose work is included in this edition.

We have greatly benefited from working with Brad Potthoff, senior editor, and Linda Stern, senior development editor, whose talent and creativity continue to impress us and who contribute much to both the vision and the details of *Good Reasons with Contemporary Arguments*. They are the best, and we much enjoyed working with them on this and other books. Linda especially provided all kinds of expert advice and specific suggestions that we capitalized on in ways too numerous to mention. Laura Newcomer provided expert assistance in locating potential selections for Part 6. We appreciate Brian C. Neff's great work in preparing the Instructor's Manual. Andrea Stefanowicz at PreMediaGlobal and Eric Jorgensen at Pearson Longman did a splendid job in preparing our book for publication. We were quite fortunate to again have Elsa van Bergen as our copyeditor, who has no peer in our experience. Finally, we thank our families, who make it all possible.

Lester Faigley
Jack Selzer

Reading and Discovering Arguments

PART 1

1 | Making an Effective Argument

MadV's *The Message* consists of a series of extremely short videos from *YouTube* members of words written on hands, similar to the one shown here.

What Exactly Is an Argument?

One of the best-known celebrities on *YouTube* is an anonymous video director who wears a Guy Fawkes mask and uses the name MadV. In November 2006 he posted a short video in which he held up his hand with the words "One World" written on his palm and invited viewers to take a stand by uploading a video to *YouTube*. They responded by the thousands, writing short messages written on their palms. MadV then compiled many of the responses in a 4-minute video titled *The Message* and posted it on *YouTube*.

MadV's project has been praised as a celebration of the values of the *YouTube* community. The common theme that we all should try to love and better understand other people is one that few oppose. Yet the video also raises the question of how any of the goals might be achieved. One hand reads "Stop Bigotry." We see a great deal of hatred in written responses to many *YouTube* videos. Slogans like "Open Mind," "Be Colorblind," "Love Is Stronger," "No More Racism," and "Yup One World" seem inadequate for the scope of the problem.

Like the ink-on-hand messages, bumper stickers usually consist of unilateral statements ("Be Green," "Save the Whales," or "Share the Road") but provide no supporting evidence or reasons for why anyone should do what they say. People committed to a particular cause or belief often assume that their reasons are self-evident, and that everyone thinks the same way. These writers know they can count on certain words and phrases to produce predictable responses.

In college courses, in public life, and in professional careers, however, written arguments cannot be reduced to signs or slogans. Writers of effective arguments do not assume that everyone thinks the same way or holds the same beliefs. They attempt to change people's minds by convincing them of the validity of new ideas or the superiority of a particular course of action. Writers of such arguments not only offer evidence and reasons to support their position but also examine the assumptions on which an argument is based, address opposing arguments, and anticipate their readers' objections.

Extended written arguments make more demands on their readers than most other kinds of writing. Like bumper stickers, these arguments often appeal to our emotions. But they typically do much more.

- They expand our knowledge with the depth of their analysis.
- They lead us through a complex set of claims by providing networks of logical relationships and appropriate evidence.
- They build on what has been written previously by providing trails of sources.

Finally, they cause us to reflect on what we read, in a process that we will shortly describe as critical reading.

Finding Good Reasons

Who's Using Up Earth's Resources?

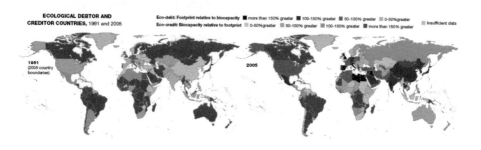

ECOLOGICAL DEBTOR AND CREDITOR COUNTRIES, 1961 and 2005

Eco-debt: Footprint relative to biocapacity ■ more than 150% greater ■ 100-150% greater ■ 50-100% greater ▨ 0-50%greater
Eco-credit: Biocapacity relative to footprint ▨ 0-50%greater ▨ 50-100% greater ■ 100-150% greater ■ more than 150% greater   ▨ Insufficient data

In the *Living Planet Report* for 2008, the World Wildlife Fund compared the ecological footprints from 1961 and 2005 for each country on Earth. The ecological footprint of a country is determined by its population, the amount of food, timber, and other resources consumed by its average citizen, the area required to produce food, fishing grounds, and the area required to absorb CO_2 emissions minus the amount absorbed by oceans.

Countries fall into four categories: ecological debtor nations (which consume more resources than they can produce), ecological creditor nations (which produce more than they consume), and two categories of ecologically balanced nations, where production and consumption are relatively balanced. In this map you can see that the United States, Mexico, Western Europe, China, India, Pakistan, Japan, and the nations of the Middle East have become ecological debtors with footprints more than 50 percent of their biocapacity—what they are able to produce. Nations such as Canada, Russia, Australia, New Zealand, and most nations in South America are ecological creditors, with footprints less than 50 percent of their biocapacity. In its entirety, the *Living Planet Report* makes the argument that nations should live in balance with what their land, rivers, lakes, and seas can support.

Write about it

1. What might be some of the causes of the differences among the ecological footprints of nations?

2. What is likely to happen in the future when some nations have enough resources (such as clean water and food) and others lack them?

3. Does the map succeed as an argument on its own? Does it contain any of the features of written arguments listed on pages 5–6?

Writing Arguments in College

Writing in college varies considerably from course to course. A lab report for a biology course looks quite different from a paper in your English class, just as a classroom observation in an education course differs from a case study report in an accounting class.

Nevertheless, much of the writing you will do in college will consist of arguments. Some common expectations about arguments in college writing extend across disciplines. For example, you could be assigned to write a proposal for a downtown light-rail system in a number of different classes—civil engineering, urban planning, government, or management. The emphasis of such a proposal would change depending on the course. In all cases, however, the proposal would require a complex argument in which you describe the problem that the light-rail system would improve, make a specific proposal that addresses the problem, explain the benefits of the system, estimate the cost, identify funding sources, assess alternatives to your plan, and anticipate possible opposition. That's a lot to think about.

Setting out a specific proposal or claim supported by reasons and evidence is at the heart of most college writing, no matter what the course. Some expectations of arguments (such as including a thesis statement) may be familiar to you, but others (such as the emphasis on finding alternative ways of thinking about a subject and finding facts that might run counter to your conclusions) may be unfamiliar.

WRITTEN ARGUMENTS...	WRITERS ARE EXPECTED TO...
State explicit claims	Make a claim that isn't obvious. The main claim is often called a **thesis**. (see pages 40–41)
Support claims with reasons	Express reasons in a **because clause** after the claim (We should do something *because* _____). (see pages 25–26)
Base reasons on evidence	Provide evidence for reasons in the form of facts, statistics, testimony from reliable sources, and direct observations. (see pages 37–38)
Consider opposing positions	Help readers understand why there are disagreements about issues by accurately representing differing views. (see pages 29–31)
Analyze with insight	Provide in-depth analysis of what they read and view. (see Chapters 6 and 7)

(continued)

WRITTEN ARGUMENTS . . .	WRITERS ARE EXPECTED TO . . .
Investigate complexity	Explore the complexity of a subject by asking "Have you thought about this?" or "What if you discard the usual way of thinking about a subject and take the opposite point of view?" (see pages 34–36)
Organize information clearly	Make the main ideas evident to readers and to indicate which parts are subordinate to others. (see pages 45–46)
Signal relationships of parts	Indicate logical relationships clearly so that readers can follow an argument without getting lost. (see page 54)
Document sources carefully	Provide the sources of information so that readers can consult the same sources the writer used. (see Chapters 20 and 21)

How can you argue responsibly?

In Washington, D.C., cars with diplomatic license plates are often parked illegally. Their drivers know they will not be towed or ticketed. People who abuse the diplomatic privilege are announcing, "I'm not playing by the rules."

When you begin an argument by saying "in my opinion," you are making a similar announcement. First, the phrase is redundant. A reader assumes that if you make a claim in writing, you believe that claim. More important, a claim is rarely *only* your opinion. Most beliefs and assumptions are shared by many people. If a claim truly is only your opinion, it can be easily dismissed. If your position is likely to be held by at least a few other people, however, then a responsible reader must consider your position seriously. You argue responsibly when you set out the reasons for making a claim and offer facts to support those reasons. You argue responsibly when you allow readers to examine your evidence by documenting the sources you have consulted. Finally, you argue responsibly when you acknowledge that other people may have positions different from yours.

How can you argue respectfully?

Our culture is competitive, and our goal often is to win. Professional athletes, top trial lawyers, or candidates for president of the United States either win big or lose. But most of us live in a world in which our opponents don't go away when the game is over.

Most of us have to deal with people who disagree with us at times but continue to work and live in our communities. The idea of winning in such situations can only be temporary. Soon enough, we will need the support of those who were on the other side of the most recent issue. You can probably think of times when a friendly argument resulted in a better understanding of everyone's views. And probably you can think of a time when an argument created hard feelings that lasted for years.

Usually, listeners and readers are more willing to consider your argument seriously if you cast yourself as a respectful partner rather than as a competitor. Put forth your arguments in the spirit of mutual support and negotiation—in the interest of finding the *best* way, not "my way." How can you be the person that your reader will want to join rather than resist? Here are a few suggestions both for your written arguments and for discussing controversial issues.

- **Try to think of yourself as engaged not so much in winning over your audience as in courting your audience's cooperation.** Argue vigorously, but not so vigorously that opposing views are vanquished or silenced. Remember that your goal is to invite a response that creates a dialogue and continuing partnership.

- **Show that you understand and genuinely respect your listener's or reader's position even if you think the position is ultimately wrong.** Remember to argue against opponents' positions, not against the opponents themselves. Arguing respectfully often means representing an opponent's position in terms that he or she would accept. Look for ground that you already share with your opponent, and search for even more. See yourself as a mediator. Consider that neither you nor the other person has arrived at a best solution. Then carry on in the hope that dialogue will lead to an even better course of action than the one you now recommend. Expect and assume the best of your listener or your reader, and deliver your best.

- **Cultivate a sense of humor and a distinctive voice.** Many textbooks about argument emphasize using a reasonable voice. But a reasonable voice doesn't have to be a dull one. Humor is a legitimate tool of argument. Although playing an issue strictly for laughs risks not being taken seriously, nothing creates a sense of goodwill quite as much as tasteful humor. A sense of humor can be especially welcome when the stakes are high, sides have been chosen, and tempers are flaring.

Arguments as Turns in a Conversation

Consider your argument as just one move in a larger process that might end up helping you. Most times we argue because we think we have something to offer. In the process of researching what has been said and written on a particular issue, however, often your own view is expanded and you find an opportunity to add your voice to the ongoing conversation.

A Case Study: The Microcredit Debate

Two women financed by microcredit sell scarves in Quito, Ecuador.

World Bank researchers reported in 2009 that 1.4 billion people—over 20 percent of the then 6.7 billion people on earth—live below the extreme poverty line of $1.25 a day, with 6 million children starving to death every year. One cause of continuing extreme poverty is the inability of poor people to borrow money because they have no cash income or assets. Banks have seldom made loans to very poor people, who have had to turn to moneylenders that charge high interest rates sometimes exceeding 100 percent a month.

In 1976, Muhammad Yunus observed that poor women in Bangladesh who made bamboo furniture could not profit from their labor because they had to borrow money at high interest rates to buy bamboo. Yunus loaned $27 to forty-two women out of his pocket. They repaid him at an interest rate of two cents per loan. The success of the experiment eventually led to Yunus securing a loan from the government to create a bank to make loans to poor people. The Grameen Bank (Village Bank) became a model for other microfinancing projects in Bangladesh, serving 7 million people, 94 percent of whom are women. For his work with the Grameen initiative, Yunus received the Nobel Peace Prize in 2006.

Microcredit now has many supporters, including Hollywood stars like Natalie Portman and Michael Douglas, companies like Benetton and Sam's Club, and former President Bill Clinton. But the success in Bangladesh has not been replicated in many other poor countries. Many critics point to the shortcomings of microcredit. This debate can be better understood if you consider the different points of view on microcredit to be different voices in a conversation.

The conversation about microcredit has led others to put new ideas on the table.

Mapping a conversation like the debate about microcredit can often help you identify how to add to the conversation. What can you add to what's been said?

Some people claim that _____.

Other people respond that _____.

Still others claim that _____.

I agree with X's and Y's points, but I maintain that _____

because _____.

Build your credibility

Know what's at stake. What you are writing about should matter to your readers. If its importance is not evident, it's your job to explain why your readers should consider it important.

LESS EFFECTIVE:

We should be concerned about two-thirds of Central and South America's 110 brightly colored harlequin frog species becoming extinct in the last twenty years. (The loss of any species is unfortunate, but the writer gives us no other reason for concern.)

MORE EFFECTIVE:

The rapid decline of amphibians worldwide due to global warming may be the advance warning of the loss of cold-weather species such as polar bears, penguins, and reindeer.

Have your readers in mind. If you are writing about a specialized subject that your readers don't know much about, take the time to explain key concepts.

LESS EFFECTIVE:

Reduction in the value of a debt security, especially a bond, results from a rise in interest rates. Conversely, a decline in interest rates results in an increase in the value of a debt security, especially bonds. (The basic idea is here, but it is not expressed clearly, especially if the reader is not familiar with investing.)

MORE EFFECTIVE:

Bond prices move inversely to interest rates. When interest rates go up, bond prices go down, and when interest rates go down, bond prices go up.

Think about alternative solutions and points of view. Readers appreciate a writer's ability to see a subject from multiple perspectives.

LESS EFFECTIVE:

We will reduce greenhouse gas and global warming only if we greatly increase wind-generated electricity. (Wind power is an alternative energy source, but it is expensive and many people don't want windmills in scenic areas. The writer also doesn't mention using energy more efficiently.)

MORE EFFECTIVE:

If the world is serious about limiting carbon emissions to reduce global warming, then along with increasing efficient energy use, all non-carbon-emitting energy sources must be considered, including nuclear power. Nuclear power now produces about 20 percent of U.S. electricity with no emissions—the equivalent of taking 58 million passenger cars off the road.

Be honest. Readers also appreciate writers who admit what they aren't sure about. Leaving readers with unanswered questions can lead them to think further about your subject.

LESS EFFECTIVE:
The decline in violent crime during the 1990s was due to putting more people in jail with longer sentences.

MORE EFFECTIVE:
Exactly what caused the decline in violent crime during the 1990s remains uncertain. Politicians point to longer sentences for criminals, but the decrease in the population most likely to commit crimes—the 16-to-35 age group—may have been a contributing factor.

Write well. Nothing impresses readers more than graceful, fluent writing that is clear, direct, and forceful. Even if readers don't agree with you in the end, they still will appreciate your writing ability.

LESS EFFECTIVE:
Nobody can live today without taking some risks, even very rich people. After all, we don't know what we're breathing in the air. A lot of food has chemicals and hormones in it. There's a big hole in the ozone, so more people will get skin cancer. And a lot of people have sexually transmitted diseases these days. (The impact of the point is lost with unfocused writing.)

MORE EFFECTIVE:
We live in a world of risks beyond our control, to the extent that it is difficult to think of anything that is risk free down to the most basic human acts—sex in an era of AIDS, eating in an era of genetically altered food, walking outside in an ozone-depleted atmosphere, drinking water and breathing air laden with chemicals whose effects we do not understand.

2 | Reading Arguments

QUICK TAKE

In this chapter, you will learn to

1. Recognize that controversies often involve many nuanced positions (see below)
2. Read an argument critically (see page 13)
3. Identify and define fallacies of logic, emotion, and language (see pages 16–19)
4. Map and summarize an argument (see pages 20–21)

Explore Controversies

People in general agree on broad goals for their society: clean water, abundant healthy food, efficient transportation, good schools, full employment, affordable health care, safe cities and neighborhoods, and peace with others near and far. However, people often disagree on how to define and achieve these goals. Controversies surround major issues and causes.

Often controversies are portrayed in the media as pro and con or even take on political labels. But if you read and listen carefully to what people have to say about a particular issue, you usually find a range of different positions on the issue, and you often discover nuances and complexities in the reasons people offer for their positions.

Find controversies

Online subject directories can help you identify the differing views on a large, general topic. Try the subject index of your library's online catalog. You'll likely find subtopics listed under large topics. Also, your library's Web site may have a link to the *Opposing Viewpoints* database.

One of the best Web subject directories for finding arguments is Yahoo's *Issues and Causes* directory. This directory provides subtopics for major issues and provides links to the Web sites of organizations interested in particular issues.

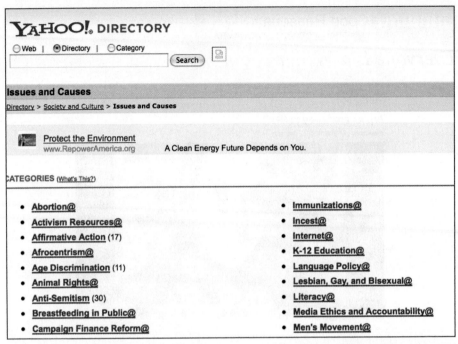

Yahoo! *Issues and Causes* directory (dir.yahoo.com/Society_and_Culture/Issues_and_Causes/)

Read Critically

After you survey the landscape of a particular issue, turn to careful reading of individual arguments, one at a time.

Before you begin reading, ask these questions

- ■ Where did the argument first appear? Was it published in a book, newspaper, magazine, or electronic source? Many items in library databases and on the Web were published somewhere else first.
- ■ Who wrote this argument? What do you know about the author?
- ■ What does the title suggest that the argument might be about?

Read the argument once without making notes to gain a sense of the content

- ■ When you finish, write one sentence that sums up the argument.

Finding Good Reasons

Everyone Is a Writer

Video blogs, known as vlogs, became a popular genre on *YouTube*.

Before the Internet was invented, readers had to make some effort to respond to writers by writing to them directly, sending a letter to the editor, or even scribbling or spray-painting a response. The Internet has changed the interaction between writers and readers by allowing readers to respond easily to writers and, in turn, changing readers into writers. Look, for example, at Amazon Web site. An incredible amount of writing surrounds any best-selling book—often an author's Web site and blog, newspaper reviews, and over a hundred readers' reviews. Or read a political, sports, culture, fashion, or parenting blog and the comments by readers of those blogs. Think about how the Internet has changed the relationship between readers and writers.

To find a blog that interests you, use a blog search engine such as *Bloglines, Google Blog Search, IceRocket,* or *Technorati.*

Write about it

1. Using a blog search engine or an online newspaper, find a blog by an author, politician, or news columnist. Answer as many of the questions for critical reading on page 15 as you can.

2. Write a summary of the blog entry.

3. What kinds of reasons do blog writers give for their responses to what they read?

4. How are blogs and online book reviews like or unlike traditional book reviews in print?

Read the argument a second and third time and make notes

- Go back through the text and underline the author's thesis.
- Do your sentence and the author's thesis match? If not, look at the text again and either adjust your sentence or check if you underlined the correct sentence.
- How is the argument organized? How are the major points arranged?
- What reasons or evidence does the writer offer in support of the thesis?
- How does the writer conclude the argument? Does the conclusion follow from the evidence presented?
- Who is the intended audience? What does the writer assume the readers know and believe?
- Do you detect a bias in the writer's position?
- Where do the writer's facts come from? Does the writer give the sources? Are the sources reliable?
- Does the writer acknowledge other views and unfavorable evidence? Does the writer deal fairly with the views of others?
- If there are images or graphics, are they well integrated and clearly labeled?

Annotate what you read

- **Mark major points and key concepts.** Sometimes major points are indicated by headings, but often you will need to locate them.
- **Connect with your experience.** Think about your own experiences and how they match up or don't match up with what you are reading.
- **Connect passages.** Notice how ideas connect to each other. Draw lines and arrows. If an idea connects to something from a few pages earlier, write a note in the margin with the page number.
- **Ask questions.** Note anything that puzzles you, including words you don't know and need to look up.

Map a controversy

Read broadly about an issue and identify three or more sources that offer different points of view on that issue. The sources may approach the issue from different angles or raise different questions instead of simply stating differing positions on the issue. Draw a map that represents the different views. The map on the next page shows some of the different positions on sustainable agriculture.

Map of different issues about sustainable agriculture.

Recognize Fallacies

Recognizing where good reasons go off track is one of the most important aspects of critical reading. What passes as political discourse is often filled with claims that lack evidence or substitute emotions for evidence. Such faulty reasoning often contains one or more **logical fallacies**. For example, politicians know that the public is outraged when the price of gasoline goes up, and they try to score political points by accusing oil companies of price gouging. This sounds good to angry voters—and it may well be true—but unless the politician defines what *price gouging* means and provides evidence that oil companies are guilty, the argument has no more validity than children calling each other bad names on the playground.

Following are some of the more common fallacies.

Fallacies of logic

■ **Begging the question** *Politicians are inherently dishonest because no honest person would run for public office.* The fallacy of begging the question occurs when the claim is restated and passed off as evidence.

It's on the Internet

Although people at times use fallacies to score political points or to gain the attention of those who feel passionately about a topic, most fallacies occur because of faulty evidence. And while the Internet is a valuable research tool because of the wealth of information available, a lot of that information is misleading or factually incorrect.

Because anyone can post on the Internet, and because many Web sites repost information without attribution, bad information can spread quickly across the Web. You may have heard of videos going viral on the Web, but the same thing can happen with misinformation. One Web site posts a story that is then reposted on several other sites. Suddenly, because a story is available on several different Web sites, it becomes "true." If an argument uses such a story to prove a point, it is employing the *common knowledge fallacy*—a variation of the *bandwagon fallacy* in which "everyone does it" is replaced by "everyone knows it's true."

After Osama bin Laden was killed in May 2011, a quotation attributed to Martin Luther King, Jr., went viral, spreading across *Facebook* and other social media sites. Unfortunately, only part of the quotation was actually something King said. The error started with a *Facebook* post in which the poster began with her own thoughts on the situation and then quoted King. The original post was quoted and reposted, but as it spread, the entire quotation was attributed to King—not just the portion of the original post that contained his actual words. An argument that made use of the quotation would be based on a fallacy.

Although the speed with which information travels across social media may be to blame for the misattribution of the *Facebook* quotation to Martin Luther King, Jr., some bad information on the Internet proliferates because it is easy to commit the fallacy of *cherry-picking the evidence*—selectively using some information and suppressing facts that do not suit the argument. If you read many articles about the local food movement, you have probably come across the claim that the food on your plate travels, on average, 1,500 miles to get to you, a claim that is repeated in numerous places around the Web. However, the study that the claim came from focused on Chicago; the distance traveled would actually differ depending on where in the country you live, a fact that has not stopped the statistic from being used in a wide range of contexts.

One of the best ways to avoid fallacies in your own arguments is to carefully evaluate your sources—especially online sources—and the validity of the information you use to construct your arguments. Chapter 18 discusses how to evaluate the sources you use in a paper.

■ **Cherry-picking the evidence** *This small sedan is as highly rated in crash tests by the Insurance Institute for Highway Safety as the most highly rated SUV.* Cherry-picking the evidence means leaving out significant facts, usually because they do not support the argument being made. In this case, the writer omits the IIHS's warning that comparisons across vehicle size groups are invalid.

- **Common knowledge fallacy** *We can't be doing that much harm to the environment. After all, alligators are thriving in the sewers of New York City.* The common knowledge fallacy assumes that stories and statistics that are widely disseminated or repeated are necessarily true. Here, the writer does not offer any facts to support the assertion about alligators.

- **Either-or** *Either we eliminate the regulation of businesses or else profits will suffer.* The either-or fallacy suggests that there are only two choices in a complex situation. Rarely, if ever, is this the case. Consider, for example, the case of Enron, which was unregulated but went bankrupt.

- **False analogies** *Japan quit fighting in 1945 when we dropped nuclear bombs on Hiroshima and Nagasaki. We should use nuclear weapons against other countries.* Analogies always depend on the degree of resemblance of one situation to another. In this case, the analogy fails to recognize that circumstances today are very different from those in 1945. Many countries now possess nuclear weapons, and we know their use could harm the entire world.

- **Hasty generalization** *We have been in a drought for three years; that's a sure sign of climate change.* A hasty generalization is a broad claim made on the basis of a few occurrences. Climate cycles occur regularly over spans of a few years. Climate trends, however, must be established with more data than one drought cycle.

- **Non sequitur** *A university that can raise a billion dollars from alumni should not have to raise tuition.* A non sequitur (a Latin term meaning "it does not follow") ties together two unrelated ideas. In this case, the argument fails to recognize that the money for capital campaigns is often donated for special purposes such as athletic facilities and is not part of a university's general revenue.

- **Oversimplification** *No one would run stop signs if we had a mandatory death penalty for doing it.* This claim may be true, but the argument would be unacceptable to most citizens. More complex, if less definitive, solutions are called for.

- **Post hoc fallacy** *The stock market goes down when the AFC wins the Super Bowl in even years.* The post hoc fallacy (from the Latin *post hoc, ergo propter hoc,* which means "after this, therefore because of this") assumes that events that follow in time have a causal relationship.

- **Rationalization** *I could have finished my paper on time if my printer had been working.* People frequently come up with excuses and weak explanations for their own and others' behavior. These excuses often avoid actual causes.

- **Slippery slope** *We shouldn't grant citizenship to illegal immigrants now living in the United States because no one will want to obey our laws.* The slippery slope fallacy maintains that one thing inevitably will cause something else to happen.

Fallacies of emotion and language

- **Bandwagon appeals** *It doesn't matter if I copy a paper off the Web because everyone else does.* This argument suggests that everyone is doing it, so why shouldn't you? But on close examination, it may be that everyone really isn't doing it—and in any case, it may not be the right thing to do.

- **Name-calling** *Every candidate running for office in this election is either a left-wing radical or a right-wing ideologue.* Name-calling is frequent in politics and among competing groups. People level accusations using names such as *radical, tax-and-spend liberal, racist, fascist, ultra-conservative extremist.* Unless these terms are carefully defined, they are meaningless.

- **Polarization** *Feminists are all man-haters.* Like name-calling, polarization exaggerates positions and groups by representing them as extreme and divisive.

- **Straw man** *Environmentalists won't be satisfied until not a single human being is allowed to enter a national park.* A straw man argument is a diversionary tactic that sets up another's position in a way that can be easily rejected. In fact, only a small percentage of environmentalists would make an argument even close to this one.

Note fallacies while you read

Marta Ramos noted a fallacy in James McWilliams's argument against locavorism. You can read her rebuttal argument on pages 188–191.

Consider fruit and vegetable production in New York. The Empire State is naturally equipped to grow a wide variety of fruits, including pears, cherries, strawberries, and some peaches. But none of these compare to its ability to grow apples and grapes, which dominate production (accounting for 94 percent of all fruit grown).

At current levels of fruit production, apples are the only crop that could currently feed New Yorkers at a level that meets the U.S. Recommended Dietary Allowances. Every other fruit that the state produces is not being harvested at a level to provide all New Yorkers with an adequate supply. Other fruits such as bananas and oranges are not produced at all because conditions are unfavorable for growing them.

What does this situation mean in terms of feeding the state with the state's own produce?

In a nutshell, <u>it means citizens would have to give up tropical fruits altogether;</u> rarely indulge in a pear, peach, or basket of strawberries; and gorge on grapes and apples— most of them in processed form (either as juice, in a can, or as concentrate).

—James E. McWilliams. *Just Food: Where Locavores Get It Wrong and How We Can Truly Eat Responsibly.* (New York: Little, Brown, 2009), 44.

McWilliams makes a straw man argument. Locavores prioritize locally produced food but don't argue that it's only what people should eat.

Map and Summarize Arguments

When you finish annotating a reading, you might want to map it.

Draw a map

Marta Ramos drew a map of James McWilliams's argument.

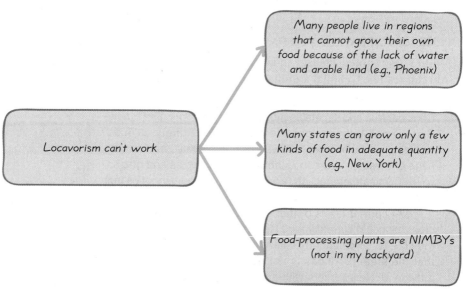

Map of the argument in James McWilliams's *Just Food.*

Write a summary

A summary should be a concise but thorough representation of the source.

- Begin your summary with the writer's name, the title of the argument, and the main point.
- Then report the key ideas. Represent the author's argument in condensed form as accurately as you can, quoting exact words for key points (see pages 254–255 for how to quote and integrate an author's words into your summary).
- Your aim is to give your readers an understanding of what the author is arguing for. Withhold judgment even if you think the author is dead wrong. Do not insert your opinions and comments. Stick to what the author is saying and what position the author is advocating.
- Usually summaries are no longer than 150 words. If your summary is longer than 150 words, delete excess words without eliminating key ideas.

McWilliams, James. *Just Food: Where Locavores Get It Wrong and How We Can Truly Eat Responsibly.* New York: Little Brown, 2009. Print.

Summary

In *Just Food,* James McWilliams argues that locavorism—the development of local food-supply systems—is an impractical goal. He offers three reasons why locavorism is not achievable. First, many people live in regions where they cannot grow their own food because of lack of water and arable land (for example, Phoenix). Second, many states can grow only a few kinds of food in adequate quantity (for example, New York), thus restricting food choices and limiting consumption to processed fruits and vegetables for much of the year. Third, many people will not like food processing plants near their homes.

3 | Finding Arguments

Although slogans printed on T-shirts often express the views of the people who wear them, the slogans usually cannot be considered arguments because they lack supporting reasons. Nevertheless, you can often supply reasons that are implied by the slogan. Think of reasons supporting the claim that bicycles make a community better.

Find Arguments in Everyday Conversations

Let's look at an example of a conversation. When the pain in his abdomen didn't go away, Jeff knew he had torn something while carrying his friend's heavy speakers up a flight of stairs. He went to the student health center and called his friend Maria when he returned home.

JEFF: I have good news and bad news. The pain is a minor hernia that can be repaired with day surgery. The bad news is that the fee we pay for the health center doesn't cover hospital visits. We should have health coverage.

MARIA: Jeff, you didn't buy the extra insurance. Why should you get it for nothing?

JEFF: Because health coverage is a right.

MARIA: No it's not. Not everyone has health insurance.

JEFF: Well, in some other countries like Canada, Germany, and Britain, they do.

MARIA: Yes, and people who live in those countries pay a bundle in taxes for the government-provided insurance.

JEFF: It's not fair in this country because some people have health insurance and others don't.

MARIA: Jeff, face the facts. You could have bought the extra insurance. Instead you chose to buy a new car.

JEFF: It would be better if the university provided health insurance because students could graduate in four years. I'm going to have to get a second job and drop out for a semester to pay for the surgery.

MARIA: Neat idea, but who's going to pay to insure every student?

JEFF: OK, all students should be required to pay for health insurance as part of their general fee. Most students are healthy, and it wouldn't cost that much more.

In this discussion, Jeff starts out by making a **claim** that students should have health coverage. Maria immediately asks him why students should not have to pay for health insurance. She wants a **reason** to accept his claim.

Distinguishing arguments from other kinds of persuasion

Scholars who study argument maintain that an argument must have a claim and one or more reasons to support that claim. Something less might be persuasive, but it isn't an argument.

A bumper sticker that says NO TOLL ROADS is a claim, but it is not an argument because the statement lacks a reason. Many reasons support an argument against building toll roads.

- We don't need new roads but should build light-rail instead.
- We should raise the gas tax to pay for new roads.
- We should use gas tax revenue only for roads rather than using it for other purposes.

When a claim has a reason attached, then it becomes an argument.

The basics of arguments

A reason is typically offered in a **because clause**, a statement that begins with the word *because* and that provides a supporting reason for the claim. Jeff's first attempt is to argue that students should have health insurance *because* health insurance is a right.

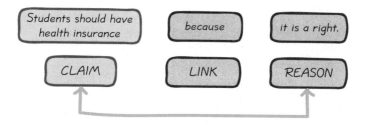

The word *because* signals a link between the reason and the claim. Every argument that is more than a shouting match or a simple assertion has to have one or more reasons. Just having a reason for a claim, however, doesn't mean that the audience will be convinced. When Jeff tells Maria that students have a right to health insurance, Maria replies that students don't have that right. Maria will accept Jeff's claim only if she accepts that his reason supports his claim. Maria challenges Jeff's links and keeps asking "So what?" For her, Jeff's reasons are not good reasons.

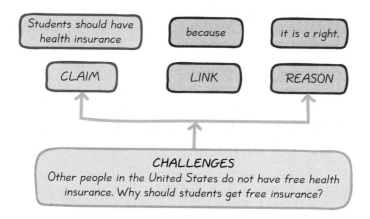

By the end of this short discussion, Jeff has begun to build an argument. He has modified his original claim and indicated how it might be implemented: All students should be required to pay for health insurance as part of their general fee. If he is to convince Maria, he will probably have to provide a series of claims that she will accept as linked to his primary claim. He will also need to find evidence to support these claims.

Benjamin Franklin observed, "So convenient a thing it is to be a rational creature, since it enables us to find or make a reason for every thing one has a mind to do." It is not hard to think of reasons. What *is* difficult is to convince your audience that your reasons are good reasons. In a conversation, you get immediate feedback that tells you whether your listener agrees or disagrees. When you are writing, you usually don't have someone you can question immediately. Consequently, you have to (1) be more specific about what you are claiming, (2) connect with the values you hold in common with your readers, and (3) anticipate what questions and objections your readers might have, if you are going to convince someone who doesn't agree with you or know what you know already.

When you write an argument, imagine a reader like Maria who is going to listen carefully to what you have to say but who is not going to agree with you automatically. Readers like Maria will expect the following.

- A **claim** that is interesting and makes them want to find out more about what you have to say
- At least one **good reason** that makes your claim worth taking seriously
- Some **evidence** that the good reason or reasons are valid
- Some acknowledgment of the **opposing views** and **limitations** of the claim

The remainder of this chapter will guide you through the process of finding a topic, making a claim, finding good reasons and evidence, and anticipating objections to your claim.

Find a Topic

When your instructor gives you a writing assignment, look closely at what you are asked to do. Assignments typically contain a great deal of information, and you have to sort through that information. First, circle all the instructions about the length, the due date, the format, the grading criteria, and anything else about the production and conventions of the assignment. This information is important to you, but it doesn't tell you what the paper is supposed to be about.

Read your assignment carefully

Often your assignment will contain key words such as *analyze, define, evaluate,* or *propose* that will assist you in determining what direction to take. *Analyze* can mean several things. Your instructor might want you to analyze a piece of writing (see Chapter 6), an image (see Chapter 7), or the causes of something (see Chapter 9).

Define usually means writing a **definition argument**, in which you argue for a definition based on the criteria you set out (see Chapter 8). *Evaluate* indicates an **evaluation argument**, in which you argue that something is good, bad, the best, or the worst in its class according to criteria that you set out (see Chapter 10). An assignment that contains the instructions *Write about an issue using your personal experience* indicates a **narrative argument** (see Chapter 11), while one that says *Take a position in regard to a reading* might lead you to write a **rebuttal argument** (see Chapter 12). *Propose* means that you should identify a particular problem and explain why your solution is the best one in a **proposal argument** (see Chapter 13).

What Is Not Arguable

- **Statements of fact.** Most facts can be verified through research. But even simple facts can sometimes be argued. For example, Mount Everest is usually acknowledged to be the highest mountain in the world at 29,028 feet above sea level. But if the total height of a mountain from base to summit is the measure, then the volcano Mauna Loa in Hawaii is the highest mountain in the world. Although the top of Mauna Loa is 13,667 feet above sea level, the summit is 31,784 above the ocean floor. Thus the "fact" that Mount Everest is the highest mountain on the earth depends on a definition of *highest*. You could argue for this definition.

- **Claims of personal taste.** Your favorite food and your favorite color are examples of personal taste. If you hate fresh tomatoes, no one can convince you that you actually like them. But many claims of personal taste turn out to be value judgments using arguable criteria. For example, if you think that *Alien* is the best science-fiction movie ever made, you can argue that claim using evaluative criteria that other people can consider as good reasons (see Chapter 10). Indeed, you might not even like science fiction and still argue that *Alien* is the best science-fiction movie ever.

- **Statements of belief or faith.** If someone accepts a claim as a matter of religious belief, then for that person, the claim is true and cannot be refuted. Of course, people still make arguments about the existence of God and which religion reflects the will of God. Whenever an audience will not consider an idea, it's possible but very difficult to construct an argument. Many people claim to have evidence that UFOs exist, but most people refuse to acknowledge that evidence as even being possibly factual.

If you remain unclear about the purpose of the assignment after reading it carefully, talk with your instructor.

Finding Good Reasons

Are Traffic Enforcement Cameras Invading Your Privacy?

Cameras that photograph the license plates and drivers of vehicles who run red lights or ride illegally in high-occupancy-vehicle (HOV) and bus lanes are currently in use in many U.S. cities and states. Cameras aimed at catching speeders, already common in Europe, are beginning to be installed in U.S. cities as well. Traffic cameras have become money machines for some communities, but they also have provoked intense public opposition and even vandalism—people have spray painted and shot cameras in attempts to disable them.

Write about it

1. How do you feel about using cameras to catch red-light runners? Illegal drivers in HOV and bus lanes? speeders? people who don't pay parking tickets? Make a list of as many possible topics as you can think of about the use of cameras to scan license plates.

2. Select one of the possible topics. Write it at the top of a sheet of paper, and then write nonstop for five minutes. Don't worry about correctness. If you get stuck, write the same sentence again.

3. When you finish, read what you have written and circle key ideas.

4. Put each key idea on a sticky note. If you think of other ideas, write them on separate sticky notes. Then look at your sticky notes. Put a star on the central idea. Put the ideas that are related next to each other. You now have the beginning of an idea map.

Thinking about what interests you

Your assignment may specify the topic you are to write about. If your assignment gives you a wide range of options and you don't know what to write about, look first at the materials for your course: the readings, your lecture notes, and discussion boards. Think about what subjects came up in class discussion.

If you need to look outside class for a topic, think about what interests you. Subjects we argue about often find us. There are enough of them in daily life. We're late for work or class because the traffic is heavy or the bus doesn't run on time. We can't find a place to park when we get to school or work. We have to negotiate through various bureaucracies for almost anything we do—making an appointment to see a doctor, getting a course added or dropped, or correcting a mistake on a bill. Most of the time we grumble and let it go at that. But sometimes we stick with a subject. Neighborhood groups in cities and towns have been especially effective in getting something done by writing about it—for example, stopping a new road from being built, getting better police and fire protection, and getting a vacant lot turned into a park.

Listing and analyzing issues

A good way to get started is to list possible issues to write about. Make a list of questions that can be answered "YES, because . . ." or "NO, because . . ." Think about issues that affect your campus, your community, the nation, and the world. Which issues interest you? About which issues could you make a contribution to the larger discussion?

Campus

- Should students be required to pay fees for access to computers on campus?
- Should smoking be banned on campus?
- Should varsity athletes get paid for playing sports that bring in revenue?
- Should admissions decisions be based exclusively on academic achievement?
- Should knowledge of a foreign language be required for all degree plans?
- Should your college or university have a computer literacy requirement?
- Is there any way to curb the dangerous drinking habits of many students on your campus?

Community

- Should people who ride bicycles and motorcycles be required to wear helmets?
- Should high schools be allowed to search students for drugs at any time?
- Should high schools distribute condoms?
- Should bilingual education programs be eliminated?
- Should bike lanes be built throughout your community to encourage more people to ride bicycles?
- Should more tax dollars be shifted from building highways to funding public transportation?

Nation/World

- Should talking on a cell phone while driving be banned?
- Should capital punishment be abolished?
- Should the Internet be censored?
- Should the government be allowed to monitor all phone calls and all e-mail to combat terrorism?
- Should assault weapons be outlawed?
- Should beef and poultry be free of growth hormones?
- Should a law be passed requiring that parents be informed before their teenage child has an abortion?
- Should people who are terminally ill be allowed to end their lives?
- Should the United States punish nations with poor human rights records?

Narrowing a list

1. Put a check beside the issues that look most interesting to write about or the ones that mean the most to you.
2. Put a question mark beside the issues that you don't know very much about. If you choose one of these issues, you will probably have to do in-depth research—by talking to people, by using the Internet, or by going to the library.
3. Select the two or three issues that look most promising. For each issue, make lists:
   - Who is most interested in this issue?
   - Whom or what does this issue affect?

- What are the pros and cons of this issue? Make two columns. At the top of the left one, write "YES, because." At the top of the right one, write "NO, because."
- What has been written about this issue? How can you find out what has been written?

Explore Your Topic

When you identify a potential topic, make a quick exploration of that topic, much as you would walk through a house or an apartment you are thinking about renting for a quick look. One way of exploring is to visualize the topic by making a map.

If you live in a state on the coast that has a high potential for wind energy, you might argue that your state should provide financial incentives for generating more electricity from the wind. Perhaps it seems like a no-brainer to you because wind power consumes no fuel and causes no air pollution. The only energy required is for the manufacture and transportation of the wind turbines and transmission lines. But your state and other coastal states have not exploited potential wind energy for three reasons:

1. **Aesthetics.** Some people think wind turbines are ugly and noisy.
2. **Hazard to wildlife.** A few poorly located wind turbines have killed birds and bats.
3. **Cost.** Wind power costs differ, but wind energy is generally more expensive than electricity produced by burning coal.

To convince other people that your proposal is a good one, you will have to answer these objections.

Possible objections to wind energy

hazard to wildlife

ugly and noisy

higher cost
$$$

The first two objections are relatively easy to address. Locating wind farms 10 kilometers offshore keeps them out of sight and sound of land and away from most migrating birds and all bats. The third objection, higher cost, is more difficult. One strategy is to argue that the overall costs of wind energy and energy produced by burning coal are comparable if environmental costs are included. You can analyze the advantages and disadvantages of each by drawing maps.

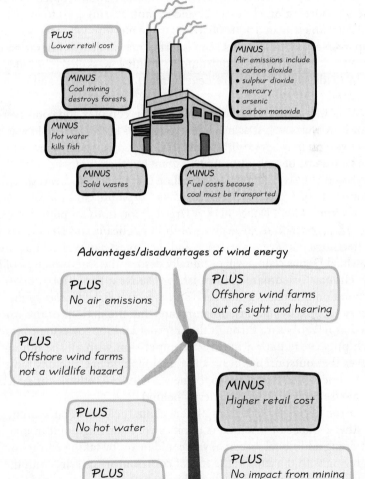

Advantages/disadvantages of coal-fired power plants

PLUS
Lower retail cost

MINUS
Coal mining
destroys forests

MINUS
Hot water
kills fish

MINUS
Solid wastes

MINUS
Fuel costs because
coal must be transported

MINUS
Air emissions include
• carbon dioxide
• sulphur dioxide
• mercury
• arsenic
• carbon monoxide

Advantages/disadvantages of wind energy

PLUS
No air emissions

PLUS
Offshore wind farms
out of sight and hearing

PLUS
Offshore wind farms
not a wildlife hazard

MINUS
Higher retail cost

PLUS
No hot water

PLUS
No wastes

PLUS
No impact from mining
and transporting fuel

These maps can help you organize an argument for providing financial incentives for wind energy.

Read About Your Topic

Much college writing draws on and responds to sources—books, articles, reports, and other material written by other people. Every significant issue discussed in today's world has an extensive history of discussion involving many people and various points of view. Before you formulate a claim about a significant issue, you need to become familiar with the conversation that's already happening by reading widely about it.

One of the most controversial and talked-about subjects in recent years is the outsourcing of white-collar and manufacturing jobs to low-wage nations. Since 2000 an estimated 400,000 to 500,000 American jobs each year have gone to cheap overseas labor markets. The Internet has made this migration of jobs possible, allowing companies to outsource not only low-skilled jobs but highly skilled jobs in fields such as software development, data storage, and even examining X-rays and MRI scans.

You may have read about this or another complex and controversial topic in one of your courses. Just as in a conversation with several people who hold different views, you may agree with some people, disagree with some, and with others agree with some of their ideas up to a point but then disagree.

Fox Business Network news anchor Lou Dobbs has been sharply critical of outsourcing. In *Exporting America: Why Corporate Greed Is Shipping American Jobs Overseas* (2006), Dobbs blames large corporations for putting profits ahead of the good of the nation. He accuses both Republicans and Democrats of ignoring the effects of a massive trade deficit and the largest national debt in American history, which Dobbs claims will eventually destroy the American way of life.

Thomas Friedman, columnist for the *New York Times*, takes a different viewpoint on outsourcing in *The World Is Flat: A Brief History of the Twenty-first Century* (2006). By *flat,* Friedman means that the nations of the world are connected as never before through the Internet and the lowering of trade barriers, which puts every nation in direct competition with all the others. Friedman believes that outsourcing is not only unstoppable but also desirable. He argues that Americans need to adapt to the new reality and rethink our system of education, or else we will be left hopelessly behind.

If you decide to write an argument about the issue of outsourcing, you might use either Dobbs's or Friedman's book as your starting point in making a claim. After doing additional research, you could begin by taking on the role of **skeptic**, disagreeing with the author; the role of **contributor**, agreeing with the author and adding another point; or the role of the **analyst**, finding some points to agree with while disagreeing with others.

The skeptic: Disagreeing with a source

It's easy to disagree by simply saying an idea is dumb, but readers expect you to be persuasive about why you disagree and to offer reasons to support your views.

X claims that _____, but this view is mistaken because _____.

Example claim for arguing against outsourcing resulting from free trade policies

Thomas Friedman claims that the world is "flat," giving a sense of a level playing field for all, but it is absurd to think that the millions of starving children in the world have opportunities similar to those in affluent countries who pay $100 for basketball shoes made by the starving children.

Example claim for arguing in favor of outsourcing resulting from free trade policies

Lou Dobbs is a patriotic American who recognizes the suffering of manufacturing workers in industries like steel and automobiles, but he neglects that the major cause of the loss of manufacturing jobs in the United States and China alike is increased productivity—the 40 hours of labor necessary to produce a car just a few years ago has now been reduced to 15.

The contributor: Agreeing with a source with an additional point

Sources should not make your argument for you. With sources that support your position, indicate exactly how they fit into your argument with an additional point.

I agree with _____ and will make the additional point that _____.

Example claim for arguing against outsourcing resulting from free trade policies

Lou Dobbs's outcry against the outsourcing of American jobs also has a related argument: We are dependent not only on foreign oil, but also on foreign clothing, foreign electronics, foreign tools, foreign toys, foreign cars and trucks—indeed, just about everything—which is quickly eroding the world leadership of the United States.

> **Example claim for arguing in favor of outsourcing resulting from free trade policies**
>
> Thomas Friedman's claim that the Internet enables everyone to become an entrepreneur is demonstrated by thousands of Americans, including my aunt, who could retire early because she developed an income stream by buying jeans and children's clothes at garage sales and selling them to people around the world on *eBay*.

The analyst: Agreeing and disagreeing simultaneously with a source

Incorporating sources is not a matter of simply agreeing or disagreeing with them. Often you will agree with a source up to a point, but you will come to a different conclusion. Or you may agree with the conclusions, but not agree with the reasons put forth.

> I agree with _____ up to a point, but I disagree with the conclusion _____ because _____.
>
> **Example claim for qualifying the argument against outsourcing resulting from free-trade policies**
>
> Lou Dobbs accurately blames our government for giving multinational corporations tax breaks for exporting jobs rather than regulating the loss of millions of jobs, but the real problem lies in the enormous appetite of Americans for inexpensive consumer products like smart phones, tablet computers, and HD televisions that is supported by borrowing money from overseas.
>
> **Example claim for qualifying the argument in favor of outsourcing resulting from free-trade policies**
>
> Thomas Friedman's central claim that the world is being "flattened" by globalization and there is not much we can do to stop this from happening is essentially correct, but he neglects the social costs of globalization around the world, where the banner of free trade has been the justification for devastating the environment, destroying workers' rights and the rights of indigenous peoples, and ignoring laws passed by representative governments.

Find Good Reasons

Get in the habit of asking these questions every time you are asked to write an argument.

Can you argue by definition?

Probably the most powerful kind of good reason is an argument from **definition**. You can think of a definition as a simple statement: _____ *is a* _____. You use these statements all the time. When you need a course to fulfill your social-science requirement, you look at the list of courses that are defined as social-science courses. You find out that the anthropology class you want to take is one of them. It's just as important when _____ *is not a* _____. Suppose you are taking College Algebra, which is a math course taught by the math department, yet it doesn't count for the math requirement. The reason it doesn't count is that College Algebra is not defined as a college-level math class. So you have to enroll next semester in Calculus I.

Many definitions are not nearly as clear-cut as the math requirement. If you want to argue that figure skaters are athletes, you will need to define what an athlete is. You start thinking. An athlete competes in an activity, but that definition alone is too broad, since many competitions do not require physical activity. Thus, an athlete must participate in a competitive physical activity and must train for it. But that definition is still not quite narrow enough, because soldiers also train for competitive physical activity. You decide to add that the activity must be a sport and that it must require special competence and precision. Your *because* clause turns out as follows: *Figure skaters are athletes because true athletes train for and compete in physical sporting competitions that require special competence and precision.*

If you can get your audience to accept your definitions, you've gone a long way toward convincing them of the validity of your claim. That is why the most controversial issues in our culture—abortion, affirmative action, gay rights, pornography, women's rights, privacy rights, gun control, the death penalty—are argued from definition. Is abortion a crime or a medical procedure? Is pornography protected by the First Amendment, or is it a violation of women's rights? Is the death penalty just or cruel and inhuman? You can see from these examples that definitions often rely on deeply held beliefs.

Because people have strong beliefs about controversial issues, they often don't care about the practical consequences. Arguing that it is much cheaper to execute prisoners who have been convicted of first-degree murder than to keep them in prison for life does not convince those who believe that it is morally wrong to kill. (See Chapter 8.)

Can you argue from value?

A special kind of argument from definition, one that often implies consequences, is the argument from value. You can support your claim with a "because clause" (or several of them) that includes a sense of evaluation. Arguments from value follow from claims like _____ *is a good* _____, *or* _____ *is not a good* _____.

Evaluation arguments usually proceed from the presentation of certain criteria. These criteria come from the definitions of good and bad, of poor and not so poor, that prevail in a given case. A great burger fulfills certain criteria; so does an outstanding movie, an excellent class, or the best laptop in your price range. Sometimes the criteria are straightforward, as in the burger example. A great burger has to have tasty meat—tender and without gristle, fresh, never frozen—a fresh bun that is the right size, and your favorite condiments.

But if you are buying a tablet computer and want to play the latest games along with doing your school tasks, you need to do some homework. The best tablet for games will have realistic graphics and a fast processor. The apps you want should be readily available. And while tablets have become affordable, you will want the best value for your money. The keys for evaluation arguments are finding the appropriate criteria and convincing your readers that those criteria are the right criteria (see Chapter 10).

Can you argue from consequence?

Another powerful source of good reasons comes from considering the possible consequences of your position: Can you sketch out the good things that will follow from your position? Can you establish that certain bad things will be avoided if your position is adopted? If so, you will have other good reasons to use.

Causal arguments take the basic form of _____ *causes* _____ (or _____ *does not cause* _____). Very often, causal arguments are more complicated, taking the form _____ *causes* _____ *which, in turn, causes* _____ *and so on*. In one famous example, environmentalist Rachel Carson in *Silent Spring* makes powerful arguments from consequence. Rachel Carson's primary claim is that *DDT should not be sprayed on a massive scale because it will poison animals and people*. The key to her argument is the causal chain that explains how animals and people are poisoned. Carson describes how nothing exists alone in nature. When a potato field is sprayed with DDT, some of that poison is absorbed by the skin of the potatoes and some washes into the groundwater, where it contaminates drinking water. Other poisonous residue is absorbed into streams, where it is ingested by insect larvae, which in turn are eaten by fish. Fish are eaten by other fish, which are then eaten by waterfowl and people. At each stage, the poisons become more concentrated. (See Chapter 9 for additional examples of causal arguments.)

Proposal arguments are future-oriented arguments from consequence. In a proposal argument, you cannot stop with naming good reasons; you also have to show that these consequences would follow from the idea or course of action that you are arguing. For example, if you are proposing designated lanes for bicycles on the streets of your city, you must argue that they will encourage more people to ride bicycles to work and school, reducing air pollution and traffic congestion for everyone. (See Chapter 13.)

Can you counter objections to your position?

Another good way to find convincing good reasons is to think about possible objections to your position. If you can imagine how your audience might counter or respond to your argument, you will probably include in your argument precisely the points that will address your readers' particular needs and objections. If you are successful, your readers will be convinced that you are right. You've no doubt had the experience of mentally saying to a writer in the course of your reading, "Yeah, but what about this other idea?"—only to have the writer address precisely this objection.

You can impress your readers if you've thought about why anyone would oppose your position and exactly how that opposition would be expressed. If you are writing a proposal argument for a computer literacy requirement for all high school graduates, you might think about why anyone would object, since computers are critical for our jobs and lives. What will the practical objections be? What about philosophical ones? Why hasn't such a requirement been put in place already? By asking such questions in your own arguments, you are likely to develop robust because clauses.

Sometimes, writers pose rhetorical questions. You might say, "But won't paying for computers for all students make my taxes go up?" Stating objections explicitly can be effective if you make the objections as those of a reasonable person with an alternative point of view. But if the objections you state are ridiculous ones, then you risk being accused of setting up a **straw man**—that is, making the position opposing your own so simplistic that no one would likely identify with it. (See Chapter 12.)

Find Evidence to Support Good Reasons

Good reasons are essential ingredients of good arguments, but they don't do the job alone. You must support or verify good reasons with evidence. Evidence consists of hard data, examples, personal experiences, episodes, or tabulations of episodes (known as statistics) that are seen as relevant to the good reasons you are putting forward. Thus, a writer of arguments puts forward not only claims and good reasons but also evidence that those good reasons are true.

How much supporting evidence should you supply? How much evidence is enough? As is usual in the case of rhetoric, the best answer is "It depends." If a reader is likely to find one of your good reasons hard to believe, then you should be aggressive in offering support. You should present detailed evidence in a patient and painstaking way. As one presenting an argument, you have a responsibility not just to *state* a case but to *make* a case with evidence. Arguments that are unsuccessful tend to fail not because of a shortage of good reasons; more often, they fail because the reader doesn't agree that there is enough evidence to support the good reason that is being presented.

If your good reason isn't especially controversial, you probably should not belabor it. Think of your own experiences as a reader. How often do you recall saying to yourself, as you read a passage or listened to a speaker, "OK! OK! I get the point! Don't keep piling up all of this evidence for me because I don't want it or need it." However, such a reaction is rare, isn't it? By contrast, how often do you recall muttering under your breath, "How can you say that? What evidence do you have to back it up?" When in doubt, err on the side of offering too much evidence. It's an error that is seldom made and not often criticized.

When a writer doesn't provide satisfactory evidence to support a because clause, readers might feel that there has been a failure in the reasoning process. In fact, in your previous courses in writing and speaking, you may have learned about various fallacies associated with faulty arguments (pages 16–19).

Strictly speaking, there is nothing false about these so-called logical fallacies. The fallacies most often refer to failures in providing evidence; when you don't provide enough good evidence to convince your audience, you might be accused of committing a fallacy in reasoning. You will usually avoid such accusations if the evidence that you cite is both *relevant* and *sufficient*.

Relevance refers to the appropriateness of the evidence to the case at hand. Some kinds of evidence are seen as more relevant than others for particular audiences. On the one hand, in science and industry, personal testimony is seen as having limited relevance, while experimental procedures and controlled observations have far more credibility. On the other hand, in writing for the general public on controversial issues such as gun control, personal experience is often considered more relevant than other kinds of data.

Sufficiency refers to the amount of evidence cited. Sometimes a single piece of evidence or a single instance will carry the day if it is especially compelling in some way—if it represents the situation well or makes a point that isn't particularly controversial. More often, people expect more than one piece of evidence if they are to be convinced of something.

If you anticipate that your audience might not accept your evidence, face the situation squarely. First, think carefully about the argument you are presenting. If you cannot cite adequate evidence for your assertions, perhaps those assertions must be modified or qualified in some way. If you remain convinced of your assertions, then think about doing more research to come up with additional evidence.

4 | Drafting Arguments

QUICK TAKE

In this chapter, you will learn to

1. Think about your purpose (see page 40)
2. State, focus, and evaluate your thesis (see page 40)
3. Appraise your readers' knowledge and attitudes (see page 42)
4. Organize your argument using a formal or working outline (see pages 45–46)
5. Write a title, an introduction, and a strong conclusion (see pages 47–48)

Some writers make detailed outlines before they begin writing. Others sketch the major sections and work from these notes. Still others start by freewriting and then identify key ideas and organize them. What is your most frequent planning strategy?

Think About Your Purpose

The first step in writing is to identify your purpose. When your instructor gives you a writing assignment, look closely at what you are being asked to do. Circle the information about the required length, the due dates, the format, and other requirements. You can attend to these details later.

Does your assignment contain words like *analyze, compare, define, evaluate, analyze causes*, or *propose* that signal your purpose? Identifying key terms can help you understand how to focus your argument. However, people rarely set out to define something in an argument just for the sake of definition, or to compare things simply for the sake of comparison. Instead, they have a purpose in mind, and they use the kinds of argument that are discussed in Chapters 8–13—most often in combination—as a means to an end. Most arguments use multiple approaches and multiple sources of good reasons.

State and Evaluate Your Thesis

Once you have identified a topic and purpose and have a good sense of how to develop your topic, the next critical step is to write a **working thesis**. Your **thesis** states your main claim. Much writing that you will do in college and later in your career will require an explicit thesis, usually placed near the beginning.

Focusing your thesis

The thesis can make or break your paper. If the thesis is too broad, you cannot do justice to the argument. Who wouldn't wish for fewer traffic accidents, better medical care, more effective schools, or a cleaner environment? Simple solutions for these complex problems are unlikely.

Stating something that is obvious to everyone isn't an arguable thesis. Don't settle for easy answers. When a topic is too broad, a predictable thesis often results. Narrow your focus and concentrate on the areas where you have the most questions. Those are likely the areas where your readers will have the most questions too.

The opposite problem is less common: a thesis that is too narrow. If your thesis simply states a commonly known fact, then it is too narrow. For example, the growth rate of the population in the United States has doubled since 1970 because of increased immigration. The U.S. Census Bureau provides reasonably accurate statistical information, so this claim is not arguable. But the policies that allow increased immigration and the effects of a larger population—more crowding and higher costs of health care, education, and transportation—are arguable.

Not arguable: The population of the United States grew faster in the 1990s than in any previous decade because Congress increased the rate of legal immigration and the government stopped enforcing most laws against illegal immigration in the interior of the country.

Arguable: Allowing a high rate of immigration helps the United States deal with the problems of an increasingly aging society and helps provide funding for millions of Social Security recipients.

Arguable: The increase in the number of visas to foreign workers in technology industries is the major cause of unemployment in those industries.

Evaluating your thesis

Once you have a working thesis, ask these questions.

- Is it arguable?
- Is it specific?
- Is it manageable given your length and time requirements?
- Is it interesting to your intended readers?

Example 1

Sample thesis

> We should take action to resolve the serious traffic problem in our city.

Is it arguable? The thesis is arguable, but it lacks a focus.

Is it specific? The thesis is too broad.

Is it manageable? Transportation is a complex issue. New highways and rail systems are expensive and take many years to build. Furthermore, citizens don't want new roads running through their neighborhoods.

Is it interesting? The topic has the potential to be interesting if the writer can propose a specific solution to a problem that everyone in the city recognizes.

When a thesis is too broad, it needs to be revised to address a specific aspect of an issue. Make the big topic smaller.

Revised thesis

> The existing freight railway that runs through the center of the city should be converted to a passenger railway because this is the cheapest and quickest way to decrease traffic congestion downtown.

Example 2
Sample thesis

> *Over 60 percent of Americans play computer games on a regular basis.*

Is it arguable? The thesis states a commonly acknowledged fact. It is not arguable.

Is it specific? The thesis is too narrow.

Is it manageable? A known fact is stated in the thesis, so there is little to research. Several surveys report this finding.

Is it interesting? The popularity of video games is well established. Nearly everyone is aware of the trend.

There's nothing original or interesting about stating that Americans love computer games. Think about what is controversial. One debatable topic is how computer games affect children.

Revised thesis

> *Computer games are valuable because they improve children's visual attention skills, literacy skills, and computer literacy skills.*

Think About Your Readers

Thinking about your readers doesn't mean telling them what they might want to hear. Instead, imagine yourself in a dialogue with your readers. What questions are they likely to have? How might you address any potential objections?

Understanding what your readers know—and do not know

Your readers' knowledge of your subject is critical to the success of your argument. If your readers are not familiar with the necessary background information, they probably won't understand your argument fully. If you know that your readers will be unfamiliar with your subject, you have to supply background information before attempting to convince them of your position. A good tactic is to tie your new information to what your readers already know. Comparisons and analogies can be very helpful in linking old and new information.

Finding Good Reasons

Should Talking While Driving Be Banned?

In a movement to improve driving safety, California, Connecticut, the District of Columbia, New Jersey, New York, Oregon, Utah, and Washington have passed laws banning the use of handheld cell phones while driving except for emergency workers and people making 911 calls. Several other states have banned cell phones while driving for drivers aged 18 and younger.

Proponents of the ban point to a National Highway Traffic Safety Administration study reporting that 25 to 30 percent of motor vehicle crashes—about 1.2 million accidents each year—are caused by driver distraction. Opponents of the ban argue that anything that distracts the driver—eating potato chips, talking with passengers, spilled coffee—can cause an accident. The answer, they say, is driver education.

Write about it

1. Write a thesis arguing in support of a ban on cell phones while driving, against a ban, or in support of a more limited position such as banning cell-phone use for drivers 18 and under.

2. Think about the audience that would tend to oppose your position. For example, if you support a ban on talking while driving, think about the likely responses of high school students, salespeople who spend much of their workday driving from place to place, and workers who receive assignments by phone. What good reasons would convince readers who hold an opposing view?

3. What reasons would people who oppose your position likely offer in response? What counterarguments could you give to answer these objections?

Understanding your readers' attitudes toward you

To get your readers to take you seriously, you must convince them that they can trust you. You need to get them to see you as

- **concerned:** Readers want you to be committed to your subject. They also expect you to be concerned about them. After all, if you don't care about them, why should they read what you write?
- **well informed:** Many people ramble on about any subject without knowing anything about it. College writing requires that you do your homework on a subject.
- **fair:** Many writers look at only one side of an issue. Readers respect objectivity and an unbiased approach.
- **ethical:** Many writers use only the facts that support their positions and often distort facts and sources. Critical readers often notice what is being left out. Don't try to conceal what doesn't support your position.

Understanding your readers' attitudes toward your subject

People have prior attitudes about controversial issues. You must take these attitudes into consideration as you write or speak. Imagine, for instance, that you are preparing an argument for a guest editorial in your college newspaper. You are advocating that your state government should provide parents with choices between public and private schools. You plan to argue that the tax dollars that now automatically go to public schools should go to private schools if parents so choose. You have evidence that the sophomore-to-senior dropout rate in private schools is less than half the rate in public schools. Furthermore, students from private schools attend college at nearly twice the rate of public school graduates. You intend to argue that one of the reasons private schools are more successful is that they spend more money on instruction and less on administration. And you believe that school choice speaks to the American desire for personal freedom.

Not everyone on your campus will agree with your position. How might the faculty at your college or university feel about this issue? How about the administrators, the staff, other students, and interested community members who read the student newspaper? What are their attitudes toward public funding of private schools? How are you going to deal with the objection that many students in private schools do better in school because they come from more affluent families?

Even when you write about a much less controversial subject, you must think carefully about your audience's attitudes toward what you have to say or write. Sometimes your audience may share your attitudes; other times, your audience may be neutral. At still other times, your audience will have attitudes that differ sharply from your own. Anticipate these various attitudes and act accordingly. If these attitudes are different from yours, you will have to work hard to counter them without insulting your audience.

Organize Your Argument

Asking a series of questions can generate a list of good reasons, but even if you have plenty, you still have to decide which ones to use and in what order to present them. Thinking about your readers' knowledge, attitudes, and values will help you to decide which reasons to present to your audience.

Writing plans often take the form of outlines, either formal outlines or working outlines. A **formal outline** typically begins with the thesis statement, which anchors the entire outline. Jenna Picchi created the following formal outline for an evaluation argument concerning organic foods. (You can read her final paper on pages 155–161.)

Organic Foods Should Come Clean

THESIS: The policy of producing and selling organic foods on a massive, industrial scale is not as good for the environment or consumers as producing and selling organic foods on a smaller scale. Although organic foods produced on an industrial scale are less expensive and more convenient, all industrial foods require massive use of fossil fuels to bring them to consumers and may be less sustainably produced.

I. Open with personal anecdote about trying to shop organic near campus. End with claim.

II. Give a specific example about issues related to industrial organic farming: the image of natural, healthy foods produced with traditional methods vs. reality of factory farms.

III. Look at industrial organic food industry:
   A. What is it?
   B. Why is it growing?
   C. What are its origins (the move from small organic to Big Organic)?

IV. State the first criterion: good organic food policy should produce healthy foods that are sustainably produced. Give reasons:
   A. Better for the environment.
   B. Better for individuals and public health.
   C. Better for taxpayers.

V. State the second criterion: good policy should protect consumers and guarantee valid organic certifications.
   A. Organic standards are hard to police.
   B. Federal investigations have found major organic milk producers breaking rules.
   C. If the organic label isn't protected, customers won't trust it.

VI. State the third criterion: good policy avoids negative effects on small farms.
    A. Industrial organic companies help define organic standards.
    B. Industrial organic companies involved in setting prices.
    C. Local farms can be held accountable about standards and sustainability, earn consumer trust.
VII. Offer conclusion and perspective.

Alternatively, Picchi could have developed a **working outline**, which is a sketch of how to arrange an essay's major sections.

Organic Foods Should Come Clean

SECTION 1: Begin by discussing why consumers buy organic food. Describe the ways that organic foods are marketed to consumers and how the packaging on organic foods appeals to people's desire for better food. Contrast this common understanding of organic foods with the reality that organic foods are often produced by large industrial producers, owned by large corporations.

SECTION 2: One concern about the new trends in organic food production is that companies are using the organic label even when they don't support organic principles. The more agribusiness becomes a part of the organic food movement, the less the labels will mean. As the business evolves, the standards need to evolve to guarantee that the foods are sustainably produced and healthy and that consumers can trust organic labeling.

SECTION 3: As the organic standards change, they are hard to police, and there are several recent examples where the standards have been an issue. Many long-time organic farmers believe the large corporate farms are working to water down existing standards.

SECTION 4: Large corporate farms can outcompete smaller farms because they are more efficient, which means it is harder for consumers to find organic products that aren't produced by agribusiness.

SECTION 5: Good organic policy should have a positive impact on small producers, and small-scale farms have to be committed to sustainable practices. Consumers should be able to trust the producers of their food.

Write an Engaging Title and Introduction

Many writers don't think much about titles, but they are very important. A good title makes the reader want to see what you have to say. Be as specific as you can in your title, and if possible, suggest your stance.

Get off to a fast start in your introduction. Convince your reader to keep reading. Cut to the chase. Think about how you can get your readers interested. Consider using one of the following strategies.

- State your thesis concisely.
- Provide a hard-hitting fact.
- Ask a question.
- Give a vivid description of a problem.
- Discuss a contradiction or paradox.
- Describe a scenario.

Jenna Picchi decided to introduce her essay by using a personal anecdote in order to grab her readers' attention and develop her credibility by demonstrating her experience with her topic.

Organic Foods Should Come Clean

As a kid growing up not far from rural communities, I took for granted the access to local produce and the farm stands my family frequented. When I moved to a college town, I assumed I would have access to an even wider variety of foods and better choices. I wanted to continue eating organic as I had at home, even though it would be more work than a campus-dining plan. I learned quickly that even in a large college town, it takes determined searching in most supermarkets to find the organic produce, bread, meat, and dairy products that are scattered in less-trafficked corners of the store. Instead of shopping at the weekly farmer's market (which I cannot attend), I choose these supermarket fruits and vegetables from the lackluster and small display of things shipped in from California and Central America. Taking a recent look at these organic departments, I noticed that almost all the products are store or national brands. It never occurred to me that living in the middle of an agricultural state my choices would be so limited. After spending much time and energy seeking out organic products in stores all around town, I wondered whether the effort is worth it. How healthy are these foods in the local supermarket? And are these national brands as good for the environment as they seem?

Write a Strong Conclusion

Restating your thesis usually isn't the best way to finish a paper. Conclusions that offer only a summary bore readers. The worst endings say something like "in my paper I've said this." Effective conclusions are interesting and provocative, leaving readers with something to think about. Give your readers something to take away besides a straight summary. Try one of these approaches.

- Issue a call to action.
- Discuss the implications.
- Make recommendations.
- Project into the future.
- Tell an anecdote that illustrates a key point.

Picchi uses a call to action to conclude her essay on organic foods. Note how her conclusion also ties back to her introduction by mentioning college students.

Small, local organic farmers are well positioned to deliver on the organic movement's original ideals of sustainably produced foods. Consumers should have a right to know where their food comes from and how organic standards are defined. In fact, as organic foods become more widely available to most consumers—even college students—it is worth questioning whether organic standards mean what they seem. Labeling foods organic cannot be just a marketing ploy, and the organic industry will continue to reach and inform more consumers if it can ensure this label has real meaning.

When you finish your conclusion, read your introduction again. The main claim in your conclusion should be closely related to the main subject, question, or claim in your introduction. If they do not match, revise the subject, question, or claim in the introduction to match the conclusion. Your thinking evolves and develops as you write, and often your introduction needs some adjusting if you wrote it first.

5 | Revising and Editing Arguments

QUICK TAKE

In this chapter, you will learn to

1. Evaluate your draft (see pages 49–51)
2. Respond to the writing of others (see pages 51, 53–54)
3. Revise your draft using outside feedback and your own analysis (see pages 54–55)
4. Edit and proofread carefully (see pages 55–56)

People frequently revise things that they own. What objects have you revised?

Evaluate Your Draft

To review and evaluate your draft, pretend you are someone who is either uninformed about your subject or informed but likely to disagree with you. If possible, think of an actual person and imagine yourself as that person.

Read your draft aloud all the way through. When you read aloud, you often hear clunky phrases and catch errors, but just put checks in the margins so you can return to them later. You don't want to get bogged down with the little stuff. What you are after in this stage is an overall sense of how well you accomplished what you set out to do.

Use the questions in the following Checklist to evaluate your draft. Note any places where you might make improvements. When you finish, make a list of your goals for the revision. You may have to write another draft before you move to the next stage.

Checklist for evaluating your draft

Does your paper or project meet the assignment?

- Look again at your assignment, especially at key words such as *analyze, define, evaluate,* and *propose.* Does your paper or project do what the assignment requires? If not, how can you change it?

- Look again at the assignment for specific guidelines including length, format, and amount of research. Does your work meet these guidelines? If not, how can you change it?

Do you have a clear focus?

- Underline your thesis. Think how you might make your thesis more precise.

- Underline the main idea of each paragraph. Check how each paragraph connects to your thesis. Think about how you can strengthen the connections.

Are your main points adequately developed?

- Put brackets around the reasons and evidence that support your main points.

- Can you explain your reasons in more detail?

- Can you add evidence to better support your main points?

Is your organization effective?

- Make a quick outline of your draft if you haven't already done so.

- Mark the places where you find abrupt shifts or gaps.

- Is the order of your main points clear?

- Are there sections or paragraphs that should be rearranged?

Do you consider your readers' knowledge and other points of view?

- Where do you acknowledge views besides your own?

- How can you make your discussion of opposing views more acceptable to readers who hold those views?

- Where do you give background if your readers are unfamiliar with your subject?

- Do you adequately define key terms that might be unfamiliar?

Do you represent yourself effectively?

- Forget for the moment that you wrote what you are reading. What is your impression of the writer?

- Is the tone of the writing appropriate for the subject?

- Are the sentences clear and properly emphatic?

- Did you choose words that convey the right connotations?

- Is the writing visually effective—easy to read with helpful headings and illustrations?

Respond to the Writing of Others

Your instructor may ask you to respond to the drafts of your classmates. Responding to other people's writing requires the same careful attention you give to your own draft. To write a helpful response, you should go through the draft more than once.

First reading

Read at your normal rate the first time through without stopping. When you finish, you should have a clear sense of what the writer is trying to accomplish. Try writing the following.

- **Main idea and purpose:** Write a sentence that summarizes what you think is the writer's main idea in the draft.
- **Purpose:** Write a sentence that states what you think the writer is trying to accomplish in the draft.

Finding Good Reasons

The Revision of Buildings and Places

The High Line operated from 1934 to 1980.

The High Line was unused for 25 years and fell into disrepair.

The first section of the new urban park opened in 2009.

In the 1930s, an elevated freight railway called the High Line was built in the industrial district of lower Manhattan to remove trains from New York City streets. The High Line cut through city blocks and ran directly through industrial buildings, where goods were loaded and unloaded without interrupting traffic. The rise of interstate trucking in the 1950s increasingly made the High Line obsolete, and in 1980, the High Line was used by a train for the last time. Some of the High Line was demolished, and surviving sections became overgrown with surprisingly adaptive weeds. In 1999, nearby residents formed Friends of the High Line and began lobbying to have the former railway converted to a park. The city, the state, and the railway owner eventually agreed to the development of the High Line as an urban park, and in 2009, the first section opened to the public. The park has been a huge success, bringing many people to visit and fostering new development in the surrounding Chelsea neighborhood.

The High Line is an example of a current trend of converting older structures such as warehouses, factories, railroads, airports, and docks that have outlived their usefulness to new uses. Rather than tearing down these structures, many are being converted to retail spaces, housing lofts, and museums. Likewise, many vacant parcels of land are being converted into parks.

Write about it

1. Identify an older building or space in your city, town, or campus that has been converted to a new use. How successful is the revision? One measure of success is how many people use the converted building or space. Not all revisions succeed. Go to the site and observe how many people visit and what they do when they get there.

2. Go to the oldest part of your city or town. Take a notebook or a tablet with you. Learn as much as you can about the history of a particular building or buildings through observing. Many buildings have visible signs of their past, such as the name of a former business on the front facade. Note as many details as you can identify. Then write about the history of the building or space from what you can infer from the details.

Second reading

In your second reading, you should be most concerned with the content, organization, and completeness of the draft. Make notes in pencil as you read.

- **Introduction:** Does the writer's first paragraph effectively introduce the topic and engage your interest?
- **Thesis:** What exactly is the writer's thesis? Is it clear? Note in the margin where you think the thesis is located.
- **Focus:** Does the writer maintain focus on the thesis? Note any places where the writer seems to wander off to another topic.
- **Organization:** Are the sections and paragraphs arranged effectively? Do any paragraphs seem to be out of place? Can you suggest a better order for the paragraphs?
- **Completeness:** Are there sections or paragraphs that lack key information or adequate development? Where do you want to know more?
- **Conclusion:** Does the last paragraph wrap up the discussion effectively?
- **Sources:** Are outside sources cited accurately? Are quotations used correctly and worked into the fabric of the draft?

Third reading

In your third reading, turn your attention to matters of audience, style, and tone.

- **Audience:** Who are the writer's intended readers? What does the writer assume the audience knows and believes?
- **Style:** Is the writer's style engaging? How would you describe the writer's voice?

■ **Tone:** Is the tone appropriate for the writer's purpose and audience? Is the tone consistent throughout the draft? Are there places where another word or phrase might work better?

When you have finished the third reading, write a short paragraph on each bulleted item above. Refer to specific paragraphs in the draft by number. Then end by answering these two questions.

■ What does the writer do especially well in the draft?
■ What one or two things would most improve the draft in a revision?

Revise Your Draft

Once you have evaluated your draft and received feedback from others, it is time to revise. Revision is one of the most important steps in the writing process. Skilled writers know that the secret to writing well is rewriting. Work through your essay in detail looking for opportunities to address the issues you identified in your evaluation.

■ **Keep your audience in mind.** Re-read the opening sentence of each paragraphs and ask yourself whether it is engaging enough to keep your readers interested. Rewrite accordingly.
■ **Sharpen your focus whenever possible.** You may have started out with a large topic but now find that most of what you write concerns only one aspect. If so, revise your thesis and supporting paragraphs.
■ **Check if key terms are adequately defined.** Locate your key terms. Are they defined precisely enough to be meaningful? Have you provided other necessary background information for your readers? Make the necessary adjustments.
■ **Develop your ideas where necessary.** Key points and claims may need more explanation and supporting evidence. Look for new evidence that you can add without being redundant.
■ **Check links between paragraphs.** Review any places where you make abrupt shifts and rewrite to make the transitions better. Make sure you signal the relationship from one paragraph to the next.
■ **Consider your title.** Many writers don't think much about titles, but they are very important. A good title makes the reader want to see what you have to say. Be as specific as you can in your title, and if possible, suggest your stance.

- **Consider your introduction.** In the introduction you want to get off to a fast start and convince your reader to keep reading. Make sure your introduction cuts right to the chase.
- **Consider your conclusions.** Restating your thesis usually isn't the best way to finish; conclusions that offer only a summary bore readers. The words endings say something like "in my paper I've said this." Effective conclusions are interesting and provocative, leaving readers with something to think about. Rework your conclusion if necessary.
- **Improve the visual aspects of your text.** Is the font you selected easy to read? Would headings and subheadings help to identify key sections? If you include statistical data, would charts be effective? Would illustrations help to establish key points?

Edit and Proofread Carefully

When you finish revising, you are ready for one final careful reading with the goals of improving your style and eliminating errors.

Edit for style

- **Check connections between sentences and paragraphs.** Notice how your sentences flow within each paragraph and from paragraph to paragraph. If you need to signal the relationship from one sentence or paragraph to the next, use a transitional word or phrase (e.g., *in addition, moreover, similarly, however, nevertheless*).
- **Check your sentences.** Often you will pick up problems with individual sentences by reading aloud. If you notice that a sentence doesn't sound right, think about how you might rephrase it. If a sentence seems too long, consider breaking it into two or more sentences. If you notice a string of short sentences that sound choppy, consider combining them.
- **Eliminate wordiness.** Look for wordy expressions such as *because of the fact that* and *at this point in time*, which can easily be shortened to *because* and *now*. Reduce unnecessary repetition such as *attractive in appearance* or *visible to the eye* to *attractive* and *visible*. Remove unnecessary words like *very, really,* and *totally*. See how many words you can remove without losing the meaning.
- **Use active verbs.** Make your style more lively by replacing forms of *be* (*is, are, was, were*) or verbs ending in *-ing* with active verbs. Sentences that begin with *There is (are)* and *It is* can often be rewritten with active verbs.

Proofread carefully

In your final pass through your text, eliminate as many errors as you can. To become an effective proofreader, you have to learn to slow down. Some writers find that moving from word to word with a pencil slows them down enough to find errors. Others read backwards to force themselves to concentrate on each word.

You can get one-on-one help in developing your ideas, focusing your topic, and revising your paper or project at your writing center.

- **Know what your spelling checker can and can't do.** Spelling checkers are the greatest invention since peanut butter. They turn up many typos and misspellings that are hard to catch. But spelling checkers do not catch wrong words (*to much* for *too much*), missing endings (*three dog*), and other similar errors.

- **Check for grammar and punctuation.** Nothing hurts your credibility more than leaving errors in what you write. Many job application letters get tossed in the reject pile because of a single, glaring error. Readers probably shouldn't make such harsh judgments when they find errors, but often they do. Keep a grammar handbook beside your computer, and use it when you are uncertain about what is correct.

Analyzing Arguments

PART

2

6 | Analyzing Written Arguments

QUICK TAKE

In this chapter, you will learn to

1. Define rhetorical analysis, including textual and contextual analysis (see below)
2. Analyze the rhetorical features of a specific argument (see page 59)
3. Analyze the appeals of logos, pathos, and ethos in a specific argument (pages 61–63)
4. Analyze the arrangement and style of a specific argument (see pages 63–64)
5. Appreciate how the rhetorical context shapes a specific argument (see pages 64–70)
6. Write an effective rhetorical analysis (see pages 70–72)

What Is Rhetorical Analysis?

To many people, the term *rhetoric* suggests speech or writing that is highly orna-mental or deceptive or manipulative. You might hear someone say, "That politi-cian is just using a bunch of rhetoric" or "The rhetoric of that advertisement is very deceiving." But *rhetoric* is also used these days in a positive or neutral sense to describe human communication; for instance, "*Silent Spring* is one of the most in-fluential pieces of environmental rhetoric ever written." When we study rhetoric, we usually associate it with effective communication, following Aristotle's classic definition of rhetoric as "the art of finding in any given case the available means of persuasion."

Rhetoric is not just a means of *producing* effective communication. It is also a way of *understanding* communication. The two aspects mutually support one another: Becoming a better writer makes you a better interpreter, and becoming a better interpreter makes you a better writer.

Rhetorical analysis is the effort to understand how people attempt to influ-ence others through language and more broadly through every kind of symbolic action—not only speeches, articles, and books, but also architecture, movies, tel-evision shows, memorials, Web sites, advertisements, photos and other images, dance, and popular songs. It might be helpful to think of rhetorical analysis as a kind of critical reading. Critical reading—rhetorical analysis, that is—involves studying carefully any kind of persuasive action in order to understand it better and to appreciate the tactics that it uses.

Build a Rhetorical Analysis

Rhetorical analysis examines how an idea is shaped and presented to an audience in a particular form for a specific purpose. There are many approaches to rhetorical analysis and no one "correct" way to do it. Generally, though, approaches to rhetorical analysis can be placed between two broad extremes—not mutually exclusive categories but extremes at the ends of a continuum.

At one end of the continuum are analyses that concentrate more on **texts** than on contexts. They typically use rhetorical concepts and terminologies to analyze the features of texts. Let's call this approach **textual analysis**. At the other extreme are approaches that emphasize **context** over text. These focus on reconstructing the cultural environment, or context, that existed when a particular rhetorical event took place. That reconstruction provides clues about the persuasive tactics and appeals. Those who undertake **contextual analysis** regard particular rhetorical acts as parts of larger communicative chains, or "conversations."

Now let's examine these two approaches in detail.

Analyze the Rhetorical Features: Textual Analysis

Just as expert teachers in every field of endeavor—from baseball to biology—devise vocabularies to facilitate specialized study, rhetoricians too have developed a set of key concepts to describe rhetorical activities. A fundamental concept in rhetoric is audience. But there are many others. Classical rhetoricians in the tradition of Aristotle, Quintilian, and Cicero developed a range of terms around what they called the canons of rhetoric in order to describe some of the actions of communicators: *inventio* (invention—the finding or creation of information for persuasive acts, and the planning of strategies), *dispostio* (arrangement), *elocutio* (style), *memoria* (the recollection of rhetorical resources that one might call upon, as well as the memorization of what has been invented and arranged), and *pronuntiatio* (delivery). These five canons generally describe the actions of any persuader, from preliminary planning to final delivery.

Over the years, as written discourse gained in prestige against oral discourse, four canons (excepting *memoria*) led to the development of concepts and terms useful for rhetorical analysis. Terms like *ethos, pathos,* and *logos*, all associated with invention, account for features of texts related to the trustworthiness and credibility of the writer or speaker (**ethos**), for the persuasive good reasons in an argument that derive from a community's mostly deeply held values (**pathos**), and for the good reasons that emerge from intellectual reasoning (**logos**). Fundamental to the classical approach to rhetoric is the concept of *decorum*, or "appropriateness": Everything within a persuasive act can be understood as reflecting a central rhetorical goal that governs consistent choices according to occasion and audience.

The statue of Castor stands at the entrance of the Piazza del Campidoglio in Rome. A textual analysis focuses on the statue itself. The size and realism of the statue makes it a masterpiece of classical Roman sculpture.

An example will make textual rhetorical analysis clearer. Let's look at the "Statement on the Articles of Impeachment" by Barbara Jordan at the end of this chapter, and at the student rhetorical analysis that follows it (pp. 73–80). In this chapter we use the fundamental concepts of rhetoric to better understand the presentation by Barbara Jordan.

Jordan's purpose and argument

What is the purpose of Jordan's speech? She presented it over forty years ago, but it remains compellingly readable because it concerns a perennial (and very contemporary) American issue: the limits of presidential power. In this case, Jordan argues in favor of bringing articles of impeachment against President Richard Nixon. She feels that the drastic step of impeachment is called for because President Nixon had violated the Constitution. Essentially, Jordan's argument comes down to this: Nixon, like any abuser of the Constitution, should be removed from office because he has been guilty of causing "the dimunition, the subversion, the destruction, of the Constitution" (para. 3 of Jordan's speech). The Founders of the nation established clear grounds for impeachment, and Nixon trespassed on those grounds by covering up crimes and by stonewalling efforts to investigate misdeeds. He "committed offenses, and planned and directed and acquiesced in a course of conduct which the Constitution will not tolerate" (para. 20). Jordan's speech amounts to a

A contextual analysis focuses on the surroundings and history of the statue. According to legend, Castor (left of staircase) and his twin brother Pollux (right of staircase), the mythical sons of Leda, assisted Romans in an early battle. Romans built a large temple in the Forum to honor them. The statues were discovered in the sixteenth century and in 1583 were brought to stand at the top of the Cordonata, a staircase designed by Michelangelo as part of a renovation of the Piazza del Campidoglio commissioned by Pope Paul III Farnese in 1536.

definition of impeachment in general, based on the Constitution, which then calls for President Nixon's impeachment in particular. And she supports that overall argument with logical, emotional, and ethical appeals—logos, pathos, and ethos.

Logos

Jordan constructs her case in favor of impeachment through a carefully reasoned process. She begins by presenting a patient account of the meaning of impeachment as it appears in the Constitution, on which her "faith is whole; it is complete; it is total" (para. 3). The Constitution defines impeachment not as conviction but as a kind of indictment of a president for misconduct; once a president is impeached, a trial then follows, conducted by the House of Representatives and judged by the Senate. Only after conviction by two-thirds of the senators, after a fair trial, could the president be removed. (President Clinton was impeached while in office, but the Senate found him not guilty.) The Constitution offers grounds for impeachment only on very general terms: Article III, section 4, explains that presidents can be removed from office for treason, bribery, or other high crimes and misdemeanors.

Do Nixon's actions qualify as impeachable? Jordan must refer to the statements that the Founders made during the ratification process for the Constitution to lay out exactly what might be considered an impeachable high crime. After a lengthy explanation of what qualifies as impeachable—"the misconduct of public men" only in "occasional and extraordinary cases," and only "if the President be connected in any suspicious manner with any person and there [are] grounds to believe he will shelter him," and only if there are "great misdemeanors" and not simple "maladministration"—she then applies the definition to Nixon's actions. Carefully and systematically she offers the evidence. She ties "misconduct," the cover-up of crimes, and the sanctioning of other misdeeds to Nixon: "the President had knowledge that these funds were being paid" (para. 15); he consorted with a range of suspicious characters and "knew about the break-in of the psychiatrist's office" (para. 16); and he "engaged in a series of public statements and actions designed to thwart the lawful investigation of government prosecutors" (para. 17). The conclusion follows rationally and inevitably. The president must be impeached.

Pathos

The logical appeals in Jordan's speech are reinforced by her emotional appeals. Her repeated references to the Constitution have a strong emotional appeal. Because Americans have a deep respect for the Constitution, any attempt to undermine it must be resisted firmly and forcefully.

Perhaps the speech's most powerful emotional moment comes in the second paragraph. By bringing up the famous "We the people" opening of the Constitution early in the speech, Jordan rouses passions and brings listeners to her side. She calls attention to how she as an African American woman was originally left out of the Constitution because it defined citizens only as white males. The appeal to fair play certainly rouses emotions in her listeners; it gains considerable sympathy for Jordan.

You can probably note many other points in the speech that carry an emotional dimension. Jordan concludes her speech by rightly saying that "it is reason, and not passion, which must guide our deliberations, guide our debate, and guide our decision." But she also brings considerable pathos to bear on her argument. Jordan appeals to the whole person.

Ethos

Why do we take Jordan's word about the legal precedents and evidence that she cites? It is because she establishes her ethos, or trustworthiness, early in the essay and sustains it throughout. Jordan's scholarship establishes her credibility as a lawyer and as a citizen. Jordan comes through as a thorough professional, as an educated lawyer who has studied constitutional law and has done her homework, and as a deeply concerned citizen. Consequently, we can trust her word and trust her judgment. Particularly effective is her citation of the historical record on impeachment.

She has sifted the records to draw from the most respected of the framers of the Constitution—notably James Madison—and from authorities later in our national history. She buttresses her trustworthiness in other ways too:

- She quotes widely, if unobtrusively: by using precise quotations, she adds a trustworthy scholarly dimension to her presentation.
- She touches lightly on her own status as an African American woman to lend firsthand authority to what she has to say.
- She demonstrates a knowledge of history and constitutional law.
- She connects herself to America generally by linking herself to traditional American values such as freedom, ethnic pride, fair play, and tolerance.

Jordan knew that Nixon's supporters were depending on being able to make the case against Nixon into a partisan matter, Democrats vs. Republicans. So in her speech Jordan goes to great lengths to avoid being placed in a partisan camp and to be regarded as fair-minded. Overall, she comes off as hard-working, honest, educated and patriotic. And definitely credible.

Jordan's arrangement

We have already said some things about the arrangement of Jordan's speech. We especially noted how the overall structure follows the pattern of most definition arguments: Jordan offers her definition of impeachment and then in the final third of the talk applies that definition to the case of Richard Nixon. Note how she begins with an introductory comment about her personal situation; the tone of the first few sentences is light hearted as she offers gentle humor to "Mr. Chairman." And then she turns to a personal anecdote about her being left out of the Constitution "by mistake." In many ways, then, Jordan organizes very conventionally—she has a clear beginning, middle, and end.

And yet in other ways the arrangement is not so conventional. Rather than sticking with a light tone, Jordan turns deadly serious in paragraph 3. In the manner of a lawyer stating a legal case, a lawyer offering a final argument after evidence has been heard, she announces that her presentation will be based solely on constitutional law, and she then follows with point after point of a formal legal brief in favor of impeachment. Note that Jordan does not announce her conclusion early; just as if she were addressing a jury, she postpones her thesis ("If the impeachment provision in the Constitution will not reach the offenses charged here, then perhaps that 18th-century Constitution should be abandoned to a 20th-century paper shredder": para. 19) until the very end. Had she begun with such an explicit statement of her thesis, had she begun by stating her conclusion early, her speech might have been dismissed as a partisan speech and not a legal case.

Jordan's style

What about Jordan's style? How is it appropriate to her purposes? Would you describe it as "lawyerly" or not?

In one sense, Jordan speaks very much as a lawyer would speak to other lawyers. Her fourth paragraph, for example, consists solely of legal language—so legal that it is difficult for a layperson to understand where these quotations come from and what they mean. And further quotations from law cases show up as the speech continues. It is as if Jordan is addressing lawyers because she repeatedly uses legal terminology: "proceed forthwith"; "obfuscation"; "the powers relating to impeachment are an essential check in the hands of the body of the legislature against and upon the encroachments of the executive"; "the framers confided in the Congress the power, if need be, to remove the President"; "a narrowly channeled exception to the separation-of-powers maxim"; and so on.

And yet in another sense, Jordan is speaking in an accessible way to a larger audience of all Americans. Rather than sustaining the legal language, she speaks in simple sentences and simple cadences from beginning to the very end—from "Today I am an inquisitor. . . . My faith in the Constitution is whole; it is complete; it is total" to "That's the question. We know that. We know the question. . . . It is reason, not passion, which must guide our deliberations, guide our debate, and guide our decision." Whenever legal jargon threatens to take over, Jordan returns to everyday language accessible to all: "The Constitution doesn't say that"; "they [the framers] did not make the accusers and the judgers the same person"; "we are trying to be big because the task before us is a big one"; "we know the nature of impeachment. We've been talking of it awhile now." In sum, Jordan's style is in keeping with her ethos. Because she wishes to come off as both a concerned citizen and a legal expert, she chooses a style that is one part newspaper reporting—simple, straightforward, unadorned (in one spot she even misspeaks, substituting "attended" for "intended")—and one part legal brief, technical and jargony, full of convolutions and qualifications.

There is more to say about the rhetorical choices that Jordan made in crafting her "Statement on the Articles of Impeachment," but this analysis is enough to illustrate our main point. Textual rhetorical analysis employs rhetorical terminology—in this case, terms borrowed from the rhetorical tradition such as ethos, pathos, logos, arrangement, style, and tone—as a way of helping us to understand how a writer makes choices to achieve certain effects. And textual analysis cooperates with contextual analysis.

Analyze the Rhetorical Context

Communication as conversation

Notice that in the previous discussion, the fact that Barbara Jordan's "Statement on the Articles of Impeachment" was originally delivered before the House Judiciary Committee did not matter much. Nor did it matter when the speech was published

(July 24, 1974), who gave it, who exactly heard the speech, what their reactions were, or what other people were saying at the time. Textual analysis can proceed as if the item under consideration "speaks for all time," as if it is a museum piece unaffected by time and space. There's nothing wrong with museums, of course; they permit people to observe and appreciate objects in an important way. But museums often fail to reproduce an artwork's original context and cultural meaning. In that sense, museums can diminish understanding as much as they contribute to it. Contextual rhetorical analysis is an attempt to understand communications through the lens of their environments, examining the rough-and-tumble, real-world setting or scene out of which any communication emerges. Contextual analysis thus complements textual analysis; the two work together.

Contextual analysis, like textual analysis, may be conducted in any number of ways. But contextual rhetorical analysis always proceeds from a description of the **rhetorical situation** that motivated the event in question. It demands an appreciation of the social circumstances that call rhetorical events into being and that orchestrate the course of those events. It regards communications as anything but self-contained.

- Every communication is a response to other communications and to other social practices.
- Communications, and social practices more generally, reflect the attitudes and values of the living communities that sustain them.
- Analysts seek evidence of how those other communications and social practices are reflected in texts.

Rhetorical analysis from a contextualist perspective understands individual pieces as parts of ongoing conversations.

The challenge is to reconstruct the conversation surrounding a specific piece of writing or speaking. Sometimes it is easy to do so. For example, sometimes there are obvious references to the context in the very words of an argument. Or sometimes you may have appropriate background information on the topic, as well as a feel for what is behind what people are writing or saying about it. People who have strong feelings these days about the environment, stem cell research, college sports, or any number of other current issues are well informed about the arguments that are converging around those topics.

But other times it takes some research to reconstruct the conversations and social practices related to a particular issue. If the issue is current, you need to study how the debate is conducted in current blogs, magazines, newspapers, talk shows, movies and TV shows, Web sites, and so forth. If the issue is from an earlier time, you must do archival research into historical collections of newspapers, magazines, books, letters, and other documentary sources in order to develop a feel for the rhetorical situation that generated the argument under analysis. Archival research usually involves libraries, special research collections, or film and television archives where it is possible to learn quite a bit about context.

Let's return now to a discussion of Jordan's "Statement" on pages 73–76. With a bit of research it is possible to reconstruct some of the "conversations" that Jordan was participating in, and the result will be an enhanced understanding of her speech as well as an appreciation for how you might do a contextual rhetorical analysis yourself. As you will see, contextual analysis will permit you to understand the challenge that any writer or speaker was facing so that you can then discover what strategies and tactics were used in order to meet that challenge. What issues and questions were swirling about in the minds of the audience members when Jordan spoke, and how did she address those issues and questions?

Jordan's life and works

You can begin by learning more about Jordan herself because ethos is not simply a textual presence; ethos also can be something that a writer or speaker brings to a performance. The headnote to her speech on page 73 "Statement on the Articles of Impeachment" provides some facts about her (e.g., that she was African American, that she went to law school, that she was elected to the U.S. House of Representatives at the age of just 36; that she came to prominence during the Watergate hearings). The speech itself suggests a few additional details: that protecting the Constitution was a special passion of hers, and that she had a reputation for doing her homework. You can learn more about Jordan by using the Internet and your library's Web site. Jordan's credibility, her ethos, is established not just by the decisions she made within her speech but also by her prior reputation.

Perhaps the most relevant information concerning Jordan that is available online is about her early political career. Jordan was a relative unknown when she gave her speech; even her colleagues in Congress did not know her well. She had recently been elected to Congress as a young woman in part because of the support of Lyndon Johnson, a fellow Texan who preceded Richard Nixon as president. Johnson then advocated for her placement on the House Judiciary Committee, chaired by Democrat Peter Rodino of New Jersey; this was a highly prized, prestigious appointment that rarely goes to someone new. Thus Jordan came to her speech with a reputation as being beholden to Johnson and the Democratic party. Her challenge therefore was to avoid the appearance of partisanship—as we will show below, that explains many of her rhetorical choices. Then again, few Americans outside Washington and Texas knew of her reputation. She essentially delivered her speech to the nation and to her congressional colleagues as a relative unknown. (Incidentally, Jordan continued to serve in Congress until 1978, when she stepped down voluntarily, for health reasons.)

The context of the speech

In one sense, the audience of Jordan's speech consisted of the other thirty-four members of the House Judiciary Committee, gathered together to decide whether or not to recommend impeachment. And yet Jordan was not at all speaking to a closed committee meeting. Her speech was heard by a national audience watching on television.

The Senate Watergate hearings had been televised the summer before Jordan's speech, from May through July of 1973. Millions of Americans had become accustomed to watching sensational testimony presented by a host of witnesses. The hearings produced charges that President Nixon may well have authorized break-ins at Democratic campaign headquarters in Washington during the 1972 election season, that he and members of his leadership team covered up their sponsorship of the break-ins, and that the White House was involved in all sorts of other dirty tricks and improprieties.

Americans remained deeply divided about these accusations until it was discovered that Nixon had himself collected possible hard evidence. He had taped many conversations in the Oval Office, tapes that could support or refute the charges against the president. But for the next year, Nixon engaged in a protracted legal battle to keep the tapes from being disclosed, on the grounds that they were private conversations protected under "executive privilege." During that time Nixon's vice president, Spiro Agnew, was forced to resign, and a number of his advisers were indicted and convicted on charges of obstructing justice. Partial and edited transcripts of the tapes were produced sporadically by the president, under pressure, but those produced only further rancor, particularly when eighteen minutes of a key conversation were mysteriously erased.

These events created a continuing national uproar and sustained headlines that fueled discussion. The House Judiciary Committee opened hearings into whether the president should be impeached beginning on May 9 of 1974. Those closed meetings moved slowly, deliberately, and inconclusively through the entire summer. On July 24, 1974, the courts ruled that Nixon had to turn over all his remaining tapes. That same day, knowing that hard evidence was now at hand, the House Judiciary Committee immediately went into session to vote whether to impeach Nixon. In keeping with the Senate Watergate hearings, these sessions were open and televised to the nation. Each member of the committee was given fifteen minutes to make an opening statement that would be carried on television to the nation. Barbara Jordan was therefore speaking not just to congressional colleagues but to millions of citizens who had never heard of her but who were very interested in what she would have to say.

Jordan was scheduled to speak at 9 p.m.—prime time. The nation was ready to listen to her argument, and she was ready to deliver: she would call for impeachment, and she would do so in a way that was absolutely principled and nonpartisan.

The larger conversation

We could offer much more contextualizing background here. We could cite a host of articles, books, news reports, and TV broadcasts in order to establish the nature of the conversation about impeachment that was raging in the nation from the summer of 1973 until President Nixon finally resigned on August 8, 1974. Such an account would establish a rather simple point: The country was bitterly divided on three related issues.

The first was a question of partisanship. His fellow Republicans naturally gave the benefit of the doubt to President Nixon, and that benefit was quite considerable, given that Nixon had won the 1972 election over George McGovern in a landslide. By contrast, Democrats controlled the Senate and the House of Representatives, and they were aggressive in pursuing a case against the president because they stood to gain politically. (Indeed, Jimmy Carter would win the presidency in the 1976 election largely because he stood as an honest anti-dote to the scandal of Watergate.) But partisanship was not supposed to be an issue in an impeachment. When Andrew Johnson was impeached by the House during 1867–1868 (and narrowly acquitted by the Senate), it was apparent that his impeachment was politically motivated. In subsequent years, it therefore was understood that impeachment should never be partisan, should never be politically motivated but based on "treason, bribery, or high crimes and misdemeanors." In the weeks leading up to July 24, supporters of President Nixon, led by his lawyer James D. St. Clair, constantly charged that his adversaries were motivated by purely political purposes. Representative David Dennis of Indiana spoke explicitly of "a political lynching," Representative Charles Sandman of New Jersey and other Republicans had emphasized partisanship earlier in the day during their own 15-minute presentations, and millions of average citizens also suspected that opponents of Nixon wanted to remove him simply to gain political power. On a practical level, since Nixon could be convicted in the Senate only by a two-thirds majority, it was essential that some Republicans come to support conviction. A purely partisan vote—Democratic vs. Republicans—could not succeed.

Barbara Jordan's task was therefore formidable. She had to take the majority, Democratic position—without seeming to take it *because* she was a Democrat. And she had to do so even though she was indeed a committed Democrat, recently installed in part through the intercession of Lyndon Johnson and embodying her Democratic credentials because of her black skin. (Nixon had swept the Southern states in the 1972 election in part because he appealed directly to white voters there.) If you scan issues of *Newsweek*, *Time*, the *Washington Post*, or the *New York Times* from the summer of 1974, you will see how frequently the Republicans were claiming that President Nixon was the victim of a "partisan vendetta." It was the strategy of his defense team to do so. By contrast, Democrats needed to get at least a half-dozen Republican members of the House Judiciary Committee to support impeachment if the actual impeachment were to succeed in the Senate.

Jordan consequently adopted a number of tactics to establish her nonpartisanship. She begins by identifying herself as a youthful, junior member of the committee, not a Democratic member, and quickly follows by claiming particular and fervent allegiance to the Constitution, not to any political party. Speaking as a custodian of "the public trust," she quotes the Constitution, its framers, and respected authorities such as Alexander Hamilton, Woodrow Wilson, James Madison of them southerners—and avoids names with a partisan identification. And she consistently and frequently uses the pronoun *we* to refer to the entire committee, Republicans and Democrats alike. In all these ways Jordan sought to address the nation on nonpartisan grounds. (And she must have succeeded: over the next three days, when the House Judiciary Committee voted in favor of three articles of impeachment—obstruction of justice, abuse of presidential power, and contempt of Congress—six of the seventeen Republican committee members voted in favor of the first, six in favor of the second, and two supported the third article. Only ten of the seventeen Republicans opposed all three articles.)

The second concern in the nation on July 24, 1974, was about hard evidence. The president's former lawyer, John Dean, had accused Nixon of obstructing justice and conspiring to give hush money to Watergate burglars; Watergate gangster Charles Colson at his sentencing hearing had recently claimed that the president obstructed justice; and many other charges had been raised. But supporting evidence was seen as circumstantial; it all appeared to be the president's word against the word of others. The conversation swirling around Barbara Jordan, therefore, was very much concerned with hard evidence, or a so-called "murder weapon" or "smoking gun." Supporters of the president, including Representatives Trent Lott and Charles Wiggins on the Judiciary Committee, constantly claimed that while the charges against Nixon were serious, they were not corroborated by irrefutable evidence. (This claim was ultimately addressed by the tapes that Nixon had collected: earlier on the very day that Jordan spoke, the Supreme Court in an 8–0 vote demanded that Nixon turn over sixty-four tapes to investigators, and those tapes provided the damning evidence that finally brought Nixon to resign two weeks later. The Supreme Court decision is alluded to in the first sentence of paragraph 13, when Jordan mentions the "new evidence that would be forthcoming" because of what happened "today.")

In her speech, Jordan addresses the evidence question explicitly, beginning in paragraph 11: "we were told that the evidence which purports to support the allegations . . . is thin . . . [and] insufficient." The paragraphs that follow rehearse hard evidence already established—evidence about the break-ins and other crimes committed by Howard Hunt as well as payments to Hunt; evidence about the payment of hush money (para. 15); evidence cited in paragraphs 16 and 17, including that "the President has made public announcements and assertions bearing on the Watergate case which . . . he knew to be false." The emphasis on evidence in Jordan's speech definitely derives from the conversations that she was enmeshed in during July 1974.

The third national concern that Jordan addressed in her speech had to do with a legal issue, one that as a lawyer Jordan was especially qualified to address: Were the actions of President Nixon serious enough to be "impeachable offenses"? As the evidence of presidential wrongdoing piled up, many Americans could see that Nixon had committed all sorts of transgressions. But were they serious enough to justify impeachment? Everyone agreed that if the president had committed a felony, he should be removed; but what about lesser offenses—how high did a crime have to reach in order to be a "high crime," and what "misdemeanors" justified impeachment? As we have already shown in our textual analysis, Jordan in paragraph 6 defines the circumstances of impeachment by quoting the framers of the Constitution directly, and in paragraph 7 concedes that a president should not be removed for incompetence (i.e., "maladministration"). The following paragraphs indicate that public officials should not be removed for "petty reasons" but only for "the grossest offenses." By agreeing that a president should be removed only for very serious offenses, and by establishing that there was indeed hard evidence of the president's guilt in serious offenses, Jordan in just ten or twelve minutes summed up for the nation the case for impeachment. And as we have seen, she did it in a language that was convincing both to her congressional colleagues and to the millions of citizens watching at home.

Barbara Jordan's specific contribution to the conversation about impeachment in 1974 could be extended for a long time—indefinitely, in fact. There is no need to belabor the point, however; our purpose has been simply to illustrate that contextual analysis of a piece of rhetoric can enrich our understanding of it.

Write a Rhetorical Analysis

Effective rhetorical analysis, as we have seen, can be textual or contextual in nature. But we should emphasize again that these two approaches to rhetorical analysis are not mutually exclusive. Indeed, many if not most analysts operate between these two extremes; they consider the details of the text, but they also attend to the particulars of context. Textual analysis and contextual analysis inevitably complement each other. Getting at what is at stake in Barbara Jordan's speech on impeachment or any other sophisticated argument takes patience and intelligence. Rhetorical analysis, as a way of understanding how people argue, is both enlightening and challenging.

Try to use elements of both kinds of analysis whenever you want to understand a rhetorical event more fully. Rhetoric is "inside" texts, but it is also "outside" them: specific rhetorical performances are an irreducible mixture of text and context, and so interpretation and analysis of those performances must account for both text and context. Remember, however, the limitations of your analysis. Realize that your analysis will always be somewhat partial and incomplete, ready to be deepened, corrected, modified, and extended by the insights of others. Rhetorical analysis can itself be part of an unending conversation—a way of learning and teaching within a community.

Steps to Writing a Rhetorical Analysis

Step 1 Select an Argument to Analyze

Find an argument to analyze—a speech or sermon, an op-ed in a newspaper, an ad in a magazine designed for a particular audience, or a commentary on a talk show.

Examples

- Editorial pages of newspapers (but not letters to the editor unless you can find a long and detailed letter)
- Opinion features in magazines such as *Time*, *Newsweek*, and *U.S. News & World Report*
- Magazines that take political positions such as *National Review*, *Mother Jones*, *New Republic*, *Nation*, and *Slate*
- Web sites of activist organizations (but not blog or newsgroup postings unless they are long and detailed)

Step 2 Analyze the Context

Who is the author?

Through research in the library or on the Web, learn all you can about the author.

- How does the argument you are analyzing repeat arguments previously made by the author?
- What motivated the author to write? What is the author's purpose for writing this argument?

Who is the audience?

Through research, learn all you can about the publication and the audience.

- Who is the anticipated audience?
- How do the occasion and forum for writing affect the argument?

What is the larger conversation?

Through research, find out what else was being said about the subject of your selection. Track down any references made in the text you are examining.

- When did the argument appear?
- What other concurrent pieces within the "cultural conversation" (e.g., TV shows, other articles, speeches, Web sites) does the item you are analyzing respond to or "answer"?
- Think of the author of the item you are analyzing as facing a "challenge": what difficulties does the author have to overcome in order to persuade his or her audience?

Step 3 Analyze the Text

Summarize the argument

- What is the main claim?
- What reasons are given in support of the claim?

- How is the argument organized? What are the components, and why are they presented in that order?

What is the medium and genre?

- What is the medium? A newspaper? a scholarly journal? a Web site?
- What is the genre? An editorial? an essay? a speech? an advertisement? What expectations does the audience have about this genre?

What appeals are used?

- Analyze the ethos. How does the writer represent himself or herself? Does the writer have any credentials as an authority on the topic? How does the writer establish reliability and trust—or fail to do so?
- Analyze the logos. Where do you find facts and evidence in the argument? What kinds of facts and evidence does the writer present? Direct observation? statistics? interviews? surveys? quotations from authorities?
- Analyze the pathos. Does the writer attempt to invoke an emotional response? Where do you find appeals to important shared values?

How would you characterize the style?

- Is the style formal, informal, satirical, or something else?
- Are any metaphors or other rhetorical figures used?

Step 4 Write a Draft

Introduction

- Describe briefly the argument you are analyzing, including where it was published, how long it is, and who wrote it.
- If the argument is about an issue unfamiliar to your readers, supply the necessary background.

Body

- Analyze the context, following Step 2.
- Analyze the text, following Step 3.

Conclusion

- Do more than simply summarize what you have said. You might, for example, end with an example that typifies the argument.
- You don't have to end by either agreeing or disagreeing with the writer. Your task in this assignment is to analyze the strategies the writer uses.

Step 5 Revise, Edit, Proofread

For detailed instructions, see Chapter 5.
For a checklist to evaluate your draft, see pages 50–51.

Barbara Jordan

Statement on the Articles of Impeachment

Barbara Jordan (1936–1996) grew up in Houston and received a law degree from Boston University in 1959. Working on John F. Kennedy's 1960 presidential campaign stirred an interest in politics, and in 1966 Jordon became the first African American woman elected to the Texas State Senate. In 1972 she was elected to the United States House of Representatives and thus became the first African American woman from the South ever to serve in Congress. Jordan was appointed to the House Judiciary Committee. Soon she was in the national spotlight when that committee considered articles of impeachment against President Richard Nixon, who had illegally covered up a burglary of Democratic Party headquarters during the 1972 election. When Nixon's criminal acts reached the Judiciary Committee, Jordan's opening speech on July 24, 1974, set the tone for the debate and established her reputation as a moral beacon for the nation. Nixon resigned as president on August 9, 1974, when it was evident that he would be impeached.

Thank you, Mr. Chairman.
Mr. Chairman, I join my colleague Mr. Rangel in thanking you for giving the junior members of this committee the glorious opportunity of sharing the pain of this inquiry. Mr. Chairman, you are a strong man and it has not been easy, but we have tried as best we can to give you as much assistance as possible.

2   Earlier today, we heard the beginning of the Preamble to the Constitution of the United States: "We, the people." It's a very eloquent beginning. But when that document was completed on the seventeenth of September in 1787, I was not included in that, the people." I felt somehow for many years that George Washington and Alexander Hamilton just left me out by mistake. But through the process of amendment, interpretation, and court decision, I have finally been included in "We, the people."

3   Today I am an inquisitor. Any hyperbole would not be fictional and would not overstate the solemnness that I feel right now. My faith in the Constitution is whole; it is complete; it is total. And I am not going to sit here and be an idle spectator to the diminution, the subversion, the destruction, of the Constitution.

4   "Who can so properly be the inquisitors for the nation as the representatives of the nation themselves?" "The subjects of its jurisdiction are those offenses which proceed from the misconduct of public men." And that's what we're talking about. In other words, [the jurisdiction comes] from the abuse or violation of some public trust.

5   It is wrong, I suggest, it is a misreading of the Constitution for any member here to assert that for a member to vote for an article of impeachment means that that member must be convinced that the President should be removed from office. The Constitution doesn't say that. The powers relating to impeachment are an essential check in the hands of the body of the legislature against and upon the encroachments of the executive. [By creating] the division between the two branches of the legislature, the House and the Senate, assigning to the one the right to accuse and to the other the right to judge, the framers of this Constitution were very astute. They did not make the accusers and the judgers the same person.

6   We know the nature of impeachment. We've been talking about it awhile now. It is chiefly designed for the President and his high ministers to somehow be called into account. It is designed to "bridle" the executive if he engages in excesses. "It is designed as a method of national inquest into the conduct of public men." The framers confided in the Congress the power, if need be, to remove the President in order to strike a delicate balance between a President swollen with power and grown tyrannical, and preservation of the independence of the executive.

7   The nature of impeachment: [it is] a narrowly channeled exception to the separation-of-powers maxim. The Federal Convention of 1787 said that. It limited impeachment to high crimes and misdemeanors and discounted and opposed the term *maladministration*. "It is to be used only for great misdemeanors," so it was said in the North Carolina ratification convention. And in the Virginia ratification convention: "We do not trust our liberty to a particular branch. We need one branch to check the other."

8   "No one need be afraid"—the North Carolina ratification convention—"No one need be afraid that officers who commit oppression will pass with immunity." "Prosecutions of impeachments will seldom fail to agitate the passions of the whole community," said Hamilton in the Federalist Papers, number 65. "We divide into parties more or less friendly or inimical to the accused." I do not mean political parties in that sense.

9   The drawing of political lines goes to the motivation behind impeachment; but impeachment must proceed within the confines of the constitutional term "high crime[s] and misdemeanors." Of the impeachment process, it was Woodrow Wilson who said that "Nothing short of the grossest offenses against the plain law of the land will suffice to give them speed and effectiveness. Indignation so great as to overgrow party interest may secure a conviction; but nothing else can."

10   Common sense would be revolted if we engaged upon this process for petty reasons. Congress has a lot to do: Appropriations, Tax Reform, Health Insurance, Campaign Finance Reform, Housing, Environmental Protection, Energy Sufficiency, Mass Transportation. Pettiness cannot be allowed to stand in the face of such overwhelming problems. So today we are not being petty. We are trying to be big, because the task we have before us is a big one.

11   This morning, in a discussion of the evidence, we were told that the evidence which purports to support the allegations of misuse of the CIA by the President is thin.

We're told that that evidence is insufficient. What that recital of the evidence this morning did not include is what the President did know on June the 23rd, 1972.

12   The President did know that it was Republican money, that it was money from the Committee for the Re-Election of the President, which was found in the possession of one of the burglars arrested on June the 17th. What the President did know on the 23rd of June was the prior activities of E. Howard Hunt, which included his participation in the break-in of Daniel Ellsberg's psychiatrist, which included Howard Hunt's participation in the Dita Beard ITT affair, which included Howard Hunt's fabrication of cables designed to discredit the Kennedy Administration.

13   We were further cautioned today that perhaps these proceedings ought to be delayed because certainly there would be new evidence forthcoming from the President of the United States. There has not even been an obfuscated indication that this committee would receive any additional materials from the President. The committee subpoena is outstanding, and if the President wants to supply that material, the committee sits here. The fact is that only yesterday, the American people waited with great anxiety for eight hours, not knowing whether their President would obey an order of the Supreme Court of the United States.

14   At this point, I would like to juxtapose a few of the impeachment criteria with some of the actions the President has engaged in. Impeachment criteria: James Madison, from the Virginia ratification convention: "If the President be connected in any suspicious manner with any person and there be grounds to believe that he will shelter him, he may be impeached."

15   We have heard time and time again that the evidence reflects the payment to the defendants of money. The President had knowledge that these funds were being paid and these were funds collected for the 1972 presidential campaign. We know that the President met with Mr. Henry Petersen 27 times to discuss matters related to Watergate, and immediately thereafter met with the very persons who were implicated in the information Mr. Petersen was receiving. The words are: "If the President is connected in any suspicious manner with any person and there be grounds to believe that he will shelter that person, he may be impeached."

16   Justice Story: "Impeachment is intended for occasional and extraordinary cases where a superior power acting for the whole people is put into operation to protect their rights and rescue their liberties from violations." We know about the Huston plan. We know about the break-in of the psychiatrist's office. We know that there was absolute complete direction on September 3rd when the President indicated that a surreptitious entry had been made in Dr. Fielding's office, after having met with Mr. Ehrlichman and Mr. Young. "Protect their rights." "Rescue their liberties from violation."

17   The Carolina ratification convention impeachment criteria: those are impeachable "who behave amiss or betray their public trust." Beginning shortly after the Watergate break-in and continuing to the present time, the President has engaged in a series of public statements and actions designed to thwart the lawful investigation by government prosecutors. Moreover, the President has made public announcements and assertions bearing on the Watergate case, which the evidence will show he knew to be false. These assertions, false assertions, impeachable, those who misbehave. Those who "behave amiss or betray the public trust."

18   James Madison again at the Constitutional Convention: "A President is impeachable if he attempts to subvert the Constitution." The Constitution charges the President
with the task of taking care that the laws be faithfully executed, and yet the President
has counseled his aides to commit perjury, willfully disregard the secrecy of grand jury
proceedings, conceal surreptitious entry, attempt to compromise a federal judge, while
publicly displaying his cooperation with the processes of criminal justice. "A President is
impeachable if he attempts to subvert the Constitution."

19   If the impeachment provision in the Constitution of the United States will not
reach the offenses charged here, then perhaps that 18th-century Constitution should
be abandoned to a 20th-century paper shredder.

20   Has the President committed offenses, and planned, and directed, and acquiesced in a course of conduct which the Constitution will not tolerate? That's the question. We know that. We know the question. We should now forthwith proceed to answer
the question. It is reason, and not passion, which must guide our deliberations, guide
our debate, and guide our decision.

21   I yield back the balance of my time, Mr. Chairman.

Sample Student Rhetorical Analysis

Jackson 1

T. Jonathan Jackson

Dr. Netaji

English 1102

11 October 2013

An Argument of Reason and Passion: Barbara Jordan's
"Statement on the Articles of Impeachment"

Barbara Jordan's July 24, 1974 speech before the U.S. House Judiciary Committee helped convince the House of Representatives, and the American public, that President Richard Nixon should be impeached. Nixon was under investigation for his role in the cover-up of the Watergate scandal. He knew about the burglary of Democratic Party headquarters, but denied having any knowledge of it and illegally shielded those responsible. Jordan used her speech to argue that the president should be impeached because his actions threatened the Constitution and the people of the United States; however, Jordan never explicitly states this position in her speech. Instead, she establishes her credibility and then uses logic to set out the evidence against the president.

> Jackson provides background information in the first paragraph and his thesis at the end.

In one sense, the audience of Jordan's speech consisted of the other 34 members of the House Judiciary Committee, gathered together to decide whether or not to recommend impeachment. And yet Jordan was not speaking just to a committee meeting; her speech was very public.

The Senate Watergate hearings had been televised during the months before her speech, and millions of Americans watched sensational testimony by a host of witnesses. The Senate hearings produced charges that Nixon authorized break-ins at Democratic campaign headquarters in Washington during the 1972 election and that the White House was involved in many political dirty tricks and improprieties.

But the accusations remained only accusations—and Americans remained deeply divided about them—until it was discovered that Nixon had himself collected possible hard evidence: he had taped many conversations in the Oval Office, tapes that could support or refute the charges against the president. Nixon engaged in a protracted legal battle to keep the tapes from being disclosed, on the grounds that they were private

Jackson 2

conversations protected under "executive privilege," and he released only partial and edited transcripts. Finally on July 24, 1974, the courts ruled that Nixon had to turn all his remaining tapes over. That same day, knowing that hard evidence was now at hand, the House Judiciary Committee immediately went into session to vote whether to impeach Nixon. Each member of the committee was given fifteen minutes for an opening statement.

Nixon was a Republican and Jordan, like the majority of the committee, was a Democrat. Jordan had to convince her audience she was not biased against the president simply because of her party affiliation. Jordan was also new to Congress, relatively unknown outside of Texas, and a low-ranking member of the committee. Consequently, she had to establish her ethos to the committee as well as to the television audience. She had to present herself as fair, knowledgeable, and intellectually mature.

> Jackson observes that Jordan had a formidable assignment in establishing her ethos in a short speech.

At the heart of Jordan's argument is her faith in the Constitution. She begins her speech from a personal perspective, pointing out that the Constitution is not perfect because it originally excluded African Americans like her. But now that the Constitution recognizes her as a citizen, Jordan says, her faith in it "is whole; it is complete; it is total." She even implies that, as a citizen, she has a moral duty to protect the Constitution, saying, "I am not going to sit here and be an idle spectator to the diminution, the subversion, the destruction of the Constitution." Jordan's emotional connection to the Constitution shows the audience that she is motivated by a love of her country, not by party loyalty. She establishes herself as someone fighting to defend and protect American values.

> Jackson analyzes how Jordan's fervent allegiance to the Constitution made her appear unbiased.

Jordan describes the Constitution as the accepted authority on the laws related to impeachment. She shows the audience how the Constitution gives her the authority to act as an "inquisitor," or judge. She depicts the Constitution and the American people as potential victims, and the president as the potential criminal. She warns of the need to remove "a President swollen with power and grown tyrannical."

The appeals to pathos and ethos in the opening of the speech establish Jordan's motivations and credibility, allowing her to next lay out her logical arguments. Jordan proceeds to explain how the Constitution defines impeachment, and she fleshes out this brief definition with

Jackson 3

evidence from several state Constitutional Conventions. She also quotes Supreme Court Justice Joseph Story. Using evidence from the North Carolina and Virginia Constitutional Conventions, Jordan shows that impeachment was intended only for "great misdemeanors," and that the branches of government were intended to act as a check upon one another.

Next Jordan uses quotations from James Madison, Justice Story, and others to define impeachable offenses. For each offense, Jordan provides an example of an act that President Nixon was known to have committed, and she shows how his actions meet the definition of impeachable offenses. She compares Nixon's meetings with Watergate suspects to Madison's statement that "if the President is connected in any suspicious manner with any person and there be grounds to believe that he will shelter that person, he may be impeached." She pairs Justice Story's statement that impeachment should "protect [citizens'] rights and rescue their liberties from violation" with Nixon's knowledge of the burglary of a private psychiatrist's office. She links Nixon's attempts to bribe a judge and thwart grand jury proceedings with Madison's statement that "a President is impeachable if he attempts to subvert the Constitution."

Throughout this section, Jordan repeats the historical quotes before and after her descriptions of the president's acts. This repetition makes the connections stronger and more memorable for the audience. Jordan also contrasts the formal, high-toned language of the Founders and the Constitution with descriptions that make President Nixon's actions sound sordid and petty: He knew about money "found in the possession of one of the burglars arrested on June the 17th," about "the break-in of Daniel Ellsberg's psychiatrist," about "the fabrication of cables designed to discredit the Kennedy Administration." Words like "burglars," "arrested," "break-in," and "fabrication" sound like evidence in a criminal trial. These words are not the kind of language Americans want to hear describing the actions of their president.

Jordan then adds another emotional appeal, implying that the Constitution is literally under attack. "If the impeachment provisions will not reach the offenses charged here," she says, "then perhaps that 18th-century Constitution should be abandoned to a 20th-century paper

[Jordan uses quotations from respected figures in American history to apply to Nixon's misdeeds.]

[Jordan had to confront a legal issue: Were the actions of President Nixon serious enough to justify impeachment?]

Jackson 4

shredder." This dramatic image encourages the audience to imagine President Nixon shredding the Constitution just as he had destroyed other evidence implicating him in the Watergate scandal. It implies that if the president is not stopped, he will commit further abuses of power. Jordan also makes the American people responsible for this possible outcome, saying that "we" may as well shred the Constitution if it cannot be used to impeach Nixon. This emotional appeal has the effect of shaming those who say they cannot or should not vote for impeachment.

> Jackson notes that the metaphor of the paper shredder adds emotional force.

   Jordan concludes her speech not by calling for impeachment, but by calling for an answer to the question, "Has the President committed offenses, and planned, and directed, and acquiesced in a course of conduct which the Constitution will not tolerate?" It almost seems like Jordan is being humble and trying not to judge by not stating her position outright. However, the reverse is true: Jordan doesn't state her position because she doesn't need to. The evidence she presented led Congress and the American public inescapably to one conclusion: President Nixon had committed impeachable offenses. Just two weeks later, Nixon resigned from office. Jordan had made her point.

> In his conclusion Jackson points out how Jordan shifts the focus to her audience in her conclusion.

Jackson 5

Works Cited

Jordan, Barbara. "Statement on the Articles of Impeachment." *American Rhetoric: Top 100 Speeches*. American Rhetoric, 25 July 1974. Web. 25 Sept. 2013.

7 | Analyzing Visual and Multimedia Arguments

QUICK TAKE

In this chapter, you will learn to

1. Distinguish how visual arguments are similar to and different from verbal arguments (see below)
2. Critically evaluate photos and videos, charts and graphs, and informational graphics used as evidence (see page 85)
3. Evaluate any specific visual argument by analyzing its context and its visual and textual elements (see pages 87–92)
4. Write an effective visual analysis (see page 92)

What Is a Visual Argument?

We live in a world flooded with images. They pull on us, compete for our attention, push us to do things. But how often do we think about how they work?

Can there be an argument without words?

Arguments in written language are visual in one sense: we use our eyes to read the words on the page. But without words, can there be a visual argument? Certainly some visual symbols take on conventional meanings. Signs in airports or other public places, for example, are designed to communicate with speakers of many languages.

Some visual symbols even make explicit claims. A one-way street sign says that drivers should travel only in the one direction. But are such signs arguments? In Chapter 3, we point out that scholars of argument do not believe that everything *is* an argument. Most scholars define an argument as a claim supported by one or more reasons. A one-way sign has a claim: All drivers should go in the same direction. But is there a reason? We all know an unstated reason the sign carries: Drivers who go the wrong way violate the law and risk a substantial fine (plus they risk a head-on collision with other drivers).

Visual arguments require viewer participation

The *Deepwater Horizon* oil spill (also known as the BP oil spill) was the largest off-shore oil spill in the history of the United States. Caused by an explosion on April 20, 2010, the spill dumped millions of gallons of oil every day for months in spite of efforts to contain it. People around the world were reminded of the spill when they turned on their televisions and saw video of the oil gushing from the well, and nearly everyone was outraged.

People interpreted the oil flowing from the pipe quite differently, inferring multiple *because* clauses. Citizens were angry for different reasons.

The *Deepwater Horizon* oil spill was a disaster because

- eleven workers were killed and seventeen were injured.
- enormous harm was done to Gulf wetlands, birds, fish, turtles, marine mammals, and other animals.
- the tourism industry suffered another major blow just five years after Hurricane Katrina.
- the fishing and shrimping industries suffered huge losses.

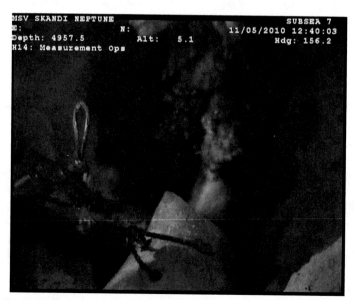

The main oil leak from the *Deepwater Horizon* wellhead.

A photo of this booth at the Taste of Chicago sent on *Twitter* enraged people in New Orleans.

- President Obama declared a moratorium on deep-water drilling, threatening the loss of jobs.
- BP and its partners were negligent in drilling the well.
- the spill was an unfortunate act of God like Hurricane Katrina.

Differing interpretations of visual arguments extended beyond the spill itself. A news producer in Chicago took a photo (above) of a booth at the Taste of Chicago festival and sent it to a friend in New Orleans, who sent it to a food writer, who posted it on *Twitter*. The mayor of New Orleans called it "disgraceful."

Talks shows in both Chicago and New Orleans ranted for a few days about the other city. One comment was perhaps telling about the source of the rage: A menu disclaimer would have been acceptable, but a prominent visual argument, even in text form, was hitting below the belt.

What Is a Multimedia Argument?

Multimedia describes the use of multiple content forms including text, voice and music audio, video, still images, animation, and interactivity. Multimedia goes far back in human history (texts and images were combined at the beginnings of writing), but digital technologies and the Web have made multimedia the fabric of our daily lives. But what exactly are multimedia arguments?

For example, games provide intense multimedia experiences, but are they arguments? Game designers such as Jane McGonigal believe they are arguments. McGonigal maintains that games make people more powerful because they connect them into larger wholes.

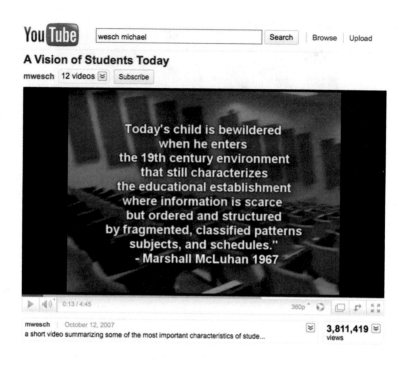

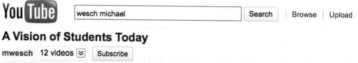

Images from Michael Wesch's *A Vision of Students Today.*

Thousands of multimedia arguments have been posted on *YouTube*. One frequently viewed video is Michael Wesch's *A Vision of Students Today*, posted in October 2007. Wesch's point is that today's education is ill-suited for most students. He enlisted his students to make the point with text and video.

Analyze Visual Evidence

Videos without narration, images, and graphics seldom make arguments on their own, but they are frequently used to support arguments.

Evaluate photographs and videos as evidence

Almost from the beginnings of photography, negatives were manipulated but realistic results required a high skill level. In the digital era anyone can alter photographs. Perhaps there's nothing wrong with using Photoshop to add absent relatives to family photographs or remove ex-boyfriends and ex-girlfriends. But where do you draw the line? Not only do many videos on *YouTube* use outright deception, but newsmagazines and networks have also been found guilty of these practices.

Ask questions about what you view.

- Who created the image or video? What bias might the creator have?
- Who published the image or video? What bias might the publisher have?
- Who is the intended audience? For example, political videos often assume that the viewers hold the same political views as the creators.
- What is being shown, and what is not being shown? For example, a video ad promoting tourism for the Gulf of Mexico will look very different from a video showing sources of pollution.
- Who is being represented, and who is not being represented? Who gets left out is as important as who gets included.

The ease of cropping digital photographs reveals an important truth about photography: A photograph represents reality from a particular viewpoint. A high-resolution picture of a crowd can be divided into many smaller images each of which says something different about the event. The act of pointing the camera in one direction and not in another shapes how photographic evidence will be interpreted. (See the examples on page 86.)

Evaluate charts and graphs

Statistical information is frequently used as evidence in arguments. The problem with giving many statistics in sentence form, however, is that readers shortly lose track of the numbers. Charts and graphs present statistics visually, allowing readers to take in trends and relationships at a glance.

A photographer's choices about whom and what to photograph shape how we see an event.

However, charts and graphs can also be misleading. For example, a chart that compares the amounts of calories in competing brands of cereal might list one with 70 calories and another with 80 calories. If the chart begins at zero, the difference looks small. But if the chart starts at 60, the brand with 80 calories appears to have twice the calories of the brand with 70. Furthermore, the chart is worthless if the data are inaccurate or come from an unreliable source. Creators of charts and graphs have an ethical obligation to present data as fairly and accurately as possible and to provide the sources of the data.

Ask these questions when you are analyzing charts and graphs

- Is the type of chart appropriate for the information presented?

 Bar and column charts make comparisons in particular categories. If two or more charts are compared, the scales should be consistent.

 Line graphs plot variables on a vertical and a horizontal axis. They are useful for showing proportional trends over time.

 Pie charts show the proportion of parts in terms of the whole. Segments must add up to 100 percent of the whole.

- Does the chart have a clear purpose?
- Does the title indicate the purpose?
- What do the units represent (dollars, people, voters, percentages, and so on)?
- What is the source of the data?
- Is there any distortion of information?

Evaluate informational graphics

Informational graphics more sophisticated than standard pie and bar charts have become a popular means of conveying information. Many are interactive, allowing viewers of a Web site to select the information they want displayed. These information graphics are a form of narrative argument, and the stories they tell have a rhetorical purpose. (See the examples on page 88.)

Build a Visual Analysis

It's one thing to construct a visual argument yourself; it's another thing to analyze visual arguments that are made by someone else. Fortunately, analyzing arguments made up of images and graphics is largely a matter of following the same strategies for rhetorical analysis that are outline in Chapter 6—except that you must analyze images instead of (or in addition to) words. To put it another way, when you analyze

Education: East Side vs. West Side

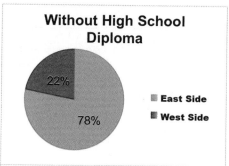

Without High School Diploma

22%

78%

- East Side
- West Side

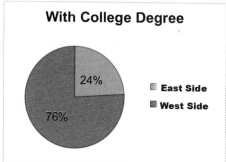

With College Degree

24%

76%

- East Side
- West Side

Starbucks Locations: East Side vs. West Side

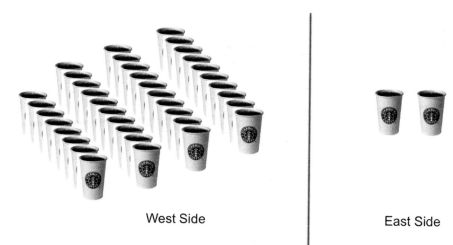

West Side

East Side

As of April 2012

Charts can make points vividly. In a comparison of the east side and west side of a city, the unequal number of Starbucks locations has a high correlation with the education level of the residents.

What does it take to be the best?

Determination and hard work, at any age, can lead to being the best. Hofstra University, just 50 years old, is already among the top ten percent of American colleges and universities in almost all academic criteria and resources.

Professionally accredited programs in such major areas as business, engineering, law, psychology and education.

A library with over 1.1 million volumes *on campus*—a collection larger than that of 95% of American universities.

Record enrollments with students from 31 states and 59 countries—with a student-faculty ratio of only 17 to 1.

The largest, most sophisticated non-commercial television facility in the East. A high technology undergraduate teaching resource with broadcast-quality production capability.

A ranking in *Barron's Guide to the Most Prestigious Colleges*—one of only 262 colleges and universities chosen from almost 4,000.

At Hofstra, determination, inspiration and hard work are qualities our faculty demands in itself and instills in our students. These qualities are what it takes to be the best. In anything.

HOFSTRA UNIVERSITY
WE TEACH SUCCESS.
50th Anniversary
Hempstead, L.I., New York 11550

Ad for Hofstra University, 1989

a visual argument, think about the image itself as well as its relationship to other images (and discourses). The arguments implied by visual images, like the arguments made through text alone, are carried both by the context and by the image.

Analyze context

A critical analysis of a visual image, like the analyses of written arguments that we discuss in the previous chapter, must include a consideration of context. Consider, for example, the above advertisement for Hofstra University. The context for the ad is not difficult to uncover through a bit of research. The ad appeared in 1989 and 1990, when Hofstra, located on Long Island 25 miles from New York City, was celebrating its fiftieth anniversary and hoping to use the occasion to enhance its esteem. At the time, Hofstra enjoyed a good reputation for its professional programs, particularly in education and business (which one-third of the 7,500 students were majoring in). However, it was not as highly regarded in the core science and humanities disciplines that are often associated with institutional prestige. In addition, Hofstra was quite well known in the New York metropolitan area—half its students were commuting to school rather than living in dormitories—but it was not attracting many students from outside the region, and its campus life was consequently regarded as mediocre. Its student body was generally well prepared, hardworking, and capable, but its most outstanding applicants were too often choosing other universities.

Feeling that its performance was exceeding its reputation and that it was capable of attracting a more diverse and talented student body, Hofstra developed a national ad campaign designed to change the opinions of prospective students and their parents, as well as the general public. It placed the ads—the ad reproduced here is one of a series—in several magazines and newspapers in order to persuade people that Hofstra was an outstanding university not just in the professions but in all fields, and that the opportunities available to its students were varied and valuable.

Analyze visual and textual elements

Ads make arguments, and the message of the Hofstra ad is something like this: "Hofstra is a prestigious, high-quality institution that brings out the best in students because of its facilities, its academic reputation, its student body, and the strength of its faculty and academic programs." The text of the Hofstra ad expresses that argument specifically: "The best" and "we teach success" are prominently displayed; the size of the print visually reinforces the message; and the fine print supports the main thesis by mentioning Hofstra's facilities (the large library with "a collection [of volumes] larger than that of 95% of American universities," the "television facility . . . with broadcast quality production capability"); its reputation (its ranking in *Barron's Guide to the Most Prestigious Colleges* and its "professionally accredited programs"); and its faculty and students. The ad works by offering good reasons and supporting arguments that are based on logical reasoning and evidence, as well as appeals to our most fervently held values. By placing the ad in prestigious publications, Hofstra enhanced its credibility even further.

In this chapter, however, we are emphasizing visuals in arguments. What kind of argument is made and supported by the image of the young girl with the flute? The photo of the girl is black and white, so that it can be printed easily and inexpensively in newspapers and magazines. But the black and white format also contributes a sense of reality and truthfulness, in the manner of black and white photos or documentary films. (Color images, on the other hand, can imply flashiness or commercialism.) Even in black and white, the image is quite arresting. In the context of an ad for Hofstra, the image is particularly intriguing. The girl is young—does she seem about 10 or 12 years of age?—and her readiness for distinguished performance suggests that she is a prodigy, a genius—in other words, the kind of person that Hofstra attracts and sustains. The ad implies that you might encounter her on the Hofstra campus sometime: if she is not a student at Hofstra now, she soon will be. Come to Hofstra, and you too can acquire the traits associated with excellence and success.

The girl is dressed up for some kind of musical performance, and the details of her costume imply that the performance is of a high order: It is not just any costume, but one associated with professional performances of the most rarefied kind, a concert that calls for only the best musicians. The delicacy and refinement of the girl are implied by the posture of her fingers, the highly polished flute that she holds with an upright carriage, and the meticulousness of her tie, shirt, and coat. The girl's expression suggests that she is serious, sober, disciplined, but comfortable—the kind of student (and faculty member) that Hofstra features. (The layout and consistent print style used in the ad reinforce that impression; by offering a balanced and harmonious placement of elements and by sticking to the same type style throughout, the ad stands for the values of balance, harmony, consistency, and order.) The girl is modest and unpretentious in expression, yet she looks directly at the viewer with supreme self-confidence. Her age suggests innocence, yet her face proclaims ambition; her age and the quasi-masculine costume (note that she wears neither a ring nor earrings) give her a sexual innocence that is in keeping with the contemplative life. Come to Hofstra, the image proclaims, and you will meet people who are sober and graceful, self-disciplined and confident, ambitious without being arrogant. The ad is supporting its thesis with good reasons implied by its central image—good reasons that we identified with logos and pathos in the previous chapter.

Speaking of pathos, what do you make of the fact that the girl is Asian? On one hand, the Asian girl's demeanor reinforces cultural stereotypes. Delicate, small, sober, controlled, even humorless, she embodies characteristics that recall other Asian American icons (particularly women), especially icons of success through discipline and hard work. On the other hand, the girl speaks to the Asian community. It is as if she is on the verge of saying, "Come and join me at Hofstra, where you too can reach the highest achievement. And read the copy below me to learn more about what Hofstra has to offer." In this way the girl participates in Hofstra's ambition to attract highly qualified, highly motivated, and high-performing minority students—as well as any other high-performing student, regardless of ethnicity or gender, who values hard work, academic distinction, and the postponement of sensual gratification in return for long-term success.

If she is Asian, the girl is also thoroughly American. She appears not to be an international student but an American of immigrant stock. Her costume, her controlled black hair, and her unmarked face and fingers identify her as achieving the American dream of material success, physical health and well being, and class advancement. If her parents or grandparents came to New York or California as immigrants, they (and she) are now naturalized—100 percent American, completely successful. The social class element to the image is unmistakable: The entire ad speaks of Hofstra's ambition to be among the best, to achieve an elite status. When the ad appeared in 1989, Hofstra was attracting few of the nation's elite students. The girl signals a change. She displays the university's aspiration to become among the nation's elite—those who enjoy material success as well as the leisure, education, and sophistication to appreciate the finest music. That ambition is reinforced by the university's emblem in the lower right-hand corner of the ad. It resembles a coat of arms and is associated with royalty. Hofstra may be a community that is strong in the professions, but it also values the arts.

No doubt there are other aspects of the image that work to articulate and to support the complex argument of the ad. There is more to be said about this ad, and you may disagree with some of the points we have offered. But consider this: By 2009, twenty years after the ad was run, Hofstra's total enrollment had climbed above 12,000, with 7,500 undergraduates. Its admissions were more selective, its student body was more diverse and less regional in character, its graduation rate had improved, its sports teams had achieved national visibility, and its minority student population had grown. Many factors contributed to the university's advancement, but it seems likely that this ad was one of them.

Write a Visual Analysis

Like rhetorical analysis, effective visual analysis takes into account the context of the image as well as its visual elements and any surrounding text. When you analyze a visual image, look carefully at its details and thoroughly consider its context. What visual elements grab your attention first, and how do other details reinforce that impression—what is most important and less important? How do color and style influence impressions? How does the image direct the viewer's eyes and reinforce what is important? What is the relationship between the image and any text that might accompany it? Consider the shapes, colors, and details of the image, as well as how the elements of the image connect with different arguments and audiences.

Consider also what you know or can learn about the context of an image and the design and text that surround it. Try to determine why and when it was created, who created it, where it appeared, and the target audience. Think about how the context of its creation and publication affected its intended audience. What elements have you seen before? Which elements remind you of other visuals?

Sample Student Visual Analysis

Discussion board posts are a frequent assignment in writing classes. Usually they are short essays, no more than 300 words. Sources of any information still need to be cited.

The assignment for this post was to find and analyze an example of a visual metaphor.

Thread: "Use Only What You Need": The Denver Water Conservation
Campaign
Author: Chrissy Yao
Posted Date: March 1, 2013 1:12 PM

Partial bus bench from Denver Water's conservation campaign

In 2006, Denver Water, the city's oldest water utility, launched
a ten-year water conservation plan based on using water efficiently
("Conservation"). Denver Water teamed up with the Sukle Advertising
firm and produced the "Use Only What You Need" campaign to help
alleviate the water crisis that the city was enduring (Samuel). The
campaign uses billboard advertising, magazine ads, and even stripped-
down cars to impart messages of water conservation and efficiency.

Clever visual metaphors are at the heart of the campaign. One
example is a park bench with available seating for only one individual.
The words, "USE ONLY WHAT YOU NEED," are stenciled on the back of the
bench. The bench, which can actually be used for sitting, conveys the
idea that if only one person were using the bench, that person would
only need a small area to sit on, not the whole thing. The bench makes
concrete the concept of water conservation.

The innovative ad campaign that uses objects in addition to
traditional advertising has proven successful. The simplicity and
minimalist style of the ads made a convincing argument about using
resources sparingly. The average water consumption of Denver dropped
between 18% and 21% annually from 2006 to 2009.

[marginal note] ...o describes the ...d campaign that ...ses the partial ...us bench.

[marginal note] ...ao analyzes the ...isual metaphor.

Works Cited

"Conservation." *Denver Water*. Denver Water, 2010. Web. 23 Feb. 2013.

Samuel, Frederick. "Denver Water." *Ad Goodness*. N.p., 16 Nov. 2006. Web. 24 Feb. 2013.

Writing Arguments

PART

3

8 | Definition Arguments

QUICK TAKE

In this chapter, you will learn to

1. Use definition arguments that set out criteria and then argue that something meets or doesn't meet those criteria (see page 96)
2. Recognize formal definitions, operational definitions, and definitions by example (see pages 96–99)
3. Analyze a definition argument (see pages 99–102)
4. Write an effective definition argument (see pages 104–105)

Graffiti dates back to the ancient Egyptian, Greek, Roman, and Mayan civilizations. Is graffiti vandalism? Or is it art? The debate has gone on for three decades. In the 1980s New York City's subways were covered with graffiti. Many New Yorkers believe that removing graffiti from subway cars was a first step toward the much-celebrated social and economic recovery of the city. For them graffiti was a sign that the subways were not safe. But at the same time, Martha Cooper and Henry Chalfant released a book titled *Subway Art*—a picture book that celebrated graffiti-covered subways as an art form. Should we appreciate graffiti as the people's art. Or should graffiti be removed as quickly as possible, as a destructive eyesore?

Understand How Definition Arguments Work

Definition arguments set out criteria and then argue that whatever is being defined meets or does not meet those criteria.

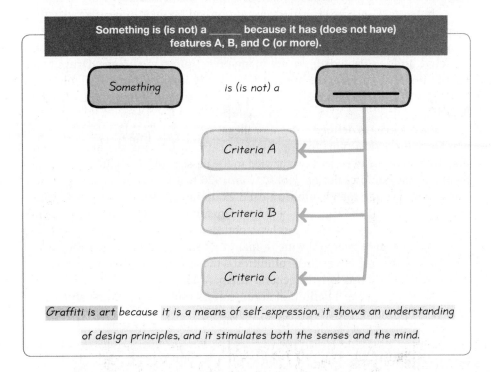

Something is (is not) a _____ because it has (does not have) features A, B, and C (or more).

Something — is (is not) a — _____

Criteria A

Criteria B

Criteria C

Graffiti is art because it is a means of self-expression, it shows an understanding of design principles, and it stimulates both the senses and the mind.

Recognize Kinds of Definitions

Rarely do you get far into an argument without having to define something. Imagine that you are writing an argument about the decades-old and largely ineffective "war on drugs" in the United States. We all know that the war on drugs is being waged against drugs that are illegal, like cocaine and marijuana, and not against the legal drugs produced by the multibillion-dollar drug industry. Our society classifies drugs into two categories: "good" drugs, which are legal, and "bad" drugs, which are illegal.

How exactly does our society arrive at these definitions? Drugs would be relatively easy to define as good or bad if the difference could be defined at the molecular level. Bad drugs would contain certain molecules that define them as bad. The history of drug use in the United States, however, tells us that this is not so simple. In the twentieth century alcohol was on the list of illegal drugs for over a decade, while opium was considered a good drug and was distributed in many patent medicines by pharmaceutical companies. Similarly, LSD and MDMA (methylenedioxymethamphetamine, better known by its street name *ecstasy*) were developed by the pharmaceutical industry but later made illegal. In a few states marijuana is now legal in small quantities and for medicinal use.

If drugs cannot be classified as good or bad by their molecular structure, then perhaps society classifies them by their effects. It might be reasonable to assume that addictive drugs are illegal, but that's not the case. Nicotine is highly addictive and is a legal drug, as are many prescription medicines. Drugs taken for the purpose of pleasure are not necessarily illegal (think of alcohol and Viagra), nor are drugs that alter consciousness or change personality (such as Prozac).

How a drug is defined as legal or illegal apparently is determined by example. The nationwide effort to stop Americans from drinking alcohol during the first decades of the twentieth century led to the passage of the Eighteenth Amendment and the ban on sales of alcohol from 1920 to 1933, known as Prohibition. Those who argued for Prohibition used examples of drunkenness, especially among the poor, to show how alcohol broke up families and left mothers and children penniless in the street. Those who opposed Prohibition initially pointed to the consumption of beer and wine in many cultural traditions. Later they raised examples of the bad effects of Prohibition—the rise of organized crime, the increase in alcohol abuse, and the general disregard for laws.

When you make a definition argument, it's important to think about what kind of definition you will use. Descriptions of three types follow.

Formal definitions

Formal definitions typically categorize an item into the next-higher classification and provide criteria that distinguish the item from other items within that classification. Most dictionary definitions are formal definitions. For example, fish are cold-blooded aquatic vertebrates that have jaws, fins, and scales and are distinguished from other cold-blooded aquatic vertebrates (such as sea snakes) by the presence of gills. If you can construct a formal definition with a specific classification and differentiating criteria that your audience will accept, then likely you will have a strong argument. The key is to get your audience to agree to your classification and criteria. Often your argument will amount to revising your audience's view of the classification or criteria (or both). For instance, imagine that you want to change your audience's view of contemporary universities. You might construct a thesis statement something like this: "While most people still think of universities as institutions of higher learning [classification] that prepare people for citizenship and the workplace [differentiating criteria], they are actually nothing more than big businesses" [revised classification].

Operational definitions

Many concepts cannot be easily defined by formal definitions. Researchers in the natural and social sciences must construct **operational definitions** that they use for their research. For example, researchers who study binge drinking among college students define a binge as five or more drinks in one sitting for a man, and four or more drinks for a woman. Some people think this standard is too low and should be raised to six to eight drinks to distinguish true problem drinkers from the general college population. No matter what the number, researchers must argue that the particular definition is one that suits the concept.

Definitions from example

Many human qualities such as honesty, courage, creativity, deceit, and love must be defined by examples that the audience accepts as representative of the concept. Few would not call the firefighters who entered the World Trade Center on September 11, 2001, courageous. Most people would describe someone with a diagnosis of terminal cancer who refuses to feel self-pity as courageous. But what about a student who declines to go to a concert with her friends so she can study for an exam? Her behavior might be admirable, but most people would hesitate to call it courageous. The key to arguing a **definition from example** is that the examples must strike the audience as typical of the concept, even if the situation is unusual.

Build a Definition Argument

Because definition arguments are so powerful, they are found at the center of some of the most important debates in American history. Definition arguments were at the heart of the abolition of slavery, for example, and many of the major arguments of the civil rights movement were based on definitions. Martin Luther King, Jr.'s, "Letter from Birmingham Jail" is one eloquent example.

King was jailed in April 1963 for leading a series of peaceful protests in Birmingham, Alabama. While he was being held in solitary confinement, Rev. King wrote a letter to eight white Birmingham clergymen. These religious leaders had issued a statement urging an end to the protests in their city. King argued that it was necessary to act now rather than wait for change. His purpose in writing the argument was to win acceptance for the protests and protestors and to make his audience see that the anti-segregationists were not agitators and rabble-rousers, but citizens acting responsibly to correct a grave injustice. A critical part of King's argument is his definition of "just" and "unjust" laws.

U.S. National Guard troops block off Beale Street in Memphis, Tennessee, as striking sanitation workers wearing placards reading "I *AM* A MAN" pass by on March 29, 1968. Rev. Martin Luther King, Jr., returned to Memphis to lead the march and was assassinated a week later on April 4.

Supporters of segregation in Birmingham had obtained a court order forbidding further protests, and the eight white clergymen urged King and his supporters to obey the courts. Our society generally assumes that laws, and the courts that enforce them, should be obeyed. King, however, argues that there are two categories of laws, and that citizens must treat one category differently from the other. Morally just laws, King argues, should be obeyed, but unjust ones should not. But how are just laws to be distinguished from unjust ones? By distinguishing two different kinds of laws, King creates a rationale for obeying some laws and disobeying others.

His argument rests on the clear moral and legal criteria he uses to define just and unjust laws. Without these criteria, people could simply disobey any law they chose, which is what King's detractors accused him of advocating. King had to show that he was in fact acting on principle, and that he and his supporters wanted to establish justice, not cause chaos. First, King states that a "just law is a man-made code that squares with the moral law of God" and "an unjust law is a code that is out of harmony with the moral law." Second, King notes that "any law that degrades human personality is unjust." Finally, King states that just laws are ones that hold for everyone because they were arrived at through democratic processes, while unjust laws are those that are inflicted on a minority that, because they were not permitted to vote, had no participation in approving them.

The definitions that King offers promote his goals. He maintains in his famous "Letter" that people have a moral responsibility to obey just laws, and, by the same logic, "a moral responsibility to disobey unjust laws." He then completes his definitional argument by showing how segregation laws fit the definition of "unjust" that he has laid out. Once his audience accepts his placement of segregation laws in the "unjust" category, they must also accept that King and his fellow protestors were right to break those laws. He answers his critics effectively through a powerful definition argument.

Note how King's three definitions all fit the structure described at the beginning of this chapter:

Something is (or is not) a ___ because it has (does not have) features A, B, and C.

Building an extended definition argument like King's is a two-step process. First, you have to establish the criteria for the categories you wish to define. In

Martin Luther King, Jr., speaking in New York City in 1967.

King's letter, consistency with moral law and uplifting of the human spirit are set forth as criteria for a just law. King provides arguments from St. Thomas Aquinas, a religious authority likely to carry significant weight with Birmingham clergymen and others who will read the letter.

Second, you must convince your audience that the particular case in question meets or doesn't meet the criteria. King cannot simply state that segregation laws are unjust; he must provide evidence showing how they fail to meet the criteria for a just law. Specifically, he notes that segregation "gives the segregator a false sense of superiority and the segregated a false sense of inferiority." These false senses of self are a distortion or degradation of the human personality.

Sometimes definition arguments have to argue for the relevance and suitability of the criteria. King, in fact, spent a great deal of his letter laying out and defending his criteria for just and unjust laws. While he addressed his letter to clergymen, he knew that it would find a wider audience. Therefore, he did not rely solely on criteria linked to moral law, or to Thomas Aquinas, or the "law of God." People who were not especially religious might not be convinced by those parts of his argument. So King presents two additional criteria for just laws that he knows will appeal to those who value the democratic process.

When you build a definition argument, often you must put much effort into identifying and explaining your criteria. You must convince your readers that your criteria are the best ones for what you are defining and that they apply to the case you are arguing.

King's Extended Definition Argument

After establishing criteria for two kinds of laws, *just* and *unjust*, King argues that citizens must respond differently to laws that are unjust, by disobeying them. He then shows how the special case of *segregation laws* meets the criteria for unjust laws. If readers accept his argument, they will agree that segregation laws belong in the category of unjust laws, and therefore must be disobeyed.

Criteria for Just Laws	Criteria for Unjust Laws	Segregation Laws
Consistent with moral law	Not consistent with moral law	✓
Uplift human personality	Damage human personality	✓
Must be obeyed by all people	Must be obeyed by some people, but not others	✓
Made by democratically elected representatives	Not made by democratically elected representatives	✓
Appropriate Response to Just Laws	**Appropriate Response to Unjust Laws**	
All citizens should obey them.	All citizens should disobey them.	✓

Finding Good Reasons

What Is Parody?

William Jennings Bryan depicted as Don Quixote in his campaign against powerful trusts in 1899.

During the 2007–2010 global financial crisis, the slogan "too big to fail" expressed anger over the government bailout of big banks at a time when individuals were losing their jobs and homes. A century earlier, Democratic presidential candidate William Jennings Bryan campaigned against *trusts*— powerful groups of companies that dominated markets. This cartoon represents Bryan as Miguel de Cervantes's character Don Quixote, fruitlessly charging windmills. The novel *Don Quixote*, published in 1605 with a sequel in 1615, is itself a parody of contemporary chivalric romances, so the cartoon is a parody using a parody.

Downfall, a German film released in 2004 about Hitler's last days, has been the basis for thousands of popular *YouTube* parodies. Every parody uses the same scene of a defeated Hitler, played by Bruno Ganz, unleashing a furious speech to his staff in German with YouTubers adding subtitles on politics, sports, popular culture, and everyday life. The owner of the rights to the film, Constantin Films, demanded that *YouTube* take down the parodies in April 2010, and *YouTube* complied for a few months. Critics of the move successfully argued that fair-use law allows a film clip, a paragraph from an article, or a short piece of music to be adapted if the purpose is to create commentary or satire.

Write about it

1. Which of the following criteria do you think must be present for a work to be considered a parody? Are there any criteria you might change or add?
   - The work criticizes a previous work
   - The work copies the same structure, details, or style of the previous work
   - The connections to the previous work are clear to the audience
   - The work is humorous
   - The title is a play on the previous work

2. Do the various uses of the *Downfall* clip meet the criteria above? Would you define them as parodies? Why or why not?

Steps to Writing a Definition Argument

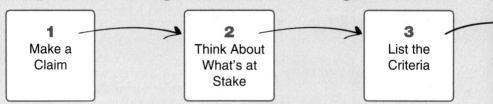

1
Make a Claim

2
Think About What's at Stake

3
List the Criteria

Step 1 Make a Claim

Make a definitional claim on a controversial issue that focuses on a key term.

Template

_____ is (or is not) a _____ because it has (or does not have) features A, B, and C (or more).

Examples

- Hate speech (or pornography, literature, films, and so on) is (or is not) free speech protected by the First Amendment because it has (or does not have) these features.
- Hunting (or using animals for cosmetics testing, keeping animals in zoos, wearing furs, and so on) is (or is not) cruelty to animals because it has (or does not have) these features.

Step 2 Think About What's at Stake

- Does nearly everyone agree with you? If so, then your claim probably isn't interesting or important. If you can think of people who disagree, then something is at stake.
- Who argues the opposite of your claim?
- Why or how do they benefit from a different definition?

Step 3 List the Criteria

- Which criteria are necessary for _____ to be a _____?
- Which are the most important?
- Does your case in point meet all the criteria?

Step 4 Analyze Your Potential Readers

- Who are your readers?
- How does the definitional claim you are making affect them?
- How familiar are they with the issue, concept, or controversy that you're writing about?
- Which criteria are they most likely to accept with little explanation, and which will they disagree with?

Step 5 Write a Draft

Introduction

- Set out the issue, concept, or controversy.
- Give the background that your intended readers need.

Body

- Set out your criteria and argue for the appropriateness of the criteria.
- Anticipate where readers might question either your criteria or how they apply to your subject.
- Address opposing viewpoints by acknowledging how their definitions differ and by showing why your definition is better.

Conclusion

- Do more than simply summarize. You can, for example, go into more detail about what is at stake or the implications of your definition.

Step 6 Revise, Edit, Proofread

- For detailed instructions, see Chapter 5.
- For a checklist to use to evaluate your draft, see pages 50–51.

Michael Pollan

Eat Food: Food Defined

Michael Pollan is a journalism professor at the University of California, Berkeley, and the author of *In Defense of Food: An Eater's Manifesto* (2008), from which this excerpt is taken. *In Defense of Food* received many prizes and was named one of the ten best books of the year by the *New York Times* and the *Washington Post*. Pollan is also the author of *Second Nature* (1991), *A Place of My Own* (1997), *The Botany of Desire: A Plant's Eye View of the World* (2001), *The Omnivore's Dilemma: A Natural History of Four Meals* (2006), *Food Rules* (2010), and *Cooked: A Natural History of Transformation* (2013). He is also a contributing writer for the *New York Times Magazine*.

Pollan asks why Americans worry so much about nutrition and yet seem so unhealthy. The title *In Defense of Food* is one of the many paradoxes that Pollan examines in the book excerpted here. After all, why should food need defending if it is plentiful and we eat so much of it? Pollan argues that the answer lies in how we define food.

Pollan begins by asking, Why does food need to be defined?

The first time I heard the advice to "just eat food" it was in a speech by Joan Gussow, and it completely baffled me. Of course you should eat food—what else is there to eat? But Gussow, who grows much of her own food on a flood-prone finger of land jutting into the Hudson River, refuses to dignify most of the products for sale in the supermarket with that title. "In the thirty-four years I've been in the field of nutrition," she said in the same speech, "I have watched real food disappear from large areas of the supermarket and from much of the rest of the eating world." Taking food's place on the shelves has been an unending stream of foodlike substitutes, some seventeen thousand new ones every year—"products constructed largely around commerce and hope, supported by frighteningly little actual knowledge." Ordinary food is still out there, however, still being grown and even occasionally sold in the supermarket, and this ordinary food is what we should eat.

Pollan claims that everything that pretends to be food really isn't food, thus establishing the need for a definition.

2 But given our current state of confusion and given the thousands of products calling themselves food, this is more easily said than done. So consider these related rules of thumb. Each proposes a different sort of map to the contemporary food landscape, but all should take you to more or less the same place.

Don't eat anything your great grandmother wouldn't recognize as food.

3 Why your great grandmother? Because at this point your mother and possibly even your grandmother is as confused as the rest of us; to be safe we need to go back at least a couple generations,

to a time before the advent of most modern foods. So depending on your age (and your grandmother), you may need to go back to your great- or even great-great grandmother. Some nutritionists recommend going back even further. John Yudkin, a British nutritionist whose early alarms about the dangers of refined carbohydrates were overlooked in the 1960s and 1970s, once advised, "Just don't eat anything your Neolithic ancestors wouldn't have recognized and you'll be OK."

Pollan's first criterion of what is food offers a simple concept.

4   What would shopping this way mean in the supermarket? Well, imagine your great grandmother at your side as you roll down the aisles. You're standing together in front of the dairy case. She picks up a package of Go-Gurt Portable Yogurt tubes—and has no idea what this could possibly be. Is it a food or a toothpaste? And how, exactly, do you introduce it into your body? You could tell her it's just yogurt in a squirtable form, yet if she read the ingredients label she would have every reason to doubt that that was in fact the case. Sure, there's some yogurt in there, but there are also a dozen other things that aren't remotely yogurt like, ingredients she would probably fail to recognize as foods of any kind, including high-fructose corn syrup, modified corn starch, kosher gelatin, carrageenan, tri-calcium phosphate, natural and artificial flavors, vitamins, and so forth. (And there's a whole other list of ingredients for the "berry bubblegum bash" flavoring, containing everything but berries or bubblegum.) How did yogurt, which in your great grandmother's day consisted simply of milk inoculated with a bacterial culture, ever get to be so complicated? Is a product like Go-Gurt Portable Yogurt still a whole food? A food of any kind? Or is it just a food product?

Another way of defining food is to define what isn't food, but what Pollan calls "food products."

5   There are in fact hundreds of foodish products in the supermarket that your ancestors simply wouldn't recognize as food: breakfast cereal bars transected by bright white veins representing, but in reality having nothing to do with, milk; "protein waters" and "nondairy creamer"; cheeselike food-stuffs equally innocent of any bovine contribution; cakelike cylinders (with creamlike fillings) called Twinkies that never grow stale. Don't eat anything incapable of rotting is another personal policy you might consider adopting.

6   There are many reasons to avoid eating such complicated food products beyond the various chemical additives and corn and soy derivatives they contain. One of the problems with the products of food science is that, as Joan Gussow has pointed out, they lie to your body; their artificial colors and flavors and synthetic sweeteners and novel fats confound the senses we rely on to assess new foods and prepare our bodies to deal with them. Foods that lie leave us with little choice but to eat by the numbers, consulting labels rather than our senses.

7   It's true that foods have long been processed in order to preserve them, as when we pickle or ferment or smoke, but

industrial processing aims to do much more than extend shelf life. Today foods are processed in ways specifically designed to sell us more food by pushing our evolutionary buttons—our inborn preferences for sweetness and fat and salt. These qualities are difficult to find in nature but cheap and easy for the food scientist to deploy, with the result that processing induces us to consume much more of these ecological rarities than is good for us. "Tastes great, less filling!" could be the motto for most processed foods, which are far more energy dense than most whole foods: They contain much less water, fiber, and micronutrients, and generally much more sugar and fat, making them at the same time, to coin a marketing slogan, "More fattening, less nutritious!"

8   The great grandma rule will help keep many of these products out of your cart. But not all of them. Because thanks to the FDA's willingness, post–1973, to let food makers freely alter the identity of "traditional foods that everyone knows" without having to call them imitations, your great grandmother could easily be fooled into thinking that that loaf of bread or wedge of cheese is in fact a loaf of bread or a wedge of cheese. This is why we need a slightly more detailed personal policy to capture these imitation foods; to wit:

What food is can also be defined by what it isn't, hence a list of criteria for what isn't food.

Avoid food products containing ingredients that are a) unfamiliar set, b) unpronounceable, c) more than five in number, or that include d) high-fructose corn syrup.

9   None of these characteristics, not even the last one, is necessarily harmful in and of itself, but all of them are reliable markers for foods that have been highly processed to the point where they may no longer be what they purport to be. They have crossed over from foods to food products.

10   Consider a loaf of bread, one of the "traditional foods that everyone knows" specifically singled out for protection in the 1938 imitation rule. As your grandmother could tell you, bread is traditionally made using a remarkably small number of familiar ingredients: flour, yeast, water, and a pinch of salt will do it. But industrial bread—even industrial whole-grain bread—has become a far more complicated product of modern food science (not to mention commerce and hope). Here's the complete ingredients list for Sara Lee's Soft & Smooth Whole Grain White Bread. (Wait a minute—isn't "Whole Grain White Bread" a contradiction in terms? Evidently not any more.)

Pollan points out that the language used for food products is as convoluted as the ingredients.

Enriched bleached flour [wheat flour, malted barley flour, niacin, iron, thiamin mononitrate (vitamin B), riboflavin (vitamin B_2), folic acid], water, whole grains [whole wheat flour, brown rice flour (rice flour, rice bran)], high fructose corn syrup [hello!], whey, wheat gluten, yeast, cellulose. Contains 2% or less of each of the following: honey, calcium sulfate, vegetable oil (soybean and/or cottonseed oils), salt, butter (cream, salt), dough conditioners (may contain one or more of the following: mono- and diglycerides, ethoxylated mono- and diglycerides, ascorbic acid, enzymes, azodicarbonamide), guar gum, calcium propionate (preservative), distilled vinegar, yeast nutrients (monocalcium phosphate, calcium sulfate, ammonium sulfate), corn starch, natural flavor, beta-carotene (color), vitamin D_3, soy lecithin, soy flour.

11   There are many things you could say about this intricate loaf of "bread," but note first that even if it managed to slip by your great grandmother (because it is a loaf of bread, or at least is called one and strongly resembles one), the product fails every test proposed under rule number two: It's got unfamiliar ingredients (monoglycerides I've heard of before, but ethoxylated monoglycerides?); unpronounceable ingredients (try "azodicarbonamide"); it exceeds the maximum of five ingredients (by roughly thirty-six); and it contains high-fructose corn syrup. Sorry, Sara Lee, but your Soft & Smooth Whole Grain White Bread is not food and if not for the indulgence of the FDA could not even be labeled "bread."

12   Sara Lee's Soft & Smooth Whole Grain White Bread could serve as a monument to the age of nutritionism. It embodies the latest nutritional wisdom from science and government (which in its most recent food pyramid recommends that at least half our consumption of grain come from whole grains) but leavens that wisdom with the commercial recognition that American eaters (and American children in particular) have come to prefer their wheat highly refined—which is to say, cottony soft, snowy white, and exceptionally sweet on the tongue. In its marketing materials, Sara Lee treats this clash of interests as some sort of Gordian knot—it speaks in terms of an ambitious quest to build a "no compromise" loaf—which only the most sophisticated food science could possibly cut.

13   And so it has, with the invention of whole-grain white bread. Because the small percentage of whole grains in the bread would render it that much less sweet than, say, all-white Wonder Bread—which scarcely waits to be chewed before transforming itself into glucose— the food scientists have added high-fructose corn syrup and honey to make up the difference; to overcome the problematic heft and toothsomeness of a real whole grain bread, they've deployed "dough conditioners," including guar gum and the aforementioned azodicarbonamide, to simulate the texture of supermarket white bread. By incorporating certain varieties of albino wheat, they've managed to maintain that deathly but apparently appealing Wonder Bread pallor.

14   Who would have thought Wonder Bread would ever become an ideal of aesthetic and gustatory perfection to which bakers would actually aspire—Sara Lee's Mona Lisa?

15   Very often food science's efforts to make traditional foods more nutritious make them much more complicated, but not necessarily any better for you. To make dairy products low fat, it's not enough to remove the fat. You then have to go to great lengths to preserve the body or creamy texture by working in all kinds of food additives. In the case of low-fat or skim milk that usually means adding powdered milk. But powdered milk contains oxidized cholesterol, which scientists believe is much worse for your arteries than ordinary cholesterol, so food makers sometimes compensate by adding antioxidants, further complicating what had been a simple one-ingredient whole food. Also, removing the fat makes it that much harder for your body to absorb the fat-soluble vitamins that are one of the reasons to drink milk in the first place.

16   All this heroic and occasionally counterproductive food science has been undertaken in the name of our health—so that Sara Lee can add to its plastic wrapper the magic words "good source of whole grain" or a food company can ballyhoo the even more magic words "low fat." Which brings us to a related food policy that may at first sound counterintuitive to a health-conscious eater:

Avoid Food Products That Make Health Claims.

17   For a food product to make health claims on its package it must first have a package, so right off the bat it's more likely to be a processed than a whole food. Generally speaking, it is only the big food companies that have the wherewithal to secure FDA-approved health claims for their products and there trumpet them to the world. Recently, however, some of the tonier fruits and nuts have begun boasting about their health-enhancing properties, and there will surely be more as each crop council scrounges together the money to commission its own scientific study. Because all plants contain antioxidants, all these studies are guaranteed to find something on which to base a health oriented marketing campaign.

18   But for the most part it is the products of food science that make the boldest health claims, and these are often founded on incomplete and often erroneous science—the dubious fruits of nutritionism. Don't forget that trans-fat-rich margarine, one of the first industrial foods to claim it was healthier than the traditional food it replaced, turned out to give people heart attacks. Since that debacle, the FDA, under tremendous pressure from industry, has made it only easier for food companies to make increasingly doubtful health claims, such as the one Frito-Lay now puts on some of its chips—that eating them is somehow good for your heart. If you bother to read the health claims closely (as food marketers make sure consumers seldom do), you will find that there is often considerably less to them than meets the eye.

19   Consider a recent "qualified" health claim approved by the FDA for (don't laugh) corn oil. ("Qualified" is a whole new category

of health claim, introduced in 2002 at the behest of industry.) Corn oil, you may recall, is particularly high in the omega-6 fatty acids we're already consuming far too many of. Very limited and preliminary scientific evidence suggests that eating about one tablespoon (16 grams) of corn oil daily may reduce the risk of heart disease due to the unsaturated fat content in corn oil.

20   The tablespoon is a particularly rich touch, conjuring images of moms administering medicine, or perhaps cod-liver oil, to their children. But what the FDA gives with one hand, it takes away with the other. Here's the small-print "qualification" of this already notably diffident health claim:

> [The] FDA concludes that there is little scientific evidence supporting this claim.
>
> To achieve this possible benefit, corn oil is to replace a similar amount of saturated fat and not increase the total number of calories you eat in a day.

Close reading of labels undercuts health claims of food products.

21   This little masterpiece of pseudoscientific bureaucratese was extracted from the FDA by the manufacturer of Mazola corn oil. It would appear that "qualified" is an official FDA euphemism for "all but meaningless." Though someone might have let the consumer in on this game: The FDA's own research indicates that consumers have no idea what to make of qualified health claims (how would they?), and its rules allow companies to promote the claims pretty much any way they want—they can use really big type for the claim, for example, and then print the disclaimers in teeny-tiny type. No doubt we can look forward to a qualified health claim for high-fructose corn syrup, a tablespoon of which probably does contribute to your health—as long as it replaces a comparable amount of, say, poison in your diet and doesn't increase the total number of calories you eat in a day.

22   When corn oil and chips and sugary breakfast cereals can all boast being good for your heart, health claims have become hopelessly corrupt. The American Heart Association currently bestows (for a fee) its heart-healthy seal of approval on Lucky Charms, Cocoa Puffs, and Trix cereals, Yoo-hoo lite chocolate drink, and Healthy Choice's Premium Caramel Swirl Ice Cream Sandwich—this at a time when scientists are coming to recognize that dietary sugar probably plays a more important role in heart disease than dietary fat. Meanwhile, the genuinely heart-healthy whole foods in the produce section, lacking the financial and political clout of the packaged goods a few aisles over, are mute. But don't take the silence of the yams as a sign that they have nothing valuable to say about health.

Pollan adds a playful touch by echoing the title of a popular movie to make a point.

Sample Student Definition Argument

Conley 1

Patrice Conley

Professor Douglas

English 101

15 Nov. 2013

Flagrant Foul: The NCAA's Definition of Student Athletes as Amateurs

Every year, thousands of student athletes across America sign the National Collegiate Athletic Association's Form 08-3a, the "Student-Athlete" form, waiving their right to receive payment for the use of their name and image (McCann). The form defines student athletes as amateurs, who cannot receive payment for playing their sports. While their schools and coaches may make millions of dollars in salaries and endorsement deals and are the highest-paid public employees in many states, student athletes can never earn a single penny from their college athletic careers. Former Nike executive Sonny Vacarro sums it up: "Everyone has a right except for the player. The player has no rights" ("Money").

Make no mistake: college athletics are big business. The most visible college sports—big-time men's football and basketball—generate staggering sums of money. For example, the twelve universities in the Southeastern Conference receive $205 million each year from CBS and ESPN for the right to broadcast their football games (Smith and Ourand). Even more money comes in from video games, clothing, and similar licenses. In 2010, the *New York Times* reported that "the NCAA's licensing deals are estimated at more than $4 billion" per year (Thamel). While the staggering executive pay at big corporations has brought public outrage, coaches' salaries are even more outlandish. Kentucky basketball coach John Calipari is paid over $4 million a year for a basketball program that makes about $35-40 million a year, more than 10% of the entire revenue. Tom Van Riper observes that no corporate CEO commands this large a share of the profits. He notes that if Steve Ballmer, the CEO at Microsoft, had Calipari's deal, Ballmer would make over $6 billion a year.

How can colleges allow advertisers, arena operators, concession owners, athletic gear manufacturers, retailers, game companies, and media moguls, along with coaches and university officials, to make millions and pay the stars of the show nothing? The answer is that colleges define

> Patrice Conley sets out the definition she is attempting to rectify: amateurs are athletes who aren't paid.

> Conley identifies what's at stake.

> Conley disputes the definition that college sports are amateur sports.

> The huge salaries paid to college coaches are comparable to those in professional sports.

nley argues
at colleges
e the defini-
n of athletes
a amateurs to
fuse to pay
em.

athletes as amateurs. Not only are student athletes not paid for playing their sport, they cannot receive gifts and are not allowed to endorse products, which may be a violation of their right to free speech. The NCAA, an organization of colleges and schools, forces student athletes to sign away their rights because, it says, it is protecting the students. If student athletes could accept money from anyone, the NCAA argues, they might be exploited, cheated, or even bribed. Taking money out of the equation is supposed to let students focus on academics and preserve the amateur status of college sports.

The definition of amateur arose in the nineteenth century in Britain, when team sports became popular. Middle-class and upper-class students in college had ample time to play their sports while working-class athletes had only a half-day off (no sports were played on Sundays in that era). Teams began to pay top working-class sportsmen for the time they had to take off from work. Middle-class and upper-class sportsmen didn't want to play against the working-class teams, so they made the distinction between amateurs and professionals. The definition of amateur crossed the Atlantic to the United States, where college sports became popular in the 1880s. But it was not long until the hypocrisy of amateurism undermined the ideal. Top football programs like Yale's had slush funds to pay athletes, and others used ringers—players who weren't students—and even players from other schools (Zimbalist 7). The Olympic Games maintained the amateur-professional distinction until 1988, but it was long evident that Communist bloc nations were paying athletes to train full-time and Western nations were paying athletes through endorsement contracts. The only Olympic sport that now requires amateur status is boxing. The college sports empire in the United States run by the NCAA is the last bastion of amateurism for sports that draw audiences large enough to be televised.

Colleges might be able to defend the policy of amateurism if they extended this definition to all students. A fair policy is one that treats all students the same. A fair policy doesn't result in some students getting paid for professional work, while other students do not. Consider the students in the Butler School of Music at the University of Texas at

Conley shows in
his paragraph
ow the defini-
ion of college
athletes as un-
paid amateurs
s based on out-
dated notions.

Conley argues
that everyone
else has dis-
carded that
old idea of
"amateurism as
unpaid," so why
won't the NCAA
discard it?

Austin, for example. Many student musicians perform at the professional level. Does the school prevent them from earning money for their musical performances? No. In fact, the school runs a referral service that connects its students with people and businesses who want to hire professional musicians. The university even advises its students on how to negotiate a contract and get paid for their performance ("Welcome").

> Comparisons show that colleges do not apply the definition of amateur consistently.

Likewise, why are student actors allowed to earn money from their work and images, while student athletes are not? Think about actor Emma Watson, who enrolled at Brown University in Rhode Island. Can you imagine the university officials at Brown telling Watson that she would have to make the next two *Harry Potter* films for free, instead of for the $5 million she was offered? Can you imagine Brown University telling Watson that all the revenue from Harry Potter merchandise bearing her likeness would have to be paid directly to the university for the rest of her life? They would if Watson were an athlete instead of an actor.

> Do you think this analogy is effective?

In fact, compared with musicians and actors, student athletes have an even greater need to earn money while they are still in college. Athletes' professional careers are likely to be much shorter than musicians' or actors'. College may be the only time some athletes have the opportunity to capitalize on their success. (Indeed, rather than focusing student athletes on their academic careers, the NCAA policy sometimes forces students to leave college early, so they can earn a living before their peak playing years are over.) Student athletes often leave school with permanent injuries and no medical insurance or job prospects, whereas student musicians and actors rarely suffer career-ending injuries on the job.

Student athletes are prevented from profiting from their name and image. The NCAA says this rule preserves their standing as amateurs and protects them from the celebrity and media frenzy surrounding professional sports stars. The rule hardly protected 2012 Heisman Trophy winner Johnny Manziel, who could not walk across his campus without being mobbed by fans. Search for a "Johnny Manziel jersey" online, and you can buy officially branded shirts bearing either his last name or his nickname, "Johnny Football," ranging in price from $24 to $89, licensed by Texas A&M. Rick Reilly observes that Manziel's school "is making the GNP of Kuwait off him in jersey sales and T-shirt sales."

Conley 4

Nobody is saying exactly how much money these jerseys have made for Nike, or for the NCAA. What we do know for sure is the amount Johnny Manziel has made off the jerseys: nothing.

Defenders of the current system argue that student athletes on scholarships are paid with free tuition, free room and board, free books, and tutoring help. The total package can be the equivalent of $120,000 over four years. For those student athletes who are motivated to take advantage of the opportunity, the lifetime benefits can be enormous. Unfortunately, too few student athletes do take advantage of the opportunity. Seldom does a major college football and men's basketball program have graduation rates at or close to that of the overall student body. A study by the University of North Carolina's College Sports Research Institute released in 2010 accuses the NCAA of playing fast and loose with graduation rates by counting part-time students in statistics for the general student body, making graduation rates for athletes look better in a comparison. Student athletes must be full-time students; thus they should be compared to other full-time students. The North Carolina Institute reports that 54.8% of major college (Football Bowl Subdivision) football players at 117 schools graduated within six years, compared with 73.7% of other full-time students. The gap between basketball players was even greater, with 44.6% of athletes graduating compared with 75.7% of the general student body (Zaiger). For the handful of talented athletes who can play in the National Football League or the National Basketball Association, college sports provide training for their future lucrative, although short-lived, profession. But as the NCAA itself points out in its ads, the great majority of student athletes "go pro in something other than sports." For the 55% of college basketball players who fail to graduate, the supposed $120,000 package is an air ball.

The NCAA would be wise to return to the older definition of amateur, which comes from Latin through old French, meaning "lover of." It doesn't necessarily have to have anything to do with money. Whether it's a jazz performer or a dancer or an athlete, an amateur ought to be considered someone in love with an activity— someone who cares deeply about the activity, studies the activity in depth, and practices in order to be highly proficient. NBA players,

[margin notes]

The example of Johnny Manziel illustrates how the definition of amateur works against college athletes.

Conley gives evidence that undercuts the argument that college athletes are compensated with a college degree.

The clever use of "air ball" reinforces Conley's argument that the NCAA's definition of amateur is outdated and unfair.

Conley concludes with her main claim. She proposes a new definition of amateur, one that would permit salaries and royalties to go to the college athlete.

Conley 5

Olympians, college athletes, high school players, and even bird watchers, star gazers, and open-source programmers: they're all amateurs. If they are lucky enough to be paid, so be it.

Conley 6

Works Cited

McCann, Michael. "NCAA Faces Unspecified Damages, Changes in Latest Anti-Trust Case." *SI.com*. Time, Inc., 21 July 2009. Web. 3 Nov. 2013.

"Money and March Madness." *Frontline*. PBS, 29 Mar. 2011. Web. 1 Nov. 2013.

National Collegiate Athletic Association. Advertisement. *NCAA.org*. NCAA, 13 Mar. 2007. Web. 3 Nov. 2013.

Reilly, Rick. "Selling Johnny Football." *ESPN.com*. ESPN, 26 Feb. 2013. Web. 2 Nov. 2013.

Smith, Michael, and John Ourand. "ESPN Pays $2.25B for SEC Rights." *SportsBusiness Journal*. Smith and Street, 25 Aug. 2008. Web. 1 Nov. 2013.

Thamel, Pete. "N.C.A.A. Fails to Stop Licensing Lawsuit." *New York Times*. New York Times, 8 Feb. 2010. Web. 1 Nov. 2013.

Van Riper, Thomas. "The Highest-Paid College Basketball Coaches." *Forbes.com*. Forbes, 8 Mar. 2010. Web. 3 Nov. 2013.

"Welcome to the Music Referral Service." *Butler School of Music*. Univ. of Texas at Austin, n.d. Web. 5 Nov. 2013.

Zaiger, Alan Scher. "Study: NCAA Graduation Rate Comparisons Flawed." *ABC News*. ABC News, 20 Apr. 2010. Web. 1 Nov. 2013.

Zimbalist, Andrew. *Unpaid Professionals: Commercialism and Conflict in Big-Time College Sports*. Princeton UP, 2001. Print.

9 Causal Arguments

QUICK TAKE

In this chapter, you will learn to

1. Identify the three basic forms of causal arguments (see page 118)
2. Understand the four methods used to identify causes (see page 119)
3. Analyze a causal argument (see pages 121–123)
4. Write an effective causal argument (see pages 124–125)

Each year, we hear that American students are falling behind their international peers. Different groups argue that the solution lies in investing more in funding for additional teacher training, or smaller classrooms, or more technology in the classroom. Yet America invests billions more in education than some nations whose students surpass American students in achievement rankings. Still others have suggested that America's problem lies in a wide-scale cultural shift that has created an American student who is less motivated than those of the past. How can America's schools become world leaders again?

Understand How Causal Arguments Work

Causal claims can take three basic forms:

1. One cause leads to one or more effects.

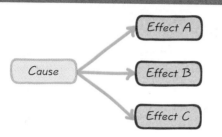

The invention of the telegraph led to the commodities market, the establishment of standard time zones, and news reporting as we know it today.

2. One effect has several causes.

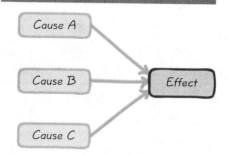

Hurricanes are becoming more financially destructive to the United States because of the greater intensity of recent storms, an increase in the commercial and residential development of coastal areas, and a reluctance to enforce certain construction standards in coastal residential areas.

3. A series of events forms a chain, where one event causes another, which then causes a third, and so on.

Making the HPV vaccination mandatory for adolescent girls will make unprotected sex seem safer, which will lead to greater promiscuity, and then ultimately to more teenage pregnancies.

Find Causes

The causal claim is at the center of the causal argument. Writing a clear claim about cause and effect can be difficult because if a cause is worth writing about, it is likely to be complex. Obvious cases of cause and effect (staying out in the sun too long without skin protection causes sunburn) usually do not require written arguments because everyone is convinced that the causal relationship exists. Many of the causal claims that most people now accept without question—smoking causes cancer, shifting plates on the Earth's crust cause earthquakes, DDT causes eggshell thinning in bald eagles—were "settled" only after long and complex arguments.

The philosopher John Stuart Mill devised four ways for an investigator to go about finding causes.

- **The Common Factor Method.** Sometimes causes can be identified because two or more similar events share a common factor. The common factor may be the cause. For example, if two people in two different states both develop a rare disease, and both of them recently traveled to Madagascar, they were probably exposed to the illness while there.

- **The Single Difference Method.** Causes can often be identified when two situations or events have different outcomes. If there is a single difference in the two scenarios, that difference may be the cause. At the 1998 Winter Olympics in Nagano, Japan, the speed skating team from the Netherlands introduced a technological innovation to the sport—clap skates, which improve skaters' performance by keeping the skate blade in contact with the ice longer. Racing against the best skaters in the world, the Dutch on their clap skates won eleven of thirty medals, five of which were gold. By the 2002 Winter Olympics, all speed skaters had switched over to the new skates, and the medal count was much more evenly distributed. That year the United States, the Netherlands, and Germany each won three gold medals, and a total of eight medals apiece. Clap skates were the most likely cause of the Netherlands' dominance four years earlier.

- **Concomitant Variation.** Some causes are discovered by observing a shared pattern of variation in a possible cause and possible effect. For example, scientists noticed that peaks in the 11-year sunspot cycle match disruptions in high-frequency radio transmission on Earth, leading them to conclude that the solar activity somehow causes the disruptions.

- **Process of Elimination.** Another way to establish causation is to identify all the possible causes of something, and then test them one by one to eliminate those that can't be the cause. When an electrical appliance stops working, electricians often trace the problem this way, by checking switches one at a time to see if current can flow across them. The switch that doesn't show a continuous flow of current is the one that needs replacing.

A frequent error of people looking for cause and effect is to mistake **correlation** for causation. Just because one event happens after or at the same time as another one, you cannot assume that the first one caused the second. Sometimes it's just a coincidence. For example, you may observe that every time the mail carrier comes to your door, your dog barks at him and then the mail carrier leaves. You might assume that your dog's barking causes the mail carrier to leave (your dog is probably convinced of this). However, the more likely cause is that the carrier has finished delivering your mail, so he goes on to the next house. Using Mills's methods will help you avoid mistaking correlation for causation in your own causal arguments.

To understand how you might use Mills's methods of identifying causes, suppose you want to research the cause of the increase in legalized lotteries in the United States. You research the history of lotteries in order to look for possible causes. You would discover that lotteries go back to colonial times but were controversial because they were run by private companies that sometimes failed to pay the winners. Laws against lotteries were passed in 1840, but after the Civil War, the defeated states of the Confederacy needed money to rebuild bridges, buildings, and schools. Southerners ran lotteries and sold tickets throughout the nation. But once again, these lotteries were run by private companies, and some of them simply took people's money without paying out winnings. Eventually, lotteries were banned again.

In 1964 New Hampshire became the first state to authorize a lottery to fund the state's educational system. Soon other states, realizing that their citizens were spending their money on lottery tickets from New Hampshire, established lotteries of their own. During the 1980s, states began approving other forms of state-run gambling such as keno and video poker. By 1993 only Hawaii and Utah had no legalized gambling of any kind.

Knowing this background, you can begin using Mills's methods to look for the causes of lotteries' recent popularity. Using the common factor method, you consider what current lotteries have in common with earlier lotteries. That factor is easy to identify: It's economic. The early colonies and later the states have turned to lotteries again and again as a way of raising money without raising taxes. But, you wonder, why have lotteries spread so quickly since 1964 and raised so little concern? The single difference method shows you the likely reason: Lotteries in the past were run by private companies, and inevitably someone took off with the money instead of paying it out. Today's lotteries are operated by state agencies or contracted under state control. While they are not immune to scandal, they are much more closely monitored than lotteries in the past.

Mills's other methods might also lead you to potential causes. If you find, for example, that lotteries grow in popularity in the aftermath of wars, this concomitant variation might lead you to suspect that the economic damage of war can be one cause of lotteries' popularity. This in turn might suggest inflation caused by the Vietnam War as a possible contributing cause to the rise of state lotteries in the 1960s and 1970s. The process of elimination could also lead you to some probable causes for lotteries' popularity, although for such a complex topic, it would be time-consuming. You might begin by making a list of all the reasons you could think of: Perhaps people these days are more economically secure and don't mind risking a few dollars on lottery tickets? Or maybe people are more desperate now, and lotteries represent one of the few ways they can accumulate wealth? Each of these possibilities would require research into history, economics, and psychology, but this might lead you to some interesting conclusions about the complex forces contributing to today's extensive lottery system.

Build a Causal Argument

Effective causal arguments move beyond the obvious to get at underlying causes. One great causal mystery today is global warming. Scientists generally agree that the average surface temperature on Earth has gone up by 1.3 degrees Fahrenheit, or 0.7 degrees Celsius, over the last hundred years and that the amount of carbon dioxide in the atmosphere has increased by 25 percent since 1960. But the causes of those phenomena are disputed. Some people argue that the rise in temperature is caused by natural climate variations and that the increase in carbon dioxide has little or nothing to do with it. Others argue that the rise in carbon dioxide traps heat in the atmosphere and has increased the Earth's temperature. They argue further that the increased carbon dioxide is the result of human activity, especially the burning of fossil fuels and the destruction of tropical forests. The debate over global warming continues because the causation at work is not simple or easy to prove.

There are many events that may be caused by global warming, and they are more dramatically evident in arctic and subarctic regions. The decade from January 2000 to December 2009 is the warmest decade since modern temperature records began in the 1880s. Arctic sea ice shrank by 14 percent—an area the size of Texas—from 2004 to 2005, and Greenland's massive ice sheet has been thinning by more than 3 feet a year.

Many scientists consider these phenomena to be effects of global warming. They argue that a single cause—the rise in the Earth's temperature—has led to many dire effects and will lead to more. If you wanted to make an argument along these lines, you would need to construct a causal chain:

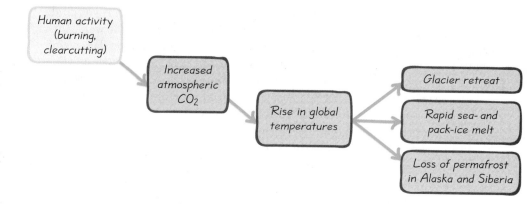

At each step, you would need to show the links between an event and its consequences, and you would need to convince readers that that link is real, not mere coincidence. You might find common factors, single differences, or concomitant variation that supports each causal link. You would also need to use a process of elimination to show that other possible causes are not in fact involved in your causal chain.

Some climate scientists have doubts about all these causal links. While the observable events—the loss of sea ice, glacier retreat, and so on—may be caused by human activity, they may be caused instead by naturally recurring cycles.

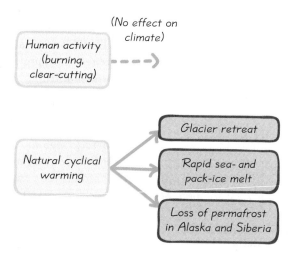

Or the effects could be caused partly by natural cycles and partly by humans.

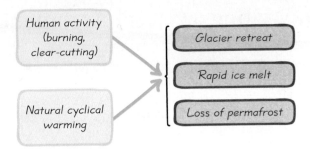

It is difficult to say for certain because much of the detailed data about the great melt in the north goes back only to the early 1990s—not long enough to rule out short-term climate cycles. However, computer models suggest a very low probability that such rapid change could occur naturally. So even if we are in a natural, short-term warming cycle, we still must ask if human activities are contributing to the documented warming and making it even worse.

Identifying the causes of global warming is important because if we do not know the real causes, we cannot make the necessary changes to stop, reduce, or reverse it. If global warming continues unabated, the economic and human costs will be disastrous. But efforts to stop it are expensive and politically risky. Thus correctly establishing the causes of global warming is a crucial first step in solving the problem.

Glaciers in many parts of the world are melting at rates faster than scientists thought possible just a few years ago. Even major oil companies have acknowledged that global warming is real. Yet the American public has taken little notice of world climate change—perhaps because it's difficult to get excited about the mean temperature rising a few degrees and the sea level rising a few feet. What would get Americans thinking seriously about global warming?

Steps to Writing a Causal Argument

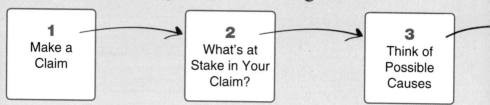

Step 1 Make a Claim

Make a causal claim on a controversial trend, event, or phenomenon.

Template

> **SOMETHING does (or does not) cause SOMETHING ELSE.**

–or–

> **SOMETHING causes SOMETHING ELSE, which, in turn, causes SOMETHING ELSE.**

Examples

- One-parent families (or television violence, bad diet, and so on) are (or are not) the cause of emotional and behavioral problems in children.
- Firearms control laws (or right-to-carry-handgun laws) reduce (or increase) violent crimes.
- Putting grade school children into competitive sports teaches them how to succeed in later life (or puts undue emphasis on winning and teaches many who are slower to mature to have a negative self-image).

Step 2 What's at Stake in Your Claim?

- If the cause is obvious to everyone, then it probably isn't worth writing about.

Step 3 Think of Possible Causes

- Which are the immediate causes?
- Which are the background causes?
- Which are the hidden causes?
- Which are the causes that most people have not recognized?

Step 4 Analyze Your Potential Readers

- Who are your readers?
- How familiar will they be with the trend, event, or phenomenon that you're writing about?
- What are they likely to know and not know?
- How likely are they to accept your causal explanation?
- What alternative explanation might they argue for?

Step 5 Write a Draft

Introduction

- Describe the controversial trend, event, or phenomenon.
- Give the background that your intended readers will need.

Body

- Explain the cause or chain of causation of a trend, event, or phenomenon that is unfamiliar to your readers.
- Set out the causes that have been offered and reject them one by one. Then you can present the cause that you think is most important.
- Treat a series of causes one by one, analyzing the importance of each.

Conclusion

- Do more than simply summarize. Consider describing additional effects beyond those that have been noted previously.

Step 6 Revise, Edit, Proofread

- For detailed instructions, see Chapter 5.
- For a checklist to use to evaluate your draft, see pages 50–51.

Finding Good Reasons

Why Are Americans Gaining Weight?

Eric Schlosser, author of *Fast Food Nation* (2001), chows down on a grilled cheese sandwich, fries, and a soda. *Fast Food Nation* traces the rise of fast-food restaurants against the background of an American culture based on the automobile. Schlosser claims that one of the effects of fast food is the increase in the number of overweight Americans.

There is no doubt that Americans have grown larger. A 2004 survey of Americans published in *JAMA: The Journal of the American Medical Association* found that nearly one-third (32.5 percent) of adults are obese and two-thirds (66.3 percent) are overweight. An especially disturbing aspect of this trend is that children are increasingly obese. The Center for Disease Control and Prevention reports that the percentage of obese children aged 6 to 11 more than quadrupled from 4 percent in 1974 to 18 percent in 2010, and the percentage of obese children aged 12 to 19 increased from 6 percent in 1974 to 18.4 percent in 2010.

Write about it

To what extent do you think fast food is the cause of the trend toward excess weight? To what extent do you think lifestyle changes and the content of food are causes? In addition to the amount of fast food Americans consume, consider the following.

- More sedentary lifestyle with more driving and less walking
- More time spent watching television, using computers, and playing video games
- Introduction of high-fructose corn syrup in many foods, from ketchup and peanut butter to chocolate milk and yogurt
- Inadequate physical education and reduced outdoor recess periods in schools
- More food advertising directed at children

**Emily
Raine**

Why Should I Be Nice to You?
Coffee Shops and the Politics
of Good Service

Emily Raine received a master's degree in communication studies at McGill University in Montreal. She writes about graffiti and street art. This article appeared in the online journal *Bad Subjects* in 2005.

In this article, Raine explains why work in a coffee chain is worse than work in other kinds of service jobs. She also outlines the causes for what she sees as a destructive dynamic in the coffee chain culture and provides a possible alternative.

> "There is no more precious commodity than the relationship of trust and confidence a company has with its employees."
> —*Starbucks Coffee Company chairman Howard Schultz*

I actually like to serve. I'm not sure if this comes from some innate inclination to mother and fuss over strangers, or if it's because the movement and sociability of service work provides a much-needed antidote to the solitude of academic research, but I've always found something about service industry work satisfying. I've done the gamut of service jobs, from fine dining to cocktail waitressing to hip euro-bistro counter work, and the only job where I've ever felt truly whipped was working as a barista at one of the now-ubiquitous specialty coffee chains, those bastions of jazz and public solitude that have spread through urban landscapes over the last ten years or so. The pay was poor, the shifts long and oddly dispersed, the work boring and monotonous, the managers demanding, and the customers regularly displayed that unique spleen that emerges in even the most pleasant people before they've had the morning's first coffee. I often felt like an aproned Coke machine, such was the effect my sparkling personality had on the clientele. And yet, some combination of service professionalism, fear of termination and an imperative to be "nice" allowed me to suck it up, smile and continue to provide that intangible trait that the industry holds above all else, good service.

Raine establishes a credible, ethical stance in her introduction.

2   Good service in coffee shops doesn't amount to much. Unlike table service, where interaction with customers spans a minimum of half an hour, the average contact with a café customer lasts less than ten seconds. Consider how specialty cafés are laid

Even before identifying the effect that she intends to analyze, Raine identifies the cause—an efficient but impersonal assembly-line approach to service.

3   out: the customer service counter is arranged in a long line that clients move along to "use" the café. The linear coffee bar resembles an assembly line, and indeed, café labor is heavily grounded in the rationalism of Fordist manufacturing principles, which had already been tested for use in hospitality services by fast food chains. Each of the café workers is assigned a specific stage in the service process to perform exclusively, such as taking orders, using the cash registers, or handing clients cups of brewed coffee.

4   The specialization of tasks increases the speed of transactions and limits the duration of any one employee's interaction with the clientele. This means that in a given visit a customer might order from one worker, receive food from the next, then brewed coffee or tea from yet another, then pay a cashier before proceeding down the line of the counter, finishing the trip at the espresso machine which is always situated at its end. Ultimately, each of the café's products is processed and served by a different employee, who repeats the same preparation task for hours and attends to each customer only as they receive that one product.

Raine argues that the assembly-line service model precludes real interaction with customers.

Needless to say, the productive work in cafés is dreary and repetitive. Further, this style of service severely curtails interaction with the clientele, and the very brevity of each transaction precludes much chance for authentic friendliness or conversation—even asking about someone's day would slow the entire operation. The one aspect of service work that can be unpredictable—people—becomes redundant, and interaction with customers is reduced to a fatiguing eight-hour-long smile and the repetition of sentiments that allude to good service, such as injunctions to enjoy their purchases or to have a nice day. Rather than friendly exchanges with customers, barista workers' good service is reduced to a quick rictus in the customer's direction between a great deal of friendly interaction with the espresso machine.

Do you agree with this description of a typical coffee shop?

5   As the hospitality industry really took off in the sixties, good service became one of the trademarks of its advertising claims, a way for brands to distinguish themselves from the rest of the pack. One needn't think too hard to come up with a litany of service slogans that holler the good graces of their personnel—at Starbucks where the baristas make the magic, at Pacific Southwest Airlines where smiles aren't just painted on, or at McDonald's where smiles are free. Employee friendliness emerged as one of the chief distinguishing brand features of personal services, which means that the workers themselves become an aspect of the product for sale.

6   Our notions of good service revolve around a series of platitudes about professionalism—we're at your service, with a smile,

where the customer's always right—each bragging the centrality of the customer to everything "we" do. Such claims imply an easy and equal exchange between two parties: the "we" that gladly serves and the "you" that happily receives. There is, however, always a third party involved in the service exchange, and that's whoever has hired the server, the body that ultimately decides just what the dimensions of good service will be.

> This "third party"—management, ownership—is the ultimate cause of the phenomenon under discussion.

7   Like most employees, a service worker sells labor to an employer at a set rate, often minimum wage, and the employer sells the product of that labor, the service itself, at market values. In many hospitality services, where gratuities make up the majority of employment revenue, the worker directly benefits from giving good service, which of course translates to good tips. But for the vast majority of service staff, and particularly those employed in venues yielding little or no gratuities—fast food outlets, café chains, cleaning and maintenance operations—this promises many workers little more than a unilateral imperative to be perpetually bright and amenable.

8   The vast majority of service personnel do not spontaneously produce an unaffected display of cheer and good will continuously for the duration of a shift. When a company markets its products on servers' friendliness, they must then monitor and control employees' friendliness, so good service is defined and enforced from above. Particularly in chains, which are premised upon their consistent reproduction of the same experience in numerous locations, organizations are obliged to impose systems to manage employees' interaction with their customers. In some chains, namely the fast food giants such as McDonald's and Burger King, employee banter is scripted into cash registers, so that as soon as a customer orders, workers are cued to offer, "would you like a dessert with that?" (an offer of dubious benefit to the customer) and to wish them a nice day. Ultimately, this has allowed corporations to be able to assimilate "good service"—or, friendly workers—into their overall brand image.

> Does your experience as a customer (or worker) at fast food chains match this description?

9   While cafés genuflect toward the notion of good service, their layouts and management styles preclude much possibility of creating the warmth that this would entail. Good service is, of course, important, but not if it interferes with throughput. What's more, these cafés have been at the forefront of a new wave of organizations that not only market themselves on service quality but also describe employees' job satisfaction as the seed from which this flowers.

10   Perhaps the most glaring example of this is Starbucks, where cheerful young workers are displayed behind elevated

counters as they banter back and forth, calling out fancy Italian drink names and creating theatre out of their productive labor. Starbucks' corporate literature gushes not only about the good service its customers will receive, but about the great joy that its "partners" take in providing it, given the company's unique ability to "provide a great work environment and treat each other with respect and dignity," and where its partners are "emotionally and intellectually committed to Starbucks success." In the epigraph to this essay, Starbucks' chairman even describes the company's relationship with its workers as a commodity. Not only does Starbucks offer good service, but it attempts to guarantee something even better: good service provided by employees that are genuinely happy to give it.

The creation of this new kind of worker is in effect a public relations gimmick.

11   Starbucks has branded a new kind of worker, the happy, wholesome, perfume-free barista. The company offers unusual benefits for service workers, including stock options, health insurance, dental plans and other perks such as product discounts and giveaways. Further, they do so very, very publicly, and the company's promotional materials are filled with moving accounts of workers who never dreamed that corporate America could care so much. With the other hand, though, the company has smashed unionization drives in New York, Vancouver and at its Seattle roaster; it schedules workers at oddly timed shifts that never quite add up to full-time hours; the company pays only nominally more than minimum wage, and their staffs are still unable to subsist schlepping lattes alone.

12   Starbucks is not alone in marketing itself as an enlightened employer. When General Motors introduced its Saturn line, the new brand was promoted almost entirely on the company's good relations with its staff. The company's advertising spots often featured pictures of and quotes from the union contract, describing their unique partnership between manufacturer, workers and union, which allowed blue-collar personnel to have a say in everything from automobile designs to what would be served for lunch. The company rightly guessed that this strategy would go over well with liberal consumers concerned about the ethics of their purchases. Better yet, Saturn could market its cars based on workers' happiness whether personnel were satisfied or not, because very few consumers would ever have the chance to interact with them.

13   At the specialty coffee chains, however, consumers have to talk to employees, yet nobody ever really asks. The café service counter runs like a smooth piece of machinery, and I found that most people preferred to pretend that they were interacting with an appliance. In such short transactions, it is exceedingly difficult

for customers to remember the humanity of each of the four to seven people they might interact with to get their coffees. Even fast food counters have one server who processes each customer's order, yet in cafés the workers just become another gadget in the well-oiled café machine. This is a definite downside for the employees—clients are much ruder to café staff than in any other sector of the industry I ever worked in. I found that people were more likely to be annoyed than touched by any reference to my having a personality, and it took no small amount of thought on my part to realize why.

14   Barista workers are hired to represent an abstract category of worker, not to act as individuals. Because of the service system marked by short customer interaction periods and a homogenous staff, the services rendered are linked in the consumer imagination to the company and not to any one individual worker. Workers' assimilation into the company image makes employees in chain service as branded as the products they serve. The chain gang, the workers who hold these eminently collegiate after-school jobs, are proscribed sales scripts and drilled on customer service scenarios to standardize interactions with customers. The company issues protocols for hair length, color and maintenance, visible piercings and tattoos as well as personal hygiene and acceptable odorific products. Workers are made more interchangeable by the use of uniforms, which, of course, serve to make the staff just that. The organization is a constant intermediary in every transaction, interjecting its presence in every detail of the service experience, and this standardization amounts to an absorption of individuals' personalities into the corporate image.

Raine spells out her thesis in this paragraph.

15   Many of the measures that chains take to secure the homogeneity of their employees do not strike us as particularly alarming, likely because similar restrictions have been in place for several hundred years. Good service today has inherited many of the trappings of the good servant of yore, including prohibitions against eating, drinking, sitting or relaxing in front the served, entering and exiting through back doors, and wearing uniforms to visually mark workers' status. These measures almost completely efface the social identities of staff during work hours, providing few clues to workers' status in their free time. Contact between service workers and their customers is thus limited to purely functional relations, so that the public only see them as workers, as makers of quality coffee, and never as possible peers.

16   Maintaining such divisions is integral to good service because this display of class distinctions ultimately underlies our

notions of service quality. Good service means not only serving well, but also allowing customers to feel justified in issuing orders, to feel okay about being served—which, in turn, requires demonstrations of class difference and the smiles that suggest servers' comfort with having a subordinate role in the service exchange.

17   Unlike the penguin-suited household servant staffs whose class status was clearly defined, service industry workers today often have much more in common from a class perspective with those that they serve. This not only creates an imperative for them to wear their class otherness on their sleeves, as it were, but also to accept their subordinate role to those they serve by being unshakably tractable and polite.

18   Faith Popcorn has rather famously referred to the four-dollar latte as a "small indulgence," noting that while this is a lot to pay for a glass of hot milk, it is quite inexpensive for the feeling of luxury that can accompany it. In this service climate, the class status of the server and the served—anyone who can justify spending this much on a coffee—is blurry, indeed. Coffee shops that market themselves on employee satisfaction assert the same happy servant that allows politically conscientious consumers, who are in many cases the workers' own age and class peers, to feel justified in receiving good service. Good service—as both an apparent affirmation of subordinate classes' desire to serve and as an enforced one-sided politeness—reproduces the class distinctions that have historically characterized servant-served relationships so that these are perpetuated within the contemporary service market.

19   The specialty coffee companies are large corporations, and for the twenty-somethings who stock their counters, barista work is too temporary to bother fighting the system. Mostly, people simply quit. Dissatisfied workers are stuck with engaging in tactics that will change nothing but allow them to make the best of their lot. These include minor infractions such as taking liberties with the uniforms or grabbing little bits of company time for their own pleasure, what Michel de Certeau calls *la perruque* and the companies themselves call "time theft." As my time in the chain gang wore on, I developed my own tactic, the only one I found that jostled the customers out of their complacency and allowed me to be a barista and a person.

20   There is no easy way to serve without being a servant, and I have always found that the best way to do so is to show my actual emotions rather than affecting a smooth display of interminable patience and good will. For café customers, bettering baristas' lots can be as simple as asking about their day, addressing them

Raine begins to shift attention to the customers' role in coffee shop culture.

by name—any little gesture to show that you noticed the person behind the service that they can provide. My tactic as a worker is equally simple, but it is simultaneously an assertion of individual identity at work, a refusal of the class distinctions that characterize the service environment and a rebuttal to the companies that would promote my satisfaction with their system: be rude. Not arbitrarily rude, of course—customers are people, too, and nobody gains anything by spreading bad will. But on those occasions when customer or management behavior warranted a zinging comeback, I would give it.

Were you expecting this "solution" to the situation Raine presents?

21   Rudeness, when it is demanded, undermines companies' claims on workers' personal warmth and allows them to retain their individuality by expressing genuine rather than affected feelings in at-work interpersonal exchanges. It is a refusal of the class distinctions that underlie consumers' unilateral prerogative of rudeness and servers' unilateral imperative to be nice. It runs contrary to everything that we have been taught, not only about service but about interrelating with others. But this seems to be the only method of asserting one's personhood in the service environment, where workers' personalities are all too easily reduced to a space-time, conflated with the drinks they serve. Baristas of the world, if you want to avoid becoming a green-aproned coffee dispensary, you're just going to have to tell people off about it.

Raine reveals her specific audience, "baristias of the world," only at the end of her argument.

Sample Student Causal Argument

Tansal 1

Armadi Tansal

Professor Stewart

English 115

29 October 2013

Modern Warfare: Video Games' Link to Real-World Violence

"John" is a nineteen-year-old college student who gets decent grades. He comes from a typical upper-middle-class family and plans to get his MBA after he graduates. John is also my friend, which is why I'm not using his real name.

John has been playing moderately violent video games since he was nine years old. I started playing video and console games around that age too, and I played a lot in junior high, but John plays more than anyone I know. John says that over the past year he has played video games at least four hours every day and "sometimes all day and night on the weekends." I have personally witnessed John play *Call of Duty: Modern Warfare 3* for six hours straight, with breaks only to use the bathroom or eat something.

I've never seen John act violently, and he's never been in trouble with the law. But new research on violent video games suggests that John's gaming habit puts him at risk for violent or aggressive behavior. Dr. Craig Anderson, a psychologist at the University of Iowa, says that "the active role required by video games . . . may make violent video games even more hazardous than violent television or cinema." When people like John play these games, they get used to being rewarded for violent behavior. For example, in the multiplayer version of *Modern Warfare 3*, if the player gets a five-kill streak, he can call in a Predator missile strike. If you kill 25 people in a row, you can call in a tactical nuclear strike. Missile strikes help you advance toward the mission goals more quickly, so the more people you kill, the faster you'll win.

> Armadi Tansal establishes a personal relationship to his subject and audience.

Along with *Modern Warfare 3*, John plays games like *League of Legends*, *Halo 4*, and versions of *Grand Theft Auto*. All these games are rated M for Mature, which according to the Entertainment Software Rating Board means they "may contain intense violence, blood and gore, sexual content and/

Tansal 2

or strong language." Some M-rated games, like *Grand Theft Auto,* feature random violence, where players can run amok in a city, beat up and kill people, and smash stuff for no reason. In others, like *Modern Warfare 3,* the violence takes place in the context of military action. To do well in all of these games, you have to commit acts of violence. But does acting violently in games make you more violent in real life?

Anderson says studies show that "violent video games are significantly associated with: increased aggressive behavior, thoughts, and affect [feelings]; increased physiological arousal; and decreased prosocial (helping) behavior." He also claims that "high levels of violent video game exposure have been linked to delinquency, fighting at school and during free play periods, and violent criminal behavior (e.g., self-reported assault, robbery)."

Being "associated with" and "linked to" violent behavior doesn't necessarily mean video games cause such behavior. Many people have argued that the links Anderson sees are coincidental, or that any effects video games might have on behavior are so slight that we shouldn't worry about them. Christopher Ferguson and John Kilburn, professors of Criminal Justice at Texas A&M International University, feel that the existing research does not support Anderson's claims. In a report published in the *Journal of Pediatrics,* they point out that in past studies, "the closer aggression measures got to actual violent behavior, the weaker the effects seen" (762).

From what I can tell, John doesn't have any more violent thoughts and feelings than most men his age. When I asked him if he thought the games had made him more violent or aggressive in real life, he said, "I'm actually less violent now. When we were kids we used to play 'war' with fake guns and sticks, chasing each other around the neighborhood and fighting commando-style. We didn't really fight, but sometimes kids got banged up. No one ever gets hurt playing a video game."

Anderson admits that "a healthy, normal, nonviolent child or adolescent who has no other risk factors for high aggression or violence is not going to become a school shooter simply because they play five hours or 10 hours a week of these violent video games" (qtd. in St. George). But just because violent video games don't turn all players into mass murderers, that doesn't mean they have no effect on a player's

---

Tansal identifies the causal question at the heart of his argument.

Direct quotations from published sources build credibility.

Tansal is careful not to accept the easy answer that video games cause everyone to be more violent.

Tansal 3

behavior and personality. For example, my friend John doesn't get into fights or rob people, but he doesn't display a lot of prosocial "helping" behaviors either. He spends most of his free time gaming, so he doesn't get out of his apartment much. Also, the friends he does have mostly play video games with him.

Here Tansal hints at his thesis, which will be explicitly stated at the end of his argument.

Even though the games restrict his interactions with other humans and condition him to behave violently onscreen, John is probably not at high risk of becoming violent in real life. But according to researchers, this low risk of becoming violent is because none of the dozens of other risk factors associated with violent behavior are present in his life (Anderson et al. 160). If John were a high school dropout, came from a broken home, or abused alcohol and other drugs, his game playing might be more likely to contribute to violent behavior.

Tansal clarifies his thesis that games can be a contributing cause of violent behavior.

Anderson contends that violent video games are a "causal risk factor" for violence and aggression—not that they cause violent aggression. In other words, the games are a small piece of a much larger problem. People like my friend John are not likely to become violent because of the video games they play. But Anderson's research indicates that some people do. Although there is no simple way to tell who those people are, we should include video games as a possible risk factor when we think about who is likely to become violent.

Even if the risk contributed by violent video games is slight for each individual, the total impact of the games on violence in society could be huge. *Call of Duty: Modern Warfare 3* enjoyed the biggest first day sales of any game ever in 2011 until it was surpassed by its successor, *Black Ops 2*, which brought over $500 million in sales to its publisher Activision on its first day in 2012. Bobby Kotick, the CEO of Activision claims that the *Call of Duty* franchise has exceeded worldwide box office receipts for the *Harry Potter* and *Star Wars* series, the two most popular movie franchises of all time (Sheer). Millions of people play this game, and games like it, and they aren't all as well-adjusted as John. If video games contribute to violent tendencies in only a small fraction of players, they could still have a terrible impact.

Tansal concludes by arguing that video games may not cause many people to become more violent, but it doesn't take many to be a big problem.

Tansal 4

Works Cited

Anderson, Craig. "Violent Video Games: Myths, Facts, and Unanswered Questions." *Psychological Science Agenda* 16.5 (2003): n. pag. Web. 6 Oct. 2013.

Anderson, Craig, et al. "Violent Video Game Effects on Aggression, Empathy, and Prosocial Behavior in Eastern and Western Countries." *Psychological Bulletin* 136 (2010): 151-73. Print.

Entertainment Software Rating Board. *Game Ratings and Descriptor Guide*. Entertainment Software Association, n.d. Web. 7 Oct. 2013.

Ferguson, Christopher J., and John Kilburn. "The Public Health Risks of Media Violence: A Meta-Analytic Review." *Journal of Pediatrics* 154.5 (2009): 759-63. Print.

John (pseudonym). Personal interview. 4 Oct. 2013.

Sheer, Matthew. "*Black Ops 2* Blasts Past $500 Million in Sales—in 24 Hours." *Christian Science Monitor*. Christian Science Monitor, 16 Nov. 2012. Web. 6 Oct. 2013.

St. George, Donna. "Study Links Violent Video Games, Hostility." *Washington Post*. Washington Post, 3 Nov. 2008. Web. 5 Oct. 2013.

10 | Evaluation Arguments

By some estimates, as many as 5 million animals are killed in shelters each year. Are "no-kill" shelters a good idea? Advocates of no-kill shelters argue that alternatives to euthanizing animals can be created by working to increase adoption demand for shelter animals. No-kill shelters also work to promote spaying and neutering to decrease the number of animals sent to shelters in the first place. Others argue that the term "no-kill" is divisive because it implies that some shelters are "kill" shelters and suggests that many shelter workers are cruel or uncaring. Are no-kill shelters an effective solution? What kind of evaluations would support or oppose the concept of the no-kill shelter? How can evaluation arguments be used to support more humane treatment of shelter animals?

People make evaluations all the time. Newspapers, magazines, and television have picked up on this love of evaluation by running "best of" polls. They ask their readers to vote on the best Chinese restaurant, the best pizza, the best local band, the best coffeehouse, the best dance club, the best neighborhood park, the best swimming hole, the best bike ride (scenic or challenging), the best volleyball court, the best place to get married, and so on. If you ask one of your friends who voted in a "best" poll why she picked a particular restaurant as the best of its kind, she might respond by saying simply, "I like it." But if you ask her why she likes it, she might start offering good reasons such as these: The food is tasty, the service prompt, the prices fair, and the atmosphere comfortable. It's really not a mystery why these polls are often quite predictable or why the same restaurants tend to win year after year. Many people think that evaluations are matters of personal taste, but when we begin probing the reasons, we often discover that different people use similar criteria to make evaluations.

The key to convincing other people that your judgment is sound is establishing the criteria you will use to make your evaluation. Sometimes it will be necessary to argue for the validity of the criteria that you think your readers should consider. If your readers accept your criteria, it's likely they will agree with your conclusions.

Understand How Evaluation Arguments Work

Evaluation arguments set out criteria and then judge something to be good or bad (or better, or best) according to those criteria.

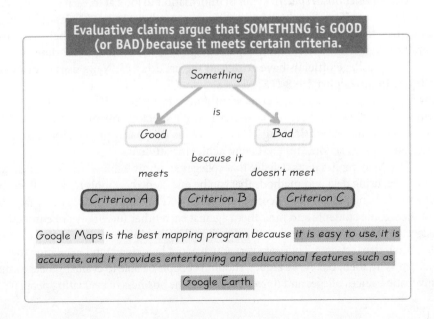

Recognize Kinds of Evaluations

Arguments of evaluation are structured much like arguments of definition. Recall that the criteria in arguments of definition are set out in *because* clauses:

SOMETHING is a _____ because it meets certain criteria.

Evaluative claims argue that

SOMETHING is GOOD (or BAD) because it meets certain criteria.

While people often agree about general criteria, they sometimes disagree about the relevance and appropriateness of specific criteria in an evaluation. Take as an example the question of which colleges are good schools. Until twenty years ago, most of the information that people used to evaluate a college came from the college itself. You could find out the price of tuition and what courses were offered, but other information was difficult to find, and it was hard to compare one college with another.

In 1983 the magazine *U.S. News & World Report* began ranking U.S. colleges and universities from a consumer's perspective. These rankings have remained controversial ever since. *U.S. News* evaluates schools using a complex set of criteria. Twenty-five percent of a school's ranking is based on a survey in which officials at each college rate the quality of schools in the same category as their own school. The results of this survey reflect the school's reputation among administrators. The remaining 75 percent is based on six kinds of statistical data. These measure retention of students, faculty resources, student selectivity, financial resources, alumni giving, and, for some schools, graduation rates (the difference between the number of students expected to graduate and the number who actually do).

U.S. News chooses specific types of information to look at in each category. For example, the category "faculty resources" is measured by the size of classes, average faculty pay, the percentage of professors with the highest degree in their field, the overall student-faculty ratio, and the percentage of faculty who are full-time.

Many college officials have criticized the criteria *U.S. News* uses to evaluate colleges. In an August 1998 *U.S. News* article, Gerhard Casper, the president of Stanford University (which is consistently near the top of the rankings), writes, "Much about these rankings—particularly their specious formulas and spurious precision—is utterly misleading." Casper argues that using graduation rates as a criterion rewards schools that pass low-achieving students.

U.S. News replies in its defense that colleges and universities themselves do a lot of ranking, using data and methods that can be questioned. Schools rank students for admission, using SAT or ACT scores, high school GPA, class rank, and other factors, and then grade students and rank them against each other once they are enrolled in college. Schools also evaluate their faculty and take great interest in the national ranking of their departments. They care very much about how they stand in relation to one another. Why, then, *U.S. News* argues, shouldn't people be able to evaluate colleges and universities, since colleges and universities are in the business of evaluating people?

The magazine and the colleges have very different ideas about what constitute fair and relevant criteria for evaluating a college. But the *U.S. News* college rankings generate a tremendous amount of income for the magazine, which suggests that students and their parents agree with the criteria and use them to help make their own decisions about college.

Some evaluation arguments rely more heavily on certain types of criteria than others. For example, a movie review (_____ is a good movie) is likely to focus most closely on aesthetic considerations: engaging characters, an exciting story, beautiful cinematography. Ethical considerations may be relevant—say, if the film is exceptionally violent or celebrates antisocial behavior—but usually don't predominate in a movie review. Practical considerations will probably be least important, since anyone reading a movie review is presumably willing to spend the price of admission to see a film. Use aesthetic, moral, and practical criteria for deciding how good or bad a person, a place, an artifact, or a policy is.

Build an Evaluation Argument

Although evaluation arguments seem very similar to definition arguments, there is a key difference. Definition arguments seek to place something in the correct category by observing its qualities. They hinge on our judgments about similarity and difference. Evaluation arguments focus instead on what we value. Because of this, the criteria you choose when making an evaluation argument are very important. If your criteria do not appeal to the values of your audience, your readers will not feel that your evaluation is accurate.

Suppose that a city task force on downtown revitalization has a plan to demolish the oldest commercial building in your city. Your neighborhood association wants to preserve the building, perhaps by turning it into a museum. To persuade officials to do this, you must show that your plan for preservation is a good one, while the task force's plan for demolition is a bad one. You might argue that a museum would attract visitors to the downtown area, bringing in revenue. You might argue that the elaborately carved stone facade of the building is a rare example of a disappearing craft. Or you might argue that it is only fair to preserve the oldest commercial building in town, since the city's oldest house and other historic buildings have been saved.

Each of these arguments uses different criteria. The argument that a museum will bring in money is based on practical considerations. The argument about the rare and beautiful stonework on the building is based on aesthetic (artistic) considerations. The argument that an old commercial building deserves the same treatment as other old buildings is based on fairness, or ethical concerns. Depending on your audience, you might use all three kinds of criteria, or you might focus more on one or two kinds. If your city is in the middle of a budget crisis, it might be wise to stress the practical, economic benefits of a museum. If several city council members are architects or amateur historians, your argument might focus

Windmills produce energy without pollution and reduce dependence on foreign oil. Do you agree or disagree with people who do not want windmills built near them because they find them ugly?

on the aesthetic criteria. You have to make assumptions about what your audience will value most as they consider your evaluation.

Evaluative arguments can look at just one case in isolation, but often they make comparisons. You could construct an argument about the fate of the old building that only describes your plan and its benefits. Or you might also directly address the demolition proposal, showing how it lacks those benefits. Then your argument might be structured like this:

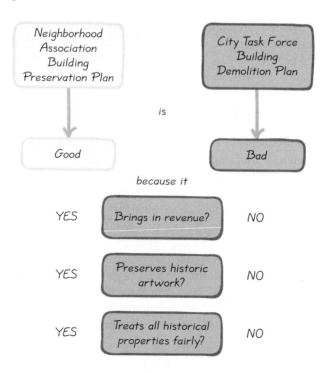

Finding Good Reasons

What's the Best Alternative Fuel?

Biodiesel is an alternative fuel source that is made from vegetable oil (or animal fats) and alcohol. While biodiesel can be used alone, it is often mixed with petroleum diesel. Blends of up to 20 percent biodiesel can be used in a standard diesel engine without modifications—meaning that many cars on the road today would be capable of using biodiesel if it were to become widely available.

But is biodiesel a realistic solution to the world's dependence on fossil fuels? Many think yes. Proponents point to the reduction in greenhouse gas emissions and the lower dependence on foreign oil that would accompany wide-scale biodiesel adoption. Detractors point to millions of acres of land, which would typically be used for food production, that would be converted to fuel production, inevitably causing shortages and an overall rise in food prices.

Write about it

1. One way to assess a complicated issue like alternative fuel technologies is to evaluate each technology against a set of common criteria. Which of the following criteria are useful for evaluating fuel-efficient cars? Why are they useful?

   - Cost of development and production
   - Sticker price of cars using the technology
   - How long it takes for cars to reach the market
   - Efficiency and reliability of cars using the technology
   - Environmental impact
   - Convenience of refueling and maintenance
   - Driver's aesthetic experience

2. Are any of the above criteria more important than the others? If so, how would you rank them? Why? Are there any criteria you would add?

Steps to Writing an Evaluation Argument

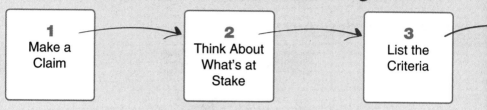

Step 1 Make a Claim

Make an evaluative claim based on criteria.

Template

> SOMETHING is good (bad, the best, the worst) if measured by certain criteria (practicality, aesthetics, ethics).

Examples

- A book or movie review
- An evaluation of a controversial aspect of sports (e.g., the current system of determining who is champion in Division I college football) or a sports event (e.g., this year's WNBA playoffs) or a team
- An evaluation of the effectiveness of a social policy or law such as restrictions on newly licensed drivers, current gun control laws, or environmental regulation

Step 2 Think About What's at Stake

- Does nearly everyone agree with you? Then your claim probably isn't interesting or important. If you can think of people who disagree, then something is at stake.
- Who argues the opposite of your claim?
- Why do they make a different evaluation?

Step 3 List the Criteria

- Which criteria make something either good or bad?
- Which criteria are the most important?
- Which criteria are fairly obvious, and which will you have to argue for?

Step 4 Analyze Your Potential Readers

- Who are your readers?
- How familiar will they be with what you are evaluating?
- Which criteria are they most likely to accept with little explanation, and which will they disagree with?

Step 5 Write a Draft

Introduction

- Introduce the person, group, institution, event, or object that you are going to evaluate. You might want to announce your stance at this point or wait until the concluding section.
- Give the background that your intended readers will need.

Body

- Describe each criterion and then analyze how well what you are evaluating meets that criterion.
- If you are making an evaluation according to the effects someone or something produces, describe each effect in detail.
- Anticipate where readers might question either your criteria or how they apply to your subject.
- Address opposing viewpoints by acknowledging how their evaluations might differ and by showing why your evaluation is better.

Conclusion

- If you have not yet announced your stance, conclude that, on the basis of the criteria you set out or the effects you have analyzed, something is good (bad, the best, the worst).
- If you have made your stance clear from the beginning, end with a compelling example or analogy.

Step 6 Revise, Edit, Proofread

- For detailed instructions, see Chapter 5.
- For a checklist to use to evaluate your draft, see pages 50–51.

Glenn Loury

A Nation of Jailers

Glenn Loury is Merton P. Stoltz Professor of the Social Sciences at Brown University and a guest on many television and radio news programs. He is the author of *One by One, From the Inside Out: Essays and Reviews on Race and Responsibility in America* (1995), *Anatomy of Racial Inequality* (2001), *Ethnicity, Social Mobility and Public Policy: Comparing the US and the UK* (2005), and over two hundred essays and reviews on racial inequality and social policy.

Instead of immediately announcing his thesis, Loury asks what are the criteria for our ideal vision of society?

The most challenging problems of social policy in the modern world are never merely technical. In order properly to decide how we should govern ourselves, we must take up questions of social ethics and human values. What manner of people are we Americans? What vision would we affirm, and what example would we set, before the rest of the world? What kind of society would we bequeath to our children? How shall we live? Inevitably, queries such as these lurk just beneath the surface of the great policy debates of the day. So, those who would enter into public argument about what ails our common life need make no apology for speaking in such terms.

In paragraph 2, Loury narrows the focus to evaluate the massive-scale imprisonment of poor Americans.

2   It is precisely in these terms that I wish to discuss a preeminent moral challenge for our time—that imprisonment on a massive scale has become one of the central aspects of our nation's social policy toward the poor, powerfully impairing the lives of some of the most marginal of our fellow citizens, especially the poorly educated black and Hispanic men who reside in large numbers in our great urban centers.

3   The bare facts of this matter—concerning both the scale of incarceration and its racial disparity—have been much remarked upon of late. Simply put, we have become a nation of jailers and, arguably, racist jailers at that. The past four decades have witnessed a truly historic expansion, and transformation, of penal institutions in the United States—at every level of government, and in all regions of the country. We have, by any measure, become a vastly more punitive society. Measured in constant dollars and taking account of all levels of government, spending on corrections and law enforcement in the United States has more than quadrupled over the last quarter century. As a result, the American prison system has grown into a leviathan unmatched in human history. This development should be deeply troubling to anyone who professes to love liberty.

4   Here, as in other areas of social policy, the United States is a stark international outlier, sitting at the most rightward end of

the political spectrum: We imprison at a far higher rate than the other industrial democracies—higher, indeed, than either Russia or China, and vastly higher than any of the countries of Western Europe. According to the International Centre for Prison Studies in London, there were in 2005 some 9 million prisoners in the world; more than 2 million were being held in the United States. With approximately one twentieth of the world's population, America had nearly one fourth of the world's inmates. At more than 700 per 100,000 residents, the U.S. incarceration rate was far greater than our nearest competitors (the Bahamas, Belarus, and Russia, which each have a rate of about 500 per 100,000.) Other industrial societies, some of them with big crime problems of their own, were less punitive than we by an order of magnitude: the United States incarcerated at 6.2 times the rate of Canada, 7.8 times the rate of France, and 12.3 times the rate of Japan.

Comparisons with other nations make a strong argument that the United States has an incarceration problem.

5   The demographic profile of the inmate population has also been much discussed. In this, too, the U.S. is an international outlier. African Americans and Hispanics, who taken together are about one fourth of the population, account for about two thirds of state prison inmates. Roughly one third of state prisoners were locked up for committing violent offenses, with the remainder being property and drug offenders. Nine in ten are male, and most are impoverished. Inmates in state institutions average fewer than eleven years of schooling.

6   The extent of racial disparity in imprisonment rates exceeds that to be found in any other arena of American social life: at eight to one, the black to white ratio of male incarceration rates dwarfs the two to one ratio of unemployment rates, the three to one non-marital child bearing ratio, the two to one ratio of infant mortality rates and the one to five ratio of net worth. More black male high school dropouts are in prison than belong to unions or are enrolled in any state or federal social welfare programs. The brute fact of the matter is that the primary contact between black American young adult men and their government is via the police and the penal apparatus. Coercion is the most salient feature of their encounters with the state. According to estimates compiled by sociologist Bruce Western, nearly 60% of black male dropouts born between 1965 and 1969 had spent at least one year in prison before reaching the age of 35.

Statistics show the degree to which the problem applies to black men.

7   For these men, and the families and communities with which they are associated, the adverse effects of incarceration will extend beyond their stays behind bars. My point is that this is not merely law enforcement policy. It is social policy writ large. And no other country in the world does it quite like we do.

8   This is far more than a technical issue—entailing more, that is, than the task of finding the most efficient crime control policies. Consider, for instance, that it is not possible to conduct a cost-benefit analysis of our nation's world-historic prison buildup over the past 35 years without implicitly specifying how the costs imposed on the persons imprisoned, and their families, are to be reckoned. Of course, this has not stopped analysts from pronouncing on the purported net benefits to "society" of greater incarceration without addressing that question! Still, how—or, indeed, whether—to weigh the costs born by law-breakers—that is, how (or whether) to acknowledge their humanity—remains a fundamental and difficult question of social ethics. Political discourses in the United States have given insufficient weight to the collateral damage imposed by punishment policies on the offenders themselves, and on those who are knitted together with offenders in networks of social and psychic affiliation.

Loury introduces an ethical criterion that imprisonment policies cause far greater costs than simply keeping criminals in jail.

9   Whether or not one agrees, two things should be clear: social scientists can have no answers for the question of what weight to put on a "thug's," or his family's, well-being; and a morally defensible public policy to deal with criminal offenders cannot be promulgated without addressing that question. To know whether or not our criminal justice policies comport with our deepest values, we must ask how much additional cost borne by the offending class is justifiable per marginal unit of security, or of peace of mind, for the rest of us. This question is barely being asked, let alone answered, in the contemporary debate.

10   Nor is it merely the scope of the mass imprisonment state that has expanded so impressively in the United States. The ideas underlying the doing of criminal justice—the superstructure of justifications and rationalizations—have also undergone a sea change. Rehabilitation is a dead letter; retribution is the thing. The function of imprisonment is not to reform or redirect offenders. Rather, it is to keep *them* away from *us*. "The prison," writes sociologist David Garland, "is used today as a kind of reservation, a quarantine zone in which purportedly dangerous individuals are segregated in the name of public safety." We have elaborated what are, in effect, a "string of work camps and prisons strung across a vast country housing millions of people drawn mainly from classes and racial groups that are seen as politically and economically problematic." We have, in other words, marched quite a long way down the punitive road, in the name of securing public safety and meting out to criminals their just deserts.

11   And we should be ashamed of ourselves for having done so. Consider a striking feature of this policy development, one that is

crucial to this moral assessment: the ways in which we now deal with criminal offenders in the United States have evolved in recent decades in order to serve expressive and not only instrumental ends. We have wanted to "send a message," and have done so with a vengeance. Yet in the process we have also, in effect, provided an answer for the question: who is to blame for the maladies that beset our troubled civilization? That is, we have constructed a narrative, created scapegoats, assuaged our fears, and indulged our need to feel virtuous about ourselves. We have met the enemy and the enemy, in the now familiar caricature, is *them*—a bunch of anomic, menacing, morally deviant "thugs." In the midst of this dramaturgy— unavoidably so in America—lurks a potent racial subplot.

12   This issue is personal for me. As a black American male, a baby-boomer born and raised on Chicago's South Side, I can identify with the plight of the urban poor because I have lived among them. I am related to them by the bonds of social and psychic affiliation. As it happens, I have myself passed through the courtroom, and the jailhouse, on my way along life's journey. I have sat in the visitor's room at a state prison; I have known, personally and intimately, men and women who lived their entire lives with one foot to either side of the law. Whenever I step to a lectern to speak about the growth of imprisonment in our society, I envision voiceless and despairing people who would have me speak on their behalf. Of course, personal biography can carry no authority to compel agreement about public policy. Still, I prefer candor to the false pretense of clinical detachment and scientific objectivity. I am not running for high office; I need not pretend to a cool neutrality that I do not possess. While I recognize that these revelations will discredit me in some quarters, this is a fate I can live with.

Loury intro- duces personal examples in support of his ethical criteria.

13   So, my racial identity is not irrelevant to my discussion of the subject at hand. But, then, neither is it irrelevant that among the millions now in custody and under state supervision are to be found a vastly disproportionate number of the black and the brown. There is no need to justify injecting race into this dis- course, for prisons are the most race-conscious public institutions that we have. No big city police officer is "colorblind" nor, arguably, can any afford to be. Crime and punishment in America have a color—just turn on a television, or open a magazine, or listen carefully to the rhetoric of a political campaign—and you will see what I mean. The fact is that, in this society as in any other, order is maintained by the threat and the use of force. We enjoy our good lives because we are shielded by the forces of law and or- der upon which we rely to keep the unruly at bay. Yet, in this soci- ety to an extent unlike virtually any other, those bearing the heavy

burden of order-enforcement belong, in numbers far exceeding their presence in the population at large, to racially defined and historically marginalized groups. Why should this be so? And how can those charged with the supervision of our penal apparatus sleep well at night knowing that it is so?

14   This punitive turn in the nation's social policy is intimately connected, I would maintain, with public rhetoric about responsibility, dependency, social hygiene, and the reclamation of public order. And such rhetoric, in turn, can be fully grasped only when viewed against the backdrop of America's often ugly and violent racial history: There is a reason why our inclination toward forgiveness and the extension of a second chance to those who have violated our behavioral strictures is so stunted, and why our mainstream political discourses are so bereft of self-examination and searching social criticism. An historical resonance between the stigma of race and the stigma of prison has served to keep alive in our public culture the subordinating social meanings that have always been associated with blackness. Many historians and political scientists—though, of course, not all—agree that the shifting character of race relations over the course of the nineteenth and twentieth centuries helps to explain why the United States is exceptional among democratic industrial societies in the severity of its punitive policy and the paucity of its social-welfare institutions. Put directly and without benefit of euphemism, the racially disparate incidence of punishment in the United States is a morally troubling residual effect of the nation's history of enslavement, disenfranchisement, segregation, and discrimination. It is not merely the accidental accretion of neutral state action, applied to a racially divergent social flux. It is an abhorrent expression of who we Americans are as a people, even now, at the dawn of the twenty-first century.

Loury again emphasizes the ethical dimension of his evaluation.

15   My recitation of the brutal facts about punishment in today's America may sound to some like a primal scream at this monstrous social machine that is grinding poor black communities to dust. And I confess that these facts do at times leave me inclined to cry out in despair. But my argument is intended to be moral, not existential, and its principal thesis is this: we law-abiding, middle-class Americans have made collective decisions on social and incarceration policy questions, and we benefit from those decisions. That is, we benefit from a system of suffering, rooted in state violence, meted out at our behest. Put differently our society—the society we together have made—first tolerates crime-promoting conditions in our sprawling urban ghettos, and then goes on to act out rituals of punishment against them as some awful form of human sacrifice.

After expressing anger Loury returns to a reasoned argument about public policy based on ethical criteria.

16   It is a central reality of our time that a wide racial gap has opened up in cognitive skills, the extent of law-abidingness, stability

of family relations, and attachment to the work force. This is the basis, many would hold, for the racial gap in imprisonment. Yet I maintain that this gap in human development is, as a historical matter, rooted in political, economic, social, and cultural factors peculiar to this society and reflective of its unlovely racial history. That is to say, *it is a societal, not communal or personal, achievement.* At the level of the individual case we must, of course, act as if this were not so. There could be no law, and so no civilization, absent the imputation to persons of responsibility for their wrongful acts. But the sum of a million cases, each one rightly judged fairly on its individual merits, may nevertheless constitute a great historic wrong. This is, in my view, now the case in regards to the race and social class disparities that characterize the very punitive policy that we have directed at lawbreakers. And yet, the state does not only deal with individual cases. It also makes policies in the aggregate, and the consequences of these policies are more or less knowable. It is in the making of such aggregate policy judgments that questions of social responsibility arise.

17   This situation raises a moral problem that we cannot avoid. We cannot pretend that there are more important problems in our society, or that this circumstance is the necessary solution to other, more pressing problems—unless we are also prepared to say that we have turned our backs on the ideal of equality for all citizens and abandoned the principles of justice. We ought to be asking ourselves two questions: Just what manner of people are we Americans? And in light of this, what are our obligations to our fellow citizens—even those who break our laws?

Loury's case is based on logic and evidence, but his strong passion is evident as well. How does he create emotion?

18   Without trying to make a full-fledged philosophical argument here, I nevertheless wish to gesture—in the spirit of the philosopher John Rawls—toward some answers to these questions. I will not set forth a policy manifesto at this time. What I aim to do is suggest, in a general way, how we ought to be thinking differently about this problem. Specifically, given our nation's history and political culture, I think that there are severe limits to the applicability in this circumstance of a pure ethic of personal responsibility, as the basis for distributing the negative good of punishment in contemporary America. I urge that we shift the boundary toward greater acknowledgment of social responsibility in our punishment policy discourse—even for wrongful acts freely chosen by individual persons. In suggesting this, I am not so much making a "root causes" argument—he did the crime, but only because he had no choice—as I am arguing that the society at large is implicated in his choices because we have acquiesced in structural arrangements which work to our benefit and his detriment, and yet which shape his consciousness and sense of identity in such a way that the choices

he makes. We condemn those choices, but they are nevertheless compelling to him. I am interested in the moral implications of what the sociologist Loïc Wacquant has called the "double-sided production of urban marginality." I approach this problem of moral judgment by emphasizing that closed and bounded social structures—like racially homogeneous urban ghettos—create contexts where "pathological" and "dysfunctional" cultural forms emerge, but these forms are not intrinsic to the people caught in these structures. Neither are they independent of the behavior of the people who stand outside of them.

19   Several years ago, I took time to read some of the nonfiction writings of the great nineteenth-century Russian novelist Leo Tolstoy. Toward the end of his life he had become an eccentric pacifist and radical Christian social critic. I was stunned at the force of his arguments. What struck me most was Tolstoy's provocative claim that the core of Christianity lies in Jesus' Sermon on the Mount: You see that fellow over there committing some terrible sin? Well, if you have ever lusted, or allowed jealousy, or envy or hatred to enter your own heart, then you are to be equally condemned! This, Tolstoy claims, is the central teaching of the Christian faith: we're all in the same fix.

> The Rawls, Wacquant, and Tolstoy references build ethos.

20   Now, without invoking any religious authority, I nevertheless want to suggest that there is a grain of truth in this religious sentiment that is relevant to the problem at hand: That is, while the behavioral pathologies and cultural threats that we see in society—the moral erosions "out there"—the crime, drug addiction, sexually transmitted disease, idleness, violence and all manner of deviance—while these are worrisome, nevertheless, our moral crusade against these evils can take on a pathological dimension of its own. We can become self-righteous, legalistic, ungenerous, stiff-necked, and hypocritical. We can fail to see the beam in our own eye. We can neglect to raise questions of social justice. We can blind ourselves to the close relationship that actually exists between, on the one hand, behavioral pathology in the so-called urban underclass of our country and, on the other hand, society-wide factors—like our greed-driven economy, our worship of the self, our endemic culture of materialism, our vacuous political discourses, our declining civic engagement, and our aversion to sacrificing private gain on behalf of much needed social investments. We can fail to see, in other words, that the problems of the so-called underclass—to which we have reacted with a massive, coercive mobilization—are but an expression, at the bottom of the social hierarchy, of a more profound and widespread moral deviance—one involving all of us.

> Loury returns to the challenge that he set out in the opening paragraph: What is our collective vision of the ideal society?

21   Taking this position does not make me a moral relativist. I merely hold that, when thinking about the lives of the disadvantaged in our society, the fundamental premise that should guide us is that we are all in this together. *Those* people languishing in the corners of our society are *our* people—they are *us*—whatever may be their race, creed, or country of origin, whether they be the crack-addicted, the HIV-infected, the mentally ill homeless, the juvenile drug sellers, or worse. Whatever the malady, and whatever the offense, we're all in the same fix. We're all in this thing together.

Loury anticipates and answers a possible objection.

22   Just look at what we have wrought. We Americans have established what, to many an outside observer, looks like a system of racial caste in the center of our great cities. I refer here to millions of stigmatized, feared, and invisible people. The extent of disparity in the opportunity to achieve their full human potential, as between the children of the middle class and the children of the disadvantaged—a disparity that one takes for granted in America—is virtually unrivaled elsewhere in the industrial, advanced, civilized, free world.

23   Yet too many Americans have concluded, in effect, that those languishing at the margins of our society are simply reaping what they have sown. Their suffering is seen as having nothing to do with us—as not being evidence of systemic failures that can be corrected through collective action. Thus, as I noted, we have given up on the ideal of rehabilitating criminals, and have settled for simply warehousing them. Thus we accept—despite much rhetoric to the contrary—that it is virtually impossible effectively to educate the children of the poor. Despite the best efforts of good people and progressive institutions—despite the encouraging signs of moral engagement with these issues that I have seen in my students over the years, and that give me hope—despite these things, it remains the case that, speaking of the country as a whole, there is no broadly based demand for reform, no sense of moral outrage, no anguished self-criticism, no public reflection in the face of this massive, collective failure.

Loury offers causal explanation for the current policy.

24   The core of the problem is that the socially marginal are not seen as belonging to the same general public body as the rest of us. It therefore becomes impossible to do just about anything with them. At least implicitly, our political community acts as though some are different from the rest and, because of their culture—because of their bad values, their self-destructive behavior, their malfeasance, their criminality, their lack of responsibility, their unwillingness to engage in hard work—they *deserve* their fate.

25   But this is quite wrongheaded. What we Americans fail to recognize—not merely as individuals, I stress, but as a political community—is that these ghetto enclaves and marginal spaces of

our cities, which are the source of most prison inmates, are products of our own making: Precisely because we do not want those people near us, we have structured the space in our urban environment so as to keep *them* away from *us*. Then, when they fester in their isolation and their marginality, we hypocritically point a finger, saying in effect: "Look at those people. They threaten to the civilized body. They must therefore be expelled, imprisoned, controlled." It is not *we* who must take social responsibility to reform our institutions but, rather, it is *they* who need to take personal responsibility for their wrongful acts. It is not we who must set our *collective* affairs aright, but they who must get their *individual* acts together. This posture, I suggest, is inconsistent with the attainment of a just distribution of benefits and burdens in society.

Having evaluated the policy as ineffective and immoral, Loury moves to the conclusion of his essay—which is to suggest a solution: civic inclusion.

26   Civic inclusion has been the historical imperative in Western political life for 150 years. And yet—despite our self-declared status as a light unto the nations, as a beacon of hope to freedom-loving peoples everywhere—despite these lofty proclamations, which were belied by images from the rooftops in flooded New Orleans in September 2005, and are contradicted by our over-crowded prisons—the fact is that this historical project of civic inclusion is woefully incomplete in these United States.

27   At every step of the way, reactionary political forces have declared the futility of pursuing civic inclusion. Yet, in every instance, these forces have been proven wrong. At one time or another, they have derided the inclusion of women, landless peasants, former serfs and slaves, or immigrants more fully in the civic body. Extending to them the franchise, educating their children, providing health and social welfare to them has always been controversial. But this has been the direction in which the self-declared "civilized" and wealthy nations have been steadily moving since Bismarck, since the revolutions of 1848 and 1870, since the American Civil War with its Reconstruction Amendments, since the Progressive Era and through the New Deal on to the Great Society. This is why we have a progressive federal income tax and an estate tax in this country, why we feed, clothe and house the needy, why we (used to) worry about investing in our cities' infrastructure, and in the human capital of our people. What the brutal facts about punishment in today's America show is that *this American project of civic inclusion remains incomplete*. Nowhere is that incompleteness more evident than in the prisons and jails of America. And this as yet unfulfilled promise of American democracy reveals a yawning chasm between an ugly and uniquely American reality, and our nation's exalted image of herself.

Loury concludes that if Americans would embrace the ideals of the United States, the conditions that lead to massive-scale imprisonment would change.

Sample Student Evaluation Argument

Picchi 1

Jenna Picchi

Professor Alameno

English 102

2 December 2013

Organic Foods Should Come Clean

As a kid growing up not far from rural communities, I took for granted the access to local produce and the farm stands that my family frequented. When I moved to a college town, I assumed I would have access to an even wider variety of foods and better choices. I wanted to continue eating organic as I had at home, even though it would be more work than a campus-dining plan. I learned quickly that even in a large college town, it takes determined searching in most supermarkets to find the organic produce, bread, meat, and dairy products that are scattered in less-trafficked corners of the store. Instead of shopping at the farmer's market (which I cannot attend), I choose these supermarket fruits and vegetables from the lackluster and small display of things shipped in from California and Central America. Taking a recent look at these organic departments, I noticed that almost all the products are store or national brands. It never occurred to me that living in the middle of an agricultural state my choices would be so limited. After spending much time and energy seeking out organic products in stores all around town, I wondered whether the effort is worth it. How healthy are these foods in the local supermarket? And are these national brands as good for the environment as they seem?

Many people shop for organic foods in the belief that they are free of pesticides, additives, and other chemicals that can harm people and the environment over time. Visit an average supermarket's organic department and you will see signs and labels confirming this idea. Organic foods are marketed as more wholesome or more humanely raised and harvested than other foods in the store. Packaging suggests organic foods are pure, natural, and simply better. But the big businesses that bring these products to consumers are anything but simple. The reality of the organic foods we find at Walmart, Target, and other major retail chains is that they are produced on a mass scale—the same industrial-sized operations that bring us cheap, "regular" products. And it may

---

Picchi introduces herself by giving personal background and explaining why she is invested in her subject.

After beginning with a personal narrative to connect with her readers, Picchi introduces her topic.

be that the policy of producing and selling organic foods on a massive, industrial scale is not as good for the environment or consumers as producing and selling organic foods on a smaller scale. Although industrially produced organic foods are convenient, they present a natural, earth-friendly image that is often not the reality. The industrial organic food industry makes many claims that deserve a closer look.

Consumers willing to pay more for organic foods might be surprised to learn that mass-produced organic foods come from farms that barely resemble the old-fashioned images on their milk carton. The majority of organic food sales come via a very large industry, not an idealistic or environmentalist movement. In fact, organic foods are the fastest-growing category in the food industry, now worth about $11 billion (Pollan 136). The way food is produced has been changing more over the past fifty years than in the previous 10,000 years (Kenner). Many organic foods are grown by big, industrial producers. These companies—often owned by large corporations—use many of the same practices as mainstream factory farms to keep costs low. They can distribute and market their products nationally, and while organic foods cost more overall, these corporations succeed because they have made organic food available to average customers (not just affluent ones). If the goal is to offer healthy choices to consumers who are trained to expect cheap, convenient options, industrial producers of organic foods have made significant contributions. The organic label works wonders in marketing, and the big corporations who produce and deliver the foods in our supermarkets are taking advantage of it.

The history of the organic food movement was originally small, locally based, and in response to the industrialization of food. The evolution away from an organic movement toward an organic food industry is fairly recent. The organic pioneers of the 1970s had "a vision of small farms, whole food, and local distribution" (Fromartz 194). They hoped to help people eat fewer processed foods, produced organically and distributed from local sources. But for some farmers the allure of reaching more consumers and national sales has led to compromises. In *Omnivore's Dilemma,* Michael Pollan traces the pressure some farmers felt in the early 1990s to "sell out" and work with agribusiness (153). Farmers like Gene Kahn, the founder of Cascadian Farm (now owned by food giant General Mills), saw that he

> Picchi gives the history of the organic food movement to show how the production of organic foods has changed.

could change and redefine the way food is grown and still reach a mass market. Even though this meant giving up on two ideals of the organic movement—local distribution and eating more whole foods—organic foods were becoming a large-scale business, bringing more naturally produced choices to more and more consumers.

One concern for Pollan and others is that the organic label is being used by companies who are not invested in organic principles. In fact, chemical farming and big agribusinesses had once been the enemy of the organic movement. Big agribusinesses changed their stance once they realized how profitable organic produce could become (Fromartz 194). As industrial organic operations grow and adopt more and more big agribusiness methods, the worry for consumers is whether the term *organic* is becoming just another marketing gimmick.

As organic foods become increasingly industrial, it is important for consumers to be able to verify whether the products they buy are defined and produced using truly organic standards. Organic standards have evolved in recent years and now regulate not just small farms but also large-scale industrial operations. But even as the standards are changing, they must at a minimum guarantee healthy foods that are sustainably produced. Organic agriculture is valuable for the way it protects the environment. Marion Nestle, a scholar on food and public health, describes research that organic farming uses less energy and leaves soils in better condition than traditional farms (213).

In addition to protecting lands from excessive chemical use, another possible benefit of organic, local farming is that it can require less use of fossil fuels. Fossil fuels are spent whenever farm supplies must be shipped or when foods are sent for processing. Foods travel long distances across the country and foods are shipped from across the world, consuming fossil fuels. But Pollan states that organic food can be produced with about one-third less fossil fuel than conventional food (183). Using fewer fossil fuels and chemicals should be a goal for any organic farmer or consumer concerned with pollution and creating a more sustainable food industry.

Less research is available to prove that organic foods are better nutritionally. Officially, Pollan says, the government takes the position that "organic food is no better than conventional food" (178). But he believes current research reveals organic foods grown in more naturally

[Margin note: Picchi introduces the criteria that she will use in her evaluation.]

[Margin note: Picchi describes how local farming can reduce energy consumption.]

[Margin note: Picchi examines the health benefits of organic foods.]

Picchi 4

fertile soil to be more nutritious. And Nestle believes organic foods may be safer than conventional foods because people who eat them will have fewer synthetic pesticides and chemicals in their bodies (213). If consumers can rely on organic foods for their health benefits, a larger good would be granted in overall public health. As a society we all benefit when people eat whole foods and organic foods as part of diets that maintain health and fight weight-related disease. Foods with an organic label should be able to guarantee these benefits to individuals and to public health.

Another benefit to taxpayers is that organic farms are far less subsidized and in particular do not receive direct government payments (Pollan 182). Many organic farms do not participate in the complicated system of paying farmers directly that mainstream farmers participate in, though Pollan points out that many industrial organic farms do benefit from less direct subsidies. For example, many states subsidize access to cheaper water and electricity to power farms. However, supporting the less subsidized farmers may bring savings to taxpayers in the end.

> Picchi argues that organic farming can cut government subsidies to farmers and thus lower overall federal spending.

Organic labels and standards are difficult but crucial to police and enforce. Consumers who are willing to pay extra for natural food choices will lose faith if it turns out the organic labels are not honest. Organic farmers traditionally set themselves up as an alternative to big agribusiness. But as Pollan explains, as giant manufacturers and chains sell more and more of the organic foods in supermarkets, organic agriculture has become more and more like the industrial food system it was supposed to challenge (151). As a result, it is more likely that without scrutiny organic standards are not being met.

Organic milk offers one example of a product where organic standards have recently been an issue. A handful of very large companies produce most of the organic milk we buy. Many chain stores have begun successfully competing, selling their own private-label organic milk. These huge private-label organic brands allow consumers to get organic goods at even lower prices. But one recent case of possible organic fraud involves Aurora Dairy, the supplier for many in-house brands of organic milk for stores such as Walmart and Costco. Aurora was discovered to have broken fourteen of the organic standards in 2007. The USDA cited it because its herds included cows that were fed inappropriate feed

> To give a concrete example, Picchi focuses on a specific organic product, milk, with which her audience will be familiar.

and because some cows had no access to pastures. It took a federal investigation to bring information about these violations to light and yet even then Aurora continued to operate without penalty (Gunther). But when organic standards are vaguely worded and unenforceable or go unmonitored at factory dairy farms, violations of organic principles are bound to happen.

The overwhelming pressure for access to foods that are cheap and convenient is something all consumers feel. But most people interested in buying organic foods do so because they believe they're doing something positive for their health, for the health of their community, and in the best interests of the environment. Often these consumers have a strong sense of the ethical importance of sustainable produced food. Because of their interest in doing what is right, these consumers are likely to be especially upset by news that the goods they're paying extra for are being misrepresented. These consumers expect and welcome organic standards that are meaningfully set and policed. Good organic agriculture policy would help ensure strong standards; without them consumers will become jaded and not trust the organic label.

Consumers interested in the monitoring of these standards might be concerned to see how standards in the past decade have changed. In crafting these rules, the government consults with some of the biggest businesses involved in organic food production. Many long-time organic farmers believe that the role of these corporations has watered down organic standards. The farmers themselves are voicing concerns that regulations should be tougher. Elizabeth Henderson, an organic farmer and member of the large organic co-op Organic Valley, spoke out in 2004 about the huge growth of organic food as coming "at an awful price, compromising standards, undercutting small farms, diluting healthy food, ignoring social justice—polluting the very ideals embodied in the word *organic*" (qtd in Fromartz 190).

In one recent example, Horizon Organic, the giant milk producer, fought for the development of USDA rules that ensure its factory farms in Idaho would not be required to give all cows a specific amount of time to graze on pasture (Pollan 157). The watered-down USDA standard Horizon helped to craft instead is very vague. The image most consumers have of organic milk coming from cows grazing in pasture is an ideal that many

---

Picchi introduces an ethical component to her argument.

Picchi gives an example of how big business has influence on organic standards.

Picchi 6

mainstream organic milk producers don't even approach. Many small dairy farmers follow older organic practices on their own, but current "organic" labels do not guarantee this.

Another challenge for consumers looking for sustainably produced organic products is that the industrial-sized producers are more efficient, which makes it hard for smaller farmers to compete. Local small farms, like personal gardens, are both "more expensive but also less efficient than larger operations in terms of transportation, labor, and materials required" (Dubner). Big organic companies can set lower prices, ship foods long distances quickly, and make distribution simpler for the supermarkets (Pollan 168). The growth of industrially produced organic foods has helped bring prices down overall. The competition is good in theory, allowing more people access to organic choices. But faced with these competing choices, perhaps only very informed consumers of organic foods may sympathize with and support their local organic farmers.

Good organic agriculture policy would ideally avoid having a negative impact on small, local producers. I would acknowledge that locally produced food is not necessarily more sustainable or by definition produced with less energy or better for the environment (McWilliams 22). The smaller-scale farm also has to be committed to sustainable practices. Local farms can be held accountable for whether they are meeting organic standards and following sustainable farming practices. A dairy farmer you can talk to at a local farmer's market can, in theory, earn trust and be held accountable to customers.

> Picchi acknowledges limits to her argument, while proposing what small, local farmers must do.

Small, local organic farmers are well positioned to deliver on the organic movement's original ideals of sustainably produced foods. Consumers should have a right to know where their food comes from and how organic standards are defined. In fact, as organic foods become more widely available to most consumers—even college students—it is worth questioning whether organic standards mean what they seem. Labeling foods organic cannot be just a marketing ploy, and the organic industry will continue to reach and inform more consumers if it can ensure this label has real meaning.

> Picchi concludes her essay with a call to arms, inspiring her audience to act.

Picchi 7

Works Cited

Dubner, Stephen J. "Do We Really Need a Few Billion Locavores?" *New York Times*. New York Times, 9 June 2008. Web. 20 Nov. 2013.

Fromartz, Samuel. *Organic, Inc.: Natural Foods and How They Grew*. New York: Houghton, 2006. Print.

Gunther, Marc. "An Organic Milk War Turns Sour." *Cornucopia Institute*. 3 Oct. 2007. Web. 20 Nov. 2013.

Kenner, Robert, dir. *Food Inc.* 2009. Magnolia Pictures. Film.

McWilliams, James E. *Just Food: Where Locavores Get It Wrong and How We Can Truly Eat Responsibly*. New York: Little, 2009. Print.

Nestle, Marion. "Eating Made Simple." *Food Inc.: How Industrial Food Is Making Us Sicker, Fatter, and Poorer—and What You Can Do About It*. Ed. Karl Weber. New York: PublicAffairs, 2009. 209-18. Print.

Pollan, Michael. *Omnivore's Dilemma: A Natural History of Four Meals*. New York: Penguin, 2006. Print.

11 | Narrative Arguments

QUICK TAKE

In this chapter, you will learn to

1. Understand how narrative arguments rely on stories rather than statistics (see page 163)
2. Recognize the kinds of narrative arguments (see pages 163–165)
3. Analyze a narrative argument (see page 165)
4. Write an effective narrative argument (see pages 166–167)

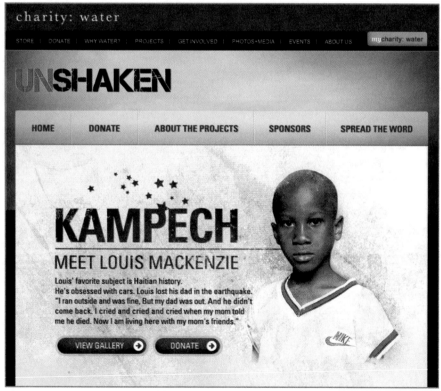

The organization *charity: water* understands the persuasive power of personal stories. Its online campaign features narratives like the story of Louis Mackenzie, a young boy who lost his father in the January 2010 earthquake in Haiti. "I cried and cried and cried when my mom told me he died," the text reads. As many organizations have learned, people often feel more compelled to donate money when they read personal stories like Louis's than when they are barraged with abstract numbers and statistics. Why are such stories effective as arguments? What makes some stories more compelling than others? © 2010 charity: water. Used with permission.

Understand How Narrative Arguments Work

A single, detailed personal story sometimes makes a stronger case than large-scale statistical evidence. The Annenberg Public Policy Center reported that an estimated 1.6 million of 17 million U.S. college students gambled online in 2005, but it was the story of Greg Hogan that made the problem real for many Americans. Hogan, the son of a Baptist minister, was an extraordinarily talented musician, who played onstage twice at Carnegie Hall by age 13. He chose to attend Lehigh University in Pennsylvania, where he was a member of the orchestra and class president. At Lehigh he also acquired an addiction to online poker. He lost $7,500, much of which he borrowed from fraternity brothers. To pay them back, he robbed a bank, only to be arrested a few hours later. Eventually, he received a long prison sentence. Hogan's story helped to influence Congress to pass the Unlawful Internet Gambling Enforcement Act, which requires financial institutions to stop money transfers to gambling sites.

Successful narrative arguments typically don't have a thesis statement but instead tell a compelling story. From the experience of one individual, readers infer a claim and the good reasons that support the claim.

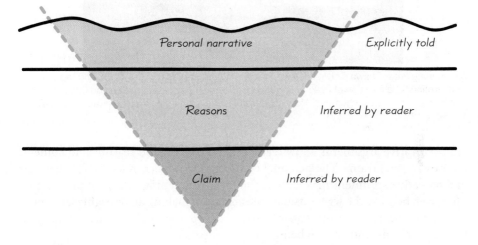

Personal narrative — Explicitly told

Reasons — Inferred by reader

Claim — Inferred by reader

Recognize Kinds of Narrative Arguments

Using narrative to make an argument is part of human nature. As far back as we have records, we find people telling stories and singing songs that argue for change. During periods of history when it is dangerous to make explicit arguments, stories allow people to safely criticize authority or imagine how life could be different. The history of folk music is a continuous recycling of old tunes, phrases, and narratives to engage new political situations. Anti-war ballads popular in Ireland in the 1840s were sung in the 1960s by Americans protesting their country's involvement in Vietnam. All the popular narrative genres—short stories, novels, movies, and theater—have been used as ways to make arguments for change.

Singer/songwriter Shawn Colvin is one of many contemporary folk, blues, rock, and rap artists who continue the tradition of making narrative arguments in their songs. Can you think of a song that makes a narrative argument? How successful is the song in making the argument? Why?

Narrative arguments allow readers to fill in the good reasons and come to their own conclusions. The personal connection readers can feel with the writer of a narrative argument makes this strategy a compelling means of persuasion. Moreover, because the writer usually refrains from making an outright claim, people reading narrative arguments are more likely to feel that they are "making up their own minds" rather than being reluctantly persuaded.

Narrative arguments can be representative anecdotes or they can be longer accounts of particular events that express larger ideas. One such story is George Orwell's account of a hanging in Burma (the country now known as Myanmar) while he was a British colonial administrator in the late 1920s. In "A Hanging," first published in 1931, Orwell narrates the story of an execution of a nameless prisoner who was convicted of a nameless crime. Everyone present quietly and dispassionately performs his job—the prison guards, the hangman, the superintendent, and even the prisoner, who offers no resistance when he is bound and led to the gallows. All is totally routine until a very small incident makes Orwell realize what is happening.

Orwell describes in detail how the prisoner, naked to the waist, walked stiff-legged with a bobbing gait, a lock of hair bouncing up and down. Even though he was being held by men on both sides, he carefully avoided stepping into a puddle on the path. This tiny act of avoiding a puddle made Orwell aware that the prisoner's brain was still thinking and reasoning as he was going to the scaffold. Orwell's sense of what was happening changed instantly. The prisoner was just like the other men at the scene with his organs working, his senses still taking in the world around him, and his mind still capable of remembering, reasoning, and foreseeing the future. Within two minutes, this mind would be removed from the human family.

Orwell writes, "It is curious, but till that moment I had never realized what it means to destroy a healthy, conscious man." Orwell's narrative leads to a dramatic moment of recognition, which gives this story its lasting power. His sudden realization of what execution means to both the prisoner and his executioners is a powerful argument to reconsider the morality of the death penalty.

Build a Narrative Argument

Because storytelling is such a familiar activity, it is easy for writers to get carried away with their narratives, and lose sight of the point they are trying to make. Readers find narrative compelling, but not if the narrative is long-winded and full of unnecessary detail, or has no obvious point. Furthermore, readers are quickly put off if they feel they are being given a lecture.

There are two keys to making effective narrative arguments: establishing that the narrative is truthful, and showing its relevance to a wider problem or question. Writing from personal experience can increase the impact of your argument, but that impact diminishes greatly if readers doubt you are telling the truth. And while the story you tell may be true, it is important that it also be representative—something that has happened to many other people or something that could happen to your readers. Narrative arguments are useful for illustrating how people are affected by particular issues or events, but they are more effective if you have evidence that goes beyond a single incident.

One rule of thumb that you can keep in mind when building a narrative argument is to start out with as much detail and as many events as you can recall, and then revise and edit heavily. It's hard to select the best details and events for your argument until you have written them all down, and often the process of writing and remembering will bring up new details that you had forgotten or hadn't seen the relevance of before. Once you can see the big picture you have painted with your narrative, it is easier to see what your readers do not need, and remove it. This strategy brings your story, and your argument, into sharper focus.

Steps to Writing a Narrative Argument

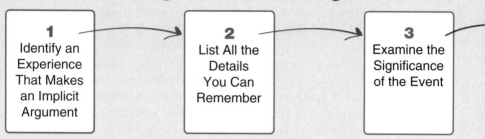

1
Identify an
Experience
That Makes
an Implicit
Argument

2
List All the
Details
You Can
Remember

3
Examine the
Significance
of the Event

Step 1 Identify an Experience That Makes an Implicit Argument

Think about experiences that made you realize that something is wrong or that things need to be changed. The experience does not have to be one that leads to a moral lesson at the end, but it should be one that makes your readers think.

Examples

- Being accused of and perhaps even arrested and hauled to jail for something you didn't do or for standing up for something you believed in
- Moving from a well-financed suburban school to a much poorer rural or urban school in the same state
- Experiencing stereotyping or prejudice in any way—for the way you look, the way you act, your age, your gender, your race, or your sexual orientation

Step 2 List All the Details You Can Remember

- When did it happen?
- How old were you?
- Why were you there?
- Who else was there?
- Where did it happen? If the place is important, describe what it looked like.
- What did it all sound like? smell like? taste like?

Step 3 Examine the Significance of the Event

- How did you feel about the experience when it happened?
- How did it affect you then?
- How do you feel about the experience now?
- What long-term effects has it had on your life?

Step 4 Analyze Your Potential Readers

- Who are your readers?
- How much will your readers know about the background of the experience you are describing?
- Would anything similar ever likely have happened to them?
- How likely are they to agree with your feelings about the experience?

Step 5 Write a Draft

- You might need to give some background first, but if you have a compelling story, often it's best to launch right in.
- You might want to tell the story as it happened (chronological order), or you might want to begin with a striking incident and then go back to tell how it happened (flashback).
- You might want to reflect on your experience at the end, but you want your story to do most of the work. Avoid drawing a simple moral lesson. Your readers should share your feelings if you tell your story well.

Step 6 Revise, Edit, Proofread

- For detailed instructions, see Chapter 5.
- For a checklist to use to evaluate your draft, see pages 50–51.

Finding Good Reasons

Can a Story Make an Argument?

A lone polar bear stands atop a small ice floe in the Arctic Ocean. The National Wildlife Federation describes the plight of the polar bear, struggling to survive in the face of a changing climate.

The National Wildlife Federation has made polar bears its featured species for advocating that nations should limit the impact of climate change. Polar bears are particularly affected by melting sea ice in the Arctic. They depend on seals for food. Because seals are much better swimmers than polar bears, the bears hunt seals from sea ice, grabbing them when they come up to breathe. The best habitat for polar bears is sea ice near land that can be reached with short swims. As sea ice shrinks, bears must either swim further and risk drowning or else find scarce food on land. Increasingly, they have turned to garbage dumps, which leads to fatal encounters with humans. Because of the loss of sea-ice cover, the U.S. Geological Survey estimates the population of polar bears will decline by two-thirds by 2050.

Write about it

1. What argument might the National Wildlife Federation be making about the state of climate change? What details reveal this argument?

2. Why might the National Wildlife Federation have chosen the polar bear to personify the effects of climate change? What other types of animals would have made good choices? poor choices?

3. How does the National Wildlife Federation's account of climate change differ from other accounts that you have heard? What is the other side of this issue? Does this story change your thinking about climate change? Why or why not?

Gregory Kristof

On the Ground with a "Gap Year"

Gregory Kristof, who attends Harvard University, has written op-eds for *The Harvard Crimson* and about education for the *Huffington Post*. In this essay, written at the invitation of his father, Pulitzer Prize–winning columnist Nicholas Kristof, he describes his experiences traveling in China during the time between high school and college. The essay first appeared in the *New York Times*.

Kristof begins with a vivid account of one of his experiences, drawing the reader in with a humorous anecdote that relates to his overall argument.

Note how Kristof uses language and dialogue to develop his main characters. Phrases like "two white dudes chillin'" and the detail about his ringtone help create a personal connection to his readers.

In paragraphs 9–12 Kristof introduces his argument, without explicitly stating it.

2   It took place on a frosty peak tucked away in the Tibetan highlands: my friend Rick and I walked in on a group of monks as they were on their knees, groaning.

3   They were performing secret rituals involving yak butter.

Peeking out from behind animal fur curtains, Rick and I hoped that they hadn't noticed us yet. They hummed and sat in rows facing a stage of yak butter candles that threw images against the walls like kicked hacky sacks. Back in the shadows, I worried: What would happen if they saw two white dudes chillin' behind the furs?

4   "Pssst," Rick said. "I think we should leave."

5   "Let's make for the door." I said.

6   I flattened myself against the back of the room, inching toward the door. Take it slow, I told myself. Don't drag your feet. Hurry up! I just had a few more feet to go. Two steps to go. Wow, I would make a great spy.

7   One step. And then—right as I was considering tacking on two zeros to the front of my name—ZINGZAMEMEM-BzerrBzerrBzerr …

8   I know, my ringtone sucks. Eyes caved in on me. I sort of just lay there on the dirt floor, not moving much, just looking up sporadically at the curious faces, and feeling sorry that I had disrupted their ritual. And yet I felt warm inside because I was here, getting caught in a mountain temple by Buddhist monks, and not where I shoulda-coulda-woulda been: listening to a PowerPoint lecture in a Boston classroom.

9   My decision to defer college for a year wasn't easy. In my New York high school, nearly every kid treads the usual path from graduation to college. Upon hearing that I would hop off the traditional academic bandwagon, some teachers, friends, and other parents would respond with "That sounds great!" while murmuring comforting remarks that I would probably turn out ok.

10   I was extremely excited about college, so it was tough to say "Not this time" to the bounty of friends and general awesomeness that my Freshman year would most assuredly bring me.

Many young people ask themselves the questions in paragraph 11, which suggests that the impetus for Kristof's experience is representative of what others his age might feel.

11   But I remember thinking how most of my great high school memories were localized capsules, like dots on paper waiting to be connected. A great weekend here, a good report card there. It was only when I extracted myself from each individual moment that I would realize that the damn picture still wouldn't come into focus. Where was I going? Where did I want to go?

12   I wanted more. I wanted to see how the other half lived, to learn the things that weren't found in books, to live a phantasmagoria of unforgettable experiences. I wanted to experience a life in which images glided by like kangaroos on rollerblades.

13   So I went to China. So far, I've rock-climbed above Buddhist grottos, showered in underground waterfalls, squeaked my way across 13th-century temples hanging halfway up cliffs, and stayed in earthquake-ravaged villages where everyone still dwells in tents. In a one-street town whose sole cab driver appeared to be blind, Rick and I went deep inside one of the world's most dazzling monasteries to party with monks (the scene was about as bangin' as what you'd expect from a group of pacifists). I've motorcycled across a frozen holy lake in the Himalayas, and I've stared into giant volcano pits on the North Korean border.

Kristof advances his argument by highlighting what he learned on his trip that he would never have learned in an American college. Note the vivid concrete details that authenticate his narrative.

14   Not all of this was safe and rosy. Rick and I spent one night fending off wild dogs with a metal bar and headlamp, after escaping from the clutches of a hawk-nosed Tibetan with a few loose screws. We finally found a place to stay (by barging into a man's tent at 5 a.m. and striking a deal with him to spend the night), but still, the Himalayan winter nearly turned us into popsicles.

15   I even learned the in's and out's of the squat toilet. Do not sink too low when you squat. Trust me.

16   And while we are on the subject of appropriate dinner table conversation, let me warn you never to pee into a strong oncoming Tibetan wind. Unless you are seeking a novel and roundabout face-washing technique. Believe me, it happened.

17   So if you are willing to unrut your wheels, if you enjoy hopscotching through the world of motorcycles and open prairie, or if you're just searching for that extra boost to send yourself hurtling down a road less traveled, then perhaps a year abroad is right for you. Think about it in particular if you're going to study a language in college: why pay expensive tuition to learn Spanish in the States when you can learn it more thoroughly and cheaply in Bolivia?

18   Even a gap year's undesired moments can have a palliative benefit. Setting off for remote mountain villages, only to discover that they have been utterly abandoned; triumphantly finding a town's only bathroom, only to discover that the mud you are now standing in is not actually mud; these are the curve balls that keep you on your toes, that preserve in your life what remains of childhood spontaneity.

19   A gap year is a larky way to mature out of youth. But if you do it right, it's also a way to keep it.

20   I nearly forgot to mention that the original purpose of traveling to China was to bolster my Chinese at Tsinghua University in Beijing. Thanks to its great program, as well as the superb Ruiwen school in Dalian, I'm now fluent. But talent in Chinese doesn't compare with talent in analyzing terrain for wild dog hangouts, or with kaleidoscopic memories that will refract experiences for a lifetime.

> The classroom experience becomes an afterthought when compared with all that Kristof has learned elsewhere.

21   So, graduating seniors, now's the time to search the Web for travel abroad programs. Check out Global Citizen Year for a mini peace corps experience. If you're less interested in a formal program, just do what I did: sign up for a foreign language school and book a flight. Because of the dollar's purchasing power, travel in China is very cheap—a rebuttal to those who think gap years are only for rich kids. I hope you choose to defer enrollment for one year, and I hope that your gap year, like mine, goes wrong in all the right ways.

22   When college does roll around, you'll already have gone through your own freshman orientation. After getting lost in a remote village because I was seeking a familiar temple but was approaching it from a completely different direction, I learned that where you are going is not all that matters. Where you are coming from matters, too.

23   It's like this: Spend time huddling for candle warmth on the Tibetan Plateau, and the C in physics ain't gonna seem so harsh.

> Kristof returns to his opening to bring closure to his narrative, while driving home the main points of his argument.

24   Eventually the dots begin to connect themselves. That's when I discovered that I got more than what I'd bargained for. I initially wanted simply to get a sense of where I was headed for the next few years. But the poverty I encountered in western China irrevocably challenged me. I felt, on the most profound of levels, the realness of others. I became just one person among very, very many. Especially since I was in China.

25   Speaking of melting into the background, that was exactly my wish that evening when my friend and I got caught in the temple.

26   "I'm just a traveler," I said. After an ungolden silence, a
monk stepped forward: "Come eat with us."

After fully establishing his argument through his narrative, Kristof concludes with a pithy statement of one of his main points.

27   Rick and I spent the rest of that evening under a temple rooftop somewhere among the Himalayan foothills—I couldn't find the place now. We and the incredibly hospitable monks traded stories and cheers over yak meat, yak cheese, and yak butter tea well past my bedtime.

28   Who says you need a classroom for an education?

12 | Rebuttal Arguments

Whaling is an ancient form of hunting that greatly expanded in the nineteenth century as the result of worldwide demand for whale oil. By 1986 the worldwide whale populations were so seriously depleted that the International Whaling Committee banned commercial whaling to allow whale populations to replenish. Limited whaling continues for scientific research, but environmental organizations such as Greenpeace insist that "science" is a guise for the continuation of commercial whaling. Greenpeace protests all whaling vigorously—both by peaceful means and by open ocean confrontations with whaling vessels. Could their protests at sea be considered a rebuttal argument?

Understand How Rebuttal Arguments Work

There are two basic approaches to rebutting an argument: you can refute the argument, or you can counterargue. In the first case, **refutation**, you demonstrate the shortcomings of the argument you wish to discredit, and you may or may not offer a positive claim of your own. In the second case, **counterargument**, you focus on the strengths of the position you support and spend little time on the specifics of the argument you are countering. There can be substantial overlap between these two tactics, and good rebuttal arguments often employ both refutation and counterargument.

Because it focuses on the shortcomings in the opposition's argument, a refutation argument often takes much of its structure from the argument being refuted.

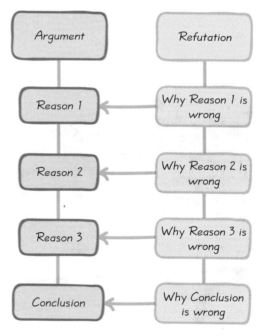

Many college students think that using technology to "multitask" makes them more productive, believing that studying, texting a friend, and listening to music all at once is an efficient use of their time. But research shows that engaging in multiple tasks is distracting, interferes with memory, and makes it difficult to switch from one task to another—all of which causes multitaskers to be less productive than people focusing on one task at a time.

Counterarguments more often take up ideas the opposing claims have not addressed at all, or they take a very different approach to the problem. By largely ignoring the specifics of the argument being countered, they make the implicit claim that the counterargument is superior.

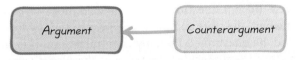

Those who argue for tariffs on goods from China claim that tariffs will protect American manufacturing jobs, but tariffs are a bad idea because they would increase prices on clothing, furniture, toys, and other consumer goods for everyone and would cause the loss of retailing jobs as well.

Recognize Kinds of Rebuttal Arguments

Refutation

A refutation can either challenge the assumptions underlying a claim or question the evidence supporting a claim. Until about five hundred years ago, people believed that the sky, and everything in it, moved, while the Earth remained still. They observed the stars moving from west to east in a regular, circular motion and concluded that all the heavenly bodies orbited around an axis between Earth and Polaris, the northern star. This theory, however, did not explain the movement of the planets. If you watch the path of Mars over several nights, for example, you will notice that it moves, like the stars, from east to west. But occasionally, it will appear to move backward, from west to east, before reversing itself and resuming an east-to-west course. This phenomenon is called retrograde motion, and it is exhibited by all the planets in our solar system. In fact, our word *planet* derives from the Greek term *planetes*, meaning "wanderer." The ancient Greeks assumed that the planets and stars orbited the Earth, but that the planets sometimes wandered from their paths.

In the second century CE, the Greek astronomer Ptolemy made precise and detailed observations of the planets and created a model to predict their retrograde motion. In his treatise, the *Almagest*, he theorized that Mars and the other "wanderers" periodically deviated from their path around the Earth, making small circles, or epicycles, before moving on again. It was a complicated system, but it predicted the movements of the planets very accurately, and so it went unchallenged for over a thousand years.

In the early sixteenth century, the Polish astronomer Nicolaus Copernicus recognized that Ptolemy's observations could be explained more simply if the Earth and other planets circled the Sun. Copernicus's theory, later confirmed by the German astronomer Johannes Kepler, eventually replaced the Ptolemaic model of the solar system as the accepted explanation for observed planetary motion.

Copernicus did not question Ptolemy's evidence—the data he had collected showing where the stars and planets appear in the sky to an Earth-bound observer. Instead, he questioned Ptolemy's central assumption that Earth is the center of the solar system. Because evidence of the planet's retrograde motion had been observed by people over such a long period of time, it was unlikely to be wrong. Instead, it was the theory Ptolemy constructed to explain his data that was incorrect.

But sometimes evidence is wrong. Sometimes, too, evidence is incomplete or not representative, and sometimes counterevidence can be found. People who are bent on persuading others may leave out information that weakens their case or employ evidence in questionable ways to try to bolster their claims. Dermatologists argue that indoor tanning is harmful to people's health because it exposes them to ultraviolet radiation, a known cause of cancer. The tanning industry, not surprisingly, disagrees, arguing that indoor tanning is safer than outdoor tanning because it assures safe levels of UV radiation exposure. While sunbathers often get sunburned, indoor tanners only get safe levels of radiation. This is an intriguing claim, but the AMA has discovered that in fact people who use tanning beds *do* get burned—as many of 50 percent of them. The tanning industry also claims indoor tanning provides people with a "protective" tan that reduces the amount of harmful UV radiation they absorb when they do go out in the sun. Doctors counter this claim by pointing out that a "base tan" provides only as much protection as a sunblock with a sun protection factor, or SPF, of 3, and that the minimum recommended SPF for sunscreen is 15. The protection offered by an indoor tan is minimal at best. Both sides continue to argue over what evidence is valid, and accurate, when assessing the safety of indoor tanning.

Counterargument

Another way to rebut is to counterargue. In a counterargument, you might acknowledge an opposing point of view, but you might not consider it in detail. Rather, you put the main effort into your own argument. A counterarguer, in effect, says, "I hear your argument. But there is more to it than that. Now listen while I explain why another position is stronger." Counterargument is an effective way of persuading audiences, but sometimes it is used as a way to avoid addressing opposing views honestly. People's tendency to be persuaded by counterargument also makes them susceptible to red herrings, when an irrelevant but dramatic detail is put forward as if it were important, and *ad hominem* attacks, where someone makes spurious accusations about an opponent instead of engaging in real debate.

The counterarguer depends on the wisdom of his or her audience members to hear all sides of an issue and make up their own minds about the merits of the case. In the following short poem, Wilfred Owen, a veteran of the horrors of World War I trench warfare, offers a counterargument to those who argue that war is noble, to those who believe along with the poet Horace that "dulce et decorum est pro patria mori"—that it is sweet and fitting to die for one's country. This poem gains in popularity whenever there is an unpopular war, for it rebuts the belief that it is noble to die for one's country in modern warfare.

Dulce et Decorum Est

Bent double, like old beggars under sacks,
Knock-kneed, coughing like hags, we cursed through sludge,
Till on the haunting flares we turned our backs
And towards our distant rest began to trudge.
Men marched asleep. Many had lost their boots
But limped on, blood-shod. All went lame; all blind;
Drunk with fatigue; deaf even to the hoots
Of tired, outstripped Five-Nines that dropped behind.

Gas! Gas! Quick, boys! — An ecstasy of fumbling,
Fitting the clumsy helmets just in time;
But someone still was yelling out and stumbling,
And flound'ring like a man in fire or lime . . .
Dim, through the misty panes and thick green light,
As under a green sea, I saw him drowning.
In all my dreams, before my helpless sight,
He plunges at me, guttering, choking, drowning.

If in some smothering dreams you too could pace
Behind the wagon that we flung him in,
And watch the white eyes writhing in his face,
His hanging face, like a devil's sick of sin;
If you could hear, at every jolt, the blood
Come gargling from the froth-corrupted lungs,
Obscene as cancer, bitter as the cud
Of vile, incurable sores on innocent tongues,
My friend, you would not tell with such high zest
To children ardent for some desperate glory,
The old Lie: Dulce et decorum est
Pro patria mori.

Owen does not summarize the argument in favor of being willing to die for one's country and then refute that argument point by point. Rather, his poem presents an opposing argument, supported by a narrative of the speaker's experience in a poison-gas attack, that he hopes will more than counterbalance what he calls "the old Lie." Owen simply ignores the reasons people give for being willing to die for one's country and argues instead that there are good reasons not to do so. And he hopes that the evidence he summons for his position will outweigh for his audience (addressed as "My friend") the evidence in support of the other side.

Rebuttal arguments frequently offer both refutation and counterargument. Like attorneys engaged in a trial, people writing rebuttals must make their own cases based on good reasons and hard evidence, but they also do what they can to undermine their opponent's case. In the end the jury—the audience—decides.

Build a Rebuttal Argument

As you prepare to rebut an argument, look closely at what your opponent says. What exactly are the claims? What is the evidence? What are the assumptions? What do you disagree with? Are there parts you agree with? Are there assumptions you share? Do you agree that the evidence is accurate?

Knowing where you agree with someone helps you focus your rebuttal on differences. Having points of agreement can also help you build credibility with your audience, if you acknowledge that your opponent makes some logical points, or makes reasonable assumptions.

Consider using counterargument if you generally agree with a claim but do not think it goes far enough, if you feel an argument proposes the wrong solution to a problem, or if you think that, while accurate, it misses the "big picture." Counterargument lets you frame your own, stronger take on the question at hand without spending a lot of time trying to find flaws in the opposing position when there may not be many in it.

If you do have serious objections to an argument, plan to refute it, and start by looking for the most important differences in your respective positions. What are the biggest "red flags" in the argument you disagree with? What are the weakest points of your opponent's argument? What are the strongest points of your own? You will probably want to highlight these differences in your rebuttal. You may find many problems with evidence and logic, in which case you will probably want to prioritize them. You do not necessarily need to point out the flaws in every single element of an argument. Direct your audience to the ones that matter the most.

You can also use counterargument in combination with refutation, first showing why an existing argument is wrong and then offering an alternative. This is one of the more common forms of rebuttal. As you examine your opponent's claims and evidence, look closely for fallacies and faulty logic (see pages 16–19). How do these distort the problem or lead the audience to mistaken conclusions? Pointing them out to your readers will strengthen your position.

Look too at sources. Check your opponent's facts. Scrutinize the experts he or she relies on. And consider the purpose and motivation behind arguments you rebut. Groups funded by major industries, political parties, and special interest groups may have hidden or not-so-hidden agendas driving the arguments they make. Pointing these out to your readers can strengthen your own position.

Finding Good Reasons

Can the Web Be Trusted for Research?

FOXTROT © 2006 Bill Amend. Reprinted with permission of UNIVERSAL UCLICK.
All rights reserved.

Most Web users are familiar with the huge and immensely popular *Wikipedia*, the online encyclopedia. What makes *Wikipedia* so different from traditional, print encyclopedias is that entries can be contributed or edited by anyone.

In 2007, Jimmy Wales, president of Wikimedia and one of its founders, debated the legitimacy of *Wikipedia* with Dale Hoiberg, editor-in-chief of *Encyclopedia Britannica*. Hoiberg's main criticism of *Wikipedia* is that its structure— an open-source wiki without the formal editorial control that shapes traditional, print encyclopedias—allows for inaccurate entries.

In response, Wales argues that *Britannica* and newspapers also contain errors, but *Wikipedia* has the advantage that they are easily corrected. Furthermore, he asserts that *Wikipedia*'s policy of using volunteer administrators to delete irrelevant entries and requiring authors of entries to cite reliable, published sources ensures quality. Nonetheless, some universities including UCLA and the University of Pennsylvania along with many instructors strongly discourage and even ban students from citing *Wikipedia* in their work. (*Wikipedia* also cautions against using its entries as a primary source for serious research.)

Write about it

1. If your college decided to ban the use of *Wikipedia* as a reference because it lacked the authority of a traditional encyclopedia, would you want to challenge it? Why or why not?

2. If you chose to challenge the college's policy, how would you do so? Would it be effective to refute the college's claims point by point, noting fallacies in logic and reasoning? Would it be effective to build a counterargument in which you examine the assumptions on which the college's claims are based? Which strategy would you choose, and why?

Steps to Writing a Rebuttal Argument

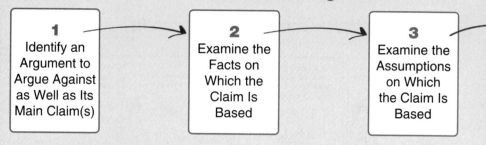

1 Identify an Argument to Argue Against as Well as Its Main Claim(s)

2 Examine the Facts on Which the Claim Is Based

3 Examine the Assumptions on Which the Claim Is Based

Step 1 Identify an Argument to Argue Against as Well as Its Main Claim(s)

- What exactly are you arguing against?
- Are there secondary claims attached to the main claim?
- Include a fair summary of your opponent's position in your finished rebuttal.

Examples

- Arguing against raising taxes for the purpose of building a new sports stadium (examine how proponents claim that a new sports facility will benefit the local economy)
- Arguing for raising the minimum wage (examine how opponents claim that a higher minimum wage isn't necessary and negatively affects small-business owners)

Step 2 Examine the Facts on Which the Claim Is Based

- Are the facts accurate, current, and representative?
- Is there another body of facts that you can present as counterevidence?
- If the author uses statistics, can the statistics be interpreted differently?
- If the author quotes from sources, how reliable are those sources?
- Are the sources treated fairly, or are quotations taken out of context?

Step 3 Examine the Assumptions on Which the Claim Is Based

- What are the primary and secondary assumptions of the claim you are rejecting?
- How are those assumptions flawed?
- Does the author resort to name-calling, use faulty reasoning, or ignore key facts (see pages 16–19)?

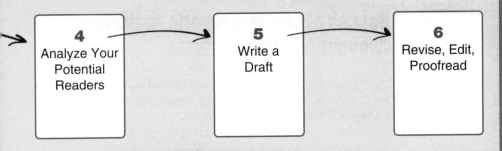

Step 4 Analyze Your Potential Readers

- To what extent do your potential readers support the claim that you are rejecting?
- If they strongly support that claim, how might you appeal to them to change their minds?
- What common assumptions and beliefs do you share with them?

Step 5 Write a Draft

Introduction
Identify the issue and the argument you are rejecting.

- Provide background if the issue is unfamiliar to most of your readers.
- Give a quick summary of the competing positions even if the issue is familiar to your readers.
- Make your aim clear in your thesis statement.

Body
Take on the argument that you are rejecting. Consider questioning the evidence that is used to support the argument by doing one or more of the following.

- Challenge the facts and the currency and relevance of examples.
- Present counterevidence and countertestimony.
- Challenge the credibility of sources cited.
- Question the way in which statistical evidence is presented and interpreted.
- Argue that quotations are taken out of context.

Conclusion
- Conclude on a firm note by underscoring your objections.
- Consider closing with a counterargument or counterproposal.

Step 6 Revise, Edit, Proofread

- For detailed instructions, see Chapter 5.
- For a checklist to use to evaluate your draft, see pages 50–51.

Ron Reagan

Speech at the Democratic National Convention, July 27, 2004

Ron Reagan is the son of the fortieth president of the United States. In August 1994, at the age of 83, President Reagan was diagnosed with Alzheimer's disease, an incurable neurological disorder that destroys brain cells, and he died of the disease in June 2004. A few months later, on July 27, Ron Reagan offered the following speech to the delegates to the Democratic National Convention and to the millions of Americans watching on television. It was countered the next day by Richard Doerflinger, whose rebuttal follows this speech.

G ood evening, ladies and gentlemen.

2 A few of you may be surprised to see someone with my last name showing up to speak at a Democratic Convention. Apparently some of you are not. Let me assure you, I am not here to make a political speech and the topic at hand should not—must not—have anything to do with partisanship.

In his first three paragraphs, Reagan makes his purpose clear.

3 I am here tonight to talk about the issue of research into what may be the greatest medical breakthrough in our or any lifetime: the use of embryonic stem cells—cells created using the material of our own bodies—to cure a wide range of fatal and debilitating illnesses: Parkinson's disease, multiple sclerosis, diabetes, lymphoma, spinal cord injuries, and much more.

4 Millions are afflicted. And every year, every day, tragedy is visited upon families across the country, around the world. Now, it may be within our power to put an end to this suffering. We only need to try.

Paragraphs 5–10 define stem cell research. Note his simple explanation and the informal tone, appropriate for a speech.

5 Some of you already know what I'm talking about when I say embryonic stem cell research. Others of you are probably thinking, that's quite a mouthful. Maybe this is a good time to go for a tall cold one. Well, wait a minute, wait a minute.

6 Let me try and paint as simple a picture as I can while still doing justice to the science, the incredible science involved. Let's say that ten or so years from now you are diagnosed with Parkinson's disease. There is currently no cure, and drug therapy, with its attendant side-effects, can only temporarily relieve the symptoms.

7 Now, imagine going to a doctor who, instead of prescribing drugs, takes a few skin cells from your arm. The nucleus of one of your cells is placed into a donor egg whose own nucleus

has been removed. A bit of chemical or electrical stimulation will encourage your cell's nucleus to begin dividing, creating new cells which will then be placed into a tissue culture. Those cells will generate embryonic stem cells containing only your DNA, thereby eliminating the risk of tissue rejection. These stem cells are then driven to become the very neural cells that are defective in Parkinson's patients. And finally, those cells—with your DNA—are injected into your brain where they will replace the faulty cells whose failure to produce adequate dopamine led to the Parkinson's disease in the first place.

8   In other words, you're cured.

9   And another thing, these embryonic stem cells, they could continue to replicate indefinitely and, theoretically, can be induced to recreate virtually any tissue in your body.

10   How'd you like to have your own personal biological repair kit standing by at the hospital? Sound like magic? Welcome to the future of medicine.

11   Now by the way, no fetal tissue is involved in this process. No fetuses are created, none destroyed. This all happens in the laboratory at the cellular level.

Anticipating an objection, he subtly but explicitly distinguishes stem cell research from abortion.

12   Now, there are those who would stand in the way of this remarkable future, who would deny the federal funding so crucial to basic research. They argue that interfering with the development of even the earliest stage embryo, even one that will never be implanted in a womb and will never develop into an actual fetus, is tantamount to murder.

13   A few of these folks, needless to say, are just grinding a political axe and they should be ashamed of themselves. But many are well-meaning and sincere. Their belief is just that, an article of faith, and they are entitled to it. But it does not follow that the theology of a few should be allowed to forestall the health and wellbeing of the many.

14   And how can we affirm life if we abandon those whose own lives are so desperately at risk? It is a hallmark of human intelligence that we are able to make distinctions.

Reagan uses the language of "life" to acknowledge and refute counterarguments.

15   Yes, these cells could theoretically have the potential, under very different circumstances, to develop into human beings—that potential is where their magic lies. But they are not, in and of themselves, human beings. They have no fingers and toes, no brain or spinal cord. They have no thoughts, no fears. They feel no pain.

16   Surely we can distinguish between these undifferentiated cells multiplying in a tissue culture and a living, breathing person—a parent, a spouse, a child.

The actor Michael J. Fox, who was diagnosed in 1991 with Parkinson's disease, spoke at the Bio International Convention in 2007. Fox appealed to scientists and investors to aggressively translate scientific research into creative treatments for debilitating diseases, including Parkinson's.

Reagan appeals to a single representative example to support his case. Why does he pick this particular example?

17   I know a child—well, she must be 13 now so I guess I'd better call her a young woman. She has fingers and toes. She has a mind. She has memories. She has hopes. She has juvenile diabetes. Like so many kids with this disease, she's adjusted amazingly well. The insulin pump she wears—she's decorated hers with rhinestones. She can handle her own catheter needle. She's learned to sleep through the blood drawings in the wee hours of the morning.

18   She's very brave. She is also quite bright and understands full well the progress of her disease and what that might ultimately mean: blindness, amputation, diabetic coma. Every day, she fights to have a future.

19   What excuse will we offer this young woman should we fail her now? What might we tell her children? Or the millions of others who suffer? That when given an opportunity to help, we turned away? That facing political opposition, we lost our nerve? That even though we knew better, we did nothing?

20   And, should we fail, how will we feel if, a few years from now, a more enlightened generation should fulfill the promise of embryonic stem cell therapy? Imagine what they would say of us who lacked the will.

21   No, we owe this young woman and all those who suffer—
we owe ourselves—better than that. We are better than that. We
are a wiser people, a finer nation.

22   And for all of us in this fight, let me say: we will prevail. The
tide of history is with us. Like all generations who have come
before ours, we are motivated by a thirst for knowledge and compelled to see others in need as fellow angels on an often difficult
path, deserving of our compassion.

23   In a few months, we will face a choice. Yes, between two
candidates and two parties, but more than that. We have a
chance to take a giant stride forward for the good of all humanity.
We can choose between the future and the past, between reason
and ignorance, between true compassion and mere ideology.

24   This—this is our moment, and we must not falter.

25   Whatever else you do come November 2, I urge you,
please, cast a vote for embryonic stem cell research.

26   Thank you for your time.

> Reagan offers his final counter-argument: inevitability. By focusing on the inevitable, he portrays those who disagree with him as stuck in the past and resistant to change.

Richard M. Doerflinger

Don't Clone Ron Reagan's Agenda

Richard M. Doerflinger is the Associate Director of Pro-Life Activities for the United States Conference of Catholic Bishops. In 2009 Doerflinger was awarded an inaugural Life Prize by the Gerard Health Foundation for his work in "preserving and upholding the sanctity of human life" in areas such as public advocacy, legal action, and outreach. A specialist in bioethics, biotechnology, and public policy, he wrote the essay that follows on July 28, 2004, in response to Ron Reagan's speech, which appears immediately before this essay.

> Does Doerflinger offer a fair summary of Reagan's argument?

Ron Reagan's speech at the Democratic convention last night was expected to urge expanded funding for stem cell research using so-called "spare" embryos—and to highlight these cells' potential for treating the Alzheimer's disease that took his father's life.

2   He did neither. He didn't even mention Alzheimer's, perhaps because even strong supporters of embryonic stem cell research say it is unlikely to be of use for that disease. (Reagan himself admitted this on a July 12 segment of MSNBC's *Hardball*.) And he didn't talk about current debates on funding research using existing embryos. Instead he endorsed the more radical agenda of

In paragraphs 2 and 3 he recontextual-izes Reagan's argument by using the word *cloning*, which never appears in Reagan's speech. He also describes Reagan's position as "radical," which makes it hard for readers to agree with Reagan.

3

human cloning—mass-producing one's own identical twins in the laboratory so they can be exploited as (in his words) "your own personal biological repair kit" when disease or injury strikes.

Politically this was, to say the least, a gamble. Americans may be tempted to make use of embryos left over from fertility clinics, but most polls show them to be against human cloning for any purpose. Other advanced nations—Canada, Australia, France, Germany, Norway—have banned the practice completely, and the United Nations may approve an international covenant against it this fall. Many groups and individuals who are "pro-choice" on abortion oppose research cloning, not least because it would re-quire the mass exploitation of women to provide what Ron Reagan casually calls "donor eggs." And the potential "therapeutic" benefits of cloning are even more speculative than those of embryonic stem cell research—the worldwide effort even to obtain viable stem cells from cloned embryos has already killed hundreds of embryos and produced exactly one stem cell line in South Korea.

Rather than at-tacking Reagan, Doerflinger praises him and therefore seems fair-minded.

4

But precisely for these reasons, Ron Reagan should be praised for his candor. The scientists and patient groups promot-ing embryonic stem cell research know that the current debate on funding is a mere transitional step. For years they have supported the mass manufacture of human embryos through cloning, as the logical and necessary goal of their agenda, but lately they have been coy about this as they fight for the more popular slogan of "stem cell research." With his speech Reagan has removed the mask and allowed us to debate what is really at stake.

5

He claimed in his speech, of course, that what is at stake in this debate is the lives of millions of patients with devastating diseases. But by highlighting Parkinson's disease and juvenile diabetes as two diseases most clearly justifying the move to human cloning, he failed to do his homework. These are two of the diseases that pro-cloning scientists now admit will probably *not* be helped by research cloning.

He rebuts Reagan's argu-ment by citing authorities to add credibility to his claims.

6

Scottish cloning expert Ian Wilmut, for example, wrote in the *British Medical Journal* in February that producing genetically matched stem cells through cloning is probably quite unneces-sary for treating any neurological disease. Recent findings sug-gest that the nervous system is "immune privileged," and will not generally reject stem cells from a human who is genetically differ-ent. He added that cloning is probably useless for auto-immune diseases like juvenile diabetes, where the body mistakenly rejects its own insulin-producing cells as though they were foreign. "In such cases," he wrote, "transfer of immunologically identical cells to a patient is expected to induce the same rejection."

7

Wilmut's observations cut the ground out from under Ron Reagan's simple-minded claim that cloning is needed to avoid tissue rejection. For some diseases, genetically matched cells are unnecessary; for others, they are useless, because they only replicate the genetic profile that is part of the problem. (Ironically, for Alzheimer's both may be true—cloning may be unnecessary to avoid tissue rejection in the brain, and useless because the cloned cells would have the same genetic defect that may lead to Alzheimer's.) Reagan declared that this debate requires us to "choose between . . . reason and ignorance," but he did not realize which side has the monopoly on ignorance.

8   That ignorance poses an obstacle to real advances that are right before our eyes. Two weeks before Ron Reagan declared that a treatment for Parkinson's may arrive "ten or so years from now," using "the material of our own bodies," a Parkinson's patient and his doctor quietly appeared before Congress to point out that this has already been done. Dennis Turner was treated in 1999 by Dr. Michel Levesque of Cedars-Sinai Medical Center in Los Angeles, using his own adult neural stem cells. Dr. Levesque did not use the Rube Goldberg method of trying to turn those cells into a cloned embryo and then killing the embryo to get stem cells—he just grew Turner's own adult stem cells in the lab, and turned them directly into dopamine-producing cells. And with just one injection, on one side of Turner's brain, he produced an almost complete reversal of Parkinson's symptoms over four years.

9   Turner stopped shaking, could eat without difficulty, could put in his own contact lenses again, and resumed his avocation of big-game photography—on one occasion scrambling up a tree in Africa to escape a charging rhinoceros.

10   Amazingly, while this advance has been presented at national and international scientific conferences and featured on ABC-TV in Chicago, the scientific establishment supporting embryonic stem cell research has almost completely ignored it, and most news media have obediently imposed a virtual news blackout on it. That did not change even after the results were presented to the Senate Commerce Subcommittee on Science, Technology and Space this month. Pro-cloning Senators on the panel actually seemed angry at the witnesses, for trying to distract them from their fixation on destroying embryos.

11   Turner also testified that his symptoms have begun to return, especially arising from the side of his brain that was left untreated, and he would like to get a second treatment. For that he will have to wait. Dr. Levesque has received insufficient appreciation and funding for his technique, and is still trying to put together the funds for broader clinical trials—as most Parkinson's foundations and NIH peer reviewers look into the starry distance of Ron Reagan's dreams about embryonic stem cells.

12   But hey, who cares about real Parkinson's patients when there's a Brave New World to sell?

Doerflinger takes a very different tone than Reagan. Which do you find more effective?

To contrast Reagan's hypothetical example, Doerflinger provides a real example of treating Parkinson's.

Compare how Doerflinger and Reagan characterize those who disagree with them. Which approach do you find more persuasive?

Sample Student Rebuttal Argument

Marta Ramos

Professor Jacobs

English 1010

30 April 2013

Oversimplifying the Locavore Ethic

James McWilliams's argument in his book *Just Food* is based on an overly simplistic understanding of the locavore ethic. His claim, that eating locally is an unrealistic goal, fails to take into account the flexibility of locavorism, the ways consumer food preferences drive the free market system, and the realities of food processing infrastructure.

> Ramos identifies the source that she will refute and the source's claim in the first paragraph.

McWilliams's criticism of locavorism would make sense if, as he implies, locavores were a single-minded group of people demanding the complete conversion of the agricultural systems to uniform, regimented local production and consumption. In fact, there is no reason that locavorism has to completely replace the existing agricultural system, and hardly any locavores advocate this. Locavorism, the practice of eating food that is grown locally and in season, is not an all-or-nothing policy. It is a direction in which individuals and communities can move. *Locavores.com*, a Web site run by the chef Jessica Prentice, who coined the term "locavore," spells out local-eating strategies:

> Ramos defines the term "locavore" and asserts that McWilliams misunderstands the movement.

> If not LOCALLY PRODUCED, then ORGANIC.
>
> If not ORGANIC, then FAMILY FARM.
>
> If not FAMILY FARM, then LOCAL BUSINESS.
>
> If not LOCAL BUSINESS, then TERROIR—foods famous for the region they are grown in. ("Guidelines")

This hierarchy of food sources prefers local sources over distant ones and prioritizes local farms and businesses to receive local food dollars. Eating locally, according to Locavores, represents "A step toward regional food self-reliance" ("Top"). Given the political instability of many areas of the world that grow our food and the way energy costs can drastically affect food prices, it makes sense to reduce our dependence on distant food sources. As Jennifer Maiser, one of the founders of the locavore movement, puts it,

> Ramos uses a direct quotation from a respected voice in the locavore community to build credibility.

Ramos 2

Locavores are people who pay attention to where their food comes from and commit to eating local food as much as possible. The great thing about eating local is that it's not an all-or-nothing venture. Any small step you take helps the environment, protects your family's health and supports small farmers in your area.

The goal is not to end completely our importation of food.

McWilliams cites Phoenix as an example of why locavorism won't work. Certainly cities like Phoenix, which lacks the water to grow much food, will always rely on external supply chains to feed their populations. But the obstacles to local eating in Phoenix should not prevent residents of San Francisco, Sarasota, or Charleston from eating locally grown foods. Locavorism doesn't have to work everywhere to be beneficial.

In addition to misrepresenting locavorism's goals, McWilliams illogically claims that it cannot meet people's food needs. "At current levels of fruit production," he warns, "apples are the only crop that could currently feed New Yorkers at a level that meets the U.S. Recommended Dietary Allowances" (44). McWilliams is wrong when he claims that if New Yorkers ate locally grown fruits, they could "rarely indulge in a pear, peach, or basket of strawberries" (44). That might be the case if New York farmers continued to grow nothing but apples and grapes. But if some of those crops were replaced with other fruits, New York could have a very diverse supply of produce that would come reasonably close to meeting the nutritional needs of its citizens. In fact, if committed locavores seek out locally grown strawberries, peaches, and pears, and are willing to pay more money for them than they do for apples, local farmers will have sound economic reasons for replacing some of their aging apple trees with peach and pear trees. McWilliams makes locavorism sound impractical because he tries to imagine it working within current agricultural realities. In fact, locavores seek to change the way food is produced and consumed. Moreover, locavorism works toward this change not, as McWilliams suggests, by advocating laws that restrict food producers but by encouraging consumers to vote with their wallets.

McWilliams's argument about New York also rests on the peculiar assumption that every person in the state has to eat the same fruits in

her refutation mos addresses McWilliams's argument int by point.

amos quotes cWilliams and en disproves e quoted claim.

Ramos 3

the same amounts in order for locavorism to work. He points out that except for apples and grapes, "every other fruit the state produces is not being harvested at a level to provide all New Yorkers with an adequate supply" (44). McWilliams implies that if you can't grow enough of a crop to supply every single person in the state, there is no point in growing it; however, the goal of locavorism is choice, not total local supply of all food, a fact McWilliams seems to willfully ignore.

> Ramos questions McWilliams's assumptions and finds them lacking.

Finally, McWilliams claims that the cost and inconvenience of processing food locally will prevent communities from moving toward local eating. He notes that "whereas the conventional system of production and distribution has in place a series of large-scale processing centers capable of handling these tasks in a handful of isolated locations," smaller communities do not (45). There are two problems with this argument. First, many of the "processing centers" McWilliams is thinking of *aren't* capable of handling the task of food production. The National Resources Defense Council reports that "from 1995 to 1998, 1,000 spills or pollution incidents occurred at livestock feedlots in ten states and 200 manure-related fish kills resulted in the death of 13 million fish" ("Facts"). In 2009, Fairbank Farms recalled over half a million pounds of ground beef after nineteen people were hospitalized and two died from E. coli bacteria in the meat (United States). Also in 2009, the King Nut Companies of Solon, Ohio, sickened over four hundred people, including three who died, by producing and distributing peanut butter infected with salmonella ("Virginia"). Large-scale processing plants are not a solution to our food security needs. They are part of the problem.

> Ramos addresses the claim that she takes greatest issue with last. She then gives it further emphasis by providing two distinct counterarguments.

Second, the cost of changing the country's food-processing system from large-scale to small-scale is not as prohibitive as McWilliams makes it sound. Factories age. Machines wear out and have to be replaced. Food production facilities are replaced all the time. Newer facilities could easily be built on a smaller, more regional scale. In fact, given the cost of recalls and lawsuits when tainted food is distributed over a large area, food producers have good reason to think about smaller, more localized production and distribution.

McWilliams either does not understand locavorism or understands it and prefers to misrepresent its goals and methods. His arguments in favor of our current food production system ignore both the very real benefits of local eating, and the considerable cost of the existing system.

> Ramos closes with an appeal to the benefits of locavorism.

Ramos 4

Works Cited

"Facts about Pollution from Livestock Farms." *Natural Resources Defense Council*. Natural Resources Defense Council, 15 July 2005. Web. 7 Apr. 2013.

"Guidelines for Eating Well." *Locavores*. Locavores, 3 June 2009. Web. 9 Apr. 2013.

Maiser, Jennifer. "10 Steps to Becoming a Locavore." *PBS: NOW*. Jump Start Productions, 2 Nov. 2007. Web. 8 Apr. 2013.

McWilliams, James E. *Just Food: Where Locavores Get It Wrong and How We Can Truly Eat Responsibly*. New York: Little, Brown, 2009.

"Top Twelve Reasons to Eat Locally." *Locavores*. Locavores, 3 June 2009. Web. 9 Apr. 2013.

United States. Dept. of Health and Human Services. "Multistate Outbreak of E. coli 0157:H7 Infections Associated with Beef from Fairbanks Farms." *Centers for Disease Control and Prevention*. Dept. of Health and Human Services, 24 Nov. 2009. Web. 8 Apr. 2013.

"Virginia, Minnesota Confirms Salmonella Deaths Related to Tainted Peanut Butter." *Fox News*. Fox News Network, 13 Jan. 2009. Web. 10 Apr. 2013.

13 | Proposal Arguments

QUICK TAKE

In this chapter, you will learn to

1. Understand how proposal arguments work (see page 193)
2. Recognize how a proposal argument identifies a problem and states a solution that readers find fair, effective, and practical (see pages 193–194)
3. Analyze a proposal argument (see pages 194–195)
4. Write an effective proposal argument (see pages 196–197)

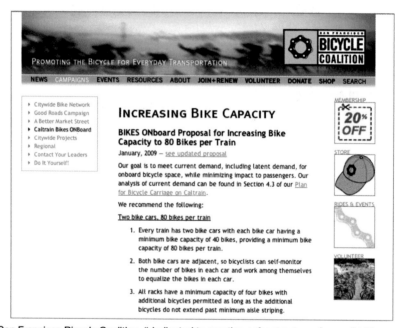

The San Francisco Bicycle Coalition, "dedicated to creating safer streets and more livable communities," is an organization whose primary goal is to build a citywide bike network in San Francisco. The success of the coalition's efforts to increase bicycle ridership for commuters created its own problem: Caltrain commuter trains ran out of room for bicycles, and riders were "bumped" because the trains' bike storage cars were filled to capacity. The coalition crafted a new proposal called Bikes On Board to persuade Caltrain to add more bike storage capacity on its trains. The coalition's proposal encourages riders to report "bumps" in order to document exactly how many times cyclists are denied rides on trains because of limited bike storage. This well-defined proposal forms part of a larger campaign and organizational mission encompassing environmental, economic, and personal fitness issues. What local issues inspire you to propose action? How would you go about crafting a proposal argument to promote interest in a cause or solution?

Understand How Proposal Arguments Work

Proposal arguments make the case that someone should do something: "The federal government should raise grazing fees on public lands." "The student union should renovate the old swimming pool in Butler Gymnasium." "All parents should secure their children in booster seats when driving, even for short distances." Proposals can also argue that something should *not* be done, or that people should stop doing something: "The plan to extend Highway 45 is a waste of tax dollars and citizens should not vote for it." "Don't drink and drive."

The challenge for writers of proposal arguments is to convince readers to take action. It's easy for readers to agree that something should be done, as long as they don't have to do it. It's much harder to get readers involved with the situation or convince them to spend their time or money trying to carry out the proposal. A successful proposal argument conveys a sense of urgency to motivate readers and describes definite actions they should take.

The key to a successful proposal is using good reasons to convince readers that if they act, something positive will happen (or something negative will be avoided). If your readers believe that taking action will benefit them, they are more likely to help bring about what you propose.

Proposal arguments take the form shown here.

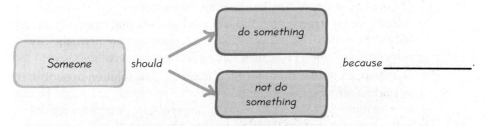

We should convert existing train tracks in the downtown areas to a light-rail system and build a new freight track around the city because we need to relieve traffic and parking congestion downtown.

Recognize Components of Proposal Arguments

Most successful proposals have four major components.

■ **Identifying and defining the problem.** Sometimes, your audience is already fully aware of the problem you want to solve. If your city frequently tears up streets and then leaves them for months without fixing them, you shouldn't have to spend much time convincing citizens that streets should be repaired more quickly. But if you raise a problem unfamiliar to your readers, first you will have to convince them that the problem is real. Citizens will not see the need to replace miles of plumbing lines running under the streets, for example, unless you convince them that the pipes are old and corroded and are a risk to everyone's safety. You will also need to define the scope of the problem—does every single pipe need to be replaced, or only those more than forty years old? Is this a job for the city, or do federal clean water regulations mean that other government officials must be involved? The clearer you are about what must be done, and by whom, the stronger your argument will be.

- **Stating a proposed solution.** A strong proposal offers a clear, definite statement of exactly what you are proposing. Vague statements that "Something must be done!" may get readers stirred up about the issue, but are unlikely to lead to constructive action. A detailed proposal also adds credibility to your argument, showing that you are concerned enough to think through the nuts and bolts of the changes to be made. You can state your proposed solution near the beginning of your argument (it's in effect your thesis statement) or introduce it later—for example, after you have considered and rejected other possible solutions.

- **Convincing readers that the proposed solution is well considered and fair.** Once your readers agree that a problem exists and a solution should be found, you have to convince them that your solution is the best one. You have to supply good reasons to favor your proposal. Perhaps you want your city to fire the planning committee members who are responsible for street repair. You will need to show that those officials are indeed responsible for the delays and that, once they are fired, the city will be able to quickly hire new, more effective planners.

- **Demonstrating that the solution is feasible.** Your solution not only has to work; it must be feasible, or practical, to implement. You might be able to raise money for street repairs by billing property owners for repairs to the streets in front of their houses, but opposition to such a proposal would be fierce. Most Americans will object to making individuals responsible for road repair costs when roads are used by all drivers.

You may also have to show how your proposal is better than other possible actions that could be taken. Perhaps others believe your city should hire private contractors to repair the streets more quickly, or reward work crews who finish quickly with extra pay or days off. If there are multiple proposed solutions, all perceived as equally good, then there is no clear course of action for your audience to work for. Very often, that means nothing will happen. Take a clear stand.

Build a Proposal Argument

At this moment, you might not think that you feel strongly enough about anything to write a proposal argument. But if you write a list of things that make you mad or at least a little annoyed, then you have a start toward writing a proposal argument.

Some things on your list are not going to produce proposal arguments that many people would want to read. If your roommate is a slob, you might be able to write a proposal for that person to start cleaning up more, but who else would be interested? Similarly, it might be annoying to you that where you live is too far from the ocean, but it is hard to imagine making a serious proposal to move your city closer to the coast. Short of those extremes, however, are many things that might make you think "Why hasn't someone done something about this?" If you believe that others have something to gain if a problem is solved, or at least that the situation can be made a little better, then you might be able to develop a good proposal argument.

For instance, suppose you are living off campus and you buy a student parking sticker when you register for courses so that you can park in the student lot. However, you quickly find out that there are too many cars and trucks for the number of available spaces, and unless you get to campus by 8:00 A.M., you aren't going to find a place to park in your assigned lot. The situation makes you angry because you believe that if you pay for a sticker, you should have a reasonable chance of finding a place to park. You see that there are unfilled lots reserved for faculty and staff next to the student parking lot, and you wonder why more spaces aren't allotted to students. You decide to write to the president of your college. You want her to direct parking and traffic services to give more spaces to students or else to build a parking garage that will accommodate more vehicles.

When you start talking to other students on campus, however, you begin to realize that the problem may be more complex than your first view of it. Your college has taken the position that if fewer students drive to campus, there will be less traffic on and around your campus. The administration wants more students to ride shuttle buses, to form car pools, or to bicycle to campus instead of driving alone. You also find out that faculty and staff members pay ten times as much as students for their parking permits, so they pay a very high premium for a guaranteed space—much too high for most students. If the president of your college is your primary audience, you first have to argue that a problem really exists. You have to convince the president that many students have no choice but to drive if they are to attend classes. You, for example, are willing to ride the shuttle buses, but they don't run often enough for you to make your classes, get back to your car that you left at home, and then drive to your job.

Next, you have to argue that your solution will solve the problem. An 8-story parking garage might be adequate to park all the cars of students who want to drive, but parking garages are very expensive to build. Even if a parking garage is the best solution, the question remains: who is going to pay for it? Many problems in life could be solved if you had access to unlimited resources, but very few people—or organizations—have such resources at their command. It's not enough to propose a solution that can resolve the problem. You have to be able to argue for the feasibility of your solution. If you want to argue that a parking garage is the solution to the parking problem on your campus, then you must also propose how to finance the garage.

Steps to Writing a Proposal Argument

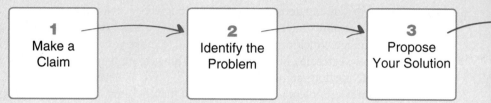

Step 1 Make a Claim

Make a proposal claim advocating a specific change or course of action.

Template

We should (or should not) do SOMETHING.

Examples

- Redesigning the process of registering for courses, getting e-mail, or making appointments to be more efficient
- Creating bicycle lanes to make cycling safer and to reduce traffic
- Streamlining the rules for recycling newspapers, bottles, and cans to encourage increased participation

Step 2 Identify the Problem

- What exactly is the problem, what causes it, and who is most affected?
- Has anyone tried to do anything about it? If so, why haven't they succeeded?
- What is likely to happen in the future if the problem isn't solved?

Step 3 Propose Your Solution

State your solution as specifically as you can, and support it with good reasons.

- What exactly do you want to achieve?
- What good consequences will follow if your proposal is adopted?
- How exactly will your solution work? Can it be accomplished quickly, or will it have to be phased in over a few years?
- Has anything like it been tried elsewhere? If so, what happened?
- If your solution costs money, how do you propose to pay for it?

Step 4 Consider Other Solutions

- What other solutions have been or might be proposed for this problem, including doing nothing?
- Why is your solution better?

Step 5 Write a Draft

Introduction

- Set out the issue or problem, perhaps by telling about your experience or the experience of someone you know.
- Argue for the seriousness of the problem.
- Give some background about the problem if necessary.
- State your proposal as your thesis.

Body

- Present your solution. Consider setting out your solution first, explaining how it will work, discussing other possible solutions, and arguing that yours is better. Or consider discussing other possible solutions first, arguing that they don't solve the problem or are not feasible, and then presenting your solution.
- Make clear the goals of your solution. Many solutions cannot solve problems completely.
- Describe in detail the steps in implementing your solution and how they will solve the problem you have identified.
- Explain the positive consequences that will follow from your proposal. What good things will happen, and what bad things will be avoided, if your advice is taken?

Conclusion

- Issue a call to action—if your readers agree with you, they will want to take action.
- Restate and emphasize exactly what readers need to do to solve the problem.

Step 6 Revise, Edit, Proofread

- For detailed instructions, see Chapter 5.
- For a checklist to use to evaluate your draft, see pages 50–51.

Finding Good Reasons

Who Should Make Decisions About Economic Development?

Cape Cod, Massachusetts, is a peninsula that extends from the southern portion of Massachusetts into the Atlantic Ocean. Famous for its beautiful shoreline, Cape Cod is a popular destination for summer vacationers. The Cape Wind project is a proposed 24-square-mile offshore wind farm that would be built beginning a little less than 5 miles off the Cape's southern coast. Proponents of the plan cite the benefits of clean energy. Strong opposition, however, has been voiced by the Alliance to Protect Nantucket Sound, which claims that the proposed wind farm will not only destroy property values, but also irrevocably damage the Cape's priceless views, threaten the vital tourist industry, dislocate necessary shipping lanes, disrupt fish populations, and pose a hazard to birds. Cape Wind has brought a prolonged battle in Massachusetts courts that no doubt will continue with a series of appeals.

Write about it

1. If you were the spokesperson for Cape Wind, what reasons would you give to the Massachusetts courts to persuade them to begin construction of the wind farm?

2. If you were the spokesperson for the Alliance to Protect Nantucket Sound, what reasons would you give to the Massachusetts courts to persuade them to block the construction of the wind farm?

3. If you were a judge on the Massachusetts Bench, what reasons might you expect to hear from these two groups? Draft a proposal that would win your vote.

Adam Gopnik

The Simple Truth About Gun Control*

Adam Gopnik (born 1956) is most commonly associated with the *New Yorker* magazine, where he has written art criticism and social commentary since 1986. His most recent book, *Through the Children's Gate: A Home in New York*, (2006), reflects on his experiences living in New York with his spouse and two children. The following essay appeared in the *New Yorker* in December, 2012, shortly after twenty children and six adult staff were massacred at Sandy Hook Elementary School in Newtown, Connecticut.

> Note how Gopnik begins with an extended analogy, one that creates a need for action.

We live, let's imagine, in a city where children are dying of a ravaging infection. The good news is that its cause is well understood and its cure, an antibiotic, easily at hand. The bad news is that our city council has been taken over by a faith-healing cult that will go to any lengths to keep the antibiotic from the kids. Some citizens would doubtless point out meekly that faith healing has an ancient history in our city, and we must regard the faith healers with respect—to do otherwise would show a lack of respect for their freedom to faith-heal. (The faith healers' proposition is that if there were a faith healer praying in every kindergarten the kids wouldn't get infections in the first place.) A few Tartuffes would see the children writhe and heave in pain and then wring their hands in self-congratulatory piety and wonder why a good God would send such a terrible affliction on the innocent—surely he must have a plan! Most of us—every sane person in the city, actually—would tell the faith healers to go to hell, put off worrying about the Problem of Evil till Friday or Saturday or Sunday, and do everything we could to get as much penicillin to the kids as quickly we could.

> References to Engel and Lewis establish that this proposal for stiffer gun laws was offered just after the Sandy Hook massacre in a Connecticut elementary school.

2   We do live in such a city. Five thousand seven hundred and forty children and teens died from gunfire in the United States, just in 2008 and 2009. Twenty more, including Olivia Engel, who was seven, and Jesse Lewis, who was six, were killed just last week. Some reports say their bodies weren't shown to their grief-stricken parents to identify them; just their pictures. The overwhelming majority of those children would have been saved with effective gun control. We know that this is so, because, in societies that *have* effective gun control, children rarely, rarely, rarely die of gunshots. Let's worry tomorrow about the problem of Evil. Let's worry more about making sure that when the Problem of Evil appears in a first-grade classroom, it is armed with a penknife.

Gopnik's proposal is supported by consequences in the form of reduced gun violence. He states that "we know that this is so" because of the experience of other nations, but will everyone accept that as evidence for the United States?

3   There are complex, hand-wringing-worthy problems in our social life: deficits and debts and climate change. Gun violence, and the work of eliminating gun massacres in schools and movie houses and the like, is not one of them. Gun control works on gun violence as surely as antibiotics do on bacterial infections. In Scotland, after Dunblane, in Australia, after Tasmania, in Canada, after the Montreal massacre—in each case the necessary laws were passed to make gun-owning hard, and in each case . . . well, you will note the absence of massacre-condolence speeches made by the Prime Ministers of Canada and Australia, in comparison with our own President.

4   The laws differ from place to place. In some jurisdictions, like Scotland, it is essentially impossible to own a gun; in others, like Canada, it is merely very, very difficult. The precise legislation that makes gun-owning hard in a certain sense doesn't really matter—and that should give hope to all of those who feel that, with several hundred million guns in private hands, there's no point in trying to make America a gun-sane country.

More argument by consequence and by analogy: If we could take effective action to curb crime in New York City, why should we not be able to take steps to curb gun violence?

5   The central insight of the modern study of criminal violence is that all crime—even the horrific violent crimes of assault and rape—is at some level opportunistic. Building a low annoying wall against them is almost as effective as building a high impenetrable one. This is the key concept of Franklin Zimring's amazing work on crime in New York; everyone said that, given the social pressures, the slum pathologies, the profits to be made in drug dealing, the ascending levels of despair, that there was no hope of changing the ever-growing cycle of violence. The right wing insisted that this generation of predators would give way to a new generation of super-predators.

6   What the New York Police Department found out, through empirical experience and better organization, was that making crime even a little bit harder made it much, much rarer. This is undeniably true of property crime, and common sense and evidence tells you that this is also true even of crimes committed by crazy people (to use the plain English the subject deserves). Those who hold themselves together enough to be capable of killing anyone are subject to the same rules of opportunity as sane people. Even madmen need opportunities to display their madness, and behave in different ways depending on the possibilities at hand. Demand an extraordinary degree of determination and organization from someone intent on committing a violent act, and the odds that the violent act will take place are radically reduced, in many cases to zero.

Gopnik uses an authority to support his case.

7   Look at Harvard social scientist David Hemenway's work on gun violence: the phrase "more guns = more homicide" tolls through it like a grim bell. The more guns there are in a country, the more gun murders and massacres of children there will be.

Even within this gun-crazy country, states with strong gun laws have fewer gun murders (and suicides and accidental killings) than states without them. (Hemenway is also the scientist who has shown that the inflated figure of guns used in self-defense every year, running even to a million or two million, is a pure fantasy, even though it's still cited by pro-gun enthusiasts. Those hundreds of thousands intruders shot by gun owners left no records in emergency wards or morgues; indeed, left no evidentiary trace behind. This is because they did not exist.) Hemenway has discovered, as he explained in an interview with *Harvard Magazine*, that what is usually presented as a case of self-defense with guns is, in the real world, almost invariably a story about an escalating quarrel. "How often might you appropriately use a gun in self-defense?" Hemenway asks rhetorically. "Answer: zero to once in a lifetime. How about inappropriately—because you were tired, afraid, or drunk in a confrontational situation? There are lots and lots of chances."

8   So don't listen to those who, seeing twenty dead six- and seven-year-olds in ten minutes, their bodies riddled with bullets designed to rip apart bone and organ, say that this is impossibly hard, or even particularly complex, problem. It's a very easy one. Summoning the political will to make it happen may be hard. But there's no doubt or ambiguity about what needs to be done, nor that, if it is done, it will work. One would have to believe that Americans are somehow uniquely evil or depraved to think that the same forces that work on the rest of the planet won't work here. It's always hard to summon up political will for change, no matter how beneficial the change may obviously be. Summoning the political will to make automobiles safe was difficult; so was summoning the political will to limit and then effectively ban cigarettes from public places. At some point, we will become a gun-safe, and then a gun-sane, and finally a gun-free society. It's closer than you think. (I'm grateful to my *New Yorker* colleague Jeffrey Toobin for showing so well that the idea that the Second Amendment assures individual possession of guns, so far from being deeply rooted in American law, is in truth a new and bizarre reading, one that would have shocked even Warren Burger.)

> Gopnik shows consistent awareness of the arguments against his position.

9   Gun control is not a panacea, any more than penicillin was. Some violence will always go on. What gun control is good at is controlling guns. Gun control will eliminate gun massacres in America as surely as antibiotics eliminate bacterial infections. Those who oppose it have made a moral choice: that they would rather have gun massacres of children continue rather than surrender whatever idea of freedom or pleasure they find wrapped up in owning guns or seeing guns owned—just as the faith

> More argument by analogy

healers would rather watch the children die than accept the reality of scientific medicine. This is a moral choice; many faith healers make it to this day, and not just in thought experiments. But it is absurd to shake our heads sapiently and say we can't possibly know what would have saved the lives of Olivia and Jesse.

10   On gun violence and how to end it, the facts are all in, the evidence is clear, the truth there for all who care to know it— indeed, a global consensus is in place, which, in disbelief and now in disgust, the planet waits for us to us to join. Those who fight against gun control, actively or passively, with a shrug of helplessness, are dooming more kids to horrible deaths and more parents to unspeakable grief just as surely as are those who fight against pediatric medicine or childhood vaccination. It's really, and inarguably, just as simple as that.

Gopnik's argument is a stereotypical proposal: A problem is dramatized; a solution is proposed; good consequences are demonstrated; opposing viewpoints are addressed.

Sample Student Proposal Argument

Lee 1

Kim Lee

Professor Patel

RHE 306

31 March 2013

Let's Make It a Real Melting Pot with Presidential Hopes for All

The image the United States likes to advertise is one of a country
that embraces diversity and creates a land of equal opportunity for
all. As the Statue of Liberty cries out, "give me your tired, your poor,
your huddled masses yearning to breathe free," American politicians
gleefully evoke such images to frame the United States as a bastion
for all things good, fair, and equal. As a proud American, however, I
must nonetheless highlight one of the cracks in this façade of equality.
Imagine that an infertile couple decides to adopt an orphaned child from
China. The couple follows all of the legal processes deemed necessary by
both countries. They fly abroad and bring home their (once parentless)
6-month-old baby boy. They raise and nurture him, and while teaching
him to embrace his ethnicity, they also teach him to love Captain Crunch,
baseball, and *The Three Stooges*. He grows and eventually attends an
ethnically diverse American public school.

One day his fifth-grade teacher tells the class that anyone can grow
up to be president. To clarify her point, she turns to the boy, knowing
his background, and states, "No, you could not be president, Stu, but
you could still be a senator. That's something to aspire to!" How do Stu's
parents explain this rule to this American-raised child? This scenario will
become increasingly common, yet as the Constitution currently reads,
only "natural-born" citizens may run for the offices of president and
vice president. Neither these children nor the thousands of hardworking
Americans who chose to make America their official homeland may aspire
to the highest political position in the land. While the huddled masses
may enter, it appears they must retain a second-class citizen ranking.

The issue arose most recently when bloggers, media personalities,
and some elected officials alleged that Barack Obama was born in Kenya,
not Hawaii, and that his birth certificate is a forgery. The release of
a certified copy of Obama's Certificate of Live Birth (the "long form")

Lee sets out
the problem
with a concrete
scenario.

Lee 2

and other evidence including birth announcements in two Hawaii newspapers in August 1961 answered Donald Trump and other prominent "birthers" (Shear). Lost in the controversy was this question: Should it matter where Obama or any other candidate was born? In a land where all citizens but American Indians are immigrants or descendants of immigrants, why should being born in the United States be considered an essential qualification for election as president?

The provision arose from circumstances very different from those of today. The "natural-born" stipulation regarding the presidency stems from the selfsame meeting of minds that brought the American people the Electoral College. During the Constitutional Convention of 1787, the Congress formulated the regulatory measures associated with the office of the president. A letter sent from John Jay to George Washington during this period reads as follows:

> Permit me to hint whether it would not be wise and seasonable to provide a strong check to the admission of foreigners into the administration of our national government; and to declare expressly that the Commander in Chief of the American army shall not be given to, nor devolve on, any but a natural-born citizen. (Mathews A1)

Shortly thereafter, Article II, Section I, Clause V, of the Constitution declared that "No Person except a natural born Citizen, or a Citizen of the United States at the time of the Adoption of this Constitution, shall be eligible to the Office of President." Jill A. Pryor states in the *Yale Law Journal* that "some writers have suggested that Jay was responding to rumors that foreign princes might be asked to assume the presidency" (881). Many cite disastrous examples of foreign rule in the eighteenth century as the impetus for the "natural-born" clause. For example, in 1772—only fifteen years prior to the adoption of the statute—Poland had been divided up by Prussia, Russia, and Austria (Kasindorf). Perhaps an element of self-preservation and not ethnocentrism led to the questionable stipulation. Nonetheless, in the twenty-first century this clause reeks of xenophobia.

The Fourteenth Amendment clarified the difference between "natural-born" and "native-born" citizens by spelling out the citizenship

Lee gives the historical background of the "natural-born" restriction.

Lee 3

status of children born to American parents outside of the United States (Ginsberg 929). This clause qualifies individuals such as Senator John McCain—born in Panama—for presidency. This change, however, is not adequate. I propose that the United States abolish the natural-born clause and replace it with a stipulation that allows naturalized citizens to run for president. This amendment would state that a candidate must have been naturalized and must have lived in residence in the United States for a period of at least twenty-five years. The present time is ideal for this change. This amendment could simultaneously honor the spirit of the Constitution, protect and ensure the interests of the United States, promote an international image of inclusiveness, and grant heretofore-withheld rights to thousands of legal and loyal United States citizens.

In our push for change, we must make clear the importance of this amendment. It would not provide special rights for would-be terrorists. To the contrary, it would fulfill the longtime promises of the nation. Naturalized citizens have been contributing to the United States for centuries. Many nameless Mexican, Irish, and Asian Americans sweated and toiled to build the American railroads. Americans have welcomed naturalized citizens such as Bob Hope, Albert Pujols, and Peter Jennings into their hearts and living rooms. Individuals such as German-born Henry Kissinger and Czechoslovakian-born Madeleine Albright have held high posts in the American government and have served as respected aides to its presidents. The amendment must make clear that it is not about one person's celebrity. Approximately seven hundred foreign-born Americans have won the Medal of Honor and over sixty thousand proudly serve in the United States military today (Siskind 5). The "natural-born" clause must be removed to provide each of these people—over half a million naturalized in 2003 alone—equal footing with those who were born into citizenship rather than having to work for it (United States).

Since the passing of the Bill of Rights, only seventeen amendments have been ratified. This process takes time and overwhelming congressional and statewide support. To alter the Constitution, a proposed amendment must pass with a two-thirds "super-majority" in both the House of Representatives and the Senate. In addition, the proposal must find favor in two-thirds (38) of state legislatures. In short,

Lee states her proposal in this paragraph.

Lee gives examples of people who are qualified to become president yet are ineligible.

Lee 4

this task will not be easy. In order for this change to occur, a grassroots campaign must work to dispel misinformation regarding naturalized citizens and to force the hands of senators and representatives wishing to retain their congressional seats. We must take this proposal to ethnicity-specific political groups from both sides of the aisle, business organizations, and community activist groups. We must convince representatives that this issue matters. Only through raising voices and casting votes can the people enact change. Only then can every American child see the possibility for limitless achievement and equality. Only then can everyone find the same sense of pride in the possibility for true American diversity in the highest office in the land.

> Lee explains the process of amending the Constitution and ends with a call for action.

Lee 5

Works Cited

Ginsberg, Gordon. "Citizenship: Expatriation: Distinction between Naturalized and Natural Born Citizens." *Michigan Law Review* 50 (1952):
926-29. *JSTOR*. Web. 6 Mar. 2013.

Kasindorf, Martin. "Should the Constitution Be Amended for Arnold?"
USA Today 2 Dec. 2004. *LexisNexis Academic*. Web. 8 Mar. 2013.

Mathews, Joe. "Maybe Anyone Can Be President." *Los Angeles Times* 2
Feb. 2005: A1. *LexisNexis Academic*. Web. 6 Mar. 2013.

Pryor, Jill A. "The Natural Born Citizen Clause and Presidential Eligibility: An Approach for Resolving Two Hundred Years of Uncertainty."
Yale Law Journal 97.5 (1988): 881-99. Print.

Shear, Michael D. "With Document, Obama Seeks to End 'Birther' Issue."
New York Times. New York Times, 27 Apr. 2011. Web. 28 Apr. 2013.

Siskind, Lawrence J. "Why Shouldn't Arnold Run?" *Recorder* 10 Dec.
2004: 5. *LexisNexis Academic*. Web. 10 Mar. 2013.

United States. Dept. of Commerce. Census Bureau. "The Fourth of July
2005." *Facts for Features*. US Dept. of Commerce, 27 June 2005.
Web. 17 Mar. 2013.

Designing and Presenting Arguments

PART

4

14 | Designing Multimedia Arguments

QUICK TAKE

In this chapter, you will learn to

1. Identify the advantages and disadvantages of different media for reaching your audience (see below)
2. Analyze how an image or a graphic communicates to an audience (see page 210)
3. Describe the argument made by an image or a graphic (see pages 210–211)
4. List the elements important to designing a print page (see pages 211–212)
5. Create effective multimedia projects involving images, Web site production, audio, and video (see pages 212–213)

A rguments do not communicate with words alone. Even written arguments that do not contain graphics or images have a look and feel that also communicate meaning. Many arguments depend on presenting information visually, in multimedia, or in images, in addition to using written language. Using effective design strategies will make your arguments more engaging and compelling.

Think About Which Media Will Reach Your Audience

Before you graduate from college, it's likely you will find occasions when you want to persuade an audience beyond your instructor, classmates, and friends—possibly for your work, possibly for an organization you belong to, or possibly because an issue concerns you. You may have a clear sense of your message and the good reasons to support that message. But no matter how good your argument, nothing will happen unless you can command the scarcest commodity in our multitasking world—the attention of your audience.

Most college assignments specify the medium, which is typically a printed paper that you submit to the instructor. In the workplace and in life outside college, the choice of medium often isn't immediately evident. For example, if you

Think about the argument a chart or graph makes

Charts and graphs are useful for visually representing statistical trends and for making comparisons. For example, the U.S. Department of Education uses a bar chart to show how a college or career school education increases your chances of making more money and having more job opportunities. This bar chart offers a direct comparison of earnings and unemployment rates for each level of education.

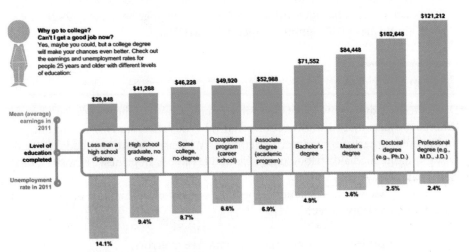

Source: Bureau of Labor Statistics, Current Population Survey, unpublished tables, 2012.

Bar chart comparing mean earnings and unemployment rates for levels of education

Design Arguments for Print

Writing on a computer gives you a range of options for designing a page that is appropriate to your assignment. Thinking about design will lead to a more effective presentation of your argument.

- **Choose the orientation, size of your page, and number of columns.** You can usually use the defaults on your computer for academic essays (remember to select double-spacing for line spacing if the default is single-spaced). For other kinds of texts you may want a horizontal rather than a vertical orientation, a size other than a standard sheet of paper, and two or more columns rather than one.

- **Divide your text into units.** The paragraph is the basic unit of extended writing, but also think about when to use lists. This list is a bulleted list. You can also use a numbered list.

- **Use left-aligned text with a ragged-right margin.** Fully justified text aligns the right margin, which gives a more formal look but can also leave unsightly rivers of extra white space running through the middle of your text. Ragged-right text is easier to read.

- **Be conscious of white space.** White space can make your text more readable and set off more important elements. Headings stand out more with white space surrounding them. Leave room around graphics. Don't crowd words too close to graphics because both the words and the visuals will become hard to read.
- **Be aware of MLA and APA design specifications.** MLA and APA styles have specifications for margins, indentions, reference lists, and other aspects of paper formatting. See the sample paper on pages 277–283 for guidelines on designing a paper using MLA style.

Design Multimedia Arguments

Digital technologies now make it possible to create on your home computer multimedia projects that formerly required entire production staffs. You can publish multimedia projects on the Internet (either as Web sites or as downloadable files), as stand-alone media distributed on CDs and DVDs, or in print with posters, brochures, and essays with images.

College viewers and listeners expect the content of multimedia projects to be high in quality. They expect

- your project to be well organized and free of errors,
- your claims to be supported with evidence,
- your analysis to be insightful,
- your sources to be documented, and
- your work to be clearly distinguished from the work of others.

Creating multimedia projects

If you decide to create a multimedia project, find out what resources are available for students on your campus. Many colleges and universities have digital media labs, which offer workshops and can provide video and audio studios, technical assistance, equipment, and software. Look for links to digital media services on your college's Web site.

Oral presentation with visuals (see Chapter 15)
Essay with images

- **Example project**: Evaluation argument concerning the poor condition of parks in your city
- Plan: Visit several parks, make notes, and take photographs.
- Produce: Write the project. Edit your images with an image editor and insert them in your project with captions.
- Edit: Revise with the comments of classmates and your instructor.

Web site production

- **Example project**: Web site making a definition argument that censorship of the Internet is a violation of the right to free speech
- Plan: Collect all the materials you will need for your site including text; digital images; graphics; and audio, video, and animation files.
- Produce: If you don't have a Web editor on your computer, find a campus lab that has Dreamweaver or similar software. Upload your site to a server. Many colleges offer server space to host student Web sites.
- Edit: Test your site to ensure that all links are working and all images and other files are showing up correctly. Edit with a Web editor.

Audio production

- **Example project**: Oral history of neighborhood residents making a causal argument about why a neighborhood declined after a freeway was built through the middle of it
- Plan: Arrange and record interviews and write a script.
- Produce: Reserve a campus audio production lab or record on your computer. Create an audio file by combining the interviews with your narration.
- Edit: Edit with an audio editor. Export the video into a format such as WAV or MP3 that you can put on the Web or share as a downloadable file.

Video production

- **Example project**: Proposal to create bike lanes on a busy street near your campus
- Plan: Identify locations, get permission to film if necessary, and write a script.
- Produce: Shoot video of the street with cars and bikes competing. Interview cyclists, drivers, and local business owners about their sense of urgency of the problem and the effects of creating bike lanes.
- Edit: Edit with a video editor. Export the video into a format such as QuickTime that you can put on the Web or share as a downloadable file.

15 | Presenting Arguments

QUICK TAKE

In this chapter, you will learn to

1. Plan an effective presentation—state a goal, identify your audience, organize your material, and assemble evidence (see below)

2. Design visuals for a presentation and use audio and video clips strategically (see pages 216–218)

3. Deliver an effective presentation (see pages 218–219)

Plan a Presentation

If you are assigned to give a presentation, look carefully at the assignment for guidance on finding a topic. Finding a topic for a presentation is similar to finding a topic for a written assignment (see Chapter 3). If your assignment requires research, you will need to document the sources of information just as you do for a research paper (see Chapters 16–19).

Start with your goal in mind

What is the real purpose of your presentation? Are you informing, persuading, or motivating? Take the elevator test. Imagine you are in an elevator with the key people who can approve or reject your ideas. Their schedule is very tight. You have only thirty seconds to convince them. Can you make your case?

This scenario is not far-fetched. One executive demanded that every new idea had to be written in one sentence on the back of a business card. What's your sentence?

It's all about your audience

Who is your audience? In college your audience is often your instructor and fellow students—an audience you know well. Many times you will not have this advantage.

Take a few minutes to answer these questions.

- Will my audience be interested in the topic?
- Why does it matter to them?
- What are they likely to know and believe about the topic?
- What are they likely not to know?
- Where are they likely to disagree?
- What do I want them to do?
- How much time do I have?
- If they remember only one thing, what should it be?

Get organized

Start with pen and paper before you begin creating slides. Post-it notes are another useful planning tool.

- **Make a list of key points.** Think about the best order for your major points.
- **Plan your introduction.** Your success depends on your introduction. You must gain the attention of your audience, introduce your topic, indicate why it's important, and give a sense of where you are headed. That's a tall order, but if you don't engage your audience in the first two minutes, you will lose them.
- **Plan your conclusion.** You want to end on a strong note. Stopping abruptly or rambling on only to tail off leaves your audience with a bad impression. Give your audience something to take away, a compelling example or an idea that captures the gist of your presentation.

Build content

Content alone does not make a presentation successful, but you cannot succeed without solid content. Support your major points with relevant evidence.

- **Facts.** Speakers who know their facts build credibility.
- **Statistics.** Effective use of statistics can tell the audience that you have done your homework. Statistics can also indicate that a particular example is representative.
- **Statements by authorities.** Quotations from credible experts can support key points.
- **Narratives.** Narratives are brief stories that illustrate key points. Narratives can hold the attention of the audience—but keep them short or they will become a distraction.

Design Visuals for a Presentation

Less is more with slides. One text-filled slide after another is mind-numbingly dull. Presentations using slides don't have to be this bad.

Keep it simple

Imagine you are making an argument that fewer animals would be euthanized at animal shelters if more people in your city knew that they could save a pet's life by adopting it. You could fill your slides with statistics alone. Or you tell your audience the facts while showing them slides that give emotional impact to your numbers.

Simple design rules! Keep in mind these principles.

- One point per slide
- Very few fonts
- Quality photos, not clipart
- Less text, more images
- Easy on the special effects

Compare the following examples.

Pet Overpopulation in the United States

- Estimated number of animals that enter shelters each year: 6–8 million
- Estimated number of animals euthanized at shelters each year: 3–4 million
- Estimated number of animals adopted at shelters each year: 3–4 million

Source: "HSUS Pet Overpopulation Estimates." *Humane Society of the U.S.* Humane Society of the U.S., 9 Nov. 2009. Web. 18 Oct. 2013.

Pet Overpopulation in the United States

- **Estimated number of animals entering shelters each year: 6–8 million**
- **Estimated number of animals euthanized at shelters each year: 3–4 million**
- **Estimated number of animals adopted at shelters: 3–4 million**

Source: "HSUS Pet Overpopulation Estimates." *Humane Society of the U.S.* Humane Society of the U.S., 9 Nov. 2009. Web. 18 Oct. 2013.

Save a pet

Which slide makes the point most effectively?

But what if you have a lot of data to show? Make a handout that the audience can study later. They can make notes on your handout, which gives them a personal investment. Keep your slides simple and emphasize the main points in the presentation.

Use audio and video clips strategically

Short audio and video clips can offer concrete examples and add some variety to your presentation. An audience appreciates hearing and even seeing the people you interview. PowerPoint, Prezi, Keynote, and other presentation software make it simple to embed the files within a presentation. Be careful, however, in using built-in sound effects such as canned applause. Most sound effects are annoying and make you come off as inexperienced.

Deliver an Effective Presentation

If you are not passionate about your subject, you will never get your audience committed to your subject, no matter how handsome your slides. Believe in what you say; enthusiasm is contagious.

It's all about you

The audience didn't come to see the back of your head in front of slides. Move away from the podium and connect with them. Make strong eye contact with individuals. You will make everyone feel as if you were having a conversation instead of giving a speech.

Prepare in advance

Practice your presentation, even if you have to speak to an empty chair. Check out the room and equipment in advance. If you are using your laptop with a projector installed in the room, make sure it connects. If the room has a computer connected to the projector, bring your presentation on a flash drive and download it to the computer.

Be professional

Pay attention to the little things.

- **Proofread carefully.** A glaring spelling error can destroy your credibility.
- **Be consistent.** If you randomly capitalize words or insert punctuation, your audience will be distracted.

- **Pay attention to the timing of your slides.** Stay in sync with your slides. Don't leave a slide up when you are talking about something else.
- **Use the "B" key.** If you get sidetracked, press the "B" key, which makes the screen go blank so the audience can focus on you. When you are ready to resume, press the "B" key again and the slide reappears.
- **Involve your audience.** Invite response during your presentation where appropriate, and leave time for questions at the end.
- **Add a bit of humor.** Humor can be tricky, especially if you don't know your audience well. But if you can get people to laugh, they will be on your side.
- **Slow down.** When you are nervous, you tend to go too fast. Stop and breathe. Let your audience take in what's on your slides.
- **Finish on time or earlier.** Your audience will be grateful.
- **Be courteous and gracious.** Remember to thank anyone who helped you and the audience for their comments. Eventually you will run into someone who challenges you, sometimes politely, sometimes not. If you remain cool and in control, the audience will remember your behavior long after the words are forgotten.

Convert a Written Text into a Presentation

The temptation when converting a written text into a presentation is to dump sentences and paragraphs onto the slides. Indeed, it's simple enough to cut and paste big chunks of text, but you risk losing your audience.

Make a list of the main points in your written text, and then decide which ones you need to show on slides and which you can tell the audience. Your voice supplies most of the information; your slides help your audience to remember and organize your presentation.

People learn better when your oral presentation is accompanied by engaging images and graphics. Slides can also add emotional involvement.

Unwanted dogs

Carlos

a playful mixed-breed pup who was recently adopted

Arrange your slides so they tell a story. For example, if you are arguing that fewer dogs would be euthanized if your city were more active in promoting adoption, you can show slides that give statistics, or you can report statistics in your presentation while letting your audience identify with individual dogs.

Researching Arguments

PART

5

16 | Planning Research

In this chapter, you will learn to

1. Analyze an assignment or research task (see below)
2. Find a subject and develop a research question (see pages 223–224)
3. Gather information through field research, including interviews, surveys, and observations (see pages 224–227)
4. Draft a working thesis to guide you through further research and the development of your argument (see page 227)

Analyze the Research Task

Research is a creative process, which is another way of saying it is a messy process. However, your results will improve if you keep the big picture in mind while you are immersed in research. When you get a research assignment, look at it closely.

Look for key words

Often the assignment will tell you what is expected.

- An assignment that asks you, for example, how the usual *definition* of intellectual property applies to *YouTube* invites you to write a definition argument (see Chapter 8).
- An *analysis of causes* requires you to write a causal argument (see Chapter 9).
- An *evaluation* requires you to make critical judgments based on criteria (see Chapter 10).
- A *proposal* requires you to assemble evidence in support of a solution to a problem or a call for the audience to do something (see Chapter 13).

Identify your potential readers

- How familiar are your readers with your subject?
- What background information will you need to supply?

- If your subject is controversial, what opinions or beliefs are your readers likely to hold?
- If some readers are likely to disagree with you, how can you convince them?

Assess the project's length, scope, and requirements

- What kind of research are you being asked to do?
- What is the length of the project?
- What kinds and number of sources or field research are required?
- Which documentation style is required such as MLA (see Chapter 20) or APA (see Chapter 21)?

Set a schedule

- Note the due dates on the assignment for drafts and final versions.
- Set dates for yourself on finding and evaluating sources, drafting your thesis, creating a working bibliography, and writing a first draft.
- Give yourself enough time to do a thorough job.

Find a Subject

One good way to begin is by browsing, which may also show you the breadth of possibilities in a topic and lead you to new topics (see Chapter 3).

You might begin browsing by doing one or more of the following.

- **Visit "Research by Subject" on your library's Web site.** Clicking on a subject such as "African and African American Studies" will take you to a list of online resources.
- **Look for topics in your courses.** Browse your course notes and readings. Are there topics you might explore in greater depth?
- **Browse a Web subject directory.** Web subject directories, including *Yahoo Directory*, are useful when you want to narrow a topic or learn what subcategories a topic might contain. In addition to the Web subject directories, your library's Web site may have a link to the *Opposing Viewpoints* database.
- **Look for topics as you read.** When you read actively, you ask questions and respond to ideas in the text. Review what you wrote in the margins or the notes you have made about something you read that interested you. You may find a potential topic.

Ask a Research Question

Often you'll be surprised by the amount of information your initial browsing uncovers. Your next task will be to identify a question for your research project within that mass of information. This **researchable question** will be the focus of the remainder of your research and ultimately of your research project or paper. Browsing on the subject of organic foods, for example, might lead you to one of the following researchable questions.

- How do farmers benefit from growing organic produce?
- Why are organic products more expensive than nonorganic products?
- Are Americans being persuaded to buy more organic products?

Once you have formulated a research question, you should begin thinking about what kind of research you will need to do to address the question.

Gather Information About the Subject

Most researchers rely partly or exclusively on the work of others as sources of information. Research based on the work of others is called **secondary research**. In the past this information was contained almost exclusively in collections of print materials housed in libraries, but today enormous amounts of information are available through library databases and on the Web (see Chapter 17).

Much research done at a university creates new data through **primary research**—experiments, examination of historical documents—and **field research**, including data-gathering surveys, interviews, and detailed observations.

Conducting field research

Sometimes you may be researching a question that requires you to gather firsthand information with field research. For example, if you are researching a campus issue such as the impact of a new fee on students' budgets, you may need to conduct interviews, make observations, and give a survey.

Interviews

College campuses are a rich source of experts in many areas, including people on the faculty and in the surrounding community. Interviewing experts on your research subject can help build your knowledge base. You can use interviews to discover what the people most affected by a particular issue are thinking, such as why students object to some fees and not others.

Arrange interviews

Before you contact anyone, think carefully about your goals. Knowing what you want to find out will help you determine whom you need to interview and what questions you need to ask. Use these guidelines to prepare for an interview.

- Decide what you want or need to know and who best can provide that information for you.
- Schedule each interview in advance, and let the person know why you are conducting the interview. Estimate how long your interview will take, and tell your subject how much time you will need.
- Choose a location that is convenient for your subject but not too chaotic or loud. An office or study room is better than a noisy cafeteria.
- Plan in advance. Write down a few questions and have a few more in mind. Background reading helps avoid unnecessary questions.
- If you want to make an audio recording, ask for permission in advance.

Conduct interviews

- Come prepared with your questions and a tablet, laptop, or paper notebook.
- Listen carefully so you can follow up on key points. Make notes when important questions are raised or answered, but don't attempt to transcribe every word the person is saying.
- When you are finished, thank your subject, and ask his or her permission to get in touch again if you have additional questions.

Surveys

Extensive surveys that can be projected to large populations, like the ones used in political polls, require the effort of many people. Small surveys, however, often can provide insight on local issues, such as what percentage of students might be affected if library hours were reduced.

Plan surveys

What information do you need for your research question? Decide what exactly you want to know, and design a survey that will provide that information. Probably you will want both close-ended questions (multiple choice, yes or no, rating scale) and open-ended questions that allow detailed responses.

- Write a few specific, unambiguous questions. People will fill out your survey quickly. If the questions are confusing, the results will be meaningless.

- Include one or two open-ended questions, such as "What do you like about X?" or "What don't you like about X?" These can be difficult to interpret, but they turn up information you had not anticipated.
- Test the questions on a few people before you conduct the survey.
- Think about how you will interpret your survey. Multiple-choice formats make data easy to tabulate, but often they miss key information. Open-ended questions will require you to figure out a way to sort responses into categories.

Administer surveys

- Decide on whom you need to survey and how many respondents your survey will require. For example, if you want to claim that the results of your survey represent the views of residents of your dormitory, your method of selecting respondents should give all residents an equal chance to be selected. Don't select only your friends.
- Decide how you will contact participants in your survey. If you are conducting your survey in person on private property, you will need permission from the property owner.
- If you e-mail your survey, include a statement about what the survey is for.

Observations

Observing can be a valuable source of data. For example, if you are researching why a particular office on your campus does not operate efficiently, observe what happens when students enter and how the staff responds to their presence.

Make observations

- Choose a place where you can observe with the least intrusion. The less people wonder about what you are doing, the better.
- Carry a tablet, laptop, or paper notebook and write extensive field notes. Record as much information as you can, and worry about analyzing it later.
- Record the date, exactly where you were, exactly when you arrived and left, and important details like the number of people present.

Analyze observations

You must interpret your observations so they make sense in the context of your argument. Ask yourself the following questions.

- What patterns of behavior did you observe?
- How was the situation you observed unique? How might it be similar to other locations?

- What constituted "normal" activity during the time when you were observing? Did anything out of the ordinary happen?
- Why were the people there? What can you determine about the purposes of the activities you observed?

Draft a Working Thesis

Once you have done some preliminary research into your question, you can begin to craft a working thesis. Let's take one topic as an example—the increasing popularity of organic products, including meat, dairy products, and produce. If you research this topic, you will discover that because of this trend, large corporations such as Walmart are beginning to offer organic products in their stores. However, the enormous demand for organic products is actually endangering smaller organic farmers and producers. As you research the question of why small farmers and producers in the United States are endangered and what small farmers and producers in other countries have done to protect themselves, a working thesis begins to emerge.

Write down your subject, research question, and working thesis, and refer to them frequently. You may need to revise your working thesis several times until the wording is precise. As you research, ask yourself, does this information tend to support my thesis? Information that does not support your thesis is still important! It may lead you to adjust your thesis or even to abandon it altogether. You may need to find another source or reason that shows your thesis is still valid.

Example

SUBJECT: Increased demand for organic products endangering smaller farmers and producers.

RESEARCH QUESTION: How can successful smaller organic farmers and producers protect themselves from becoming extinct?

WORKING THESIS: In order to meet the increasing demand for organic products that has been created by larger corporations such as Walmart, smaller organic farmers and producers should form regional co-ops. These co-ops will work together to supply regional chains, much as co-ops of small farmers and dairies in Europe work together, thereby cutting transportation and labor costs and ensuring their survival in a much-expanded market.

17 | Finding Sources

QUICK TAKE

In this chapter, you will learn to

1. Develop a search strategy, including using keywords, to find quality sources faster (see below)
2. Find sources in library databases (see pages 229–231)
3. Use search engines to find reliable Web sources, including government, online reference, and interactive media sources (see pages 232–235)
4. Identify search engines and Web sites for multimedia sources, including images, videos, podcasts, and graphics (see pages 236–237)
5. Find library print sources such as books and journals (see pages 237–238)

Develop Strategies for Finding Sources

The Internet makes available vast quantities of searchable facts and data. Nevertheless, libraries still contain many resources not available on the Web. Even more important, libraries have professional research librarians who can help you locate sources quickly.

Determine where to start looking

Searches using *Google* or *Yahoo!* turn up thousands of items, many of which are often not useful for research. Considering where to start is the first step.

Scholarly books and articles in scholarly journals often are the highest-quality sources, but the lag in publication time makes them less useful for very current topics. Newspapers cover current issues, but often not in the depth of books and scholarly journals. Government Web sites and publications are often the best for finding statistics and are also valuable for researching science and medicine.

Learn the art of effective keyword searches

Keyword searches take you to the sources you need. Start with your working thesis and generate a list of possible keywords for researching your thesis.

First, think of keywords that make your search more specific. For example, a search for sources related to Internet privacy issues might focus more specifically on privacy *and*

Internet
cookies
data retention
social media
photographs

You should also think about more general ways to describe what you are doing. What synonyms can you think of for your existing terms? Other people may have discussed the topic using those terms instead. Instead of relying on "privacy," you can also try keywords like

identity theft
data protection
electronic records

You can even search using terms that refer to related people, events, or movements that you are familiar with.

Facebook
Google
phishing

Many databases have a thesaurus that can help you find more keywords.

Find Sources in Databases

Sources found through library **databases** have already been filtered for you by professional librarians. They will include some common sources like popular magazines and newspapers, but the greatest value of database sources are the many journals, abstracts, studies, e-books, and other writing produced by specialists whose work has been scrutinized and commented on by other experts. When you read a source from a library database, chances are you are hearing an informed voice in an important debate.

Locate databases

You can find databases on your library's Web site. Sometimes you will find a list of databases. Sometimes you select a subject, and then you are directed to databases. Sometimes you select the name of a database vendor such as *EBSCOhost* or *ProQuest*. The vendor is the company that provides databases to the library.

Use databases

Your library has a list of databases and indexes by subject. If you can't find this list on your library's Web site, ask a **reference librarian** for help. Follow these steps to find articles.

1. Select a database appropriate to your subject or a comprehensive database like *Academic Search Complete, Academic Search Premier,* or *LexisNexis Academic.*
2. Search the database using your list of keywords.
3. Once you have chosen an article, print or e-mail to yourself the complete citation to the article. Look for the e-mail link after you click on the item you want.
4. Print or e-mail to yourself the full text if it is available. The full text is better than cutting and pasting because you might lose track of which words are yours, which could lead to unintended plagiarism.
5. If the full text is not available, check the online library catalog to see if your library has the journal.

Your library will probably have printed handouts or online information that tells you which database to use for a particular subject. Ask a librarian who works at the reference or information desk to help you.

If you wish to get only full-text articles, you can filter your search by checking that option. Full-text documents give you the same text you would find in print. Sometimes the images are not reproduced in the HTML versions, but the PDF versions show the actual printed copy. Get the PDF version if it is available. Articles in HTML format usually do not contain the page numbers.

Common Databases	
Academic OneFile	Indexes periodicals from the arts, humanities, sciences, social sciences, and general news, with full-text articles and images. (Formerly *Expanded Academic ASAP*)
Academic Search Premier and Complete	Provides full-text articles for thousands of scholarly publications, including social sciences, humanities, education, computer sciences, engineering, language and linguistics, literature, medical sciences, and ethnic-studies journals.

(Continued)

Common Databases

ArticleFirst	Indexes journals in business, the humanities, medicine, science, and social sciences.
EBSCOhost Research Databases	Gateway to a large collection of EBSCO databases, including *Academic Search Premier* and *Complete, Business Source Premier* and *Complete, ERIC,* and *Medline.*
Factiva	Provides full-text articles on business topics, including articles from the *Wall Street Journal.*
Google Books	Allows you to search within books and gives you snippets surrounding search terms for copyrighted books. Many books out of copyright have the full text. Available for everyone.
Google Scholar	Searches scholarly literature according to criteria of relevance. Available for everyone.
General OneFile	Contains millions of full-text articles about a wide range of academic and general-interest topics.
LexisNexis Academic	Provides full text of a wide range of newspapers, magazines, government and legal documents, and company profiles from around the world.
Opposing Viewpoints Resource Center	Provides full-text articles representing differing points of view on current issues.
ProQuest Databases	Like *EBSCOhost, ProQuest* is a gateway to a large collection of databases with over 100 billion pages, including the best archives of doctoral dissertations and historical newspapers.

Find Sources on the Web

Because anyone can publish on the Web, there is no overall quality control and there is no system of organization—two strengths we take for granted in libraries. Nevertheless, the Web offers you some resources for current topics that would be difficult or impossible to find in a library. The key to success is knowing where you are most likely to find current and accurate information about the particular question you are researching and knowing how to access that information.

Use search engines wisely

Search engines designed for the Web work in ways similar to library databases and your library's online catalog but with one major difference. Databases typically do some screening of the items they list, but search engines potentially take you to everything on the Web—millions of pages in all. Consequently, you have to work harder to limit searches on the Web or you can be deluged with tens of thousands of items.

Kinds of search engines

A search engine is a set of programs that sort through millions of items at incredible speed. There are four basic kinds of search engines.

1. **Keyword search engines** (e.g., *Bing, Google, Yahoo!*). Keyword search engines give different results because they assign different weights to the information they find.
2. **Meta-search engines** (e.g., *Dogpile, MetaCrawler, Surfwax*). Meta-search engines allow you to use several search engines simultaneously. While the concept is sound, metasearch agents are limited because many do not access *Google* or *Yahoo!*
3. **Web directories** (e.g., Britannica.com, *Yahoo! Directory*). Web directories classify Web sites into categories and are the closest equivalent to the cataloging system used by libraries. On most directories professional editors decide how to index a particular Web site. Web directories also allow keyword searches.
4. **Specialized search engines** are designed for specific purposes:

   - regional search engines (e.g., *Baidu* for China)
   - medical search engines (e.g., *WebMD*)
   - legal search engines (e.g., *Lexis*)
   - job search engines (e.g., Monster.com)
   - property search engines (e.g., *Zillow*)

Advanced searches

Search engines often produce too many hits and are therefore not always useful. If you look only at the first few items, you may miss what is most valuable. The alternative is to refine your search. Most search engines offer you the option of an advanced search, which gives you the opportunity to limit numbers.

Google searches can be focused by using the "Search tools" option. You can specify the time range from the past hour to the past year to a custom date range. You can also specify that *Google* finds the exact phrase you type in with the Verbatim option under "All results." Another useful way of limiting searches is to specify the domain, e.g., **site:.gov**.

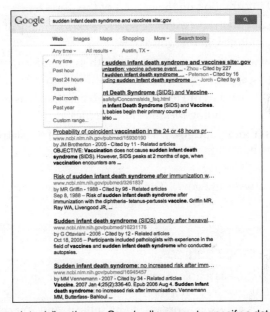

The "Search tools" option on *Google* allows you to specify a date range.

The **OR** operator is useful if you don't know exactly which term will get the results you want, especially if you are searching within a specific site. For example, you could try this search: "face-to-face OR f2f site:webworkerdaily.com."

You can also exclude terms by putting a minus sign before the term. If you want to search for social network privacy, but not *Facebook*, try "social network privacy–Facebook."

Find online government sources

The federal government has made many of its publications available on the Web. Also, many state governments now publish important documents on the Web. Often the most current and most reliable statistics are government statistics. Among the more important government resources are the following.

- **Bureau of Labor Statistics** (www.bls.gov/). Source for official U.S. government statistics on employment, wages, and consumer prices
- **Census Bureau** (www.census.gov/). Contains a wealth of links to sites for population, social, economic, and political statistics, including the *Statistical Abstract of the United States* (www.census.gov/compendia/statab/)
- **Centers for Disease Control** (www.cdc.gov/). Authoritative and trustworthy source for health statistics
- **CIA World Factbook** (www.cia.gov/library/publications/the-world-factbook/). Resource for geographic, economic, demographic, and political information on the nations of the world
- **Library of Congress** (www.loc.gov/). Access to many of the resources of the largest library in the world
- **NASA** (www.nasa.gov/). A rich site with much information and images concerning space exploration and scientific discovery
- **National Institutes of Health** (www.nih.gov/). Extensive health information including *MedlinePlus* searches
- **Thomas** (thomas.loc.gov/). The major source of legislative information, including bills, committee reports, and voting records of individual members of Congress
- **USA.gov** (www.usa.gov/). The place to start when you are not sure where to look for government information

Find online reference sources

Your library's Web site has a link to reference sites, either on the main page or under another heading like "research tools."

Reference sites are usually organized by subject, and you can find resources under the subject heading.

- **Business information** (links to business databases and sites like *Hoover's* that profiles companies)
- **Dictionaries** (including the *Oxford English Dictionary* and various subject dictionaries and language dictionaries)
- **Education** (including *The College Blue Book* and others)
- **Encyclopedias** (including *Britannica* and others)
- **Government information** (links to federal, state, and local Web sites)
- **Reference books** (commonly used books like atlases, almanacs, biographies, handbooks, and histories)
- **Statistics and demographics** (links to federal, state, and local government sites; *FedStats* [www.fedstats.gov/] is a good place to start)

Search interactive media

The Internet allows you to access other people's opinions on thousands of topics. Millions of people post messages on discussion lists and groups, *Facebook* groups, blogs, RSS feeds, *Twitter*, and so on. Much of what you read on interactive media sites is undocumented and highly opinionated, but you can still gather important information about people's attitudes and get tips about other sources, which you can verify later.

Several search engines have been developed for interactive media. *Facebook* and *Twitter* also have search engines for their sites.

Discussion list search engines

- **Big Boards** (www.big-boards.com). Tracks over two thousand of the most active discussion forums
- **Google Groups** (groups.google.com). Archives discussion forums dating back to 1981
- **Yahoo! Groups** (groups.yahoo.com). A directory of groups by subject

Blog search engines

- **Bloglines** (www.bloglines.com). Web-based aggregator that delivers RSS feeds
- **Google Blog Search** (blogsearch.google.com). Searches blogs in several languages besides English
- **IceRocket** (blogs.icerocket.com). Searches blogs, *MySpace*, and *Twitter*
- **Technorati** (www.technorati.com). Searches blogs and other user-generated content

Know the limitations of *Wikipedia*

Wikipedia is a valuable resource for current information and for popular culture topics that are not covered in traditional encyclopedias. You can find out, for example, that SpongeBob SquarePants's original name was "SpongeBoy," but the name had already been copyrighted.

Nevertheless, many instructors and the scholarly community in general do not consider *Wikipedia* a reliable source of information for a research paper. The fundamental problem with *Wikipedia* is stability, not whether the information is correct or incorrect. *Wikipedia* and other wikis constantly change. The underlying idea of documenting sources is that readers can consult the same sources that you consulted. Consult other sources to confirm what you find on *Wikipedia* and cite those sources. Often the *Wikipedia* entry includes a list of references that you can use as a starting point for your own research.

Find Multimedia Sources

Massive collections of images; audio files including music, speeches, and podcasts; videos; maps, charts, and graphs; and other resources are now available on the Web.

Find images

The major search engines for images include the following.

- **Bing Images** (www.bing.com/images/)
- **Google Image Search** (images.google.com/)
- **Picsearch** (www.picsearch.com/)
- **Yahoo! Image Search** (images.search.yahoo.com)

Libraries and museums also offer large collections of images that may help you in your research. For example, the *American Memory* collection in the Library of Congress offers an important visual record of the history of the United States (memory.loc.gov/ammem/).

Find videos

- **Bing Videos** (www.bing.com/videos/)
- **blinkx** (www.blinkx.com/)
- **Google Videos** (video.google.com/)
- **Vimeo** (vimeo.com)
- **Yahoo! Video Search** (video.search.yahoo.com)
- **YouTube** (www.youtube.com)

Find podcasts

- **iTunes Podcast Resources** (www.apple.com/itunes/podcasts/)
- **PodcastDirectory.com** (www.podcastdirectory.com/)

Find charts, graphs, and maps

You can find statistical data represented in charts and graphs on many government Web sites.

- **Statistical Abstract of the United States** (www.census.gov/compendia/statab/)
- **Google Earth** (earth.google.com/)

- **National Geographic Map Machine**
  (mapmachine.nationalgeographic.com/)
- **Perry Casteñada Map Collection, University of Texas**
  (www.lib.utexas.edu/maps/map_sites/map_sites.html)

Respect copyright

Just because images, videos, and other multimedia files are easy to download from the Web does not mean that everything is available for you to use. Look for the creator's copyright notice and suggested credit line. This notice will tell you if you can reproduce the multimedia file. Include properly formatted citations for each electronic resource you include in your paper.

Find Print Sources

Print sources may seem "old fashioned" if you grew up with the Internet. You might even feel a little bit intimidated by them. But they are the starting point for much of the research done by experts. In college and beyond, they are indispensable. No matter how current the topic you are researching, you will likely find information in print sources that is simply not available online.

Print sources have other advantages as well.

- Books are shelved according to subject, which allows for easy browsing.
- Books often have bibliographies, directing you to other research on the subject.
- You can search for books in multiple ways: author, title, subject, or call letter.
- The majority of print sources have been evaluated by scholars, editors, and publishers, who decided whether they merited publication.

Find books

Nearly all libraries now shelve books according to the Library of Congress Classification System, which uses a combination of letters and numbers to give you the book's unique location in the library. The Library of Congress call number begins with a letter or letters that represent the broad subject area into which the book is classified.

Locating books in your library

The floors of your library where books are shelved are referred to as the stacks. The call number will enable you to find the item in the stacks. You will need to consult the locations guide for your library, which gives the level and section where an item is shelved.

Locating e-books

Use your library's online catalog to find e-books the same way you find printed books. You'll see on the record "e-book" or "electronic resource." Click on the link and you can read the book and often download a few pages or the entire book.

Find journal articles

Like books, **scholarly journals** provide in-depth examinations of subjects. The articles in scholarly journals are written by experts, and they usually contain lists of references that can guide you to other research on a subject.

Popular journals are useful for gaining general information. Articles in popular magazines are usually short with few, if any, source references and are typically written by journalists. Some instructors frown on using popular magazines, but these journals can be valuable for researching current opinion on a particular topic.

Many scholarly journals and popular magazines are available on your library's Web site. Find them the same way you look for books, using your library's online catalog. Databases increasingly contain the full text of articles, allowing you to read and copy the contents onto your computer. If the article you are looking for isn't available online, the paper copy will be shelved with the books in your library.

18 | Evaluating and Recording Sources

QUICK TAKE

In this chapter, you will learn to

1. Use the working thesis to decide a source's relevance (see below)
2. Distinguish among sources: anonymous versus edited, popular versus scholarly, and primary versus secondary sources (see pages 240–241)
3. Evaluate library database and print sources (see page 242)
4. Evaluate the quality of Web sources (see pages 243–244)
5. Keep track of sources, including recording all the information you need to cite a source (see pages 245–247)

Determine the Relevance of Sources

Whether you use print or online sources, a successful search will turn up many more items than you can expect to use in your final product. You have to make a series of decisions as you evaluate your material. Use your research question and working thesis to create guidelines for yourself about importance and relevance.

If you ask a research question about contemporary events such as the NCAA's policy on compensating student athletes (see pages 155–161), you will need to find both background information and current information. You will need to know, for example, the most recent statistics on how many scholarship athletes actually graduate because the NCAA's main defense of not paying scholarship athletes is that they get a free education.

Use these guidelines to determine the importance and relevance of your sources to your research question.

- Does your research question require you to consult primary or secondary sources?
- Does a source you have found address your question?
- Does a source support or disagree with your working thesis? (You should not throw out work that challenges your views. Representing opposing views accurately enhances your credibility.)
- Does a source add significant information?

- Is the source current? (For most topics try to find the most up-to-date information.)
- What indications of possible bias do you note in the source?

Determine the Quality of Sources

In the digital era, we don't lack for information, but we do lack filters for finding quality information. Two criteria will help you to make a beginning assessment of quality: individual vs. edited sources and popular vs. scholarly sources.

Distinguish individual and anonymous sources from edited sources

Anyone with a computer and Internet access can put up a Web site. Furthermore, people can put up sites anonymously or under an assumed name. It's no wonder that so many Web sites contain misinformation or are intentionally deceptive.

In general, sources that have been edited and published in scholarly journals, scholarly books, major newspapers, major online and print magazines, and government Web sites are considered of higher quality than what an individual might put on a personal Web site, on a *Facebook* page, in a user review, or in a blog.

Edited sources can have biases, and indeed some are quite open about their perspectives. *National Review* offers a conservative perspective, the *Wall Street Journal* is pro-business, and the *Nation* is a liberal voice. The difference from individual and anonymous sites is that we know the editorial perspectives of these journals, and we expect the editors to check the facts. On self-published Web sites and in self-published books, anything goes.

Distinguish popular sources from scholarly sources

Scholarly books and **scholarly journals** are published by and for experts. Scholarly books and articles published in scholarly journals undergo a **peer review** process in which a group of experts in a field reviews them for their scholarly soundness and academic value. Scholarly books and articles in scholarly journals include

- author's name and academic credentials and
- a list of works cited.

Newspapers, popular books, and **popular magazines** vary widely in quality. Newspapers and popular magazines range from highly respected publications such as the *Los Angeles Times, Scientific American,* and the *Atlantic Monthly* to the sensational tabloids at grocery-store checkouts. Popular sources are not peer reviewed and require more work on your part to determine their quality. *EBSCOhost* databases allow you to limit searches to scholarly journals.

Distinguish primary sources from secondary sources

Another key distinction for researchers is primary versus secondary sources. In the humanities and fine arts, **primary sources** are original, creative works and original accounts of events written close to the time they occurred. **Secondary sources** interpret creative works and primary sources of events.

In the sciences, primary sources are the factual results of experiments, observations, and clinical trials, and other factual data. Secondary sources analyze and interpret those results.

Read sources critically

Evaluating sources requires you to read critically, which includes the following.

- Identifying the source, which is not always easy on the Web
- Identifying the author and assessing the author's credentials
- Understanding the content—what the text says
- Recognizing the author's purpose—whether the author is attempting to reflect, inform, or persuade
- Recognizing biases in the choices of words, examples, and structure
- Recognizing what the author does not include or address
- Developing an overall evaluation that takes into account all of the above

Evaluate the quality of visual sources

Evaluating the quality of visual sources involves skills similar to critical reading skills. As in critical reading, you should

- identify and assess the source,
- identify the creator,
- identify the date of creation,
- describe the content,
- assess the purpose, and
- recognize how the purpose influences the image, graphic, or video.

For visuals including charts and graphs, pay attention to the source of any data presented and see that the data are presented fairly.

Evaluate Database and Print Sources

Books are expensive to print and distribute, so book publishers generally protect their investment by providing some level of editorial oversight. Printed and online materials in your library undergo another review by professional librarians who select them for their collections.

This initial screening doesn't free you, however, from the responsibility of evaluating the quality of the sources. Many printed and database sources contain their share of inaccurate, misleading, and biased information. Also, all sources carry the risk of becoming outdated if you are looking for current information.

Checklist for evaluating database and print sources

Over the years librarians have developed a set of criteria for evaluating sources, and you should apply them in your research.

1. **Source.** Who published the book or article? Enter the publisher's name on *Google* or another search engine to learn about the publisher. Scholarly books and articles in scholarly journals are generally more reliable than popular magazines and books, which tend to emphasize what is sensational or entertaining at the expense of accuracy and comprehensiveness.

2. **Author.** Who wrote the book or article? Enter the author's name on *Google* or another search engine to learn more about him or her. What are the author's qualifications? Does the author represent an organization?

3. **Timeliness.** How current is the source? If you are researching a fast-developing subject such as treating ADHD, then currency is very important, but even historical topics are subject to controversy or revision.

4. **Evidence.** Where does the evidence come from—facts, interviews, observations, surveys, or experiments? Is the evidence adequate to support the author's claims?

5. **Biases.** Can you detect particular biases of the author? How do the author's biases affect the interpretation offered?

6. **Advertising.** For print sources, is advertising a prominent part of the journal or newspaper? How might the ads affect the credibility or the biases of the information that gets printed?

Evaluate Web Sources

Researching on the Web has been compared to drinking from a fire hose. The key to success is not only getting the torrent down to the size of a glass, but also making sure the water in the glass is pure enough to drink.

Pay attention to domain names

Domain names can give you clues about the quality of a Web site.

- **.com** Commercial site. The information on a .com site is generally about a product or company. While the information may be accurate, keep in mind that the purpose of the site may be to sell a product or service.
- **.edu** Educational institution. The suffix tells you the site is on a school server, ranging from kindergarten to higher education. If the information is from a department or research center, it is generally credible, but if the site is an individual's, treat it as you would other kinds of self-published information.
- **.gov** Government. If you see this suffix, you're viewing a federal or state government site. Most government sites are considered credible sources.
- **.org** Nonprofit organization. Initially, nonpartisan organizations like the Red Cross used this domain, but increasingly partisan political groups and commercial interests have taken the .org suffix. Evaluate these sites carefully.
- **.mil** Military. This domain suffix is owned by the various branches of the armed forces.
- **.net** Network. Anyone can use this domain. Seek out information about the site's origin.

Be alert for biased Web sites

Nearly every large company and political and advocacy organization has a Web site. We expect these sites to represent the company or the point of view of the organization. Many sites on the Web, however, are not so clearly labeled.

For example, if you do a search for "Sudden Infant Death Syndrome (SIDS)" and "vaccines," you'll find near the top of the list an article titled "Vaccines and Sudden Infant Death Syndrome: Is There a Link?" The article concludes that vaccines cause SIDS. If you look at the home page, you'll find that the site's sponsor, Global Vaccine Institute, opposes all vaccinations of children.

Always look for other objective sources for verification of your information. The U.S. Centers for Disease Control and Prevention publishes fact sheets with the latest information about diseases and their prevention (www.cdc.gov/vaccinesafety/

Concerns/sids_faq.html). The fact sheet on SIDS and vaccines reports that people associate sudden infant death syndrome with vaccinations because babies are given vaccinations when they are between 2 and 4 months old, the same age babies die of SIDS. There is no scientific evidence that vaccines cause SIDS.

Checklist for evaluating Web sources

Web sources present special challenges for evaluation. When you find a Web page by using a search engine, you will often go deep into a complex site without having any sense of the context for that page. To evaluate the credibility of the site, you would need to examine the home page, not just the specific page you get to first. Use the following criteria for evaluating Web sites.

1. **Source.** What organization sponsors the Web site? Look for the site's owner at the top or bottom of the home page or in the Web address. Enter the owner's name on *Google* or another search engine to learn about the organization. If a Web site doesn't indicate ownership, then you have to make judgments about who put it up and why.

2. **Author.** Is the author identified? Look for an "About Us" link if you see no author listed. Enter the author's name on *Google* or another search engine to learn more about the author. Often Web sites give no information about their authors other than an e-mail address, if that. In such cases, it is difficult or impossible to determine the author's qualifications. Be cautious about information on an anonymous site.

3. **Purpose.** Is the Web site trying to sell you something? Many Web sites are infomercials that might contain useful information, but they are no more trustworthy than other forms of advertising. Is the purpose to entertain? to inform? to persuade?

4. **Timeliness.** When was the Web site last updated? Look for a date on the home page. Many Web pages do not list when they were last updated; thus you cannot determine their currency.

5. **Evidence.** Are sources of information listed? Any factual information should be supported by indicating where the information came from. Reliable Web sites that offer information will list their sources.

6. **Biases.** Does the Web site offer a balanced point of view? Many Web sites conceal their attitude with a reasonable tone and seemingly factual evidence such as statistics. Citations and bibliographies do not ensure that a site is reliable. Look carefully at the links and sources cited, and peruse the "About Us" link if one is available.

Keep Track of Sources

As you begin to collect your sources, make sure you get full bibliographic information for everything you might want to use in your project. Your instructor likely will tell you which documentation style you will use. (Two major documentation styles—MLA and APA—are explained in detail in Chapters 20 and 21.)

Locate elements of a citation in database sources

For any sources you find on databases, MLA style requires you to provide the full print information, the name of the database in italics, the medium of publication (Web), and the date you accessed the database. If page numbers are not included, use "n. page." Do not include the URL of the database.

See pages 263–264 for detailed coverage.

Author's name	Shaughnessy, Dan
Title of article	"They've Had Some Chief Concerns"
Publication information	
Name of periodical	*Boston Globe*
Date of publication	12 Oct. 2007
Section and page number	C5
Database information	
Name of database	*LexisNexis Academic*
Medium of publication	Web
Date you accessed the site	19 Apr. 2013

Citation in MLA-style list of works cited

Shaughnessy, Dan. "They've Had Some Chief Concerns." *Boston Globe* 12 Oct. 2007: C5. *LexisNexis Academic*. Web. 19 Apr. 2013.

Many databases include a feature that shows you how to cite the source; some have a built-in citation generator. Double-check the format before you include the citation in your paper to ensure accuracy.

Locate elements of a citation in online sources

As you conduct your online research, make sure you collect the necessary bibliographic information for everything you might want to use as a source. Because of the potential volatility of online sources (they can and do disappear overnight), their citations require extra information. Depending on the citation format you use, you'll arrange this information in different ways.

See page 264 for detailed coverage.

Author's name	Zaiger, Alan Scher
Title of work	"Study: NCAA Graduation Rate Comparisons Flawed"
Title of the overall Web site	*ABC News*
Publication information	
Publisher or sponsor	ABC News
Date of publication	20 Apr. 2010
Medium of publication	Web
Date you accessed the site	1 Nov. 2013

Citation in MLA-style list of works cited

Zaiger, Alan Scher. "Study: NCAA Graduation Rate Comparisons Flawed." *ABC News*. ABC News, 20 Apr. 2010. Web. 1 Nov. 2013.

Locate elements of a citation in print sources

For books you will need, at minimum, the following information, which can typically be found on the front and back of the title page.

See pages 262–263 for detailed coverage.

Author's name	Fleitz, David L.
Title of the book	Louis Sockalexis: The First Cleveland Indian
Publication information	
Place of publication	Jefferson
Name of publisher	McFarland
Date of publication	2002
Medium of publication	Print

Citation in MLA-style list of works cited

Fleitz, David L. *Louis Sockalexis: The First Cleveland Indian*. Jefferson: McFarland, 2002. Print.

19 | Writing the Research Project

QUICK TAKE

In this chapter, you will learn to

1. Assess the thesis for your research project and determine your contribution and main points (see below)
2. Understand what is considered plagiarism in college writing (see pages 249–251)
3. Avoid plagiarism in quoting sources (see pages 252–253)
4. Avoid plagiarism in summarizing and paraphrasing (see pages 254–255)
5. Decide when to quote and when to paraphrase (see page 256)
6. Integrate quotations into your text, including using signal phrases and block quotations (see pages 257–258)

Review Your Goals and Plan Your Organization

If you have chosen a subject you're interested in, asked questions about it, and researched it thoroughly, you have a wealth of ideas and information to communicate to your audience.

Review your assignment and thesis

Before you begin writing a research project, review the assignment to remind yourself of the purpose of your argument, your potential readers, and the requested length of the finished paper.

By now you should have formulated a **working thesis**, which will be the focus of your project. You also should have located, read, evaluated, and taken notes on enough source material to write your project, and perhaps have conducted field research. At this stage in the writing process, your working thesis may be rough and may change as you write your draft, but having a working thesis will help keep your project focused.

Determine your contribution

A convincing and compelling source-based argument does not make claims based solely on the word of you, the writer. To be persuasive, it must draw on the expertise and reputations of others as well. However, you must also demonstrate that you have thought about and synthesized the evidence you have gathered from your sources, and you must show your readers which elements of your project represent your original thinking.

Determine exactly what you are adding to the larger conversation about your subject by answering these questions.

- Whom do you agree with?
- Whom do you disagree with?
- Which positions do you agree with but can add an additional point or example to?
- What original analysis or theorizing do you have to offer?

See pages 32–34 for examples of how to identify your contribution in relation to your sources.

Determine your main points

Look back over your notes on your sources and determine how to group the ideas you researched. Decide what your major points will be and how those points support your thesis. Group your research findings so that they match up with your major points.

Now it is time to create a working outline. Always include your thesis at the top of your outline as a guiding light. Some writers create formal outlines with roman numerals and the like; others compose the headings for the paragraphs of their project and use them to guide their draft; still others may start writing and then determine how they will organize their draft when they have a few paragraphs written. Experiment and decide which method works best for you.

Avoid Plagiarism

Plagiarism means claiming credit for someone else's intellectual work no matter whether it's to make money or get a better grade. Intentional or not, plagiarism has dire consequences. Reputable authors have gotten into trouble through carelessness by copying passages from published sources without acknowledging those sources. A number of famous people have had their reputations tarnished by accusations of plagiarism, and several prominent journalists have lost their jobs and careers for copying the work of other writers and passing it off as their own.

Deliberate plagiarism

If you buy a paper on the Web, copy someone else's paper word for word, or take an article off the Web and turn it in as yours, it's plain stealing, and people who take that risk should know that the punishment can be severe—usually failure for the course and sometimes expulsion. Deliberate plagiarism is easy for your instructors to spot because they recognize shifts in style, and it is easy for them to use search engines to find the sources of work stolen from the Web.

Patch plagiarism

The use of the Web has increased instances of plagiarism in college. Some students view the Internet as a big free buffet where they can grab anything, paste it in a file, and submit it as their own work. Other students intend to submit work that is their own, but they commit patch plagiarism because they aren't careful in taking notes to distinguish the words of others from their own words.

What you are not required to acknowledge

Fortunately, common sense governs issues of academic plagiarism. The standards of documentation are not so strict that the source of every fact you cite must be acknowledged. You do not have to document the following.

- **Facts available from many sources.** For example, many reference sources report that the death toll of the sinking of the *Titanic* on April 15, 1912, was around 1,500.
- **Results of your own field research.** If you take a survey and report the results, you don't have to cite yourself. You do need to cite interviews that you conduct.

What you are required to acknowledge

The following sources should be acknowledged with an in-text citation and an entry in the list of works cited (MLA style) or the list of references (APA style).

- **Quotations.** Short quotations should be enclosed within quotation marks, and long quotations should be indented as a block. See page 257 for how to integrate quotations with signal phrases.
- **Summaries and paraphrases.** Summaries represent the author's argument in miniature as accurately as possible. Paraphrases restate the author's argument in your own words.
- **Facts that are not common knowledge.** For facts that are not easily found in general reference works, cite the source.
- **Ideas that are not common knowledge.** The sources of theories, analyses, statements of opinion, and arguable claims should be cited.
- **Statistics, research findings, examples, graphs, charts, and illustrations.** As a reader you should be skeptical about statistics and research findings when the source is not mentioned. When a writer does not cite the sources of statistics and research findings, there is no way of knowing how reliable the sources are or whether the writer is making them up.

Plagiarism in college writing

If you find any of the following problems in your academic writing, you may be guilty of plagiarizing someone else's work. Because plagiarism is usually inadvertent, it is especially important that you understand what constitutes using sources responsibly. Avoid these pitfalls.

- **Missing attribution.** Make sure the author of a quotation has been identified. Include a lead-in or signal phrase that provides attribution to the source, and identify the author in the citation.

- **Missing quotation marks.** You must put quotation marks around material quoted directly from a source.

- **Inadequate citation.** Give a page number to show where in the source the quotation appears or where a paraphrase or summary is drawn from.

- **Paraphrase that relies too heavily on the source.** Be careful that the wording or sentence structure of a paraphrase does not follow the source too closely.

- **Distortion of meaning.** Don't allow your paraphrase or summary to distort the meaning of the source, and don't take a quotation out of context so that the result is a change of meaning.

- **Missing works-cited entry.** The Works Cited page must include all the works cited in the project.

- **Inadequate citation of images.** A figure or photo must appear with a caption and a citation to indicate the source of the image. If material includes a summary of data from a visual source, an attribution or citation must be given for the graphic being summarized.

Avoid plagiarism when taking notes

The best way to avoid unintentional plagiarism is to take care to distinguish source words from your own words. Don't mix words from the source with your own words.

- **Create a working bibliography and make separate files for content notes.** Create a file for each source and label it clearly with the author's name. If you work on paper, use a separate page for each source. At the top of each page, write down all the information you need for a list of works cited or a list of references in your working bibliography.

- **If you copy anything from a source when taking notes, place those words in quotation marks and note the page number(s) where those words appear.** If you copy words from an online source, take special care to note the source. You could easily copy online material and later not be able to find where it came from.

■ **Print out the entire source or e-mail it to yourself so you can refer to it later.** Having a complete copy allows you to double-check later that you haven't used words from the source by mistake and that any words you quote are accurate.

Avoid Plagiarism When Quoting Sources

Effective research writing builds on the work of others. You can summarize or paraphrase the work of others, but often it is best to let the authors speak in your text by quoting their exact words. Indicate the words of others by placing them inside quotation marks.

Most people who get into plagiarism trouble lift words from a source and use them without quotation marks. Look carefully at this example to see where the line is drawn. In the following passage, Steven Johnson takes sharp issue with the metaphor of surfing applied to the Web:

> The concept of "surfing" does a terrible injustice to what it means to navigate around the Web. . . .What makes the idea of cybersurf so infuriating is the implicit connection drawn to television. Web surfing, after all, is a derivation of channel surfing—the term thrust upon the world by the rise of remote controls and cable panoply in the mid-eighties. . . . Applied to the boob tube, of course, the term was not altogether inappropriate. Surfing at least implied that channel-hopping was more dynamic, more involved, than the old routine of passive consumption. Just as a real-world surfer's enjoyment depended on the waves delivered up by the ocean, the channel surfer was at the mercy of the programmers and network executives. The analogy took off because it worked well in the one-to-many system of cable TV, where your navigational options were limited to the available channels.
>
> But when the term crossed over to the bustling new world of the Web, it lost a great deal of precision. . . . Web surfing and channel surfing are genuinely different pursuits; to imagine them as equivalents is to ignore the defining characteristics of each medium. Or at least that's what happens in theory. In practice, the Web takes on the greater burden. The television imagery casts the online surfer in the random, anesthetic shadow of TV programming, roaming from site to site like a CD player set on shuffle play. But what makes the online world so revolutionary is the fact that there *are* connections between each stop on a Web itinerant's journey. The links that join those various destinations are links of association, not randomness. A channel surfer hops back and forth between different channels because she's bored. A Web surfer clicks on a link because she's interested.

—Steven Johnson, *Interface Culture: How New Technology Transforms the Way We Create and Communicate* (New York: Harper, 1997), 107–109.

If you were writing a paper or creating a Web site that concerns Web surfing, you might want to mention the distinction that Johnson makes between channel surfing and surfing on the Web.

Quoting directly

If you quote directly, you must place quotation marks around all words you take from the original.

> One observer marks this contrast: "A channel surfer hops back and forth between different channels because she's bored. A Web surfer clicks on a link because she's interested" (Johnson 109).

Notice that the quotation is introduced and not just dropped in. This example follows MLA style, where the citation—(Johnson 109)—goes outside the quotation marks but before the final period. In MLA style, source references are made according to the author's last name, which refers you to the full citation in the list of works cited at the end. Following the author's name is the page number where the quotation can be located. (Notice that there is no comma after the name.)

Attributing every quotation

If the author's name appears in the sentence, cite only the page number, in parentheses.

> According to Steven Johnson, "A channel surfer hops back and forth between different channels because she's bored. A Web surfer clicks on a link because she's interested" (109).

Quoting words that are quoted in your source

Use single quotation marks to quote material that is already quoted in your source.

> Steven Johnson uses the metaphor of a Gothic cathedral to describe a computer interface: "'The principle of the Gothic architecture,' Coleridge once said, 'is infinity made imaginable.' The same could be said for the modern interface" (42).

Avoid Plagiarism When Summarizing and Paraphrasing

Summarizing

When you summarize, you state the major ideas of an entire source or part of a source in a paragraph or perhaps even a sentence. The key is to put the summary in your own words. If you use words from the source, you must put those words within quotation marks.

Plagiarized

> Steven Johnson argues in *Interface Culture* that the concept of "surfing" is misapplied to the Internet because channel surfers hop back and forth between different channels because they're bored, but Web surfers click on links because they're interested.

[Most of the words are lifted directly from the original; see page 252.]

Acceptable summary

> Steven Johnson argues in *Interface Culture* that the concept of "surfing" is misapplied to the Internet because users of the Web consciously choose to link to other sites while television viewers mindlessly flip through the channels until something catches their attention.

Paraphrasing

When you paraphrase, you present the idea of the source in your own words at about the same length as the original. You still need to include the reference to the source of the idea. The following example illustrates an unacceptable paraphrase.

Plagiarized

> Steven Johnson argues that the concept of "surfing" does a terrible injustice to what it means to navigate around the Web. What makes the idea of Web surfing infuriating is the association with television. Surfing is not a bad metaphor for channel hopping, but it doesn't fit what people do on the Web. Web surfing and channel surfing are truly different activities; to imagine them as the same is to ignore their defining characteristics. A channel surfer skips around because she's bored while a Web surfer clicks on a link because she's interested (107-09).

Even though the source is listed, this paraphrase is unacceptable. Too many of the words in the original are used directly here, including much or all of entire sentences. When a string of words is lifted from a source and inserted without quotation marks, the passage is plagiarized. Changing a few words in a sentence is not a paraphrase. Compare these two sentences.

Source

Web surfing and channel surfing are genuinely different pursuits; to imagine them as equivalents is to ignore the defining characteristics of each medium.

Unacceptable paraphrase

Web surfing and channel surfing are truly different activities; to imagine them as the same is to ignore their defining characteristics.

The paraphrase takes the structure of the original sentence and substitutes a few words. It is much too similar to the original.

A true paraphrase represents an entire rewriting of the idea from the source.

Acceptable paraphrase

Steven Johnson argues that "surfing" is a misleading term for describing how people navigate on the Web. He allows that "surfing" is appropriate for clicking across television channels because the viewer has to interact with what the networks and cable companies provide, just as the surfer has to interact with what the ocean provides. Web surfing, according to Johnson, operates at much greater depth and with much more consciousness of purpose. Web surfers actively follow links to make connections (107-09).

Even though this paraphrase contains a few words from the original, such as *navigate* and *connections*, these sentences are original in structure and wording while accurately conveying the meaning of the source.

Decide When to Quote and When to Paraphrase

The general rule in deciding when to include direct quotations and when to para-phrase lies in the importance of the original wording.

- If you want to refer to an idea or fact and the original wording is not critical, make the point in your own words.
- Save direct quotations for language that is memorable or conveys the character of the source.

Use quotations effectively

Quotations are a frequent problem area in research projects. Review every quota-tion to ensure that each is used effectively and correctly.

- **Limit the use of long quotations.** If you have more than one block quotation on a page, look closely to see if one or more can be paraphrased or summarized. Use direct quotations only if the original wording is important.
- **Check that each quotation is supporting your major points rather than making major points for you.** If the ideas rather than the original wording are what's important, paraphrase the quotation and cite the source.
- **Check that each quotation is introduced and attributed.** Each quotation should be introduced and the author or title named. Check for signal phrases, which point to a quotation: Smith *claims*, Jones *argues*, Brown *states*.
- **Check that each quotation is properly formatted and punctuated.** Prose quotations longer than four lines (MLA) or forty words (APA) should be indented 1 inch in MLA style or 1/2 inch in APA style. Shorter quotations should be enclosed within quotation marks.
- **Check that you cite the source for each quotation.** You are required to cite the sources of all direct quotations, paraphrases, and summaries.
- **Check the accuracy of each quotation.** It's easy to leave out words or mistype a quotation. Compare what is in your project to the original source. If you need to add words to make the quotation grammatical, make sure the added words are in brackets. Use ellipses to indicate omitted words.
- **Read your project aloud to a classmate or a friend.** Each quotation should flow smoothly when you read your project aloud. Put a check beside rough spots as you read aloud so you can revise later.

Use signal phrases

Signal verbs often indicate your stance toward a quotation. Introducing a quotation with "X says" or "X believes" tells your readers nothing. Find a livelier verb that suggests how you are using the source. For example, if you write "X contends," your reader is alerted that you likely will disagree with the source. Be as precise as possible.

Signal phrases that report information or a claim

X argues that . . .

X asserts that . . .

X claims that . . .

X observes that . . .

As X puts it, . . .

X reports that . . .

As X sums it up, . . .

Signal phrases when you agree with the source

X affirms that . . .

X has the insight that . . .

X points out insightfully that . . .

X theorizes that . . .

X verifies that . . .

Signal phrases when you disagree with the source

X complains that . . .

X contends that . . .

X denies that . . .

X disputes that . . .

X overlooks that . . .

X rejects that . . .

X repudiates that . . .

Signal phrases in the sciences

Signal phrases in the sciences often use the past tense, especially for interpretations and commentary.

X described . . .

X found . . .

X has suggested . . .

Introduce block quotations

Long direct quotations, called **block quotations**, are indented from the margin instead of being placed in quotation marks. In MLA style, a quotation longer than four lines should be indented 1 inch. A quotation of forty words or longer is indented 1/2 inch in APA style. In both MLA and APA styles, long quotations are double-spaced. You still need to integrate a block quotation into the text of your project by mentioning who wrote or said it.

- No quotation marks appear around the block quotation.
- Words quoted in the original retain the double quotation marks.
- The page number appears in parentheses after the period at the end of the block quotation.

It is a good idea to include at least one or two sentences following the quotation to describe its significance to your thesis.

Double-check quotations

Whether they are long or short, you should double-check all quotations you use to be sure they are accurate and that all words belonging to the original are set off with quotation marks or placed in a block quotation. If you wish to leave out words from a quotation, indicate the omitted words with ellipses (. . .), but make sure you do not alter the meaning of the original quotation. If you need to add words of your own to a quotation to make the meaning clear, place your words in square brackets.

Write a Draft

Some writers begin by writing the title, first paragraph, and concluding paragraph.

Write a specific title

A bland, generic title says to readers that you are likely to be boring.

Generic

> Good and Bad Fats

Specific titles are like tasty appetizers; if you like the appetizer, you'll probably like the main course.

Specific

> The Secret Killer: Hydrogenated Fats

Write an engaging introduction

Get off to a fast start. If, for example, you want to alert readers to the dangers of partially hydrogenated oils in the food we eat, you could begin by explaining the difference in molecular structure between natural unsaturated fatty acids and trans-fatty acids. And you would probably lose your readers by the end of the first paragraph.

Instead, let readers know what is at stake along with giving some background and context; consider dramatizing a problem that your paper will address. State your thesis early on. Then go into the details in the body of your project.

Write a strong conclusion

The challenge in writing ending paragraphs is to leave the reader with something provocative, something beyond pure summary of the previous paragraphs. Connect back to your thesis, and use a strong concluding image, example, question, or call to action to leave your readers with something to remember and think about.

Review and Revise

After you've gone through the peer editing process or assessed your own draft, sit down with your project and consider the changes you need to make. Start from the highest level, reorganizing paragraphs and possibly even cutting large parts of your project and adding new sections. If you make significant revisions, likely you will want to repeat the overall evaluation of your revised draft when you finish (see Chapter 5).

When you feel your draft is complete, begin the editing phase. Use the guidelines on pages 55–56 to revise style and grammatical errors. Finally, proofread your project, word by word, checking for mistakes.

20 | Documenting Sources in MLA Style

QUICK TAKE

In this chapter, you will learn to

1. Describe the elements of MLA documentation, including in-text references and the works-cited list (see below)
2. Identify the basic patterns for MLA in-text citations (see pages 265–268)
3. Identify the basic patterns for MLA works-cited entries, including entries for books, periodicals, databases, online sources, and nonprint sources (see pages 268–276)
4. Format research papers using MLA style (see pages 277–283)

The two styles of documentation used most frequently are APA style and MLA style. APA stands for American Psychological Association, which publishes a style manual used widely in the social sciences and education (see Chapter 21). MLA stands for the Modern Language Association, and its style is the norm for the humanities and fine arts, including English and rhetoric and composition. If you have questions that this chapter does not address, consult the *MLA Handbook for Writers of Research Papers*, Seventh Edition (2009), and the *MLA Style Manual and Guide to Scholarly Publishing*, Third Edition (2008).

Elements of MLA Documentation

Citing a source in your paper

Citing sources is a two-part process. When readers find a reference to a source (called an in-text or parenthetical citation) in the body of your paper, they can turn to the works-cited list at the end and find the full publication information. Place the author's last name and the page number inside parentheses at the end of the sentence.

Anticipating the impact of *Google*'s project of digitally scanning books in major research libraries, one observer predicts that "the real magic will come in the second act, as each word in each book is cross-linked, clustered, cited, extracted, indexed, analyzed, annotated, remixed, reassembled and woven deeper into the culture than ever before" (Kelly 43).

Author not mentioned in text

If you mention the author's name in the sentence, you do not have to put the name in the parenthetical reference at the end. Just cite the page number.

> Anticipating the impact of *Google*'s project of digitally scanning books in major research libraries, Kevin Kelly predicts that "the real magic will come in the second act, as each word in each book is cross-linked, clustered, cited, extracted, indexed, analyzed, annotated, remixed, reassembled and woven deeper into the culture than ever before" (43).

Author mentioned in text

The corresponding entry in the works-cited list at the end of your paper would be as follows.

Works Cited

> Kelly, Kevin. "Scan This Book!" *New York Times* 14 May 2006, late ed., sec. 6: 43+. Print.

Entry in the works-cited list

Citing an entire work, a Web site, or another electronic source

If you wish to cite an entire work (a book, a film, a performance, and so on), a Web site, or an electronic source that has no page numbers or paragraph numbers, MLA style instructs that you mention the name of the person (for example, the author or director) in the text with a corresponding entry in the works-cited list. You do not need to include the author's name in parentheses. If you cannot identify the author, mention the title in your text.

> Joel Waldfogel discusses the implications of a study of alumni donations to colleges and universities, observing that parents give generously to top-rated colleges in the hope that their children's chances for admission will improve.

Author mentioned in text

Works Cited

> Waldfogel, Joel. "The Old College Try." *Slate.* Washington Post Newsweek Interactive, 6 July 2007. Web. 27 Jan. 2014.

MLA style requires the medium of publication (print, Web, performance, etc.) to be included in each citation.

Creating an MLA-style works-cited list

To create your works-cited list, go through your paper and find every reference to the sources you consulted during your research. Each in-text reference must have an entry in your works-cited list. Do not include any sources on your works-cited list that you do not refer to in your paper.

Organize your works-cited list alphabetically by authors' last names or, if no author is listed, by the first word in the title other than *a*, *an*, or *the*. (See pages 282–283 for a sample works-cited list.) MLA style uses four basic forms for entries in the works-cited list: books, periodicals (scholarly journals, newspapers, magazines), online library database sources, and other online sources (Web sites, discussion forums, blogs, online newspapers, online magazines, online government documents, and e-mail messages). There are also specific formats for citation of interviews, images, music, and film.

Works-cited entries for books

Entries for books have three main elements.

> Pollan, Michael. *In Defense of Food: An Eater's Manifesto*. New York: Penguin, 2008. Print.

1. Author's name.
- List the author's name with the last name first, followed by a period.

2. *Title of book.*
- Find the exact title on the title page, not the cover.
- Separate the title and subtitle with a colon.
- Italicize the title and put a period at the end.

3. Publication information.
- Give the city of publication and a colon.
- Give the name of the publisher, using accepted abbreviations, and a comma.
- Give the date of publication, followed by a period.
- Give the medium of publication (Print), followed by a period.

Works-cited entries for periodicals

Entries for periodicals (scholarly journals, newspapers, magazines) have three main elements.

Pilgrim, Sarah, David Smith, and Jules Pretty. "A Cross-Regional Assessment of the Factors Affecting Ecoliteracy: Implications for Policy and Practice." *Ecological Applications* 17.6 (2007): 1742-51. Print.

1. Author's name.
  - List the author's name with the last name first, followed by a period.

2. "Title of article."
  - Place the title of the article inside quotation marks.
  - Insert a period before the closing quotation mark.

3. Publication information.
  - Italicize the title of the journal.
  - Give the volume number and, if there is one, the issue number.
  - List the date of publication, in parentheses, followed by a colon.
  - List the page numbers, followed by a period. (Note: MLA uses hyphens in page spans and does not use full numbers.)
  - Give the medium of publication (Print), followed by a period.

Works-cited entries for library database sources

Basic entries for library database sources have four main elements.

Damiano, Jessica. "Growing Vegetables in Small Spaces: Train Them up Trellises and Plant Crops in Succession." *Newsday* 2 May 2010: G107. *LexisNexis Academic*. Web. 8 Apr. 2013.

1. Author's name.
  - List the author's name with the last name first, followed by a period.

2. "Title of article."
  - Place the title of the article inside quotation marks.
  - Insert a period before the closing quotation mark.

3. Print publication information
  - Give the print publication information in standard format, in this case for a periodical (see pages 271–273).

4. Database information
- Italicize the name of the database, followed by a period.
- List the medium of publication, followed by a period. For all database sources, the medium of publication is Web.
- List the date you accessed the source (day, month, and year), followed by a period.

Works-cited entries for other online sources

Basic entries for online sources (Web sites, discussion forums, blogs, online newspapers, online magazines, online government documents, and e-mail messages) have three main elements. Sometimes information such as the author's name or the date of publication is missing from the online source. Include the information you are able to locate.

There are many formats for the different kinds of electronic publications. Here is the format of an entry for an online article.

Jacobs, Ruth. "Organic Garden Gives Back." *Colby Magazine* 99.1 (2013): n. pag. Web. 2 Apr. 2013.

1. Author's name.
- List the author's name with the last name first, followed by a period.

2. "Title of work"; Title of the overall Web site
- Place the title of the work inside quotation marks if it is part of a larger Web site.
- Italicize the name of the overall site if it is different from the title of the work.
- Some Web sites are updated periodically, so list the version if you find it (e.g., 2014 edition).

3. Publication information.
- List the publisher or sponsor of the site, followed by a comma. If not available, use N.p. (for "no publisher").
- List the date of publication if available; if not, use n.d. (for "no date")
- List the medium of publication (Web).
- List the date you accessed the source (day, month, and year).

MLA In-Text Citations

1. Author named in your text

Put the author's name in a signal phrase in your sentence. Put the page number in parentheses at the end of the sentence.

> Sociologist Daniel Bell called this emerging U.S. economy the "postindustrial society" (3).

2. Author not named in your text

Put the author's last name and the page number inside parentheses at the end of the sentence.

> In 2012, the Gallup poll reported that 56% of adults in the United States think secondhand smoke is "very harmful," compared with only 36% in 1994 (Saad 4).

3. Work by a single author

The author's last name comes first, followed by the page number. There is no comma.

> (Bell 3)

4. Work by two or three authors

The authors' last names follow the order of the title page. If there are two authors, join the names with *and*. If there are three authors, use a comma between the first two names and a comma with *and* before the last name.

> (Francisco, Vaughn, and Lynn 7)

5. Work by four or more authors

You may use the phrase *et al.* (meaning "and others") for all names but the first, or you may write out all the names. Make sure you use the same method for both the in-text citations and the works-cited list.

> (Abrams et al. 1653)

6. Work by an unnamed author

Use a shortened version of the title that includes at least the first important word. Your reader will use the shortened title to find the full title in the works-cited list.

> A review in the *New Yorker* of Ryan Adams's new album focuses on the artist's age ("Pure" 25).

Notice that "Pure" is in quotation marks because it is the shortened title of an article. If it were a book, the short title would be in italics.

7. Work by a group or organization

Treat the group or organization as the author, but try to identify the group author in the text and place only the page number in parentheses.

> According to the *Irish Free State Handbook*, published by the Ministry for Industry and Finance, the population of Ireland in 1929 was approximately 4,192,000 (23).

8. Quotations longer than four lines

When using indented (block) quotations of more than four lines, place the period *before* the parentheses enclosing the page number.

> In her article "Art for Everybody," Susan Orlean attempts to explain the popularity of painter Thomas Kinkade:
>> People like to own things they think are valuable. ...
>> The high price of limited editions is part of their appeal:
>> it implies that they are choice and exclusive, and that
>> only a certain class of people will be able to afford
>> them. (128)
>
> This same statement could possibly also explain the popularity of phenomena like PBS's *Antiques Road Show*.

If the source is longer than one page, provide the page number for each quotation, paraphrase, and summary.

9. Online sources including Web pages, blogs, podcasts, tweets, social media, wikis, videos, and other multimedia sources

Give the author's name in the text instead of in parentheses.

> Andrew Keen ironically used his own blog to claim that "blogs are boring to write (yawn), boring to read (yawn) and boring to discuss (yawn)."

If you cannot identify the author, mention the title in your text.

> The podcast "Catalina's Cubs" describes the excitement on Catalina Island when the Chicago Cubs went there for spring training in the 1940s.

10. Work in an anthology

Cite the name of the author of the work within an anthology, not the name of the editor of the collection. Alphabetize the entry in the list of works cited by the author, not the editor.

> In "Beard," Melissa Jane Hardie explores the role assumed by Elizabeth Taylor as the celebrity companion of gay actors including Rock Hudson and Montgomery Clift (278-79).

11. Two or more works by the same author

When an author has two or more items in the works-cited list, distinguish which work you are citing by using the author's last name and then a shortened version of the title of each source.

> The majority of books written about coauthorship focus on partners of the same sex (Laird, *Women* 351).

Note that *Women* is italicized because it is the name of a book; if an article were named, quotation marks would be used.

12. Different authors with the same last name

If your list of works cited contains items by two or more different authors with the same last name, include the initial of the first name in the parenthetical reference.

> Web surfing requires more mental involvement than channel surfing (S. Johnson 107).

Note that a period follows the initial.

13. Two or more sources within the same sentence

Place each citation directly after the statement it supports.

> In the 1990s, many sweeping pronouncements were made that the Internet is the best opportunity to improve education since the printing press (Ellsworth xxii) or even in the history of the world (Dyrli and Kinnaman 79).

14. Two or more sources within the same citation

If two sources support a single point, separate them with a semicolon.

> (McKibbin 39; Gore 92)

15. Work quoted in another source

When you do not have access to the original source of the material you wish to use, put the abbreviation *qtd. in* ("quoted in") before the information about the indirect source.

> National governments have become increasingly what Ulrich Beck, in a 1999 interview, calls "zombie institutions"—institutions that are "dead and still alive" (qtd. in Bauman 6).

16. Literary works

To supply a reference to a literary work, you sometimes need more than a page number from a specific edition. Readers should be able to locate a quotation in any edition of the book. Give the page number from the edition that you are using, then a semicolon and other identifying information.

> "Marriage is a house" is one of the most memorable lines in *Don Quixote* (546; pt. 2, bk. 3, ch. 19).

MLA Works-Cited List: Books

One author

17. Book by one author

The author's last name comes first, followed by a comma, the first name, and a period.

> Doctorow, E. L. *The March*. New York: Random, 2005. Print.

18. Two or more books by the same author

In the entry for the first book, include the author's name. In the second entry, substitute three hyphens and a period for the author's name. List the titles of books by the same author in alphabetical order.

> Grimsley, Jim. *Boulevard*. Chapel Hill: Algonquin, 2002. Print.
> ---. *Dream Boy*. New York: Simon, 1995. Print.

Multiple authors

19. Book by two or three authors

Second and subsequent authors' names appear first name first. A comma separates the authors' names.

Chapkis, Wendy, and Richard J. Webb. *Dying to Get High: Marijuana as Medicine*. New York: New York UP, 2008. Print.

20. Book by four or more authors

You may use the phrase *et al.* (meaning "and others") for all authors but the first, or you may write out all the names. Use the same method in the in-text citation as you do in the works-cited list.

Zukin, Cliff, et al. *A New Engagement? Political Participation, Civic Life, and the Changing American Citizen*. New York: Oxford UP, 2006. Print.

Anonymous and group authors

21. Book by an unknown author

Begin the entry with the title.

Encyclopedia of Americana. New York: Somerset, 2001. Print.

22. Book by a group or organization

Treat the group as the author of the work.

United Nations. *The Charter of the United Nations: A Commentary*. New York: Oxford UP, 2000. Print.

23. Religious texts

Do not italicize the title of a sacred text, including the Bible, unless you are citing a specific edition.

King James Text: Modern Phrased Version. New York: Oxford UP, 1980. Print.

Imprints, reprints, and undated books

24. Book with no publication date

If no year of publication is given but can be approximated, put a *c.* ("circa") and the approximate date in brackets: [c. 2009]. Otherwise, put *n.d.* ("no date"). For works before 1900, you do not need to list the publisher.

O'Sullivan, Colin. *Traditions and Novelties of the Irish Country Folk*. Dublin, [c. 1793]. Print.

James, Franklin. *In the Valley of the King*. Cambridge: Harvard UP, n.d. Print.

25. Reprinted works

For works of fiction that have been printed in many different editions or reprints, give the original publication date after the title.

> Wilde, Oscar. *The Picture of Dorian Gray*. 1890. New York: Norton, 2001. Print.

Parts of books

26. Introduction, foreword, preface, or afterword

Give the author and then the name of the specific part being cited. Next, name the book. Then, if the author for the whole work is different, put that author's name after the word *By*. Place inclusive page numbers at the end.

> Benstock, Sheri. Introduction. *The House of Mirth*. By Edith Wharton. Boston: Bedford-St. Martin's, 2002. 3-24. Print.

27. Single chapter written by same author as the book

> Ardis, Ann L. "Mapping the Middlebrow in Edwardian England." *Modernism and Cultural Conflict: 1880-1922*. Cambridge: Cambridge UP, 2002. 114-42. Print.

28. Selection from an anthology or edited collection

> Sedaris, David. "Full House." *The Best American Nonrequired Reading 2004*. Ed. Dave Eggers. Boston: Houghton, 2004. 350-58. Print.

29. Article in a reference work

You can omit the names of editors and most publishing information for an article from a familiar reference work. Identify the edition by date. There is no need to give the page numbers when a work is arranged alphabetically. Give the author's name, if known.

> "Utilitarianism." *The Columbia Encyclopedia*. 6th ed. 2001. Print.

Editions and translations

30. Book with an editor

List an edited book under the editor's name if your focus is on the editor. Otherwise, cite an edited book under the author's name as shown in the second example below.

> Lewis, Gifford, ed. *The Big House of Inver*. By Edith Somerville and Martin Ross. Dublin: Farmar, 2000. Print.

Somerville, Edith, and Martin Ross. *The Big House of Inver*. Ed. Gifford Lewis. Dublin: Farmar, 2000. Print.

31. Book with a translator

Benjamin, Walter. *The Arcades Project*. Trans. Howard Eiland and Kevin McLaughlin. Cambridge: Harvard UP, 1999. Print.

32. Second or subsequent edition of a book

Hawthorn, Jeremy, ed. *A Concise Glossary of Contemporary Literary Theory*. 3rd ed. London: Arnold, 2001. Print.

Multivolume works

33. Multivolume work

Identify both the volume you have used and the total number of volumes in the set.

Samuel, Raphael. *Theatres of Memory*. Vol. 1. London: Verso, 1999. 2 vols. Print.

If you refer to more than one volume, identify the specific volume in your in-text citations, and list the total number of volumes in your list of works cited.

Samuel, Raphael. *Theatres of Memory*. 2 vols. London: Verso, 1999. Print.

MLA Works-Cited List: Periodicals

Journal articles

34. Article by one author

Ekotto, Frieda. "Against Representation: Countless Hours for a Professor." *PMLA* 127.4 (2012): 968-72. Print.

35. Article by two or three authors

Miller, Thomas P., and Brian Jackson. "What Are English Majors For?" *College Composition and Communication* 58.4 (2007): 825-31. Print.

36. Article by four or more authors

You may use the phrase *et al.* (meaning "and others") for all authors but the first, or you may write out all the names.

> Breece, Katherine E., et al. "Patterns of mtDNA Diversity in Northwestern North America." *Human Biology* 76.1 (2004): 33-54. Print.

Pagination in journals

37. Article in a scholarly journal

List the volume and issue number after the name of the journal.

> Bernard-Donals, Michael. "Synecdochic Memory at the United States Holocaust Memorial Museum." *College English* 74.5 (2012): 417-36. Print.

38. Article in a scholarly journal that uses only issue numbers

List the issue number after the name of the journal.

> McCall, Sophie. "Double Vision Reading." *Canadian Literature* 194 (2007): 95-97. Print.

Magazines

39. Monthly or seasonal magazines

Use the month (or season) and year in place of the volume. There is no comma before the date. Abbreviate the names of all months except May, June, and July.

> Barlow, John Perry. "Africa Rising: Everything You Know about Africa Is Wrong." *Wired* Jan. 1998: 142-58. Print.

40. Weekly or biweekly magazines

Give both the day and the month of publication, as listed on the issue.

> Brody, Richard. "A Clash of Symbols." *New Yorker* 25 June 2007: 16. Print.

Newspapers

41. Newspaper article by one author

The author's last name comes first, followed by a comma and the first name.

> Marriott, Michel. "Arts and Crafts for the Digital Age." *New York Times* 8 June 2006, late ed.: C13. Print.

42. Article by two or three authors

The second and subsequent authors' names are printed in regular order, first name first:

> Schwirtz, Michael, and Joshua Yaffa. "A Clash of Cultures at a Square in Moscow." *New York Times* 11 July 2007, late ed.: A9. Print.

43. Newspaper article by an unknown author

Begin the entry with the title.

> "The Dotted Line." *Washington Post* 8 June 2006, final ed.: E2. Print.

Reviews, editorials, letters to the editor

44. Review

If there is no title, just name the work reviewed.

> Mendelsohn, Daniel. "The Two Oscar Wildes." Rev. of *The Importance of Being Earnest*, dir. Oliver Parker. *The New York Review of Books* 10 Oct. 2002: 23-24. Print.

45. Editorial

> "Hush-hush, Sweet Liberty." Editorial. *Los Angeles Times* 7 July 2007: A18. Print.

46. Letter to the editor

> Doyle, Joe. Letter. *Direct* 1 July 2007: 48. Print.

MLA Works-Cited List: Library Database Sources

47. Work from a library database

Begin with the print publication information, then the name of the database (italicized), the medium of publication (*Web*), and the date of access.

> Snider, Michael. "Wired to Another World." *Maclean's* 3 Mar. 2003: 23-24. *Academic Search Premier*. Web. 14 Jan. 2013.

MLA Works-Cited List: Online Sources

Web publications

When do you list a URL? MLA style no longer requires including URLs of Web sources. URLs are of limited value because they change frequently and they can be specific to an individual search. Include the URL as supplementary information only when your readers probably cannot locate the source without the URL.

48. Publication by a known author

> Boerner, Steve. "Leopold Mozart." *The Mozart Project: Biography*. The Mozart Project, 21 Mar. 1998. Web. 30 Oct. 2013.

49. Publication by a group or organization

If a work has no author's or editor's name listed, begin the entry with the title.

> "State of the Birds." *Audubon*. National Audubon Society, 2012. Web. 19 Aug. 2013.

50. Article in a scholarly journal on the Web

Some scholarly journals are published on the Web only. List articles by author, title, name of journal in italics, volume and issue number, and year of publication. If the journal does not have page numbers, use *n. pag.* in place of page numbers. Then list the medium of publication (*Web*) and the date of access (day, month, and year).

> Fleckenstein, Kristie. "Who's Writing? Aristotelian Ethos and the Author Position in Digital Poetics." *Kairos* 11.3 (2007): n. pag. Web. 6 Apr. 2013.

51. Article in a newspaper on the Web

The first date is the date of publication; the second is the date of access.

> Brown, Patricia Leigh. "Australia in Sonoma." *New York Times*. New York Times, 5 July 2008. Web. 3 Aug. 2013.

52. Article in a magazine on the Web

> Brown, Patricia Leigh. "The Wild Horse Is Us." *Newsweek*. Newsweek, 1 July 2008. Web. 12 Dec. 2013.

53. E-book on Kindle, iPad, or another device

> Morrison, Toni. *Home*. New York: Vintage, 2013. Kindle file.

Other online sources

54. Blog entry
If there is no sponsor or publisher for the blog, use *N.p.*

> Arrington, Michael. "Think Before You Voicemail." *TechCrunch*. N.p., 5 July
> 2008. Web. 10 Sept. 2013.

55. E-mail
Give the name of the writer, the subject line, a description of the message, the date, and the medium of delivery (*E-mail*).

> Ballmer, Steve. "A New Era of Business Productivity and Innovation."
> Message to Microsoft Executive E-mail. 30 Nov. 2010. E-mail.

56. Video on the Web
Video on the Web often lacks a creator and a date. Begin the entry with a title if you cannot find a creator. Use *n.d.* if you cannot find a date.

> Wesch, Michael. *A Vision of Students Today*. *YouTube*. YouTube, 2007.
> Web. 28 May 2013.

57. Posting on social media
Many organizations now use *Facebook* and other social media. Give the author, title, name of the organization, the name of the site, the sponsor (*Facebook*), the date, the medium (*Web*), and the date of access.

> Eklund, Doug. "Dedicated to Myself." *Metropolitan Museum of Art*. Facebook,
> 14 Mar. 2013. Web. 18 Mar. 2013.

58. Posting on *Twitter*
Include the entire tweet and the date and time of publication. Conclude with the medium (*Tweet*).

> Obama, Barack (BO). "It should not be a partisan issue." Utah business
> leaders urge their representative to move on #immigration reform.
> 27 Aug. 2013. 12:02 p.m. Tweet.

59. Wiki entry

A wiki is a collaborative writing and editing tool. Although some topic-specific wikis are written and carefully edited by recognized scholars, the more popular wiki sites—such as *Wikipedia*—are often considered unreliable sources for academic papers.

"Snowboard." *Wikipedia*. Wikimedia Foundation, 2014. Web. 30 Jan. 2014.

60. Podcast

Sussingham, Robin. "All Things Autumn." No. 2. *HighLifeUtah*. N.p., 20 Nov. 2006. Web. 28 Feb. 2014.

MLA Works-Cited List: Other Sources

61. Sound recording

McCoury, Del, perf. "1952 Vincent Black Lightning." By Richard Thompson. *Del and the Boys*. Ceili, 2001. CD.

62. Film

Begin with the title in italics. List the director, the distributor, the date, and the medium. Other information, such as the names of the screenwriters and performers, is optional.

Wanted. Dir. Timur Bekmambetov. Perf. James McAvoy, Angelina Jolie, and Morgan Freeman. Universal, 2008. Film.

63. DVD

No Country for Old Men. Dir. Joel Coen and Ethan Coen. Perf. Tommy Lee Jones, Javier Bardem, and Josh Brolin. Paramount, 2007. DVD.

64. Television or radio program

"Kaisha." *The Sopranos*. Perf. James Gandolfini, Lorraine Bracco, and Edie Falco. HBO. 4 June 2006. Television.

65. Personal interview

Andrews, Michael. Personal interview. 25 Sept. 2013.

Sample MLA paper

Brian Witkowski

Professor Mendelsohn

RHE 309K

3 May 2013

Need a Cure for Tribe Fever?

How about a Dip in the Lake?

Everyone is familiar with the Cleveland Indians' Chief Wahoo logo—and I do mean everyone, not just Clevelanders. Across America people wear the smiling mascot on Cleveland Indians caps and jerseys, and recent trends in sports merchandise have popularized new groovy multicolored Indians sportswear. Because of lucrative contracts between Major League Baseball and Little League, youth teams all over the country don Cleveland's famous (or infamous) smiling Indian each season as fresh-faced kids scamper onto the diamonds looking like mini major leaguers (Liu). Various incarnations of the famous Chief Wahoo—described by writer Ryan Zimmerman as "a grotesque caricature grinning idiotically through enormous bucked teeth"—have been around since the 1940s. Now redder and even more cartoonish than the original hook-nosed, beige Indian with a devilish grin, Wahoo often passes as a cheerful baseball buddy like the San Diego Chicken or the St. Louis Cardinals' Fredbird.

Though defined by its distinctive logo, Cleveland baseball far preceded its famous mascot. The team changed from the Forest Citys to the Spiders to the Bluebirds/Blues to the Broncos to the Naps and finally to the Indians. Dubbed the Naps in 1903 in honor of its star player and manager Napoleon Lajoie, the team gained its current appellation in 1915. After Lajoie was traded, the team's president challenged sportswriters to devise a suitable "temporary" label for the floundering club. Publicity material claims that the writers decided on the Indians to celebrate Louis Sockalexis, a Penobscot Indian who played for the team from 1897 to 1899. With a high batting average and the notability of being the first Native American in professional baseball, Sockalexis was immortalized by the new Cleveland label (Schneider 10-23). (Contrary to popular lore, some cite alternative—and less reverent—motivations behind the team's

Margin notes:

A style does [not] require a [title] page. Ask [you]r instructor [wh]ether you [need] one.

[Us]e 1" margins [all] around. [Do]uble-space [ev]erything.

[Som]e publications [use] the name of [the] author (or [aut]hors).

[In]dent each [pa]ragraph [.]2" on [the] ruler in [you]r word [pro]cessing [pr]ogram.

Include your last name and page number as page header, beginning with the first page, 1/2" from the top.

Center your title. Do not put the title in quotation marks or type it in all capital letters.

naming and point to a lack of Sockalexis publicity in period newspaper articles discussing the team's naming process [Staurowsky 95-97].) A century later, the "temporary" name continues to raise eyebrows, in both its marketability and its ideological questionability.

Today the logo is more than a little embarrassing. Since the high-profile actions of the American Indian Movement (AIM) in the 1970s, sports teams around the country—including the Indians—have been criticized for their racially insensitive mascots. Native American groups question these caricatured icons—not just because of grossly stereotyped mascots, but also because of what visual displays of team support say about Native American culture. Across the country, professional sporting teams, as well as high schools and colleges, perform faux rituals in the name of team spirit. As Tim Giago, publisher of *The Lakota Times*, a weekly South Dakotan Native American newspaper, has noted,

> The sham rituals, such as the wearing of feathers, smoking of so-called peace pipes, beating of tomtoms, fake dances, horrendous attempts at singing Indian songs, the so-called war whoops, and the painted faces, address more than the issues of racism. They are direct attacks upon the spirituality of the Indian people. (qtd. in Wulf)

Controversy over such performances still fuels the fire between activists and alumni at schools such as the University of Illinois at Champaign-Urbana, where during many decades of football halftimes fans cheered the performance of a student (often white) dressed as Chief Illiniwek. In March of 2007, the University of Illinois board of trustees voted in a nearly unanimous decision to retire the mascot's name, regalia, and image ("Illinois").

Since 1969, when Oklahoma disavowed its "Little Red" mascot, more than six hundred school and minor league teams have followed a more ethnically sensitive trend and ditched their "tribal" mascots (Price). High-profile teams such as Stanford, St. Johns University, and Miami (Ohio) University have changed their team names from the Indians to the Cardinal (1972), the Redmen to the Red Storm (1993), and the Redskins to the Redhawks (1996), respectively. In 2005, the NCAA officially ruled that "colleges whose nicknames or mascots refer to American Indians will not be permitted to hold National Collegiate Athletic Association tournament events" (Wolverton). The University of North Dakota was one of the last holdouts, but in 2012, the citizens of North Dakota voted overwhelmingly to allow the University of North Dakota to drop its controversial "Fighting Sioux" nickname ("UND").

Cleveland's own Chief Wahoo has far from avoided controversy. Multiple conflicts between Wahoo devotees and dissenters occur annually during the baseball season. At the opening game of 1995, fifty Native Americans and supporters took stations around Jacobs Field to demonstrate against the use of the cartoonish smiling crimson mascot (Kropk). Arrests were made in 1998 when demonstrators from the United Church of Christ burned a three-foot Chief Wahoo doll in effigy ("Judge"). Opinions on the mascot remain mixed. Jacoby Ellsbury, outfielder for the Boston Red Sox and a member of the Colorado River Indian Tribes, said in 2007, "I'm not offended [by the mascot]. You can look at it two different ways. You can look at it that it's offensive or you can look at it that they are representing Native Americans. Usually I'll try to take the positive out of it" (Shaughnessy). Nonetheless, Ellsbury still acknowledges that he "can see both sides of [the controversy]" (Shaughnessy). Wedded to their memorabilia, fans proudly stand behind their Indian as others lobby vociferously for its removal, splitting government officials, fans, and social and religious groups.

In 2000, Cleveland mayor Michael White came out publicly against the team mascot, joining an already established group of religious leaders, laypersons, and civil rights activists who had demanded Wahoo's retirement. African American religious and civic leaders such as Rev. Gregory A. Jacobs pointed to the absurdity of minority groups who embrace the Wahoo symbol. "Each of us has had to fight its [sic] own battle, quite frankly," Jacobs stated. "We cannot continue to live in this kind of hypocrisy that says, Yes, we are in solidarity with my [sic] brothers and sisters, yet we continue to exploit them" (qtd. in Briggs).

This controversy also swirls outside of the greater Cleveland area. In 2009, the image of Wahoo was removed from the team's training complex in Goodyear, Arizona ("Cleveland"), while the *Seattle Times* went so far as to digitally remove the Wahoo symbol from images of the Cleveland baseball cap ("Newspaper"). As other teams make ethnically sensitive and image-conscious choices to change their mascots, Cleveland stands firm in its resolve to retain Chief Wahoo. Despite internal division and public ridicule fueled by the team icon, the city refuses to budge.

Cleveland's stubbornness on the issue of Wahoo runs contrary to the city's recently improved image and downtown revitalization. As a native of Cleveland, I understand the power of "Tribe Fever" and the unabashed pride one feels when wearing Wahoo garb during a winning (or losing) season. Often it is not until we leave northeastern Ohio that we realize the negative image that Wahoo projects. What then can Cleveland do to simultaneously save face and bolster its burgeoning positive city image? I propose that the team finally change the "temporary" Indians label. In a city so proud of its diverse ethnic heritage—African American, Italian American, and Eastern European American to name a few examples—why stand as a bearer of retrograde ethnic politics? Cleveland should take this opportunity to link its positive Midwestern image to the team of which it is so proud. I propose changing the team's name to the Cleveland Lakers.

The city's revival in the last twenty years has embraced the geographic and aesthetic grandeur of Lake Erie. Disavowing its "mistake on the lake" moniker of the late 1970s, Cleveland has traded aquatic pollution fires for a booming lakeside business district. Attractions such as the Great Lakes Science Center, the Rock and Roll Hall of Fame, and the Cleveland Browns Stadium take advantage of the beauty of the landscape and take back the lake. Why not continue this trend through one of the city's biggest and highest-profile moneymakers: professional baseball? By changing the team's name to the Lakers, the city would gain national advertisement for one of its major selling points, while simultaneously announcing a new ethnically inclusive image that is appropriate to our wonderfully diverse city. It would be a public relations triumph for the city.

Of course this call will be met with many objections. Why do we have to buckle to pressure? Do we not live in a free country? What fans and citizens alike need to keep in mind is that ideological pressures would not be the sole motivation for this move. Yes, retiring Chief Wahoo would take Cleveland off AIM's hit list. Yes, such a move would promote a kinder and gentler Cleveland. At the same time, however, such a gesture would work toward uniting the community. So much civic division exists over this issue that a renaming could help start to heal these old wounds.

Additionally, this type of change could bring added economic prosperity to the city. First, a change in name will bring a new wave of team merchandise. Licensed sports apparel generates more than a 10-billion-dollar annual retail business in the United States, and teams have proven repeatedly that new uniforms and logos can provide new capital. After all, a new logo for the Seattle Mariners bolstered severely slumping merchandise sales (Lefton). Wahoo devotees need not panic; the booming vintage uniform business will keep him alive, as is demonstrated by the current ability to purchase replica 1940s jerseys with the old Indians logo. Also, good press created by this change will possibly help increase tourism in Cleveland. If the goodwill created by the Cleveland Lakers can prove half as profitable as the Rock and Roll Hall of Fame, then local businesses will be humming a happy tune. Finally, if history repeats itself, a change to a more culturally inclusive logo could, in and of itself, prove to be a cash cow. When Miami University changed from the Redskins to the Redhawks, it saw alumni donations skyrocket (Price). A less divisive mascot would prove lucrative to the ball club, the city, and the players themselves. (Sluggers with inoffensive logos make excellent spokesmen.)

Perhaps this proposal sounds far-fetched: Los Angeles may seem to have cornered the market on Lakers. But where is their lake? (The Lakers were formerly the Minneapolis Lakers, where the name makes sense in the "Land of 10,000 Lakes.") Various professional and collegiate sports teams—such as baseball's San Francisco Giants and football's New York Giants—share a team name, so licensing should not be an issue. If Los Angeles has qualms about sharing the name, perhaps Cleveland could persuade Los Angeles to become the Surfers or the Stars; after all, Los Angeles players seem to spend as much time on the big and small screens as on the court.

Witkowski 6

Now is the perfect time for Cleveland to make this jump. Perhaps a new look will help usher in a new era of Cleveland baseball and a World Series ring to boot. Through various dry spells, the Cleveland Indians institution has symbolically turned to the descendants of Sockalexis, asking for goodwill or a latter-generation Penobscot slugger (Fleitz 3). Perhaps the best way to win goodwill, fortunes, and the team's first World Series title since 1948 would be to eschew a grinning, life-size Chief Wahoo for the new Cleveland Laker, an oversized furry monster sporting water wings, cleats, and a catcher's mask. His seventh-inning-stretch show could include an air-guitar solo with a baseball bat as he quietly reminds everyone that the Rock Hall is just down the street.

Witkowski 7

Works Cited

Center "Works Cited" on a new page.

Briggs, David. "Churches Go to Bat against Chief Wahoo." *Cleveland Plain Dealer* 25 Aug. 2000: 1A. *LexisNexis Academic*. Web. 19 Apr. 2013.

Double-space all entries. Indent all but the first line in each entry one-half inch.

"Cleveland Indians' Chief Wahoo Logo Left Off Team's Ballpark, Training Complex in Goodyear, Arizona." *Cleveland.com*. Cleveland Plain Dealer, 12 Apr. 2009. Web. 23 Apr. 2013.

Fleitz, David L. *Louis Sockalexis: The First Cleveland Indian*. Jefferson: McFarland, 2002. Print.

"Illinois Trustees Vote to Retire Chief Illiniwek." *ESPN*. ESPN Internet Ventures, 13 Mar. 2007. Web. 26 Apr. 2013.

"Judge Dismisses Charges against City in Wahoo Protest." *Associated Press* 6 Aug. 2001. *LexisNexis Academic*. Web. 19 Apr. 2013.

Alphabetize entries by the last names of the authors or by the first important word in the title if no author is listed.

Kropk, M. R. "Chief Wahoo Protestors Largely Ignored by Fans." *Austin American Statesman* 6 May 1995: D4. Print.

Lefton, Terry. "Looks Are Everything: For New Franchises, Licensing Battles Must Be Won Long before the Team Even Takes the Field." *Sport* 89 (May 1998): 32. Print.

Witkowski 8

Liu, Caitlin. "Bawl Game." *Portfolio.com*. Condé Nast, 21 Oct. 2008.
    Web. 28 Apr. 2013.

"Newspaper Edits Cleveland Indian Logo from Cap Photo." *Associated
    Press* 31 Mar. 1997. *LexisNexis Academic*. Web. 27 Apr. 2013.

Price, S. L. "The Indian Wars." *Sports Illustrated* 4 Mar. 2002: 66+.
    Academic OneFile. Web. 20 Apr. 2013.

Schneider, Russell. *The Cleveland Indians Encyclopedia*. Philadelphia:
    Temple UP, 1996. Print.

Shaughnessy, Dan. "They've Had Some Chief Concerns." *Boston Globe* 12
    Oct. 2007: C5. *LexisNexis Academic*. Web. 19 Apr. 2013.

Staurowsky, Ellen J. "Sockalexis and the Making of the Myth at the Core
    of the Cleveland's 'Indian' Image." *Team Spirits: The Native Ameri-
    can Mascots Controversy*. Ed. C. Richard King and Charles Fruehling
    Springwood. Lincoln: U of Nebraska P, 2001. 82-106. Print.

"UND OK to Drop Fighting Sioux Name." *ESPN.com*. ESPN, 14 June 2012.
    Web. 16 Apr. 2013.

Wolverton, Brad. "NCAA Restricts Colleges with Indian Nicknames
    and Mascots." *Chronicle of Higher Education* 2 Sept. 2005: A65.
    ProQuest. Web. 25 Apr. 2013.

Wulf, Steve. "A Brave Move." *Sports Illustrated* 24 Feb. 1992: 7. Print.

Zimmerman, Ryan. "The Cleveland Indians' Mascot Must Go." *Christian
    Science Monitor* 15 Oct. 2007: 5. *LexisNexis Academic*. Web. 19 Apr.
    2013.

cize the titles
ooks and
odicals.

eck to make
e all the
urces you
ve cited in
ur text are in
list of works
ed.

21 | Documenting Sources in APA Style

QUICK TAKE

In this chapter, you will learn to

1. Describe the elements of APA documentation style, including in-text citations and the References list (see below)
2. Identify the basic patterns for APA in-text citations (see pages 287–289)
3. Identify the basic patterns for APA References entries, including entries for books, periodicals, databases, online sources, and nonprint sources (see pages 289–293)

Papers written for the social sciences, including government, linguistics, psychology, sociology, and education, frequently use the APA documentation style. For a detailed treatment of APA style, consult the *Publication Manual of the American Psychological Association*, sixth edition (2010).

Elements of APA Documentation

Citing a source in your paper

APA style emphasizes the date of publication. When you cite an author's name in the body of your paper, always include the date of publication. Notice too that APA style includes the abbreviation for page (*p.*) in front of the page number. A comma separates each element of the citation.

> Zukin (2004) observes that teens today begin to shop for themselves at age 13 or 14, "the same age when lower-class children, in the past, became apprentices or went to work in factories" (p. 50).

If the author's name is not mentioned in the sentence, cite the author, date, and page number inside parentheses.

> One sociologist notes that teens today begin to shop for themselves at age 13 or 14, "the same age when lower-class children, in the past, became apprentices or went to work in factories" (Zukin, 2004, p. 50).

The corresponding entry in the references list would be as follows.

Zukin, S. (2004). *Point of purchase: How shopping changed American culture.*
New York, NY: Routledge.

Creating an APA-style references list

To create your references list, go through your paper and find every reference to the sources you consulted during your research. Each in-text citation must have an entry in your references list.

Organize your references list alphabetically by authors' last names or, if no author is listed, by the first word in the title other than *a, an,* or *the*. APA style uses three basic forms for entries in the references list: books, periodicals (scholarly journals, newspapers, magazines), and online sources.

Increasingly, books and articles are accessed online. Because URLs frequently change, many scholarly publishers have begun to use a Digital Object Identifier (DOI), a unique alphanumeric string that is permanent. If a DOI is available, use the DOI. APA now recommends listing DOIs as URLs. Use the new format if available: http://dx.doi.org/10.XXXX/JXXXX.

References entries for books

Orum, A. M., & Chen, X. (2003). *The world of cities: Places in comparative and historical perspective.* Malden, MA: Blackwell.

1. **Author's or editor's name.**
   - List the author's name with the last name first, followed by a comma and the author's initials.
   - Join two authors' names with an ampersand.
   - For an editor, put (Ed.) after the name: Kavanaugh, P. (Ed.).

2. **(Year of publication).**
   - Give the year of publication in parentheses. If no year of publication is given, write (n.d.) ("no date") : Smith, S. (n.d.).
   - If it is a multivolume edited work, published over a period of more than one year, put the time span in parentheses: Smith, S. (1999–2001).

3. ***Title of book.***
   - Italicize the title.
   - Capitalize only the first word, proper nouns, and the first word after a colon.
   - If the title is in a foreign language, copy it exactly as it appears on the title page.

4. Publication information.
- For all books list the city with a two-letter state abbreviation (or full country name) after the city name. If more than one city is given on the title page, list only the first.
- Do not shorten or abbreviate words like *University* or *Press*. Omit words such as *Co.*, *Inc.*, and *Publishers*.

References entries for periodicals

Lee, E. (2007). Wired for gender: Experientiality and gender-stereotyping in computer-mediated communication. *Media Psychology, 10,* 182–210.

1. Author's name.
- List the author's name, last name first, followed by the author's initials.
- Join two authors' names with a comma and an ampersand.

2. (Year of publication).
- Give the year the work was published in parentheses.

3. Title of article.
- Do not use quotation marks. If there is a book title in the article title, italicize it.
- Capitalize only the first word of the title, the first word of the subtitle, and any proper nouns in the title.

4. Publication information.
- Italicize the journal name.
- Capitalize all nouns, verbs, and pronouns, and the first word of the journal name. Do not capitalize any article, preposition, or coordinating conjunction unless it is the first word of the title or subtitle.
- Put a comma after the journal name.
- Italicize the volume number and follow it with a comma.
- If each issue of the journal begins on page 1, give the issue number in parentheses, followed by comma. See sample references 18 and 24.
- Give page numbers of the article (see sample references 20 and 21 for more on pagination). Note: APA provides the full numbers for page spans.

References entries for online sources

Department of Justice. Federal Bureau of Investigation. (2004). Hate crime
statistics 2004: Report summary. Retrieved from http://www.fbi.gov/
ucr/hc2004/openpage.htm

1. Author's name, associated institution, or organization.
- List the author's name, if given, with the last name first,
  followed by the author's initials.
- If the only authority you find is a group or organization (as in
  this example), list its name as the author.
- If the author or organization is not identified, begin the
  reference with the title of the document.

2. (Date of publication).
- List the date the site was produced, last revised, or copyrighted.

3. Title of page or article.
- If you are citing a page or article that has a title, treat the title
  like an article in a periodical. If you are citing an entire Web
  site, treat the name like a book.
- If the Web site has no title, list it by author or creator.

4. Retrieval information
- If your source has been assigned a DOI (Digital Object Identifier), list
  it at the end in the format that appears in your source (alphanumeric
  string or URL). Do not add a period at the end of a DOI.
- If the source does not have a DOI, list the URL of the journal's
  home page.

APA In-Text Citations

1. Author named in your text

Influential sociologist Daniel Bell (1973) noted a shift in the United States
to the "postindustrial society" (p. 3).

2. Author not named in your text

In 2012, the Gallup poll reported that 56% of adults in the United States
think secondhand smoke is "very harmful," compared with only 36% in 1994
(Saad, 1997, p. 4).

3. Work by a single author

(Bell, 1973, p. 3)

4. Work by two authors
Notice that APA uses an ampersand (&) with multiple authors' names rather than *and*.

(Suzuki & Irabu, 2013, p. 404)

5. Work by three to five authors
The authors' last names follow the order of the title page.

(Francisco, Vaughn, & Romano, 2012, p. 7)

Subsequent references can use the first name and *et al.*

(Francisco et al., 2013, p. 17)

6. Work by six or more authors
Use the first author's last name and *et al.* for all in-text references.

(Swallit et al., 2014, p. 49)

7. Work by a group or organization
Identify the group author in the text and place only the page number in parentheses.

The National Organization for Women (2001) observed that this "generational shift in attitudes towards marriage and childrearing" will have profound consequences (p. 325).

8. Work by an unknown author
Use a shortened version of the title (or the full title if it is short) in place of the author's name. Capitalize all key words in the title. If it is an article title, place it in quotation marks.

("Derailing the Peace Process," 2003, p. 44)

9. Quotations of 40 words or longer

Indent long quotations 1/2 inch and omit quotation marks. Note that the period appears before the parentheses in an indented block quote.

> Orlean (2001) has attempted to explain the popularity of the painter Thomas Kinkade:
>> People like to own things they think are valuable. . . . The high price of limited editions is part of their appeal; it implies that they are choice and exclusive, and that only a certain class of people will be able to afford them. (p. 128)

APA References List: Books

10. Book by one author

The author's last name comes first, followed by a comma and the author's initials.

> Gladwell, M. (2012). *Outliers: The story of success.* New York, NY: Back Bay Books.

If an editor, put (Ed.) in parentheses after the name.

> Kavanagh, P. (Ed.). (1969). *Lapped furrows.* New York, NY: Hand Press.

11. Book by two authors

Join two authors' names with a comma and ampersand.

> Hardt, M., & Negri, A. (2000). *Empire.* Cambridge, MA: Harvard University Press.

For editors, use *(Eds.)* after the names.

> McClelland, D., & Eismann, K. (Eds).

12. Book by three or more authors

List last names and initials for up to seven authors, with an ampersand between the last two names. For works with eight or more authors, list the first six names, then an ellipsis, then the last author's name.

> Anders, K., Child, H., Davis, K., Logan, O., Petersen, J., Tymes, J., . . . Johnson, S.

13. E-book with DOI assigned

> Chaffe-Stengel, P., & Stengel, D. (2012). *Working with sample data:*
> *Exploration and inference.* doi:10.4128/9781606492147

14. E-book with no DOI assigned

> Burton, R. (1832). *The anatomy of melancholy.* Retrieved from http://etext.
> library.adelaide.edu.au/b/burton/robert/melancholy

15. Chapter in an edited collection

Add *In* after the selection title and before the names of the editor(s).

> Howard, A. (1997). Labor, history, and sweatshops in the new global
>   economy. In A. Ross (Ed.), *No sweat: Fashion, free trade, and the rights*
>   *of garment workers* (pp. 151–172). New York, NY: Verso.

16. Government document

When the author and publisher are identical, use *Author* as the name of the publisher.

> U.S. Environmental Protection Agency. (2002). *Respiratory health effects of*
>   *passive smoking: Lung cancer and other disorders.* (EPA Publication No.
>   600/6-90/006 F). Washington, DC: Author.

APA References List: Periodicals

17. Article by one author

> Goolkasian, P. (2012). Research in visual pattern recognition: The enduring
>   legacy of studies from the 1960s. *American Journal of Psychology, 125,*
>   155–163.

18. Article by multiple authors

Write out all of the authors' names, up to seven authors. For works with eight or more authors, list the first six names, then an ellipsis, then the last author's name.

> Blades, J., & Rowe-Finkbeiner, K. (2006). The motherhood manifesto. *The*
>   *Nation, 282*(20), 11–16.

19. Article by a group or organization

> National Organization for Women (2002). Where to find feminists in Austin. *The NOW guide for Austin women.* Austin, TX: Chapter Press.

20. Article in a journal with continuous pagination

Include the volume number and the year, but not the issue number.

> Engen, R., & Steen, S. (2000). The power to punish: Discretion and sentencing reform in the war on drugs. *American Journal of Sociology, 105,* 1357–1395.

21. Article in a journal paginated by issue

List the issue number in parentheses (not italicized) after the volume number with no intervening space (see entry 18). For a popular magazine that does not commonly use volume numbers, use the season or date of publication.

> McGinn, D. (2006, June 5). Marriage by the numbers. *Newsweek,* 40–48.

22. Monthly publication

> Barlow, J. P. (1998, January). Africa rising: Everything you know about Africa is wrong. *Wired,* 142–158.

23. Newspaper article

> Hagenbaugh, B. (2005, April 25). Grads welcome an uptick in hiring. *USA Today,* p. A1.

APA References List: Library Database Sources

24. Document from a library database

APA no longer requires listing the names of well-known databases. The article below was retrieved from the PsycARTICLES database, but there is no need to list the database, the retrieval date, or the URL if the DOI is listed.

> Erdfelder, E. (2008). Experimental psychology: Good news. *Experimental Psychology, 55*(1), 1–2. doi:0.1027/1618-3169.55.1.1

APA References List: Online Sources

25. Article with DOI assigned

You may need to click on a button labeled "Article" or "PubMed" to find the DOI.

> Sharpless, B. A. (2013). Kierkegaard's conception of psychology. *Journal of Theoretical and Philosophical Psychology, 33*(2), 90–106. doi:10.1037/a0029009

26. Article with no DOI assigned

> Brown, B. (2004). The order of service: The practical management of customer interaction. *Sociological Research Online, 9*(4). Retrieved from http://www.socresonline.org.uk/9/4/brown.html

27. Online publication by a group or organization

If the only authority you find is a group or organization, list its name as the author.

> Girls Inc. (2013). Girls' bill of rights. Retrieved from http://www.girlsinc.org/about/girls-bill-of-rights/

28. Article in an online newspaper

> Slevin, C. (2005, April 25). Lawmakers want to put limits on private toll roads. *Boulder Daily Camera*. Retrieved from http://www.dailycamera.com

29. Article in an online magazine

> Pein, C. (2005, April 20). Is Al-Jazeera ready for prime time? *Salon*. Retrieved from http://www.salon.com

APA References List: Other Sources

30. Television program

> Winter, T. (Writer). (2012). Resolution. [Television series episode]. In T. Winter (Producer), *Boardwalk empire*. New York: HBO.

31. Film, Video, or DVD

Boal, M. (Writer), & Bigelow, K. (Director). (2012). *Zero dark thirty* [DVD]. United States: Columbia Pictures.

32. Musical recording

List both the title of the song and the title of the album or CD. In the in-text citation, include side or track numbers.

Lowe, N. (2001). Lately I've let things slide. On *The convincer* [CD]. Chapel Hill, NC: Yep Roc Records.

33. Social media (e.g., *Facebook*) page or note

The Daily Show. (2013, March 18). Political speeches contain much more than empty promises. [Facebook page]. Retrieved July 29, 2013, from https://www.facebook.com/thedailyshow

34. Twitter update or tweet

Collins, F. S. (2013, April 30). Check out my NPR interview this afternoon with Marketplace's @kairyssdal about #NIH research. [Twitter post]. Retrieved from https://twitter.com/NIH

Contemporary Arguments

PART

6

22 | Sustainability

Environmentalism and Sustainability

Most people agree that the modern environmental movement emerged from the work of two people: Aldo Leopold, who outlined a "land ethic" in his 1948 book

Dams on the Klamath River in Oregon provide water to power plants, which in turn supply clean electricity. But dams also affect fish and other wildlife, farmers, and Native Americans who live along the river. When people decide to build a dam, whose priorities should be considered?

A Sand County Almanac; and Rachel Carson, whose 1962 book *Silent Spring* sounded a national alarm against pesticides commonly used in the agriculture industry, particularly DDT. Together Leopold and Carson argued persuasively for a new sense of our relationship to our environment, for the conviction that we should be living in balance with nature, not in domination over it. Both books ultimately influenced not only agricultural practice but also efforts to protect endangered species, to regulate population growth, and to clean up our air and water resources. When President Richard Nixon created the Environmental Protection Agency in 1973, environmental concern became institutionalized in the United States; most states created their own departments of natural resources or environmental protection soon afterward.

In part, Aldo Leopold and Rachel Carson were successful because their appeals struck a chord deep within many Americans. In a very real sense environmentalism is anything but modern. Ingrained deep within the American character, it derives from a respect for the land—the American Eden—that is evident in the legend of Rip Van Winkle, in the work of Hudson River painters such as Thomas Cole, in the landscape architecture of Frederick Law Olmsted, in Henry David Thoreau's *Walden* and in Ralph Waldo Emerson's transcendentalist writings in the 1850s, in John

> We are the most dangerous species of life on the planet, and every other species, even the earth itself, has cause to fear our power to exterminate. But we are also the only species which, when it chooses to do so, will go to great effort to save what it might destroy.
>
> —WALLACE STEGNER

Muir's testimonials about Yosemite, and in Theo-
dore Roosevelt's withdrawals into the Badlands and
his campaign to begin a system of national parks. Of
course, the exploitation of the American green world
for profit is also ingrained in our national character.
Even as some Americans were revering the land as a
special landscape that sustained them physically and
spiritually, pioneers moving westward were subduing
it for their own purposes, in the process spoiling rivers and air and virgin forests—and decimating native
peoples—in the name of development.

    Today, tensions between preserving nature
and using nature are as high as they have ever been.
The BP oil spill of 2010, as well as continuing concerns about global warming and climate change, has
brought new urgency to all the debates related to the
environment, particularly when population increases
are factored in. According to the U.S. Census Bureau,

In this photograph of an environmental rally in Washington,
D.C., what images evoke
environmental themes?

the human population reached 7 billion in 2012 and is expected to reach 9 billion by 2050. Most of the population increase will be in economically "developing"
nations like India and China or in Africa and South America, in nations where
citizens are aspiring to the living standards common in the Western democracies.
Those living standards have traditionally required the consumption (and waste) of
increasing amounts of water, energy, breathable air, and other resources. The combination of rapid population increase in the developing world and unsustainable
consumption levels in the developed world poses a stark challenge, a challenge
that many are taking up through what has become known as the sustainability
movement.

    Many scientists are concerned that humans are already living beyond
the carrying capacity of the Earth. If the "ecological footprint" of humans—
that is, the quantity that each human being consumes—exceeds the carrying
capacity of the Earth, then humanity is on a disastrous course that cannot be
sustained without dire consequences to the quality of life. In the short run,
deficits can temporarily be made up by mining the reserves built up in the
past (for example, by drilling for fossil fuels that are destined to run out) or
by borrowing from the future (for example, by overfishing the seas until fish
supplies run dry or by running up debt). But in the long run such practices
cannot succeed.

    What is the responsibility of every human being for the happiness and pros-
perity of future generations? That question now animates citizens involved in the
growing sustainability movement, which takes as its goal the promotion of environmental, social, and economic practices that will assure the long-term viability
of human life—and all life—on Earth.

Contemporary Arguments

A key concept in the sustainability community is stewardship: How can people make use of the Earth's bounty without destroying the planet? How can citizens be good stewards of the advantages they have inherited? Those committed to sustainability are currently intent on ameliorating all kinds of destructive habits—debilitating farming practices, damaging or ineffectual methods of energy production and conservation, even human overpopulation. Deeply involved in arguments about ethics, sustainability advocates are promoting diverse and healthy ecosystems, the renewal of forests and wetlands, a resistance to the use of fossil fuels, concern for climate change, and the redesign of urban and suburban living spaces. On the one hand, sustainability advocates seek to reduce the human impact on ecosystems; they draw from experts in conservation biology, environmental science, agricultural science, even philosophy and religion. On the other hand, sustainability advocates seek to manage and limit the consumption of resources; they draw from experts in economics, law, public policy, energy production, sanitation engineering, urban planning, and transportation engineering, among other fields.

As these lists imply, those attracted to the sustainability ideal come from across the political spectrum. Both radical and reformist principles are present in the movement; deeply conservative, libertarian, even reactionary impulses can be found within the sustainability movement. Some contend that capitalism itself is unsustainable, while others believe that free enterprise and competition hold the key to creating a more sustainable world. Arguments within the movement are often as fierce, therefore, as arguments directed against people who resist or even ridicule the entire sustainability movement.

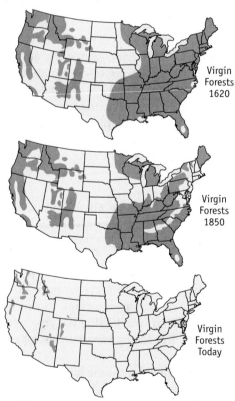

How virgin forests have diminished in the continental United States

Source: Atlas of the Historical Georgraphy of the United States, ed. C. O. Paullin.

A United Nations commission, on March 20, 1987, declared that "sustainable development is development that meets the needs of the present without compromising the ability of future generations to meet their own needs." Since then, the "three pillars" of the sustainability movement have been environmental quality, social equality, and economic reform. But exactly what kinds of reform?

The sustainability movement offers an expansive but conflicted social agenda that challenges nearly every human practice. True, some standards have been drafted—the Rainforest Alliance and Fair Trade certification programs and the Common Code for the Coffee Community are well-known examples—but the three pillars have been incompletely accepted and variously interpreted.

- What exactly is meant by "sustainability"?
- What should be the specific goals and methods of the movement?
- Does sustainability require a radical restructuring of political systems and the destruction of multinational corporations?
- Or does it call for more gradual reforms or for personal changes in individual human desires and appetites?

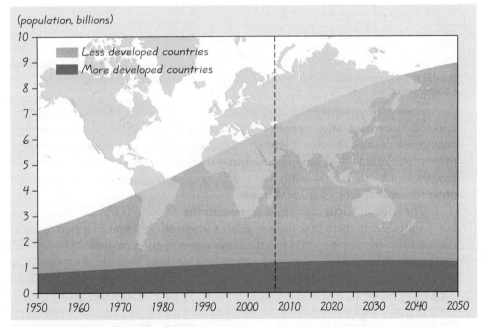

Projected Worldwide Population Growth.
The world's population is expected to reach 9.1 billion by 2050, with virtually all population growth occurring in less-developed countries.

Source: Finance and Development (Sept 2006, vol 43, no. 3) published by the International Monetary Fund.

Here we include a selection of arguments related to such questions. Wendell Berry, one of the esteemed high priests of the sustainability effort, begins by articulating the moral and philosophical arguments underpinning many sustainability practices. But Berry's positions and his withering criticisms of capitalism do not stand unchallenged. As a partial response to the sustainability movement's distrust of large corporations, we offer the decorated scientist Jared Diamond's 2009 essay "Will Big Business Save the Earth?" As a further rejoinder to sustainability enthusiasms, one with direct implications for colleges

Brown pelicans are common along the coasts of the South and California, but they were headed toward extinction by 1970 because the pesticide DDT caused their eggs to be too thin to support developing chicks to maturity. Although DDT was banned in the United States, many countries continue to use it for agricultural spraying and malaria control even though insects and mosquitoes have developed resistance to it.

and college students, we then provide the conservative National Association of Scholars statement "Fixing Sustainability," issued in 2011. Then Mark Bittman offers an argument that first appeared in 2009 in the *New York Times*; he urges his readers to complicate their attitudes toward what counts as "organic" food and farming.

Finally, we conclude this chapter with an Issue in Focus: Making Cities Sustainable. Since population growth of the past century has been accompanied by a concurrent rush to the city, it is particularly important that people in exploding urban populations find ways of sustaining their urban environments. But how? Exactly which deeply held habits and practices must be changed or ameliorated in order to ward off ecological catastrophe?

The Issue in Focus offers four arguments that in various ways touch on some possibilities. All of them in some way relate to controlling "sprawl," which refers to the tendency of people to move to the outer edges of cities in order to escape the environmental problems associated with urban life. Kaid Benfield, founder of the Smart Growth America Coalition, argues that urban planners must think beyond the simple prevention of urban sprawl if we are to have sustainable urban spaces. Greg LeRoy, a well-known critic of unsustainable urban practices, supports Benfield's argument with an essay that is strongly critical of urban tax policies, especially when those policies not only encourage sprawl but also disproportionately

Hiroshi Takatsuki/Japan for Sustainability

affect the poor. David Resnick explores the ways that smart growth policies can address the problems of urban sprawl, why some oppose such policies, and how using the techniques of deliberative democracy can help bring communities to consensus. Finally, we offer the introductory segment from a sustainability Web site, Original Green, that offers the quirky but intriguing proposition that a building is sustainable only if it is also "lovable."

How serious is our current environmental predicament? Are some of our cultural practices truly unsustainable and destructive? What are the best ways to ensure that future generations will inherit a planet able to sustain happiness and prosperity? Must we give up many creature comforts in order to survive in a sustainable environment? Must population controls be instituted in order to stave off mass starvation? What compromises must we make to balance economic growth, technological advancement and innovation, the preservation of green spaces, environmental quality, and biodiversity—and what should be our priorities? Together the selections should enlighten you about what sustainability advocates promise and stimulate you to take up your own arguments about the matter.

Wendell E. Berry

"It All Turns on Affection": 2012 Jefferson Lecture

A writer and teacher who grew up on a farm in Kentucky (he still lives on one), Wendell Berry has been living out sustainability principles since his birth in 1934 and promoting them in a long-running series of widely read and admired essays and poems. In articles such as "What Are People For?" and "Why I Am Not Going to Buy a Computer" and in the poems collected in *Sabbaths* and *The Country of Marriage*, Berry has long explored the ties that connect people and has advocated a simple lifestyle, at odds with new technologies that threaten agrarian ways. In 2012, Berry was invited by the National Endowment for the Humanities to give the prestigious annual Jefferson Lecture, a lecture that was subsequently published in a book of his essays and that is excerpted here. Berry used the occasion to argue eloquently for sustainability principles and practices.

"Because a thing is going strong now, it need not go strong for ever," [Margaret] said. "This craze for motion has only set in during the last hundred years. It may be followed by a civilization that won't be a movement, because it will rest upon the earth."

—E. M. Forster, *Howards End* (1910)[1]

One night in the winter of 1907, at what we have always called "the home place" in Henry County, Kentucky, my father, then six years old, sat with his older brother and listened as their parents spoke of the uses they would have for the money from their 1906 tobacco crop. The crop was to be sold at auction in Louisville on the next day. They would have been sitting in the light of a kerosene lamp, close to the stove, warming themselves before bedtime. They were not wealthy people. I believe that the debt on their farm was not fully paid, there would have been interest to pay, there would have been other debts. The depression of the 1890s would have left them burdened. Perhaps, after the income from the crop had paid their obligations, there would be some money that they could spend as they chose. At around two o'clock the next morning, my father was wakened by a horse's shod hooves on the stones of the driveway. His father was leaving to catch the train to see the crop sold.

2   He came home that evening, as my father later would put it, "without a dime." After the crop had paid its transportation to market and the commission on its sale, there was nothing left. Thus began my father's lifelong advocacy, later my brother's and my own, and now my daughter's and my son's, for small farmers and for land-conserving economies.

3   The economic hardship of my family and of many others, a century ago, was caused by a monopoly, the American Tobacco Company, which had eliminated all competitors and thus was able to reduce as it pleased the prices it paid to farmers. The American Tobacco Company was the work of James B. Duke of Durham, North Carolina, and

New York City, who, disregarding any other consideration, followed a capitalist logic to absolute control of his industry and, incidentally, of the economic fate of thousands of families such as my own.

4   My effort to make sense of this memory and its encompassing history has depended on a pair of terms used by my teacher, Wallace Stegner. He thought rightly that we Americans, by inclination at least, have been divided into two kinds: "boomers" and "stickers." Boomers, he said, are "those who pillage and run," who want "to make a killing and end up on Easy Street," whereas stickers are "those who settle, and love the life they have made and the place they have made it in."[2] "Boomer" names a kind of person and a kind of ambition that is the major theme, so far, of the history of the European races in our country. "Sticker" names a kind of person and also a desire that is, so far, a minor theme of that history, but a theme persistent enough to remain significant and to offer, still, a significant hope.

5   The boomer is motivated by greed, the desire for money, property, and therefore power. James B. Duke was a boomer, if we can extend the definition to include pillage *in absentia*. He went, or sent, wherever the getting was good, and he got as much as he could take.

6   Stickers on the contrary are motivated by affection, by such love for a place and its life that they want to preserve it and remain in it. Of my grandfather I need to say only that he shared in the virtues and the faults of his kind and time, one of his virtues being that he was a sticker. He belonged to a family who had come to Kentucky from Virginia, and who intended to go no farther. He was the third in his paternal line to live in the neighborhood of our little town of Port Royal, and he was the second to own the farm where he was born in 1864 and where he died in 1946.

7   We have one memory of him that seems, more than any other, to identify him as a sticker. He owned his farm, having bought out the other heirs, for more than fifty years. About forty of those years were in hard times, and he lived almost continuously in the distress of debt. Whatever has happened in what economists call "the economy," it is generally true that the land economy has been discounted or ignored. My grandfather lived his life in an economic shadow. In an urbanizing and industrializing age, he was the wrong kind of man. In one of his difficult years he plowed a field on the lower part of a long slope and planted it in corn. While the soil was exposed, a heavy rain fell and the field was seriously eroded. This was heartbreak for my grandfather, and he devoted the rest of his life, first to healing the scars and then to his obligation of care. In keeping with the sticker's commitment, he neither left behind the damage he had done nor forgot about it, but stayed to repair it, insofar as soil loss can be repaired. My father, I think, had his father's error in mind when he would speak of farmers attempting, always uselessly if not tragically, "to plow their way out of debt." From that time, my grandfather and my father were soil conservationists, a commitment that they handed on to my brother and to me.

8   It is not beside the point, or off my subject, to notice that these stories and their meanings have survived because of my family's continuing connection to its home place. Like my grandfather, my father grew up on that place and served as its caretaker. It has now belonged to my brother for many years, and he in turn has been its caretaker. He and I have lived as neighbors, allies, and friends. Our long conversation has often taken its themes from the two stories I have told, because we have been

continually reminded of them by our home neighborhood and topography. If we had not lived there to be reminded and to remember, nobody would have remembered. If either of us had lived elsewhere, both of us would have known less. If both of us, like most of our generation, had moved away, the place with its memories would have been lost to us and we to it—and certainly my thoughts about agriculture, if I had thought of it at all, would have been much more approximate than they have been.

9   Because I have never separated myself from my home neighborhood, I cannot identify myself to myself apart from it. I am fairly literally flesh of its flesh. It is present in me, and to me, wherever I go. This undoubtedly accounts for my sense of shock when, on my first visit to Duke University, and by surprise, I came face-to-face with James B. Duke in his dignity, his glory perhaps, as the founder of that university. He stands imperially in bronze in front of a Methodist chapel aspiring to be a cathedral. He holds between two fingers of his left hand a bronze cigar. On one side of his pedestal is the legend: INDUSTRIALIST. On the other side is another single word: PHILANTHROPIST. The man thus commemorated seemed to me terrifyingly ignorant, even terrifyingly innocent, of the connection between his industry and his philanthropy. But I did know the connection. I felt it instantly and physically. The connection was my grandparents and thousands of others more or less like them. If you can appropriate for little or nothing the work and hope of enough such farmers, then you may dispense the grand charity of "philanthropy."

10   After my encounter with the statue, the story of my grandfather's 1906 tobacco crop slowly took on a new dimension and clarity in my mind. I still remembered my grandfather as himself, of course, but I began to think of him also as a kind of man standing in thematic opposition to a man of an entirely different kind. And I could see finally that between these two kinds there was a failure of imagination that was ruinous, that belongs indelibly to our history, and that has continued, growing worse, into our own time.

11   The term "imagination" in what I take to be its truest sense refers to a mental faculty that some people have used and thought about with the utmost seriousness. The sense of the verb "to imagine" contains the full richness of the verb "to see." To imagine is to see most clearly, familiarly, and understandingly with the eyes, but also to see inwardly, with "the mind's eye." It is to see, not passively, but with a force of vision and even with visionary force. To take it seriously we must give up at once any notion that imagination is disconnected from reality or truth or knowledge. It has nothing to do either with clever imitation of appearances or with "dreaming up." It does not depend upon one's attitude or point of view, but grasps securely the qualities of things seen or envisioned.

12   I will say, from my own belief and experience, that imagination thrives on contact, on tangible connection. For humans to have a responsible relationship to the world, they must imagine their places in it. To have a place, to live and belong in a place, to live from a place without destroying it, we must imagine it. By imagination we see it illuminated by its own unique character and by our love for it. By imagination we recognize with sympathy the fellow members, human and nonhuman, with whom we share our place. By that local experience we see the need to grant a sort of preemptive sympathy to all the fellow members, the neighbors, with whom we share the world. As

imagination enables sympathy, sympathy enables affection. And it is in affection that we find the possibility of a neighborly, kind, and conserving economy.

13   Obviously there is some risk in making affection the pivot of an argument about economy. The charge will be made that affection is an emotion, merely "subjective," and therefore that all affections are more or less equal: people may have affection for their children and their automobiles, their neighbors and their weapons. But the risk, I think, is only that affection is personal. If it is not personal, it is nothing; we don't, at least, have to worry about governmental or corporate affection. And one of the endeavors of human cultures, from the beginning, has been to qualify and direct the influence of emotion. The word "affection" and the terms of value that cluster around it—love, care, sympathy, mercy, forbearance, respect, reverence—have histories and meanings that raise the issue of worth. We should, as our culture has warned us over and over again, give our affection to things that are true, just, and beautiful. When we give affection to things that are destructive, we are wrong. A large machine in a large, toxic, eroded cornfield is not, properly speaking, an object or a sign of affection.

14   My grandfather knew, urgently, the value of money, but only of such comparatively small sums as would have paid his debts and allowed to his farm and his family a decent prosperity. He certainly knew of the American Tobacco Company. He no doubt had read and heard of James B. Duke, and could identify him as the cause of a hard time, but nothing in his experience could have enabled him to imagine the life of the man himself.

15   James B. Duke came from a rural family in the tobacco country of North Carolina. In his early life he would have known men such as my grandfather. But after he began his rise as an industrialist, the life of a small tobacco grower would have been to him a negligible detail incidental to an opportunity for large profits. In the minds of the "captains of industry," then and now, the people of the land economies have been reduced to statistical numerals. Power deals "efficiently" with quantities that affection cannot recognize.

16   It may seem plausible to suppose that the head of the American Tobacco Company would have imagined at least that a dependable supply of raw material to his industry would depend upon a stable, reasonably thriving population of farmers and upon the continuing fertility of their farms. But he imagined no such thing. In this he was like apparently all agribusiness executives. They don't imagine farms or farmers. They imagine perhaps nothing at all, their minds being filled to capacity by numbers leading to the bottom line. Though the corporations, by law, are counted as persons, they do not have personal minds, if they can be said to have minds. It is a great oddity that a corporation, which properly speaking has no self, is by definition selfish, responsible only to itself. This is an impersonal, abstract selfishness, limitlessly acquisitive, but unable to look so far ahead as to preserve its own sources and supplies. The selfishness of the fossil fuel industries by nature is self-annihilating; but so, always, has been the selfishness of the agribusiness corporations. Land, as Wes Jackson has said, has thus been made as exhaustible as oil or coal.

17   . . . Corporate industrialism has tended to be, and as its technological and financial power has grown it has tended increasingly to be, indifferent to its sources in what Aldo Leopold called "the land-community": the land, all its features and "resources," and all its members, human and nonhuman, including of course the humans who do, for better or worse, the

work of land use.[3] Industrialists and industrial economists have assumed, with permission from the rest of us, that land and people can be divorced without harm. If farmers come under adversity from high costs and low prices, then they must either increase their demands upon the land and decrease their care for it, or they must sell out and move to town, and this is supposed to involve no ecological or economic or social cost. Or if there are such costs, then they are rated as "the price of progress" or "creative destruction."

18   But land abuse *cannot* brighten the human prospect. There is in fact no distinction between the fate of the land and the fate of the people. When one is abused, the other suffers. The penalties may come quickly to a farmer who destroys perennial cover on a sloping field. They *will* come sooner or later to a land-destroying civilization such as ours.

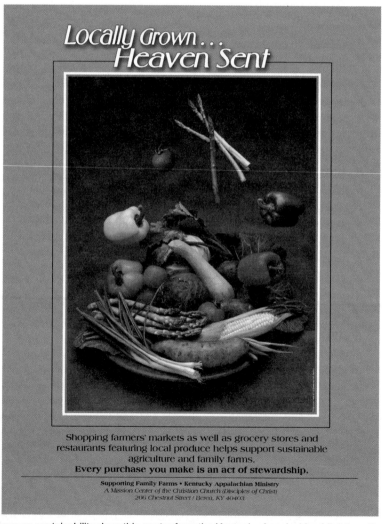

What views on sustainability does this poster from the Kentucky Appalachian Ministry articulate?

19   And so it has seemed to me less a choice than a necessity to oppose the boomer enterprise with its false standards and its incomplete accounting, and to espouse the cause of stable, restorative, locally adapted economies of mostly family-sized farms, ranches, shops, and trades. Naïve as it may sound now, within the context of our present faith in science, finance, and technology—the faith equally of "conservatives" and "liberals"—this cause nevertheless has an authentic source in the sticker's hope to abide in and to live from some chosen and cherished small place—which, of course, is the agrarian vision that Thomas Jefferson spoke for, a sometimes honored human theme, minor and even fugitive, but continuous from ancient times until now. Allegiance to it, however, is not a conclusion but the beginning of thought.

20   . . . Economy in its original—and, I think, its proper—sense refers to household management. By extension, it refers to the husbanding of all the goods by which we live. An authentic economy, if we had one, would define and make, on the terms of thrift and affection, our connections to nature and to one another. Our present industrial system also makes those connections, but by pillage and indifference. Most economists think of this arrangement as "the economy." Their columns and articles rarely if ever mention the land-communities and land-use economies. They never ask, in their professional oblivion, why we are willing to do permanent ecological and cultural damage "to strengthen the economy."

21   In his essay, "Notes on Liberty and Property," Allen Tate gave us an indispensable anatomy of our problem. His essay begins by equating, not liberty and property, but liberty and *control* of one's property. He then makes the crucial distinction between ownership that is merely legal and what he calls "effective ownership." If a property, say a small farm, has one owner, then the one owner has an effective and assured, if limited, control over it as long as he or she can afford to own it, and is free to sell it or use it, and (I will add) free to use it poorly or well. It is clear also that effective ownership of a small property is personal and therefore can, at least possibly, be intimate, familial, and affectionate. If, on the contrary, a person owns a small property of stock in a large corporation, then that person has surrendered control of the property to larger shareholders. The drastic mistake our people made, as Tate believed and I agree, was to be convinced "that there is *one* kind of property— just *property*, whether it be a thirty-acre farm in Kentucky or a stock certificate in the United States Steel Corporation." By means of this confusion, Tate said, "Small ownership . . . [Berry's ellipsis] has been worsted by big, dispersed ownership—the giant corporation."[4] (It is necessary to append to this argument the further fact that by now, owing largely to corporate influence, land ownership implies the right to destroy the land-community entirely, as in surface mining, and to impose, as a consequence, the dangers of flooding, water pollution, and disease upon communities downstream.)

22   Tate's essay was written for the anthology, *Who Owns America?*, the publication of which was utterly without effect. With other agrarian writings before and since, it took its place on the far margin of the national dialogue, dismissed as anachronistic, retrogressive, nostalgic, or (to use Tate's own term of defiance) reactionary in the face of the supposedly "inevitable" dominance of corporate industrialism. *Who Owns America?* was published in the Depression year of 1936. It is at least ironic that talk of "effective

property" could have been lightly dismissed at a time when many rural people who had migrated to industrial cities were returning to their home farms to survive.

23   In 1936, when to the dominant minds a thirty-acre farm in Kentucky was becoming laughable, Tate's essay would have seemed irrelevant as a matter of course. At that time, despite the Depression, faith in the standards and devices of industrial progress was nearly universal and could not be shaken.

24 But now, three-quarters of a century later, we are no longer talking about theoretical alternatives to corporate rule. We are talking with practical urgency about an obvious need. Now the two great aims of industrialism—replacement of people by technology and concentration of wealth into the hands of a small plutocracy—seem close to fulfillment. At the same time the *failures* of industrialism have become too great and too dangerous to deny. Corporate industrialism itself has exposed the falsehood that it ever was inevitable or that it ever has given precedence to the common good. It has failed to sustain the health and stability of human society. Among its characteristic signs are destroyed communities, neighborhoods, families, small businesses, and small farms. It has failed just as conspicuously and more dangerously to conserve the wealth and health of nature. No amount of fiddling with capitalism to regulate and humanize it, no pointless rhetoric on the virtues of capitalism or socialism, no billions or trillions spent on "defense" of the "American dream," can for long disguise this failure. The evidences of it are everywhere: eroded, wasted, or degraded soils; damaged or destroyed ecosystems; extinction of species; whole landscapes defaced, gouged, flooded, or blown up; pollution of the whole atmosphere and of the water cycle; "dead zones" in the coastal waters; thoughtless squandering of fossil fuels and fossil waters, of mineable minerals and ores; natural health and beauty replaced by a heartless and sickening ugliness. Perhaps its greatest success is an astounding increase in the destructiveness, and therefore the profitability, of war.

25   In 1936, moreover, only a handful of people were thinking about sustainability. Now, reasonably, many of us are thinking about it. The problem of sustainability is simple enough to state. It requires that the fertility cycle of birth, growth, maturity, death, and decay—what Albert Howard called "the Wheel of Life"—should turn continuously in place, so that the law of return is kept and nothing is wasted. For this to happen in the stewardship of humans, there must be a cultural cycle, in harmony with the fertility cycle, also continuously turning in place. The cultural cycle is an unending conversation between old people and young people, assuring the survival of local memory, which has, as long as it remains local, the greatest practical urgency and value. This is what is meant, and is all that is meant, by "sustainability." The fertility cycle turns by the law of nature. The cultural cycle turns on affection. . . .

26 In my reading of the historian John Lukacs, I have been most instructed by his understanding that there is no knowledge but human knowledge, that we are therefore inescapably central to our own consciousness, and that this is "a statement not of arrogance but of humility. It is yet another recognition of the inevitable limitations of mankind."[5] We are thus isolated within our uniquely human boundaries, which we certainly cannot transcend or escape by means of technological devices.

27   But as I understand this dilemma, we are not *completely* isolated. Though we cannot by our own powers escape our limits, we are subject to correction from, so to

speak, the outside. I can hardly expect everybody to believe, as I do (with due caution), that inspiration can come from the outside. But inspiration is not the only way the human enclosure can be penetrated. Nature too may break in upon us, sometimes to our delight, sometimes to our dismay.

28   As many hunters, farmers, ecologists, and poets have understood, Nature (and here we capitalize her name) is the impartial mother of all creatures, unpredictable, never entirely revealed, not my mother or your mother, but nonetheless our mother. If we are observant and respectful of her, she gives good instruction. As Albert Howard, Wes Jackson, and others have carefully understood, she can give us the right patterns and standards for agriculture. If we ignore or offend her, she enforces her will with punishment. She is always trying to tell us that we are not so superior or independent or alone or autonomous as we may think. She tells us in the voice of Edmund Spenser that she is of *all* creatures "the equall mother, / And knittest each to each, as brother unto brother."[6] Nearly three and a half centuries later, we hear her saying about the same thing in the voice of Aldo Leopold: "In short, a land ethic changes the role of *Homo sapiens* from conqueror of the land-community to plain member and citizen of it."[7]

29   We cannot know the whole truth, which belongs to God alone, but our task nevertheless is to seek to know what is true. And if we offend gravely enough against what we know to be true, as by failing badly enough to deal affectionately and responsibly with our land and our neighbors, truth will retaliate with ugliness, poverty, and disease. The crisis of this line of thought is the realization that we are at once limited and unendingly responsible for what we know and do.

30   The discrepancy between what modern humans presume to know and what they can imagine—given the background of pride and self-congratulation—is amusing and even funny. It becomes more serious as it raises issues of responsibility. It becomes fearfully serious when we start dealing with statistical measures of industrial destruction.

31   To hear of a thousand deaths in war is terrible, and we "know" that it is. But as it registers on our hearts, it is not more terrible than one death fully imagined. The economic hardship of one farm family, if they are our neighbors, affects us more painfully than pages of statistics on the decline of the farm population. I can be heartstruck by grief and a kind of compassion at the sight of one gulley (and by shame if I caused it myself), but, conservationist though I am, I am not nearly so upset by an accounting of the tons of plowland sediment borne by the Mississippi River. Wallace Stevens wrote that "Imagination applied to the whole world is vapid in comparison to imagination applied to a detail"[8]—and that appears to have the force of truth . . .

32   . . . The losses and damages characteristic of our present economy cannot be stopped, let alone restored, by "liberal" or "conservative" tweakings of corporate industrialism, against which the ancient imperatives of good care, homemaking, and frugality can have no standing. The possibility of authentic correction comes, I think, from two already-evident causes. The first is scarcity and other serious problems arising from industrial abuses of the land-community. The goods of nature so far have been taken for granted and, especially in America, assumed to be limitless, but their diminishment, sooner or later unignorable, will enforce change.

33   A positive cause, still little noticed by high officials and the media, is the by now well-established effort to build or rebuild local economies, starting with economies of

food. This effort to connect cities with their surrounding rural landscapes has the advantage of being both attractive and necessary. It rests exactly upon the recognition of human limits and the necessity of human scale. Its purpose, to the extent possible, is to bring producers and consumers, causes and effects, back within the bounds of neighborhood, which is to say the effective reach of imagination, sympathy, affection, and all else that neighborhood implies. An economy genuinely local and neighborly offers to localities a measure of security that they cannot derive from a national or a global economy controlled by people who, by principle, have no local commitment.

34   . . . By now all thoughtful people have begun to feel our eligibility to be instructed by ecological disaster and mortal need. But we endangered ourselves first of all by dismissing affection as an honorable and necessary motive. Our decision in the middle of the last century to reduce the farm population, eliminating the allegedly "inefficient" small farmers, was enabled by the discounting of affection. As a result, we now have barely enough farmers to keep the land in production, with the help of increasingly expensive industrial technology and at an increasing ecological and social cost. Far from the plain citizens and members of the land-community, as Aldo Leopold wished them to be, farmers are now too likely to be merely the land's exploiters.

35   I don't hesitate to say that damage or destruction of the land-community is morally wrong, just as Leopold did not hesitate to say so when he was composing his essay, "The Land Ethic," in 1947. But I do not believe, as I think Leopold did not, that morality, even religious morality, is an adequate motive for good care of the land-community. The *primary* motive for good care and good use is always going to be affection, because affection involves us entirely. And here Leopold himself set the example. In 1935 he bought an exhausted Wisconsin farm and, with his family, began its restoration. To do this was morally right, of course, but the motive was affection. Leopold was an ecologist. He felt, we may be sure, an informed sorrow for the place in its ruin. He imagined it as it had been, as it was, and as it might be. And a profound, delighted affection radiates from every sentence he wrote about it.

36   Without this informed, practical, and *practiced* affection, the nation and its economy will conquer and destroy the country . . .

NOTES

1. *Everyman's Library*, Alfred A. Knopf, New York, 1991, page 355.
2. *Where the Bluebird Sings to the Lemonade Springs*, Random House, New York, 1992, pages xxii & 4.
3. *A Sand County Almanac*, Oxford University Press, New York, 1966, pages 219–220.
4. *Who Owns America?* edited by Herbert Agar and Allen Tate, ISI Books, Wilmington, DE, 1999, pages 109–114. (First published by Houghton Mifflin Company, Boston, 1936.)
5. *Last Rites*, Yale University Press, New Haven and London, 2009, pages 31 and 35.
6. *The Faerie Queene*, VII, vii, stanza XIV.
7. *A Sand County Almanac*, pages 219–220.
8. *Opus Posthumous*, edited, with an Introduction by Samuel French Morse, Alfred A. Knopf, New York, 1957, page 176.

JARED **DIAMOND**

Will Big Business Save the Earth?

Jared Diamond (born 1937) is well known as the best-selling author of *Guns, Germs, and Steel* (1997) and *Collapse* (2005), two books that are fundamentally concerned with issues of sustainability. He is an interdisciplinary scientist whose work draws from physiology, anthropology, evolutionary biology, and geography. Diamond is adept at connecting the general public with science by means of his clear and readable prose, as the following essay indicates. It appeared in the *New York Times* in December 2009.

There is a widespread view, particularly among environmentalists and liberals, that big businesses are environmentally destructive, greedy, evil and driven by short-term profits. I know—because I used to share that view.

2   But today I have more nuanced feelings. Over the years I've joined the boards of two environmental groups, the World Wildlife Fund and Conservation International, serving alongside many business executives.

3   As part of my board work, I have been asked to assess the environments in oil fields, and have had frank discussions with oil company employees at all levels. I've also worked with executives of mining, retail, logging and financial services companies. I've discovered that while some businesses are indeed as destructive as many suspect, others are among the world's strongest positive forces for environmental sustainability.

4   The embrace of environmental concerns by chief executives has accelerated recently for several reasons. Lower consumption of environmental resources saves money in the short run. Maintaining sustainable resource levels and not polluting saves money in the long run. And a clean image—one attained by, say, avoiding oil spills and other environmental disasters—reduces criticism from employees, consumers and government.

5   What's my evidence for this? Here are a few examples involving three corporations—Walmart, Coca-Cola and Chevron—that many critics of business love to hate, in my opinion, unjustly.

6   Let's start with Walmart. Obviously, a business can save money by finding ways to spend less while maintaining sales. This is what Walmart did with fuel costs, which the company reduced by $26 million per year simply by changing the way it managed its enormous truck fleet. Instead of running a truck's engine all night to heat or cool the cab during mandatory 10-hour rest stops, the company installed small auxiliary power units to do the job. In addition to lowering fuel costs, the move eliminated the carbon dioxide emissions equivalent to taking 18,300 passenger vehicles off the road.

7   Walmart is also working to double the fuel efficiency of its truck fleet by 2015, thereby saving more than $200 million a year at the pump. Among the efficient prototypes now being tested are trucks that burn biofuels generated from waste grease at Walmart's delis. Similarly, as the country's biggest private user of electricity, Walmart is saving money by decreasing store energy use.

8   Another Walmart example involves lowering costs associated with packaging materials. Walmart now sells only concentrated liquid laundry detergents in North America, which has reduced the size of packaging by up to 50 percent. Walmart stores also have machines called bailers that recycle plastics that once would have been discarded. Walmart's eventual goal is to end up with no packaging waste.

9   One last Walmart example shows how a company can save money in the long run by buying from sustainably managed sources. Because most wild fisheries are managed unsustainably, prices for Chilean sea bass and Atlantic tuna have been soaring. To my pleasant astonishment, in 2006 Walmart decided to switch, within five years, all its purchases of wild-caught seafood to fisheries certified as sustainable.

10   Coca-Cola's problems are different from Walmart's in that they are largely long-term. The key ingredient in Coke products is water. The company produces its beverages in about 200 countries through local franchises, all of which require a reliable local supply of clean fresh water.

11   But water supplies are under severe pressure around the world, with most already allocated for human use. The little remaining unallocated fresh water is in remote areas unsuitable for beverage factories, like Arctic Russia and northwestern Australia.

12   Coca-Cola can't meet its water needs just by desalinizing seawater, because that requires energy, which is also increasingly expensive. Global climate change is making water scarcer, especially in the densely populated temperate-zone countries, like the United States, that are Coca-Cola's main customers. Most competing water use around the world is for agriculture, which presents sustainability problems of its own.

13   Hence Coca-Cola's survival compels it to be deeply concerned with problems of water scarcity, energy, climate change and agriculture. One company goal is to make its plants water-neutral, returning to the environment water in quantities equal to the amount used in beverages and their production. Another goal is to work on the conservation of seven of the world's river basins, including the Rio Grande, Yangtze, Mekong and Danube—all of them sites of major environmental concerns besides supplying water for Coca-Cola.

14   These long-term goals are in addition to Coca-Cola's short-term cost-saving environmental practices, like recycling plastic bottles, replacing petroleum-based plastic in bottles with organic material, reducing energy consumption and increasing sales volume while decreasing water use.

15   The third company is Chevron. Not even in any national park have I seen such rigorous environmental protection as I encountered in five visits to new Chevron-managed oil fields in Papua New Guinea. (Chevron has since sold its stake in these properties to a New Guinea-based oil company.) When I asked how a publicly traded company could justify to its shareholders its expenditures on the environment, Chevron employees and executives gave me at least five reasons.

16   First, oil spills can be horribly expensive: it is far cheaper to prevent them than to clean them up. Second, clean practices reduce the risk that New Guinean landowners become angry, sue for damages and close the fields. (The company has been sued for problems in Ecuador that Chevron inherited when it merged with Texaco in 2001.) Next, environmental standards are becoming stricter around the world, so building clean facilities now minimizes having to do expensive retrofitting later.

17   Also, clean operations in one country give a company an advantage in bidding on leases in other countries. Finally, environmental practices of which employees are proud improve morale, help with recruitment and increase the length of time employees are likely to remain at the company.

18   In view of all those advantages that businesses gain from environmentally sustainable policies, why do such policies face resistance from some businesses and many politicians? The objections often take the form of one-liners.

- We have to balance the environment against the economy. The assumption underlying this statement is that measures promoting environmental sustainability inevitably yield a net economic cost rather than a profit. This line of thinking turns the truth upside down. Economic reasons furnish the strongest motives for sustainability, because in the long run (and often in the short run as well) it is much more expensive and difficult to try to fix problems, environmental or otherwise, than to avoid them at the outset.

19   Americans learned that lesson from Hurricane Katrina in August 2005, when, as a result of government agencies balking for a decade at spending several hundred million dollars to fix New Orleans's defenses, we suffered hundreds of billions of dollars in damage—not to mention thousands of dead Americans. Likewise, John Holdren, the top White House science adviser, estimates that solving problems of climate change would cost the United States 2 percent of our gross domestic product by the year 2050, but that not solving those problems would damage the economy by 20 percent to 30 percent of G.D.P.

- Technology will solve our problems. Yes, technology can contribute to solving problems. But major technological advances require years to develop and put in place, and regularly turn out to have unanticipated side effects—consider the destruction of the atmosphere's ozone layer by the nontoxic, nonflammable chlorofluorocarbons initially hailed for replacing poisonous refrigerant gases.
- World population growth is leveling off and won't be the problem that we used to fear. It's true that the rate of world population growth has been decreasing. However, the real problem isn't people themselves, but the resources that people consume and the waste that they produce. Per-person average consumption rates and waste production rates, now 32 times higher in rich countries than in poor ones, are rising steeply around the world, as developing countries emulate industrialized nations' lifestyles.
- It's futile to preach to us Americans about lowering our standard of living: we will never sacrifice just so other people can raise their standard of living. This conflates consumption rates with standards of living: they are only loosely correlated, because so much of our consumption is wasteful and doesn't contribute to our quality of life. Once basic needs are met, increasing consumption often doesn't increase happiness.
- Replacing a car that gets 15 miles per gallon with a more efficient model wouldn't lower one's standard of living, but would help improve all of our lives by reducing the political and military consequences of our dependence on

imported oil. Western Europeans have lower per-capita consumption rates than Americans, but enjoy a higher standard of living as measured by access to medical care, financial security after retirement, infant mortality, life expectancy, literacy and public transport.

20   Not surprisingly, the problem of climate change has attracted its own particular crop of objections.

- Even experts disagree about the reality of climate change. That was true 30 years ago, and some experts still disagreed a decade ago. Today, virtually every climatologist agrees that average global temperatures, warming rates and atmospheric carbon dioxide levels are higher than at any time in the earth's recent past, and that the main cause is greenhouse gas emissions by humans. Instead, the questions still being debated concern whether average global temperatures will increase by 13 degrees or "only" by 4 degrees Fahrenheit by 2050, and whether humans account for 90 percent or "only" 85 percent of the global warming trend.

- The magnitude and cause of global climate change are uncertain. We shouldn't adopt expensive countermeasures until we have certainty. In other spheres of life — picking a spouse, educating our children, buying life insurance and stocks, avoiding cancer and so on — we admit that certainty is unattainable, and that we must decide as best we can on the basis of available evidence. Why should the impossible quest for certainty paralyze us solely about acting on climate change? As Mr. Holdren, the White House adviser, expressed it, not acting on climate change would be like being "in a car with bad brakes driving toward a cliff in the fog."

- Global warming will be good for us, by letting us grow crops in places formerly too cold for agriculture. The term "global warming" is a misnomer; we should instead talk about global climate change, which isn't uniform. The global average temperature is indeed rising, but many areas are becoming drier, and frequencies of droughts, floods and other extreme weather events are increasing. Some areas will be winners, while others will be losers. Most of us will be losers, because the temperate zones where most people live are becoming drier.

- It's useless for the United States to act on climate change, when we don't know what China will do. Actually, China will arrive at this week's Copenhagen climate change negotiations with a whole package of measures to reduce its "carbon intensity."

21   While the United States is dithering about long-distance energy transmission from our rural areas with the highest potential for wind energy generation to our urban areas with the highest need for energy, China is far ahead of us. It is developing ultra-high-voltage transmission lines from wind and solar generation sites in rural western China to cities in eastern China. If America doesn't act to develop innovative energy technology, we will lose the green jobs competition not only to Finland and Germany (as we are now) but also to China.

22   On each of these issues, American businesses are going to play as much or more of a role in our progress as the government. And this isn't a bad thing, as corporations know they have a lot to gain by establishing environmentally friendly business practices.

23   My friends in the business world keep telling me that Washington can help on two fronts: by investing in green research, offering tax incentives and passing cap-and-trade legislation; and by setting and enforcing tough standards to ensure that companies with cheap, dirty standards don't have a competitive advantage over those businesses protecting the environment. As for the rest of us, we should get over the misimpression that American business cares only about immediate profits, and we should reward companies that work to keep the planet healthy.

The United States faces the challenge of recycling or disposing of almost 2.5 million tons of used electronics generated by Americans each year.

National Association of Scholars

Fixing Sustainability and Sustaining Liberal Education

The National Association of Scholars (NAS) is a professional association of college teachers that is dedicated to the principles of reasoned public debate and academic freedom. (Academic freedom involves the practice of free inquiry and the belief that scholars have the freedom to teach and learn as they see fit, without being targeted for harassment or repression.) Generally conservative in its positions on social issues, the NAS issued the following statement about sustainability in 2011.

"Sustainability" is one of the key words of our time. We are six years along in the United Nations' "Decade of Education for Sustainable Development." In the United States, 677 colleges and universities presidents have committed themselves to a sustainability-themed "Climate Commitment." Sustainability is, by a large measure, the most popular social movement today in American higher education. It is, of course, not just a campus movement, but also a ubiquitous presence in the K-12 curriculum, and a staple of community groups, political platforms, appeals to consumers, and corporate policy.

2 In view of the broad popularity of the idea, we realize that a dissenting opinion may be dismissed out of hand. Yet sustainability ought not to be held exempt from critical scrutiny. And the campus movement built around the word "sustainability," is, in our view, very much in need of such scrutiny. This statement presents the National Association of Scholars' considered view of nine ways that the campus sustainability movement has gone wrong. And we offer a proposal for how it can be set right.

3 We came to compose this statement after three years of studying the campus sustainability movement. We have at this point published over one hundred online articles, reports, and interviews on the topic; attended sustainability events; presented findings at academic meetings; and devoted a special issue of our quarterly journal *Academic Questions* to scholarly analyses of the movement's origins and claims. Our policy statement distills what we have learned from this investigation.

1. A MISAPPROPRIATED WORD

4 Our dissent does not aim at the whole of "sustainability." We regard good stewardship of natural and institutional resources and respect for the environment as excellent principles. We have nothing against colleges and universities attempting to trim their budgets by saving energy. But wholesome words standing for wholesome principles do not always stay put. They can be appropriated by political movements seeking to mask unattractive or unworthy ideas.

5 Words can be twisted, and on our campuses this is what has happened to "sustainability." We've seen this before. "Diversity," for example, appealed to tolerance, but

was twisted into a rationalization for special privilege and coercive policy. "Multicultural-ism" initially seemed a call to appreciate other cultures, but turned out to be primarily an attack on our own. "Sustainability" has followed this crooked path, appealing initially to our obligation to give future generations a clean and healthy planet, but quickly turn-ing into a thicket of ideological prescriptions.

6   In its career as a politically correct euphemism, sustainability has begun to cause some serious mischief.

2. MISTAKING SCARCITY

7   The sustainability movement by and large mistakes the fundamental problem dealt with by the discipline of economics: scarcity. Economics has shown us that scarcity of material goods is basic. Humans can respond to scarcity in many ways, including hoarding, theft, war, and oligarchy. But among the most constructive responses are trade, substitution, the development of markets, and technological innovation.

8   The sustainability movement, however, embraces the notion that the best ap-proach to the problem of scarcity is generally the maximal conservation of existing resources. That can be accomplished only by curtailing use, and in the effort to achieve sharp reductions in the use of resources, the sustainability movement favors govern-ment regulation as key. The sustainability movement is, in its essence, neo-Malthusian. (It supposes that, short of intervention, population growth will outstrip resources.)

9   There are, to be sure, advocates of sustainability who are friendlier towards the roles of innovation and markets in addressing future needs, but they do not represent the mainstream of the movement.

3. MALIGNING PROGRESS

10   Historically, progress has depended on finding means to do more with less, or do more by converting the previously unusable into a source of value. Because the sustainability movement has so little confidence in the power of technological innovation, it is essen-tially anti-progress. Indeed some sustainability advocates openly declare their hostility to the industrialization of the West and the spread of advanced economic structures to the rest of the world. Instead of progress, the sustainability movement prefers control. Progress proceeds through innovation; sustainability through regulation.

11   While not inherently at cross-purposes with progress, regulation can thwart it by replacing market mechanisms with planned allocation, thereby diminishing the in-centives for invention. The trade-offs between regulation and innovation will vary from case to case and need to be specifically analyzed. But turning sustainability, as often happens, into a moral imperative, a public icon, a matter of unquestioned doctrine, frustrates rational canvass.

4. MISLEADING ASSUMPTIONS

12   The sustainability movement often simply assumes what it cannot show. Is the world running out of key resources? Has consumption in developed countries reached "un-sustainable" levels? In view of global warming or climate change, do we need to insti-tute dramatic changes in the world economy? Such questions, if asked at all, tend to

be asked rhetorically, as if the answers were self-evident. Or if the situation requires an answer, we are met with spurious declarations of authority: the Intergovernmental Panel on Climate Change says this; the "consensus" of scientists says that.

13 Sustainability in this sense is becoming a means of question-begging, of preempting discussion about the best ways of dealing with the problem of scarcity.

14 To be sure, the National Association of Scholars does not have its own answers to these important questions. To the extent that the questions are really questions and not just rhetorical devices, they are beyond our scope as an organization to answer. But it is not beyond our scope to insist on respect for the scientific method and conclusions based on the best available evidence, not mere assumptions packaged to look like science.

5. STIFLING INQUIRY

15 The sustainability movement's aversion to progress and its tendency to assume rather than argue its basic propositions runs against the spirit of higher education. Our institutions of higher learning have long been great centers of inquiry. They have helped to drive technological progress for more than four centuries, and have been instrumental as well in driving economic development. To transform sustainability into mindless mantra—absorbed by students, faculty, and staff through catchword repetition—risks replacing the West's traditional optimism with a reflexive self-denial. That shouldn't be the vocation of America's higher educators.

6. MISUSING AUTHORITY

16 The sustainability movement arrived on campuses mainly at the invitation of college presidents and administrative staff in areas such as student activities and residence life. That means that it largely escaped the scrutiny of faculty members and that it continues to enjoy a position of unearned authority. In many instances, the movement advances by administrative fiat, backed up by outside advocacy groups and students recruited for their zeal in promoting the cause. Agenda-driven organizations—such as the Association for the Advancement of Sustainability in Higher Education (AASHE) and the American College and University Presidents' Climate Commitment (ACUPCC)—have taken advantage of academic sensibilities to turn sustainability into what is in many cases, a campus fetish. Sustainability also gets promoted by resort to pledges, games, competitions, and a whole variety of psychological gimmicks that bypass serious intellectual inquiry.

17 Some results are relatively trivial. For example, at certain institutions, cafeteria trays have been banned to save food, water, and energy, leaving students and staff to juggle dishes, cups, and utensils as they move between counters and tables. Many campuses have also banned the sale of disposable water bottles to reduce plastic waste. Yet however laughable, such petty annoyances have a sinister penumbra. They advertise a willingness to bully that creates a more generalized climate of intimidation, spilling over into other domains.

7. ABUSING FREEDOM

18 One of these is academic freedom, and here the news is worse. As with diversity, some institutions have been pressuring faculties to incorporate "sustainability" across-the-

curriculum, requiring reports about the ways in which individual instructors have redesigned their teaching. Quite apart from the practical difficulties this creates in fields like music or philology, it invades the pivotal right of faculty members to interpret their subject matter freely. Belief in the imminence of environmental crisis, or the imperative of laying aside other intellectual priorities to address it, should not be a requirement for teaching or scholarship, or a standard of good academic citizenship. That it threatens to become so reflects a serious disturbance in the academic climate, to say nothing of being a tell-tale sign of the kind of hubris that infects ideologically empowered administrators.

8. IDEOLOGICAL AGGREGATION

19 When we hear the word "sustainability," most of us think of the environment, but for a long time many sustainability advocates have been staking claims to larger territory. They see sustainability as not just about the environment but also about economics and social justice. The movement takes as its unofficial logo a Venn diagram of three overlapping circles labeled accordingly. And many in the movement believe that to achieve a sustainable society, we must make coordinated radical changes in all three areas. In practice, this means that sustainability is used as a means of promoting to students a view that capitalism and individualism are "unsustainable," morally unworthy, and a present danger to the future of the planet.

20   Many sustainability advocates, particularly those situated in, or allied to, offices of student life, now contend that since moral choices inevitably produce a cascade of environmental consequences, moral reeducation is needed to ensure sustainability. Much of this is directed, at least implicitly, against traditional moral values. Having an affirmative attitude toward homosexuality, for instance, is reinterpreted so as to bear

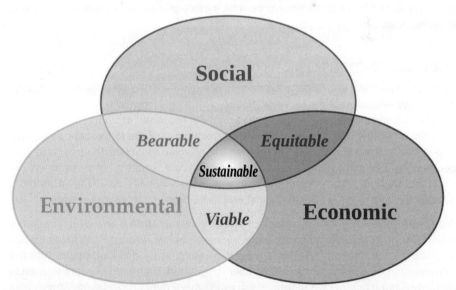

The Venn diagram demonstrates what sustainability advocates see as the relationships between the environmental, economic, and social spheres.

a positive environmental significance. Obviously, moral principles are an entirely valid topic for debate, on campus or off. In a university setting we would prefer this debate—to the degree it is under official auspices—to occur in those courses where it's materially relevant. Needless to say, students should also be completely free to discuss these questions outside the classroom. What should not happen, but nonetheless does, is for the debate to be stage-managed by dormitory-based bureaucrats, under the pretext of furthering the university's educational responsibilities.

9. MYSTIC DOOM

21 Fascination with decline and ruin are nothing new in Western thought. The sustainability movement combines a bureaucratic and regulatory impulse with an updated version of the Romantics' preoccupation with the end of civilization, and with hints of the Christian apocalyptic tradition. These are the "end times" in the view of some sustainability advocates—or potentially so in the eyes of many others. The movement has its own versions of sin and redemption, and in many other respects has a quasi-religious character. For some of the adherents, the earth itself is treated as a sentient deity; others content the mselves with the search for the transcendent in Nature.

22 As a creed among creeds, sustainability constitutes an upping of the ideological ante. Feminism, Afro-centrism, gay-liberation, and various other recent fads and doctrines, whatever else they were, were secular, speaking merely to politics and culture. The sustainability movement reaches beyond that, having nothing less than the preservation of life on earth at its heart.

23 The religious creeds of faculty members and students are their own business, but we have reason for concern when dogmatic beliefs are smuggled into the curriculum and made a basis for campus programs as though they were mere extensions of scientific facts.

RECOMMENDATIONS

24 Our list of nine ways in which the sustainability movement has gone wrong, of course, reflects our view of what the university ideally should be. Universities at their best adhere to reasoned discourse and scientific method: reasoned discourse in welcoming all serious perspectives, scientific method in subjecting them to the canons of logic and evidence. Universities are founded on the premise that clear thought must precede action. The sustainability movement as it is now assaults all of these ideals.

25 We can imagine, however, ways in which sustainability could play a far more constructive role in the university. To that end, NAS urges colleges and universities to:

Treat sustainability as an object of inquiry rather than a set of precepts. A great deal of worthwhile scientific work, research in engineering, and investigation in fields such as economics, for example, remains to be done on points that the movement in its current form tends to take for granted. Some of this work is already underway, but it is crowded together with much more dubious "research" that is little more than ideological touting. Universities have an obligation to distinguish legitimate inquiry from its counterfeits. This is where the reform of sustainability should begin.

Restore the debate. The sustainability movement poses as though many long-disputed matters are now settled. This isn't true. For sustainability to play a genuinely constructive part in the intellectual life of the nation's universities, it must submit to both cross-examination and to open dialog. The neo-Malthusian component of the movement (the idea that the world's population is outstripping its resources) is especially in need of the questioning that open debate can provide.

Level the playing field. It won't be much of a debate if sustainability advocates enjoy all the advantages of administrative favor. Advocates of alternative "narratives," such as those who emphasize progress through technological innovation, need comparable levels of support.

Get off the bandwagon. Signing statements like the "American College and University Presidents' Climate Commitment" preempts discussion of matters that should rightly be open for debate and for robust expression of different opinions. Efforts to collectivize opinion and to settle open questions by appealing to the prestige of signatories are, at bottom, anti-intellectual as well as a threat to academic freedom.

Quit bullying the skeptics. Even tenured faculty members complain of the heavy-handed tactics of sustainability advocates in their attempts to silence dissent. Matters are much worse for undergraduate students who often come under the gaze of "sustainabullies"—those students who, often with the encouragement of their colleges, take it upon themselves to enforce the ideology.

Promote intellectual freedom. Sustainability would be a much more attractive idea shorn of its coercive aspect. College and university officials should take care not to turn optional campus activities themed on sustainability into de facto requirements. Making sustainability part of freshman orientation, for example, preempts most students from ever risking the expression of an independent opinion. Advocacy of causes about which individuals can reasonably disagree should always take place in a manner in which disagreement can be voiced without fear of official sanction.

Respect pedagogical freedom. Recent efforts at some colleges and universities to quiz faculty members in every department about their contributions to sustainability in all their classes are another instance of administrative overreach. If sustainability is to thrive as one perspective among many it must be set free from such meddling. Faculty members must be free to interpret course content, and to exclude content they don't believe falls within the purview of their fields. Sustainability is not a subject that should be imposed across the curriculum.

Remember the mission. Make sound education rather than enthusiasm for social causes the essence of the academic mission. Good causes beckon every day. But even the best of social causes is, in the end, a diversion from the real purpose of the university.

26   We encourage college and university presidents, who have so often taken the lead in bringing the sustainability movement to campus, to take the lead again in correcting the excesses of the movement. We also encourage trustees, alumni, faculty members, administrators, and students to raise the pertinent questions and stand fast in their expectations of fair-minded debate.

WHAT'S NEXT

27   At the beginning of this statement we acknowledged that we are critiquing a movement that enjoys widespread popularity. We have no illusions that in setting out a brief summary of that movement's flaws we will prompt an equally widespread reassessment. It is human nature that once people invest themselves in a system of belief, they defend it with vigor and turn away from it only reluctantly and after numerous disappointments. The academy is no exception. Though it espouses in principle the rules of rational inquiry and reliance on unbiased evidence, academics too are prey to the dynamics of ideological conviction.

28   In that light, what purpose does our critique serve? We offer it in the spirit of a constructive alternative. We are far from dismissing the importance of environmental issues or the complicated connections between the environment, economic structures, and social conditions. Our overriding concern is that a movement that is in haste to promote its preferred solutions to what it sees as urgent problems has deflected higher education from its proper role. We seek to remind all those concerned with the future of American higher education what that role is, and to summon the responsible authorities back to their primary work.

29   We do this knowing that a large number of faculty members as well as members of the general public harbor misgivings about the sustainability movement but have all too often found themselves shut out of debate and unable even to find a forum in which to express their doubts. This statement offers those who are already skeptical encouragement. It offers those who have reserved judgment an invitation to embark on their own critical examination of the topic. And it offers those who are currently committed to the sustainability movement a challenge to their settled assumptions and a path to the exit when they are ready to rethink.

30   That rethinking is inevitable. The sustainability movement is, in a word, unsustainable. It runs too contrary to the abiding purposes of higher education; it is too rife with internal contradictions; and it is too contrary to the environmental, economic, and social facts to endure indefinitely. When it begins to sink, we trust that this document will be remembered as offering a useful map for finding higher—and firmer— ground

How "Green" Is Your T-Shirt?

Cotton is cheaper and takes less energy to manufacture than synthetic fibers. But over its lifetime, a cotton T-shirt requires twice the energy that is necessary to manufacture and maintain a polyester blouse. The main difference: Polyester garments can be washed at a lower temperature, can hang dry, and need no ironing.

The list below shows energy used over the lifetime of the garment, in kilowatt-hours.★

	COTTON T-SHIRT	POLYESTER BLOUSE
Raw material	4	9
Manufacturing	7	3
Transportation	2	1
Use	18	2

Use assumes 25 washes per garment. The cotton T-shirt is washed at 140 degrees Fahrenheit, followed by tumble-drying and ironing. The polyester blouse is washed at 104 degrees Fahrenheit, hung dry, and not ironed.

★The energy of one kilowatt-hour will operate a 40-watt lightbulb for a full day or a 19-inch color television for about four hours.

(*Source:* University of Cambridge Institute for Manufacturing)

MARK **BITTMAN**

Eating Food That's Better for You, Organic or Not

If you like food, you may have already encountered Mark Bittman (born 1950) through his cookbooks or through observing his efforts as a judge on the Food Network television show *Chopped* or through his appearances on the *Today Show* or NPR. But he is also a writer whose work appears often in the *New York Times*, where the following essay appeared in March 2009.

In the six-and-one-half years since the federal government began certifying food as "organic," Americans have taken to the idea with considerable enthusiasm. Sales have at least doubled, and three-quarters of the nation's grocery stores now carry at least some organic food. A Harris poll in October 2007 found that about 30 percent of Americans buy organic food at least on occasion, and most think it is safer, better for the environment and healthier.

2   "People believe it must be better for you if it's organic," says Phil Howard, an assistant professor of community, food and agriculture at Michigan State University.

3   So I discovered on a recent book tour around the United States and Canada.

4   No matter how carefully I avoided using the word "organic" when I spoke to groups of food enthusiasts about how to eat better, someone in the audience would inevitably ask, "What if I can't afford to buy organic food?" It seems to have become the magic cure-all, synonymous with eating well, healthfully, sanely, even ethically.

5   But eating "organic" offers no guarantee of any of that. And the truth is that most Americans eat so badly—we get 7 percent of our calories from soft drinks, more than we do from vegetables; the top food group by caloric intake is "sweets"; and one-third of nation's adults are now obese—that the organic question is a secondary one. It's not unimportant, but it's not the primary issue in the way Americans eat.

6   To eat well, says Michael Pollan, the author of "In Defense of Food," means avoiding "edible food-like substances" and sticking to real ingredients, increasingly from the plant kingdom. (Americans each consume an average of nearly two pounds a day of animal products.) There's plenty of evidence that both a person's health—as well as the environment's—will improve with a simple shift in eating habits away from animal products and highly processed foods to plant products and what might be called "real food." (With all due respect to people in the "food movement," the food need not be "slow," either.)

7   From these changes, Americans would reduce the amount of land, water and chemicals used to produce the food we eat, as well as the incidence of lifestyle diseases linked to unhealthy diets, and greenhouse gases from industrial meat production. All without legislation.

8   And the food would not necessarily have to be organic, which, under the United States Department of Agriculture's definition, means it is generally free of synthetic substances; contains no antibiotics and hormones; has not been irradiated or fertilized with sewage sludge; was raised without the use of most conventional pesticides; and contains no genetically modified ingredients.

9   Those requirements, which must be met in order for food to be labeled "U.S.D.A. Organic," are fine, of course. But they still fall short of the lofty dreams of early organic farmers and consumers who gave the word "organic" its allure—of returning natural nutrients and substance to the soil in the same proportion used by the growing process (there is no requirement that this be done); of raising animals humanely in accordance with nature (animals must be given access to the outdoors, but for how long and under what conditions is not spelled out); and of producing the most nutritious food possible (the evidence is mixed on whether organic food is more nutritious) in the most ecologically conscious way.

10   The government's organic program, says Joan Shaffer, a spokeswoman for the Agriculture Department, "is a marketing program that sets standards for what can be certified as organic. Neither the enabling legislation nor the regulations address food safety or nutrition."

11   People don't understand that, nor do they realize "organic" doesn't mean "local." "It doesn't matter if it's from the farm down the road or from Chile," Ms. Shaffer said. "As long as it meets the standards it's organic."

12   Hence, the organic status of salmon flown in from Chile, or of frozen vegetables grown in China and sold in the United States—no matter the size of the carbon footprint left behind by getting from there to here.

13   Today, most farmers who practice truly sustainable farming, or what you might call "organic in spirit," operate on small scale, some so small they can't afford the requirements to be certified organic by the government. Others say that certification isn't meaningful enough to bother. These farmers argue that, "When you buy organic you don't just buy a product, you buy a way of life that is committed to not exploiting the planet," says Ed Maltby, executive director of the Northeast Organic Dairy Producers Alliance.

3   But the organic food business is now big business, and getting bigger. Professor Howard estimates that major corporations now are responsible for at least 25 percent of all organic manufacturing and marketing (40 percent if you count only processed organic foods). Much of the nation's organic food is as much a part of industrial food production as midwinter grapes, and becoming more so. In 2006, sales of organic foods and beverages totaled about $16.7 billion, according to the most recent figures from Organic Trade Association.

14   Still, those sales amounted to slightly less than 3 percent of overall food and beverage sales. For all the hoo-ha, organic food is not making much of an impact on the way Americans eat, though, as Mark Kastel, co-founder of The Cornucopia Institute, puts it: "There are generic benefits from doing organics. It protects the land from the ravages of conventional agriculture," and safeguards farm workers from being exposed to pesticides.

15   But the questions remain over how we eat in general. It may feel better to eat an organic Oreo than a conventional Oreo, but, says Marion Nestle, a professor at New York University's department of nutrition, food studies and public health, "Organic junk food is still junk food."

16   Last week, Michelle Obama began digging up a patch of the South Lawn of the White House to plant an organic vegetable garden to provide food for the first family and, more important, to educate children about healthy, locally grown fruits and vegetables at a time when obesity and diabetes have become national concerns.

17   But Mrs. Obama also emphasized that there were many changes Americans can make if they don't have the time or space for an organic garden.

18   "You can begin in your own cupboard," she said, "by eliminating processed food, trying to cook a meal a little more often, trying to incorporate more fruits and vegetables."

19   Popularizing such choices may not be as marketable as creating a logo that says "organic." But when Americans have had their fill of "value-added" and overprocessed food, perhaps they can begin producing and consuming more food that treats animals and the land as if they mattered. Some of that food will be organic, and hooray for that. Meanwhile, they should remember that the word itself is not synonymous with "safe," "healthy," "fair" or even necessarily "good."

Making Cities Sustainable

For the first time ever, most people on Earth now live in cities. Not only that, nearly 60 million people migrate to cities each year, and the World Health Organization estimates that seven out of ten people will live in an urban area by 2050. Thirty million people live in and around Tokyo; 20 million in Delhi, Jakarta, and Mexico City; 15 million in Moscow, London, and Cairo. In the United States, 20 million people are gathered in and around New York City, 15 million in the greater Los Angeles area, and almost 10 million in the Chicago metropolitan area. As cities' populations expand, urban areas are spreading outward to accommodate these larger populations as well as the movement of urban dwellers to the edges of cities, motivated by the search for healthier, cleaner, and less densely populated environments. The result is urban sprawl on the fringes of urban areas, which in turn is accompanied by increased use of automobiles, the loss of open spaces, and general environmental decay. How can communities cope with the rapid urban population increase and the urban sprawl that accompanies it? How can cities become more sustainable?

Though "megacities" (metropolitan areas with a population of more than 10 million) have captured much of the attention, urban population growth often presents an even greater challenge to smaller towns and cities because they are less equipped to cope with the phenomenon. Sprawl in particular is a multidimensional challenge involving issues related to jobs, housing, transportation, water, and sewage, and as a result both its consequences and potential solutions

Top 10 Most Sprawling U.S. Metro Regions

1. Riverside-San Bernardino, CA
2. Greensboro-Winston-Salem-High Point, NC
3. Raleigh-Durham, NC
4. Atlanta, GA
5. Greenville-Spartanburg, SC
6. West Palm Beach-Boca Raton-Delray Beach, FL
7. Bridgeport-Stamford-Norwalk-Danbury, CT
8. Knoxville, TN
9. Oxnard-Ventura, CA
10. Fort Worth-Arlington, TX

Source: Ewing R, Pendall R, Chen D, 2002. Measuring Sprawl and Its Impact. The Character and Consequences of Metropolitan Expansion. Washington, D.C.: Smart Growth America.

are themselves multifaceted. For example, as cities grow and people seek housing in suburbs, the vehicle-miles traveled per day grow too: people living and working on Manhattan island, for instance, may depend on convenient public transit; however, their friends who work in Manhattan but live in the suburbs must often commute part or all of the way by car. The result is a spike in vehicular emissions—pollutants that foul the air, damage people's health, and contribute to climate change. Other environmental problems associated with population growth include garbage disposal, the destruction of wildlife habitat, and pollution of streams, rivers, and beaches. In response to these challenges, more and more people are asking how their urban living spaces might become more sustainable.

In recent years, the concept of "smart growth" has gained popularity as one possible solution. The objective of smart growth is to revitalize existing urban communities so that people are less inclined to leave them to move to lower-density residences on the urban fringe. Common smart-growth projects include expanding public transit; preserving urban green spaces; creating walkable, mixed-use areas (which allow residents to shorten or eliminate some trips and enjoy the cultural advantages of urban life); implementing energy-efficient building strategies; reducing noise; and cultivating distinctive, place-based urban identities. Cities throughout the nation—notably Portland, Oregon, but also notoriously sprawled cities such as Atlanta, Georgia—have begun to implement a number of smart-growth policies.

Here we present several arguments that connect with smart-growth values. Kaid Benfield proposes what he calls "great people habitats" within urban environments. The cofounder of Smart Growth America, a nationwide coalition that promotes urban sustainability efforts, Benfield argues for a reconceptualization of smart-growth metrics, asserting that "smart growth shouldn't be considered smart if it doesn't show respect to our historic buildings and local culture." Then, in an article first published in *Race, Poverty, and the Environment*, a periodical from the progressive group Urban Habitat, the activist Greg LeRoy points out that economic development subsidy programs (such as property tax abatements, corporate income tax credits, and low-interest loans) have essentially become subsidies for sprawl—subsidies that disadvantage the poor. Next, you will find an argument first published in the *American Journal of Public Health* by bioethicist David Resnick of the National Institute of Environmental Health Sciences. He explores how smart growth policies can address the problems of urban sprawl, why some people oppose such policies, and how using the tactics of deliberative democracy can help to bring communities to consensus on issues related to urban growth. Last, we offer a manifesto of sorts—"Lovable Green"—that was produced by Original Green, an organization advocating for traditional building practices that work with the environment, not against it.

Are there arguments being mounted in your community that dovetail with those of the smart growth advocates represented here? How will your community and your university or college manage itself in a sustainable way? And how might you develop your own written contributions to the ongoing debate?

Kaid Benfield

Why Smart Growth Can't Be the Only Answer

T he smart growth agenda has become a bit formulaic and even clinical.

2 I was lucky enough to be there at the beginning, when we first started using the phrase "smart growth" to describe an alternative to suburban sprawl, a better way of accommodating a growing population and economy with less damage to the environment. It did indeed represent, in a way, part of the "new environmentalism" . . . in that it was affirmative, a philosophy not opposed to development, but of making it better.

3 Most readers probably know the smart growth fundamentals: by building homes, shops and services on vacant and underutilized land left in our older communities by decades of disinvestment, and by building in more compact development patterns with more efficient transportation links, we can reduce the spread of environmental harm and growth in emissions while conserving valuable wilderness and rural land outside of the development footprint. More than anything else, smart growth was—and remains—about a more deliberate and sensible allocation of land and development.

4 We now have oodles of research quantifying the benefits of smart growth to the environment. If we build this way, we will reduce carbon emissions, air pollution, land consumption, and water runoff compared to a continuation of the sprawl paradigm that shaped our landscape in the last half of the 20th century. We have to do this.

5 And yet. Something has been nagging me about smart growth for years. I believe that, at least for those of us in the policy world, the smart growth agenda has become a bit formulaic and even clinical: we tell ourselves and others, for example, that we must increase settlement density, which we measure in dwelling units per acre or the ratio of building floor space to lot space; that we must reduce driving, which we measure by vehicle miles traveled; that we must reduce carbon emissions, which we measure by metric tons. And so on. If we're looking at a growth scenario, we may measure these things on a per capita basis.

6 We judge potential policy measures by how well they will produce these outcomes. When a new government action allows us to project out the numbers favorably, we rightfully applaud it. Often I'll be among the cheerleaders.

7 But, as I have opined before, the fact that we are increasing dwelling units per acre, reducing vehicle miles traveled per capita, and reducing tons of carbon emissions compared to sprawl does not mean that we are making great people habitat. We may be creating smart growth, while in some cases doing little for people or doing less for the natural environment than we could be. I believe that achieving the *fact* of smart growth,

Urban growth issues often pit bicycle and public transit advocates against those in favor of unrestricted automobile use. What are the arguments for and against each mode of transportation? What kind of policy might take the needs of both groups into account?

where we have it, is no longer enough, and may not warrant our enthusiasm as much as it did, say, a decade ago. It is time to focus more on the *quality* of what we are building.

8 Smart growth shouldn't be considered smart if it doesn't show respect to our historic buildings and local culture.

9 To an extent, we have become slaves to measurable outcomes. In the nonprofit world, our sources of funding demand it. Increasingly, so do our managers and never-ending strategic planning exercises. (I am so tempted to go into a detailed rant here but, really, this isn't the place.)

10 But what if we produce urban density that saves land and reduces carbon emissions, but overwhelms people with its scale, looks mediocre and, by the way, creates hotspots of environmental impacts? Should we still be applauding? Because, to my eye, that is exactly what has happened in some places.

11 I've been beating a drum on this cause for a while now. I've argued that so-called smart growth shouldn't be considered smart if it doesn't include green buildings and green infrastructure, if it doesn't show respect to our historic buildings and local culture, if it doesn't foster public health, if it isn't equitable. And these are just the more familiar topics. My colleagues in the smart growth world don't disagree with me about these things, but after they nod their heads in a meeting they go right back to work on urban density and transportation issues, because they must to fulfill obligations.

12   For a long while I thought the right tack was to reform smart growth from within, adding the concerns (such as green infrastructure and food) that weren't at the forefront when the movement was founded. Some leaders in our field are, in fact, convening a process to that end. There have been a couple of preliminary meetings. Maybe something good will come of this.

13   But my nagging feeling won't go away. Even if we add some neglected categories and tweak some others, we're still stuck in a box that makes it all about defined issues and, to a great extent, measurable outcomes. We remain fixated on things that can be accomplished through broad policy initiatives. That remains vitally important, but I don't think it's enough.

14   I've now come to the conclusion that smart growth is critical to a sustainable future, but it can only get us part way there. The truth is that much of what can make people habitat great cannot be quantified or put into identifiable categories. The process of creating a better, more sustainable world—anchored by better, more sustainable places—is as much art as science.

15   Our communities of the future must not only reduce carbon emissions, save land, and encourage use of transit, walking and bicycling. They must also contain beauty, warmth, places of solitude and reflection. They must be significantly more dense than sprawl, but also sometimes forego additional increments of density in order to maintain light, limit noise, provide privacy, and respect a human scale. They must be conducive to engaging the intellect and the spirit. When we pursue these things, we are out of the realm of smart growth *per se*, and into the realm of placemaking. I have become convinced that the two overlap but should not be mistaken for the same thing. In other words, sustainability in our built environment requires both smart growth *and* great placemaking.

16   If that's too mushy for you, I'll give you a more strategic reason. Those of us who are advocates of smart growth—and I've been one for going on twenty years—often make our case with numbers: amounts of pollution avoided, dollars saved in infrastructure expenses, acres of land conserved, and so on. Our opponents don't do that, at least not much (in part because the numbers are not on their side). They appeal to emotion: do you really want, they ask the public, to live in or amidst tall buildings? Don't you want a big yard for your kids or dog? Don't you want to keep the freedom that your car gives you? Those are not unreasonable questions.

17   If our preferences don't include not just good places but great ones, beautiful ones, lovable ones—places that provide what people seek but in a setting that is more sustainable—we lose in that set of arguments. People are naturally resistant to change and must be inspired in order to embrace it.

18   I don't think smart growth by itself gets us there. We need to stop thinking of smart growth as a goal but instead as a tool to achieving the more demanding goal of creating better, greener, more sustainable people habitat. If we want to win hearts as well as minds, we need to start paying much more attention to placemaking, to the quality of what we advocate. In fact, I would go further. If we want to *deserve* to win, we need to pay a lot more attention to making great places. It's not just about the numbers: to paraphrase [the poet] Gil Scott-Heron, the revolution will not be quantified.

A decades-long project in Boston put the multi-lane I-93 *(top)* underground and replaced it at ground level with green spaces and more pedestrian-friendly streets *(bottom)*. In what became known as The Big Dig, Bostonians invested heavily in a more livable cityscape to discourage suburban sprawl.

GREG **LEROY**

Subsidizing Sprawl: Economic Development Policies That Deprive the Poor of Transit, Jobs

Economic development subsidy programs—such as property tax abacements, corporate income cut credits and low-interest loans—were originally justified in the name of poverty reduction. Initiated as far back as the 1930s and accelerated in the 1950s, many of these programs were targeted to older areas and pockets of poverty that needed revitalization.

2   But over time, more and more of the 1,500 development subsidy programs nationwide have become part of the problem instead of the solution. Subsidies originally meant to rebuild older urban areas are being perverted into subsidies for suburban sprawl. Wal-Mart and other big box retailers are getting subsidies that allow them to simply pirate sales from existing merchants. Upscale residential and golf course projects are getting subsidies from programs originally designed to serve law-income neighborhoods.

Street Maps at the Same Scale

(Venice, Italy)   (Downtown Los Angeles, CA)   (Irvine, CA)

The more intersections per square mile, the more walkable the city. In his book, *Great Streets*, architect and city planner Allan Jacobs maps three cities—Venice, Italy; Downtown Los Angeles; and Irvine, California—at the same scale. In which city is walking probably the most enjoyable? Why would you expect more intersections to translate to more enjoyable walking?

3   The net effect has been to worsen sprawl and all of its disparate harms to communities of color: the outmigration of urban jobs, the growth of jobs in areas that are nor accessible by public transportation, and the resulting concentration of unemployment and poverty.

Deconstructing Sprawl Development

4   "Suburban sprawl" usually refers to development characterized by low density, a lack of transportation options, strict separation of residential from non-residential property, and job growth in newer suburbs with job decline in older areas. Sprawl causes increased dependence on automobiles and longer average commuting times, deteriorating air quality, and rapid consumption of open space in outlying areas. It also results in disinvestment of central city infrastructure and services, and strains city budgets at the core (due to a declining tax base) and in some suburbs.

5   The decentralization of jobs means work becomes scarce for low-skilled workers who are concentrated at the core. Many suburbs lack affordable housing and many suburban jobs are not accessible by public transit—either because a suburb has opposed the entry of transit lines or because jobs are thinly spread out far from transit routes. So sprawl effectively cuts central city residents off from regional labor markets. That means greater poverty for residents of core areas, who are disproportionately people of color.

6   What causes sprawl? Urban experts cite many factors, including some people's preference for low-density housing; white flight; lack of effective regional planning; competition between cities for jobs and tax base; "redlining" or geographic and racial discrimination against older areas by banks and insurance companies; crime and perceptions of crime; declining quality of central city schools; contaminated land or "brownfields;" exclusionary suburban zoning that blocks apartment construction; federal capital gains rules that encourage people to buy ever-larger homes; the historically low price of gasoline; and federal highway spending that far exceeds public transportation spending.

7   But another important factor is economic development subsidies like tax increment financing (TIF) and enterprise zones that have gone awry and are being abused in ways their creators never intended.

Sprawl Subsidy #1: TIF

8   Originally conceived to help revitalize depressed inner-city areas, tax increment financing, or TIF, allows a city to designate a small TIF district and say that the area will get redeveloped so property values will go up and property taxes will rise. When that happens, the tax revenue gets split into two streams. The first stream, set at the "base value" before redevelopment, continues to go where it always has: to schools, police, fire departments and other public services. The second stream is diverted back into the TIF district to subsidize the redevelopment. This diversion can last 15, 23, even 40 years—i.e., a lot of money for a long time.

9   Many states originally restricted TIF to truly needy areas with high rates of distress such as property abandonment, building code violations or poverty. Today TIF is allowed in 47 states and Washington, D.C. Over the year, about a third of the states have loosened their TIF rules so that even affluent areas qualify. The wealthy Chicago suburb of Lake Forest, for example, has a TIF district—and a Ferrari dealership. Pennsylvania's TIF statute allows a trout stream near Pittsburgh called Deer Creek to be TIFed because the land has "economically or socially undesirable land uses."

10   Worse still, a few states allow the sales tax increment to be "TIFed" on top of the property tax increment. That results in a perverse incentive to overbuild sprawling retail. A study by PriceWaterhouseCoopers about "greyfields"—the euphemism for dead malls—found that 7 percent of regional malls were already greyfields, and another 12 percent are "potentially moving towards greyfield status in the next five years." That would mean 389 dead malls by 2009.

11   Missouri, which allows sales tax TIF, is learning this lesson the hard way. The state has had a raging four-year debate about how to reform its TIF program before it subsidizes any more unnecessary new stores. State Senator Wayne Goode, D-St. Louis County, if the primary sponsor of a reform bill, "Putting public money into retail in a big metropolitan, area doesn't make any sense at all," Goode says. "It just moves retail sales around." About one-third of the 90-odd municipalities in St. Louis County collect "point of sale" sales tax, he explains. In other words, cities get to keep a portion of the sales tax if a purchase happens within their borders. The other two thirds of cities in the county pool their revenue. So the one-third fight each other for sales—and pirate sales from the two-thirds—often using TIF. Area developers go to great lengths to block reforms because the TIF is so lucrative.

12   As the *St. Louis Post-Dispatch* editorialized: "With towns handing out TIF like bubble gum, St. Louis may be getting over-stored, while developments are under-taxed. Projects that make no sense get built because of tax breaks."

13   Subsidizing new retail is almost always bad economics, and terrible public policy. Retail packs a lousy bang for the buck compared to manufacturing or almost any other activity. The "upstream" inputs do little for the local economy (think of all those goods from China at Wal-Mart), and the "down-stream" ripple effects are terrible because retail jobs are overwhelmingly part-time and poverty-wage, with no health care.

14   Suburban areas with the greatest numbers of high-income households will always have plenty of shopping opportunities. Supply chases demand. The only situation where retail can be legitimately called economic development—and therefore deserving of a subsidy—is in an older, disinvested neighborhood that is demonstrably underserved, and lacking basic retail amenities such a groceries, drugs and clothing.

Sprawl Subsidy #2: Enterprise Zones

15   Enterprise zones, another geographically targeted program intended to help poor inner-city areas, have also been weakened in many states so that affluent areas get multiple zone subsidies.

16   New York, for example, allows zones to be gerrymandered non-contiguously. So Buffalo's two original enterprise zones have morphed into more than 130 non-contiguous areas, raising questions about political favoritism. A scathing *Buffalo News* investigative series found that "[t]he program, crafted to create business in distressed areas and jobs for the down-and-out, has transmuted here into a subsidy program for the up-and-in"—including even downtown law firms.

17   In an episode that gives new meaning to the term "Philadelphia lawyer," law firms there are moving a few blocks into a "Keystone Opportunity Zone," which will make the law firm partners exempt from state income tax! Meanwhile, the city's African-American and Latino neighborhoods continue to suffer catastrophic rates of abandonment and unemployment.

18   Ohio has a large number of enterprise zones and they have a controversial history. A study from Policy Matters Ohio found that "[t]he very areas [that zones were] initially designed to help are now disadvantaged by the program. An aging infrastructure, a low tax base, weak education systems, and numerous costly social challenges place poor urban areas in a weak position relative to their wealthier suburban neighbors. Ohio's [zone program] has succeeded in making the playing field even more tilted against urban areas by extending to wealthier suburbs an additional fiscal tool with which to compete for firms."

Discriminatory Development

19   TIF and enterprise zones are just the tip of the iceberg when it comes to explaining how pro-sprawl development subsidies undermine jobs for the truly needy. A recent study by Good Jobs First, *Missing the Bus*, finds that not one of the 1,500, total state development programs nationwide requires—or even encourages—a company getting a subsidy in a metro area to locate the jobs at a site served by public transportation.

20   In other words, despite all the anti-poverty rhetoric that most programs come draped in, states are typically indifferent to whether they create jobs that low-income people can get to. Research has shown that African-American households are about three and a half times more likely than white families to not own a car, and Latino households are about two and a half times more likely. Given those facts, the discriminatory bias of economic development in the United States today could not be clearer.

DAVID B. **RESNIK**

Urban Sprawl, Smart Growth, and Deliberative Democracy

In the last two decades, public health researchers have demonstrated how the built environment—homes, roads, neighborhoods, workplaces, and other structures and spaces created or modified by people—can affect human health adversely.[1–7] Urban sprawl, a pattern of uncontrolled development around the periphery of a city, is an increasingly common feature of the built environment in the United States and other industrialized nations.[8] Although there is considerable evidence that urban sprawl has adverse environmental impacts and contributes to a variety of health problems—including obesity, diabetes, cardiovascular disease, and respiratory disease[9]—implementation of policies designed to combat sprawl, such as smart growth, has proven to be difficult.[10–17] One of the main difficulties obstructing the implementation of smart-growth policies is the considerable controversy these policies generate. Such controversy is understandable, given the fact that the stakeholders affected by urban-planning policies have conflicting interests and divergent moral and political viewpoints.[4] In some of these situations, deliberative democracy—an approach to resolving controversial public-policy questions that emphasizes open, deliberative debate among the affected parties as an alternative to voting—would be a fair and effective way to resolve urban-planning issues.

URBAN SPRAWL

2   Urban sprawl in the United States has its origins in the flight to the suburbs that began in the 1950s. People wanted to live outside of city centers to avoid traffic, noise, crime, and other problems, and to have homes with more square footage and yard space.[8,9] As suburban areas developed, cities expanded in geographic size faster than they grew in population. This trend has produced large metropolitan areas with low population densities, interconnected by roads.

3   Residents of sprawling cities tend to live in single-family homes and commute to work, school, or other activities by automobile.[8,9] People who live in large metropolitan areas often find it difficult to travel even short distances without using an automobile, because of the remoteness of residential areas and inadequate availability of mass transit, walkways, or bike paths. In 2002, the 10 worst US metropolitan areas for sprawl were Riverside–San Bernardino, CA; Greensboro–Winston-Salem–High Point, NC; Raleigh–Durham, NC; Atlanta, GA; Greenville–Spartanburg, SC; West Palm Beach–Boca Raton–Delray Beach, FL; Bridgeport–Stamford–Norwalk–Danbury, CT; Knoxville, TN; Oxnard–Ventura, CA; and Fort Worth–Arlington, TX.[8]

4   There is substantial evidence that urban sprawl has negative effects on human health and the environment.[4,7,9,19] An urban development pattern that necessitates automobile use will produce more air pollutants, such as ozone and airborne particulates, than a pattern that includes alternatives to automotive transportation. The relationship between air pollution and respiratory problems, such as asthma and lung cancer, is well documented.[4] Cities built around automobile use also provide fewer opportunities to exercise than cities that make it easy for people to walk or bike

to school, work, or other activities.[4] Exercise has been shown to be crucial to many different aspects of health, such as weight control, cardiovascular function, stress management, and so on.[20,21]

5   Because socioeconomically disadvantaged people in sprawling cities may have less access to exercise opportunities and healthy food than do wealthier people, sprawl may also contribute to health inequalities.[22] Urban sprawl can reduce water quality by increasing the amount of surface runoff, which channels oil and other pollutants into streams and rivers.[4] Poor water quality is associated with a variety of negative health outcomes, including diseases of the gastrointestinal tract, kidney disease, and cancer.[23] In addition to air and water pollution, adverse environmental impacts of sprawl include deforestation and disruption of wildlife habitat.[4]

SMART GROWTH

6   Many public health advocates have recommended smart growth as a potential solution to the problem of urban sprawl.[4,7, 9,20] Smart growth can be defined as a policy framework that promotes an urban development pattern characterized by high population density, walkable and bikeable neighborhoods, preserved green spaces, mixed-use development (i.e., development projects that include both residential and commercial uses), available mass transit, and limited road construction.[4,7,11] Smart growth was originally conceptualized as an aesthetically pleasing alternative to urban

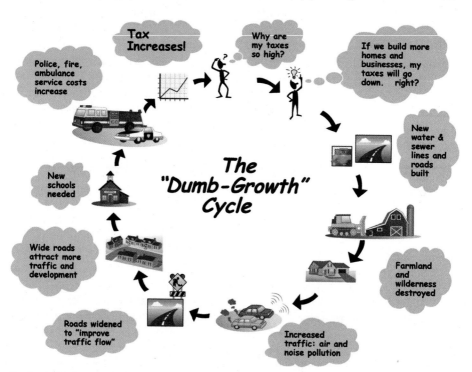

RochesterEnvironment.com aims to encourage dialogue on environmental issues in the area of Rochester, New York. What is the aim of these diagrams? How effective are they?

sprawl that would offer residents a high quality of life and the convenience of local amenities,[24] but it also has many potential health benefits, such as diminished air pollution, fewer motor vehicle accidents, lower pedestrian mortality, and increased physical exercise.[4,7] Smart growth is different from the concept of "garden suburbs" because it addresses issues of population density and transportation, not just availability of green space and preservation of agricultural land.[4]

7   In the 1970s, Portland, Oregon, was the first major city in the United States to establish smart growth urban planning by limiting urban growth to an area around the inner city.[11] Since the 1990s, many other urban areas have encouraged the development of planned communities in which people can live, shop, work, go to school, worship, and recreate without having to travel great distances by automobile. An example of one of these planned communities is Southern Village, situated on 300 acres south of Chapel Hill, North Carolina. Launched in 1996, Southern Village features apartments, townhouses, single-family homes, and a conveniently located town center with a grocery store, restaurants, shops, a movie theater, a dry cleaner, common areas, offices, health care services, a farmer's market, a day-care center, an elementary school, and a church. Southern Village is a walkable community with sidewalks on both sides of the streets and a 1.3-milegreenway running through the middle of town. Southern Village residents have access to mass transit via Chapel Hill's bus system and can enjoy free outdoor concerts in the common areas. More than 3,000 people live in Southern Village.[25]

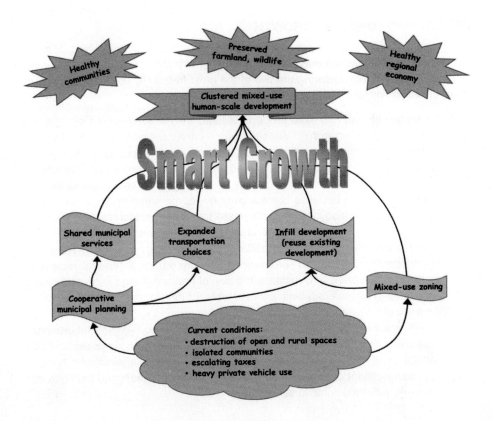

8   Urban sprawl has occurred largely because land owners and developers have made choices that promote their own economic and personal interests, which do not necessarily coincide with the public good.[18,25] Many community leaders have found it necessary to engage in centralized urban planning to promote smartgrowth.[11] Various laws and regulations can help to control land use and development. One of the most useful land-use policy tools is to change zoning laws to promote mixed-use development.[18] Zoning laws that forbid commercial development in residential areas promote sprawl because they require residents to travel greater distances to buy groceries, shop for clothes, and so on. Zoning laws can also be written to encourage high-density development and to require sidewalks and bike lanes.

9   Another important policy tool for promoting smart growth is to take steps to prevent development outside of a defined urban area, such as forbidding new housing construction on rural land, or setting administrative boundaries for city services, such as water and sewer connections.[18] The government can also use economic incentives to promote smart growth. Developers that follow smart-growth principles can be deemed eligible for reduced fees that help offset the costs of smart growth development, such as environmental impact fees. Conversely, developers that do not follow smart-growth principles can be subjected to higher fees.[18] Finally, governments can also invest public funds in projects and land uses that facilitate smart growth, such as mass-transit systems, recreation areas, and schools conveniently situated in neighborhoods.[2]

OBJECTIONS TO SMART GROWTH

10   Although smart growth appears to be a promising alternative to urban sprawl that could benefit public health and the environment, it has met with stiff resistance in some communities.[11,13,15,18,26] The following are five of the most frequently voiced objections to smart growth philosophies and policies:

1. Smart growth can decrease property values.[11–13] Property values may be adversely affected when high-density housing units are built in an area where low-density housing prevails because the increase in population density may exacerbate local traffic, congestion, and crime, which reduces property values. Property values may also be negatively affected by commercial development in a residential area, because commercial development can increase traffic and crime. Crime may also increase when mass transit connects a residential area to a location where crime is more prevalent, such as the inner city.
2. Smart growth can decrease the availability of affordable housing.[14,15] Requiring developers to build planned communities with mixed uses, sidewalks, recreation areas, and bike paths may increase the cost of housing. Also, setting aside large undeveloped spaces can limit land available for development, which drives up the price of housing.
3. Smart growth restricts property owners' use of their land.[10,17,27,28] Suburbanites have complained that laws requiring residential areas to have sidewalks and bike paths deprive them of lawn space. Farmers have protested against laws that prevent development of large portions of agricultural and forestland because this interferes with their rights to sell the land.

4. Smart growth can disrupt existing communities.[11,12,29,30] Low-density, quiet, noncommercial living areas may become high-density, noisy, and commercial. Historically low-income minority communities may be displaced to make room for high-rise, smart-growth housing complexes and upscale commercial development.

5. Smart growth may increase sprawl instead of decreasing it.[11,14] Some opponents of smart growth have argued that it often fails to achieve its intended effect and can actually exacerbate sprawl, traffic, congestion, pollution, and other urban problems.

11   Proponents of smart growth have responded to these and other objections at meetings of county planning boards and city councils, but opposition remains strong. Though smart growth has been a popular buzzword in real estate and urban development since the1990s, some leaders of the movement worry that it has lost momentum.[13,16] One reason why smart growth has stalled is that key stakeholders involved in the debate—real estate developers, land owners, environmentalists, public health advocates, and people living in metropolitan areas affected by smart-growth projects—have divergent interests, and the political process has often been unable to resolve these conflicts.[18]

DELIBERATIVE DEMOCRACY

12   One approach to resolving controversial public-policy questions that may be able to help loosen the smart-growth gridlock is a procedure known as deliberative democracy. Democracy is a form of government in which citizens wield political power by directly voting on issues, as in referendums, or by electing representatives to make decisions on their behalf.[31] Deliberative democracy emphasizes public deliberation on controversial issues as an alternative to voting.[31–34] In deliberative democracy, public deliberation should meet five conditions[31–34]:

1. Political legitimacy. The parties to the deliberation view the democratic process as a source of political legitimacy and are willing to abide by the decision that is reached.

2. Mutual respect. The parties are committed to respecting each other's diverging interests, goals, and moral, political, or religious viewpoints.

3. Inclusiveness. All parties with an interest in the issue can participate in the deliberative process, and a special effort is made to include those parties who often lack political influence because of socioeconomic status, lack of education, or other factors.

4. Public reason. Parties involved in the deliberation are committed to giving publicly acceptable arguments for their positions, drawing on publicly available evidence and information.

5. Equality. All parties to the deliberation have equal standing to defend and criticize arguments; there is no hierarchy or presumed line of authority.

13   Deliberative democracy was originally proposed as a method for resolving disagreements on controversial topics for which interested parties have conflicting interests and incompatible moral or political viewpoints, such as abortion, euthanasia, and

capital punishment. Proponents of deliberative democracy have argued that public deliberation about controversial topics can be more fair and effective than can traditional democratic procedures, which can be manipulated by powerful interest groups.[31-34] Critics of deliberative democracy have argued that it is an idealized theory of political decision-making whose conditions are often not met in the real world.[35] However, deliberative democracy may be worth trying when other approaches have failed to resolve controversial issues.

14   The debate about smart growth appears to be a good candidate for application of a deliberative approach because the parties have conflicting interests and divergent moral and political viewpoints.[10,11,18,28] Proponents of smart growth typically argue that collective action must be taken to promote common goods, such as public health, environmental integrity, or overall quality of life.[4,5,7] This type of argument is utilitarian in form because it asserts that public policies should promote the overall good of society.[36,37] Many of the property owners who oppose smart growth assume a libertarian perspective and argue that individual rights may be restricted only to prevent harm to others, not to promote the good of society.[18] According to libertarianism, the role of the state is to protect individual rights to life, liberty, or property; thus, government authority should not be used to redistribute wealth or advance social causes.[38,39] Critics who are concerned that smart growth may reduce the availability of affordable housing or adversely affect minority neighborhoods may subscribe to an egalitarian philosophy, such as Rawls's theory of justice, which holds that public policies should promote the interests of the least advantaged people in society and should not undermine equality of opportunity.[40,41] If smart growth benefits society as a whole at the expense of harming its least advantaged members by reducing the availability of affordable housing or disrupting minority neighborhoods, then it would violate Rawls's egalitarian principles of justice. Thus, the debate about smart growth can be viewed as a conflict among three competing visions of social justice: utilitarianism, libertarianism, and egalitarianism.

DELIBERATING ABOUT SMART GROWTH

15   Smart growth is an important strategy for combating the adverse public health, environmental, and aesthetic effects of urban sprawl. Because proponents and opponents of smart growth have conflicting interests and divergent moral and political viewpoints, deliberative democracy may be a fair and effective procedure for addressing some of the controversies surrounding policy proposals designed to counteract urban sprawl. To implement a deliberative approach, governments should sponsor open community forums on issues related to sprawl and smart growth, such as focus groups, public debates, and town-hall meetings. The deliberations that occur at these public forums should supplement the discussions that take place on county planning board or city council meetings. The goal of these public forums should be to foster open debate, information sharing, constructive criticism, and mutual understanding. Forums should be well-publicized and open to all parties with an interest in the proceedings. A special effort should be made to invite participants from groups that lack political influence.[42] Many communities have already held open forums on smart growth that embody some of the principles of deliberative democracy, but many others have not.[11,18,26] Communities that have not tried the deliberative approach should attempt it; those that have already held open forums should continue deliberating.

REFERENCES

1. Fitzpatrick K. *Unhealthy Places*. New York, NY: Routledge; 2000.

2. Frank L, Engelke P, Schmid T. *Health and Community Design: The Impact of the Built Environment on Physical Activity*. Washington, DC: Island Press; 2003.

3. Jackson RJ. The impact of the built environment on health: an emerging field. *Am J Public Health*. 2003; 93(9): 1382–1384.

4. Frumkin H, Frank L, Jackson R. *Urban Sprawl and Public Health*. Washington, DC: Island Press; 2004.

5. Corburn J. Confronting the challenges in reconnecting urban planning and public health. *Am J Public Health*. 2004; 94(4): 541–546.

6. Rao M, Prasad S, Adshead F, Tissera H. The built environment and health. *Lancet*. 2007; 370(9593): 1111–1113.

7. Jackson R, Kochtitzky C. Creating a healthy environment: the impact of the built environment on public health. Atlanta, GA: Centers for Disease Control and Prevention; 2009. Available at: http://www.cdc.gov/healthyplaces/articles/Creating%20A%20Healthy%20Environment.pdf. Accessed July 12, 2009.

8. Ewing R, Pendall R, Chen D. Sprawl scores for 83 metropolitan regions. Washington, DC: Smart Growth America; 2002. Available at: http://www.smartgrowthamerica.org/sprawlindex/chart.pdf. Accessed July 24, 2009.

9. Frumkin H. Urban sprawl and public health. *Public Health Rep*. 2002; 117(3): 201–217.

10. Whoriskey P. Planners' brains vs. public's brawn: neighbors' hostility to dense projects impairs Md. land preservation. *Washington Post*. August 10, 2004:A1. Available at: http://www.washingtonpost.com/wp-dyn/articles/A52900-2004Aug9.html. Accessed December 10, 2009.

11. Harris J, Evans J. Sprawl brawl: battle lines drawn in smart growth debate. *Real Estate Issues*, April 2000. Available at: http://recenter.tamu.edu/pdf/1371.pdf. Accessed July 26, 2009.

12. Waite D. It's not smart growth. *Gainesville Sun*. May 22, 2009. Available at: http://www.gainesville.com/article/20090522/NEWS/905229984. Accessed July 25, 2009.

13. Ward B. Report: smart growth failing. *Carroll County Times*. March 11, 2009. Available at: http://www.carrollcountytimes.com/article_4e9dc828-6126-5ffb-9fbf-33a673b3a924.html. Accessed July 26, 2009.

14. Staley S. The peril and promise of smart growth: is Ohio ready for regional planning? Columbus, OH: Buckeye Institute; July 2004. Available at: http://www.buckeyeinstitute.org/docs/smartgrowth72304.pdf. Accessed December 10, 2009.

15. Orski C, Shaw J. Smart growth? Sprawl-reducing policies suffer setback. *Rocky Mountain News*. July 9, 2005. Available at: http://www.perc.org/articles/article575.php. Accessed December 10, 2009.

16. Hirschhorn J. Why the smart growth movement will fail. Planetizen Web site. Available at: http://www.planetizen.com/node/55. Published June 17, 2002. Accessed December 10, 2009.

17. Berg N. Suburban officials try to build sidewalks amid local opposition. Planetizen Web site. Available at: http://www.planetizen.com/node/26436. Published August 21, 2007. Accessed December 10, 2009.

18. Ramirez de la Cruz E. Local political institutions and smart growth: an empirical study of the politics of compact development. *Urban Aff Rev*. 2009; 45(2): 218–246.

19. Frumkin H. Health, equity, and the built environment. *Environ Health Perspect.* 2005; 113(5): A290–A291.

20. Committee on Environmental Health, Tester JM. The built environment: designing communities to promote physical activity in children. *Pediatrics.* 2009; 123(6): 1591–1598.

21. Sallis JF, Glanz K. Physical activity and food environments: solutions to the obesity epidemic. *Milbank Q.* 2009; 87(1): 123–154.

22. Gordon-Larsen P, Nelson M, Page P, Popkin B. Inequality in the built environment underlies key health disparities in physical activity and obesity. Pediatrics. 2006; 117(2): 417–424.

23. Barzilay J, Weinberg W, Eley J. *The Water We Drink: Water Quality and Its Effects on Health.* Piscataway, NJ: Rutgers University Press; 1999.

24. Fox W, ed. *Ethics and the Built Environment.* New York, NY: Routledge; 2000.

25. Southern Village Web site. Southern Village: a new old neighborhood. Available at: http://www.southernvillage.com/images/sv_history.pdf. Published November 12, 2006. Accessed July 24, 2009.

26. Downs A. Smart growth: why we discuss it more than we do it. *J Am Plann Assoc.* 2005;71(4):367–378.

27. Gilroy L. The human face of smart growth opposition. Reason Foundation Web site. Available at: http://reason.org/news/show/the-human-face-of-smartgrowth. Published September 13, 2002. Accessed December 11, 2009.

28. Utt R. Can both sides of the sprawl debate find common ground on property rights? Heritage Foundation Web site. Available at: http://www.heritage.org/research/smartgrowth/wm730.cfm. Published April 25, 2005. Accessed July 26, 2009.

29. Campbell C. Faulty towers? Construction revives gentrification fears. *Chapel Hill News.* March 4, 2009:A1.

30. Campbell C. Vandals try to fight Greenbridge condos. *News and Observer.* April 28, 2009:B1.

31. Gutmann A, Thompson D, eds. *Why Deliberative Democracy?* Princeton, NJ: Princeton University Press; 2004.

32. Gutmann A, Thompson D. *Democracy and Disagreement.* Cambridge, MA: Harvard University Press; 1998.

33. Cohen J. *Philosophy, Politics, Democracy.* Cambridge, MA: Harvard University Press; 2009.

34. Rawls J. *Political Liberalism.* New York, NY: Columbia University Press; 1993.

35. Fishkin J, Laslett P. *Debating Deliberative Democracy.* Somerset, NJ: Wiley-Blackwell; 2003.

36. Mill J. *Utilitarianism.* 2nd ed. Indianapolis, IN: Hackett; 2002.

37. Singer P. *Practical Ethics.* 2nd ed. Cambridge, UK: Cambridge University Press; 1999.

38. Nozick R. *Anarchy, State, and Utopia.* New York, NY: Basic Books; 1974.

39. Boaz D. *Libertarianism: A Primer.* New York, NY: Free Press; 1998.

40. Rawls J. *A Theory of Justice.* Cambridge, MA: Harvard University Press; 1971.

41. Daniels N. *Just Health.* Cambridge, UK: Cambridge University Press; 2007.

42. Shrader-Frechette K. *Environmental Justice.* New York, NY: Oxford University Press; 2002.

Original Green

Lovable

Any serious conversation about sustainable buildings must begin with the issue of Lovability. If a building cannot be loved, then it is likely to be demolished and carted off to the landfill in only a generation or two. All of the embodied energy of its materials is lost (if they are not recycled.) And all of the future energy savings are lost, too. Buildings continue to be demolished for no other reason except that they cannot be loved. Even an architectural landmark as celebrated as the Boston City Hall is in danger of this fate because only an architect could love it. It is not possible for a building to be considered sustainable when its parts reach a landfill in a generation or two.

2   The popular green community is now advocating that every building should have a plan for its eventual demolition and recycling. At first, this seems like an honorable goal. But in reality, it is an admission of the inability to build in a lovable fashion. Our ancestors once built for the ages, and the best of their buildings could last for a thousand years or more. Even the everyday buildings lining every street regularly lasted for centuries. And they lasted because they could be loved.

3   Many ask today how it is possible to know what other people love, and some are even offended at the proposition that we might know what future generations might love. This suspicion is built upon the notion that beauty is in the eye of the beholder, and is predicated upon the model of architecture as fashion.

4   But architecture can do so much better than that. Because that which is the most intensely of our time today is also the most quickly out-of-date tomorrow. If we focus on what it means to be human rather than just what is popular in this moment, then it is clear that some things have resonated with humans throughout the ages. These include shapes that reflect the basic arrangement of the human body, which has a head, a body, and feet, or a cap, a shaft, and a base. The human body also is arranged horizontally with equal members on either side, at least externally, although our internal organs are arranged simply to do their jobs properly. And the exterior symmetry can be very relaxed, like when someone is sprawled out on a couch, or may be very rigid, like a soldier standing at attention.

5   Humans also resonate both with proportions found in the human body, and with a set of mathematical proportions that are both rational (1:1, 4:3, 3:2, etc.) and irrational (the square root of 2, the Golden Mean, etc.). Humans also resonate with natural laws,

such as the law of gravity. In other words, they don't just expect for things to stand up, but also to look like they are capable of standing up. Nobody except an architect wants to walk into a building built so thinly that it appears to be in imminent danger of collapse.

6   So while it is not possible to guess what architectural fashions might be like in 20 or 30 human generations (or not even next year, for that matter,) it most certainly is possible to stack the deck in our favor by building things that incorporate patterns that reflect timeless aspects of our humanity. Doing so extends the efficiency of what we build today into the distant future.

FROM READING TO WRITING

1. Analyze the paired arguments by either Wendell Berry and the National Association of Scholars, or by Berry and Jared Diamond: How is each argument the product of its audience and purpose? What sources of argument (ethical appeals, emotional appeals, and logical appeals) does each author choose and why? (See Chapter 6 for more on rhetorical analysis.)

2. Compare the various photos and charts that appear in this chapter. What visual argument does each photo seem to make? (See Chapter 7 for guidance on analyzing visuals.)

3. Write an argument that makes its point by defining a key term related to environmental concerns. You might choose to change someone's attitude toward a particular practice or concept in order to defend or challenge it, for instance, by defining it in a certain way. For example, you might start with the claim that "Green clothes are just a marketing ploy for the fashion industry to cash in on consumers' increased environmental awareness" or "Global warming is actually a blessing in disguise for some of the world." (See Chapter 8 for strategies for writing definition arguments.)

4. Propose a change in policy related to an environmental issue in your community. (See Chapter 13 for help with writing a proposal argument.)

5. Write a rebuttal of an article related to the environment in your local or school newspaper. Imitate, as appropriate, the moves you see in the statement by the National Association for Scholars, and see Chapter 12 for advice on rebuttals. Consider whether you wish to show the weaknesses in the article, whether you wish to counterargue, or both.

6. Write an essay that recounts a personal experience of yours to make an argumentative point related to the environment. It could be a story about camping or hiking, for example, or a tale of your encounter with some environmental problem or challenge. (See Chapter 11 for advice on writing narrative arguments.)

23 | Education

Joe Heller/Cagle Cartoons, Inc.

Education in American Society

Why have Americans always been so passionate about issues related to education? For one thing, education issues affect every American in a personal way because no other people strive for universal education with the zeal that Americans do. True, there is a strong anti-intellectual strain in American life, and true, not everyone appreciates the mandate for universal education; but it is also true that Americans do pursue with a passion the ideal of "education for all" both as a means of self-improvement and as the source of the enlightened citizenry required by democratic institutions. For another thing, education issues in America are decided locally and immediately. The relatively decentralized nature of our educational "system" (not that American education is as monolithic as the term *system* implies) encourages continuing and passionate public discussion among citizens interested in shaping the policies and practices of local schools.

What principles should guide educational policy in the United States? That fundamental question, which lies behind most of the debates about education, has been restated in a compelling way by the American philosopher and educational reformer John Dewey: *Should society be a function of education,* or *should education be a function of society?* In other words, should educational institutions be developed to perpetuate American institutions and values and to develop a skilled workforce for the American economy ("education as a function of society")? Or should educational institutions be developed chiefly in order to critique and reform American institutions in the interest of creating a more just and equitable society ("society as a function of education")? To put it yet another way: Should schools emphasize mastery of bodies of knowledge, "what every educated citizen needs to know"? Or instead should they emphasize practical learning skills—problem-solving ability, flexibility, independent thinking, and resourcefulness? Most people would answer "Both": Education should equip people both with practical, vocational abilities and with the critical and communication skills necessary to make for a vibrant, resourceful, just society. Yet that answer only complicates the issue, for in what proportion should schools develop creative criticizers and questioners versus efficient and adjusted workers?

Contemporary Arguments

The arguments included in this chapter bear directly on the issue of "education as a function of society" and "society as a function of education." While considerable controversy today concerns the goals of primary and secondary education— so that matters such as school choice, charter schools, No Child Left Behind legislation, and a host of reform proposals remain topics of heated debate in the United States—here we include arguments that are specifically related to higher education. What should a college student be and do? And how might college students learn most effectively and efficiently?

The selections that follow address those basic and vital questions. Andrew Delbanco opens the chapter by defining higher education in a way that protects its traditional function of preparing students for full citizenship—that is, preparing them to live productive lives in both an economic sense and a cultural sense. Delbanco promotes a college experience that will offer graduates marketable abilities as well as the intellectual skills needed to shape an effective American society. Next Salman Khan proposes changes in the college experience (and the learning experience more broadly) that are as explicitly practical as they are revolutionary: He aims to fundamentally remake the college experience by emphasizing practicality. Two arguments then take up the implications of online learning and specifically the advent of MOOCs (Massive Open Online Courses). You've heard of MOOCs, the online courses that are being made available for free to anyone with access to a computer; will they completely remake higher education and replace the traditional college experience by offering cost-effective and learning-effective course experiences that extend throughout our lives? Kevin Carey provides an informed defense of MOOCs that is attentive to practical issues, while Scott

Carlson maintains that residential colleges will incorporate MOOC offerings in a manner that preserves colleges' traditional functions, values, and value. And David Brooks, the respected newspaper columnist, has advice for how college students might learn to improve social cohesion and interpersonal cooperation.

The chapter concludes with an Issue in Focus: Is College Worth the Price? With college tuition rates spiking and the U.S. economy struggling to recover its vitality, critics are questioning the wisdom of encouraging so many people to attend college. The Issue in Focus not only confronts the controversy directly but also offers practical alternatives to college that most high school students might not have considered—and that might be easier for state legislatures to finance.

Taken together, the readings you encounter in this chapter should give you a better understanding of the issues that you and your classmates are grappling with right now. As you read, remember that the perennial nature of debates about education can be frustrating, especially to educational leaders. Hard questions rarely go away. But the very relentlessness of the debates probably brings out the best feature of a democratic society: the freedom of citizens to shape policy through open, public, and passionate debate.

ANDREW DELBANCO

College at Risk

Andrew Delbanco (born 1952) teaches American Studies and humanities courses at Columbia University. Described by *Time* in 2001 as "America's best social critic," he is a celebrated scholar with many books to his credit, including works on Puritan America, Herman Melville, and nineteenth-century religious and social history. He has articulated his views on higher education in *Required Reading: Why Our American Classics Matter Now* (1997) and in his 2012 defense of the four-year college education model, *College: What It Was, Is, and Should Be.* In "College at Risk," which appeared on February 26, 2012, in the *Chronicle of Higher Education,* Delbanco argues for "an abiding attachment to the college ideal" because it promotes both the advancement of individuals and the improvement of society as a whole.

I f there's one thing about which Americans agree these days, it's that we can't agree. Gridlock is the name of our game. We have no common ground.

2   There seems, however, to be at least one area of cordial consensus—and I don't mean bipartisan approval of the killing of Osama bin Laden or admiration for former Rep. Gabrielle Giffords's courage and grace.

3   I mean the public discourse on education. On that subject, Republicans and Democrats speak the same language—and so, with striking uniformity, do more and more college and university leaders. "Education is how to make sure we've got a workforce that's productive and competitive," said President Bush in 2004. "Countries that outteach us today," as President Obama put it in 2009, "will outcompete us tomorrow."

4   What those statements have in common—and there is truth in both—is an instrumental view of education. Such a view has urgent pertinence today as the global "knowledge economy" demands marketable skills that even the best secondary schools no longer adequately provide. Recent books, such as *Academically Adrift: Limited Learning on College Campuses*, by Richard Arum and Josipa Roksa, and *We're Losing Our Minds: Rethinking American Higher Education*, by Richard P. Keeling and Richard H. H. Hersh, marshal disturbing evidence that our colleges and universities are not providing those skills, either—at least not well or widely enough. But that view of teaching and learning as an economic driver is also a limited one, which puts at risk America's most distinctive contribution to the history and, we should hope, to the future of higher education. That distinctiveness is embodied, above all, in the American college, whose mission goes far beyond creating a competent workforce through training brains for this or that functional task.

5   College, of course, is hardly an American invention. In ancient Greece and Rome, young men attended lectures that resembled our notion of a college course, and gatherings of students instructed by settled teachers took on some of the attributes we associate with modern colleges (libraries, fraternities, organized sports). By the Middle Ages, efforts were under way to regulate the right to teach by issuing licenses, presaging the modern idea of a faculty with exclusive authority to grant degrees. In that broad sense, college as a place where young people encounter ideas and ideals from teachers, and debate them with peers, has a history that exceeds two millennia.

6   But in several important respects, the American college is a unique institution. In most of the world, students who continue their education beyond secondary school are expected to choose their field of specialization before they arrive at university. In America there has been an impulse to slow things down, to extend the time for second chances and defer the day when determinative choices must be made. When, in 1851, Herman Melville wrote in his great American novel *Moby-Dick* that "a whaleship was my Yale College and my Harvard," he used the word "college" as a metaphor for the place where, as we would say today, he "found himself." In our own time, a former president of Amherst College writes of a young man experiencing in college the "stirring and shaping, perhaps for the first time in his life, [of] actual convictions—not just gut feelings—among his friends and, more important, further down, in his own soul."

7   In principle, if not always in practice, this transformative ideal has entailed the hope of reaching as many citizens as possible. In ancient Greece and Rome, where women were considered inferior and slavery was an accepted feature of society, the study of *artes liberates* was reserved for free men with leisure and means. Conserved by medieval scholastics, renewed in the scholarly resurgence we call the Renaissance and again in the Enlightenment, the tradition of liberal learning survived in the Old World but remained largely the possession of ruling elites. But in the New World, beginning in the Colonial era with church-sponsored scholarships for promising schoolboys, the story of higher education has been one of increasing inclusion. That story continued in the early national period through the founding of state colleges, and later through the land-grant colleges created by the federal government during the Civil War. In the 20th century, it accelerated with the GI Bill, the "California plan" (a tiered system designed to provide virtually universal postsecondary education), the inclusion of women and minorities in previously all-male or all-white institutions, the growth of

community colleges, and the adoption of "need-based" financial-aid policies. American higher education has been built on the premise that human capital is widely distributed among social classes and does not correlate with conditions of birth or social status.

8   Seen in that long view, the distinctive contribution of the United States to the history of liberal education has been to deploy it on behalf of the cardinal American principle that all persons have the right to pursue happiness, and that "getting to know," in Matthew Arnold's much-quoted phrase, "the best which has been thought and said in the world" is helpful to that pursuit. That understanding of what it means to be educated is sometimes caricatured as elite or effete, but in fact it is neither, as Arnold makes clear by the (seldom-quoted) phrase with which he completes his point: "and through this knowledge, turning a stream of fresh and free thought upon our stock notions and habits." Knowledge of the past, in other words, helps citizens develop the capacity to think critically about the present—an indispensable attribute of a healthy democracy.

9   These ideals and achievements are among the glories of our civilization, and all Americans should be alarmed as they come to be regarded as luxuries unaffordable for all but the wealthy few. A former director of the for-profit University of Phoenix put it this way in an interview on *Frontline*: "I'm happy that there are places in the world where people sit down and think. We need that. But that's very expensive. And not everybody can do that." Meanwhile, too many selective nonprofit colleges are failing to enroll significant numbers of students from low-income families, and those colleges are thereby reinforcing rather than ameliorating the discrepancies of wealth and opportunity in American society. Yet even at selective nonprofit colleges, where students come overwhelmingly from affluent families and are still invited to "sit down and think," they are more and more likely to choose fields of study for their preprofessional utility—on the assumption that immersing themselves in learning for the sheer joy of it, with the aim of deepening their understanding of culture, nature, and, ultimately, themselves, is a vain indulgence.

10   One of the difficulties in making the case for liberal education against the rising tide of skepticism is that it is almost impossible to persuade doubters who have not experienced it for themselves. The Puritan founders of our oldest colleges would have called it "such a mystery as none can read but they that know it."

11   Testimony by converts can help. One student, born and educated in China, who came to the United States recently to attend Bowdoin College, encountered the modern version of the Puritan principle that no communicants should "take any ancient doctrine for truth till they have examined it" for themselves. "Coming from a culture in which a 'standard answer' is provided for every question, I did not argue with others even when I disagreed. However, Bowdoin forced me to reconsider 'the answer' and reach beyond my comfort zone. In my first-year seminar, 'East Asian Politics,' I was required to debate with others and develop a habit of class engagement," he said in an interview with the Web site *Inside Higher Ed* about a book he and two other Chinese students wrote for an audience in China, about their liberal-arts educations in America.

12   "One day we debated what roles Confucianism played in the development of Chinese democracy. Of the 16 students in the classroom, 15 agreed that Confucianism impeded China's development; but I disagreed. I challenged my classmates. Bowdoin made me consistently question the 'prescribed answer.'"

13   That kind of education does not lack for eloquent exponents. A current roster would include, among many others, Martha C. Nussbaum (in her books *Not For Profit: Why Democracy Needs the Humanities*, 2010, and *Cultivating Humanity: A Classical Defense of Reform in Liberal Education*, 1997, as well as in an essay in *The Chronicle*, "The Liberal Arts Are Not Elitist"), Anthony T. Kronman (*Educations End: Why Our Colleges and Universities Have Given Up on the Meaning of Life*, 2007), Mark William Roche (*Why Choose the Liberal Arts*, 2010), and, most recently, in *The Chronicle*, Nannerl O. Keohane, "The Liberal Arts as Guideposts in the 21st Century." But in our time of economic retrenchment, defenders of the faith are sounding beleaguered. Everyone who is honest about academe knows that colleges and universities tend to be wasteful and plagued by expensive redundancies. The demand for greater efficiency is reasonable and, in some respects, belated. The cost of college must be reined in, and its "productivity"—in the multiple senses of student proficiency, graduation rates, and job attainment—must be improved. The trouble is that many reforms, and most efficiencies, whether achieved through rational planning or imposed by the ineluctable process of technological change, are at odds with practices that are essential if liberal education is to survive and thrive.

14   High on the list of such practices is the small-class experience that opened the mind of the Chinese student at Bowdoin. One of the distinctive features of the American college has always been the idea that students have something to learn not only from their teachers but also from each other. That idea of lateral learning originates from the Puritan conception of the gathered church, in which the criterion for membership was the candidate's "aptness to edifie another." The idea persists to this day in the question that every admissions officer in every selective college is supposed to ask of every applicant: "What would this candidate bring to the class?" It underlies the opinion by Justice Lewis Powell in the landmark case of Regents of the University of California v. Bakke (1978), in which the Supreme Court ruled that considering a candidate's race is constitutional for the purpose of ensuring "the interplay of ideas and the exchange of views" among students from different backgrounds. Those are modern reformulations of the ancient (by American standards) view that a college, no less than a church, exists fundamentally as what one scholar of Puritanism calls the "interaction of consciences."

15   A well-managed discussion among peers of diverse interests and talents can help students learn the difference between informed insights and mere opinionating. It can provide the pleasurable chastisement of discovering that others see the world differently, and that their experience is not replicable by, or even reconcilable with, one's own. It is a rehearsal for deliberative democracy.

16   Unfortunately, at many colleges, as fiscal imperatives overwhelm educational values, this kind of experience is becoming the exception more than the rule. The educational imperative is clear: A class should be small enough to permit every student to participate in the give-and-take of discussion under the guidance of an informed, skilled, and engaged teacher. But the economic imperative is also clear: The lower the ratio between students and faculty, the higher the cost. One obvious way to mitigate the cost is to put fewer full-time tenured or tenure-track faculty in the classroom, and to replace them with underpaid, overworked part-timers—something that is happening at a frightening pace across the nation.

17   An even more promising strategy for cost containment is to install one or another technological "delivery system" in place of the cumbersome old system of teachers mentoring students. On that matter, the academic community is divided among true

believers, diehard opponents, and those trying to find some middle ground in the form of "hybrid" or "blended" learning, whereby students are instructed and assessed through electronic means but do not entirely lose face-to-face human contact with their teachers and with one another.

18   Those of us who have trouble imagining how technology can advance liberal learning are liable to be charged with mindless obedience to what the English classicist F. M. Cornford famously called the first law of academe: "Nothing should ever be done for the first time." No doubt there is some truth to that charge. But as a more recent English scholar, Alison Wolf, puts it in her book *Does Education Matter? Myths About Education and Economic Growth*, "We have not found any low-cost, high-technology alternatives to expert human teachers." At least not yet.

19   Meanwhile, American academic leaders, long accustomed to assuming that their institutions are without peer abroad, are looking nervously over their collective shoulder at the rising universities of Asia, as well as at "the Bologna process" in Europe—the movement to make degree requirements compatible across national borders, so that, for example, a baccalaureate in chemistry earned in a French university will qualify the holder for further study or skilled employment in, say, Belgium. They are watching, too, those countries—notably China and Germany—that have a long tradition of standardized national examinations by which students are evaluated quite apart from whatever academic credentials they hold.

20   The standardized-testing regime (along with the mania for institutional rankings) is spreading throughout the world and making inroads in the historically decentralized education system of the United States. With it arises the specter that our colleges will be subject to some version of what, in our elementary and secondary schools, has come to be known as the No Child Left Behind (NCLB) assessment program. There is no reason to doubt President Bush's good intentions when, on behalf of minority children in weak schools, he called for the imposition of enforceable standards to put an end to "the soft bigotry of low expectations." But there is mounting evidence that the law has had little positive effect, while driving "soft" subjects such as art and music to the margins or out of the curriculum altogether.

21   There is also no reason to doubt President Obama's deep understanding—as anyone will recognize who has read his prepresidential writings—of the immense and immeasurable value of a liberal education. But as the distinguished psychologist Robert J. Sternberg, provost of Oklahoma State University, wrote recently in an open letter to the president published in *Inside Higher Ed*, there is reason to worry that blunt "metrics for progress" of the NCLB type would "undermine liberal education in this country." So far President Obama's plans are not yet sharply defined. His initial emphasis has been on the cost of education, the promise of technology, and the establishment of standards for the transition from school to college. As a strategy emerges in more detail for holding colleges accountable for cost and quality, we need to keep in mind that standardized tests—at least those that exist today—are simply incapable of measuring the qualities that should be the fruits of a true liberal education: creativity, wisdom, humility, and insight into ethical as well as empirical questions.

22   As we proceed into the future, fantasies of retrieving an irretrievable past won't help. College is our American pastoral. We imagine it as a verdant world where the harshest

sounds are the reciprocal thump of tennis balls or the clatter of cleats as young bodies trot up and down the field-house steps. Perhaps our brains are programmed to edit out the failures and disappointments—the botched exams, missed free throws, unrequited loves—that can make college a difficult time for young people struggling to grow up.

23   In fact, most college students today have nothing like the experience preserved in myth and selective memory. For a relatively few, college remains the sort of place that Kronman, a former dean of Yale Law School, recalls from his days at Williams College, where his favorite class took place at the home of a philosophy professor whose two golden retrievers slept on either side of the fireplace "like bookends beside the hearth" while the sunset lit the Berkshire hills "in scarlet and gold." But for many more students, college means the anxious pursuit of marketable skills in overcrowded, underresourced institutions, where little attention is paid to that elusive entity sometimes called the "whole person." For still others, it means traveling by night to a fluorescent-lit office building or to a classroom that exists only in cyberspace.

24   It is a pipe dream to imagine that every student can have the sort of experience that our richest colleges, at their best, still provide. But it is a nightmare society that affords the chance to learn and grow only to the wealthy, brilliant, or lucky few. Many remarkable teachers in America's community colleges, unsung private colleges, and underfinanced public colleges live this truth every day, working to keep the ideal of liberal education for all citizens alive.

25   It seems beyond doubt that the American college is going through a period of truly radical, perhaps unprecedented, change. It is buffeted by forces—globalization; economic instability; the continuing revolution in information technology; the increasingly evident inadequacy of elementary and secondary education; the elongation of adolescence; the breakdown of faculty tenure as an academic norm; and, perhaps most important, the collapse of consensus about what students should know—that make its task more difficult and contentious than ever before.

26   Moreover, students tend to arrive in college already largely formed in their habits and attitudes, or, in the case of the increasing number of "nontraditional" (that is, older) students, preoccupied with the struggles of adulthood: finding or keeping a job, making or saving a marriage, doing right by their children. Many college women, who now outnumber men, are already mothers, often single. And regardless of age or gender or social class, students experience college—in the limited sense of attending lectures, writing papers, taking exams—as a smaller part of daily life than did my generation, which came of age in the 1960s and 70s. They live in an ocean of digital noise, logged on, online, booted up, as the phrase goes, 24/7, linked to one another through an arsenal of gadgets that are never powered down.

27   As we try to meet those challenges, it would be folly to dismiss as naïveté or nostalgia an abiding attachment to the college ideal—however much or little it ever conforms to reality. The power of this ideal is evident at every college commencement in the eyes of parents who watch their children advance into life. What parents want for their children is not just prosperity but happiness. And though it is foolish to deny the linkage between the two, they are not the same thing.

28   As the literary scholar Norman Foerster once put it, the American college has always sought to prepare students for more than "pecuniary advantage over the unprepared." To succeed in sustaining college as a place where liberal learning still takes place will be very costly. But in the long run, it will be much more costly if we fail.

29   A few years ago, when I was beginning to work on my book about the American college, I came across a manuscript diary kept in the early 1850s by a student at a small Methodist college in southwest Virginia. One spring evening, after attending a sermon by the college president that left him troubled and apprehensive, he made the following entry: "Oh that the Lord would show me how to think and how to choose." That sentence, poised somewhere between a wish and a plea, sounds archaic today. But even if the religious note is dissonant to some of us, it seems hard to come up with a better formulation of what a college should strive to be: an aid to reflection, a place and process whereby young people take stock of their talents and passions and begin to sort out their lives in a way that is true to themselves and responsible to others. "Show me how to think and how to choose."

Garry B. Trudeau

Teaching Is Dead

Garry B. Trudeau (born 1948) is one of America's most influential (and controversial) political and social commentators. His vehicle is the comic strip "Doonesbury," which appears in more than 850 newspapers and whose audience may top 100 million readers. What exactly does this cartoon argue about the nature of current higher education?

Salman Khan

What College Could Be Like: Imagining an Optimized Education Model

Born in 1976 in New Orleans, Salman Khan quit his position as a hedge fund entrepreneur in 2009 in order to turn his attention to education. He is best known for founding the Khan Academy, a free online education service, and in 2012 he was named one of *Time's* Most Influential People in the World for his contributions to education. The following essay is adapted from Khan's 2012 book, *The One World Schoolhouse: Education Reimagined.*

Between 2000–2001 and 2010–2011, prices for undergraduate tuition, room, and board at public institutions rose 42%, and prices at private not-for-profit institutions rose 31%, after adjustment for inflation.[1] With rising costs, large numbers of graduates are leaving college with huge debts and are struggling to find work. Fifty-three percent of recent college graduates are jobless or underemployed, the highest in eleven years.[2] The core value proposition of higher education is under increasing scrutiny, in part because of the disconnect between student's expectations, the traditional classroom experience, and the ever-growing need for active creators in the marketplace.

2   There is a basic divide between most students' expectations for college—a means to employment first and a good intellectual experience second; and what universities believe their value is—an intellectual and social experience first, with only secondary consideration to employment. At the same time, existing credentials carry very little information for employers to really decide who has the skills and talents they need.

3   So let us face this as an openended design problem: Is it possible to craft a university experience that bridges the gap between students' expectations, universities' strengths, and employers' needs? One that provides the rich social and intellectual atmosphere of a good existing college, while at the same time exposing students to those intellectual but also practical fields that will make them valuable to the world. Where "microcredentials" could be earned and maintained in intellectual and vocational fields to prove to the world what a student can do. And now let's be ambitious: Might there be a sustainable way to make this experience free or even pay the students to participate?

4   Computer science is a good place to start. I know the field reasonably well and I also have a sense for the job market—which is tight and growing tighter every day. It is a field where degrees can be valuable, but the ability to design and execute on open-ended, complex projects is paramount; 17-year-olds with unusual creativity and intellect have been known to get six-figure salaries. Because of the demand for talent and the recognition that college degrees and high GPAs are not the best predictor of creativity, intellect, or passion, top employers have begun to treat summer internships as something of a farm league. They observe students actually working and make offers to those who perform the best. Employers know that working with a student is an infinitely better assessment than any degree or transcript.

5   Students have also begun to recognize something very counterintuitive: that they are more likely to get an intellectual grasp of computer science—which is really the logical and algorithmic side of mathematics—by working at companies like Google, Microsoft, or Facebook or trying to create their own mobile applications than by reading textbooks or sitting in lecture halls. They see the real-world projects as being more intellectually challenging and open-ended than the somewhat artificial projects given in classrooms. Even more, they know that the product of their efforts has the potential to touch millions of people instead of just being graded by a teaching assistant and thrown away.

6   So, to be clear, in software engineering, the internship and self-directed projects have become far more valuable to the students, as an intellectual learning experience, than any university class. And they have become more valuable to employers, as a signal of student ability, than any formal credential, class taken, or grade point average.

7   When it comes to internships, I want to emphasize that these are very different from the ones many people remember having even 20 years ago. There is no getting coffee for the boss, sorting papers or doing other types of busywork. The projects are not just cute things to work on that have no impact on real people. In fact, the best way to differentiate between forward-looking, 21st century industries and old-school, backward-looking ones is to see what interns are doing. At top Internet companies, interns might be creating patentable artificial intelligence algorithms or even creating new lines of business. By contrast, at a law firm, government office, or publishing house, they will be doing paperwork, scheduling meetings, and proofreading text. This trivial work will be paid accordingly, if at all, whereas pay scales at the new-style internships reflect the seriousness of the work involved.

8   Given the increasing importance of real-world projects in terms of both intellectual enrichment and enhancement of job prospects, why do traditional colleges tend to limit them to summers, pushing them aside to cater to the calendar needs of lectures and homework? The answer is simple inertia—this is how it has always been done, so people have not really questioned it.

9   Actually, some universities have. Despite being founded not even 60 years ago, the University of Waterloo is generally considered to be Canada's top engineering school. Walk down a hallway at Microsoft or Google and you will find as many Waterloo grads as those from MIT, Stanford, or Berkeley—despite the fact that, because of work visa issues, it is a significant hassle for U.S. employers to hire Canadian nationals. And this is not some attempt to get low-cost labor from across the border—Waterloo graduates are commanding salaries as high as the very best American grads. What is Waterloo doing right?

10   For one thing, Waterloo recognized the value of internships long ago (they call them co-ops) and has made them an integral part of its students' experience. By graduation, a typical Waterloo grad will have spent six internships lasting a combined 24 months at major companies—often American. The typical U.S. college graduate will have spent about 36 months in lecture halls and a mere three to six months in internships.

11   This past winter—not summer—all of the interns at the Khan Academy, and probably most of the interns in Silicon Valley, were from Waterloo because it is the only school that views internships as an integral part of students' development outside of the summer. While the students at most colleges are taking notes in lecture halls and cramming for winter exams, the Waterloo students are pushing themselves intellectually by working on real projects with experienced professionals. They are also getting valuable time with

employers and pretty much guaranteeing several job offers once they graduate. On top of that, some are earning enough money during their multiple high-paying internships to pay for their tuition (which is about 1/6th to 1/3rd the cost of a comparable American school) and then some. So Waterloo students graduate with valuable skills, broad intellectual development, high-paying jobs, and potential savings after four or five years.

12   Compare this to the typical American college grad with tens or hundreds of thousands of dollars in debt, no guarantee of an intellectually challenging job, and not much actual experience with which to get a job.

13   Waterloo has already proven that the division between the intellectual and the useful is artificial; I challenge anyone to argue that Waterloo co-op students are in any way less intellectual or broad thinking than the political science or history majors from other elite universities. If anything, based on my experience with Waterloo students, they tend to have a more expansive worldview and are more mature than typical new college graduates—arguably due to their broad and deep experience base.

14   So let us imagine optimizing the model that schools like Waterloo have already begun. Imagine a new university in Silicon Valley—it does not have to be there but it will help to make things concrete. I am a big believer that inspiring physical spaces and rich community really does elevate and develop one's thinking. So we will put in dormitories, nicely manicured outdoor spaces, and as many areas that facilitate interaction and collaboration as possible. Students would be encouraged to start clubs and organize intellectual events. So far, this is not so different from the typical residential college.

15   What is completely different is where and how the students spend their days. Rather than taking notes in lectures halls, these students will be actively learning through real-world, intellectual projects. A student could spend five months at Google optimizing a search algorithm. She might spend another six months at Microsoft working on human speech recognition. The next four months could be spent apprenticing under a designer at Apple, followed by a year of building her own mobile applications. Six months could be spent doing biomedical research at a startup or even at another university like Stanford. Another four months could be spent prototyping and patenting an invention. Students could also apprentice with venture capitalists and successful entrepreneurs, eventually leading to attempts to start their own businesses. One of the primary roles of the college itself would be ensure the internships are challenging and intellectual; that they truly do support a student's development. The college will also provide a scaffold of shared, physical experiences, but they will not be passive lectures. They will be active interactions between teachers and students.

16   All of this will be tied together with a self-paced academic scaffold through something like EdX (Harvard, MIT, and Berkeley's "MOOC") or Khan Academy. Students will also still be expected to have a broad background in the arts and deep proficiency in the sciences; it will just be done in a more natural way. They will be motivated to formally learn about linear algebra when working on a computer graphics apprenticeship at Pixar or Electronic Arts. They will want to learn accounting when working under the CFO of a publicly traded company. Ungraded seminars will be held regularly during nights and weekends when students can enjoy and discuss great works of literature and art. If the students decide they want to prove their academic ability within a domain—like algorithms or French history—they can sign up for rigorous assessments leading to microcredentials that are valued by employers and graduate schools.

17   This thought experiment envisions a school focused on engineering, design, and entrepreneurship in Silicon Valley. We placed it there so that it could take advantage of the local ecosystem, but why not a school of finance or journalism located in New York or London, or a school focused on energy in Houston? Even better, why can't they all be affiliated so that a student can experience multiple cities and industries, all while having a residential and intellectual support network?

18   Will this be for everyone? Absolutely not. But majoring in literature or accounting at a traditional university is not for everyone either. There should be more options, and this could be one of them—an option that introduces diversity of thought and practice into a higher education world that has not changed dramatically in hundreds of years.

19   It also should be noted that this does not necessarily have to be a new university. Existing campuses could move in this direction by de-emphasizing or eliminating lecture-based courses, having their students more engaged in research and co-ops in the broader world, and having more faculty with broad backgrounds that show a deep desire to mentor students.

Notes

1. U.S. Department of Education, National Center for Education Statistics. Digest of Education Statistics, 2011 (NCES 2012-001), 2012, Chapter 3.
2. Yen, H. Half of recent college grads underemployed or jobless, analysis says. Cleveland.com. Associated Press (Apr. 23, 2012); http://www.cleveland.com/business/index.ssf/2012/04/half_of_recent_college_grads_u.html.

KEVIN **CAREY**

Into the Future with MOOCs

Kevin Carey is the director of the Education Policy Program at the New America Foundation, a nonprofit public policy institute. A frequent contributor to publications such as the *New York Times*, the *American Prospect*, *Slate*, and the *New Republic* and a frequent guest on C-SPAN, CNN, and NPR, Carey also writes a monthly column for the *Chronicle of Higher Education* and is editor of the *Washington Monthly College Guide*, an annual publication. "Into the Future with MOOC's" was published in the *Chronicle* in September 2012.

I n the spring of my freshman year in college, I took "Principles of Microeconomics" in Lecture Hall 1, a 400-seat auditorium. The professor was an economist and thus possessed a certain perspective on human nature. On the first day of class, he explained that our grades would be based on two midterms and a final. If we skipped the first midterm, the second would count double. If we skipped them both, the final would count for 100 percent of our grade. I may or may not have waited until the hour ended before walking out the back door of Lecture Hall 1 toward the nearest bar.

2   Fifteen weeks later, suddenly mindful of various dire warnings from my father about passing grades, continuing financial support, and the strong connection between them, I cracked my econ textbook and began a five-day cram session

fueled by youthful energy and caffeine. When I walked down to the bottom of Lecture Hall 1 to turn in my final exam, one of the teaching assistants told me to place it in a pile corresponding to my course section. I never attended a course section, I replied. I'll always remember the look of resignation and disgust that crossed his face.

3   A few weeks later, I received a letter informing me that I had received a C on the final and thus the course. Accordingly, Binghamton University, a prestigious, regionally accredited research institution, awarded me four academic credits, which I applied toward a bachelor's degree that I hold today.

4   Last fall, more than 100,000 people enrolled in a free online version of the renowned Stanford roboticist Sebastian Thrun's artificial-intelligence course. Many didn't finish. But some did, and among them, some performed just as well on the assignments and exams as the whip-smart students in Palo Alto who took the course in person. For this, the online students received no official academic credits of any kind.

5   That doesn't make any sense.

6   Over the last year, massive open online courses, or MOOCs, have quickly traversed the cultural cycle of hype, saturation, backlash, and backlash-to-the-backlash. Like blogs, MOOCs are interesting, important, and stuck with an absurdly unserious name. But don't let the silly-sounding moniker fool you. Some new things are praised to the skies because people have a weakness for the shiny and novel. Others are hyped because they will obviously change the world, and it always takes the world a little while to adjust. MOOCs are of the latter kind.

7   This became clear not when Thrun and his colleagues enrolled vast legions of learners from around the world. The online Rubicon wasn't truly crossed until Harvard, which had been studiously ignoring the free online course movement, jumped aboard the bandwagon to become a partner in MIT's MOOC venture, edX. University officials in Cambridge were clearly anxious about missing the next big thing. Then, a few weeks later, the University of Virginia's Board of Visitors fired its president after reading about MOOCs in the *Wall Street Journal*.

8   Good intentions come and go. Status anxiety, by contrast, is the great motivating force in elite higher education, and where elite colleges go, others follow. In a stroke, the public perception of online higher education shifted from down-market for-profit colleges to the most famous universities in the world. It's hard to overstate how important that will be to acceptance of this burgeoning educational form.

9   Indeed, the future is so clearly one of universal access to free, high-quality, impeccably branded online courses that their presence can be simply assumed. The interesting questions now revolve around financing, quality assurance, and—most important—credit.

10   At the moment, colleges have a monopoly on the sale of college credits, the only units of learning that can be assembled into credentials with wide acceptance in the labor market. Monopolies are valuable things to control, and monopolists tend not to relinquish them voluntarily. But the MOOC explosion will accelerate the breakup of the college credit monopoly.

11   Someone scoring in the top 1 percent of students in a course taught by a world-famous scholar and endorsed by a world-famous university deserves no credit, while some slacker freshman who ekes out a C deserves four credits? The most obscure, perpetually-on-probation, nobody-ever-heard-of-it college can grant credits, but not

edX, backed by MIT, Harvard, and now Berkeley? Students can get credits from for-profit higher-education corporations that buy up failing accredited colleges and turn them into giant online student-loan-processing machines, but not from Coursera, where online courses are designed by hand-picked professors from universities including Princeton, Duke, Caltech, and Penn?

12   That kind of crazy cognitive dissonance can't last forever. When it breaks, and it will, we're headed for a world that looks something like this:

13   Some accredited colleges—don't forget, there are thousands of them—will start accepting MOOC certificates as transfer credit. They'll see it as a tool for marketing and building enrollment. This is already starting to happen. The nonprofit Saylor Foundation recently struck a deal whereby students completing its free online courses can, for a small fee, take exams to earn credit at Excelsior College, a regionally accredited nonprofit online institution.

14   Pressure to accept MOOC credits will build and gradually move up the higher-education food chain. Public officials eager to offer credible low-cost options to parents and students fed up with rising college prices will pile on. Many will question the quality of MOOCs, but that's the great thing about empiricism—courses can be evaluated and knowledge assessed.

15   Some organizations will develop businesses devoted exclusively to credible, secure assessments of what MOOC students have learned. Security and integrity will always be issues for online learning (although I don't remember anyone checking my ID when I took my econ final, or any final for that matter). But these are solvable problems. Thrun's MOOC company, Udacity, is forming a partnership with the textbook giant Pearson's VUE testing-center service for exactly this reason.

16   Other companies will sell services designed specifically to support learning online. This, too, is already happening. The tech company Piazza, for example, provides online spaces for instructors and students to ask and answer questions about course concepts and assignments, for traditional and online classes. Piazza's offices are in Palo Alto, just up the street from Stanford. That's not a coincidence; as new modes of online higher education develop, the ecosystem of start-up capital and innovation in Silicon Valley will organize around them.

17   All of this points toward a world where the economics of higher education are broken down and restructured around marginal cost. The cost of serving the 100,000th student who enrolls in a MOOC is essentially zero, which is why the price is zero, too. Open-source textbooks and other free online resources will drive the prices of supporting materials toward the zero line as well.

18   The cost of administering an exam to the 100,000th student in a secure testing center, by contrast, isn't zero, so students will end up paying for that. One-on-one access to an expert or teaching assistant also costs money, so students who need those services will pay for them as well.

19   Meanwhile, the dominant higher-education pricing model, in which different students pay a single price for a huge package of services they may or may not need, will come under increasing stress. Colleges of all kinds will need to re-examine exactly what value they provide to students, what it costs, and what price the market will bear.

20   I'm far from the first person to make these predictions. MOOCs just make the future seem more certain—and less distant—than ever before.

SCOTT **CARLSON**

For Making the Most of College, It's Still Location, Location, Location

Scott Carlson is a senior writer at the *Chronicle of Education*, where he runs his Buildings & Grounds Blog. A former technology reporter, he now writes about campus planning and college management as well as energy, architecture, and sustainability. He is also contributing writer for *Urbanite*, a Baltimore-based magazine focused on city living, and a regular contributor to *Grist*, an environmental news site. The following article was published in the *Chronicle* in 2013.

I n late December, a set of articles and essays in the *New York Times* focused on the public library as a place, and on the changing meaning of that place with the rise of electronic books and the demise of brick-and-mortar bookstores like Borders.

2 As librarians "struggle with the task of redefining their roles and responsibilities in a digital age," said the lead article, their libraries are "reinventing themselves as vibrant town squares, showcasing the latest best sellers, lending Kindles loaded with e-books, and offering grass-roots technology-training centers." A related commentary prodded readers with a provocative question: "Do We Still Need Libraries?"

3 For me it was déjà vu. Back in 2001, I wrote an article in the *Chronicle*, "The Deserted Library," which reported that libraries would change in the face of the Internet and electronic materials. Some people, like Mark C. Taylor, a professor of religion at Columbia University, predicted an inevitable decline of the physical library with the advent of the Internet. My own conclusion, and what I reinforced in follow-up pieces, was that while deserted libraries tended to be outdated, unimaginative, and sterile places, the libraries that stayed vibrant—and busier than ever—were the ones that found ways to appeal to people's sensibilities and needs (including caffeine).

4 And they continue to be. I write many of my *Chronicle* stories from a seat in Goucher College's new library, and it is buzzing, even in the middle of the day. People, especially young people, want to be around other people, even if they don't want to interact. The library, as someone once put it, is one of few places you can go to be alone in public.

5 This conversation about place versus the Internet continues, but now it has grown to encompass the fate of the college campus itself. Online learning and MOOCs have arrived, the argument goes, so place doesn't matter. The campus will become a relic, bound for desertion, like the ruins of Shelley's Ozymandias. Many of these predictions come with barely concealed indignation over the college building boom of the past 15 years. Pundits see a reckoning for the luxurious climbing-wall colleges—"Disneyland for Geeks," as Nathan Harden, in the latest issue of the *American Interest*, calls it.

6 Within the next 50 years, Mr. Harden declares in his essay, half of American colleges will succumb to mounting financial pressures and shut down. The problem is not student debt or a flaccid hiring market, he argues. Big changes are coming because "the college classroom is about to go virtual."

7 "Recent history shows us that the Internet is a great destroyer of any traditional business that relies on the sale of information," he continues. "Nostalgia won't stop the

unsentimental beast of progress from wreaking havoc on old ways of doing things. If a faster, cheaper way of sharing information emerges, history shows us that it will quickly supplant what came before. People will not continue to pay tens of thousands of dollars for what technology allows them to get for free."

8   I'm not buying it—at least not the way that Mr. Harden lays it out. Online classes will surely play some role in supplanting some classroom teaching—they already do. And certainly colleges face challenges—like burdensome debt and deferred maintenance—that may hobble or kill off a number of them. In the next 50 years, we could see major geopolitical, environmental, or socioeconomic mayhem, which could push weak colleges over the cliff.

9   But will campuses and traditional teaching disappear because we now have MOOCs? No, because that defies the human yearning for meaningful places and the real benefits that come with them. We see it in the migration to cities and in walkable neighborhoods. We see it most of all on college campuses.

"PLACE IS EVERYTHING"

10   Such yearning may sound nostalgic, which is how Mr. Harden characterizes it. But even evangelists of disruption acknowledge the intangible, serendipitous, and sometimes even uncomfortable educational opportunities that colleges offer by bringing different kinds of people together in one place.

11   Andrew Delbanco, a professor of humanities at Columbia and author of *College: What It Was, Is, and Should Be*, lauds the value of "lateral learning" between student peers who share a place. Mr. Harden, of all people, should understand this: *Sex and God at Yale*, his recent book about his experiences with promiscuity and political correctness on that campus, is a memoir made possible by being there.

12   "I think place is everything, and that's not to say that virtual learning can't enhance place," says Jonathan Brand, president of Cornell College, in Iowa. "You see how much students learn from each other sitting in the classroom, how much they learn sitting together in the dining hall—more than from their professor. It's hard to imagine replicating that virtually."

13   Look around, and you see the way people value place in education, even where you might not expect it. Goddard College did away with its traditional campus program and now offers low-residency programs mostly for adults, who spend only a week per semester on the campus. But those students regard the campus experience as a sacred time, when long walks and late nights on the old Vermont estate yield new ideas and new connections.

14   The so-called digital natives, who are too young for nostalgia, get it: Last fall, at a sustainability conference, a prominent environmental entrepreneur presented her vision for virtual classes designed to replace face-to-face classes. Undergraduates in the audience lined up at the microphones to tell her it was a bad idea, because they valued place and what it offered.

15   Many of these in-person-versus-online comparisons have a classist streak, as my colleague Goldie Blumenstyk and I discussed in a *Chronicle* essay in December. Mr. Harden, while briefly acknowledging that the virtualized classroom "can never duplicate the experience of the student with the good fortune to get into Yale," says it provides the wisdom of the Ivy League to "anyone who can access the Internet—at a

public library, for instance—no matter how poor or disadvantaged or isolated or uneducated he or she may be."

16   He draws a simile: "Online education is like using online dating Web sites—15 years ago it was considered a poor substitute for the real thing, even creepy; now it's ubiquitous." Perhaps it's more like online sex—missing out on the intimacy, but offering something to those who have fewer options.

LOCAL GEOGRAPHY

17   Take a lesson from recent history: Just as with libraries, campuses that are dismal, disconnected, and underutilized as places will suffer, while the ones that are vital will have a shot at succeeding. Colleges will need to find ways—preferably creative and inexpensive—to make their places relevant: Link to local communities. Use those communities as places where students can apply their education to fix problems or enhance strengths. Find the unique characteristics of the local geography, and incorporate them into lessons. Provide spaces where students can connect both intellectually and physically with one another, and with their college work.

18   People who predicted the death of the library made the mistake of thinking that libraries were merely useful for information distribution—an understandable error, given that libraries' central role involved passing around books and journals. But pundits now make the same mistake when thinking about the college campus. If college were merely about the "sale of information," the enterprise would have gone the way of Borders a long time ago.

DAVID **BROOKS**

Sam Spade at Starbucks

David Brooks, born in 1961, raised in New York City, and educated at the University of Chicago, is a popular social columnist whose work appears regularly in the *New York Times* and on PBS. He has also written for the *Wall Street Journal*, *Newsweek*, and other magazines, and his books include *Bobos in Paradise: The New Upper Class and How They Got There* (2000), *On Paradise Drive* (2004), and *The Social Animal: The Hidden Sources of Love, Character, and Achievement* (2011). The following essay appeared in the *New York Times* and many other newspapers on April 12, 2012.

If you attend a certain sort of conference, hang out at a certain sort of coffee shop or visit a certain sort of university, you've probably run into some of these wonderful young people who are doing good. Typically, they've spent a year studying abroad. They've traveled in the poorer regions of the world. Now they have devoted themselves to a purpose larger than self.

2   Often they are bursting with enthusiasm for some social entrepreneurship project: making a cheap water-purification system, starting a company that will empower Rwandan women by selling their crafts in boutiques around the world.

3   These people are refreshingly uncynical. Their hip service ethos is setting the moral tone for the age. Idealistic and uplifting, their worldview is spread by enlightened advertising campaigns, from Benetton years ago to everything Apple has ever done.

4   It's hard not to feel inspired by all these idealists, but their service religion does have some shortcomings. In the first place, many of these social entrepreneurs think they can evade politics. They have little faith in the political process and believe that real change happens on the ground beneath it.

5   That's a delusion. You can cram all the nongovernmental organizations you want into a country, but if there is no rule of law and if the ruling class is predatory then your achievements won't add up to much.

6   Furthermore, important issues always spark disagreement. Unless there is a healthy political process to resolve disputes, the ensuing hatred and conflict will destroy everything the altruists are trying to build.

7   There's little social progress without political progress. Unfortunately, many of today's young activists are really good at thinking locally and globally, but not as good at thinking nationally and regionally.

8   Second, the prevailing service religion underestimates the problem of disorder. Many of the activists talk as if the world can be healed if we could only insert more care, compassion and resources into it.

9   History is not kind to this assumption. Most poverty and suffering—whether in a country, a family or a person—flows from disorganization. A stable social order is an artificial accomplishment, the result of an accumulation of habits, hectoring, moral stricture and physical coercion. Once order is dissolved, it takes hard measures to restore it.

10   Yet one rarely hears social entrepreneurs talk about professional policing, honest courts or strict standards of behavior; it's more uplifting to talk about microloans and sustainable agriculture.

11   In short, there's only so much good you can do unless you are willing to confront corruption, venality and disorder head-on. So if I could, presumptuously, recommend a reading list to help these activists fill in the gaps in the prevailing service ethos, I'd start with the novels of Dashiell Hammett or Raymond Chandler, or at least the movies based on them.

12   The noir heroes like Sam Spade in "The Maltese Falcon" served as models for a generation of Americans, and they put the focus squarely on venality, corruption and disorder and how you should behave in the face of it.

13   A noir hero is a moral realist. He assumes that everybody is dappled with virtue and vice, especially himself. He makes no social-class distinction and only provisional moral distinctions between the private eyes like himself and the criminals he pursues. The assumption in a Hammett book is that the good guy has a spotty past, does spotty things and that the private eye and the criminal are two sides to the same personality.

14   He (or she—the women in these stories follow the same code) adopts a layered personality. He hardens himself on the outside in order to protect whatever is left of the finer self within.

15   He is reticent, allergic to self-righteousness and appears unfeeling, but he is motivated by a disillusioned sense of honor. The world often rewards the wrong things, but each job comes with obligations and even if everything is decaying you should still take pride in your work. Under the cynical mask, there is still a basic sense of good order, that crime should be punished and bad behavior shouldn't go uncorrected. He knows he's not going to be uplifted by his work; that to tackle the hard jobs he'll have to risk coarsening himself, but he doggedly plows ahead.

16   This worldview had a huge influence as a generation confronted crime, corruption, fascism and communism. I'm not sure I can see today's social entrepreneurs wearing fedoras and trench coats. But noir's moral realism would be a nice supplement to today's prevailing ethos. It would fold some hardheadedness in with today's service mentality. It would focus attention on the core issues: order and rule of law. And it would be necessary. Contemporary Washington, not to mention parts of the developing world, may be less seedy than the cities in the noir stories, but they are equally laced with self-deception and self-dealing.

ISSUE IN FOCUS

Is College Worth the Price?

"It's an old story," says Anthony P. Carnevale, director of Georgetown University's Center on Education and the Workforce and one of the authors featured in this section: "When economic downturns hit, unemployment rates spiral and tales of college graduates forced to tend bar or mop floors proliferate."

But is the story really so old? According to the National Center for Education Statistics, fifty-some years ago, about 45 percent of 1.7 million high school graduates went to college. By fall 2011, according to the Bureau of Labor Statistics, that number had more than doubled, with 68.3 percent of the year's 3.1 million high school graduates enrolled in colleges or universities. The dramatic upsurge in college enrollment is driven both by increases in the college age population and rising enrollment rates overall. The end result is that more people—many more—than ever before are attending college before entering the workforce.

Despite growing enrollment rates, not everyone is convinced that a college education is worth the rising tuition costs and student loan debt that increasingly accompany getting a college degree. In some ways, this debate is nothing new. According to the *Concise Encyclopedia of Economics*, opinions about the necessity of a college degree have fluctuated for decades, often in correspondence with increases or decreases in the average salaries of college graduates. The intensity of the debate has escalated in recent years thanks in large part to the Great Recession of 2008 and the rising unemployment rates that have accompanied it, even among college graduates.

Many believe college's Golden Age has come and gone. College, they say, is now the virtual equivalent of high school: As college attendance becomes more common, the degree loses its value—even as it becomes more expensive to attain. College tuition prices are sky-rocketing, leaving more and more college graduates in debt—and without the employment opportunities to pay back their loans. Meanwhile, statistics suggest that salary disparities between college and high school graduates are shrinking and that there are now more college graduates than there are jobs requiring a college degree.

These statistics fuel the argument that college is hardly a guarantee of personal advancement. In fact, critics of the "college education for all" approach argue that the idea that a college diploma is necessary for successful entry into the job market is a myth. While few if any would advocate for the complete abolition of the American university system, some people do argue that college degrees are appropriate mostly for the few people who markedly stand to benefit from them.

Not so fast, say others. Proponents of the college experience often discredit the statistics cited by naysayers. They argue that college graduates remain in high demand and consistently earn more than those who entered the work force directly after high school. In fact, more employers than ever require post-secondary degrees (whether two- or four-year) as a condition for employment consideration. The demand for advanced degrees has grown as technology advances and, concurrently, countries around the world become increasingly interconnected. Present-day employers seek out applicants who are literate in the use of digital technologies and able to communicate across cultural boundaries.

Then there are the social benefits derived from a college-educated population. According to the Solutions for Our Future Project (an organization dedicated to educating the public about the social benefits of higher education), "Individuals who have had the opportunity to go to college have a greater probability of having the resources to develop into productive and engaged citizens." Although the costs of higher education are undeniably high (perhaps even to a discriminatory extent), the societal costs of a primarily uneducated citizenship might be even higher.

Advocates for some form of middle ground assert that "degrees" and "education" are not necessarily the same thing. While *degrees* may not be worth the costs incurred by college tuition, the principle of *education* is—but in order to honor it, we need to switch the university system's focus to cultivating well-rounded, culturally literate individuals as opposed to churning out diplomas. Rather than adopting a black-and-white approach to higher education—that college is categorically worth it or it is not—perhaps college should be approached on a case-by-case basis, pursued only if it enhances an individual's goals or is the necessary means to working in a particular career.

In this Issue in Focus, we present arguments representing many of these divergent viewpoints. First, in a January 2011 essay published in *Inside Higher Ed*, Anthony Carnevale argues that college is still very much worth it, primarily from an economic perspective. Richard Vedder, an economist, counters Carnevale's argument directly, asserting that college is not a wise investment for the majority of high school graduates. Then the historian and Harvard professor Niall Ferguson, in an essay that first appeared in *Newsweek*, argues that the American university system has become a tool for promoting an insular, elite class and for maintaining a modern caste system. Finally, we feature an "infographic" from the *Atlantic* that supports the persistent value of an investment in higher education, even in the face of tuition hikes.

Will a college degree be "worth it" in your life? As you read, pay attention not only to the claims that are made but also to *how* they are supported: Do the authors cite statistics, and if so, how might the data be skewed or interpreted in ways

THE NON-TUITION
COSTS OF EDUCATION

High school grads often look at the bill for their upcoming 4 years of college in disbelief. Thankfully, student loans often cover the cost of actually getting them into the classroom, but what about all the additional expenses that come along with their four years away from home? Living on their own for the first time is costly, especially in the fast-paced world of the college social scene.

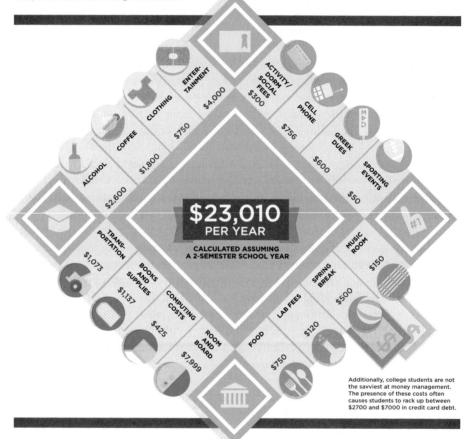

ENTERTAINMENT $4,000

CLOTHING $750

ACTIVITY/DORM/SOCIAL FEES $300

CELL PHONE $756

COFFEE $1,800

GREEK DUES $600

ALCOHOL $2,600

SPORTING EVENTS $50

$23,010 PER YEAR
CALCULATED ASSUMING A 2-SEMESTER SCHOOL YEAR

TRANSPORTATION $1,073

MUSIC ROOM $150

BOOKS AND SUPPLIES $1,137

SPRING BREAK $500

COMPUTING COSTS $425

LAB FEES $120

ROOM AND BOARD $7,999

FOOD $750

Additionally, college students are not the savviest at money management. The presence of these costs often causes students to rack up between $2700 and $7000 in credit card debt.

that support seemingly divergent arguments? Do you find statistical evidence to be more compelling than personal anecdotes, expert interviews, or rhetorical reasoning? Should the worth of a college education be determined purely by employment and salary data, or does a college education offer more intangible (and perhaps even more important) benefits? Should everybody go to college, or should college be reserved only for the few? Are there alternative paths to education that are just as viable and as valuable as college, or is a college degree still a necessity? These are issues to confront as you contemplate the beginning of your college experience.

ALCOHOL
Don't let their schedules fool you, college kids always find time to party. In fact, partying is such a staple of the college like that the average student spends $2,600/year on beer.

COFFEE
Between exciting social life, class projects, studying, and part time work, a daily dose of caffeine is nearly required to function. All those morning Starbucks lattés can add up to $1,800/year.

CLOTHING
College is a chance to redefine oneself, to transform one's image, and of course, to get dates with style. To that end, college students spend around $750/year on new clothes.

ENTERTAINMENT
And where do they take all the new dates you meet at college? To the movies, concerts, plays, resturants, and on and on. In fact, the average college student spends around $4,000 per year on entertainment.

BOOKS AND SUPPLIES
The national average cost of books and class supplies for the 2010 - 2011 school year was $1,137.

COMPUTING COSTS
The average retail price of a new laptop for college is around $1700. This works out to about $425/year in computing costs.

ROOM AND BOARD
Room and board fees cover the cost of on-campus housing and a meal plan for food served in the school cafeteria. In 2008 these costs stood around $7999/year average.

TRANSPORATION
Between exploring their new city and traveling home on the holidays, students living on-campus from the 2010 - 2011 school year spent an average of $1,073 on transportation.

ACTIVITY/DORM SOCIAL FEES
Many students decide to join a fraternity or sorority to take advantage of the social life. Greek life isn't free however – dues can cost about $600/year.

CELL PHONE
A cell phone is a survival tool in college. The average cell phone bill is around $63/month.

GREEK DUES
Many students decide to join a fraternity or sorority to take advantage of the social life. Greek life isn't free however – dues can cost about $600/year.

SPORTING EVENTS
Each year, college students throw on their face paint, don big foam fingers, and support their school at at least one sports game. The average cost of a college football game is around $50.

FOOD
Of course, not every meal can be eaten on campus, especially with all those late nights exploring the new city. Assuming the student eats the majority of their meals on campus, extra food costs typically run around $750 per year.

LAB FEES
Most degrees require students to take at least one science class and/or art class. Lab fees for such classes typically run around $60/semester per class.

SPRING BREAK
If ever there was a reason to crack open beers at 9 AM on a beach, spring break at college is it. The average cost of a trip to any of the popular spring break destinations is $500.

MUSIC ROOM
Students who take music classes need to rent practice rooms to rehearse. This generally costs about $75 per semester, depending on the school.

Sources: www.collegeboard.com; abcnews.go.com; walletpop.com; college.lovetoknow.com; collegeboard .com; youngadults.about.com; mainstreet.com; degreecentral.com; icsellinghope.com; campuscalm.com; blog .oregonlive.com

ANTHONY P. **CARNEVALE**

College Is Still Worth It

It's an old story: when economic downturns hit, unemployment rates spiral and tales of college graduates forced to tend bar or mop floors proliferate. So, too, do the assertions of experts and budget-constrained political leaders that young people don't need costly postsecondary education in a job market that has little use for college degrees.

2   Those who make the "skip college" argument [1] often bolster their arguments with official state and national Bureau of Labor Statistics (BLS) data suggesting that the U.S. higher education system has been turning out far more college grads than current or future job openings require.

3   To a public wary of paying steep tuition bills in a depressed economy, it all sounds alarming and—with the backing of national and state government BLS data—authoritative.

4   There's just one problem with the official BLS statistics: they're wrong.

5   BLS data assigns occupations a "required" education level. Their numbers assert that 16.6 percent of jobs, or nearly 25 million jobs, require a bachelor's; in reality, over 30.7 million jobs, or 20.4 percent are filled with workers who have a bachelor's.

6   The BLS also holds that 6.1 million jobs (4.1 percent) require an associate degree, when 14 million jobs across the economy are actually filled by those with associate-degree holders. The BLS data, therefore, imply that Americans are overeducated.

7   The most persuasive evidence that the BLS numbers are wrong are earnings data, which show that employers across the country pay a "wage premium" to college graduates, even in occupations that BLS does not consider "college" jobs. This simply means that businesses pay more money to workers with degrees than to those without because employers believe that postsecondary educated workers are more valuable.

8   And employers aren't just hiring degrees. Over the decades, this premium has ebbed and flowed, but the longer-term trend in demand for college graduates has risen consistently. The college wage premium over high school graduates dropped significantly in the 1970s when vast numbers of college-educated Baby Boomers and males who went to college instead of Vietnam flooded the job market.

9   When the baby boomers aged beyond their prime college age years and the Vietnam draft ended, most expected a plunge in college-going. The rate of college-going did fall off, but not nearly as much as most experts predicted. Instead, a sharp upswing in the demand for college-educated workers kept college enrollments growing. Moreover, since the early 1980s, college completion has been unable to keep pace with employer demand. As a result, the college wage premium over high school degrees skyrocketed from roughly 30 percent to 74 percent at present. Hardly a sign of an oversupply of college talent.

10   To dismiss the significance of wage data requires a belief that employers across the country have systematically hired overqualified workers for their job openings and then grossly overpaid them for the past three decades. Consider the implications: It would mean that employers followed the law of supply and demand in the 1970s by cutting back the wage premium, but completely cast it aside in subsequent years by inexplicably throwing extra money at college-educated workers.

11   It would mean that, by 2008, more than a *third* of all workers with postsecondary education were receiving an appreciable economic benefit from their degrees that reasonable employers should never have paid. In short, if all of this is true, then chaos reigns: economic markets don't work, employers are irrational, and preparing children for college is naive for all but a select few.

12   There is a better explanation for the puzzling official data that suggest we are producing too many college graduates.

Official Education Demand Numbers Have Serious Flaws

13   Bureau of Labor Statistics data, as mentioned, underpin the argument that America overproduces college graduates by the millions. Among the chronically overqualified and overpaid are 43 percent of nuclear technicians who have attained more than the "required" associate degree, and the 80 percent of commercial pilots who hold more than their "required" certificate.

14   While we have high regard for the BLS, and believe that its national and state-level occupational and employment data are unimpeachable, we cannot say the same for its education numbers. They are an offhand byproduct of its other data—and of substantially lower quality.

15   One significant flaw in the BLS method is that it categorizes occupations as either "college" or "non-college," a methodology that is both subjective and static. A better approach, typical of mainstream economic analysis, is to track actual earnings of college graduates to determine the demand for postsecondary education. We reason that if the wages of college-educated workers within an occupation are high and/or rising relative to people with high school diplomas or less, that reflects a tangible advantage conferred by postsecondary education. People with college degrees in these occupations, therefore, are not overeducated because they are actually gaining value in return for their educational investment. While all degrees may not produce equal returns, in virtually every case, the return is far greater than the cost of obtaining the diploma.

16   In contrast, we do not define the "college labor market" as the BLS does, with its set of "college" occupations that cover the traditional white-collar and professional jobs. The official BLS data assign an education level to an occupation based on the lowest level of education attainment necessary to access the occupation. This approach is remarkably static and fails to adjust to changing economic realities.

17   For one, it misses the shift toward increased postsecondary requirements within occupations that are not traditionally deemed "college jobs." Labor economists agree that there has been a consistent shift toward increased postsecondary requirements across a growing share of occupations that previously did not require two- or four-year college degrees. Examples in the white-collar world include increasing demand for college degrees among managers, health care workers, and a wide variety of office workers, from insurance agents to building inspectors. Examples in the blue- and pink-collar world include increasing degree requirements among production workers, health care technicians, and utility and transportation workers.

Technology Drives Ongoing Demand for Better-Educated Workers

18   The standard explanation in the economic literature for such shifts is "skill-biased technology change." The core mechanism behind this concept in our current economy is the computer, which automates repetitive tasks and increases the relative value of non-repetitive tasks in individual occupations. Performing these more sophisticated tasks successfully typically requires more skill, training and education.

19   Wage data show that employers have tended to hire workers with postsecondary credentials for these more complex positions—and pay a wage premium to get them. As a result, we view a "college job" as any position that gives substantial earnings returns to a college degree, irrespective of occupation, whether an individual is an insurance agent or a rocket scientist.

20   Our method for tracking education demand is also careful to minimize counting statistical outliers such as bartenders, cab drivers and janitors with BAs and graduate degrees. These kinds of mismatches between degrees and low-skilled jobs—a phenomenon sometimes called "over-education"—are relatively small in number and don't matter much in an economy of nearly 150 million jobs. In addition, most such workers

won't stay in those positions long-term. They eventually move on to better-paying jobs. Over a 10-year period, each cashier job has 13 incumbents who permanently leave the occupation; among medical doctors, that replacement rate is only one.

21   People rarely leave jobs that require a college education because they have the best earnings, benefits and working conditions. There are many more brain surgeons who used to be cashiers than there are cashiers who used to be brain surgeons. A brain surgeon never starts as a brain surgeon, but would have likely had all types of jobs before entering college and medical school. Most jobs people hold in high school are in retail, food services, and other low-skill, low-wage jobs, and future brain surgeons are no exception.

22   In addition, low-skill, non-college positions tend to be greatly overrepresented in the official jobs data because so many of them are part-time. Although low-wage, low-skill jobs make up 20 percent of all jobs in a single year, they only make up 14 percent of the hours worked. Jobs that require a BA or better make up 30 percent of all jobs, but 75 percent of those are full-time, full-year jobs, compared with 64 percent of jobs that require a high school diploma or less.

23   There are, then, a number of serious flaws with the BLS education demand numbers, ranging from the designation of college and non-college occupations to their failure to reflect rising education requirements across virtually every occupational category. Still, because the BLS has a stellar—and deserved—reputation for its employment data, its static and misleading metrics on education requirements are treated with undue credibility. BLS numbers are widely used by social scientists to gauge education demand, and yet their accuracy receives little serious scrutiny.

Census Numbers Offer Valuable Test of BLS Education Demand Projections

24   As it turns out, though, there is an effective test to gauge the validity of education demand projections based on BLS data. The Census Bureau actually counts the number of workers with college degrees in the workforce and tracks their earnings on the job. As time passes and the Census data catch up with the BLS projections, we can determine if those projections were accurate. To get to the punch line: BLS projections always under-predict demand for college educations.

25   For instance, when we compare the BLS projections for 2006 and the actual count of people in the labor force with degrees during that year, we see that the Bureau undercounted the true number of postsecondary-educated workers by 17 million in 2006, or roughly 30 percent, and by 22 million, or 40 percent in 2008. The alternative method we introduced in Help Wanted [2] missed by just 4 percent.

26   The bottom line is that the BLS predictions didn't even come close to what actually happened in the economy. The only way to reconcile those projections with real life is to assert that the Bureau's projections reflect the number of college degrees employers actually *require,* not the actual numbers of college-educated workers they decide to hire. If this is the case, then employers not only hired millions of overqualified workers in 2006 and 2008, but paid wage premiums of more than 70 percent for the privilege— a notion, as we said earlier, that requires a belief that business owners across the nation and economic markets as a whole have taken leave of their senses.

Spate of Media Stories on Value of College Fuels Needless Fears

27   And yet, much of the media coverage of the issue would have us believe college isn't worth it.

28   Stories on the value of college tend to follow the business cycle, and when the cycle is down, journalists often find it easy to write a story that bucks the conventional wisdom. Headlines that suggest postsecondary education no longer pays off in the labor market are news because they play into middle-class parents' fears that they will not be able to give their children the advantages they had. The bad advice gets more and more pointed as the recession deepens.

29   This year, the *New York Times* offered "Plan B: Skip College," while the *Washington Post* ran "Parents Crunch the Numbers and Wonder, Is College Still Worth It?" Even the *Chronicle of Higher Education* has succumbed, [3] recently running "Here's Your Diploma. Now Here's Your Mop."—a story about a college graduate working as a janitor that implies a college degree may not be worthwhile in today's economic climate.

30   And if college educated workers were overpaid by 75 percent and oversupplied by 40 percent, why wouldn't they be the first fired and last hired in these tough times? It is true that unemployment rates are relatively high among college grads. When it rains long enough and hard enough, everyone gets wet. But the unemployment rate for all workers with college degrees is a quarter the rate for high school graduates.

31   And it's true, as the *New York Times* pointed out in an editorial [4] on December 13, that the unemployment rate for freshly minted college grads was 9.2 percent, not much different from the 9.8 percent unemployment rate for all workers. But the *Times* didn't bother to mention that the unemployment rate for freshly minted high school graduates was 35 percent.

32   The current recession isn't the first to produce such gloom. The *New York Times* and other prominent newspapers were printing similar stories in the early 1980s, during the last severe recession. At that time, the *Times* ran headlines like "The Underemployed: Working for Survival Instead of Careers."

33   And it's not just the journalists who get gloomy. The *New York Times* quoted Ronald Kutscher, associate commissioner at the Bureau of Labor Statistics in 1984, as saying, "We are going to be turning out about 200,000 to 300,000 too many college graduates a year in the '80s." Yet the 1980s was a decade that saw an unprecedented rise in the wage premium for college-educated workers over high school-educated workers. The wage premium for college degrees over high school degrees increased from 30 percent to more than 80 percent—evidence that the postsecondary system was under-producing college graduates, not that, as Kutscher went on to say, "the supply far exceeds the demand."

34   The gloomy stories, the high unemployment among college graduates and the misleading official data are unlikely to keep many middle- and upper-class youth from going to college. Higher education is a value that such families are unlikely to abandon, regardless of economic pressures. Instead, the real tragedy of these headlines is the message they send to less privileged youth for whom college is not an assumed path. The negative press on college fuels pre-existing biases among working families that college is neither accessible nor worth the cost and effort. Moreover, the bad press and worse data strengthen the hand of elitists [5] who argue that college should be the exclusive preserve of those born into the right race, ethnicity and bank account.

35   It is important to note that current evidence demonstrates increasing demand for college graduates, and the future promises more of the same. By 2018, our own projections from the "Help Wanted" study show that 63 percent of jobs nationwide will require some form of postsecondary degree. Moreover, postsecondary education has

become the only way to secure middle-class earnings in America and, for the least advantaged among us, is now the only way to escape poverty. In 1970, about 60 percent of Americans who attained middle-class status were high school graduates or dropouts. Today, only 46 percent can be found there. In contrast, 44 percent of the top three income deciles had postsecondary education in 1970; today, 81 percent do.

36   The press coverage and expert stumbles don't reflect the empirical reality, but they are symptomatic of a mundane human instinct. People tend to project what's happening in the present into the distant future. If housing prices are great, they'll be that way forever! If job creation is slow, it will be that way forever! If college graduates have to work as bartenders in the depth of a recession, their degrees will never get them ahead! The reality is that jobs come and go with economic cycles. But what lies beneath the economic cycles, and what has remained constant, is the relentless engine of technological change that demands more skilled workers. There is no indication that the trend has suddenly reversed itself.

College Is Still the Best Safe Harbor in Bad Economic Times

37   Meanwhile, when jobs disappear, college is the best safe harbor for waiting out the recession and improving your hiring prospects in anticipation of the recovery. Indeed, college-educated workers are much more likely to be employed than their high school-educated counterparts, even during a recession.

38   Irrespective of the current economic conditions, individuals need to consider college as a lifelong investment decision. Likewise, the investment horizon for economic development needs to be measured in decades, not annual budget cycles. Skipping or shortening college on the basis of a headline or even a few years of bad economic news is foolish for individuals whose careers will span 40 or more years of working life. On average, skipping an associate degree will cost a high school graduate half a million dollars in earnings, and skipping a bachelor's degree will cost $1 million in potential earnings over a lifetime.

39   Many argue that the value of college is declining as tuition rises. [6] However, while it is true that the sticker price cost of going to college has risen faster than the inflation rate, the college wage premium has risen even faster, both in terms of the cost of going to college and the inflation rate. The best measure of the value of college is the net present value of going to college. Here we discount the lifetime earnings by the real interest rate, and discount the principal and interest payments from taking out a college loan (a $60,000 loan). Once we've done that, the most accurate estimation of the average value of a college education over a high school education is still $1 million dollars (net present value).

40   Our own forthcoming research shows that we have under-produced college graduates by almost 10 million since 1983. We also find in Help Wanted that through 2018, at least three million jobs that require postsecondary education and training will be unfilled due to lack of supply. The share of jobs for those with a high school education or less is shrinking. In 1973, high school graduates and dropouts accounted for 72 percent of jobs, while by 2007 it was 41 percent. The opposite has happened for those with at least some college: the share of jobs has increased from 28 percent in 1973 to 59 percent in 2007, and is projected to be 63 percent by 2018. Likewise, the share of national wage income from college-educated workers has increased from 38 percent to 73 percent since 1970, and there is every reason to believe that this trend will continue.

41   We believe there is no doubt about the requirements of our fast-approaching economic future: we need more college graduates, not fewer. But at the very time we

need our higher-education system to kick into high gear, it is under pressure to apply the brakes instead.

42   While the economics of higher education are clear, the politics are not. The economy's lackluster demand in recession, coupled with media stories questioning the value of college, makes it easier to excuse cuts in public funding for postsecondary education. In the short term, federal stimulus funds have helped fill the gaps for post-secondary cuts driven by declining state revenues. But the stimulus funds will be unavailable after 2011, and federal money can't make up the difference indefinitely. In fact, it's an easy target for the chopping block. Higher education is especially vulnerable in the debate about public priorities because it lacks the core constituency and the immediacy of such issues as Social Security or homeland security.

43   Still, it's clear that reducing funding for postsecondary education is both bad economic and social policy. The consequences of slashing higher education budgets is a decision that will effect inequality for the next several decades by determining who gets access to middle-class careers. And, slowing the stream of college graduates into the economy threatens to leave employers without the skilled workers they need to thrive in a fiercely competitive economy.

44   While doubts about spending on higher education are understandable in the depths of a catastrophic recession, the potential consequences of succumbing to gloom and relying on flawed data to inform decisions about the value of postsecondary education are ruinous.

45   Bad numbers on the economic value of college encourage disinvestment in college both by individuals and government. And disinvestment in higher education is bad news not only for our higher education system, but for our economy—and for the lives and futures of millions of Americans.

Links

1. http://www.nebhe.org/2010/11/30/the-real-education-crisis-are-35-of-all-college-degrees-in-new-england-unnecessary/
2. http://cew.georgetown.edu/jobs2018/
3. http://chronicle.com/article/Heres-Your-Diploma-Now/124982/
4. http://www.nytimes.com/2010/12/14/opinion/14tue1.html
5. http://www.aei.org/article/101207
6. http://www.insidehighered.com/news/2008/04/07/miller

RICHARD **VEDDER**

For Many, College Isn't Worth It

In this space last Friday, Anthony Carnevale strongly and lengthily argued [1] that "college is still worth it." He implicitly criticized those, including me [2], who rely on U.S. Bureau of Labor Statistics (BLS) data showing that the number of college graduates exceeds the number of available jobs that require a college degree. While he says many things, he has two main points. First, "There's just one problem with the official BLS statistics: they're wrong." Second, he notes that "the most persuasive evidence that the BLS numbers are wrong are earnings data which show employers across the country pay a 'wage premium' for college graduates. . . . "

2   I will argue that the BLS data are, in fact, pretty good, and that while Carnevale is factually correct about the earnings data, his interpretation of it is, at the minimum, misleading. Moreover, I will further argue that what is involved here is a classic application of what economists over the age of 50 call "Say's Law" (i.e., the theory suggesting that supply creates its own demand; economists under 50 are largely ignorant of it because they have no knowledge of the evolution of their own discipline, reflecting the general abandonment of thorough teaching of the history of economic thought).

3   Furthermore, I will argue that diplomas are a highly expensive and inefficient screening device used by employers who are afraid to test potential employee skills owing to a most unfortunate Supreme Court decision and related legislation. Finally, I will assert that Carnevale and others who argue "college has a high payoff" are comparing apples with oranges—i.e., they are making totally inappropriate comparisons that lead to skewed conclusions.

4   An even-handed interpretation of the data is that college *is* "worth it" for some significant number of young people, but is a far more problematic investment for others. The call by President Obama, the Lumina and Gates Foundations, and many higher education advocates to rapidly and radically increase the number of college graduates is fundamentally off-base.

The BLS Data

5   Carnevale essentially argues that the BLS data are pretty bad, mainly because earnings data show that employers pay workers with college degrees a wage premium, which would be irrational if the education associated with a college degree were not valuable for the job in question. Indeed, "a better approach" to this question, according to Carnevale, would be "to track actual earnings of college graduates to determine the demand for postsecondary education." Additionally, Carnevale accurately notes that there are some variations within skills required within some of the BLS occupational categories, and it is possible that for some jobs a college degree would be necessary or highly desirable, while for others it would not be.

6   However, Carnevale's overall description of the BLS data and its system for categorizing education requirements is far from accurate. For instance, Carnevale blandly declares that "[t]he official BLS data assign an education level to an occupation based on the lowest level of education attainment necessary to access the occupation." Actually, as the BLS makes quite clear on its website [3], it "assign[s] what [its] research suggests was the most significant source of education or training" for each occupation. (Apparently Carnevale confuses a proposed change to the BLS category system—and one which isn't going to be implemented [4] at that—with the system currently in place.) Furthermore, the BLS also noted that its data do in some cases understate educational requirements, but in others they overstate it, suggesting that, in the aggregate, the BLS data can be viewed as reasonably sound.

7   Another problem with Carnevale's critique of the BLS data is that, in reality, the BLS dataset is arguably superior to that developed by Carnevale and his colleagues.

This point was made a couple of months ago by Paul E. Harrington and Andrew M. Sum [5] when they observed that taking Carnevale's approach "assumes a world where no under-employment or mal-employment of college graduates exists." On the other hand, the BLS dataset is robust enough to account for underemployment, albeit perhaps imperfectly.

8   Carnevale's criticism of the BLS data is nothing, however, compared to that of Cliff Adelman of the Institute for Higher Education Policy, who, in commenting on Carnevale's article, said "the base data are bizarre," claiming the statistics misrepresented the numbers in some occupations (he focused on solar panel installers and like occupations) by a huge magnitude. Adelman simply misread the data—badly—as Carnevale himself has indicated in a response.

9   Before turning to Carnevale's earnings-based argument, I want to comment on his remark about "statistical outliers such as bartenders, cab drivers and janitors with B.A.s and graduate degrees. . . . These kinds of mismatches between degrees and low-skilled jobs . . . are relatively small in number and don't matter much. . . . "

10   Hogwash. The BLS tells us that for waiters and waitresses alone, there are more than one-third of a million who hold B.A. degrees or more—not an inconsequential number. And the BLS data would indicate that, in total, about 17 million college graduates have jobs that do not require a college degree. Not only is that 11 percent or so of the total labor force, hardly a "relatively small" number, but, more relevantly, it constitutes well over 30 percent of the working college graduates in the U.S.—a number of mammoth proportions.

11   Carnevale argues that a large portion of these persons are short-term in these jobs, and that they typically move on into more appropriate jobs later on. I am the first to admit the turnover rate of waiters is greater than that of physicians, but so what? If roughly one-third of college graduates in general are in jobs not requiring college-level training, that is far more than frictional unemployment—workers temporarily taking a low paying job while awaiting more permanent employment. And that certainly is not simply a function of the recession, although that phenomenon no doubt has aggravated the problem.

The Earnings Data

12   Carnevale is absolutely correct that college graduates on average earn more than those with lesser formal educational certifications. And I would agree that on average college graduates have a higher productivity per worker (justifying the higher pay) than those merely possessing high school diplomas. Therefore, for many, going to college is a good personal investment decision.

13   But to a considerable extent, the reason college graduates have higher pay has little to do with what they learned in college *per se*. Suppose an employer has two applicants, who in personal interviews seemed similar in quality. The employer likely will choose the college graduate over the high school graduate because, on average, college graduates have higher levels of cognitive skills (as measured by IQ tests or similar instruments), are more likely to have relatively high levels of motivation and discipline developed before attending college, have more general knowledge about the world in which we live, etc. Hence such employees are often offered a wage premium, since the anticipated level of performance of the college graduate is perceived to be higher. The

diploma serves as a screening device that allows businesses to narrow down the applicant pool quickly and almost without cost to the employer, but with a huge financial cost to the individual earning the diploma (often at least $100,000), and to society at large in the form of public subsidies.

14   For the past several decades, moreover, the ability of employers to find other means of certifying competence and skills has been severely circumscribed by judicial decisions and laws. In *Griggs v. Duke Power* (1971), the U.S. Supreme Court essentially outlawed employer testing of prospective workers where the test imparted a "disparate impact" on members of minority groups. Cautious employers have sharply reduced such testing, and are now forced to rely on other measures of competence, namely the possession of a college diploma.

15   This perception that college is primarily a screening device rather than the source of a true vocationally relevant curriculum is supported by a good deal of data that show college students spend relatively little time in academic studies (e.g., the Time Use Survey [6] data of the BLS). The most notable recent effort, utilizing detailed data from the National Survey of Student Engagement, is examined in Richard Arum and Josipa Roksa's new book *Academically Adrift: Limited Learning on College Campuses* [7], just released by the University of Chicago Press. "How much are students actually learning in contemporary higher education? The answer for many undergraduates, we have concluded, is not much," write Arum and Roksa.

Say's Law and Credential Inflation

16 The economist Jean Baptiste Say, writing in 1803, formulated his "law of markets," which can be roughly summarized as: "supply creates its own demand." In the context of American higher education, colleges have supplied millions of graduates over recent decades—more than needed to fill jobs that historically have been considered ones requiring the skills associated with a college education. Therefore, employers are flooded with applicants who possess college degrees, and given the inherently better character and intellectual traits that college graduates on average have, the employers demand a diploma for a job. The rise in the supply of diplomas created the demand for them, not the other way around.

17   Jobs that have not changed much over time, such as serving as a mail carrier or restaurant manager, now have large numbers of college graduates filling them, relative to the past. This is almost certainly mainly a manifestation of what might be termed "credential inflation." To be sure, the quality of high school graduates may have declined over time somewhat owing to the mediocre state of our public schools, but it is hard to believe this is important in explaining the rise in, say, college-educated mail carriers.

Apples and Oranges: Risk-Taking in Attending College

18 A huge problem in any analysis such as that performed by Carnevale is that it ignores the vast number of students who enter college and do not complete a degree. While I am the first to admit there are some problems with the underlying IPEDS data used to measure dropout rates, it is probably nonetheless true that at least two out of every five persons entering college full-time fail to graduate within *six* years. There is a huge risk associated with enrolling in college: you might not graduate. A person considering a $100,000 investment in 1,000 shares of XYZ Corporation common stock at $100

a share is assured that he or she will have those 1,000 shares, although there are some risks associated with the shares declining in value over time. A person making a $100,000 investment in a B.A. degree is *not* assured that he or she will obtain the investment—i.e., actually graduate in a timely fashion.

19   For years, economists have written that the rate of return on college investments tends to be high—10 percent is an oft-cited estimate, greater than the average investor is likely to earn in alternatives such as stocks, bonds or real estate. Thus the studies have concluded that going to college typically makes sense, independent of any non-pecuniary advantages college offers. Yet these studies have failed to account for the added risk associated with it—the probability of dropping out.

20   Two new studies have attempted to correct for this problem, one by Gonzalo Castex and the other by Kartik Athreya and Janice Eberly [8]. They suggest that the reported superior rate of return on investing in college disappears when investments are adjusted for risk.

21   At the individual student level, it is possible to reasonably estimate the risk. A student who was at the top of her class at a top-flight suburban high school, had a composite SAT score of 1500, and plans to attend a private college with relatively low dropout rates is probably going to get a reasonable return on her investment, although even that is no certainty. By contrast, a student who is below average in his graduating class from a mediocre high school, has a combined SAT score of 850, and is considering a college with high dropout rates is very likely not to graduate even in six years, and probably will get a very low return on his college investment. That student might well do much better by going to a certificate program at a career college, learning to be a truck driver, or becoming a barber, for example.

22   In short, a good maxim is "different strokes for different folks." A one-size-fits-all solution does not work as long as human beings have vastly different aptitudes, skills, motivations, etc. On balance, we are probably over-invested in higher education, not under-invested. The earnings data reflect less about human capital accumulation imparted to college graduates by their collegiate experiences than the realities of information costs associated with job searches.

23   With fewer public subsidies of higher education, I suspect much or all of the problem would disappear: College enrollments would reach levels consistent with the needs of our economy and the personal economic welfare of those attending.

Links

1. http://www.insidehighered.com/views/2011/01/14/carnevale_college_is_still_worth_it_for_americans
2. http://collegeaffordability.blogspot.com/search/label/underemployment
3. http://www.bls.gov/emp/ep_education_tech.htm
4. http://www.bls.gov/emp/ep_propedtrain.htm
5. http://www.nebhe.org/2010/11/08/college-labor-shortages-in-2018/
6. http://www.bls.gov/tus/charts/students.htm
7. http://www.insidehighered.com/news/2011/01/18/study_finds_large_numbers_of_college_students_don_t_learn_much
8. http://www.aeaweb.org/aea/2011conference/program/preliminary.php?search_string=eberly&search_type=last_name&search=Search

...FOR THE NEXT THIRTY YEARS

NIALL **FERGUSON**

Who Needs College?

School is in the air. It is the time of year when millions of apprehensive young people are crammed into their parents' cars along with all their worldly gadgets and driven off to college.

2   The rest of the world looks on with envy. American universities are the best in the world—22 out of the world's top 30, according to the Graduate School of Education at Shanghai Jiao Tong University. Once it was Oxford or Cambridge that bright young Indians dreamed of attending; now it is Harvard or Stanford. Admission to a top U.S. college is the ultimate fast track to the top.

3   Little do the foreigners know that all is far from well in the groves of American academe.

4   Let's start with the cost. According to the College Board, average tuition and fees for in-state residents at a sample of public colleges have soared by 25 percent since 2008–09. A key driver has been the reduction in funding as states have been forced to adopt austerity measures. In the same time frame, tuition and fees at private universities rose by less (13 percent), but still by a lot more than inflation.

5   According to the Consumer Financial Protection Bureau, total student debt (which includes private loans and federal loans) climbed to more than $1 trillion. It is the only form of consumer debt that has continued to grow even as households pay off

mortgages, credit cards, and auto loans. In real terms, students are borrowing twice what they did a decade ago.

6   It's not only Facebook stock that Silicon Valley superstar Peter Thiel is selling. He's shorting higher education, too, arguing that college is the new asset bubble—the natural successor to subprime. Remember when we all believed that a home was an investment that would never lose money? Now, Thiel argues, exactly the same thing is being said about a degree. To back up his point, Thiel is paying 20 of the country's most promising students $100,000 to walk away from their studies and become entrepreneurs.

7   Thiel is not alone in his skepticism. "President Obama once said he wants everybody in America to go to college. What a snob!" Rick Santorum famously declared. "There are good, decent men and women who go out and work hard every day . . . that aren't taught by some liberal college professor trying to indoctrinate them."

8   The irony is that Thiel himself was a star student at Stanford, with degrees in philosophy and law, while Santorum himself has no fewer than three degrees.

9   Come to think of it, you probably do need a degree to get through the recent, voluminous literature on this subject. Start with Andrew Hacker and Claudia Dreifus's *Higher Education? How Colleges Are Wasting Our Money and Failing Our Kids*, which slams professors at the "Golden Dozen" top U.S. colleges. Apparently, we neglect our students, while university bureaucrats squander gazillions on sports facilities with no academic value. Despite being an alumnus of Brown, Michael Ellsberg, author of *The Education of Millionaires*, believes that college "can actually hold you back." And in *Academically Adrift*, Richard Arum and Josipa Roksa argue that students' skills scarcely improve in college, while their motivation may actually decline.

10   But doesn't a degree improve your chances of getting a job? Not anymore. Recent graduates are just as likely as anyone to be out of a job right now. Globalization and technology aren't just destroying unskilled jobs; many of the functions previously performed by graduates are now being off-shored.

11   As a professor, I can see much that is wrong with our system—but not so much that I would advise a smart 18-year-old to skip college. The real problem is not that our college system is failing. The problem is that it is succeeding all too well—at ranking and sorting each cohort of school-leavers by academic performance.

11   As Charles Murray has pointed out, our highly competitive admissions system has become a mechanism for selecting a "cognitive elite." In 1997, just over a hundred elite colleges, which admitted fewer than a fifth of all freshmen, also accounted for three quarters of the ones with SAT or ACT scores in the top 5 percent.

12   Meritocracy in action? The problem is that this cognitive elite has become self-perpetuating: they marry one another, live in close proximity to one another, and use every means, fair or foul, to ensure that their kids follow in their academic footsteps (even when Junior is innately less smart than Mom and Dad).

13   Paradoxically, our universities now offer social mobility mostly to foreigners. For Americans, they risk creating a new caste system.

NICOLE **ALLAN** AND DEREK **THOMPSON**

The Myth of the Student-Loan Crisis

This month, college-admission letters are being accompanied by national anxiety over the growing "student-debt crisis." The cost of college has spiked 150 percent since 1995, compared with a 50 percent increase in the cost of other goods and services. Last year, outstanding student loans soared to nearly $1 trillion—a 300 percent jump since 2003. College is an undeniably risky investment, seemingly more so than ever. But are rising debt levels a national crisis?

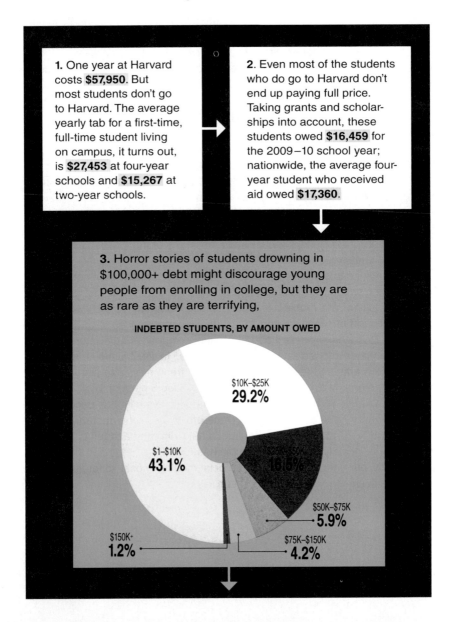

1. One year at Harvard costs **$57,950**. But most students don't go to Harvard. The average yearly tab for a first-time, full-time student living on campus, it turns out, is **$27,453** at four-year schools and **$15,267** at two-year schools.

2. Even most of the students who do go to Harvard don't end up paying full price. Taking grants and scholarships into account, these students owed **$16,459** for the 2009–10 school year; nationwide, the average four-year student who received aid owed **$17,360**.

3. Horror stories of students drowning in $100,000+ debt might discourage young people from enrolling in college, but they are as rare as they are terrifying,

INDEBTED STUDENTS, BY AMOUNT OWED

$10K–$25K
29.2%

$1–$10K
43.1%

$25K–$50K
16.5%

$50K–$75K
5.9%

$150K+
1.2%

$75K–$150K
4.2%

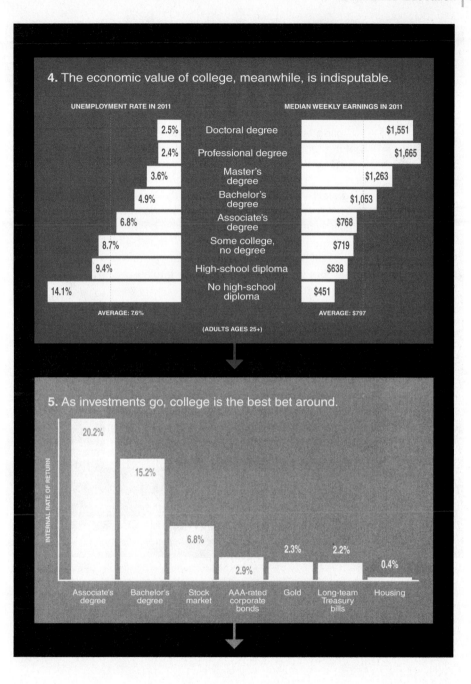

4. The economic value of college, meanwhile, is indisputable.

UNEMPLOYMENT RATE IN 2011 | | MEDIAN WEEKLY EARNINGS IN 2011

2.5%	Doctoral degree	$1,551
2.4%	Professional degree	$1,665
3.6%	Master's degree	$1,263
4.9%	Bachelor's degree	$1,053
6.8%	Associate's degree	$768
8.7%	Some college, no degree	$719
9.4%	High-school diploma	$638
14.1%	No high-school diploma	$451
AVERAGE: 7.6%		AVERAGE: $797

(ADULTS AGES 25+)

5. As investments go, college is the best bet around.

INTERNAL RATE OF RETURN

- Associate's degree: 20.2%
- Bachelor's degree: 15.2%
- Stock market: 6.8%
- AAA-rated corporate bonds: 2.9%
- Gold: 2.3%
- Long-team Treasury bills: 2.2%
- Housing: 0.4%

6. College is such a good investment, in fact, that it might even justify *more* student debt. A 2012 study found that **1 in 6** full-time students at four-year schools who were eligible for government loans weren't taking advantage of them. Another found that low-income families are likely to overestimate the cost of college, and suggested that they may be scared off by the complexity of financial-aid forms. But for students from these families, not going to college can be more expensive than going to college.

7. Each of the 6.7 million Americans ages 16 to 24 who are neither employed nor in school costs the country **$37,450** a year in lost wages, lost tax revenue, and higher public spending. Compared with this figure, the cost of college is a bargain—for students and for taxpayers.

1. Harvard University; National Center for Education Statistics. 2. National Center for Education Statistics. 3. Federal Reserve Bank of New York, 4. Bureau of Labor Statistics. 5. Brookings Institution, 6. Brian C. Cadena, University of Colorado at Boulder, and Benjamin J. Keys, University of Chicago; Eric Bettinger et al., National Bureau of Economic Research. 7. Clive R. Belfield et al., Civic Enterprises.

FROM READING TO WRITING

1. There are several explicit rebuttals in this chapter: Salman Khan in effect refutes Andrew Delbanco, for example, and Richard Vedder directly answers the argument of Anthony Carnevale. Find an essay in a local publication that is related to education issues and that you disagree with, and then compose a rebuttal. (Consult Chapter 12 on writing a rebuttal.)

2. Notice that several essays in this chapter make their arguments at least in part by referencing a personal experience. Write a narrative of your own experiences that supports your point of view about a specific educational practice or policy that operates at your college or in your community. (For more on narrative arguments, see Chapter 11.)

3. Evaluate some policy or practice related to education in your community; it could be a teacher, an academic department, the food, the athletic program, Greek life, admissions practices, tuition rates, or anything else. Be sure to base your evaluation on specific criteria, such as those described in Chapter 10.

4. Chapter 7 reproduces an ad from Hofstra University (page 89). Locate other ads for colleges (in magazines, in newspapers, or on college Web sites), and analyze the nature of the arguments presented. How do those ads present and support their arguments? Look carefully as well at the cartoons in this chapter. What specific arguments are offered in those cartoons, and what good reasons are offered in support?

5. Education arguments frequently depend on definitions. "Higher education is nothing but a big business," someone might say, for example. Or "Liberal arts education is turning into vocational education." Several essays in this chapter also offer definitions: Delbanco's definition of liberal education, for example, or Carey's definition of a MOOC. Compose your own argument that defines or redefines some concept or topic related to education—"general education" or "writing across the curriculum," for example; or Greek life; or charter schools, or whatever. For advice on definition arguments, see Chapter 8.

6. Imagine that Andrew Delbanco, Salman Khan, David Brooks, and Scott Carlson were involved in a conversation about the nature and goals of education. Considering the essays by those four thinkers that are reproduced in this chapter, do you think they would have any areas of agreement, any common ground? And what issues would separate them?

7. Would you say that a particular school or university that you are familiar with has markedly improved or deteriorated over the years? If so, what caused that advance or decline? (For advice on causal arguments, see Chapter 9.)

24 | Globalization

America meets the world as the iconic golden arches mix with Japanese characters at the world's busiest McDonald's restaurant in Tokyo. Is the world becoming more like America, or is America becoming more global?

America's Place in the World—and the World's Place in America

The place of America and Americans in relation to the rest of the world has always been an important topic in the national conversation. A product itself of globalization (embodied in the figure of Christopher Columbus) and created through the force of European colonialism, the United States has taken an increasing role in international affairs since its founding. But globalization has only grown more important, it seems, since the end of the Cold War (which seemed to leave the United States as the world's only superpower); since the development of economic reforms in China, in the European Union, and in other parts of the world (which are challenging the primacy of American economic power); and especially since the events of September 11 and the subsequent wars in Iraq and Afghanistan (which have underscored the limits of the American military and compromised our will to work cooperatively with traditional allies).

Indeed, according to a survey released by the Pew Research Center for the People and the Press, the American public has a divided, even paradoxical opinion about the place of the United States in the world. On the one hand, Americans agree that the United States has assumed a more powerful role as a world leader, but on the other hand, they concede that America also seems less respected around the world. Americans reject the role of the United States as a single world leader, but they also reject the pull toward isolation. More generally, then, Americans are confronting the issue of what has come to be known as globalization—that is, the general impact of various nations on each other, particularly the impact of American culture on other nations and cultures and the impact of those nations' cultures on the United States.

Some of that impact is economic, as the United States outsources manufacturing jobs to other nations and shifts in the direction of a service economy. Other effects are military and political, as leaders and citizens debate the wisdom of various options. For example, should our nation behave as a kind of American empire, free to impose its wishes and will on others? Should our foreign policy be an effort to export democracy, even at the point of a gun? Or should we cooperate more broadly with allies, cultivate new friends, and respect the right of each nation to self-determination? Should the United States close off its borders, literally and figuratively, to follow a kind of neo-isolationism?

Still other effects are broadly cultural, as Americans import some of the cultural practices and values of others, as in popular songs, films, restaurants, and fashions, and export our own cultural values and traditions to others. U.S. culture inevitably absorbs the values of immigrant populations and exports its ideologies (for example, representative democracy, women's rights, resistance to sweatshop labor, pluralistic religious tolerance). This chapter of *Good Reasons with Contemporary Arguments* offers arguments about one or another aspect of these questions related to globalization.

Contemporary Arguments

The arguments in this chapter focus on the exchange of capital and cultural goods between the United States and other nations. To contextualize the readings in the chapter and to offer perspective on globalization more generally, we first present Thomas Friedman, who explains approvingly the new "flat world" that globalization is creating. Richard Florida counters Friedman by arguing that the world is actually not "flat" but "spiky." Robyn Meredith and Suzanne Hoppough tout the economic benefits of globalization. And Sadanand Dhume interprets the Best Picture of 2008, *Slumdog Millionaire*, as the product of a thoroughly globalized mentality and as "a metaphor for India in the age of globalization."

Then, in the Issue in Focus section, we turn to specific analyses of popular culture in the United States that demonstrate the effects of globalization. How is American culture altering the cultures of other nations, and how is American culture being affected by globalization?

While the topics discussed in this chapter are varied, all of the readings bring up similar questions about the movement between cultures—of people, goods, values, images, and communication. What are the effects of globalization here and abroad? Where are those effects visible in our communities? What do you think about American importation of cultural forms from other nations? What about the exportation of American culture that is welcomed—even sought out—by people in other nations? Is this importation and exportation dangerous, enriching, or some complicated mixture of the two?

Thomas Friedman

Why the World Is Flat

Thomas Friedman is a syndicated columnist, whose work appears in the *New York Times*, as well as the author of a number of books on America in the world today, including *Longitudes and Attitudes: Exploring the World after September 11* (2002), *The World Is Flat: A Brief History of the Twenty-First Century* (2005), and *That Used to Be Us: How America Fell Behind in the World It Invented and How We Can Come Back* (2012). The online magazine *Wired* published the following interview in May 2005. Daniel Pink, the author of several books himself on globalization, as well as numerous articles in the *New York Times*, conducted the interview since he is a contributing editor for *Wired*.

Thirty-five years ago this summer, the golfer Chi Chi Rodriguez was competing in his seventh U.S. Open, played that year at Hazeltine Country Club outside Minneapolis. Tied for second place after the opening round, Rodriguez eventually finished 27th, a few strokes ahead of such golf legends as Jack Nicklaus, Arnold Palmer, and Gary Player. His caddy for the tournament was a 17-year-old local named Tommy Friedman.

2   Rodriguez retired from golf several years later. But his caddy—now known as Thomas L. Friedman, foreign affairs columnist for the *New York Times* and author of the new book *The World Is Flat: A Brief History of the Twenty-First Century*—has spent his career deploying the skills he used on the golf course: describing the terrain, shouting warnings and encouragement, and whispering in the ears of big players. After ten years of writing his twice-weekly foreign affairs column, Friedman has become the most influential American newspaper columnist since Walter Lippmann.

3   One reason for Friedman's influence is that, in the mid-'90s, he staked out the territory at the intersection of technology, financial markets, and world trade, which the foreign policy establishment, still focused on cruise missiles and throw weights, had largely ignored. "This thing called globalization," he says, "can explain more things in more ways than anything else."

4   Friedman's 1999 book, *The Lexus and the Olive Tree: Understanding Globalization*, provided much of the intellectual framework for the debate. "The first big book on globalization that anybody actually read," as Friedman describes it, helped make him a fixture on the Davos-Allen Conference-Renaissance Weekend circuit. But it

also made him a lightning rod. He's been accused of "rhetorical hyperventilation" and dismissed as an "apologist" for global capital. The columnist Molly Ivins even dubbed top-tier society's lack of concern for the downsides of globalization "the Tom Friedman Problem."

5 After 9/11, Friedman says, he paid less attention to globalization. He spent the next three years traveling to the Arab and Muslim world trying to get at the roots of the attack on the U.S. His columns on the subject earned him his third Pulitzer Prize. But Friedman realized that while he was writing about terrorism, he missed an even bigger story: Globalization had gone into overdrive. So in a three-month burst last year, he wrote *The World Is Flat* to explain his updated thinking on the subject.

6 Friedman enlisted some impressive editorial assistance. Bill Gates spent a day with him to critique the theory. Friedman presented sections of the book to the strategic planning unit at IBM and to Michael Dell. But his most important tutors were two Indians: Nandan Nilekani, CEO of Infosys, and Vivek Paul, a top executive at Wipro. "They were the guys who really cracked the code for me."

7 *Wired* sat down with Friedman in his office at the *Times'* Washington bureau to discuss the flattening of the world.

8 **WIRED: What do you mean the world is flat?**
FRIEDMAN: I was in India interviewing Nandan Nilekani at Infosys. And he said to me, "Tom, the playing field is being leveled." Indians and Chinese were going to compete for work like never before, and Americans weren't ready. I kept chewing over that phrase—"the playing field is being leveled"—and then it hit me: Holy mackerel, the world is becoming flat. Several technological and political forces have converged, and that has produced a global, Web-enabled playing field that allows for multiple forms of collaboration without regard to geography or distance—or soon, even language.

9 **So, we're talking about globalization enhanced by things like the rise of open source?**
This is Globalization 3.0. In Globalization 1.0, which began around 1492, the world went from size large to size medium. In Globalization 2.0, the era that introduced us to multinational companies, it went from size medium to size small. And then around 2000 came Globalization 3.0, in which the world went from being small to tiny. There's a difference between being able to make long distance phone calls cheaper on the Internet and walking around Riyadh with a PDA where you can have all of Google in your pocket. It's a difference in degree that's so enormous it becomes a difference in kind.

10 **Is that why the Netscape IPO is one of your "10 flatteners"? Explain.**
Three reasons. Netscape brought the Internet alive with the browser. They made the Internet so that Grandma could use it and her grandchildren could use it. The second thing that Netscape did was commercialize a set of open transmission protocols so that no company could own the Net. And the third is that Netscape triggered the dotcom boom, which triggered the dotcom bubble, which triggered the overinvestment of a trillion dollars in fiber-optic cables.

11 **Are you saying telecommunications trumps terrorism? What about September 11? Isn't that as important?**
There's no question flattening is more important. I don't think you can understand 9/11 without understanding flattening.

12　This is probably the first book by a major foreign affairs thinker that talks about the world-changing effects of . . . supply chains.

[*Friedman laughs.*]

The 10 Great Levelers

1. **Fall of the Berlin Wall**
   The events of November 9, 1989, tilted the worldwide balance of power toward democracies and free markets.

2. **Netscape IPO**
   The August 9, 1995, offering sparked massive investment in fiber-optic cables.

3. **Work flow software**
   The rise of apps from PayPal to VPNs enabled faster, closer coordination among far-flung employees.

4. **Open-sourcing**
   Self-organizing communities, à la Linux, launched a collaborative revolution.

5. **Outsourcing**
   Migrating business functions to India saved money *and* a third world economy.

6. **Offshoring**
   Contract manufacturing elevated China to economic prominence.

7. **Supply-chaining**
   Robust networks of suppliers, retailers, and customers increased business efficiency. See Walmart.

8. **Insourcing**
   Logistics giants took control of customer supply chains, helping mom-and-pop shops go global. See UPS and FedEx.

9. **In-forming**
   Power searching allowed everyone to use the Internet as a "personal supply chain of knowledge." See Google.

10. **Wireless**
    Like "steroids," wireless technologies pumped up collaboration, making it mobile and personal

13 **Why are supply chains so important?**

They're incredible flatteners. For UPS to work, they've got to create systems with customs offices around the world. They've got to design supply chain algorithms so when you take that box to the UPS Store, it gets from that store to its hub and then out. Everything they are doing is taking fat out of the system at every joint. I was in India after the nuclear alert of 2002. I was interviewing Vivek Paul at Wipro shortly after he'd gotten an email from one of their big American clients saying, "We're now looking for an alternative to you. We don't want to be looking for an alternative to you. You don't *want* us to be looking for an alternative to you. Do something about this!" So I saw the effect that India's being part of this global supply chain had on the behavior of the Indian business community, which eventually filtered up to New Delhi.

14 **And that's how you went from your McDonald's Theory of Conflict Prevention—two countries that have a McDonald's will never go to war with each other—to the Dell Theory of Conflict Prevention.**

Yes. No two countries that are both part of a major global supply chain like Dell's will fight against each other as long as they are both part of that supply chain. When I'm managing your back room, when I'm managing your HR, when I'm doing your accounting—that's way beyond selling you burgers. We are intimately in bed with each other. And that has got to affect my behavior.

15 **In some sense, then, the world is a gigantic supply chain. And you don't want to be the one who brings the whole thing down.**

Absolutely.

16 **Unless your goal is to bring the whole thing down. Supply chains work for al Qaeda, too, don't they?**

Al Qaeda is nothing more than a mutant supply chain. They're playing off the same platform as Walmart and Dell. They're just not restrained by it. What is al Qaeda? It's an open source religious political movement that works off the global supply chain. That's what we're up against in Iraq. We're up against a suicide supply chain. You take one bomber and deploy him in Baghdad, and another is manufactured in Riyadh the next day. It's exactly like when you take the toy off the shelf at Walmart and another is made in Shen Zhen the next day.

17 **The book is almost dizzily optimistic about India and China, about what flattening will bring to these parts of the world.**

I firmly believe that the next great breakthrough in bioscience could come from a 15-year-old who downloads the human genome in Egypt. Bill Gates has a nice line: He says, 20 years ago, would you rather have been a B-student in Poughkeepsie or a genius in Shanghai? Twenty years ago you'd rather be a B-student in Poughkeepsie. Today?

18 **Not even close.**

Not even close. You'd much prefer to be the genius in Shanghai because you can now export your talents anywhere in the world.

19 **As optimistic as you are about that kid in Shanghai, you're not particularly optimistic about the US.**

I'm worried about my country. I love America. I think it's the best country in the world. But I also think we're not tending to our sauce. I believe that we are in what Shirley Ann Jackson [president of Rensselaer Polytechnic Institute] calls a "quiet crisis." If we don't change course now and buckle down in a flat world, the kind of competition our kids will face will be intense and the social implications of not repairing things will be enormous.

20 **You quote a CEO who says that Americans have grown addicted to their high salaries, and now they're going to have to earn them. Are Americans suffering from an undue sense of entitlement?**
Somebody said to me the other day that—I wish I had this for the book, but it's going to be in the paperback—the entitlement we need to get rid of is our sense of entitlement.

21 **Let's talk about the critics of globalization. You say that you don't want the antiglobalization movement to go away. Why?**
I've been a critic of the antiglobalization movement, and they've been a critic of me, but the one thing I respect about the movement is their authentic energy. These are not people who don't care about the world. But if you want to direct your energy toward helping the poor, I believe the best way is not throwing a stone through a McDonald's window or protesting World Bank meetings. It's through local governance. When you start to improve local governance, you improve education, women's rights, transportation.

22 **It's possible to go through your book and conclude it was written by a US senator who wants to run for president. There's a political agenda in this book.**
Yes, absolutely.

23 **You call for portable benefits, lifelong learning, free trade, greater investment in science, government funding for tertiary education, a system of wage insurance. Uh, Mr. Friedman, are you running for president?**
[*Laughs loudly*.] No, I am not running for president!

24 **Would you accept the vice presidential nomination?**
I just want to get my Thursday column done!

25 **But you are outlining an explicit agenda.**
You can't be a citizen of this country and not be in a hair-pulling rage at the fact that we're at this inflection moment and nobody seems to be talking about the kind of policies we need to get through this flattening of the world, to get the most out of it and cushion the worst. We need to have as focused, as serious, as energetic, as sacrificing a strategy for dealing with flatism as we did for communism. This is the challenge of our day.

26 **Short of Washington fully embracing the Friedman doctrine, what should we be doing? For instance, what advice should we give to our kids?**
When I was growing up, my parents told me, "Finish your dinner. People in China and India are starving." I tell my daughters, "Finish your homework. People in India and China are starving for your job."

27 **Think about your own childhood for a moment. If a teenage Tommy Friedman could somehow have been transported to 2005, what do you think he would have found most surprising?**
That you could go to PGA.com and get the scores of your favorite golfer in real time. That would have been amazing.

Patrick Chappatte/Cagle Cartoons, Inc.

RICHARD **FLORIDA**

The World in Numbers:
The World Is Spiky

Richard Florida (born 1957) is a professor at the University of Toronto, but he is also a prominent and respected public intellectual who writes for a broad readership. In addition to several books, he has written many articles about global trends and economic development strategies for the *New York Times*, the *Wall Street Journal*, and other newspapers and magazines, and he appears frequently as a commentator on CNN, PBS, and CBS. Since 2011 he has been a senior editor for the *Atlantic* (a leading magazine on culture and literature since its founding before the Civil War), where the following article appeared in 2005. Among other things, it is a response to Thomas Friedman's argument that "the world is flat."

The World Is Spiky

*Globalization has changed the economic
playing field, but hasn't leveled it*

Ⓐ POPULATION
*Urban areas house half of all the
world's people, and continue to grow
in both rich and poor countries.*

The world, according to the title
of the *New York Times* columnist Thomas Friedman's book, is flat.
Thanks to advances in technology, the
global playing field has been leveled,
the prizes are there for the taking, and
everyone's a player—no matter where
on the surface of the earth he or she
may reside. "In a flat world," Friedman
writes, "you can innovate without having to emigrate."

Friedman is not alone in this belief:
for the better part of the past century
economists have been writing about
the leveling effects of technology.
From the invention of the telephone,
the automobile, and the airplane to the
rise of the personal computer and the
Internet, technological progress has
steadily eroded the economic importance of geographic place—or so the
argument goes.

But in partnership with colleagues
at George Mason University and the
geographer Tim Gulden, of the Center
for International and Security Studies, at the University of Maryland, I've
begun to chart a very different economic topography. By almost any
measure the international economic
landscape is not at all flat. On the contrary, our world is amazingly "spiky."
In terms of both sheer economic horse-
power and cutting-edge innovation,

PEAKS, HILLS, AND VALLEYS

When looked at through the lens of economic production, many cities
with large populations are diminished and some nearly vanish. Three
sorts of places make up the modern economic landscape. First are
the cities that generate innovations. These are the tallest peaks; they
have the capacity to attract global talent and create new products and
industries. They are few in number, and difficult to topple. Second are
the economic "hills"—places that manufacture the world's established
goods, take its calls, and support its innovation engines. These hills
can rise and fall quickly; they are prosperous but insecure. Some, like
Dublin and Seoul, are growing into innovative, wealthy peaks; others
are declining, eroded by high labor costs and a lack of enduring competitive advantage. Finally there are the vast valleys—places with little
connection to the global economy and few immediate prospects.

surprisingly few regions truly matter in today's global economy. What's
more, the tallest peaks—the cities and
regions that drive the world economy—are growing ever higher, while
the valleys mostly languish.

The most obvious challenge to
the flat-world hypothesis is the
explosive growth of cities worldwide.
More and more people are cluster-
ing in urban areas—the world's demographic mountain ranges, so to speak.
The share of the world's population
living in urban areas, just three percent in 1800, was nearly 30 percent
by 1950. Today it stands at about 50
percent; in advanced countries three
out of four people live in urban areas.
Map A shows the uneven distribution

of the world's population. Five megacities currently have more than 20
million inhabitants each. Twenty-four
cities have more than 10 million inhabitants, sixty more than 5 million, and
150 more than 2.5 million. Population
density is of course a crude indicator
of human and economic activity. But it
does suggest that at least some of the
tectonic forces of economics are concen-
trating people and resources, and pushing up some places more than others.

Still, differences in population density vastly understate the spikiness of
the global economy; the continuing
dominance of the world's most productive urban areas is astounding. When
it comes to actual economic output,
the ten largest U.S. metropolitan areas
combined are behind only the United

Source: Center for International Earth Science Information Network, Columbia University; and Centro
Internacional de Agricultura Tropical. (Reprinted by permission of *The Atlantic Monthly*)

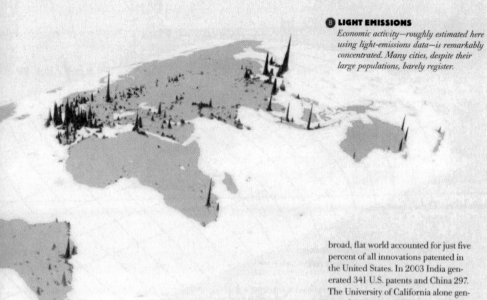

SOURCE: U.S. DEFENSE METEROLOGICAL SATELLITE PROGRAM

B LIGHT EMISSIONS

Economic activity—roughly estimated here using light-emissions data—is remarkably concentrated. Many cities, despite their large populations, barely register.

States as a whole and Japan. New York's economy alone is about the size of Russia's or Brazil's, and Chicago's is on a par with Sweden's. Together New York, Los Angeles, Chicago, and Boston have a bigger economy than all of China. If U.S. metropolitan areas were countries, they'd make up forty-seven of the biggest 100 economies in the world.

Unfortunately, no single, comprehensive information source exists for the economic production of all the world's cities. A rough proxy is available, though. Map B shows a variation on the widely circulated view of the world at night, with higher concentrations of light—indicating higher energy use and, presumably, stronger economic production—appearing in greater relief. U.S. regions appear almost Himalayan on this map. From their summits one might look out on a smaller mountain range stretching across Europe, some isolated peaks in Asia, and a few scattered hills throughout the rest of the world.

Population and economic activity are both spiky, but it's innovation—the engine of economic growth—that is most concentrated. The World Intellectual Property Organization recorded about 300,000 patents from resident inventors in more than a hundred nations in 2002 (the most recent year for which statistics are available). Nearly two thirds of them went to American and Japanese inventors. Eighty-five percent went to the residents of just five countries (Japan, the United States, South Korea, Germany, and Russia).

Worldwide patent statistics can be somewhat misleading, since different countries follow different standards for granting patents. But patents granted in the United States—which receives patent applications for nearly all major innovations worldwide, and holds them to the same strict standards—tell a similar story. Nearly 90,000 of the 170,000 patents granted in the United States in 2002 went to Americans. Some 35,000 went to Japanese inventors, and 11,000 to Germans. The next ten most innovative countries—including the usual suspects in Europe plus Taiwan, South Korea, Israel, and Canada—produced roughly 25,000 more. The rest of the broad, flat world accounted for just five percent of all innovations patented in the United States. In 2003 India generated 341 U.S. patents and China 297. The University of California alone generated more than either country. IBM accounted for five times as many as the two combined.

This is not to say that Indians and Chinese are not innovative. On the contrary, AnnaLee Saxenian, of the University of California at Berkeley, has shown that Indian and Chinese entrepreneurs founded or co-founded roughly 30 percent of all Silicon Valley startups in the late 1990s. But these fundamentally creative people had to travel to Silicon Valley and be absorbed into its innovative ecosystem before their ideas became economically viable. Such ecosystems matter, and there aren't many of them.

Map C—which makes use of data from both the World Intellectual Property Organization and the U.S. Patent and Trademark Office—shows a world composed of innovation peaks and valleys. Tokyo, Seoul, New York, and San Francisco remain the front-runners in the patenting competition. Boston, Seattle, Austin, Toronto, Vancouver, Berlin, Stockholm, Helsinki, London, Osaka, Taipei, and Sydney also stand out.

Map D shows the residence of the 1,200 most heavily cited scientists in leading fields. Scientific advance is even more concentrated than patent

Just a few places produce most of the world's innovations. Innovation remains difficult without a critical mass of financiers, entrepreneurs, and scientists, often nourished by world-class universities and flexible corporations.

THE GEOGRAPHY OF INNOVATION

Commercial innovation and scientific advance are both highly concentrated—but not always in the same places. Several cities in East Asia—particularly in Japan—are home to prolific business innovation but still depend disproportionately on scientific breakthroughs made elsewhere. Likewise, some cities excel in scientific research but not in commercial adaptation. The few places that do both well are very strongly positioned in the global economy. These regions have little to fear, and much to gain, from continuing globalization.

production. Most occurs not just in a handful of countries but in a handful of cities—primarily in the United States and Europe. Chinese and Indian cities do not even register. As far as global innovation is concerned, perhaps a few dozen places worldwide really compete at the cutting edge.

Concentrations of creative and talented people are particularly important for innovation, according to the Nobel Prize–winning economist Robert Lucas. Ideas flow more freely, are honed more sharply, and can be put into practice more quickly when large numbers of innovators, implementers, and financial backers are in constant contact with one another, both in and out of the office. Creative people cluster not simply because they like to be around one another or they prefer cosmopolitan centers with lots of amenities, though both those things count. They and their companies also cluster because of the powerful pro-

ductivity advantages, economies of scale, and knowledge spillovers such density brings.

So although one might not *have* to emigrate to innovate, it certainly appears that innovation, economic growth, and prosperity occur in those places that attract a critical mass of top creative talent. Because globalization has increased the returns to innovation, by allowing innovative products and services to quickly reach consumers worldwide, it has strengthened the lure that innovation centers hold for our planet's best and brightest, reinforcing the spikiness of wealth and economic production.

The main difference between now and even a couple of decades ago is not that the world has become flatter but that the world's peaks have become slightly more dispersed—and that the world's hills, the industrial and service centers that produce mature products and support innovation centers, have proliferated and shifted. For the

better part of the twentieth century the United States claimed the lion's share of the global economy's innovation peaks, leaving a few outposts in Europe and Japan. But America has since lost some of those peaks, as such industrial-age powerhouses as Pittsburgh, St. Louis, and Cleveland have eroded. At the same time, a number of regions in Europe, Scandinavia, Canada, and the Pacific Rim have moved up.

The world today looks flat to some because the economic and social distances between peaks worldwide have gotten smaller. Connection between peaks has been strengthened by the easy mobility of the global creative class—about 150 million people worldwide. They participate in a global technology system and a global labor market that allow them to migrate freely among the world's leading cities. In a Brookings Institution study the demographer Robert Lang and the world-cities expert Peter Taylor identify a relatively small group of leading city-regions—London, New York, Paris, Tokyo, Hong Kong, Singapore, Chicago, Los Angeles, and San Francisco among them—that are strongly connected to one another.

But Lang and Taylor also identify a much larger group of city-regions that are far more locally oriented. People in spiky places are often more connected

Source: World Intellectual Property Organization; U.S. Patent and Trademark Office. (Reprinted by permission of *The Atlantic Monthly*)

to one another, even from half a world away, than they are to people and places in their veritable back yards.

The flat-world theory is not completely misguided. It is a welcome supplement to the widely accepted view (illustrated by the Live 8 concerts and Bono's forays into Africa, by the writings of Jeffrey Sachs and the UN Millennium project) that the growing divide between rich and poor countries is the fundamental feature of the world economy. Friedman's theory more accurately depicts a developing world with capabilities that translate into economic development. In his view, for example, the emerging economies of India and China combine cost advantages, high-tech skills, and entrepreneurial energy, enabling those countries to compete effectively for industries and jobs. The tensions set in motion as the playing field is leveled affect mainly the advanced countries, which see not only manufacturing work but also higher-end jobs, in fields such as software development and financial services, increasingly threatened by offshoring.

But the flat-world theory blinds us to far more insidious tensions among the world's growing peaks, sinking valleys, and shifting hills. The innovative, talent-attracting "have" regions seem increasingly remote from the talent-exporting "have-not" regions. Second-tier cities, from Detroit and Wolfsburg to Nagoya and Mexico City, are entering an escalating and potentially devastating competition for jobs, talent, and investment. And inequality is growing across the world and within countries.

This is far more harrowing than the flat world Friedman describes, and a good deal more treacherous than the old rich-poor divide. We see its effects in the political backlash against globalization in the advanced world. The recent rejection of the EU constitution by the French, for example, resulted in large part from high rates of "no" votes in suburban and rural quarters, which understandably fear globalization and integration.

But spiky globalization also wreaks havoc on poorer places. China is seeing enormous concentrations of talent and innovation in centers such as Shanghai, Shenzhen, and Beijing, all of which are a world apart from its vast, impoverished rural areas. According to detailed polling by Richard Burkholder, of Gallup, average household incomes in urban China are now triple those in rural regions, and they've grown more than three times as fast since 1999; perhaps as a result, urban and rural Chinese now have very different, often conflicting political and lifestyle values. India is growing even more divided, as Bangalore, Hyderabad, and parts of New Delhi and Bombay pull away from the rest of that enormous country, creating destabilizing political tensions. Economic and demographic forces are sorting people around the world into geographically clustered "tribes" so different (and often mutually antagonistic) as to create a somewhat Hobbesian vision.

We are thus confronted with a difficult predicament. Economic progress requires that the peaks grow stronger and taller. But such growth will exacerbate economic and social disparities, fomenting political reactions that could threaten further innovation and economic progress. Managing the disparities between peaks and valleys worldwide—raising the valleys without shearing off the peaks—will be among the top political challenges of the coming decades. —*RICHARD FLORIDA*

Richard Florida, the author of The Flight of the Creative Class, *is the Hirst Professor of Public Policy at George Mason University.*

urce: Michael Batty, Centre for Advanced Spatial Analysis, University College London. (Reprinted by ·rmission of *The Atlantic Monthly*)

Robyn Meredith and Suzanne Hoppough

Why Globalization Is Good

Robyn Meredith is author of the best-selling book *The Elephant and the Dragon: The Rise of India and China and What It Means for All of Us*. She and her colleague at *Forbes* magazine, Suzanne Hoppough, collaborated on the following excerpt from *The Elephant and the Dragon* and published it in *Forbes* on April 16, 2007.

A ragtag army of save-the-world crusaders has spent years decrying multinational corporations as villains in the wave of globalization overwhelming the Third World. This ominous trend would fatten the rich, further impoverish and oppress the poor, and crush local economies.

2 The business-bashing group Public Citizen argued as much in a proclamation signed by almost 1,500 organizations in 89 countries in 1999. Whereupon hundreds of protesters rioted outside a conference of the World Trade Organization in Seattle, shattering windows, blocking traffic, and confronting cops armed with tear gas and pepper spray. Six hundred people were arrested.

3 Cut to 2007, and the numbers are in: The protesters and do-gooders are just plain wrong. It turns out that globalization is good—and not just for the rich, but *especially* for the poor. The booming economies of India and China—the Elephant and the Dragon—have lifted 200 million people out of abject poverty in the 1990s as globalization took off, the International Monetary Fund says. Tens of millions more have catapulted themselves far ahead into the middle class.

4 It's remarkable what a few container ships can do to make poor people better off. Certainly more than $2 trillion of foreign aid, which is roughly the amount (with an inflation adjustment) that the U.S. and Europe have poured into Africa and Asia over the past half-century.

5 In the next eight years almost a billion people across Asia will take a Great Leap Forward into a new middle class. In China middle-class incomes are set to rise threefold, to $5,000, predicts Dominic Barton, a Shanghai managing partner for McKinsey & Co.

6 As the Chindia revolution spreads, the ranks of the poor get smaller, not larger. In the 1990s, as Vietnam's economy grew 6% a year, the number of people living in poverty (42 million) fell 7% annually; in Uganda, when GDP growth passed 3%, the number fell 6% per year, says the World Bank.

7 China unleashed its economy in 1978, seeding capitalism first among farmers newly freed to sell the fruits of their fields instead of handing the produce over to Communist Party collectives. Other reforms let the Chinese create 22 million new businesses that now employ 135 million people who otherwise would have remained peasants like the generations before them. Foreign direct investment, the very force so virulently opposed by the do-gooders, has helped drive China's gross domestic product to a more than tenfold increase since 1978. Since the reforms started, $600 billion has flooded into the country, $70 billion of it in the past year. Foreigners built hundreds

of thousands of new factories as the Chinese government built the coal mines, power grid, airports, and highways to supply them.

8   As China built infrastructure, it created Special Economic Zones where foreign companies willing to build modern factories could hire cheap labor, go years without paying any taxes, and leave it to government to build the roads and other infrastructure they needed. All of that, in turn, drove China's exports from $970 million to $974 billion in three decades. Those container loads make Americans better off, too. You can get a Chinese DVD at Walmart for $28, and after you do you will buy some $15 movies made in the U.S.A.

9   Per-person income in China has climbed from $16 a year in 1978 to $2,000 now. Wages in factory boomtowns in southern China can run $4 a day—scandalously low in the eyes of the protesters, yet up from pennies a day a generation ago and far ahead of increases in living costs. Middle-class Chinese families now own TVs, live in new apartments, and send their children to private schools. Millions of Chinese have traded in their bicycles for motorcycles or cars. McDonald's has signed a deal with Sinopec, the huge Chinese gasoline retailer, to build drive-through restaurants attached to gas stations on China's new roads.

10   Today 254 Starbucks stores serve coffee in the land of tea, including one at the Great Wall and another at the Forbidden Palace. (The latter is the target of protesters.) In Beijing 54 Starbucks shops thrive, peddling luxury lattes that cost up to $2.85 a cup and paying servers $6 for an 8-hour day. That looks exploitative until you peek inside a nearby Chinese-owned teahouse where the staff works a 12-hour day for $3.75. Says one woman, 23, who works for an international cargo shipper in Beijing: "My parents were both teachers when they were my age, and they earned 30 yuan [$3.70] a month. I earn 4,000 yuan ($500) a month, live comfortably, and feel I have better opportunities than my parents did."

11   Tony Ma, age 51, was an unwilling foot soldier in Mao's Cultural Revolution. During that dark period from 1966 to 1976 universities were closed, and he was sent at age 16 to work in a steel mill for $2 a month. He cut metal all day long for seven years and feared he might never escape. When colleges reopened, he landed a spot to study chemistry, transferred to the U.S., got a Ph.D. in biochemistry, and signed on with Johnson & Johnson at $45,000 a year. Later he returned to the land he fled and now works for B.F. Goodrich in Hong Kong. The young college grads in China today wouldn't bother immigrating to the U.S. for a job that pays $45,000, he says—because now they have better opportunities at home.

12   Capitalism alone, however, isn't enough to remake Third World economies— globalism is the key. A big reason India trails behind its bigger neighbor to the northeast in lifting the lower classes is that, even after embracing capitalism, it kept barriers to the flow of capital from abroad. Thus 77% of Indians live on $2 a day or less, the Asian Development Bank says, down only nine percentage points from 1990. A third of the population is illiterate. In 1980 India had more of its population in urban centers than China did (23% versus 20% for China). But by 2005 China had 41% in cities, where wages are higher; India's urbanites had grown to only 29%.

13   Freed of British colonial rule in 1947 and scarred by its paternalistic effects, India initially combined capitalism with economic isolationism. It thwarted foreign companies intent on investing there and hampered Indian firms trying to sell abroad. This hurt

Indian consumers and local biz: A $100 Microsoft operating system got slapped with duties that brought the price to $250 in India, putting imported software and computers further from reach for most people and businesses. Meanwhile, the government granted workers lavish job protections and imposed heavy taxes and regulations on employers. Government jobs usually were by rote and paid poorly, but they guaranteed lifetime employment. They also ensured economic stagnation.

14   Financial crisis struck in 1991. Desperate for cash, India flew a planeload of gold reserves to London and began, grudgingly, to open its economy. Import duties were lowered or eliminated, so India's consumers and companies could buy modern, foreign-made goods and gear. Overseas firms in many industries were allowed to own their subsidiaries in India for the first time since 1977. India all but banned foreign investment until 1991. Since then foreign companies have come back, but not yet on the scale seen in China. Foreign companies have invested $48 billion in India since 1991—$7.5 billion of that just in the last fiscal year—the same amount dumped into China every six weeks. By the mid-1990s the economy boomed and created millions of jobs.

15   By the late 1990s U.S. tech companies began turning to India for software design, particularly in the Y2K crunch. The Indians proved capable and cheap, and the much-maligned offshoring boom began. Suddenly Indian software engineers were programming corporate America's computers. New college graduates were answering America's customer service phone calls. Builders hired construction workers to erect new high-rise buildings suddenly in demand as American and European firms rushed to hire Indian workers. The new college hires, whose older siblings had graduated without finding a job, tell of surpassing their parents' salaries within five years and of buying cell phones, then motorcycles, then cars and even houses by the time they were 30. All of that would have been impossible had India failed to add globalization to capitalism.

16   Today, despite its still dilapidated airports and pothole-riddled highways, the lumbering Elephant now is in a trot, growing more than 7% annually for the last decade. In 2005, borrowing from the Chinese, India began a five-year, $150 billion plan to update its roads, airports, ports, and electric plants. India is creating free trade zones, like those in China, to encourage exports of software, apparel, auto parts and more. S. B. Kutwal manages the assembly line where Tata Motors builds Safari SUVs. He remembers how, in the 1980s, people waited five years to buy a scooter and cars were only for the rich. "Since we've liberated the economy, lots of companies have started coming into India," says Kutwal. "People couldn't afford cars then. Now the buying power is coming."

17   In Mumbai (formerly Bombay), Delhi, Bangalore, and other big cities, shopping malls have sprung up, selling everything from Levi's jeans to Versace. India still has raggedy street touts, but when they tap on car windows at stoplights, instead of peddling cheap plastic toys, they sell to the new India: copies of *Vogue* and *House & Garden* magazines. Western restaurants are moving in, too: Domino's Pizza and Ruby Tuesday's have come to India, and 107 McDonald's have sprung up, serving veggie burgers in the land where cattle are sacred.

18   None of this gives pause to an entity called International Forum on Globalization. The group declares that globalism's aim is to "benefit transnational corporations over workers; foreign investors over local businesses; and wealthy countries over developing

nations. While promoters . . . proclaim that this model is the rising tide that will lift all boats, citizen movements find that it is instead lifting only yachts."

19   "The majority of people in rich and poor countries aren't better off" since the World Trade Organization formed in 1995 to promote global trade, asserts Christopher Slevin, deputy director of Global Trade Watch, an arm of Ralph Nader's Public Citizen. "The breadth of the opposition has grown. It's not just industrial and steel workers and people who care about animal rights. It includes high-tech workers and the offshoring of jobs, also the faith-based community."

20   While well-off American techies may be worried, it seems doubtful that an engineer in Bangalore who now earns $40,000 a year, and who has just bought his parents' house, wants to ban foreign investment.

21   Slevin's further complaint is that globalism is a creature of WTO, the World Bank and other unelected bodies. But no, the people do have a voice in the process, and it is one that is equivocal on the matter of free market capitalism. The Western World's huge agriculture subsidies—$85 billion or more annually, between the U.S., Japan, and the European Union—are decreed by democratically elected legislatures. The EU pays ranchers $2 per cow in daily subsidies, more than most Indians earn. If these farmers weren't getting handouts, and if trade in farm products were free, then poor farmers in the Third World could sell more of their output, and could begin to lift themselves out of poverty.

Sadanand Dhume

Slumdog Paradox

Sadanand Dhume is a writer who is based in Washington, D.C. Having lived in Asia from 1999 to 2004, he is an expert on Asian affairs and the author of *My Friend the Fanatic: Travels with a Radical Islamist*, a travel narrative about the rise of Muslim fundamentalism in Indonesia. His writing has been published in the *Washington Post, Forbes, Commentary*, and *YaleGlobal Online*, where the following essay appeared on February 9, 2009.

The unexpected international success of *Slumdog Millionaire* has pleased some Indians while provoking unusually strong protests from others. The critical and commercial success of the film, contrasted with sharp criticism and a lackluster run in Indian theaters, captures the inherent contradictions of an increasingly globalized country. India basks in the glow of international recognition, but resents the critical scrutiny that global exposure brings.

2   Not since Sir Richard Attenborough's *Gandhi* has a film about India captured the world's imagination as strongly as *Slumdog Millionaire*, director Danny Boyle's gritty yet uplifting

drama about a boy from the slums of Mumbai who makes good as a game-show contestant on the Indian version of *Who Wants to Be a Millionaire*. The low-budget production—which cost $15 million to make, a pittance in Hollywood terms—has garnered both commercial and critical success, grossing $96 million worldwide as of February 1st, and picking up four Golden Globe awards and 10 Oscar nominations. In one among a raft of glowing reviews, the *Wall Street Journal*'s Joe Morgenstern hailed *Slumdog* as "the world's first globalized masterpiece."

3   In India, however, the response to the film has been ambivalent. Commercially, it has failed to replicate its American success. Despite a wave of publicity and an ambitious nationwide rollout, *Slumdog* is showing in half-empty theaters. It trails the box-office receipts of an obscure Hindi horror movie released the same day. And though some Indian reviewers praised the film for everything from inspired casting to an improbable Bollywoodish storyline, it also attracted its share of brickbats. On his blog, Bollywood star Amitabh Bachchan struck a populist note: "If SM projects India as [a] third-world, dirty, underbelly developing nation and causes pain and disgust among nationalists and patriots, let it be known that a murky underbelly exists and thrives even in the most developed nations." The critic Meenakshi Shedde dismissed the film as "a laundry list of India's miseries." Interviewed in the

Young Jamal (Ayush Mahesh Khedekar) runs through the alleys of Mumbai in a scene from *Slumdog Millionaire* (2008).

Los Angeles Times, film professor Shyamal Sengupta called the film "a white man's imagined India."

4   In many ways, *Slumdog Millionaire* is a metaphor for India in the age of globalization. The director, Danny Boyle, and screenwriter, Simon Beaufoy, are British. The male lead, Dev Patel, who plays the part of the quiz-show contestant Jamal, is a Gujarati whose family migrated to London from Nairobi. His love interest, Latika, is played by Freida Pinto, a Catholic girl from Mumbai, India's most cosmopolitan city. The novel upon which the film is loosely based, *Q and A,* was written by an Indian diplomat currently stationed in South Africa. The television game show *Who Wants to Be a Millionaire,* which supplies the film's narrative backbone, is another British creation. Adapted in more than 50 countries, the show is recognizable to audiences from Beijing to Buenos Aires.

5   The film's success also underscores India's emergence on the world stage. Indeed, the superficial similarities with Ang Lee's *Crouching Tiger, Hidden Dragon,* the 2001 blockbuster set in Qing dynasty China, are striking. Both films draw on the talents of a widespread diaspora: Michelle Yeoh, Dev Patel. Like *Crouching Tiger*, *Slumdog* taps into Western curiosity about a country whose weight is increasingly felt in ordinary lives. Service workers in the West worry about being "Bangalored," or losing their jobs to less expensive competitors in India. Credit-card and consumer-appliance users routinely deal with customer-service professionals in Gurgaon or Hyderabad. In America, one no longer has to live in a big city to be familiar with yoga or chicken tikka masala. An Indian company, Tata Motors, owns the iconic automobile brands Jaguar and Land Rover. India-born professionals helm Pepsi and Citibank. Salman Rushdie and Jhumpa Lahiri occupy a similarly exalted place in fiction. To sum up, it seems unlikely that a story set in the slums of Manila or Jakarta would find nearly as large an audience in Boston or Baton Rouge.

6   For India, one of the most autarkic and culturally inward-looking countries in Asia until the advent of economic reforms in 1991, the benefits of globalization are easily apparent. In purchasing power parity terms, per capita income more than doubled from $1,400 in 1991 to $3,800 in 2006. The ranks of the middle class, broadly defined, have swelled to more than 250 million people. More Indians buy cell phones each month than any other people.

7   The same story can be told on the corporate and macroeconomic level. Since liberalization, a dozen Indian firms—spanning banking, pharmaceuticals, software, and services—have listed on the New York Stock Exchange, and three on the technology-heavy

NASDAQ. The United Nations Conference on Trade and Development estimates that a record $36.7 billion of foreign direct investment flowed into India in 2008. Foreign-exchange reserves stand at a robust $250 billion.

8   There are less tangible changes as well. For generations after independence from Britain in 1947, more or less the only way for an Indian to make a mark on the world stage was to emigrate. A. R. Rahman, the Chennai-based composer of the *Slumdog* soundtrack, has not needed to change the color of his passport to snag a Golden Globe or multiple Oscar nominations. In a broader sense, the same holds true for many of the scientists and engineers who work for General Electric or Microsoft in Bangalore, or for the employees of a clutch of ambitious homegrown pharmaceutical companies with global ambition. India may not quite be center-stage—its contribution to world trade remains a slender 1.5 percent—but neither is it off-stage anymore. If an ambitious government target is met, the country's share of world trade will more than triple to 5 percent by 2020.

9   Notwithstanding the giant strides made over the past 18 years, Indian criticism of *Slumdog* also reveals the chasm between the country's self-perception and projection and any reasonable measure of its achievements. India may boast homegrown programs in space exploration and nuclear power, but—as

Jamal Malik (Dev Patel) appears on the game show *Who Wants to Be a Millionaire?* in a scene from *Slumdog Millionaire* (2008).

a first time visitor to India immediately notices and as the film mercilessly reveals—it also struggles to provide its people with electricity, sanitation, and drinking water. About half of Indian women are illiterate, a higher percentage than in Laos, Cambodia, or Myanmar. It is at number 122—between Nepal and Lesotho—on the World Bank index that measures ease of doing business, and 85 on the global corruption index maintained by the anti-graft NGO Transparency International. To put it bluntly, the squalor of the slums depicted in *Slumdog* is closer to reality than an elaborately choreographed Bollywood dance sequence shot on location in Switzerland.

10   To sum up, by jettisoning socialism and embracing globalization India has become more prosperous than at any time in more than six decades of independence. But the effects of failed policies pursued between 1947 and 1991 cannot be erased overnight. As *Slumdog* reveals, India is doing better than ever only when benchmarked against its own dismal past. When compared to the West, or to East Asian countries that have truly transformed themselves—Japan, Taiwan, and Korea—the gap between India's rhetoric and its reality remains jarring. *Slumdog* may wound national pride, but the answer is more openness not less. As long as chronic poverty remains a central fact of Indian life, the spotlight that globalization brings will shine on India's software success as well as on its slums.

ISSUE IN FOCUS

Exporting American Culture

"The United States, which began as Europe's collective fantasy, built a civilization to deliver the goods for playing, feeling, and meaning." So writes culture critic Todd Gitlin, in an essay in this section of *Good Reasons with Contemporary Arguments*.

And indeed, in many ways American culture does seem to be conquering the globe. If our efforts to spread American-style democracy through wars in Iraq and Afghanistan have led to imperfect results, our less conscious and less direct efforts to spread American values have been quite successful for some time. Critics of the exportation of American culture call this "cultural imperialism": influencing other

In what sense is America a cultural beacon in the world?

nations to adopt our values by promoting those values through popular media. Indeed, the fingerprints of American influence can be found nearly everywhere in the world, from the McDonald's golden arches that gleam in Tokyo to the American movies and movie stars, and the music and music icons, that are so iconic around the globe.

Though much of the United States' impact on other countries is economic, some of it involves cultural values, including representative democracy, women's rights, and even a resistance to sweatshop labor; these values can often change national identities in ways that approximate American norms. According to one argument, about 80 percent of the world's Internet home pages are presented in English, and so U.S. cultural values pass easily into other societies. For better or for worse.

This process of "Americanization" is so striking that many commentators have come to equate Americanization with globalization. It's not that the world is becoming more globalized, they argue, but that the world is becoming distinctly more American. Those who approve point to positive American exports and improving economic conditions in underdeveloped nations. But critics of the "globalization of Americanization" accuse the United States of exerting its widespread influence on other countries in order to further a kind of global empire.

Critics of cultural imperialism might seem to hold the moral high ground—they are, after all, seeking to preserve local identities and lifestyles—yet these critics are not without critics of their own. Opponents of the "globalization = Americanization" camp argue that it is arrogant and ignorant to assume that globalization is unidirectional. While American culture may be visible (and popular) around the globe, the same is true in reverse: Americans are increasingly consuming and assimilating the media, foods, fashions, and consumer products of cultures from all over the world. (Look at the popularity of Japanese *anime* among American youth or the regular presence of Mexican *telenovelas* on American cable.) In fact, though America exports its entertainment and its products on a huge scale, it also *imports* more goods and services than it exports to foreign countries.

If the world is becoming more American, then America is also incorporating the values of other nations and is becoming more multiculturally literate. Globalization goes both ways.

The complex nature of globalization perhaps explains why the American public has a divided opinion about the role of the United States in the world. On the one hand, according to surveys conducted by the Pew Research Center for the People and the Press in 2009, Americans agree that the United States has assumed a powerful leadership role. On the other hand, they concede that America also seems less respected around the world. If more and more Americans are rejecting the role of the United States as a single world leader, they are also rejecting the pull toward isolation. Americans are suspicious of immigration, resistant to adopting cultural practices from elsewhere, and protective of English as a national language. But they also acknowledge our history as a nation of immigrants, travel around the world in huge numbers, and are delightfully curious about other peoples and their cultures.

American ambivalence about "Americanization" is apparent in the selections in this Issue in Focus. First, we present "Under the Sign of Mickey Mouse & Co.," an excerpt from Gitlin's book, *Media Unlimited: How the Torrent of Images and Sounds Overwhelms Our Lives*. His essay uses iconic American cultural signs to argue that the global village today has a distinctly American flavor—though that flavor blends in with and changes its new environments. Then in "Walmart vs. Pyramids," the policy analyst Laura Carlsen chronicles the conflict between Walmart's expansion into Mexico and Mexicans' right to retain their distinctive cultural heritage. Carlsen's essay can profitably be read alongside the article by Meredith and Hoppough presented earlier in the chapter. Finally, we include Robert McCrum's 2011 *Newsweek* essay "Glob-ish," which meditates on the implications of English having become "the world's language," a language that is shaped as much by nonnative English speakers as by native English speakers.

Together, the selections are designed to enhance your own knowledge of the ways in which the United States currently interacts with global cultures and to stimulate you to think and write about the roles that American culture should play around the world.

Todd Gitlin

Under the Sign of Mickey Mouse & Co.

Everywhere, the media flow defies national boundaries. This is one of its obvious, but at the same time amazing, features. A global torrent is not, of course, the master metaphor to which we have grown accustomed. We're more accustomed to Marshall McLuhan's *global village*. Those who resort to this metaphor casually often forget that if the world is a global village, some live in mansions on the hill, others in huts. Some dispatch images and sounds around town at the touch of a button; others collect them at the touch of *their* buttons. Yet McLuhan's image reveals an indispensable half-truth. If there is a village, it speaks American. It wears jeans, drinks Coke, eats at the golden arches, walks on swooshed shoes, plays electric guitars, recognizes Mickey Mouse, James Dean, E.T., Bart Simpson, R2-D2, and Pamela Anderson.

2   At the entrance to the champagne cellar of Piper-Heidsieck in Reims, in eastern France, a plaque declares that the cellar was dedicated by Marie Antoinette. The tour is narrated in six languages, and at the end you walk back upstairs into a museum featuring photographs of famous people drinking champagne. And who are they? Perhaps members of today's royal houses, presidents or prime ministers, economic titans or Nobel Prize winners? Of course not. They are movie stars, almost all of them American—Marilyn Monroe to Clint Eastwood. The symmetry of the exhibition is obvious, the premise unmistakable: Hollywood stars, champions of consumption, are the royalty of this century, more popular by far than poor doomed Marie.

3   Hollywood is the global cultural capital—capital in both senses. The United States presides over a sort of World Bank of styles and symbols, an International

AISLIN
THE GAZETTE
Montreal
CANADA

Aislin Terry/Montreal Gazette/Cartoonists and Writers Syndicate

Cultural Fund of images, sounds, and celebrities. The goods may be distributed by American-, Canadian-, European-, Japanese-, or Australian-owned multinational corporations, but their styles, themes, and images do not detectably change when a new board of directors takes over. Entertainment is one of America's top exports. In 1999, in fact, film, television, music, radio, advertising, print publishing, and computer software together *were* the top export, almost $80 billion worth, and while software alone accounted for $50 billion of the total, some of that category also qualifies as entertainment—video games and pornography, for example. Hardly anyone is exempt from the force of American images and sounds. French resentment of Mickey Mouse, Bruce Willis, and the rest of American civilization is well known. Less well known, and rarely acknowledged by the French, is the fact that *Terminator 2* sold 5 million tickets in France during the month it opened—with no submachine guns at the heads of the customers. The same culture minister, Jack Lang, who in 1982 achieved a moment of predictable notoriety in the United States for declaring that *Dallas* amounted to cultural imperialism, also conferred France's highest honor in the arts on Elizabeth Taylor and Sylvester Stallone. The point is not hypocrisy pure and simple but something deeper, something obscured by a single-minded emphasis on American power: dependency. American popular culture is the nemesis that hundreds of millions—perhaps billions—of people love, and love to hate. The antagonism and the dependency are inseparable, for the media flood—essentially American in its origin, but virtually unlimited in its reach—represents, like it or not, a common imagination.

4   How shall we understand the Hong Kong T-shirt that says "I Feel Coke"? Or the little Japanese girl who asks an American visitor in all innocence, "Is there really a Disneyland in America?" (She knows the one in Tokyo.) Or the experience of a German television reporter sent to Siberia to film indigenous life, who after flying out of Moscow and then traveling for days by boat, bus, and jeep, arrives near the Arctic Sea where live a tribe of Tungusians known to ethnologists for their bearskin rituals. In the community store sits a grandfather with his grandchild on his knee. Grandfather is dressed in traditional Tungusian clothing. Grandson has on his head a reversed baseball cap.

5   American popular culture is the closest approximation today to a global lingua franca, drawing the urban and young in particular into a common cultural zone where they share some dreams of freedom, wealth, comfort, innocence, and power—and perhaps most of all, youth as a state of mind. In general, despite the rhetoric of "identity," young people do not live in monocultures. They are not monocular. They are both local and cosmopolitan. Cultural bilingualism is routine. Just as their "cultures" are neither hard-wired nor uniform, so there is no simple way in which they are "Americanized," though there are American tags on their experience—low-cost links to status and fun. Everywhere, fun lovers, efficiency seekers, Americaphiles, and Americaphobes alike pass through the portals of Disney and the arches of McDonald's wearing Levi's jeans and Gap jackets. Mickey Mouse and Donald Duck, John Wayne, Marilyn Monroe, James Dean, Bob Dylan, Michael Jackson, Madonna, Clint Eastwood, Bruce Willis, the multicolor chorus of Coca-Cola, and the next flavor of the month or the universe are the icons of a curious sort of one-world sensibility, a global semiculture. America's bid for global unification surpasses in reach that of the Romans, the British, the Catholic

John Wayne in a scene from *The Searchers* (1956), directed by John Ford, a film widely considered to be one of the greatest Westerns of all time.

Church, or Islam; though without either an army or a God, it requires less. The Tungusian boy with the reversed cap on his head does not automatically think of it as "American," let alone side with the U.S. Army.

6   The misleadingly easy answer to the question of how American images and sounds became omnipresent is: American imperialism. But the images are not even faintly force-fed by American corporate, political, or military power. The empire strikes from inside the spectator as well as from outside. This is a conundrum that deserves to be approached with respect if we are to grasp the fact that Mickey Mouse and Coke are everywhere recognized and often enough *enjoyed.* In the peculiar unification at work throughout the world, there is surely a supply side, but there is not only a supply side. Some things are true even if multinational corporations claim so: there is demand.

7   What do American icons and styles mean to those who are not American? We can only imagine—but let us try. What young people graced with disposable income encounter in American television shows, movies, soft drinks, theme parks, and American-labeled (though not American-manufactured) running shoes, T-shirts, baggy pants, ragged jeans, and so on, is a way of being in the world, the experience of a flow of ready feelings and sensations bobbing up, disposable, dissolving, segueing to the next and the next after that. It is a quality of immediacy and casualness not so different from what Americans desire. But what the young experience in the video game arcade or the music megastore is more than the flux of sensation. They flirt with a loose sort of social membership that requires little but a momentary (and monetary) surrender. Sampling American goods, images, and sounds, they affiliate with an empire of informality.

Consuming a commodity, wearing a slogan or a logo, you affiliate with disaffiliation. You make a limited-liability connection, a virtual one. You borrow some of the effervescence that is supposed to emanate from this American staple, and hope to be recognized as one of the elect. When you wear the Israeli version that spells *Coca-Cola* in Hebrew, you express some worldwide connection with unknown peers, or a sense of irony, or both—in any event, a marker of membership. In a world of ubiquitous images, of easy mobility and casual tourism, you get to feel not only local or national but global—without locking yourself in a box so confining as to deserve the name "identity."

8   We are seeing on a world scale the familiar infectious rhythm of modernity. The money economy extends its reach, bringing with it a calculating mentality. Even in the poor countries it stirs the same hunger for private feeling, the same taste for disposable labels and sensations on demand, the same attention to fashion, the new and the now, that cropped up earlier in the West. Income beckons; income rewards. The taste for the marketed spectacle and the media-soaked way of life spreads. The culture consumer may not like the American goods in particular but still acquires a taste for the media's speed, formulas, and frivolity. Indeed, the lightness of American-sponsored "identity" is central to its appeal. It imposes few burdens. Attachments and affiliations coexist, overlap, melt together, form, and re-form.

After World War II, the U.S. State Department sponsored jazz tours, including a 27-city tour of Africa by the jazz musician and singer Louis "Satchmo" Armstrong, to introduce other nations to American culture and values. (Image courtesy of the *New York World-Telegram & Sun* Photography Collection, Library of Congress Prints and Photographs Division, LC-USZ62-127236.)

9   Marketers, like nationalists and fundamentalists, promote "identities," but for most people, the melange is the message. Traditional bonds bend under pressure from imports. Media from beyond help you have your "roots" and eat them, too. You can watch Mexican television in the morning and American in the afternoon, or graze between Kurdish and English. You can consolidate family ties with joint visits to Disney World—making Orlando, Florida, the major tourist destination in the United States, and the Tokyo and Marne-la-Vallée spin-offs massive attractions in Japan and France. You can attach to your parents, or children, by playing oldie music and exchanging sports statistics. You plunge back into the media flux, looking for—what? Excitement? Some low-cost variation on known themes? Some next new thing? You don't know just what, but you will when you see it—or if not, you'll change channels.

10   As devotees of Japanese video games, Hong Kong movies, and Mexican *telenovelas* would quickly remind us, the blends, juxtapositions, and recombinations of popular culture are not just American. American and American-based models, styles, and symbols are simply the most far-flung, successful, and consequential. In the course of a century, America's entertainment corporations succeeded brilliantly in cultivating popular expectations for entertainment—indeed, the sense of a *right* to be entertained, a right that belongs to the history of modernity, the rise of market economies and individualism. The United States, which began as Europe's collective fantasy, built a civilization to deliver the goods for playing, feeling, and meaning. Competitors ignore its success at their own peril, financial and otherwise.

Laura Carlsen

Walmart vs. Pyramids

The showdown is rife with symbolism. Walmart's expansion plans in Mexico have brought about a modern-day clash of passions and principles at the site of one of the earth's first great civilizations.

2   Several months ago Walmart, the world's largest retail chain, quietly began constructing a new store in Mexico—the latest step in a phenomenal takeover of Mexico's supermarket sector. But the expansion north of Mexico City is not just part of Walmart's commercial conquest of Mexico. It is infringing on the cultural foundations of the country. The new store is just 3,000 meters from the Pyramid of the Sun, the tallest structure in the ancient city of Teotihuacan.

3   The Teotihuacan Empire is believed to have begun as early as 200 B.C. Its dominion stretched deep into the heart of Mayan country in Guatemala and throughout present-day Mexico. At its peak, Teotihuacan was a thriving city of about 200,000 inhabitants, but the civilization declined in 700 A.D. under circumstances still shrouded in mystery.

4   Since then, other tribes and civilizations, including the Aztecs and contemporary Mexican society, have claimed

the "City of the Gods" as their heritage. The grand human accomplishment it represents and the power of its architectural, historical and, for many, spiritual legacy is central to Mexico's history and culture.

5   While little is known for certain about the rise and fall of Teotihuacan, much is known about the rise of the Walmart empire. From a store in Rogers, Arkansas founded by the Walton brothers in 1962, the enterprise grew in the breathtakingly short period of 42 years into the world's largest company.

6   In Mexico, its conquest of the supermarket sector began by buying up the nation's extensive chain, Aurrerá, beginning in 1992. Today, with 657 stores, Mexico is home to more Walmarts and their affiliates than any other country outside the United States. Walmart is now Mexico's largest private employer, with over 100,000 employees. But recent studies in the United States, where resistance to the megastores has been growing, show that job creation is often job displacement, because Walmarts put local stores out of business, leading to net job losses.

7   Walmart has revolutionized the labor and business world by working cheap and growing big. Labor costs are held down through anti-union policies, the hiring of undocumented workers in the United States, alleged discrimination against women and persons with disabilities, and cutbacks in benefits. Prices paid suppliers are driven down by outsourcing competition. Buoyed by $244.5 billion dollars in annual net sales, the chain can afford to make ever deeper incursions into Mexico's retail sector.

8   A diverse group of local merchants, artists, actors, academics and indigenous organizations are leading the opposition, protesting that the store damages Mexico's rich cultural heritage. Through ceremonies, hunger strikes, demonstrations and press coverage, the movement to defend the site has kept the conflict in the public eye and heightened the public-opinion costs to Walmart. Now opponents have taken their concerns to the Mexican Congress and UNESCO.

9   Some ancient ruins have already been found on the store's new site, and Walmart construction workers told the national daily, *La Jornada,* that they had orders to hide any archaeological relics they found. Normally, the presence of relics requires that further excavation be carried out painstakingly or halted altogether. But the booming Walmart corporation clearly has no time for such delays.

10   The dispute in Teotihuacan today is not a battle between the past and the future. It is a struggle over a country's right to define itself. For defenders of the ancient site, the foremost symbol of the nation's cultural heritage also constitutes part of its contemporary integrity. Modern Mexico is still a country that

defines itself by legends, and whose collective identity—unlike its neophyte northern neighbor—reaches back thousands of years.

11   In this context, Walmart is a symbol of the cultural insensitivity of rampant economic integration. While its actions may be technically legal, in the end Walmart could pay a high price for this insensitivity . . . and if there is anything Walmart hates, it is high prices.

ROBERT McCRUM

Glob-ish

The alumni of the vast people's University of China are typical of the post–Mao Zedong generation. Every Friday evening several hundred gather informally under the pine trees of a little square in Beijing's Haidian district, in the so-called English Corner, to hold "English conversation." Chatting together in groups, they discuss football, movies, and celebrities like Victoria Beckham and Paris Hilton in awkward but enthusiastic English. They also like to recite simple slogans such as Barack Obama's 2008 campaign catchphrases—"Yes, we can" and "Change we can believe in."

2   This scene, repeated on campuses across China, demonstrates the dominant aspiration of many contemporary, educated Chinese teenagers: to participate in the global community of English-speaking nations. Indeed, China offers the most dramatic example of a near-global hunger for English that has brought the language to a point of no return as a lingua franca. More vivid and universal than ever, English is now used, in some form, by approximately 4 billion people on earth—perhaps two thirds of the planet—including 400 million native English speakers. As a mother tongue, only Chinese is more prevalent, with 1.8 billion native speakers—350 million of whom also speak some kind of English.

3   Contagious, adaptable, populist, and subversive, the English language has become as much a part of the global consciousness as the combustion engine. And as English gains momentum as a second language all around the world, it is morphing into a new and simplified version of itself—one that responds to the 24/7 demands of a global economy and culture with a stripped-down vocabulary of words like "airplane," "chat room," "taxi," and "cell phone." Having neatly made the transition from the Queen's English to the more democratic American version, it is now becoming a worldwide power, a populist tool increasingly known as Globish.

4   The rise of Globish first became obvious in 2005, when an obscure Danish newspaper called *The Jutland Post* published a sequence of satirical cartoons poking fun at the Prophet Muhammad. The Muslim world exploded, with riots across Afghanistan, Nigeria, Libya, and Pakistan; in all, 139 people died. But perhaps the most bizarre response was a protest by fundamentalist Muslims outside the Danish Embassy in

London. Chanting in English, the protesters carried placards with English slogans like BUTCHER THOSE WHO MOCK ISLAM; FREEDOM OF EXPRESSION GO TO HELL; and (my favorite) DOWN WITH FREE SPEECH.

5   This collision of the Islamic jihad with the Oxford English Dictionary, or perhaps of the Quran with *Monty Python*, made clear (at least to me) the dramatic shift in global self-expression asserting itself across a world united by the Internet. What more sur-real—and telling—commentary on the Anglicization of modern society than a demon-stration of devout Muslims, in London, exploiting an old English freedom expressed in the English language, to demand the curbing of the libertarian tradition that actually legitimized their protest?

6   I wasn't alone in noticing this change. In 2007 I came across an article in the *International Herald Tribune* about a French-speaking retired IBM executive, Jean-Paul Nerrière, who described English and its international deployment as "the worldwide dialect of the third millennium." Nerrière, posted to Japan with IBM in the 1990s, had noticed that non-native English speakers in the Far East communicated in English far more successfully with their Korean and Japanese clients than British or American executives. Standard English was all very well for Anglophones, but in the developing

The Internet has accelerated the use of English as a second language across much of the world, as this sign in Hong Kong shows. Because it exists alongside so many other languages these days, in many cases, English is influenced by local language practices.

world, this non-native "decaffeinated English"—full of simplifications like "the son of my brother" for "nephew," or "words of honor" for "oath"—was becoming the new global phenomenon. In a moment of inspiration, Nerrière christened it "Globish."

7 The term quickly caught on within the international community. The (London) *Times* journalist Ben Macintyre described a conversation he had overheard while waiting for a flight from Delhi between a Spanish U.N. peacekeeper and an Indian soldier. "The Indian spoke no Spanish; the Spaniard spoke no Punjabi," he says. "Yet they understood one another easily. The language they spoke was a highly simplified form of English, without grammar or structure, but perfectly comprehensible, to them and to me. Only now do I realize that they were speaking 'Globish,' the newest and most widely spoken language in the world."

8 For Nerrière, Globish was a kind of linguistic tool, a version of basic or so-called Easy English with a vocabulary of just 1,500 words. As I saw it, however, "Globish" was the newly globalized lingua franca, essential English merged with the terminology of the digital age and the international news media. I knew from my work in the mid-1980s on a PBS series called *The Story of English* that British English had enjoyed global supremacy throughout the 19th-century age of empire, after centuries of slow growth from Chaucer and Shakespeare, through the King James Bible to the establishment of the Raj in India and the great Imperial Jubilee of 1897. The map of the world dominated by the Union Jack answered to the Queen's English; Queen Victoria, in her turn, was the first British monarch to address her subjects worldwide through the new technology of recorded sound, with a scratchy, high-pitched "Good evening!" In this first phase, there was an unbreakable link between imperialism and language that inhibited further development.

9 In the second phase, the power and influence of English passed to the United States, largely through the agency of the two world wars. Then, throughout the Cold War, Anglo-American culture became part of global consciousness through the mass media—movies, newspapers, and magazines. Crucially, in this second phase, the scope of English was limited by its troubled association with British imperialism and the Pax Americana. But the end of the Cold War and the long economic boom of the 1990s distanced the Anglo-American hegemony from its past, setting the language free in the minds of millions. Now you could still hate George W. Bush and burn the American flag while simultaneously idolizing American pop stars or splashing out on Apple computers.

10 With the turn of the millennium, it appeared that English language and culture were becoming rapidly decoupled from their contentious past. English began to gain a supranational momentum that made it independent of its Anglo-American origins. And as English became liberated from its roots, it began to spread deeper into the developing world. In 2003 both Chile and Mongolia declared their intention to become bilingual in English. In 2006 English was added to the Mexican primary-school curriculum as a compulsory second language. And the formerly Francophone state of Rwanda adopted English as its official language in 2009.

11 In China, some 50 million people are enrolled in a language program, known colloquially as "Crazy English," conducted by "the Elvis of English," Li Yang, who often teaches groups of 10,000 or more, under the slogan "Conquer English to make China strong." Li Yang is part preacher, part drill sergeant, part pedagogue. He gathers his students in football stadiums, raucously repeating everyday phrases. "How are you?" he yells through a bullhorn. "How are you?" repeats the crowd. "I'm in the pink!" he

responds. "I'm in the pink!" they reply—ironically, using an arcane bit of Edwardian slang for "feeling good." Li Yang has even published a memoir called *I Am Crazy, I Succeed.*

12   The viral nature of Globish means that it's bottom-up, not top-down. The poet Walt Whitman once wrote that English was not "an abstract construction of dictionary makers" but a language that "has its basis broad and low, close to the ground." Ever since English was driven underground by the Norman Conquest in 1066, it has been the language of Everyman and the common people. That's truer than ever today.

13   The fact is that English no longer depends on the U.S. or U.K. It's now being shaped by a world whose second language is English, and whose cultural reference points are expressed in English but without reference to its British or American origins. Films like the 2009 Oscar-winning *Slumdog Millionaire* hasten the spread of Globish— a multilingual, multicultural cast and production team creating a film about the collision of languages and cultures, launched with an eye toward Hollywood. The dialogue may mix English, Hindi, and Arabic, but it always falls back on Globish. When the inspector confronts Amir on suspicion of cheating, he asks in succinct Globish: "So. Were you wired up? A mobile or a pager, correct? Some little hidden gadget? No? A coughing accomplice in the audience? Microchip under the skin, huh?"

14   Globish is already shaping world events on many fronts. During last year's Iranian elections, the opposition used Globish to transmit its grievances to a worldwide audience. Cell-phone images of crude slogans like GET AWAY ENGLAND and FREE, FAIR VOTING NOW, and innumerable tweets from Westernized Iranians communicated the strength of the emergency to the West.

15   In the short term, Globish is set to only grow. Some 70 to 80 percent of the world's Internet home pages are in English, compared with 4.5 percent in German and 3.1 percent in Japanese. According to the British Council, by 2030 "nearly one third of the world's population will be trying to learn English at the same time." That means ever more voices adapting the English language to suit their needs, finding in Globish a common linguistic denominator.

16   The distinguished British educator Sir Eric Anderson tells a story that illustrates the growing life-and-death importance of Globish. On the morning of the 7/7 bombings in London, an Arab exchange student tried to take the Underground from southwest London to his daily class in the City. When he found his station inexplicably closed, he boarded a bus. During his journey his mobile phone rang. It was a Greek friend in Athens who was watching the news of the bombings on CNN. Communicating urgently in the Globish jargon of international TV, he described the "breaking news" and warned that London's buses had become terror targets. As a result of this conversation, the student disembarked from the bus. A minute later it was destroyed by a suicide bomber, with the loss of many lives.

17   This is not the end of Babel. The world, "flatter" and smaller than ever before, is still a patchwork of some 5,000 languages. Native speakers still cling fiercely to their mother tongues, as they should. But when an Indian and a Cuban want to commission medical research from a lab in Uruguay, with additional input from Israeli technicians— as the Midwestern U.S. startup EndoStim recently did—the language they will turn to will be Globish.

FROM READING TO WRITING

1. Analyze one of the arguments in this chapter, for example, by Gitlin, Carlson, or Dhume; how is that argument the product of its audience and purpose? How would the argument be presented differently if it were directed to a different readership or published in a different forum? How would the argument be different if it were rewritten on this very day? (See Chapter 6 for advice on rhetorical analysis.)

2. Examine the various photos, charts, and other illustrations that accompany the selections in this chapter. What visual argument does each one make? (See Chapter 7 for guidance on analyzing visuals.)

3. Write your own argument about some aspect of globalization. Do you see its effects on your campus or in your community? How has globalization affected your community and your university? (See Chapter 9 for advice on writing causal arguments.)

4. Propose your own solution to a problem associated with globalization, a problem that you have some firsthand experience with. It could be a problem related to local misunderstandings among people, or something connected with your local economy (such as the outsourcing of jobs in a local industry), or a difficulty associated with immigration—or something else. (See Chapter 13 for advice on writing proposals.)

5. Is there a current proposal being considered by the federal government or your state government that is related to globalization? Write an essay in support or opposition to the legislation.

6. Or write an essay refuting the argument of someone who is proposing or supporting the legislation. (See Chapter 12 for advice on writing rebuttals.) Consider whether you wish to show the weaknesses in that other argument, or whether you wish to counterargue, or whether you want to do both.

7. Do you have firsthand experience of "Americanization" in other countries—maybe in your birth country or a country you've traveled to? Write a narrative argument related to Americanization that is based on, and generalizes from, your own experiences. (See Chapter 11 for advice on writing narrative arguments.)

8. What exactly is "globalization," anyway? Write an essay that defines the term in such a way that persuades readers to sympathize with it—or to resist it. (See Chapter 8 for advice on writing definition arguments.)

The Ethics of Science and Technology

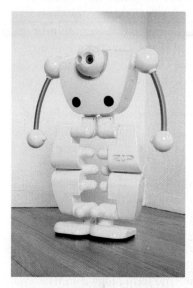

How does the Nuvo robot's appearance meet—or not meet—your notions of what a household robot might look like? What are some of the ethical concerns associated with having robots "living" in the home?

Item: In November 2004, couples with a family history of cancer were given an unusual permission by the Human Fertilization and Embryology Authority in Great Britain—they were allowed to select for human fertilization embryos free of cancer-causing genes. Critics immediately complained about this effort to create "designer babies." They drew comparisons with Adolph Hitler's interest in creating a "super-race" of genetically enhanced Aryans and raised concerns about the possibility that "better" human beings might have advantages over "natural" people.

Item: Early in 2005 in the United States, members of the National Academy of Sciences were finishing a recommendation report on the legal and ethical status of "chimeras"—hybrid creatures created by implanting one animal's stem cells into the fetal matter of a different species. Several living creatures have been "invented" and patented in recent years, raising the question of the possibility of others—mice with human brains? Pigs bioengineered to produce human blood? Or even a genetically plausible hybrid between humans and chimpanzees?

Item: One Thanksgiving Day, teenager Shawn Woolley committed suicide after (his mother claims) weeks of 12-hour stints playing the online role-playing game *EverQuest* addled his neurochemical condition. Do electronically mediated experiences like playing *EverQuest*—not to mention similar experiences that may soon make the transition from science fiction to reality—have mind-and-body effects on the human condition? What about the widespread use of Prozac and other mind-altering drugs: Do they threaten to change our sense of what human nature is at its

> "Twenty-first century technologies—genetics, nanotechnology, and robotics—are so powerful they can spawn whole new classes of accidents and abuses."
>
> —BILL JOY, SUN MICROSYSTEMS

core? No wonder science fiction movies and narratives are so popular—characters like the Terminator (hybrids of human and nonhuman) seem possible in the not-so-very-distant future.

These three items, brought to our attention by Jeffrey Pruchnic, highlight some of the ethical issues related to science and technology that people are grappling with these days. Still other issues have emerged with the new technology known as nanotechnology. MIT researcher K. Eric Drexler coined the term because *nano* literally means "one billionth"; nanotechnology refers to the science of creating molecule-sized materials and machines. Occupying the space between biology and engineering, nanotechnologists promise to create new things that fundamentally change the ways we work and live. As *Spiderman, Star-Trek: The Next Generation*, and popular magazines such as *Forbes* and *Wired* all indicate, nanotechnology promises to be the Next Big Thing. Nano skin creams are on the market, nano-enhanced tennis balls are used in the Davis Cup, microscopic silicon chips run computer games, and nanotechnologists are developing other micromachines that might radically improve water quality, benefit agriculture, clean up toxic waste, or make obsolete our reliance on oil by improving the efficiency of solar power. Nanomaterials hundreds of times stronger than steel might make possible 10-pound automobiles or airplanes. But is nanotechnology safe? Could dangerous nanoparticles escape and cause great damage? And what about nanotechnology's implications for the way human beings think of themselves?

Science and technology, as central enterprises in our culture, have always raised difficult moral and ethical questions. Science fiction stories and films have frequently addressed those same questions. Whether it is environmental protection (the subject of Chapter 22), energy, medicine, genetic engineering (including stem cell research and cloning), animal rights, the teaching of evolution, computer technologies, space exploration, or military weapons technology, science and technology command our attention and our committed arguments because they challenge our assumptions about what is possible and push the limits of what we think of as ethical.

Contemporary Arguments

Many new technologies are calling into question "the nature of nature," including our human nature. Is the natural world really "natural" when genetic engineers construct new species of plants and animals? And what are we to make of scientific developments that offer the potential for tremendous human benefits if they also have the potential to change our very human natures? Here we include arguments on several especially important and compelling developments related to science and human nature.

The first is energy. As we indicated in Chapter 22, an expanding human population and concerns over climate change have together created an expanding thirst for new sources of energy. In the United States, large new deposits of natural gas have been located in Pennsylvania, New York, Ohio, West Virginia, and several areas of the western United States and Canada, and those deposits promise tremendous economic benefits. But as recent films such as *Gasland* and *Promised Land* indicate, many citizens are concerned about the safety of mining those deposits through the method known as fracking. Here we offer arguments by Jay Lehr, Mike Gemmell, and Joseph Bast, and by Elizabeth Royte that articulate the possibilities and problems associated with energy production.

A second issue is robotics. According to Bill Gates, robots have the potential to become as ubiquitous as computers—although he acknowledges that there are as many naysayers about today's robotics developments as there once were about the possibilities of bringing computers into nearly every home. In "A Robot in Every Home," Gates discusses the potential for robotics with enthusiasm, but detractors (represented here by Paul Marks) are raising questions about the ethics of replacing humans and human labor with robots and robotic labor. The rise of robotics lends an almost science-fiction quality to technology and gives rise in the popular imagination to sci-fi's greatest dreams and fears. Will robots turn on their creators, as the Frankenstein monster turned on its? Or will they remain friendly as pets, like C3PO and R2D2?

Third, we invite you to meditate on bioethics. How do we ethically balance the risks and responsibilities of tampering with the "natural"? No doubt you have read and heard a great deal about stem cell research because of highly publicized

New scientific advances are creating new ethical issues for consideration. What are the ethical consequences of pursuing genetic engineering or creating robots with humanlike intelligence?

Doug Savage/Savage Chickens

appeals on its behalf by very public people: Michael J. Fox (who suffers from Parkinson's disease); Christopher Reeve (who suffered paralyzing, ultimately fatal spine damage in a horseback riding accident); Nancy Reagan (who cared for former president Ronald Reagan during his battle with Alzheimer's); former Senator Arlen Specter (who died of cancer in 2012); and, at the Democratic National Convention in 2004, the ex-president's son, Ron Reagan.

And yet there are many others who find stem cell research in particular and genetic engineering more generally to be dangerous and/or unethical, and who find claims of potential miracle cures to be highly exaggerated (and sometimes motivated by the prospect of grant money). Some people fear that stem cell research, the harvesting of human organs, the manipulation of animals for the benefit of humans, and other biotechnologies, if approved, would lead to a catalog of horrors. Here we offer a sample of the arguments involved, both pro and con: Sally Satel advocates the sale of human organs (under controlled conditions) in order to increase the supply available for transplant, and Carl Zimmer explores the wisdom of bring extinct species back to life.

Finally, we close with an Issue in Focus, on genetically modified food—the fourth science-and-ethics controversy represented here. Perhaps you too have personal, moral, religious, or occupational reasons to be concerned about one or another of these controversies. Read the selections that follow with care—and then develop and express your own considered views.

Jay Lehr, Mike Gemmell, and Joseph Bast

An Open Letter to the Oil and Gas Industry: The Ethical Case for Fracking

The Heartland Institute, based in Chicago, is a nonprofit think tank that promotes "free-market solutions to social and economic problems" (according to its Web site). It typically offers conservative perspectives on climate change, health care, and energy policy. On December 12, 2011, three members of The Heartland Institute released the following "open letter." Jay Lehr is the Heartland Institute's science director; Mike Gemmell, a hydrogeologist, specializes in groundwater contamination studies; and Joseph Bast is president of The Heartland Institute.

Those of you in the oil and gas industry are no doubt familiar with the U.S. Environmental Protection Agency's claim that fracking is a potential source of groundwater contamination, and that a moratorium on the use of fracking should be enacted until EPA can study it to death. (*Note: For lay people, hydraulic fracturing, or "fracking," is a technique used to increase oil and gas yields in petroleum-bearing formations. It involves injecting fluids at high pressure into the formation to increase its transmission properties.*)

2   This step—one EPA has been hinting about for months—will be another nail in the energy industry's coffin if its representatives do not step up and oppose this utterly unwarranted accusation. Will you rise to the challenge?

3   EPA and its allies in the environmental movement and media are claiming there is *now* a reason to believe fracking has contaminated the groundwater in certain wells in Wyoming, even though the use of fracking was generally considered safe and noncontroversial for the past 50 years. This is an out-and-out fabrication, which in time will be exposed. But if a moratorium is imposed before the truth comes out, energy production in the United States will suffer another serious setback. Lifting the moratorium may take years and millions of dollars in campaign contributions.

4   If the energy industry doesn't step up—in a specific way, this time—EPA will probably get away with this. The scientific data supporting the safety of fracking are overwhelming, but science alone is not enough to stop the "what if . . . what if . . . what ifs" of the environmental lobby. There are innumerable ways to twist and distort scientific and economic data to advance the environmental activists' agenda, stop fracking, and continue their attempts, via EPA, to cripple energy production in the United States.

5   The specific argument needed is an unequivocal ethical stand defending the use of fracking technology, *thereby taking the high ground away from the environmental lobby*. Only philosophical or ethical arguments can cut off this sort of nonsense at its root.

6   The ethical arguments are based on truth-telling and fairness. A moratorium on fracking is justified only as a way to slow or stop the development of new energy resources in America. It has nothing to do with protecting human health. Those reporting the story and those advocating a ban on fracking must be confronted with that truth again and again. The other side is cynical and willing to say anything to advance its anti-energy campaign.

7   Because it is impossible to "prove a negative," the energy industry cannot prove beyond any doubt that fracking is "safe," any more than car, cell phone, or soap manufacturers can prove their products are "perfectly safe." It is profoundly unfair to hold producers to impossible standards. It is profoundly unethical to pretend to be protecting human health when the true objectives of those mounting the anti-fracking campaign are entirely different.

8   The philosophical arguments for fracking are based on the role of energy and freedom in creating and preserving a prosperous society. The energy industry must not apologize for the products and services it produces, but instead must educate the public that energy is the Master Resource (as Julian Simon wrote); it makes possible virtually all other goods and services that we need to prosper. Energy is at the root of all production, and inexpensive energy is the way out of poverty for millions of people.

9   The attack on fracking is a naked attack on energy, and an attack on energy is an attack on America's prosperity and the free-enterprise system that helped bring it about. The other side knows this; it is their rationale and motivation. Shutting down fracking is a means to this end. Their allies in the media know this and hide the true agenda from their readers. It is up to industry to make the argument itself, repeatedly and in every possible venue. Because if the attack on fracking is *not* about public health, as the other side says, *what is it about?* It is, in fact, an ideologically driven campaign against our lifestyles, our values, and our future.

10   This administration is out of control; there is no need to belabor that point. We can't be everywhere at once trying to put our fingers in the dike to keep the dam from bursting. However, each of us *can* put our fingers in the dike in areas we specialize in, and the energy industry *MUST* now do this in its area of expertise.

ELIZABETH **ROYTE**

Fracking Our Food Supply

The following article was published in the *Nation* on December 17, 2012. (The *Nation*, for the past century, has been publishing resolutely left-of-center arguments on politics, culture, and the arts.) Elizabeth Royte is a noted science writer with several books to her credit—as well as articles in *Smithsonian*, *New York Times Magazine*, *Harper's*, *National Geographic*, and the *New Yorker*. "Fracking Our Food Supply" was produced in collaboration with the Food and Environment Reporting Network, an investigative reporting nonprofit focusing on food, agriculture, and environmental health.

In a Brooklyn winery on a sultry July evening, an elegant crowd sips rosé and nibbles trout plucked from the gin-clear streams of upstate New York. The diners are here, with their checkbooks, to support a group called Chefs for the Marcellus, which works to protect the foodshed upon which hundreds of regional farm-to-fork restaurants depend. The foodshed is coincident with the Marcellus Shale, a geologic formation that arcs northeast from West Virginia through Pennsylvania and into New York State. As everyone invited here knows, the region is both agriculturally and energy rich, with vast quantities of natural gas sequestered deep below its fertile fields and forests.

2   In Pennsylvania, the oil and gas industry is already on a tear—drilling thousands of feet into ancient seabeds, then repeatedly fracturing (or "fracking") these wells with millions of gallons of highly pressurized, chemically laced water, which shatters the surrounding shale and releases fossil fuels. New York, meanwhile, is on its own natural-resource tear, with hundreds of newly opened breweries, wineries, organic dairies and pastured livestock operations—all of them capitalizing on the metropolitan area's hunger to localize its diet.

3   But there's growing evidence that these two impulses, toward energy and food independence, may be at odds with each other.

4   Tonight's guests have heard about residential drinking wells tainted by fracking fluids in Pennsylvania, Wyoming and Colorado. They've read about lingering rashes, nosebleeds and respiratory trauma in oil-patch communities, which are mostly rural, undeveloped, and lacking in political influence and economic prospects. The trout nibblers in the winery sympathize with the suffering of those communities. But their main concern tonight is a more insidious matter: the potential for drilling and fracking operations to contaminate our food. The early evidence from heavily fracked regions, especially from ranchers, is not reassuring.

5   Jacki Schilke and her sixty cattle live in the top left corner of North Dakota, a windswept, golden-hued landscape in the heart of the Bakken Shale. Schilke's neighbors love her black Angus beef, but she's no longer sharing or eating it—not since fracking began on thirty-two oil and gas wells within three miles of her 160-acre ranch and five of her cows dropped dead. Schilke herself is in poor health. A handsome 53-year-old with a faded blond ponytail and direct blue eyes, she often feels lightheaded when she ventures outside. She limps and has chronic pain in her lungs, as well as rashes that have lingered for a year. Once, a visit to the barn ended with respiratory distress and a trip to the emergency room. Schilke also has back pain linked with overworked kidneys, and on some mornings she urinates a stream of blood.

6   Ambient air testing by a certified environmental consultant detected elevated levels of benzene, methane, chloroform, butane, propane, toluene and xylene—compounds associated with drilling and fracking, and also with cancers, birth defects and organ damage. Her well tested high for sulfates, chromium, chloride and strontium; her blood tested positive for acetone, plus the heavy metals arsenic (linked with skin lesions, cancers and cardiovascular disease) and germanium (linked with muscle weakness and skin rashes). Both she and her husband, who works in oilfield services, have recently lost crowns and fillings from their teeth; tooth loss is associated with radiation poisoning and high selenium levels, also found in the Schilkes' water.

7   State health and agriculture officials acknowledged Schilke's air and water tests but told her she had nothing to worry about. Her doctors, however, diagnosed her with neurotoxic damage and constricted airways. "I realized that this place is killing me and my cattle," Schilke says. She began using inhalers and a nebulizer, switched to bottled water, and quit eating her own beef and the vegetables from her garden. (Schilke sells her cattle only to buyers who will finish raising them outside the shale area, where she presumes that any chemical contamination will clear after a few months.) "My health improved," Schilke says, "but I thought, 'Oh my God, what are we doing to this land?'"

8   Schilke's story reminds us that farmers need clean water, clean air and clean soil to produce healthful food. But as the largest private landholders in shale areas across the nation, farmers are disproportionately being approached by energy companies eager to extract oil and gas from beneath their properties. Already, some are regretting it.

9   Earlier this year, Michelle Bamberger, an Ithaca veterinarian, and Robert Oswald, a professor of molecular medicine at Cornell's College of Veterinary Medicine, published the first (and, so far, only) peer-reviewed report to suggest a link between fracking and illness in food animals. The authors compiled case studies of twenty-four farmers in six shale-gas states whose livestock experienced neurological, reproductive and acute gastrointestinal problems. Exposed either accidentally or incidentally to fracking chemicals in the water or air, scores of animals have died. The death toll is insignificant when measured against the nation's livestock population (some 97 million beef cattle go to market each year), but environmental advocates believe these animals constitute an early warning.

10   Exposed animals "are making their way into the food system, and it's very worrisome to us," Bamberger says. "They live in areas that have tested positive for air, water and soil contamination. Some of these chemicals could appear in milk and meat products made from these animals."

11   In Louisiana, seventeen cows died after an hour's exposure to spilled fracking fluid. (Most likely cause of death: respiratory failure.) In north central Pennsylvania, 140 cattle were exposed to fracking wastewater when an impoundment was breached. Approximately seventy cows died; the remainder produced eleven calves, of which only three survived. In western Pennsylvania, an overflowing waste pit sent fracking chemicals into a pond and a pasture where pregnant cows grazed: half their calves were born dead. The following year's animal births were sexually skewed, with ten females and two males, instead of the usual 50-50 or 60-40 split.

12   In addition to the cases documented by Bamberger, hair testing of sick cattle that grazed around well pads in New Mexico found petroleum residues in fifty-four of fifty-six animals. In North Dakota, wind-borne fly ash, which is used to solidify the waste from drilling holes and contains heavy metals, settled over a farm: one cow, which either inhaled or ingested the caustic dust, died, and a stock pond was contaminated with arsenic at double the accepted level for drinking water.

13   Cattle that die on the farm don't make it into the nation's food system. (Though they're often rendered to make animal feed for chickens and pigs—yet another cause for concern.) But herd mates that appear healthy, despite being exposed to the same compounds, do: farmers aren't required to prove their livestock are free of fracking contaminants before middlemen purchase them. Bamberger and Oswald consider these animals sentinels for human health. "They're outdoors all day long, so they're constantly exposed to air, soil and groundwater, with no break to go to work or the supermarket," Bamberger says. "And they have more frequent reproductive cycles, so we can see toxic effects much sooner than with humans."

14   Fracking a single well requires up to 7 million gallons of water, plus an additional 400,000 gallons of additives, including lubricants, biocides, scale and rust inhibitors, solvents, foaming and defoaming agents, emulsifiers and de-emulsifiers, stabilizers and breakers. About 70 percent of the liquid that goes down a borehole eventually comes up—now further tainted with such deep-earth compounds as sodium, chloride, bromide, arsenic, barium, uranium, radium and radon. (These substances occur naturally, but many of them can cause illness if ingested or inhaled over time.) This super-salty

"produced" water, or brine, can be stored on-site for reuse. Depending on state regulations, it can also be held in plastic-lined pits until it evaporates, is injected back into the earth, or gets hauled to municipal wastewater treatment plants, which aren't designed to neutralize or sequester fracking chemicals (in other words, they're discharged with effluent into nearby streams).

15   At almost every stage of developing and operating an oil or gas well, chemicals and compounds can be introduced into the environment. Radioactive material above background levels has been detected in air, soil and water at or near gas-drilling sites. Volatile organic compounds—including benzene, toluene, ethylene and xylene—waft from flares, engines, compressors, pipelines, flanges, open tanks, spills and ponds. (The good news: VOCs don't accumulate in animals or plants. The bad news: inhalation exposure is linked to cancer and organ damage.)

16   Underground, petrochemicals can migrate along fissures through abandoned or orphaned wells or leaky well casings (the oil and gas industry estimates that 60 percent of wells will leak over a thirty-year period). Brine can spill from holding ponds or pipelines. It can be spread, legally in some places, on roadways to control dust and melt ice. Truck drivers have also been known to illegally dump this liquid in creeks or fields, where animals can drink it or lick it from their fur.

17   Although energy companies don't make a habit of telling potential lease signers about the environmental risks they might face, the Securities and Exchange Commission requires them to inform potential investors. In a 2008 filing, Cabot

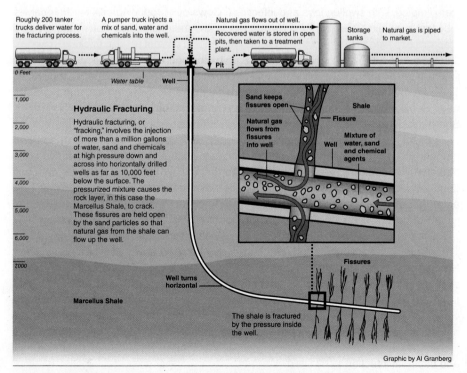

Roughly 200 tanker trucks deliver water for the fracturing process.

A pumper truck injects a mix of sand, water and chemicals into the well.

Natural gas flows out of well.

Recovered water is stored in open pits, then taken to a treatment plant.

Storage tanks

Natural gas is piped to market.

0 Feet

Water table   Well

Pit

1,000

Hydraulic Fracturing

Hydraulic fracturing, or "fracking," involves the injection of more than a million gallons of water, sand and chemicals at high pressure down and across into horizontally drilled wells as far as 10,000 feet below the surface. The pressurized mixture causes the rock layer, in this case the Marcellus Shale, to crack. These fissures are held open by the sand particles so that natural gas from the shale can flow up the well.

2,000

3,000

4,000

5,000

6,000

7,000

Sand keeps fissures open

Shale

Natural gas flows from fissures into well

Fissure

Mixture of water, sand and chemical agents

Well

Well turns horizontal

Fissures

Marcellus Shale

The shale is fractured by the pressure inside the well.

Graphic by Al Granberg

Hydraulic fracturing is a process used for extracting natural gas from shale.

Industries cited "well site blowouts, cratering and explosions; equipment failures; uncontrolled flows of natural gas, oil or well fluids; fires; formations with abnormal pressures; pollution and other environmental risks." In 2011, oil companies in North Dakota reported more than 1,000 accidental releases of oil, drilling wastewater or other fluids, with many more releases likely unreported. Between 2008 and 2011, drilling companies in Pennsylvania reported 2,392 violations of law that posed a direct threat to the environment and safety of communities.

18 Schilke looks left and right, twice, for oncoming tanker trucks, then scoots down a gravel road in her camo-patterned four-wheeler. She parks alongside a leased pasture about a mile from her house and folds her body through a barbed-wire fence. "These guys are much healthier than those I've got at home," she says, puffing as she hikes up a straw-colored hill. "There's Judy ... that's Buttercup ... those are my little bulls." The black-faced animals turn to face her; some amble through the tall grass and present their foreheads for rubbing. "We're upwind of the drill rigs here," Schilke says. "They're high enough to miss some of the road dust, and they've got good water." Ever since a heater-treater unit, which separates oil, gas and brine, blew out on a drill pad a half-mile upwind of Schilke's ranch, her own creek has been clogged with scummy growth, and it regularly burps up methane. "No one can tell me what's going on," she says. But since the blowout, her creek has failed to freeze, despite temperatures of forty below. (Testing found sulfate levels of 4,000 parts per million: the EPA's health goal for sulfate is 250 parts per million.)

19 Schilke's troubles began in the summer of 2010, when a crew working at this site continued to force drilling fluid down a well that had sprung a leak. Soon, Schilke's cattle were limping, with swollen legs and infections. Cows quit producing milk for their calves; they lost from sixty to eighty pounds in a week; and their tails mysteriously dropped off. (Lab rats exposed to the carcinogen 2-butoxyethanol, a solvent used in fracking, have lost their tails, but a similar connection with cattle hasn't been shown. In people, breathing, touching or consuming enough of the chemical can lead to pulmonary edema and coma.)

20 An inveterate label reader who obsessively tracks her animals' nutritional intake, Schilke couldn't figure out what was wrong. Neither could local veterinarians. She nursed individual cows for weeks and, with much sorrow, put a $5,000 bull out of its misery with a bullet. Upon examination, the animal's liver was found to be full of tunnels and its lungs congested with pneumonia. Before the year was out, five cows had died, in addition to several cats and two dogs. (Hair testing of Schilke's cats and dogs revealed elevated selenium levels, while water tests showed sulfate at levels high enough, Schilke's vet told her, to cause polio in cattle.) Inside Schilke's house today, where the china cabinets are kept empty for fear of a shattering drill-site explosion, nearly a dozen cats sneeze and cough, some with their heads tilted at a creepy angle.

21 Before the drilling started, two cars a day traveled down Schilke's gravel road. Now, it's 300 trucks hauling sand, fresh water, wastewater, chemicals, drill cuttings and drilling equipment. Most of the tankers are placarded for hazardous or radioactive material. Drilling and fracking a single well requires 2,000 truck trips, and each pass of a vehicle sends a cyclone of dust and exhaust fumes into the air. Mailbox numbers are obliterated, conversations are choked off, and animals die of "dust pneumonia." (More formally known as bovine respiratory disease, the illness is associated with viral, fungal and bacterial infection.)

22   Ordinarily, Schilke hauls her calves to auction when they're eight months old. "Buyers come from everywhere for Dakota cows," she says. The animals are then raised on pasture or in feedlots until they are big enough for slaughter. No longer Schilke cattle, they're soon part of the commodity food system: anonymous steaks and chops on supermarket shelves. Now, Schilke is diffident about selling her animals. "I could get good money for these steers," she says, cocking her head toward a pair of sleek adolescents. "They seem to be in very good shape and should have been butchered. But I won't sell them because I don't know if they're OK."

23   Nor does anyone else. By design, secrecy shrouds the hydrofracking process, casting a shadow that extends over consumers' right to know if their food is safe. Federal loopholes crafted under former Vice President Dick Cheney have exempted energy companies from key provisions of the Clean Air, Clean Water and Safe Drinking Water Acts, the Toxics Release Inventory, the Resource Conservation and Recovery Act, and the National Environmental Policy Act, which requires a full review of actions that may cause significant environmental impacts. If scientists and citizens can't find out precisely what is in drilling or fracking fluids or air emissions at any given time, it's difficult to test whether any contaminants have migrated into the water, soil or food—and whether they can harm humans. It gets even more complicated: without information on the interactions between these chemicals and others already existing in the environment, an animal's cause of death, Bamberger says, "is anyone's guess."

24   Fracking proponents criticize Bamberger and Oswald's paper as a political, not a scientific, document. "They used anonymous sources, so no one can verify what they said," Steve Everley, of the industry lobby group Energy In Depth, says. The authors didn't provide a scientific assessment of impacts—testing what quaternary ammonium compounds might do to cows that drink it, for example—so treating their findings as scientific, he continues, "is laughable at best, and dangerous for public debate at worst." (Bamberger and Oswald acknowledge this lack of scientific assessment and blame the dearth of funding for fracking research and the industry's use of nondisclosure agreements.)

25   No one doubts that fracking fluids have the potential to do serious harm. Theo Colborn, an environmental health analyst and former director of the World Wildlife Fund's wildlife and contaminants program, identified 632 chemicals used in natural-gas production. More than 75 percent of them, she said, could affect sensory organs and the respiratory and gastrointestinal systems; 40 to 50 percent have potential impacts on the kidneys and on the nervous, immune and cardiovascular systems; 37 percent act on the hormone system; and 25 percent are linked with cancer or mutations.

26   Thanks to public pressure, several states have started to tighten regulations on the cement casings used to line wells, and the Obama administration recently required energy companies to disclose, on the industry-sponsored website fracfocus.org, the fracking chemicals used on public land. (States regulate fracking on private land and set different requirements.) Still, information about quantities and concentrations of the chemicals remains secret, as do compounds considered proprietary. Further, no state requires a company to disclose its ingredients until a fracking job is complete. At that point, it's easy to blame the presence of toxins in groundwater on a landowner's use of pesticides, fertilizers or even farm equipment.

27   Clearly, the technology to extract gas from shale has advanced faster, and with a lot more public funding, than has the study of its various effects. To date, there have been no systematic, peer-reviewed, long-term studies of the health effects of hydraulic fracturing for oil and gas production (one short-term, peer-reviewed study found that fracking emissions may contribute to acute and chronic health problems for people living near drill sites). And the risks to food safety may be even more difficult to parse.

28   "Different plants take up different compounds," says John Stolz, an environmental microbiologist at Duquesne University. For example, rice and potatoes take up arsenic from water, but tomatoes don't. Sunflowers and rape take up uranium from soil, but it's unknown if grasses do. "There are a variety of organic compounds, metals and radioactive material that are of human health concern when livestock meat or milk is ingested," says Motoko Mukai, a veterinary toxicologist at Cornell's College of Veterinary Medicine. These "compounds accumulate in the fat and are excreted into milk. Some compounds are persistent and do not get metabolized easily."

29   Veterinarians don't know how long the chemicals may remain in animals, and the Food Safety Inspection Service, part of the US Department of Agriculture, isn't looking for them in carcasses. Inspectors in slaughterhouses examine organs only if they look diseased. "It's gross appearance, not microscopic," Bamberger says of the inspections—which means that animals either tainted or sickened by those chemicals could enter the food chain undetected.

30   "The USDA focuses mostly on pathogens and pesticide residues," says Tony Corbo, a senior lobbyist for Food and Water Watch. "We need to do risk assessments for these fracking chemicals and study tolerance levels." The process, he adds, could take more than five years. In the meantime, fractivists are passing around a food-pyramid chart that depicts chemicals moving from plants into animals, from animals into people, and from people into . . . zombies.

31   The relatively small number of animals reported sick or dead invites the question: If oil and gas operations are so risky, why aren't there more cases? There likely are, but few scientists are looking for them. ("Who's got the money to study this?" Colborn asks rhetorically.) Rural vets won't speak up for fear of retaliation. And farmers aren't talking for myriad reasons: some receive royalty checks from the energy companies (either by choice or because the previous landowner leased their farm's mineral rights); some have signed nondisclosure agreements after receiving a financial settlement; and some are in active litigation. Some farmers fear retribution from community members with leases; others don't want to fall afoul of "food disparagement" laws or get sued by an oil company for defamation (as happened with one Texan after video of his flame-spouting garden hose was posted on the Internet. The oil company won; the homeowner is appealing).

32   And many would simply rather not know what's going on. "It takes a long time to build up a herd's reputation," says rancher Dennis Bauste, of Trenton Lake, North Dakota. "I'm gonna sell my calves, and I don't want them to be labeled as tainted. Besides, I wouldn't know what to test for. Until there's a big wipeout, a major problem, we're not gonna hear much about this." Ceylon Feiring, an area vet, concurs. "We're just waiting for a wreck to happen with someone's cattle," she says. "Otherwise, it's just one-offs"—a sick cow here and a dead goat there, easy for regulators, vets and even farmers to shrug off.

33   The National Cattlemen's Beef Association takes no position on fracking, nor has it heard from members either concerned by or in favor of the process. And yet it's ranchers and farmers—many of them industry-supporting conservatives—who are, increasingly, telling their stories to the media and risking all. These are the people who have watched helplessly as their livestock suffer and die. "It's not our breeding or nutrition destroying these animals," Schilke says, her voice rising in anger. "It's the oilfield industry."

34   However, some institutions that specialize in risk have started to connect the dots. Nationwide Mutual Insurance, which sells agricultural insurance, recently announced that it would not cover damages related to fracking. Rabobank, the world's largest agricultural bank, reportedly no longer sells mortgages to farmers with gas leases. And in the boldest move yet by a government official, Christopher Portier, director of the National Center for Environmental Health at the Centers for Disease Control and Prevention, called for studies that "include all the ways people can be exposed, such as through air, water, soil, plants and animals." While the EPA is in the midst of a $1.9 million study of fracking's impact on water, no government agency has taken up Portier's challenge to study plants and animals.

35   The possibility of chemical contamination aside, oil and gas operations have already affected food producers. "I lost six acres of hayfields when the gas company put roads in," says Terry Greenwood, a rancher in western Pennsylvania. "Now I have to buy more feed for my cattle." (Like other farmers hurt by drilling and fracking, he still pays taxes on his unproductive land.) Others have lost the use of stock ponds or creeks to brine spills.

36   "We've got 12,000 wells in the Bakken, and they each take up six acres," says Mark Trechock, former director of the Dakota Resource Council. "That's 72,000 acres right there, without counting the waste facilities, access roads, stored equipment and man camps that go along with the wells." Before the drilling boom, that land might have produced durum wheat, barley, oats, canola, flax, sunflowers, pinto beans, lentils and peas. In Pennsylvania, where nearly 6,500 wells have been drilled since 2000, the Nature Conservancy estimates that thirty acres are directly or indirectly affected for every well pad.

37   East of the Rockies, intensive drilling and fracking have pushed levels of smog, or ground-level ozone, higher than those of Los Angeles. Ozone significantly diminishes crop yields and reduces the nutritional value of forage. Flaring of raw gas can acidify soil and send fine particulate matter into the air; long-term exposure to this material has been linked to human heart and lung diseases and disruption to the endocrine system. Earlier this year, the Environmental Protection Agency finalized standards that require reductions in airborne emissions from gas wells, although the industry has more than two years to comply.

38   Besides clean air, farmers need clean water—lots of it. But some farmers now find themselves competing with energy companies for this increasingly precious resource. At water auctions in Colorado, the oil and gas industry has paid utilities up to twenty times the price that farmers typically pay. In Wyoming, ranchers have switched from raising beef to selling their water. Unwilling to risk her animals' health to creek water that's possibly tainted, Schilke spent $4,000 last summer hauling safe water from

town to her ranch. "I'd wait in line for hours," she says, "usually behind tanker trucks buying water to frack wells."

39   Given the absence of studies on the impacts of drilling and fracking in plants and animals, as well as inadequate inspection and scant traceability in the food chain, it's hard to know what level of risk consumers face when drinking milk or eating meat or vegetables produced in a frack zone. Unless, of course, you're Jacki Schilke, and you feel marginally healthier when you quit eating the food that you produced downwind or downstream from drill rigs. But many consumers—those intensely interested in where and how their food is grown—aren't waiting for hard data to tell them what is or isn't safe. For them, the perception of pollution is just as bad as the real thing. Ken Jaffe, who raises grass-fed cattle in upstate New York, says, "My beef sells itself. My farm is pristine. But a restaurant doesn't want to visit and see a drill pad on the horizon."

40   Nor do the 16,200 members of the Park Slope Food Co-op in Brooklyn, which buys one cow per week from Jaffe. "If hydrofracking is allowed in New York State, the co-op will have to stop buying from farms anywhere near the drilling because of fears of contamination," says Joe Holtz, general manager of the co-op. That's $4 million in direct sales, with economic multipliers up and down the local food chain, affecting seed houses, creameries, equipment manufacturers and so on.

41   Already, wary farmers in the Marcellus are seeking land away from the shale. The outward migration is simultaneously raising prices for good farmland in the Hudson River Valley, which lies outside the shale zone, and depressing the price of land over the Marcellus. According to John Bingham, an organic farmer in upstate New York who is involved in regional planning, lower prices entice absentee investors to buy up farmland and gain favorable "farm rate" tax breaks, even as they speculate on the gas boom. "Fracking is not a healthy development for food security in regions near fracking or away from it," Bingham concludes.

42   Only recently has the Northeast's local-foods movement reached a critical mass, to the point where colleges and caterers trip over themselves in the quest for locally sourced and sustainably grown products. (New York has the fourth-highest number of organic farms in the nation.) But the movement's lofty ideals could turn out to be, in shale-gas areas, a double-edged sword. "People at the farmers' market are starting to ask exactly where this food comes from," says Stephen Cleghorn, a Pennsylvania goat farmer.

43   With a watchful eye on Pennsylvania's turmoil, many New York farmers have started to test their water pre-emptively, in the event that Governor Andrew Cuomo lifts the state's current moratorium on fracking. And in the commercial kitchens of a city obsessed with the provenance of its prosciutto, chefs like Heather Carlucci-Rodriguez, a founder of Chefs for the Marcellus and the executive pastry chef at Manhattan's Print Restaurant, are keeping careful tabs on their regional suppliers.

44   "I have a map of the Marcellus and my farmers on my office wall," Carlucci-Rodriguez says at the Brooklyn winery event. "So far, I haven't stopped buying from anyone. But I'm a believer in the precautionary principle." She nods to a colleague who's dishing up summer squash with peach slices and ricotta. "We shouldn't have to be defending our land and water," she says with a sigh. "We should be feeding people."

BILL **GATES**

A Robot in Every Home

From 1995 to 2009, Bill Gates had been ranked by *Forbes* magazine as the richest person in the world (he has now "fallen" to number 2). Best known for his role with Microsoft, the company he cofounded with Paul Allen, Gates now serves as the primary stockholder for that corporation. He spends most of his time doing philanthropic work with the Gates Foundation, which he and his wife, Melinda, founded in 2000. In "A Robot in Every Home," which first appeared in the December 2006 issue of *Scientific American*, Gates waxes enthusiastic and optimistic about the prospect of bringing robotics into every American household—much as Microsoft did with personal computers.

I magine being present at the birth of a new industry. It is an industry based on groundbreaking new technologies, wherein a handful of well-established corporations sell highly specialized devices for business use and a fast-growing number of start-up companies produce innovative toys, gadgets for hobbyists and other interesting niche products. But it is also a highly fragmented industry with few common standards or platforms. Projects are complex, progress is slow, and practical applications are relatively rare. In fact, for all the excitement and promise, no one can say with any certainty when—or even if—this industry will achieve critical mass. If it does, though, it may well change the world.

2   Of course, the paragraph above could be a description of the computer industry during the mid-1970s, around the time that Paul Allen and I launched Microsoft. Back then, big, expensive mainframe computers ran the back-office operations for major companies, governmental departments and other institutions. Researchers at leading universities and industrial laboratories were creating the basic building blocks that would make the information age possible. Intel had just introduced the 8080 microprocessor, and Atari was selling the popular electronic game Pong. At homegrown computer clubs, enthusiasts struggled to figure out exactly what this new technology was good for.

3   But what I really have in mind is something much more contemporary: the emergence of the robotics industry, which is developing in much the same way that the computer business did 30 years ago. Think of the manufacturing robots currently used on automobile assembly lines as the equivalent of yesterday's mainframes. The industry's niche products include robotic arms that perform surgery, surveillance robots deployed in Iraq and Afghanistan that dispose of roadside bombs, and domestic robots that vacuum the floor. Electronics companies have made robotic toys that can imitate people or dogs or dinosaurs, and hobbyists are anxious to get their hands on the latest version of the Lego robotics system.

4   Meanwhile some of the world's best minds are trying to solve the toughest problems of robotics, such as visual recognition, navigation and machine learning. And they are succeeding. At the 2004 Defense Advanced Research Projects Agency (DARPA) Grand Challenge, a competition to produce the first robotic vehicle capable of navigating autonomously over a rugged 142-mile course through the Mojave Desert, the top competitor managed to travel just 7.4 miles before breaking down. In 2005, though,

five vehicles covered the complete distance, and the race's winner did it at an average speed of 19.1 miles an hour. (In another intriguing parallel between the robotics and computer industries, DARPA also funded the work that led to the creation of Arpanet, the precursor to the Internet.)

5   What is more, the challenges facing the robotics industry are similar to those we tackled in computing three decades ago. Robotics companies have no standard operating software that could allow popular application programs to run in a variety of devices. The standardization of robotic processors and other hardware is limited, and very little of the programming code used in one machine can be applied to another. Whenever somebody wants to build a new robot, they usually have to start from square one.

6   Despite these difficulties, when I talk to people involved in robotics—from university researchers to entrepreneurs, hobbyists and high school students—the level of excitement and expectation reminds me so much of that time when Paul Allen and I looked at the convergence of new technologies and dreamed of the day when a computer would be on every desk and in every home. And as I look at the trends that are now starting to converge, I can envision a future in which robotic devices will become a nearly ubiquitous part of our day-to-day lives. I believe that technologies such as distributed computing, voice and visual recognition, and wireless broadband connectivity will open the door to a new generation of autonomous devices that enable computers to perform tasks in the physical world on our behalf. We may be on the verge of a new era, when the PC will get up off the desktop and allow us to see, hear, touch and manipulate objects in places where we are not physically present.

From Science Fiction to Reality

7   The word "robot" was popularized in 1921 by Czech playwright Karel Capek, but people have envisioned creating robot-like devices for thousands of years. In Greek and Roman mythology, the gods of metalwork built mechanical servants made from gold. In the first century A.D., Heron of Alexandria—the great engineer credited with inventing the first steam engine—designed intriguing automatons, including one said to have the ability to talk. Leonardo da Vinci's 1495 sketch of a mechanical knight, which could sit up and move its arms and legs, is considered to be the first plan for a humanoid robot.

8   Over the past century, anthropomorphic machines have become familiar figures in popular culture through books such as Isaac Asimov's *I, Robot*, movies such as *Star Wars* and television shows such as *Star Trek*. The popularity of robots in fiction indicates that people are receptive to the idea that these machines will one day walk among us as helpers and even as companions. Nevertheless, although robots play a vital role in industries such as automobile manufacturing—where there is about one robot for every 10 workers—the fact is that we have a long way to go before real robots catch up with their science-fiction counterparts.

9   One reason for this gap is that it has been much harder than expected to enable computers and robots to sense their surrounding environment and to react quickly and accurately. It has proved extremely difficult to give robots the capabilities

that humans take for granted—for example, the abilities to orient themselves with respect to the objects in a room, to respond to sounds and interpret speech, and to grasp objects of varying sizes, textures and fragility. Even something as simple as telling the difference between an open door and a window can be devilishly tricky for a robot.

10 But researchers are starting to find the answers. One trend that has helped them is the increasing availability of tremendous amounts of computer power. One megahertz of processing power, which cost more than $7,000 in 1970, can now be purchased for just pennies. The price of a megabit of storage has seen a similar decline. The access to cheap computing power has permitted scientists to work on many of the hard problems that are fundamental to making robots practical. Today, for example, voice-recognition programs can identify words quite well, but a far greater challenge will be building machines that can understand what those words mean in context. As computing capacity continues to expand, robot designers will have the processing power they need to tackle issues of ever greater complexity.

11 Another barrier to the development of robots has been the high cost of hardware, such as sensors that enable a robot to determine the distance to an object as well as motors and servos that allow the robot to manipulate an object with both strength and delicacy. But prices are dropping fast. Laser range finders that are used in robotics to measure distance with precision cost about $10,000 a few years ago; today they can be purchased for about $2,000. And new, more accurate sensors based on ultrawideband radar are available for even less.

12 Now robot builders can also add Global Positioning System chips, video cameras, array microphones (which are better than conventional microphones at distinguishing a voice from background noise) and a host of additional sensors for a reasonable expense. The resulting enhancement of capabilities, combined with expanded processing power and storage, allows today's robots to do things such as vacuum a room or help to defuse a roadside bomb—tasks that would have been impossible for commercially produced machines just a few years ago.

A BASIC Approach

13 In February 2004 I visited a number of leading universities, including Carnegie Mellon University, the Massachusetts Institute of Technology, Harvard University, Cornell University and the University of Illinois, to talk about the powerful role that computers can play in solving some of society's most pressing problems. My goal was to help students understand how exciting and important computer science can be, and I hoped to encourage a few of them to think about careers in technology. At each university, after delivering my speech, I had the opportunity to get a firsthand look at some of the most interesting research projects in the school's computer science department. Almost without exception, I was shown at least one project that involved robotics.

14 At that time, my colleagues at Microsoft were also hearing from people in academia and at commercial robotics firms who wondered if our company was doing any work in robotics that might help them with their own development efforts. We were not, so we decided to take a closer look. I asked Tandy Trower, a member of my strategic

staff and a 25-year Microsoft veteran, to go on an extended fact-finding mission and to speak with people across the robotics community. What he found was universal enthusiasm for the potential of robotics, along with an industry-wide desire for tools that would make development easier. "Many see the robotics industry at a technological turning point where a move to PC architecture makes more and more sense," Tandy wrote in his report to me after his fact-finding mission. "As Red Whittaker, leader of [Carnegie Mellon's] entry in the DARPA Grand Challenge, recently indicated, the hardware capability is mostly there; now the issue is getting the software right."

15   Back in the early days of the personal computer, we realized that we needed an ingredient that would allow all of the pioneering work to achieve critical mass, to coalesce into a real industry capable of producing truly useful products on a commercial scale. What was needed, it turned out, was Microsoft BASIC. When we created this programming language in the 1970s, we provided the common foundation that enabled programs developed for one set of hardware to run on another. BASIC also made computer programming much easier, which brought more and more people into the industry. Although a great many individuals made essential contributions to the development of the personal computer, Microsoft BASIC was one of the key catalysts for the software and hardware innovations that made the PC revolution possible.

16   After reading Tandy's report, it seemed clear to me that before the robotics industry could make the same kind of quantum leap that the PC industry made 30 years ago, it, too, needed to find that missing ingredient. So I asked him to assemble a small team that would work with people in the robotics field to create a set of programming tools that would provide the essential plumbing so that anybody interested in robots with even the most basic understanding of computer programming could easily write robotic applications that would work with different kinds of hardware. The goal was to see if it was possible to provide the same kind of common, low-level foundation for integrating hardware and software into robot designs that Microsoft BASIC provided for computer programmers.

17   Tandy's robotics group has been able to draw on a number of advanced technologies developed by a team working under the direction of Craig Mundie, Microsoft's chief research and strategy officer. One such technology will help solve one of the most difficult problems facing robot designers: how to simultaneously handle all the data coming in from multiple sensors and send the appropriate commands to the robot's motors, a challenge known as concurrency. A conventional approach is to write a traditional, single-threaded program—a long loop that first reads all the data from the sensors, then processes this input and finally delivers output that determines the robot's behavior, before starting the loop all over again. The shortcomings are obvious: if your robot has fresh sensor data indicating that the machine is at the edge of a precipice, but the program is still at the bottom of the loop calculating trajectory and telling the wheels to turn faster based on previous sensor input, there is a good chance the robot will fall down the stairs before it can process the new information.

18   Concurrency is a challenge that extends beyond robotics. Today as more and more applications are written for distributed networks of computers, programmers have struggled to figure out how to efficiently orchestrate code running on many different

servers at the same time. And as computers with a single processor are replaced by machines with multiple processors and "multicore" processors—integrated circuits with two or more processors joined together for enhanced performance—software designers will need a new way to program desktop applications and operating systems. To fully exploit the power of processors working in parallel, the new software must deal with the problem of concurrency.

19   One approach to handling concurrency is to write multi-threaded programs that allow data to travel along many paths. But as any developer who has written multi-threaded code can tell you, this is one of the hardest tasks in programming. The answer that Craig's team has devised to the concurrency problem is something called the concurrency and coordination runtime (CCR). The CCR is a library of functions—sequences of software code that perform specific tasks—that makes it easy to write multithreaded applications that can coordinate a number of simultaneous activities. Designed to help programmers take advantage of the power of multicore and multiprocessor systems, the CCR turns out to be ideal for robotics as well. By drawing on this library to write their programs, robot designers can dramatically reduce the chances that one of their creations will run into a wall because its software is too busy sending output to its wheels to read input from its sensors.

20   In addition to tackling the problem of concurrency, the work that Craig's team has done will also simplify the writing of distributed robotic applications through a technology called decentralized software services (DSS). DSS enables developers to create applications in which the services—the parts of the program that read a sensor, say, or control a motor—operate as separate processes that can be orchestrated in much the same way that text, images and information from several servers are aggregated on a Web page. Because DSS allows software components to run in isolation from one another, if an individual component of a robot fails, it can be shut down and restarted—or even replaced—without having to reboot the machine. Combined with broadband wireless technology, this architecture makes it easy to monitor and adjust a robot from a remote location using a Web browser.

21   What is more, a DSS application controlling a robotic device does not have to reside entirely on the robot itself but can be distributed across more than one computer. As a result, the robot can be a relatively inexpensive device that delegates complex processing tasks to the high-performance hardware found on today's home PCs. I believe this advance will pave the way for an entirely new class of robots that are essentially mobile, wireless peripheral devices that tap into the power of desktop PCs to handle processing-intensive tasks such as visual recognition and navigation. And because these devices can be networked together, we can expect to see the emergence of groups of robots that can work in concert to achieve goals such as mapping the seafloor or planting crops.

22   These technologies are a key part of Microsoft Robotics Studio, a new software development kit built by Tandy's team. Microsoft Robotics Studio also includes tools that make it easier to create robotic applications using a wide range of programming languages. One example is a simulation tool that lets robot builders test their applications in a three-dimensional virtual environment before trying them out in the real world. Our goal for this release is to create an affordable, open platform that allows robot developers to readily integrate hardware and software into their designs.

Robots like this vacuum by IRobot are already in use in households around the world.

Should We Call Them Robots?

23 How soon will robots become part of our day-to-day lives? According to the International Federation of Robotics, about two million personal robots were in use around the world in 2004, and another seven million will be installed by 2008. In South Korea the Ministry of Information and Communication hopes to put a robot in every home there by 2013. The Japanese Robot Association predicts that by 2025, the personal robot industry will be worth more than $50 billion a year worldwide, compared with about $5 billion today.

24 As with the PC industry in the 1970s, it is impossible to predict exactly what applications will drive this new industry. It seems quite likely, however, that robots will play an important role in providing physical assistance and even companionship for the elderly. Robotic devices will probably help people with disabilities get around and extend the strength and endurance of soldiers, construction workers and medical professionals. Robots will maintain dangerous industrial machines, handle hazardous materials and monitor remote oil pipelines. They will enable health care workers to diagnose and treat patients who may be thousands of miles away, and they will be a central feature of security systems and search-and-rescue operations.

25 Although a few of the robots of tomorrow may resemble the anthropomorphic devices seen in *Star Wars*, most will look nothing like the humanoid C-3PO. In fact, as mobile peripheral devices become more and more common, it may be increasingly difficult to say exactly what a robot is. Because the new machines will be so specialized and ubiquitous—and look so little like the two-legged automatons of science fiction—we probably will not even call them robots. But as these devices become affordable to consumers, they could have just as profound an impact on the way we work, communicate, learn and entertain ourselves as the PC has had over the past 30 years.

PAUL **MARKS**

Armchair Warlords and Robot Hordes

Paul Marks is a technology correspondent for *New Scientist*, an international weekly science magazine and Web site that covers issues in science and technology. In 2007, Marks won the BT IT Security Journalist of the Year Award. His portfolio included the article below, published in *New Scientist* on October 28, 2006, which examines the development of lethal robot soldiers and the risks attached to their use.

It sounds like every general's dream: technology that allows a nation to fight a war with little or no loss of life on its side. It is also a peace-seeking citizen's nightmare. Without the politically embarrassing threat of soldiers returning home in flag-wrapped coffins, governments would find it far easier to commit to military action. The consequences for countries on the receiving end—and for world peace—would be immense.

2   This is not a fantasy scenario. Over the coming years, the world's most powerful military machine, the U.S. Department of Defense, aims to replace a large proportion of its armed vehicles and weaponry with robotized technologies. By 2010, a third of its "deep-strike" aircraft will be unmanned aerial vehicles (UAVs), according to a Congressional Research Service report issued in July (http://tinyurl.com/yafoht). In a further five years a similar proportion of the U.S. army's ground combat vehicles will be remote-controlled robots varying in size from supermarket carts to trucks. The U.S. navy, too, will have fleets of uncrewed boats and submarines.

3   The U.S. military is already using robots in various roles. In November 2002, for example, an armed UAV destroyed a car in Yemen carrying the suspected chief of Al-Qaida in that country, killing him and five others. In Iraq and Afghanistan, robots are proving highly successful in neutralizing roadside bombs and other small-scale explosives.

4   This is only the start. One of the next steps is to give robotic ground vehicles the attack power of UAVs, arming them with weapons such as machine guns, grenade launchers and anti-tank rockets (*New Scientist,* 21 September, p. 28). They could then be sent into places that were particularly dangerous for troops, such as booby-trapped or ambush-vulnerable buildings.

5   After that the plan is to take things to a whole new level, with unmanned planes and ground robots able to communicate with each other and act in concert. A reconnaissance UAV could signal swarms of robots to attack an enemy position, for example, or an unmanned ground vehicle might call in an air strike from UAVs.

6   All uncrewed vehicles are remote-controlled at present, but the Pentagon's Office of Naval Research is planning to develop technology that it hopes will enable a robot to determine whether a person it comes across is a threat, using measures such as the remote sensing of their heartbeat—though whether these kinds of methods can be made reliable is highly questionable.

7   "Teleoperation [remote control] is the norm, but semi-autonomous enhancements are being added all the time," says Bob Quinn of Foster-Miller, a technology firm in Waltham, Massachusetts, owned by the UK defense research company Qinetiq.

Foster-Miller, like its main rival iRobot, was set up by roboticists from the Massachusetts Institute of Technology. The company's armed robot, dubbed Swords, has just received U.S. army safety certification. Nevertheless, doubts remain over how reliable armed robotic devices will be, especially if they end up operating autonomously. What happens when the software fails?

8   Such fears have persuaded the military to go slow on the use of autonomous weaponry. An early version of one of Foster-Miller's robots was designed to de-mine beaches autonomously but was later converted to remote control at the navy's request. It is feasible that as safety concerns are addressed, autonomous devices will become increasingly popular, though experts in robotics point out that might be a long time away. An armed robot will not only need to be fail-safe, it must also be able to identify friend and foe just as well as a soldier.

9   Despite these fears, the rise of armed robots seems inevitable. Quinn tells the story of a group of U.S. marines impressed by a Swords robot armed with a machine gun being tested at a U.S. army base. "If they could have, they would have put that robot in their trunk, because they were off to Ramadi, Iraq, and they wanted that robot to [help them] stay alive. When you see that passion, I have no philosophical problems about this technology whatsoever," he says.

10   Outside the military, however, plenty of people beg to differ. Ultimately, these developments will allow the U.S., as well as several NATO countries that are also keen on the technology, to fight wars without suffering anywhere near as many casualties. The idea that warfare can be "clinical" has been found wanting time and again in recent years—think of the current conflicts in Iraq and Afghanistan, and Israel's recent bombardment of Lebanon—but there's no question that reliable autonomous robots deployed on a large scale could make fighting wars a great deal less risky for those that own them.

11   And therein lies the great danger. What are the chances of a less violent world when the powerful nations can make their mark on the less powerful at the flick of a switch? As Quinn puts it: "We are not trying to create a level battlefield here, we are trying to do the opposite: create a very un-level battlefield."

SALLY **SATEL**

Organs for Sale

Sally Satel is a practicing psychiatrist, lecturer at the Yale University School of Medicine, and resident scholar at the American Enterprise Institute for Public Policy Research, a nonpartisan, nonprofit institution committed to research and education on issues of government, politics, economics, and social welfare. Her work focuses on mental health policy and political trends in medicine. She is the author of several books, including *When Altruism Isn't Enough: The Case for Compensating Kidney Donors*. Her argument below appeared in the *Journal of the American Enterprise Institute* on October 14, 2006.

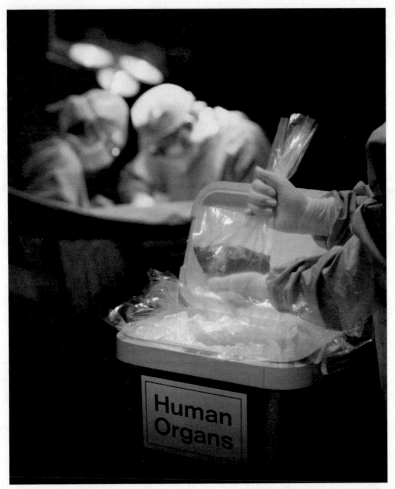

How should we resolve the ever-increasing demand for organs to aid those in need of transplants?

A year ago, I was searching the Internet for something rare and valuable: a human kidney. In August 2004, I learned I had end-stage renal disease and would need a transplant. At the time, my prospects for a donation from family or friends looked bleak, and I would soon have to begin dialysis. I would be hooked up to a machine three days a week for four hours at a time. This would continue for at least five years—the time it would take for a kidney from a deceased donor to become available. Even with dialysis, the kidneys of many sick people deteriorate so quickly that time runs out. An average of 11 Americans die each day waiting for a renal transplant.

2   Waiting for a kidney from a deceased donor is such a risky business that some people try publicly to convince strangers to give them live organs. Some put up billboards ("I NEED A KIDNEY, CAN YOU HELP? Call . . . "), start websites (GordyNeedsAKidney .org, whose opening page carries the plaintive headline, "Please Help Our Dad"), or go

overseas to become "transplant tourists" on the Chinese black market with the frightful knowledge that the organ they get will almost surely come from an executed political prisoner. The desperation, as I found myself, is perfectly understandable. I have no siblings. Several friends said they would look into it—donors don't need to be genetically related—but they turned out to have disqualifying medical problems or spouses who objected, or they grew scared.

3   Last fall, I turned to a website called MatchingDonors.com—which "matches" mostly prospective kidney donors with recipients—and quickly found a prospective donor. But six weeks later, he changed his mind. Then my wonderful friend Virginia Postrel came along. We are both healthy after a transplant operation on March 4 at the Washington Hospital Center. If Virginia had not donated her kidney, I could have languished on dialysis for years. Indeed, when I joined the national queue in January 2005, there were about 60,000 other people ahead of me, according to the nonprofit United Network for Organ Sharing (UNOS), which maintains the list under a monopoly contract with the federal government.

4   Today, there are 67,600 people waiting for a posthumous kidney. In big cities, where the ratio of needy patients to available organs is highest, the wait—spent on dialysis, a procedure that circulates your blood through a machine that purifies it and returns it to your body—is up to eight years. Last year, only 16,470 people received kidneys; roughly half of the donors were deceased, and half were living. Meanwhile, 4,100 died waiting. By 2010, the wait will be at least ten years, exceeding the average length of time that adults on dialysis survive.

5   Despite decades of public education about the virtues of donating organs at death, the level of such gifts has remained disappointingly steady. Only about one-third of Americans have designated themselves as donors on their driver's licenses or on state-run donor registries. For the rest, the decision to donate organs will fall to family members, who about half the time deny the requests of hospitals. More important, however, is that very few of the Americans who die, perhaps 13,000 a year (or less than 1 percent of all deaths), possess organs healthy enough for transplanting—so even if every family consented, the need for thousands of kidneys would go unmet.

6   The chasm between the number of available kidneys and the number of people needing one will widen each year. This is due to our misplaced faith in the power of altruism. The "transplant community," as it is called—organizations that encourage funding and gifts of organs, and many surgeons and nephrologists—expects people, both living donors and loved ones of the deceased, to give a body part and to receive nothing in return. In fact, it is illegal in the United States to receive money or anything of value ("valuable consideration") in exchange for an organ, a principle set down by Congress in 1984 in the National Organ Transplantation Act.

7   Don't get me wrong. Altruism is a beautiful thing—it's the reason I have a new kidney—but altruism alone cannot resolve the organ shortage. For that reason, more and more physicians, ethicists, economists, and legal scholars are urging the legalization of payments for organs in order to generate more kidneys for transplantation. One doesn't need to be Milton Friedman to know that a price of zero for anything virtually guarantees its shortage.

8   "Is it wrong for an individual . . . who wishes to utilize part of his body for the benefit of another [to] be provided with financial compensation that could obliterate a

life of destitution for the individual and his family?" asked Dr. Richard Fine, president of the American Society of Transplantation, in his address to the World Transplant Congress this year. Supporters of experimenting with a market for organs encounter an array of objections, theoretical and practical. One popular argument, first advanced by Richard M. Titmuss, professor of social administration at the London School of Economics, is that altruism is the sole legitimate impulse behind organ donation. In 1971, Titmuss, a dedicated socialist and member of the Fabian Society, published *The Gift Relationship: From Human Blood to Social Policy*, which rapidly became a U.S. bestseller. He argued that altruistic acts are among the most sensitive indicators of the quality of human relationships and values in a society. Capitalism, on the other hand, is morally bankrupt.

9   This ethic is very much alive among the bureaucrats that run the United Network for Organ Sharing, which manages the transplant list. "Organ transplantation is built upon altruism and public trust. If anything shakes that trust, then everyone loses," says the UNOS website. Yet the trust is already badly rattled. "The current system has degenerated into an equal opportunity to die on the waiting list," observes nephrologist Benjamin Hippen, who advocated compensating donors (or perhaps they should be called "vendors") before the President's Council on Bioethics this summer.

10   Another theoretical objection to compensating donors is the notion that it will "commodify" the body and thus dehumanize the rest of us, let alone the person who gives his kidney in exchange for "valuable consideration." Yet with proper respect for donors and informed consent, it strikes me that careful engagement in financial arrangements is far less distasteful than allowing people to suffer and die. These are not abstract people, mind you, like the ones who may well be helped by stem cell discoveries years down the road, but live humans like the 49-year-old former secretary from the Pentagon I met last summer. For four years now, every Monday, Wednesday, and Friday, she has been sitting in Chair No. 7 in the dialysis center a few blocks from our offices.

11   Others go so far as to reject the very premise that saving lives is a paramount goal of medicine. "If we turn organ procurement into a crusade, we make of death simply a problem to be solved rather than an event to be endured as best we can, with whatever resources of mind and spirit are available to us,"[1] says Gilbert Meilaender, professor of theological ethics at Valparaiso University and a member of the President's Council on Bioethics. Now, it is one thing to question whether we should prolong the life of a vegetative patient, but quite another to abandon treatments for renal failure under circumstances in which a well-established remedy (transplantation) already exists—a remedy whose economic cost to society is lower than the cost of the less effective alternative, dialysis.

12   This is a good time to point out that the live donor—or vendor—of a kidney is exposed to only minor risks, the most significant being those associated with anesthesia and surgery itself—0.03% mortality—comparable to any other operation. Because the surgery is done using a laparoscopic approach, the visible scar is only 2 to 3 inches long. My donor, Virginia, was out of the hospital in three days and back to writing her magazine column a week later.

13   Long-term risks are also low. Typical is a 1997 study from Norway that followed 1,332 kidney donors for an average of 32 years. It found no difference in mortality rates

between people who give kidneys and the general population. A 25-year follow-up of 70 donors conducted by the Cleveland Clinic found that the renal function is "well preserved" and that the overall incidence of hypertension was comparable to that of nondonors. The truth is that a normal person can get along perfectly well with one kidney. The risk a donor runs is that his single functioning kidney will become diseased or injured, and he'll need a transplant himself—a highly unlikely event.

14 Perhaps the most vocal critic of compensating donors is the National Kidney Foundation. It is offended by the idea that a donor might benefit in ways other than the psychic reward of pure giving. States NKF chairman Charles Fruit, "Families decide to donate the organs of a loved one for altruistic reasons. Payment is an affront to those who have already donated."[2] Virginia, a take-no-prisoners journalist, responded pointedly to Fruit on her website, Dynamist, "The argument that paying organ donors is 'an affront' to unpaid donors is disgusting. Are unpaid donors giving organs to save lives or just to make themselves feel morally superior? Even in the latter case, they shouldn't care if *other* people get paid."

15 In the end, moral objections such as these put us at a standoff. I doubt I could change the mind of Professor Meilaender, who sincerely believes that organ donation violates what it means to be human. And there's nothing he can say to dissuade me from believing that free, informed, and willing individuals should be able to participate in a regulated exchange involving valuable consideration. Thus, the meaningful question becomes how both sides can honor their moral commitments.

16 The best answer is by creating a market arrangement to exist in parallel with altruistic giving. Within such a framework, any medical center or physician who objects to the practice of compensating donors can simply opt out of performing transplants that use such organs. Recipients on the list are free to turn down a paid-for organ and wait for one given altruistically. Choice for all—donors, recipients, and physicians—is enhanced. And it is choice in the greater service of diminishing sickness and death. Paradoxically, the current system based on altruism-or-else undermines the individual autonomy that is at the heart of the most widely held values in bioethics.

17 Not all objections to donor compensation, however, are abstract. A common concern is the potential for exploiting donors—especially low-income donors, who, as the critics reasonably claim, will be the most likely to find incentives attractive. Without question, protecting donors is enormously important. That is why any plan for compensation should be regulated. Potential donors must receive education about what it means to donate a kidney and the risks they run. They must undergo careful medical and psychological screening and receive quality follow-up care.

18 Critics often point to the horror stories from transplant black markets overseas and hold them up as cautionary tales. But the catastrophists have it exactly backward. It is when payment is not an above-board part of the medical system that black markets lead to minimal education of prospective donors, poor post-operative and follow-up care, and failure to honor agreements for payment.

19 Finally, some critics argue we have no evidence that an incentive system would work. True. So we need experimentation. Frankly, I don't know what the perfect kidney market would look like, but let's assume that Congress makes a bold and common-sense move and amends current law to permit the exchange of money or something of value for a kidney. Here are several alternative market systems:

1. A FORWARD MARKET FOR CADAVER ORGANS:

20 Economist Lloyd Cohen proposed one of the first market-based models to increase the number of cadaver organs. Potential donors would either (1) be paid a small amount today by the government or insurance companies to join the current donor registry, or (2) register today in return for the possibility of a much larger payment to their estates should the organs be used at death.

21 The advantage of such a forward-looking approach is that the decision-making burden is taken off family members at a painful time—when they are sitting in the emergency room learning that someone they love is now brain-dead. And, of course, there is no worry of exploiting the donor. A forward market could also help satisfy the 23,000 people waiting for livers, hearts, and lungs.

22 But deceased donors cannot meet the need for kidneys. In addition, kidneys from live donors are healthier than those obtained after death and survive, typically, for 10 to 20 years (or one-third longer). Thus, to mitigate the shortage of kidneys, we must consider offering incentives to people amenable to relinquishing one while they are alive.

2. THE CENTRALIZED SINGLE COMPENSATOR:

23 In this approach, the federal government or a designated agency acts as the only authority with the power to buy and allocate organs for transplants. As is currently the case with cadaver organs, kidneys obtained through compensated donors would be matched with the next best candidate waiting on the national list.

24 Under this scheme, Medicare would underwrite the incentives in light of the fact that it already pays for dialysis treatment under the 1972 End Stage Renal Disease (ESRD) amendment to the Social Security Act. This entitlement provides care for Americans with terminal renal failure regardless of age if they have met required work credits for Social Security. Last year, the ESRD program spent about $16 billion on dialysis, or about $66,000 per patient annually. Since a 35-year-old spends about nine years on dialysis, the total cost is around $600,000; for a 64-year-old, about four years at $300,000. Compare these expenses with the cost of a transplant operation—approximately $75,000 in all for the one-time cost of the surgeries and hospital stays of the donor and recipient, plus the first year of follow-up medical care (including medicine).

25 In most cases, these savings would easily pay for a lifetime supply of the expensive immunosuppressant drugs to prevent rejection of the new kidney. The drugs cost $15,000 to $20,000 a year, and every recipient must take them every day for life. Medicare pays for transplant surgery but stops reimbursing for the drugs, at 80 percent of full price, three years post-transplant if the patient goes back to work.

26 What kinds of compensation should be offered? A reasonable case could be made for an outright payment—after all, it is hard to argue that an individual is competent enough to sell an organ yet unfit to manage the money he receives in exchange for it—but I am partial to a compromise approach in order to defuse those who say that people will sell their organs for quick cash or use it to buy something frivolous. For example, the donor could choose from a menu of options, including a deposit to a 401(k) retirement plan, tax credits, tuition vouchers for the donor's children, long-term nursing care, family health coverage, life and nonfatal injury insurance, a charitable contribution in the donor's name, or cash payments stretched over time.

27   Donor protection is the linchpin of any compensation model. Standard guidelines for physical and psychological screening, donor education, and informed consent could be formulated by a medical organization, such as the American Society of Transplant Surgeons, or another entity designated by the federal Department of Health and Human Services. A "waiting period" of three to six months could be built in to ensure the prospective donor has ample time to think it through. Monitoring donor health post-transplant is important as well. One idea is to provide lifetime health insurance, through Medicare or a private insurer for the donor. He would receive annual physicals, routine medical screening, and long-term follow-up in addition to standard health coverage. A federally sponsored registry of donors could help us study long-term outcomes for donors and vendors and take steps to remedy physical or psychological difficulties that arise.

3. MULTIPLE COMPENSATORS:

28   In this scheme, donors, compensators (that is, the entities that pay for the transplants), and medical centers (that perform them) would be coordinated with one another through an intermediary broker. Medicare would be one of several possible compensators, along with private insurers, charitable foundations, or a fund established perhaps through a surcharge added to the cost paid by insurers and foundations.

4. PRIVATE CONTRACTS:

29   The easiest way to start a market for organs is simply to change the law to allow someone who needs an organ and someone who wants to sell one to make their own arrangements through contract—as infertile couples currently do with surrogate mothers. But such a system would inevitably attract criticism because it appears to favor well-off sick people over poor.

30   While private contracts may seem unfair because only those with means will be able to purchase directly, poor people who need kidneys would be no worse off—and, very likely, considerably better off—than under the current system. First, a stranger interested in selling a kidney is unlikely to give it away for free to the next person on the list (only 88 donors last year made such anonymous gifts); thus, few poor people would be deprived of kidneys they would otherwise have gotten voluntarily. Second, anyone who gets a kidney by contract is removed from the waiting list, and everyone behind him benefits by moving up. Third, private charities could offer to help subsidize the cost for a needy patient or pay outright.

31   These broad proposals, and variants on them, need considerable elaboration. Many questions remain: How would prices be determined? Would each available kidney be allotted to the next well-matched person on the list? Or should living organs be preferentially allocated to the healthiest people on the list—that is, those who will get the most "life" out of the organ? Could noncitizens be paid donors? Also, could people have a say in who would receive their kidneys? As it currently stands, most living donors give altruistically because they are trying to help a friend or relative, not a stranger. But it is surely possible that the decision of an ambivalent friend could tip in the direction of giving with the promise of compensation. And since each patient on dialysis is functionally "attached" to a Medicare entitlement, perhaps the recipient could direct a portion of "his" Medicare allotment to his friend as payment.

32   There is no denying the political and practical challenges that come with introducing payment into a 20-year-old scheme built on the premise that generosity is the only
legitimate motive for giving. Yet as death and suffering mount, constructing a market-
based incentive program to increase the supply of transplantable organs has become a
moral imperative. Its architects must give serious consideration to principled reservations
and to concerns about donor safety, but repugnance and caution are not in themselves
arguments against innovation. They are only reasons for vigilance and care.

NOTES

1. Gilbert Meilaender, "Gifts of the Body," *New Atlantis*, Number 13 (Summer
    2006): 25–35.
2. Letters in response to Richard Epstein, "Kidney Beancounters," *Wall Street Jour-
    nal*, May 15, 2006 (May 26, 2006).

CARL **ZIMMER**

Bringing Them Back to Life

Carl Zimmer (born 1966) is an award-winning science writer with a special interest in mat-
ters related to evolution. His articles and blogs have appeared in *Discover*, the *New York
Times*, and many other publications, and he is frequently interviewed on National Public
Radio. The following essay appeared in *National Geographic* in April 2013.

O   n July 30, 2003, a team of Spanish and French scientists reversed time. They
       brought an animal back from extinction, if only to watch it become extinct again.
       The animal they revived was a kind of wild goat known as a *bucardo,* or Pyr-
enean ibex. The bucardo *(Capra pyrenaica pyrenaica)* was a large, handsome creature,
reaching up to 220 pounds and sporting long, gently curved horns. For thousands of
years it lived high in the Pyrenees, the mountain range that divides France from Spain,
where it clambered along cliffs, nibbling on leaves and stems and enduring harsh winters.

2   Then came the guns. Hunters drove down the bucardo population over several
centuries. In 1989 Spanish scientists did a survey and concluded that there were only
a dozen or so individuals left. Ten years later a single bucardo remained: a female nick-
named Celia. A team from the Ordesa and Monte Perdido National Park, led by wildlife
veterinarian Alberto Fernández-Arias, caught the animal in a trap, clipped a radio collar
around her neck, and released her back into the wild. Nine months later the radio collar let out a long, steady beep: the signal that Celia had died. They found her crushed
beneath a fallen tree. With her death, the bucardo became officially extinct.

3   But Celia's cells lived on, preserved in labs in Zaragoza and Madrid. Over the
next few years a team of reproductive physiologists led by José Folch injected nuclei
from those cells into goat eggs emptied of their own DNA, then implanted the eggs
in surrogate mothers. After 57 implantations, only seven animals had become pregnant. And of those seven pregnancies, six ended in miscarriages. But one mother—a

hybrid between a Spanish ibex and a goat—carried a clone of Celia to term. Folch and his colleagues performed a cesarean section and delivered the 4.5-pound clone. As Fernández-Arias held the newborn bucardo in his arms, he could see that she was struggling to take in air, her tongue jutting grotesquely out of her mouth. Despite the efforts to help her breathe, after a mere ten minutes Celia's clone died. A necropsy later revealed that one of her lungs had grown a gigantic extra lobe as solid as a piece of liver. There was nothing anyone could have done.

4   The dodo and the great auk, the thylacine and the Chinese river dolphin, the passenger pigeon and the imperial woodpecker—the bucardo is only one in the long list of animals humans have driven extinct, sometimes deliberately. And with many more species now endangered, the bucardo will have much more company in the years to come. Fernández-Arias belongs to a small but passionate group of researchers who believe that cloning can help reverse that trend.

5   The notion of bringing vanished species back to life—some call it de-extinction—has hovered at the boundary between reality and science fiction for more than two decades, ever since novelist Michael Crichton unleashed the dinosaurs of Jurassic Park on the world. For most of that time the science of de-extinction has lagged far behind the fantasy. Celia's clone is the closest that anyone has gotten to true de-extinction. Since witnessing those fleeting minutes of the clone's life, Fernández-Arias, now the head of the government of Aragon's Hunting, Fishing and Wetlands department, has been waiting for the moment when science would finally catch up, and humans might gain the ability to bring back an animal they had driven extinct.

6   "We are at that moment," he told me.

7   I met Fernández-Arias last autumn at a closed-session scientific meeting at the National Geographic Society's headquarters in Washington, D.C. For the first time in history a group of geneticists, wildlife biologists, conservationists, and ethicists had gathered to discuss the possibility of de-extinction. Could it be done? Should it be done? One by one, they stood up to present remarkable advances in manipulating stem cells, in recovering ancient DNA, in reconstructing lost genomes. As the meeting unfolded, the scientists became increasingly excited. A consensus was emerging: De-extinction is now within reach.

8   "It's gone very much further, very much more rapidly than anyone ever would've imagined," says Ross MacPhee, a curator of mammalogy at the American Museum of Natural History in New York. "What we really need to think about is why we would want to do this in the first place, to actually bring back a species."

9   In Jurassic Park dinosaurs are resurrected for their entertainment value. The disastrous consequences that follow have cast a shadow over the notion of de-extinction, at least in the popular imagination. But people tend to forget that Jurassic Park was pure fantasy. In reality the only species we can hope to revive now are those that died within the past few tens of thousands of years and left behind remains that harbor intact cells or, at the very least, enough ancient DNA to reconstruct the creature's genome. Because of the natural rates of decay, we can never hope to retrieve the full genome of Tyrannosaurus rex, which vanished about 65 million years ago. The species theoretically capable of being revived all disappeared while humanity was rapidly climbing toward world domination. And especially in recent years we humans were the ones who wiped them out, by hunting them, destroying their habitats, or spreading diseases. This suggests another reason for bringing them back.

Though the revival of dinosaur species in Michael Crichton's *Jurassic Park* is fantasy, scientists face the very real possibility of bringing back species that, like *Capra pyrenaica,* became extinct within the last few tens of thousands of years. Do the pros of de-extinction outweigh the cons?

10   "If we're talking about species we drove extinct, then I think we have an obligation to try to do this," says Michael Archer, a paleontologist at the University of New South Wales who has championed de-extinction for years. Some people protest that reviving a species that no longer exists amounts to playing God. Archer scoffs at the notion. "I think we played God when we exterminated these animals."

11   Other scientists who favor de-extinction argue that there will be concrete benefits. Biological diversity is a storehouse of natural invention. Most pharmaceutical drugs, for example, were not invented from scratch—they were derived from natural compounds found in wild plant species, which are also vulnerable to extinction. Some extinct animals also performed vital services in their ecosystems, which might benefit from their return. Siberia, for example, was home 12,000 years ago to mammoths and other big grazing mammals. Back then, the landscape was not moss-dominated tundra but grassy steppes. Sergey Zimov, a Russian ecologist and director of the Northeast Science Station in Cherskiy in the Republic of Sakha, has long argued that this was no coincidence: The mammoths and numerous herbivores maintained the grassland

by breaking up the soil and fertilizing it with their manure. Once they were gone, moss took over and transformed the grassland into less productive tundra.

12   In recent years Zimov has tried to turn back time on the tundra by bringing horses, muskoxen, and other big mammals to a region of Siberia he calls Pleistocene Park. And he would be happy to have woolly mammoths roam free there. "But only my grandchildren will see them," he says. "A mouse breeds very fast. Mammoths breed very slow. Be prepared to wait."

13   When Fernández-Arias first tried to bring back the bucardo ten years ago, the tools at his disposal were, in hindsight, woefully crude. It had been only seven years since the birth of Dolly the sheep, the first cloned mammal. In those early days scientists would clone an animal by taking one of its cells and inserting its DNA into an egg that had been emptied of its own genetic material. An electric shock was enough to get the egg to start dividing, after which the scientists would place the developing embryo in a surrogate mother. The vast majority of those pregnancies failed, and the few animals that were born were often beset with health problems.

14   Over the past decade scientists have improved their success with cloning animals, shifting the technology from high-risk science to workaday business. Researchers have also developed the ability to induce adult animal cells to return to an embryo-like state. These can be coaxed to develop into any type of cell—including eggs or sperm. The eggs can then be further manipulated to develop into full-fledged embryos.

15   Such technical sleights of hand make it far easier to conjure a vanished species back to life. Scientists and explorers have been talking for decades about bringing back the mammoth. Their first—and so far only—achievement was to find well-preserved mammoths in the Siberian tundra. Now, armed with the new cloning technologies, researchers at the Sooam Biotech Research Foundation in Seoul have teamed up with mammoth experts from North-Eastern Federal University in the Siberian city of Yakutsk. Last summer they traveled up the Yana River, drilling tunnels into the frozen cliffs along the river with giant hoses. In one of those tunnels they found chunks of mammoth tissue, including bone marrow, hair, skin, and fat. The tissue is now in Seoul, where the Sooam scientists are examining it.

16   "If we dream about it, the ideal case would be finding a viable cell, a cell that's alive," says Sooam's Insung Hwang, who organized the Yana River expedition. If the Sooam researchers do find such a cell, they could coax it to produce millions of cells. These could be reprogrammed to grow into embryos, which could then be implanted in surrogate elephants, the mammoth's closest living relatives.

17   Most scientists doubt that any living cell could have survived freezing on the open tundra. But Hwang and his colleagues have a Plan B: capture an intact nucleus of a mammoth cell, which is far more likely to have been preserved than the cell itself. Cloning a mammoth from nothing but an intact nucleus, however, will be a lot trickier. The Sooam researchers will need to transfer the nucleus into an elephant egg that has had its own nucleus removed. This will require harvesting eggs from an elephant—a feat no one has yet accomplished. If the DNA inside the nucleus is well preserved enough to take control of the egg, it just might start dividing into a mammoth embryo. If the scientists can get past that hurdle, they still have the formidable task of transplanting the embryo into an elephant's womb. Then, as Zimov cautions, they will need patience. If all goes well, it will still be almost two years before they can see if the elephant will give birth to a healthy mammoth.

18   "The thing that I always say is, if you don't try, how would you know that it's impossible?" says Hwang.

19   In 1813, while traveling along the Ohio River from Hardensburgh to Louisville, John James Audubon witnessed one of the most miraculous natural phenomena of his time: a flock of passenger pigeons *(Ectopistes migratorius)* blanketing the sky. "The air was literally filled with Pigeons," he later wrote. "The light of noon-day was obscured as by an eclipse, the dung fell in spots, not unlike melting flakes of snow; and the continued buzz of wings had a tendency to lull my senses to repose."

20   When Audubon reached Louisville before sunset, the pigeons were still passing overhead—and continued to do so for the next three days. "The people were all in arms," wrote Audubon. "The banks of the Ohio were crowded with men and boys, incessantly shooting at the pilgrims… . Multitudes were thus destroyed."

21   In 1813 it would have been hard to imagine a species less likely to become extinct. Yet by the end of the century the red-breasted passenger pigeon was in catastrophic decline, the forests it depended upon shrinking, and its numbers dwindling from relentless hunting. In 1900 the last confirmed wild bird was shot by a boy with a BB gun. Fourteen years later, just a century and a year after Audubon marveled at their abundance, the one remaining captive passenger pigeon, a female named Martha, died at the Cincinnati Zoo.

22   The writer and environmentalist Stewart Brand, best known for founding the *Whole Earth Catalog* in the late 1960s, grew up in Illinois hiking in forests that just a few decades before had been aroar with the sound of the passenger pigeons' wings. "Its habitat was my habitat," he says. Two years ago Brand and his wife, Ryan Phelan, founder of the genetic-testing company DNA Direct, began to wonder if it might be possible to bring the species back to life. One night over dinner with Harvard biologist George Church, a master at manipulating DNA, they discovered that he was thinking along the same lines.

23   Church knew that standard cloning methods wouldn't work, since bird embryos develop inside shells and no museum specimen of the passenger pigeon (including Martha herself, now in the Smithsonian) would likely contain a fully intact, functional genome. But he could envision a different way of re-creating the bird. Preserved specimens contain fragments of DNA. By piecing together the fragments, scientists can now read the roughly one billion letters in the passenger pigeon genome. Church can't yet synthesize an entire animal genome from scratch, but he has invented technology that allows him to make sizable chunks of DNA of any sequence he wants. He could theoretically manufacture genes for passenger pigeon traits—a gene for its long tail, for example—and splice them into the genome of a stem cell from a common rock pigeon.

24   Rock pigeon stem cells containing this doctored genome could be transformed into germ cells, the precursors to eggs and sperm. These could then be injected into rock pigeon eggs, where they would migrate to the developing embryos' sex organs. Squabs hatched from these eggs would look like normal rock pigeons—but they would be carrying eggs and sperm loaded with doctored DNA. When the squabs reached maturity and mated, their eggs would hatch squabs carrying unique passenger pigeon traits. These birds could then be further interbred, the scientists selecting for birds that were more and more like the vanished species.

25   Church's genome-retooling method could theoretically work on any species with a close living relative and a genome capable of being reconstructed. So even if the Sooam team fails to find an intact mammoth nucleus, someone might still bring the species back. Scientists already have the technology for reconstructing most of the genes it takes to make a mammoth, which could be inserted into an elephant stem cell. And there is no shortage of raw material for further experiments emerging from the Siberian permafrost.

"With mammoths, it's really a dime a dozen up there," says Hendrik Poinar, an expert on mammoth DNA at McMaster University in Ontario. "It's just a matter of finances now."

26 Though the revival of a mammoth or a passenger pigeon is no longer mere fantasy, the reality is still years away. For another extinct species, the time frame may be much shorter. Indeed, there's at least a chance it may be back among the living before this story is published.

27 The animal in question is the obsession of a group of Australian scientists led by Michael Archer, who call their endeavor the Lazarus Project. Archer previously directed a highly publicized attempt to clone the thylacine, an iconic marsupial carnivore that went extinct in the 1930s. That effort managed to capture only some fragments of the thylacine's DNA. Wary of the feverish expectations that such high-profile experiments attract, Archer and his Lazarus Project collaborators kept quiet about their efforts until they had some preliminary results to offer.

28 That time has come. Early in January, Archer and his colleagues revealed that they were trying to revive two closely related species of Australian frog. Until their disappearance in the mid-1980s, the species shared a unique—and utterly astonishing—method of reproduction. The female frogs released a cloud of eggs, which the males fertilized, whereupon the females swallowed the eggs whole. A hormone in the eggs triggered the female to stop making stomach acid; her stomach, in effect, became a womb. A few weeks later the female opened her mouth and regurgitated her fully formed babies. This miraculous reproductive feat gave the frogs their common names: the northern *(Rheobatrachus vitellinus)* and southern *(Rheobatrachus silus)* gastric brooding frogs.

29 Unfortunately, not long after researchers began to study the species, they vanished. "The frogs were there one minute, and when scientists came back, they were gone," says Andrew French, a cloning expert at the University of Melbourne and a member of the Lazarus Project.

30 To bring the frogs back, the project scientists are using state-of-the-art cloning methods to introduce gastric brooding frog nuclei into eggs of living Australian marsh frogs and barred frogs that have had their own genetic material removed. It's slow going, because frog eggs begin to lose their potency after just a few hours and cannot be frozen and revived. The scientists need fresh eggs, which the frogs produce only once a year, during their short breeding season.

31 Nevertheless, they've made progress. "Suffice it to say, we actually have embryos now of this extinct animal," says Archer. "We're pretty far down this track." The Lazarus Project scientists are confident that they just need to get more high-quality eggs to keep moving forward. "At this point it's just a numbers game," says French.

32 The matchless oddity of the gastric brooding frogs' reproduction drives home what we lose when a species becomes extinct. But does that mean we should bring them back? Would the world be that much richer for having female frogs that grow little frogs in their stomachs? There are tangible benefits, French argues, such as the insights the frogs might be able to provide about reproduction—insights that might someday lead to treatments for pregnant women who have trouble carrying babies to term. But for many scientists, de-extinction is a distraction from the pressing work required to stave off mass extinctions.

33 "There is clearly a terrible urgency to saving threatened species and habitats," says John Wiens, an evolutionary biologist at Stony Brook University in New York. "As far as I can see, there is little urgency for bringing back extinct ones. Why invest mil-

lions of dollars in bringing a handful of species back from the dead, when there are millions still waiting to be discovered, described, and protected?"

34   De-extinction advocates counter that the cloning and genomic engineering technologies being developed for de-extinction could also help preserve endangered species, especially ones that don't breed easily in captivity. And though cutting-edge biotechnology can be expensive when it's first developed, it has a way of becoming very cheap very fast. "Maybe some people thought polio vaccines were a distraction from iron lungs," says George Church. "It's hard in advance to say what's distraction and what's salvation."

35   But what would we be willing to call salvation? Even if Church and his colleagues manage to retrofit every passenger pigeon–specific trait into a rock pigeon, would the resulting creature truly be a passenger pigeon or just an engineered curiosity? If Archer and French do produce a single gastric brooding frog—if they haven't already—does that mean they've revived the species? If that frog doesn't have a mate, then it becomes an amphibian version of Celia, and its species is as good as extinct. Would it be enough to keep a population of the frogs in a lab or perhaps in a zoo, where people could gawk at it? Or would it need to be introduced back into the wild to be truly de-extinct?

36   "The history of putting species back after they've gone extinct in the wild is fraught with difficulty," says conservation biologist Stuart Pimm of Duke University. A huge effort went into restoring the Arabian oryx to the wild, for example. But after the animals were returned to a refuge in central Oman in 1982, almost all were wiped out by poachers. "We had the animals, and we put them back, and the world wasn't ready," says Pimm. "Having the species solves only a tiny, tiny part of the problem."

37   Hunting is not the only threat that would face recovered species. For many, there's no place left to call home. The Chinese river dolphin became extinct due to pollution and other pressures from the human population on the Yangtze River. Things are just as bad there today. Around the world frogs are getting decimated by a human-spread pathogen called the chytrid fungus. If Australian biologists someday release gastric brooding frogs into their old mountain streams, they could promptly become extinct again.

38   "Without an environment to put re-created species back into, the whole exercise is futile and a gross waste of money," says Glenn Albrecht, director of the Institute for Social Sustainability at Murdoch University in Australia.

39   Even if de-extinction proved a complete logistical success, the questions would not end. Passenger pigeons might find the rebounding forests of the eastern United States a welcoming home. But wouldn't that be, in effect, the introduction of a genetically engineered organism into the environment? Could passenger pigeons become a reservoir for a virus that might wipe out another bird species? And how would the residents of Chicago, New York, or Washington, D.C., feel about a new pigeon species arriving in their cities, darkening their skies, and covering their streets with snowstorms of dung?

40   De-extinction advocates are pondering these questions, and most believe they need to be resolved before any major project moves forward. Hank Greely, a leading bioethicist at Stanford University, has taken a keen interest in investigating the ethical and legal implications of de-extinction. And yet for Greely, as for many others, the very fact that science has advanced to the point that such a spectacular feat is possible is a compelling reason to embrace de-extinction, not to shun it.

41   "What intrigues me is just that it's really cool," Greely says. "A saber-toothed cat? It would be neat to see one of those."

Is Genetically Modified Food a Boon or a Risk?

Each month, the United States Food and Drug Administration lists on its Web site its latest "food alerts": foods recalled by sellers because of fears about their safety. In the first two weeks of May 2010 alone, the FDA alerted Americans to concerns about certain apricots, breads, sunflower seeds, cheeses, lettuce, bread, and Amish pumpkin butter.

In one sense, fears about food safety have been around since time immemorial; ever since the Garden of Eden, consumers have worried about what they were putting into their mouths. Nevertheless, out of necessity early humans began experimenting with various species to tame for agricultural purposes so that today, just over 100 crop species are grown intensively around the world, and only a handful of these supply us with most of what we now eat. Through a process of trial and error, farmers and scientists developed processes of selection and cross-breeding (or "hybridization") to combine desirable traits from several varieties into elite cross-bred species. When desired characteristics were unavailable in the crop species, farmers introduced genes from wild species into the cultivated plants. The result, as in the case of corn and dairy cows, is the production of highly productive food species that people born two centuries ago could not have envisioned.

And so in a sense the modern use of gene transfer techniques in the development of genetically modified (GM) crops is but a logical extension of a practice that has existed in agriculture for thousands of years. While GM crops are initially more costly to produce, they eventually save farmers money due to the efficiencies created by greater yields and resistance to insects. Biotechnology, its proponents maintain, further benefits our food supply because genetic modification reduces harmful toxic compounds that exist either naturally or unnaturally in the food we eat. Biotechnology may also allow farmers to produce plants that are tolerant to low temperatures, that thrive in poor soil conditions, and that have a longer shelf life—all of which could benefit the world's hungry.

And yet modern GM processes are decidedly different from their forebears. While the development of new cultivars through classical breeding processes generally takes ten to fifteen years, changes from new gene transfer methods can occur within one generation. And while traditional cross-breeding transfers genes only between similar plants, modern bioengineering can isolate a gene from one type of organism and combine it with the DNA of dissimilar species. Given what is still unknown about the effects of such dramatic transformation, critics express concern over the rapidity with which GM foods are spreading across the globe. Critics of GM also worry about losses of crop biodiversity—essential for species resilience and the health of surrounding ecosystems—as the popularity of high-yielding varieties limits the genetic variation found in major crops. Should not new species be tested carefully over a long period of time in order that potential risks to health, safety, society, and the environment can be fully assessed?

In the following pages, we present several arguments related to genetically modified food. James Freeman defends GM in an essay that originally appeared in *USA Today* in February 2000. Freeman maintains that biotechnology is nothing more than a highly developed breeding tool, and he labels its opponents "scare mongers" with a limited understanding of the realities of biotechnology and its benefits. Does Jeffrey Smith's essay, which follows Freeman's, fit the description of "scare mongering"? (Smith is the author of *Genetic Roulette: The Documented Health Risks of Genetically Modified Foods*.) Freeman's views are then reinforced by James McWilliams, an environmentalist and proponent of natural and organic foods who nevertheless supports (cautiously) the development of genetically modified foods. In an essay published in the online magazine *Slate* in 2009, McWilliams offers the possibility that genetically modified foods can benefit the environment. What follows is an excerpt from an FDA Consumer Health Information booklet, *FDA's Role in Regulating Safety of GE Foods*, which includes a diagram of how genetic modification works. Finally, we offer Gregory Jaffe's advice on how to "Lessen the Fear of Genetically Engineered Crops." An expert on consumer issues relating to agricultural biotechnology, Jaffe suggests in his essay (which appeared August 8, 2001, in the *Christian Science Monitor*) that "sensible measures" must be developed to ensure that GM foods are safe for public consumption.

So in the end is it ethical and practical for scientists to modify living organisms, to tamper with the food supply? Is the genetic modification of crops

How was your food grown? If you are living in the United States, it is likely that you are consuming genetically modified foods on a regular basis.

inherently hazardous? Could we unwittingly be making our foods and our world unsafe? And what about the long-term consequences of producing and consuming GM foods? Do GM crops affect the environment or the wild ecosystem, reducing crop biodiversity and the persistence of beneficial insects? (Some suspect that the revered monarch butterfly is being compromised by new varieties of corn.) Could new crops lead to the development of noxious "superweeds"? And what about genetic pollution? Should we be concerned that GM genes might be transferred to other organisms, even to humans and other animals? How can scientists allay public concerns considering the complexities of the issues involved?

James Freeman

You're Eating Genetically Modified Food

There's no escape. You are consuming mass quantities of genetically modified food. The milk on your Cheerios this morning came from a genetically modified cow, and the Cheerios themselves featured genetically modified whole grain goodness. At lunch you'll enjoy french fries from genetically modified potatoes and perhaps a bucket of genetically modified fried chicken. If you don't have any meetings this afternoon, maybe you'll wash it all down with the finest genetically modified hops, grains, and barley, brewed to perfection—or at least to completion if you're drinking Schaefer.

2   Everything you eat is the result of genetic modification. When a rancher in Wyoming selected his stud bull to mate with a certain cow to produce the calf that ultimately produced the milk on your breakfast table, he was manipulating genes. Sounds delicious, doesn't it? Sorry, but you get the point.

3   Long before you were ever born, farmers were splicing genes and manipulating seeds to create more robust plants. Genetic modification used to be called "breeding," and people have been doing it for centuries. Thomas Jefferson did it at Monticello, as he experimented in his gardens with literally hundreds of varieties of fruits and vegetables. (Hmm, Thomas Jefferson and genes. . . . This column is going to disappoint a lot of people doing Web searches.)

4   Anyway, to return to the topic at hand, breeding isn't a scary word, so people who oppose technology call it "genetic modification." They want to cast biotechnology, which is just a more precise and effective breeding tool, as some kind of threat to our lives, instead of the blessing that it is.

5   Have you ever seen corn in its natural state without genetic modification? It's disgusting. We're talking about that nasty, gnarled, multi-colored garbage used as

ornamentation in Thanksgiving displays. The fear mongers should eat that the next time they want to criticize technology. In fact, the fear mongers are waging a very successful campaign against biotechnology, especially in Europe where they've lobbied to limit the availability of "genetically modified" foods. Even in the United States, where we generally embrace technology and its possibilities, the fear is spreading—not because of some horrible event related to the food supply, but because of more aggressive spinning of the media. In fact, you've been enjoying foods enhanced by biotechnology for most of the last decade. And the news is all good—lower prices and more abundant food.

6   As for the future, the potential to eliminate human suffering is enormous. Right now, according to the World Health Organization, more than a million kids die every year because they lack vitamin A in their diets. Millions more become blind. WHO estimates that more than a billion people suffer from anemia, caused by iron deficiency. What if we could develop rice or corn plants with all of the essential vitamins for children? Personally, I'd rather have an entire day's nutrition bio-engineered into a Twinkie or a pan pizza, but I recognize the benefits of more-nutritious crops. Reasonable people can disagree on the best applications for this technology.

7   Still, the critics want to talk about the dangers of genetically modified crops. The Environmental Protection Agency wants to regulate the use of certain bio-engineered corn seeds because they include a resistance to pests. Specifically, the seeds are bred to include a toxin called BT that kills little creatures called corn borers, so farmers don't need to spray pesticides. Turns out, according to the EPA, that the toxin in the corn can kill monarch butterflies, too. The butterflies don't eat corn, but the EPA is afraid that the corn pollen will blow over and land on a milkweed and stick to it and then confused monarch caterpillars will inadvertently eat the pollen. Not exactly the end of the world, but it sounds bad—until you consider the alternatives. According to Professor Nina Fedoroff, "A wide-spectrum pesticide sprayed from a plane is going to kill a lot more insects than will be killed by an in-plant toxin."

8   Of course, the anti-tech crowd will say that they don't like pesticides either. They promote organic farming—meaning we use more land to produce our food and we clear more wilderness. We also pay more for food, since we're not using the efficiencies that come from technology. Maybe that's not a problem for you or me, but it's bad news for those millions of malnourished kids around the world. Says Fedoroff, "I think that most inhabitants of contemporary urban societies don't have a clue about how tough it is to grow enough food for the human population in competition with bacteria, fungi, insects, and animals and in the face of droughts, floods, and other climatic variations." That may be true, but I do think that most Americans understand the positive impact of technology. And that's why they'll ultimately reject the scare campaign against biotechnology.

Jeffrey Smith

Another Reason for Schools to Ban Genetically Engineered Foods

Before the Appleton, Wisconsin high school replaced their cafeteria's processed foods with wholesome, nutritious food, the school was described as out-of-control. There were weapons violations, student disruptions, and a cop on duty full-time. After the change in school meals, the students were calm, focused, and orderly. There were no more weapons violations, and no suicides, expulsions, dropouts, or drug violations. The new diet and improved behavior has lasted for seven years, and now other schools are changing their meal programs with similar results.

2   Years ago, a science class at Appleton found support for their new diet by conducting a cruel and unusual experiment with three mice. They fed them the junk food that kids in other high schools eat everyday. The mice freaked out. Their behavior was totally different than the three mice in the neighboring cage. The neighboring mice had good karma; they were fed nutritious whole foods and behaved like mice. They slept during the day inside their cardboard tube, played with each other, and acted very mouse-like. The junk food mice, on the other hand, destroyed their cardboard tube, were no longer nocturnal, stopped playing with each other, fought often, and two mice eventually killed the third and ate it. After the three month experiment, the students rehabilitated the two surviving junk food mice with a diet of whole foods. After about three weeks, the mice came around.

3   Sister Luigi Frigo repeats this experiment every year in her second grade class in Cudahy, Wisconsin, but mercifully, for only four days. Even on the first day of junk food, the mice's behavior "changes drastically." They become lazy, antisocial, and nervous. And it still takes the mice about two to three weeks on unprocessed foods to return to normal. One year, the second graders tried to do the experiment again a few months later with the same mice, but this time the animals refused to eat the junk food.

4   Across the ocean in Holland, a student fed one group of mice genetically modified (GM) corn and soy, and another group the non-GM variety. The GM mice stopped playing with each other and withdrew into their own parts of the cage. When the student tried to pick them up, unlike their well-behaved neighbors, the GM mice scampered around in apparent fear and tried to climb the walls. One mouse in the GM group was found dead at the end of the experiment.

5   It's interesting to note that the junk food fed to the mice in the Wisconsin experiments also contained genetically modified ingredients. And although the Appleton school lunch program did not specifically attempt to remove GM foods, it happened anyway. That's because GM foods such as soy and corn and their derivatives are largely found in processed foods. So when the school switched to unprocessed alternatives, almost all ingredients derived from GM crops were taken out automatically.

6   Does this mean that GM foods negatively affect the behavior of humans or animals? It would certainly be irresponsible to say so on the basis of a single student mice experiment and the results at Appleton. On the other hand, it is equally irresponsible to say that it doesn't.

7   We are just beginning to understand the influence of food on behavior. A study in *Science* in December 2002 concluded that "food molecules act like hormones, regulating body functioning and triggering cell division. The molecules can cause mental imbalances ranging from attention-deficit and hyperactivity disorder to serious mental illness." The problem is we do not know which food molecules have what effect. The bigger problem is that the composition of GM foods can change radically without our knowledge.

8   Genetically modified foods have genes inserted into their DNA. But genes are not Legos; they don't just snap into place. Gene insertion creates unpredicted, irreversible changes. In one study, for example, a gene chip monitored the DNA before and after a single foreign gene was inserted. As much as 5 percent of the DNA's genes changed the amount of protein they were producing. Not only is that huge in itself, but these changes can multiply through complex interactions down the line.

9   In spite of the potential for dramatic changes in the composition of GM foods, they are typically measured for only a small number of known nutrient levels. But even if we *could* identify all the changed compounds, at this point we wouldn't know which might be responsible for the antisocial nature of mice or humans. Likewise, we are only beginning to identify the medicinal compounds in food. We now know, for example, that the pigment in blueberries may revive the brain's neural communication system, and the antioxidant found in grape skins may fight cancer and reduce heart disease. But what about other valuable compounds we don't know about that might change or disappear in GM varieties?

10   Consider GM soy. In July 1999, years after it was on the market, independent researchers published a study showing that it contains 12–14 percent less cancer-fighting phytoestrogens. What else has changed that we don't know about? [Monsanto responded with its own study, which concluded that soy's phytoestrogen levels vary too much to even carry out a statistical analysis. They failed to disclose, however, that the laboratory that conducted Monsanto's experiment had been instructed to use an obsolete method to detect phytoestrogens—one that had been replaced due to its highly variable results.]

11   In 1996, Monsanto published a paper in the *Journal of Nutrition* that concluded in the title, "The composition of glyphosate-tolerant soybean seeds is equivalent to that of conventional soybeans." The study only compared a small number of nutrients and a close look at their charts revealed significant differences in the fat, ash, and carbohydrate content. In addition, GM soy meal contained 27 percent more trypsin inhibitor, a well-known soy allergen. The study also used questionable methods. Nutrient comparisons are routinely conducted on plants grown in identical conditions so that variables such as weather and soil can be ruled out. Otherwise, differences in plant composition could be easily missed. In Monsanto's study, soybeans were planted in widely varying climates and geography.

12   Although one of their trials *was* a side-by-side comparison between GM and non-GM soy, for some reason the results were left out of the paper altogether. Years later, a medical writer found the missing data in the archives of the *Journal of Nutrition* and made them public. No wonder the scientists left them out. The GM soy showed significantly lower levels of protein, a fatty acid, and phenylalanine, an essential amino acid. Also, toasted GM soy meal contained nearly twice the amount of a lectin that may block the body's ability to assimilate other nutrients. Furthermore, the toasted GM soy contained as much as seven times the amount of trypsin inhibitor, indicating that the allergen may survive cooking more in the GM variety. (This might explain the 50 percent jump in soy allergies in the UK, just after GM soy was introduced.)

13   We don't know all the changes that occur with genetic engineering, but certainly GM crops are not the same. Ask the animals. Eyewitness reports from all over North America describe how several types of animals, when given a choice, avoided eating GM food. These included cows, pigs, elk, deer, raccoons, squirrels, rats, and mice. In fact, the Dutch student mentioned above first determined that his mice had a two-to-one preference for non-GM before forcing half of them to eat only the engineered variety.

14   Differences in GM food will likely have a much larger impact on children. They are three to four times more susceptible to allergies. Also, they convert more of the food into body-building material. Altered nutrients or added toxins can result in developmental problems. For this reason, animal nutrition studies are typically conducted on young, developing animals. After the feeding trial, organs are weighed and often studied under magnification. If scientists used mature animals instead of young ones, even severe nutritional problems might not be detected. The Monsanto study used mature animals instead of young ones.

15   They also diluted their GM soy with non-GM protein 10- or 12-fold before feeding the animals. And they never weighed the organs or examined them under a microscope. The study, which is the only major animal feeding study on GM soy ever published, is dismissed by critics as rigged to avoid finding problems.

16   Unfortunately, there is a much bigger experiment going on—an uncontrolled one which we are all a part of. We're being fed GM foods daily, without knowing the impact of these foods on our health, our behavior, or our children. Thousands of schools around the world, particularly in Europe, have decided not to let their kids be used as guinea pigs. They have banned GM foods.

17   The impact of changes in the composition of GM foods is only one of several reasons why these foods may be dangerous. Other reasons may be far worse (see www.seedsofdeception.com). With the epidemic of obesity and diabetes and with the results in Appleton, parents and schools are waking up to the critical role that diet plays. When making changes in what kids eat, removing GM foods should be a priority.

JAMES E. McWILLIAMS

The Green Monster: Could Frankenfoods Be Good for the Environment?

I'm sitting at my desk examining a $10.95 jar of South River Miso. The stuff is delicious, marked by a light, lemony tang. The packaging, by contrast, is a heavy-handed assurance of purity. The company is eager to tell me that the product I've purchased is certified organic, aged for three weeks in wood (sustainably harvested?), unpasteurized, made with "deep well water," handcrafted, and—the designation that most piques my interest—*GMO free*.

2   GMO refers to "genetically modified organisms." A genetically modified crop results from the laboratory insertion of a gene from one organism into the DNA sequence of another in order to confer an advantageous trait such as insect resistance, drought

tolerance, or herbicide resistance. Today almost 90 percent of soy crops and 80 percent of corn crops in the United States sprout from genetically engineered seeds. Forty-five million acres of land worldwide contain genetically engineered crops. From the perspective of commercial agriculture, the technology has been seamlessly assimilated into traditional farming routines.

3   From the perspective of my miso jar, however, it's evident that not all consumers share the enthusiasm. It's as likely as not that you know GMOs by their stock term of derision: *Frankenfoods*. The moniker reflects a broad spectrum of concerns: Some anti-biotech activists argue that these organisms will contaminate their wild cousins with GM pollen and drive native plants extinct. Others suggest that they will foster the growth of "superweeds"—plants that develop a resistance to the herbicides many GMOs are engineered to tolerate. And yet others fear that genetic alterations will trigger allergic reactions in unsuspecting consumers. Whether or not these concerns collectively warrant a ban on GMOs—as many (most?) environmentalists would like to see—is a hotly debated topic. The upshot to these potential pitfalls, however, is beyond dispute: A lot of people find this technology to be creepy.

4   Whatever the specific cause of discontent over GM crops, popular resistance came to a head in 2000, when the National Organic Program solicited public input on the issue of whether they should be included. In response, sustainable-food activists deluged officials with a rainforest's worth of letters—275,000, to be exact—beating the measure into oblivion. Today, in the same spirit, environmentalists instinctively deem GMOs the antithesis of environmental responsibility.

5   Many scientists, and even a few organic farmers, now believe the 2000 rejection was a fatal rush to judgment. Most recently, Pamela Ronald, a plant pathologist and chair of the Plant Genomics Program at the University of California-Davis, has declared herself one such critic. In *Tomorrow's Table: Organic Farming, Genetics, and the Future of Food*, she argues that we should, in fact, be actively merging genetic engineering and organic farming to achieve a sustainable future for food production. Her research—which she conducts alongside her husband, an organic farmer—explores genetically engineered crops that, instead of serving the rapacity of agribusiness, foster the fundamentals of sustainability. Their endeavor, counterintuitive as it seems, points to an emerging green biotech frontier—a hidden realm of opportunity to feed the world's impending 9 billion a diet produced in an environmentally responsible way.

6   To appreciate how "responsible genetic modification" isn't an oxymoron, consider grass-fed beef. Cows that eat grass are commonly touted as the sustainable alternative to feedlot beef, a resource-intensive form of production that stuffs cows with a steady diet of grain fortified with antibiotics, growth hormones, steroids, and appetite enhancers that eventually pass through the animals into the soil and water. One overlooked drawback to grass-fed beef, however, is the fact that grass-fed cows emit four times more methane—a greenhouse gas that's more than 20 times as powerful as carbon dioxide—as regular, feedlot cows. That's because grass contains lignin, a substance that triggers a cow's digestive system to secrete a methane-producing enzyme. An Australian biotech company called Gramina has recently produced a genetically modified grass with lower amounts of lignin. Lower amounts of lignin mean less methane, less methane means curbed global warming emissions, and curbed emissions means environmentalists can eat their beef without hanging up their green stripes.

7   Another area where sustainable agriculture and genetic modification could productively overlap involves nitrogen fertilizer. A plant's failure to absorb all the nutrients from the fertilizer leads to the harmful accumulation of nitrogen in the soil. From there it leaches into rivers and oceans to precipitate dead zones so choked with algae that other marine life collapses. In light of this problem, Syngenta and other biotech companies are in the process of genetically engineering crops such as potatoes, rice, and wheat to improve their nitrogen uptake efficiency in an effort to diminish the negative consequences of nitrogen fertilization. Early results suggest that rice farmers in Southeast Asia and potato farmers in Africa might one day have the option of planting crops that mitigate the harmful effects of this long-vilified source of agricultural pollution.

8   Animals, of course, are just as modifiable as plants. Livestock farmers have been genetically tinkering with their beasts for centuries through the hit-or-miss process of selective breeding. They've done so to enhance their animals' health, increase their weight, and refine their fat content. Breeding animals to reduce environmental impact, however, hasn't been a viable option with the clunky techniques of conventional breeding. But such is not the case with genetic engineering.

9   Case in point: Canadian scientists have recently pioneered the "enviropig," a genetically modified porker altered to diminish the notoriously high phosphorous level of pig manure by 60 percent. Like nitrogen, phosphorous runoff is a serious pollutant with widespread downstream consequences. But with the relatively basic insertion of a gene (from E. coli bacteria) that produces a digestive enzyme called phytase, scientists have provided farmers with yet another tool for lessening their heavy impact on the environment.

10   When commercial farmers hear about GM grass, increased nitrogen uptake, and cleaner pigs, they're excited. And when they hear about other products in the

How effective is the illustration in conveying a point of view on the genetic modification of livestock? Why?

works—genetically modified sugar beets that require less water and have higher yields than cane sugar; a dust made from genetically modified ferns to remove heavy metals from the soil; genetically modified and *edible* cotton seeds that require minimal pesticide use—they're also excited. And they're excited not only because these products have the potential to streamline production, but also because GM technology allows them to play a meaningful role in reducing their carbon footprint.

11   However, with the exception of the modified sugar beets, the GMOs mentioned in this article are not currently on the market. The cutting-room floors of research laboratories all over the world, in fact, are littered with successful examples of genetically engineered products that have enormous potential to further the goals of sustainable agriculture. Demand for these products remains high among farmers—it almost always does—but food producers fear the bad publicity that might come from anti-GMO invective.

12   Given the potential of these products to reduce the environmental impact of farming, it's ironic that traditional advocates for sustainable agriculture have led a successful campaign to blacklist GMOs irrespective of their applications. At the very least, they might treat them as legitimate ethical and scientific matters deserving of a fair public hearing. Such a hearing, I would venture, would not only please farmers who were truly concerned about sustainability, but it would provide the rest of us—those of us who do not grow food for the world but only think about it—a more accurate source of scientific information than the back of a miso jar.

U.S. Food and Drug Administration

FDA's Role in Regulating Safety of GE Foods

Foods from genetically engineered organisms, also known as biotech foods and referred to by some as food from genetically modified organisms (GMOs), have been in our food supply for about 20 years.

2   Genetic engineering refers to certain methods that scientists use to introduce new traits or characteristics to an organism. For example, plants may be genetically engineered to produce characteristics that enhance the growth or nutritional value of food crops.

3   Using a science-based approach, the Food and Drug Administration (FDA) regulates foods and ingredients made from genetically engineered plants to help ensure that they are safe to eat.

4   Since people have been modifying plants for thousands of years through breeding and selection, FDA uses the term "genetically engineered," or "GE," to distinguish plants that have been modified using modern biotechnology from those modified through traditional breeding.

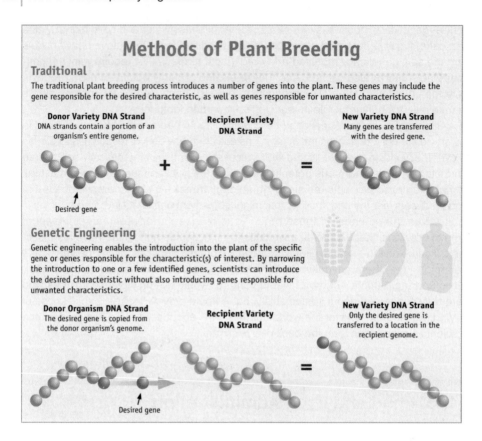

Methods of Plant Breeding

Traditional

The traditional plant breeding process introduces a number of genes into the plant. These genes may include the gene responsible for the desired characteristic, as well as genes responsible for unwanted characteristics.

Donor Variety DNA Strand
DNA strands contain a portion of an organism's entire genome.

Recipient Variety DNA Strand

New Variety DNA Strand
Many genes are transferred with the desired gene.

+   =

Desired gene

Genetic Engineering

Genetic engineering enables the introduction into the plant of the specific gene or genes responsible for the characteristic(s) of interest. By narrowing the introduction to one or a few identified genes, scientists can introduce the desired characteristic without also introducing genes responsible for unwanted characteristics.

Donor Organism DNA Strand
The desired gene is copied from the donor organism's genome.

Recipient Variety DNA Strand

New Variety DNA Strand
Only the desired gene is transferred to a location in the recipient genome.

=

Desired gene

5   FDA regulates food from GE crops in conjunction with the U.S. Department of Agriculture (USDA) and the Environmental Protection Agency (EPA). USDA's Animal and Plant Health Inspection Service is responsible for protecting agriculture from pests and disease, including making sure that all new GE plant varieties pose no pest risk to other plants. EPA regulates pesticides, including those bioengineered into food crops, to make sure that pesticides are safe for human and animal consumption and do not pose unreasonable risks of harm to human health or the environment.

GREGORY **JAFFE**

Lessen the Fear of Genetically Engineered Crops

Protesters carrying signs stating "Biocide is Homicide" and shouting concerns about the risks of eating genetically engineered foods recently demonstrated outside the biotechnology industry's annual convention. Inside the convention center, industry extolled the safety of genetically engineered foods and the benefits of future crops like "golden rice."

2   Neither corporate hyperbole nor radical slogans do much to inform the public. What is needed is the shaping of sensible measures to ensure that genetically engineered foods are safe. The first few first engineered crops are already providing remarkable benefits. Cotton modified to kill insects has greatly diminished farmers' use of toxic insecticides, thereby reducing costs, increasing yields, and, presumably, reducing harm to nontarget species. Likewise, biotech soybeans facilitate no-till farming, which reduces soil erosion and water pollution.

3   Despite such benefits, agricultural biotechnology is under siege for reasons good and bad. Activists have burned fields and bombed labs. Farmers will not plant genetically engineered sweet corn, sugar beets, and apples, for fear of consumer rejection. And countries in Europe and Asia refuse to import U.S.-grown genetically engineered crops. Some countries now require labeling of foods containing engineered ingredients. Those requirements have spurred food processors, who want to avoid negative-sounding labels, to eliminate bioengineered ingredients.

4   Buffeted by the polarized debate, many Americans oppose biotech foods, in part because farmers and seed companies get the benefits while consumers bear the risk. If anti-genetically engineered sentiment increases, U.S. farmers may be forced to forgo the advantages of engineered crops. And most public and private investment in agricultural biotechnology would dry up.

5   To reap the benefits of agricultural biotechnology, minimize the risks, and boost public confidence, the U.S. must upgrade its flawed regulatory system. Currently, the Food and Drug Administration (FDA) does not formally approve any genetically engineered crops as safe to eat. Instead, it reviews safety data provided voluntarily by seed companies. That consultation process, which the FDA admits is "not a comprehensive scientific review of the data," culminates with the FDA stating only that it has "no further questions . . . at this time." Although no health problems with genetically engineered crops have been detected, that industry-driven process is weak insurance. The recent FDA proposal requiring a formal notification before marketing a biotech food is an improvement.

6   All biotech foods should go through a mandatory approval process with specific testing and data requirements. The National Academy of Sciences should be commissioned to recommend a precise method of assessment.

7   Genetically engineered crops also raise environmental concerns. They could lead to pesticide-resistant insects and weeds and might contaminate plants that are close relatives of the crops. To safeguard our ecosystem, the current laws need fixing. Congress should close regulatory gaps to ensure that all future applications of biotechnology, ranging from fast-growing fish to corn plants that produce industrial chemicals, receive thorough environmental reviews. Also, the Environmental Protection Agency must enforce restrictions it has imposed on bioengineered crops to help prevent emergence of insecticide-resistant pests.

8   Although strong regulations would minimize environmental and safety risks, nothing would boost public confidence more than engineered products that benefit consumers. No beneficial products currently exist.

9   Worldwide acceptance of biotechnology will occur only when other countries reap benefits from this technology. Instead of spending millions of dollars on feel-good

advertising campaigns, the biotech industry should train developing-country scientists and fund research in those countries. Companies—and universities—should donate patented crops and processes to developing countries. Agricultural biotechnology is not a panacea for all agricultural problems here or abroad, nor is it free from risk. But, with adequate safeguards, it could provide tremendous benefits for an ever-populous, pesticide-drenched, and water-deficient globe.

FROM READING TO WRITING

1. In this section, you read essays by Jay Lehr, Mike Gemmell, and Joseph Bast, and by Elizabeth Royte on the ethics of hydraulic fracking. In essence, these are evaluation essays. What evaluative criteria are used in each essay? Do the authors work from the same criteria, or do their conclusions arise from differing premises? Do they stay on moral ground, or consider as well practicality or even aesthetics? (See Chapter 10 for information on how evaluation arguments work.)

2. In his essay, Bill Gates writes glowingly of the potential for robots to benefit human society. Yet, as you have also seen (in the argument put forth by Marks), robots are not without their critics. Exactly what is a robot, anyway? What differentiates robots from other machines? Write an essay that shows your attitude toward robots by defining them in a particular way. (For advice on writing definitions, see Chapter 8.)

3. One of the major methods for convincing people of the need for organ donor compensation or stem cell research is the use of personal examples—narratives—about people who might benefit. Beginning from your own informed beliefs, write a story that illustrates your position on a particular scientific issue—stem cell, organ donation, genetically modified foods, or some other controversial process or technology. If possible, draw from your personal experience with the subject at hand. (For advice on narrative arguments, see Chapter 11.)

4. Conduct a rhetorical analysis of one of the arguments in this chapter, perhaps the one by Carl Zimmer or by Elizabeth Royte. How is the argument a product of the particular rhetorical situation that the writer found himself or herself in? How might the writer have presented the argument if he or she had appeared before another readership or in a different forum or in a speech? (See Chapter 6 for advice on rhetorical analysis.)

5. Using the guidelines in Chapter 13, write a proposal argument that defends or undermines the practice of genetic modification of food crops *from a human rights perspective*. Is genetic engineering the solution to world hunger (or at least a part of that solution)? Or will it only exacerbate the existing polarization between the "haves" and the "have-nots"? Conduct your own research prior to constructing your argument.

26 | Privacy

New Challenges to Personal Privacy

The student pictured here doesn't seem too worried about privacy: she's seated outside, in the open, and she's hiding herself and her work from no one. But should she be so unconcerned? Is she being watched without knowing it? Should her Facebook presence and the surveillance cameras that might be trained on her give her reason for concern?

> "You have zero privacy now— get over it."
>
> —Scott McNealy, CEO of Sun Microsystems

Item: In 2012, Apple's App Store released a new iPhone and iPad app called Girls Around Me. As reported in Michael Faris's doctoral dissertation, it provided users with a map of their surrounding area with pictures of local women plotted onto the map. (Alternatively, a user could opt to use it to find men instead of women.) By tapping onto a profile picture plotted onto the map, a user could see someone's publicly available *Facebook* photo and name and send a message to the person's *Facebook* account. When a number of people wrote about the app, however, they emphasized the potential dangers of the app and the need for readers to educate their friends about privacy settings on social network sites: The developers of Girls Around Me had probably imagined it as a harmless app that did not violate Apple's policies for the App Store, but could Girls Around Me not be used as well by stalkers and sexual

How does a new bathroom design, like this colored glass structure in the middle of an apartment, reflect (or push for) new attitudes about privacy?

predators? After several articles pointed out the problems with Girls Around Me, Apple subsequently removed the app from the App Store.

Item: The Dog Poop Girl (as she came to be known) was riding the subway in Seoul, South Korea, one day when her dog decided to "take care of business." According to a *Washington Post* story written by Jonathan Krim on July 7, 2005, the woman (a university student) made no move to clean up the mess, so fellow passengers grew agitated. One of them recorded the scene on a cell phone camera and then posted photos on a Web site. Web surfers came upon the photos and began referring to her as Dog Poop Girl. One thing led to another, and soon her privacy was completely gone: People revealed her true name, began asking for and sharing more information about her, launched blogs commenting about her and her relatives, and generally crackled with gossip about her and her behavior. Ultimately she became the subject of sermons and online discussions, and her story made the national news. In humiliation, Dog Poop Girl withdrew from her university.

Item: According to an American Civil Liberties Union (ACLU) Web posting in May 2010, the Department of Justice was seeking to obtain the contents of a *Yahoo!* e-mail account without the e-mailer's permission and without a search warrant. Government investigators in the process of building a criminal case were maintaining that because the *Yahoo!* e-mail had been accessed by the user, it no longer qualified as "in electronic storage" (protected as private property under the Stored Communications Act). But *Yahoo!* asked a federal court judge to block the government attempt, and the company was supported by the ACLU, the Electronic Frontier Foundation (EFF), Google, and many other public interest organizations. "The government is trying to evade federal privacy law and the Constitution," said EFF Senior Staff Attorney Kevin Bankston. "The Fourth Amendment protects these stored e-mails, just like it does our private papers. We all have a reasonable expectation of privacy in the contents of our e-mail accounts, and the government should have to make a showing of probable cause to a judge before it rifles through our private communications."

These three incidents illustrate some of the new challenges to personal privacy that have been raised in response to new technology developments and concerns about security that are one legacy of the September 11, 2001, attacks. There is no doubt that electronic technologies have given people a new degree of personal freedom; handheld computers, cell phones, e-mail, and Web shopping are now routine time-savers. *Facebook* has become a routine and nearly free form of entertainment. But there is also no doubt that a price has been paid for that freedom: That price is the surveillance side of the Internet and other technologies. In the wake of September 11, other terrorist attacks, and the increased attention to security that has ensued, privacy issues have been an increasing concern in American life. Law enforcement officials seek access to information about potential conspiracies, parents are placing devices on their children in order to keep tabs on their whereabouts, concerns have been raised about Facebook's corporate Data Use Policy, and businesses increasingly gather information about people to individualize marketing campaigns, keep an eye out for good (and bad) credit risks, and customize customers. (Businesses and police also increasingly spy on their own employees.)

A biometric measuring instrument at Busch Gardens helps staff make sure the same person uses the same ticket each day.

One emerging technology—biometrics—measures physical and behavioral data, such as fingerprints or keystroke patterns, in order to identify individual human beings. Biometric recognition provides a deeply personalized means of identification that enhances security, say its supporters, but a national biometric database also raises questions of privacy, say its detractors. What would it mean in terms of national security and surveillance to store citizens' inherently unique characteristics in a nationwide database?

And when is freedom too much freedom? If bloggers act as a posse, tracking down criminals and turning them over to law enforcement, is that appropriate action or vigilante action? What about efforts to replicate what was done to the Dog Poop Girl? Should laws prevent people from publicizing and branding people who seem undesirable? Is too much sharing going on via *Facebook*? Should people who wish to share secrets—whether the secrets are true or not—have the anonymity and apparent protection afforded by the Internet? Must e-mail users simply accept as a fact of life that they are bombarded by hundreds of unauthorized, unsolicited spam messages? And what are the limits of what government officials should be able to do to inspect the personal records of citizens?

Contemporary Arguments

Is it possible, in other words, to have both security and freedom in the United States? What is the proper balance of the two?

While surveillance cameras may be designed to provide security, the devices may also intrude on individuals' privacy, even without their knowledge.

On the one hand, some people support a national ID card (like those already used, incidentally, in several European nations) or sign up for in-vehicle security systems such as OnStar (always on the watch!) as a safety feature. They root for police to pursue potential terrorists, they use E-ZPass without giving a thought to the fact that they are giving out their whereabouts, they approve when cameras are mounted to watch over high-crime areas, they wink when Internet service providers disclose customer records to government agents if they feel that a crime is being committed, and they appreciate being notified that convicted felons have moved into the neighborhood. On the other hand, they protest when police use wiretaps without explicit legal permission, worry about the ability of global positioning systems to snoop on people from satellites (especially by zeroing in on cell phones or implanted homing devices), and protest when roving surveillance cameras are mounted in stores and at street corners, in public parks and on school playgrounds.

Everyone these days seems to be monitored or monitoring. Online data collectors record which Web sites people visit; airlines record data on people's travels; companies routinely perform background checks on potential employees; bus and train companies check passenger lists against records of "suspicious" characters; businesses seek to develop systems that can deliver customized marketing information to particular households and commuters; and supermarkets record purchases in order to fine-tune their stocking patterns. In the future, some say, we can look forward to smart cars, smart airports, smart TVs, smart credit cards, and smart homes—all designed to give us certain freedoms, even if at the price of losing some of our privacy.

The arguments in this chapter discuss all these questions related to privacy. Adam Penenberg's "The Surveillance Society" overviews the brave new world that is now developing (for better or for worse), and the selections that follow argue about aspects of technology that undermine our privacy. Robert Cringely sounds an alert about *Facebook*. Jonathan Locker worries about OnStar. Dahlia Lithwick questions the ethics of sexting. And Adam Cohen makes a plea for citizens to be able to walk down the street without being monitored by cameras—to be able to enjoy what he calls "locational privacy." These are just a small sample of the issues that are facing Americans as it becomes easier and easier for us to watch each other.

Because the emerging field of biometrics effectively illustrates the tensions between protection and privacy, we look in detail at this emerging technology in the Issue in Focus. The selections reproduced there describe the technologies (such as signature analysis, keystroke patterns, and vein biometric systems) and dramatize the excitement—and the fears—that accompany them. On one hand, biometric technologies hold out the promise of improved crime fighting and national security. On the other, such technologies inevitably encroach on individuals' privacy and may even open the door to DNA identify theft. What price are we willing to pay for privacy (or security)? At what point does it make sense to forfeit private information for protection and convenience?

ADAM **PENENBERG**

The Surveillance Society*

Adam L. Penenberg (born 1962) is an investigative journalist who currently edits PandoDaily, a technology news site. He is the author of several books, including *Spooked: Espionage in Corporate America* and *Viral Loop: From Facebook to Twitter, How Today's Smartest Businesses Grow Themselves*. Formerly senior editor at *Forbes*, Penenberg has also written for *Inc.*, the *New York Times*, *Slate*, *Playboy*, *Mother Jones*, and *Wired*, in which the following article appeared in December 2001, shortly after 9-11.

W ithin hours of the attacks on the World Trade Center and the Pentagon, as federal officials shut down airports and U.S. strategists began plotting a military response, Attorney General John Ashcroft was mobilizing his own forces. In meetings with top aides at the FBI's Strategic Information and Operations Center—during which the White House as well as the State and Defense departments dialed in via secure videoconference—Ashcroft pulled together a host of anti-terrorism measures. Days later, the attorney general sent to Capitol Hill a bill (the Patriot Act) that would make it easier for the government to tap cell phones and pagers, give the Feds broad authority to monitor email and Web browsing, strengthen money-laundering laws, and weaken immigrants' rights. There were whispers of a national identity card and of using face-recognition software and retinal scans at airports and in other public spaces. And high above it all would sit an Office of Homeland Security, run by former Pennsylvania Governor Tom Ridge, who would report directly to the Oval Office.

2 Such talk usually generates fractious debate between privacy hawks and security hounds. By now, most of us can recite the familiar *Nightline* arguments and counterarguments. But this time the acrimony has been muted. The terrorist assault

Surveillance cameras have become a part of the urban landscape.

on America shifted the balance between privacy and security. What was considered Orwellian one week seemed perfectly reasonable—even necessary—the next. Politicians who routinely clash were marching in lockstep. "When you're in this type of conflict—when you're at war—civil liberties are treated differently," said Senate Republican Trent Lott. "This event will change the balance between freedom and security," echoed House Democrat Richard Gephardt. "There's a whole range of issues that we're going to be grappling with in the next month that takes us to this basic trade-off."

3   Almost immediately, there were unmistakable signs that new surveillance tools would be a linchpin in the war on terrorism. The FBI met with AOL, EarthLink, and other large ISPs, and there was renewed talk of using DCS 1000 to let the FBI monitor email traffic. Visionics—a maker of face-recognition software used in surveillance cameras in London and Tampa, Florida, and in the databases of close to a dozen state law enforcement agencies—reported that its switchboards were jammed. The stock prices of some companies in the security business spiked as the rest of the market crumbled.

4   But truth be told, the U.S. was embracing the Surveillance Society well before September 11. In the name of safety, we have grown increasingly comfortable with cameras monitoring us whenever we stop to buy a Slurpee, grab cash from an ATM, or park in a downtown lot. And in the name of convenience, we've happily accepted a range of products and services, from cell phones to credit cards to Web browsers, that

make our lives easier and have the secondary effect of permitting us to be tracked. They're not spy technologies—but they might as well be.

5   Americans don't seem to be spooked by these incursions. "Apparently, consumers don't feel their privacy is threatened," says Barbara Bellissimo, owner of a now-defunct dotcom that offered anonymous Web browsing. "That's why there are no profitable privacy companies." (It might also be why millions of Americans watch reality-based television shows like *Survivor* that package round-the-clock surveillance as entertainment.)

6   Just how vast is the new surveillance world? Let's start with cameras. More than 60 communities in a dozen states have set up traffic-light cameras that ticket drivers for running red lights or speeding. Casinos in Las Vegas zoom in on the cards we hold at the blackjack table. Cameras are mounted on police cars, they hang from trees in public parks, they're affixed to the walls in sports stadiums and shopping malls. David Brin, author of *The Transparent Society,* postulates a "Moore's law of cameras." He sees them roughly "halving in size, and doubling in acuity and movement capability and sheer numbers, every year or two."

7   The surveillance net also has a digital arm. With computers home to the data entrails of half a billion bank accounts, just as many credit card accounts, and hundreds of millions of medical claims, mortgages, and retirement funds, there exists a significant cache of online data about each of us.

8   Then there's the matter of monitoring our daily travels. Debit cards like New York's E-ZPass deduct a fee as commuters zip through tollbooths *and* track our comings and goings on the road; transit cards chart riders' subway journeys; employee ID cards can show when we arrived at work, when we left, and where we went within the office complex. Phone cards mark who we call and, often, from where. Credit card records etch us in time and space more reliably than any eyewitness. So do airline tickets—even if you pay cash. And as for the cell phone: "If you turn it on, you can be tracked," says Jim Atkinson, a countersurveillance expert who is president of Granite Island Group in Gloucester, Massachusetts.

9   OnStar, GM's onboard communications system, offers a GPS service to its 1.5 million customers. That means that at any given moment, OnStar can locate each of those 1.5 million cars. (OnStar will track a car only at the request of the driver or, in some instances, the police; the company keeps no historical database of car locations, though if it had the inclination—or was pressured—to gather and store reams of data, it could.) Mercedes' TeleAid and Ford's Wingcast provide similar services. As does AirIQ, which Hertz, Avis, and Budget use for their premium fleets: If a car is abandoned, AirIQ can locate it; if it's stolen, the company can disable its motor.

10   For now, the information about each of us resides in dozens of separate databases owned by the credit card companies and the phone carriers, the rental car agencies and police departments, the ISPs and the IRS. But the aftermath of September 11 could change all that by creating in many of us an appetite for information and a willingness to be monitored. And this raises a disquieting possibility: Will the disparate elements of our surveillance society be assembled into a surveillance web? Will the private companies and the government agencies come together to create a superdatabase accessible to . . . who? Will it strip us not just of personal privacy—we seem resigned, even OK, with that—but of public anonymity?

11   Worrying is a waste of time. Surveillance is here. It was inevitable. But the surveillance state is not.

12   A few days after September 11, Akram Jaber was driving his Chevy Suburban over the pothole-strewn streets of Chicago's south side. With his 15-month-old son in the backseat, he was heading to the liquor store he owns to lock up for the night. A battered Chevy Caprice sped by, then stopped in front of him at a red light. Two men emerged; one pointed a gun at Jaber. "Take it easy," Jaber called out. "I have my son in the car." He left the keys in the ignition, unhitched his son, and turned over the $50,000 vehicle.

13   As the carjackers sped away, Jaber whipped out his cell phone to dial 911. Then he called an operator at OnStar. (He had been paying $16.95 a month for the basic Safety & Security plan: roadside and emergency assistance, remote lock and unlock, and stolen vehicle tracking.) He gave his name, license plate number, and four-digit PIN. The operator called Jaber's vehicle and requested GPS data, then updated the car's position by pinging it every minute. The operator relayed the car's heading to the police officer on the scene, who forwarded it to a dispatcher. Within minutes, officers swooped in on the vehicle and arrested the men. "The police were amazed at how easy it was," say Jaber, who himself was awfully pleased.

14   What's really amazing is just how many similar tools are becoming available to law enforcement. A suspect's alibi can be checked out by looking at the location data trail created by use of his tollbooth pass, transit card, or credit card. Surveillance cameras capture images that authorities can cross-check against a database of criminals through the use of face-recognition software. And cell phones have become the digital equivalent of Hansel and Gretel's bread crumbs.

15   When a cell phone is turned on, it broadcasts an identification number to the closest antennas, which allow the carrier to chart its customers. It's a simple matter—known as triangulation—to track the signal as it arrives at different towers, then calculate the location of the phone based on time differences. The police have taken full advantage of this tracking trick, though—technically, at least—they need a court order to access the information. Earlier this year, Timothy Crosby, 40, was busted for raping and robbing a Brooklyn woman after the police located him by homing in on his cell phone signal. In November 2000, authorities pursued Kofi Apea Orleans-Lindsay for allegedly killing a Maryland state trooper during a buy-and-bust operation. Police used cell data to track Orleans-Lindsay to Brooklyn, where they arrested him.

16   Then there was the case of Christopher Stewart, a New York subway employee whose alibi in the March slaying of his ex-girlfriend crumbled when police subjected his MetroCard transit pass to detailed analysis (MetroCard use can be traced by a serial number). Stewart had claimed he was boarding a Staten Island ferry at the time she was killed. But data from the MetroCard, still in his possession, had him exiting a subway station near the crime scene just before the murder. He was arrested and indicted by a grand jury. MetroCard records were also used against Marco Valencia, who was charged in the December 1999 assault and robbery of a supermarket manager in Manhattan. Valencia claimed he was in Staten Island, but his MetroCard told a different tale, and when confronted, he pleaded guilty.

17   In light of the way cell phones and transit cards are being used to track criminals, video cameras seem remarkably, well, obvious. But they're a cornerstone of the
surveillance society, and they've proved an important weapon in law enforcement's
arsenal. Prior to September 11, such cameras stirred up controversy. When the Tampa
Police Department installed face-recognition software in its network last June, the
public was outraged, and House majority leader Dick Armey joined with civil rights
groups to protest. There was similar push-back in Britain in 1996, when authorities
installed 300 cameras in the East London neighborhood of Newham in an effort to
gather intelligence on suspected IRA bombings. The cameras didn't help much in the
fight on terrorism, but overall crime rates fell 30 percent after they were deployed,
according to city figures. Crime dropped an additional 34 percent in 1998, after the
cameras were equipped with Visionic's face-recognition software. Last year, illegal activities in surrounding areas increased between 10 and 20 percent, but Newham's
inched up less than half a percent. The program has been so successful that Visionics
has been retained to hook up closed-circuit TV cameras in five more nearby London
neighborhoods.

18   Although face-recognition surveillance systems are not foolproof, most Brits
now view "spy" cameras as a part of everyday life, and polls indicate a majority of
citizens support their use. England already boasts about 1.5 million police surveillance
cameras—more than any other country—and the government plans to double that
number within three years. With so many cams, the average city denizen can expect to
be taped every five minutes, according to *The Times* of London.

19   Even as new surveillance technologies increase the amount of information
available about each of us, there's something reassuring in the fact that this data is
extremely far-flung. It would, today, take a considerable amount of sleuthing and multiple search warrants for anyone—individuals, private companies, public agencies—to
aggregate the fruits of the surveillance web in any useful way.

20   But there are signs that in the future it might be much easier to access disparate
data about individuals—where they've been, what they bought, who they were with,
what they were wearing, who they called, what Web sites they visited, what they wrote
in email. After all, the information exists, and from a technical perspective, it's easy to
tap (cell phones, credit cards, ATMs, tollbooth passes—all are part of the same bit-
stream of 0s and 1s). The legal protections that might have prevented access to this
data are eroding. And as the line between the public and private sectors blurs, the data
will likely flow in ways it never has before.

21   So what do we get? Think of all these factoids residing not in some static
database but in a dynamic environment in which strands of information can be pulled
together from a huge variety of sources based on a user's request. It's not Microsoft
Outlook, it's Google. In fact, researchers at Applied Systems Intelligence in Roswell,
Georgia, are working on just such software. Called Karnac (Knowledge Aided Retrieval in Activity Context), the program would scan everything from gun registrations
and credit card records to newspapers and Web sites. While Karnac or a similar program may be a long way off, more modest developments provide a glimpse into where
we could be headed. In the weeks following the attacks, airport authorities hatched
plans for security systems that would link biometric techniques like iris scans with a

government database of known or suspected terrorists. Such systems could easily migrate to other public spaces, motivated by a concern for community safety and a desire to catch criminals.

22   Eventually, surveillance cameras in every mom-and-pop store could use face-recognition software and network databases to link you to your Social Security number, consumer profile, credit report, home and work addresses, and criminal and driving records. Networked street cams could track your location—and keep the digital footage on file.

23   The gated communities of tomorrow will be monitored by cameras, motion detectors, and sensors of all kinds embedded in the walls, floors—every surface. Such systems, hyped as smart-house technologies, are already in beta at universities and corporate labs across the country. Tools such as Bluetooth and 802.11 will turn every object and street corner into a node of the wireless Web, aware of and communicating with the Net-connected PDA and cell of every passerby. Like transit cards and tollbooth passes, the wireless Web isn't a surveillance technology per se, but it will have that effect.

24   Look out a few more years and nano-cameras as small as grains of sand will create a world in which the wind has eyes. Fingerprint-scanning doorknobs and steering wheels could know their users by touch.

25   There will be limits, of course—legal mechanisms like search warrants that protect individuals from undue surveillance. But those safeguards will change with the times. In an effort to bring wiretapping laws into the cellular age, Attorney General Ashcroft proposed—and Congress approved—"roving wiretaps" to give the government authority to monitor a suspect's calls from any phone and any jurisdiction. As communications technologies continue to multiply and blur, it will be increasingly difficult to say where the telephone network ends and the Web begins. Cell phones send messages to pagers. Cars log on to the Internet. The search warrants of the surveillance era will need to span multiple technologies and will likely be written with increasingly broad language.

26   If all this raises the specter of Big Brother, well, that's understandable. But it's also wrong. Even as we trade privacy for security and convenience, we're hardly headed toward totalitarianism. Orwell's greatest error, says Peter Huber, author of *Orwell's Revenge,* was his view that the government had a monopoly on surveillance technologies. Says Huber: "If the Thought Police use telescreens, so can others—that's just the way telescreens work, if they work at all."

27   Indeed, citizens have already learned to use surveillance tools to keep government accountable. When motorist Rodney King was beaten by Los Angeles police officers in 1991, a bystander caught the incident on video. Though the subsequent trial ended in acquittal of the officers, it proved the potency of videotape as evidence. "Video cameras create a potential counterbalance—a kind of ombudsman," says Sam Gregory, a program coordinator for Witness, a New York nonprofit that lends video equipment to human rights activists around the world. "They let citizens protect themselves and hold the state accountable." Recent projects sponsored by Witness include *Operation Fine Girl,* which documents rape as a weapon of war in Sierra Leone, and *Behind the Labels,* an exposé of the clothing-industry sweatshops in Saipan.

28   In Orange County, California, the sheriff's department mounted video cameras on its patrol cars with the idea that footage of arrests could be used to protect against false accusations of excessive force. Not surprisingly, those tapes have been used against the police officers themselves. In June, Robert Delgiudice, who was beaten by police for resisting arrest, had his case dismissed when the video showed that the officer had lied in his police report and preliminary hearing testimony. (Delgiudice is now planning a civil suit.) As Don Landis Jr., the Orange County deputy public defender who argued Delgiudice's case, puts it: "The cameras bring accountability."

29   They also bring transparency, which is almost always a good thing. An antidote to corruption, it keeps financial markets strong, governments honest, and corporations accountable. In public institutions and on city streets, the more transparency the better. Sometimes the reverse is true: The darkness of privacy is essential to the conversations between doctor and patient, to the personal information sent by letter, and to the things we do and say within our bedrooms. In those cases, privacy must be staunchly defended.

30   "Just about the only Fourth Amendment concern that the Supreme Court protects, year after year, decision after decision, is a U.S. citizen's privacy in his own home," says Landis. Earlier this year, the court upheld this principle again, deciding that the police in Florence, Oregon, had violated the Fourth Amendment when, without a warrant, they used thermal imaging technology to detect the heat lamps inside the house of a man they suspected of growing marijuana. Any technology that enables law enforcement to see or hear through walls, the court decreed, required a search warrant; without a warrant, the practice amounted to an unreasonable search.

31   The Constitution itself, therefore, stands in the way of Big Brother. OK, privacy is eroding. But liberty, and the safeguards inherent in due process, remain strong. The government can collect megabytes of information about us, but where and when they do and how that information is used is still subject to the laws designed to keep the state from abusing its power. And of course, even as Congress and the judicial system struggle to maintain the balance of privacy and security, citizens will continue to take technology into their own hands.

32   "Look at all the cameras and cell phones, a gazillion of them, that documented everything on September 11," says David Brin. "The powers of vision and information are expanding exponentially in the hands of the people, far faster than they are being acquired by government." In the long run, Brin predicts, it will be people— empowered by the surveillance web—who thwart the thugs, the tyrants, and even the terrorists.

Mike Luckovich's Pulitzer Prize–winning political cartoons appear in the *Atlanta Journal-Constitution* and are frequently reprinted. This one appeared first on May 27, 2010, just after Facebook founder Mark Zuckerberg announced that he was taking steps, in response to criticism, to protect the privacy of Facebook participants.

By permission of Mike Luckovich and Creators Syndicate, Inc.

Robert X. Cringely	# Facebook Puts Your Privacy on Parade

From 1987 to 1995 Robert X. Cringely wrote the "Notes from the Field" column in *InfoWorld*, a weekly computer trade newspaper. More recently, his writing has appeared in the *New York Times*, *Newsweek*, *Forbes*, *Upside*, *Success*, and *Worth*, among other publications. The argument printed here originally appeared on InfoWorld's Web site in January 2010. In May 2010, *Facebook* responded to its critics by altering its privacy controls (see the cartoon above), but the criticism has not stopped.

Once again Facebook is involved in a privacy imbroglio, and once again it's because boy-founder Mark Zuckerberg opened his yap and stuck his Keds-clad foot inside.

2   Last week at The Crunchies, the annual awards party thrown by TechCrunch doyenne Michael Arrington, Zuckerberg got on stage briefly and made the following statement (per Gawker):

When I got started in my dorm room at Harvard, the question a lot of people asked was "why would I want to put any information on the Internet at all? Why would I want to have a website?"

And then in the last 5 or 6 years, blogging has taken off in a huge way and all these different services that have people sharing all this information. People have really gotten comfortable not only sharing more information and different kinds, but more openly and with more people. That social norm is just something that's evolved over time.

We view it as our role in the system to constantly be innovating and be updating what our system is to reflect what the current social norms are.

So now, a lot of companies would be trapped by the conventions and their legacies of what they've built, [and so] doing a privacy change for 350 million users is not the type of thing that a lot of companies would do. But we viewed that as a really important thing, to always keep a beginner's mind and think: what would we do if we were starting the company now, and starting the site now, and we decided that these would be the social norms now and we just went for it.

3   Allow me to translate. By "innovating and updating" his system, Zuckerberg means the modifications to user privacy settings Facebook unveiled a few weeks ago that made Facebookers' information more easily accessible by Google et al. by default. And by "current social norms," Zuckerberg means "stuff we think we can get away with today that we couldn't get away with three or four years ago."

Facebook founder Mark Zuckerberg at the company's Palo Alto, California, headquarters.

4   Interestingly, after Facebook's default settings changed, Zuckerberg's personal profile went from being virtually inaccessible (unless you were the CEO's friend) to nearly wide open, allowing any Facebooker to view the 290 photos he'd posted. These included several of Zucky the Party Animal (the worst of which Gawker happily scooped up and republished). A couple of days later those photos were mysteriously inaccessible again.

5   So much for social norms.

6   After those changes, ten privacy groups banded together and filed a protest with the FTC about Facebook's sudden open-book privacy policy. In response, Facebook also made a few small tweaks to restore some (but not all) of its previous privacy settings.

7   Zuckerberg's comments last week just re-ignited the Facebook privacy debate, including the inevitable responses from knuckleheads like Arrington "that privacy is already really, really dead. . . . We don't really care about privacy anymore. And Facebook is just giving us exactly what we want." (There is, however, no truth to the rumor that Zuckerberg is planning to publish nude pix of himself on his profile as part of Facebook's new "bare it and share it" campaign.)

8   It's almost always the case that people who like to say "privacy is dead, get over it," (a) have a financial interest in buying and selling personal information, and (b) guard their own personal information zealously, even if they live otherwise very public lives. For example: I'm still waiting for Arrington to share his Social Security number with the world, like the Lifelock CEO he seems to like so much, or to post pix from his vacation at that nudist colony (I'm making that last bit up—I hope). Even if he did, that doesn't mean other people should.

9   People may not give a damn about some kinds of personal information, but they care a great deal about other information. The stuff they care about just varies from person to person. In fact, it's usually the most public of us that have the greatest need for privacy. Exotic dancers may take their clothes off in public (or on MySpace), but they don't usually use their real names or broadcast their home address. Their bodies may be public, but not their identities.

10   Likewise, just because women shared their bra colors on Facebook to raise awareness of breast cancer doesn't mean they want to share that information with the marketers at Victoria's Secrets. (Facebook is not explicitly doing this, but opening up people's status updates to searches makes that possible.)

11   I think people want the ability to easily control what information is and isn't private. While Facebook offers a lot of control—you

might even say a confusing amount for most people—it's still doing its best to encourage you to share early and often. If you can't easily determine how someone wants a particular piece of information to be treated, you should assume it is private, not that they want to share it with the world. The latter is the assumption Facebook is making and Zuckerberg was defending.

12   What people really want is not what Facebook is giving us. As Read Write Web's Marshall Fitzpatrick points out, Facebook's popularity stems in part from how carefully it protected its members' information—at first limiting access to college students, then just to your networks of friends. Now it seems to have forgotten all of that, to its detriment.

13   Why? In a word, money. You can't easily monetize data that's private. The more data you can share with the world, the more revenue you can generate. Facebook isn't trying to give users what they want or to conform with "social norms." It's trying to make a buck out of each and every one of its 350 million users, over and over again. Nothing wrong with that, except perhaps how you go about it.

Jonathan Locker

OnStar: Big Brother's Eye in the Sky

Jonathan I. Locker contributed the following article to the Web site *The Truth About Cars,* which presents automotive news, reviews, and editorials. The article appeared February 14, 2008.

Ever since the Model T hit the silver screen, evading the long arm of the law has been a cinematic theme. From the General Lee locomotive outrunning Boss Hogg, to Smokey being outwitted by Burt Reynolds' mustache, the public imagination has always associated fast cars with police pursuit. While the majority of motorists would never dream of trying to outrun the long arm of the law, soon, they won't have to. It'll be resting on their shoulder.

2   Consider OnStar.

3   OnStar is a telemetry system providing a central data bank with real-time data on virtually every system in your car, including GPS. OnStar's computer knows where you were, when you were there, and how fast you went. It knows if and when you applied the brakes, if and when the air bags deployed, and what speed you were going at the time. It knows if and when your car

was serviced. OnStar operators can determine if you have a passenger in the front seat (airbag detection). All interactions with OnStar's operators are automatically recorded (hence the commercials). By the same token, under certain conditions, OnStar can switch on your GM car's microphone remotely and record any and all sounds within the vehicle (i.e., conversations).

4 But wait, there's more. As of 2009, customers who upgrade to OnStar's "Safe & Sound" plan automatically receive the "Stolen Vehicle Slowdown" service. (Yes, it's an "opt out" deal.) If the OnStar-equipped vehicle is reported stolen and law enforcement has "established a clear line of sight of the stolen vehicle," the police may ask OnStar to slow it down remotely.

5 Many customers find OnStar immensely reassuring; it's their guardian e-angel. No question: OnStar has saved lives and provided its customers with valuable services. Otherwise, they wouldn't be in business.

6 But what if the police are investigating a crime. They ask OnStar where your car was on a certain date and time, to corroborate an alibi. Or what if you're in a crash and the other guy's attorney would like to know how fast you were driving when you ran the red light? Would OnStar surrender the information? GM notes that "OnStar is required to locate the car to comply with legal requirements, including valid court orders showing probable cause in criminal investigations." And OnStar may use gathered information to "protect the rights, property, or safety of you or others."

7 Imagine the following scenario. The FBI shows up at OnStar master command and tells them your car's been stolen by a terrorist, who may be using it to commit a crime at this very moment. Contacting the owner is out of the question; the owner may also be a terrorist. What does OnStar do? They cooperate with the FBI and give them everything they've got on your car. No warrant needed and no notification to you. Hell, you may not even have the service enabled. In other words, you not only have to trust OnStar to protect your privacy, you have to trust the police not to ask the questions in the first place.

8 The Constitution of the United States protects us from the heavy hand of government. However, when it comes to protection from private entities, it does little. Into this void, multiple privacy laws have entered, creating a farrago of local, state, and federal laws which provide limited and haphazard protection to citizens. Whatever privacy protection these laws provide are usually nullified when companies violate them in "good faith" (e.g., while assisting the authorities).

9 So who is going to stop the government from monitoring your car? The Bill of Rights protects you from an unreasonable

search and seizure; the government cannot take what belongs to you without a warrant. OnStar can owns the information they collect about your car. In short, there is nothing to stop the police or OnStar from using the information you paid for against you.

10   And the next step is even more insidious. Imagine GPS speed limiters which only allow you to go the speed limit based upon a map uploaded into your car's navigation system. Now Sammy Hagar will only be driving 55 no matter how hard he stomps on the go pedal. This is the ultimate assault on piston-heads. The only place where driving will be fun will be on the track—if OnStar and/or the car's manufacturer (e.g., the Japanese GT-R) let you.

11   There's only one sensible response to this trend: boycott vehicles equipped with OnStar, even if you don't sign up for the service. (Remember: it can be remotely enabled.) If customers actively avoid vehicles that spy on them, manufacturers will have to stop installing the monitoring software and hardware. And law enforcement agencies and prosecutors will have to get their information and apprehend criminals the old-fashioned way: through legally-sanctioned police work.

12   In short, I don't buy OnStar, and neither should you.

DAHLIA **LITHWICK**

Teens, Nude Photos and the Law

Dahlia Lithwick is a contributing editor at *Newsweek* and senior editor at *Slate*, an online current affairs and culture magazine, for which she writes "Supreme Court Dispatches" and "Jurisprudence." Her work has also appeared in the *New Republic*, *ELLE*, the *New York Times*, the *Ottawa Citizen*, and the *Washington Post*. A product of Stanford University's law school, Lithwick worked for a family law firm and clerked for Judge Procter Hug on the United States Court of Appeals for the Ninth Circuit, before turning to a career as a writer. The following article appeared in *Newsweek* in February 2009.

A sk yourself: should the police be involved when tipsy teen girls e-mail their boyfriends naughty Valentine's Day pictures?

2   Say you're a middle-school principal who confiscated a cell phone from a 14-year-old boy, only to discover that it contains a nude photo of his 13-year-old girlfriend. Do you (a) call the boy's parents in despair; (b) call the girl's parents in despair; or (c) call the police? More and more, the answer is (d) all of the above. Which could

result in criminal charges for both of your students, and their eventual designation as sex offenders. "Sexting" is the clever new name for the act of sending, receiving, or forwarding naked photos via your cell phone, and I wasn't fully convinced that America was facing a sexting epidemic, as opposed to a journalists-writing-about-sexting epidemic, until I saw a new survey done by the National Campaign to Prevent Teen and Unplanned Pregnancy. One teenager in five reported having sent or posted naked photos of themselves. Whether all this reflects a new child-porn epidemic, or is just a new iteration of the old teen narcissism epidemic, remains unclear.

3   Last month, three girls (ages 14 or 15) in Greensburg, Pa., were charged with disseminating child pornography for sexting their boyfriends. The boys who received the images were charged with possession. A teenager in Indiana faces felony obscenity charges for sending a picture of his genitals to female classmates. A 15-year-old girl in Ohio and a 14-year-old girl in Michigan were charged with felonies for sending nude images of themselves to classmates. Some of these teens have pleaded guilty to lesser charges. Others have not. If convicted, these young people may have to register as sex offenders, in some cases for a decade or two. Similar charges have been brought in cases reported in Alabama, Connecticut, Florida, New Jersey, New York, Pennsylvania, Texas, Utah, and Wisconsin.

4   Want one quick clue that the criminal-justice system is probably not the best venue for addressing sexting? A survey of the charges brought in these cases reflects that—depending on the jurisdiction—prosecutors have charged the senders of smutty photos, the recipients of smutty photos, those who save the smutty photos, and the hapless forwarders of smutty photos with the same crime: child pornography. Who is the victim here? Everybody and nobody.

5   There may be an argument for police intervention in cases that involve a genuine threat or cyberbullying, such as a recent Massachusetts incident in which the picture of a naked 14-year-old girl was allegedly sent to more than 100 cell phones, or a New York case involving a group of boys who turned a nude photo of a 15-year-old girl into crude animations and PowerPoint presentations. But ask yourself whether those cases are the same as the cases in which tipsy teen girls send their boyfriends naughty Valentine's Day pictures.

6   The argument for hammering every such case seems to be that sending naked pictures might have serious consequences, so let's charge these kids with felonies, which will surely have serious consequences. In the Pennsylvania case a police captain explained that the charges were brought because "it's very dangerous. Once it's on a cell phone, that cell phone can be put on the Internet where everyone in the world can get access to that juvenile picture." The argument that we must prosecute kids as the producers and purveyors of kiddie porn because they are too dumb to understand that their seemingly innocent acts can harm them goes beyond paternalism. Child-pornography laws intended to protect children should not be used to prosecute and then label children as sex offenders. We seem to forget that kids can be as tech-savvy as Bill Gates but as gullible as Bambi. Even in the age of the Internet, young people fail to appreciate that naked pictures want to roam free.

7   The real problem with criminalizing teen sexting as a form of child pornography is that the great majority of these kids are not predators. They just think they're being brash and sexy. And while some of the reaction to sexting reflects legitimate concerns

about children as sex objects, some also perpetuates legal stereotypes and fallacies. A recent *New York Times* article quotes the Family Violence Prevention Fund, a nonprofit domestic-violence-awareness group, as saying that the sending of nude pictures, even if done voluntarily, constitutes "digital dating violence." But do we truly believe that one in five teens is participating in an act of violence? Experts insist the sexting trend hurts teen girls more than boys, fretting that they feel "pressured" to take and send naked photos. Paradoxically, the girls in the Pennsylvania case were charged with "manufacturing, disseminating, or possessing child pornography" while the boys were merely charged with possession. If the girls are the real victims, why are we treating them more harshly than the boys?

8   Judging from the sexting prosecutions in Pennsylvania, Ohio, and Indiana this year, it's clear that the criminal-justice system is too blunt an instrument to resolve a problem that reflects more about the volatile combination of teens and technology than about some national cybercrime spree. Parents need to remind their teens that a dumb moment can last a lifetime in cyberspace. But judges and prosecutors need to understand that a lifetime of cyberhumiliation shouldn't be grounds for a lifelong real criminal record.

ADAM **COHEN**

A Casualty of the Technology Revolution: "Locational Privacy"

Adam Cohen is a member of the *New York Times* editorial board; before that he was a senior writer at *Time*. Since he holds a law degree, he naturally writes on legal issues, particularly when they involve technology. Among other things, he is the author of *Nothing to Fear: FDR's Inner Circle* and *American Pharaoh: Mayor Richard J. Daley.* The editorial printed below was published by the *New York Times* in September 2009.

When I woke up the other day, I went straight to my computer to catch up on the news and to read e-mail. About 20 minutes later, I walked half a block to the gym, where I exercised for 45 minutes. I took the C train to The New York Times building, and then at the end of the day, I was back on the C train. I had dinner on my friends' (Elisabeth and Dan's) rooftop, then walked home seven blocks.

2   I'm not giving away any secrets here—nothing I did was secret to begin with. Verizon online knows when I logged on, and New York Sports Club knows when I swiped my membership card. The M.T.A. could trace (through the MetroCard I bought with a credit card) when and where I took the subway, and *The Times* knows when I used my ID to enter the building. AT&T could follow me along the way through my iPhone. There may also be videotape of my travels, given the ubiquity of surveillance cameras in New York City. There are thousands of cameras on buildings and lampposts around Manhattan, according to the New York Civil Liberties Union, many near my home and office. Several may have been in a position to film my dinner on Elisabeth and Dan's roof.

3   A little-appreciated downside of the technology revolution is that, mainly without thinking about it, we have given up "locational privacy." Even in low-tech days, our movements were not entirely private. The desk attendant at my gym might have recalled seeing me, or my colleagues might have remembered when I arrived. Now the information is collected *automatically and often stored indefinitely.*

Location-aware cell phones, iPads, and other mobile devices make it easy for anyone to track your location and movements. Privacy advocates are concerned; are you?
© 2010 Google-Map Data © Google, Sanborn

4   Privacy advocates are rightly concerned. Corporations and the government can keep track of what political meetings people attend, what bars and clubs they go to, whose homes they visit. It is the fact that people's locations are being recorded "pervasively, silently, and cheaply that we're worried about," the Electronic Frontier Foundation said in a recent report.

5   People's cellphones and E-ZPasses are increasingly being used against them in court. If your phone is on, even if you are not on a call, you may be able to be found (and perhaps picked up) at any hour of the day or night. As disturbing as it is to have your private data breached, it is worse to think that your physical location might fall into the hands of people who mean you harm.

6   This decline in locational privacy, from near-absolute to very little in just a few years, has not generated much outrage, or even discussion. That is partly because so much of it is a side-effect of technology that people like. Drivers love E-ZPasses. G.P.S. enables all sorts of cool smart phone applications, from driving directions and find-a-nearby-restaurant features to the ever-popular "Take Me to My Car."

7   And people usually do not know that they are being monitored. The transit authority does not warn buyers that their MetroCards track their subway use (or that the police have used the cards in criminal investigations). Cameras that follow people on the street are placed in locations that are hard to spot. It is difficult for cellphone users

to know precisely what information their devices are sending about their current location, when they are doing it, and where that information is going. Some privacy advocates were upset by recent reports that the Palm Pre, which has built-in G.P.S., has a feature that regularly sends its users' location back to Palm without notifying them at the time.

8   What can be done? As much as possible, location-specific information should not be collected in the first place, or not in personally identifiable form. There are many ways, as the Electronic Frontier Foundation notes, to use cryptography and anonymization to protect locational privacy. To tell you about nearby coffee shops, a cellphone application needs to know where you are. It does not need to know who you are.

9   In addition, when locational information is collected, people should be given advance notice and a chance to opt out. Data should be erased as soon as its main purpose is met. After you pay your E-ZPass bill, there is no reason for the government to keep records of your travel.

10   The idea of constantly monitoring the citizenry's movements used to conjure up images of totalitarian states. Now, technology does the surveillance—generally in the name of being helpful. It's time for a serious conversation about how much of our privacy of movement we want to give up.

ISSUE IN FOCUS

Biometrics: Measuring the Body for Identity

The 1997 film *Gattaca,* starring Ethan Hawke and Uma Thurman, features the supposedly futuristic plot of a "natural" man stealing genetic information to pose as an elite citizen—someone who was genetically engineered before birth. Using stolen biometric identifiers, Hawke's character poses as another person, but the film's final message just may be that the "natural" man still triumphs: spirit trumps technology. A more recent film, *Minority Report* (2002), starring Tom Cruise, also involves biometric technologies. Cruise's character takes someone else's retinas in order to clear his name of a crime he supposedly commits in the future. Like *Gattaca, Minority Report* employs futuristic biometric technologies that today are not entirely feasible but are no longer beyond the realm of possibility. Indeed, both films characterize the possibilities—fascinating and frightening—of biometrics that no longer belong exclusively to the realm of science fiction.

Biometrics encompasses a variety of identification strategies. You've seen them on TV shows like *CSI* and *NCIS*. Biometric devices can record physical characteristics such as irises, retinas, fingerprints, hands, knuckles, palms, veins, faces, DNA, sweat, pores, lips, odors, and voices. In addition, biometric technologies can analyze human behavior patterns such as signatures, keyboard keystroke patterns, and gaits. Some of these technologies are more advanced and more feasible than others, but the goal of biometrics is to conclusively determine individual identity and thus remove the element

Tom Cruise in *Minority Report* (2002)

of human error that comes with lost, stolen, hacked, copied, or shared passwords and tokens. Biometrics helps us bypass these pitfalls by securing data that belongs exclusively to one person—since that data is actually part of the person.

There are more everyday problems with biometrics than *CSI* and *NCIS, Gattaca,* and *Minority Report* suggest. For one thing, in large-scale uses of biometrics, there are likely to be portions of the population for whom some facets of the technology simply don't work, as well as small percentages of overlap that make identity difficult to determine. In addition to concerns about the cleanliness and safety of the machinery used to collect and measure biometric data, some detractors raise concerns about security and privacy: if biometric data are stolen, individuals can be permanently vulnerable because, unlike passwords and tokens, biometric information is difficult, if not impossible, to change. Furthermore, biometrics incites fears that individuals who protect valuable property with biometrics might be physically harmed or endangered if someone tries to steal the property. These concerns about biometrics extend beyond the cost and logistics to the ways in which we use, store, and manipulate our bodies for security's sake.

The reading selections in this section describe the range of types and uses of biometrics and argue about advantages and disadvantages that accompany this emerging technology. Because biometric recognition technologies effectively illustrate the tensions between protection and privacy, we include images and articles that dramatize the excitement and fear surrounding them.

The section opens with an article by Steven C. Bennett, a partner in a law firm who teaches a course in privacy law at Hunter College. He gives an even-handed discussion of the pros and cons of biometric technologies and goes on to argue that the biometrics industry should set standards that protect the privacy of individuals. Less even-handed is a page from the FBI Web site, which extols the benefits of these technologies. Paul Saffo, Managing Director of Foresight at Discern Analytics and teacher at Stanford, is a writer whose essays have appeared in *Fortune,* the

Harvard Business Review, the *Los Angeles Times, Newsweek,* the *New York Times,* the *Washington Post*, and *Wired*. He explains the not-so-science-fiction possibility of DNA identity theft and cautions against blind faith in biometrics. We conclude with Ben Goldacre lamenting "the biometric blues"; a physician and medical researcher in Britain, Goldacre contributes frequently to the British national newspaper the *Guardian*—especially in a regular column entitled "Bad Science."

As you read and analyze the texts and images, consider the desirability of biometrics—a technology that started as science fiction but has been studied and advanced by the U.S. military in efforts to secure the nation and catch terrorists. What about this technology captivates our imaginations in so many different ways? What balance are we willing to strike between personal privacy and national security, or even personal protection? How does biometrics alter our sense of ourselves as unique individuals—both in terms of what information we would share publicly and in terms of identity theft? These selections introduce you to a complex and significant technological advance, and they can prompt further thinking, reading, research, and writing as you enter this important contemporary debate about security and privacy.

STEVEN C. BENNETT

Privacy Implications of Biometrics

B roadly speaking, biometrics is a term for any measurement of individuals used either to identify or authenticate their claimed identity. Fingerprints and wanted posters, for example, are well-established biometric methods used by law enforcement to track down, identify, and authenticate suspects. Modern information technology has added a number of new machine-based identification techniques, such as facial scanning and recognition, and improved the older techniques. These mechanical innovations offer a host of benefits, chiefly speed, efficiency, and vast analytical power. Several nations, including the United States and most of Europe, have begun to take advantage of the security benefits of these advances by issuing passports and other forms of identification encoded with biometric information. With such benefits, however, may come significant risks to the privacy and data security rights of consumers, workers, and citizens at large. The development of "best practices" in managing the use of biometrics is essential to strike an appropriate balance, ensuring proper use of these techniques and safeguards against abuse. If industry does not develop and follow such guidelines, more stringent regulations may be imposed.

2   A prime example of both the potential benefits and the threats of rapidly evolving biometric technology appears in the use of facial scanning technology at several recent NFL Superbowls. Before the 2001 Superbowl in Tampa, over 30 closed-circuit television cameras were installed to monitor the crowd and compare images of spectators to images of known criminals. Approximately 20 matches were made, several during the game. There was a widespread outcry, including dramatic media accounts labeling the game the "Snooper Bowl," disparaging the Orwellian overtones, after this use of biometrics became public knowledge. These complaints were muted at the New Orleans Superbowl in 2002, perhaps as a consequence of the September 11th attacks. Nonetheless, the use of facial recognition technology during the Superbowl has since been abandoned.

WHAT IS BIOMETRICS?

3   Essentially, biometrics is the use of human physical characteristics as identifiers. While any trait can be used, several specific types have proven to be most useful. The three most common genres of biometric identifiers are appearance, physiography, and bio-dynamics. Physical appearance is primarily judged through the use of photographs or other still images, but can also be validated through written descriptions of an individual's height, weight, coloration, hair, and visible markings. Physiography, on the other hand, requires some form of measurement—such as fingerprints, dental measurements, optical scans of the retina or iris, hand geometry, or DNA testing. As opposed to these two static characteristics, bio-dynamics measures patterned active behavior—voice fluctuation, keystroke tendencies, manner of writing a signature, and habituated body signals such as gait.

4   To perform the task of identification or authentication, biometrics relies on the comparison of live data supplied—voluntarily or not—by the subject to a dataset or template containing pre-existing information. The prime difference between the objectives of identification and authentication lies in the scope of pre-existing information required for each task. Identification can assign a name or other value to a previously anonymous person by comparing the live data to a large number of samples, a "1:N search," to determine whether there is a match. Authentication, on the other hand, merely requires confirmation that individuals are who they claim to be. The comparison, then, is between the live data and previously supplied data from a single individual, or a "1:1 search." Both searches can either be positive or negative; they can ensure either that a person is already within the database and permitted access (positive) or, as in the Superbowl example, that a person is not within a database and therefore permitted access (negative).

5   Basic forms of biometrics are all around us. The typical driver's license or state identification card, for example, contains a photograph and some form(s) of physical description (such as height and eye color). The license often also contains a sample signature from the individual; and the individual's address. All of these, in some ways, are forms of biometrics:

- The photograph may be compared to the individual carrying the license;
- The physical characteristics described on the license may also be compared to those of the individual;
- The individual may be asked for a signature sample, and that sample compared to the license sample;
- The individual may be asked to recall (unaided) his or her address, and that answer compared to the license information.

What Is Different About Machine Biometrics?

6   Biometrics standing alone are just characteristics; they neither protect nor threaten individual privacy. As the license example suggests, the use of biometrics has been accepted and commonplace for over 100 years. It is how biometric technologies are used that determines their effect on privacy. The rise of mechanical biometric technology, especially computers and computerized databases, and the consequent automation of

the identification process have radically increased both the ability to identify individuals biometrically and the potential for abuse of biometrics. These changes extend to almost every aspect of biometrics—data capture, analysis, communication, and storage—and must be understood before analyzing their implications for privacy and data security rights of individuals.

Data Capture

7   Technological advances now allow for involuntary or unknowing capture of biometric characteristics. The Superbowl provides an example—if the security firm had chosen to store the captured images rather than merely test and destroy them, it would have created the possibility for biometric identification of all who attended the game. Even when the submission of information is voluntary, many biometrics are very difficult for a human to gather unaided. For example, scanning the retina of the human eye requires light-producing and magnification devices, and meaningful analysis of the results requires imaging and comparison technology. These techniques, however, may offer highly individualized identification when used properly. Even biometric methods that can be performed competently by humans (such as fingerprint or hand shape identification) can be greatly improved through machine operation.

Data Analysis

8   Though Moore's law of increasing computer capacity is only observational, the exponential growth of computing power has allowed for ever more rapid identification searches, even as databases expand. Fingerprinting technology provides the perfect lens through which to view this growth. Originally, fingerprinting could only be used to authenticate the identity of criminals who had left their prints at a crime scene, noting any 1:1 matches. Gradually, a classification system (the Henry system) developed, which allowed for identification searches, but these searches required significant amounts of time to perform. By 1971, the FBI possessed over 200 million paper fingerprint files, including records on 30 million criminals, and J. Edgar Hoover had unsuccessfully promoted universal fingerprinting. The true technological shift, however, came in the 1990s, when new fingerprint scanners cut the time to identify prints from months to hours.

Data Communication

9   Many forms of biometrics were impossible to communicate until recently. Before the creation of reasonably high quality photographs and copies, accurate re-creation of most biometrics via transmission was impossible. The year 1924 witnessed the first transmission of fingerprints from Australia to Scotland Yard via telegraph. Since then, modern communication has dramatically enhanced the efficiency of biometrics. Just as computational analysis has followed the predictions of Moore's law, so too the field of communications has lived up to the even more aggressive predictions of the "Photon Law"—that bandwidth will more than double every year. As bandwidth increases, more biometrics can be transmitted, and data transfer is faster. This allows for linkage of varied biometric data sets, as well as non-biometric information.

Data Storage

10 Finally, the ability to reduce biometrics to electronic datasets of relatively small size has allowed for construction of large, searchable electronic databases. As a result of the falling costs of electronic data storage and the rising ability to transmit that data rapidly across long distances, technological shifts have allowed for creation of massive inter-linked databases of biometric information. The FBI's Integrated Automated Fingerprint Identification System ("IAFIS") is the largest biometric database in the world, containing the fingerprints and related criminal history of over 47 million individuals. Remote electronic submissions for criminal inquiries can receive a response from IAFIS within two hours. The IAFIS data illustrate a final observational law of technology, Metcalfe's law, which states that the power of a network increases (exponentially, though this value is debated) as every node is added. Thus, the ability to integrate and store information from many different databases dramatically increases the value of biometric data.

THE VALUE OF MACHINE BIOMETRICS

11 The efficiency gained from mechanization of biometrics is clear. Fingerprint searches that a decade ago took three months to complete now can be completed in under two hours. Biometrics also has an intrinsic value in its ability to function as (potentially) the most effective security safeguard, restricting access to sensitive information or physical areas. To secure such access, authorization (or identity) must be validated. The rise in identity theft demonstrates the weakness of validating systems based purely on possession of particular information about the individual. These faults have caused many in business to turn to biometrics as a more secure method of identifying or authenticating individuals.

12 In response to digital hackers, many password systems now require frequent changes or the use of special symbols and non-repetitive character strings. These shifts, designed to protect security, tend instead to undermine it as users often write their passwords on a sticky note by their desks. Relying on access cards is equally problematic—such cards can be lost, stolen, or left right by the computer to which they provide access. A recent survey, moreover, found that 70 percent of Americans, in response to an unsolicited email or phone call, would share information such as an account number, or provide the answer to a security code question. A majority also indicated they would not want their accounts locked after three failed attempts to verify the identity of someone trying to gain access. More than two-thirds of respondents in this survey were open to using biometric technologies—they want technology that is as secure as it is convenient.

13 The weaknesses and security lapses in other validation mechanisms have increasingly caused industry innovators to turn to biometrics. Banco Azteca was created in 2001 by the massive Grupo Elektra, to target the previously untapped 70 percent of Mexico's population that did not use banks at all. One of the problems the new bank confronted in enrolling customers in underserved communities was the lack of any form of secure identification papers, driver's licenses, or the like. In response, the bank turned to biometrics and fingerprint scans. Over seven million Banco Azteca customers have enrolled in the biometric identification program; more than 75 percent of the bank's business comes from customers who have dealt with a bank for the first time due to this program.

HOW CAN MACHINE BIOMETRICS THREATEN PRIVACY?

14   Although biometrics techniques may provide new opportunities for security, these techniques also present the potential for abuse. Biometric information is inherently linked to individuality and functions as a unique identifier in a way that would make its loss irreplaceable. The potentially unrestrained scope of data collecting, sharing, linking, and warehousing also may invite misuse. Finally, the potential for pervasive monitoring of movement and activities may chill discourse and protest.

15   Identity theft in a biometric world may be particularly problematic. When a check is lost or stolen, one immediately requests a stop payment order. When a credit card is taken, one calls the company to freeze the account and order a new card. What does one do when biometric information is stolen? Once biometric information is reduced to electronic data, that data can be captured or altered by hackers. Hackers can then reproduce the data in a way that convinces biometric scanners that they are authorized, and thereby gain access to supposedly secure information or locations. Essentially, biometrics are the equivalent of a PIN that is impossible to change. The theft of biometric information amounts to permanent identity theft, and thus may be extremely difficult to counteract.

16   Use of biometrics also risks the problem of data creep, in which information given voluntarily to one recipient for one purpose may be transferred, without permission or knowledge, to another recipient, linked with other data, or applied to a new purpose. The average American's personal information is now available in approximately 50 different commercial databases. Linkage of such information could permit discrimination based on physical characteristics that might otherwise remain unknown.

17   Followed to its logical extreme, moreover, the linkage of digital images into a single database with facial recognition technology would permit the tracking of everyone's movements. The possibility of such tracking, however remote, epitomizes the threat that widespread use of biometrics poses for personal privacy. If an organization or government can monitor movement and actions, it could discriminate against individuals based on their associations. As anonymous behavior becomes less possible, dissent may be suppressed.

WHAT FORM OF REGULATION IS APPROPRIATE?

18   Individual autonomy is the cornerstone of the American legal and social structure. The free flow of information, however, is equally essential to a functioning democracy. The challenge of regulating biometrics lies in resolving the tension between the rights to privacy, free speech, and information security.

19   Americans generally disfavor broad government regulation of industry practices regarding personal information. Congress prefers to rely on industry self-regulation when possible. Nevertheless, the government will step in to regulate a market when the market clearly has failed to provide adequate safeguards. Notable examples of such government intervention include the Child Online Protection Act, the Graham-Leach-Bliley Act, and the Health Insurance Portability and Accountability Act. If the biometrics industry wishes to avoid potentially strict sector-specific government regulations, it must self-regulate, to harmonize the tensions between the fundamental benefits of biometrics while limiting the potential for abuse. In establishing such best practices, the industry must proceed from two basic principles: notice and security.

Notice

20 Individuals must know when data collection occurs. A notice requirement recognizes the importance of individual autonomy and enables people to choose whether to participate. Notice, however, means more than simply saying "surveillance cameras are in use," when police apply facial recognition software at the Superbowl. When any biometric system is used, there should ideally be an open statement of its scope, purpose, function, and application, including the system's potential uses. The evaluation of potential uses is beneficial because biometric systems rarely threatens abuse in themselves. The true threat to privacy comes from the mission creep permitted by latent capabilities. Biometric systems should be narrowly tailored to the job they are to perform. Participation, if at all possible, should be optional. Any change in scope once in use should have the same public disclosure, and participants should be given the option to unenroll from the system.

21 While enrolled within a system, participants should be able to access and correct their personal information contained within the system. Failure to provide for access and correction will increase error in the program and may violate privacy principles.

22 The final notice element of a good self-regulatory program is third-party oversight. Some independent oversight should be implemented to ensure conformity with "best practices," and to suggest other improvements. Periodic audits of the scope and operation of the system coupled with public disclosure of the results of the audits may provide particular deterrence against abuse.

Security

23 To ensure adequate security of biometric information requires both limits on construction of system capabilities as well as protections for data use. System operators should inform participants of the different security measures a biometric identification system will undertake.

24 Data collected should be protected by techniques such as encryption, data hashing, and the use of closed networks and secure facilities. Wireless transmissions of data, even when encrypted, should be avoided. To the extent possible, data should not be stored in a warehouse or database but rather with the individual participant, by means of an encrypted smart card. If storage is necessary, the initial collection of biometric data should be used to generate templates of authorized people and not linked to any one individual.

Government Oversight

25 If the biometrics industry establishes adequate notice and security practices, it may avoid potentially more restrictive governmental regulations. Some system of enforcement of best practice principles may be necessary. The Federal Trade Commission's power to prosecute unfair, deceptive, or fraudulent business activities may help prevent violations of security procedures or unannounced expansions of a biometric system's purview. The FTC already leads in the data protection field, having developed its own set of information practice principles.

WHAT IS THE FUTURE OF BIOMETRICS?

26 A decade ago, Bill Gates forecast that biometrics would be among "the most important IT innovations of the next several years." Technological innovation has dramatically

increased the breadth, depth, and speed with which disparate data sets can be connected and analyzed. Recent developments demonstrate the widespread growth and potential power of biometrics. Use of this technology will certainly continue to grow in the next decade. Taken on its own, biometrics is neither a friend nor a foe to privacy rights; their relationship depends on the manner in which the technology is used.

27   If the biometrics industry wishes to maintain its current flexibility and avoid overly stringent regulations, it must respond to the potential threats to privacy by formulating and adopting best practice principles, keeping in mind the essential need for notice and security. Such self-regulation in managing the use of biometrics will allow the market to strike an appropriate balance between the rights to privacy, free speech, and effective use of information technology.

PAUL SAFFO

A Trail of DNA and Data

If you're worried about privacy and identity theft, imagine this:

2   The scene: Somewhere in Washington. The date: April 3, 2020.

3   You sit steaming while the officer hops off his electric cycle and walks up to the car window. "You realize that you ran that red light again, don't you, Mr. Witherspoon?" It's no surprise that he knows your name; the intersection camera scanned your license plate and your guilty face, and matched both in the DMV database. The cop had the full scoop before you rolled to a stop.

4   "I know, I know, but the sun was in my eyes," you plead as you fumble for your driver's license.

5   "Oh, don't bother with that," the officer replies, waving off the license while squinting at his hand-held scanner. Of course. Even though the old state licensing system had been revamped back in 2014 into a "secure" national program, the new licenses had been so compromised that the street price of a phony card in Tijuana had plummeted to five euros. In frustration, law enforcement was turning to pure biometrics.

6   "Could you lick this please?" the officer asks, passing you a nanofiber blotter. You comply and then slide the blotter into the palm-sized gizmo he is holding, which reads your DNA and runs a match against a national genomic database maintained by a consortium of drug companies and credit agencies. It also checks half a dozen metabolic fractions looking for everything from drugs and alcohol to lack of sleep.

7   The officer looks at the screen, and frowns, "Okay. I'll let you off with a warning, but you really need more sleep. I also see that your retinal implants are past warranty, and your car tells me that you are six months overdue on its navigation firmware upgrade. You really need to take care of both or next time it's a ticket."

8   This creepy scenario is all too plausible. The technologies described are already being developed for industrial and medical applications, and the steadily dropping cost and size of such systems will make them affordable and practical police tools well before 2020. The resulting intrusiveness would make today's system of search warrants and wiretaps quaint anachronisms.

9   Some people find this future alluring and believe that it holds out the promise of using sophisticated ID techniques to catch everyone from careless drivers to bomb-toting terrorists in a biometric dragnet. We have already seen places such as Truro, Mass., Baton Rouge, La. and Miami ask hundreds or thousands of citizens to submit to DNA mass-testing to catch killers. Biometric devices sensing for SARS symptoms are omnipresent in Asian airports. And the first prototypes of systems that test in real time for SARS, HIV and bird flu have been deployed abroad.

10   The ubiquitous collection and use of biometric information may be inevitable, but the notion that it can deliver reliable, theft-proof evidence of identity is pure science fiction. Consider that oldest of biometric identifiers—fingerprints. Long the exclusive domain of government databases and FBI agents who dust for prints at crime scenes, fingerprints are now being used by electronic print readers on everything from ATMs to laptops. Sticking your finger on a sensor beats having to remember a password or toting an easily lost smart card.

11   But be careful what you touch, because you are leaving your identity behind every time you take a drink. A Japanese cryptographer has demonstrated how, with a bit of gummi bear gelatin, some cyanoacrylic glue, a digital camera and a bit of digital fiddling, he can easily capture a print off a glass and confect an artificial finger that foils fingerprint readers with an 80 percent success rate. Frightening as this is, at least the stunt is far less grisly than the tale, perhaps apocryphal, of some South African crooks who snipped the finger off an elderly retiree, rushed her still-warm digit down to a government ATM, stuck it on the print reader and collected the victim's pension payment. (Scanners there now gauge a finger's temperature, too.)

12   Today's biometric advances are the stuff of tomorrow's hackers and clever crooks, and anything that can be detected eventually will be counterfeited. Iris scanners are gaining in popularity in the corporate world, exploiting the fact that human iris patterns are apparently as unique as fingerprints. And unlike prints, iris images aren't left behind every time someone gets a latte at Starbucks. But hide something valuable enough behind a door protected by an iris scanner, and I guarantee that someone will figure out how to capture an iris image and transfer it to a contact lens good enough to fool the readers. And capturing your iris may not even require sticking a digital camera in your face—after all, verification requires that the representation of your iris exist as a cloud of binary bits of data somewhere in cyberspace, open to being hacked, copied, stolen and downloaded. The more complex the system, the greater the likelihood that there are flaws that crooks can exploit.

13   DNA is the gold standard of biometrics, but even DNA starts to look like fool's gold under close inspection. With a bit of discipline, one can keep a card safe or a PIN secret, but if your DNA becomes your identity, you are sharing your secret with the world every time you sneeze or touch something. The novelist Scott Turow has already written about a hapless sap framed for a murder by an angry spouse who spreads his DNA at the scene of a killing.

14   The potential for DNA identity theft is enough to make us all wear a gauze mask and keep our hands in our pockets. DNA can of course be easily copied—after all, its architecture is designed for duplication—but that is the least of its problems. Unlike a credit card number, DNA can't be retired and swapped for a new sequence if it falls

into the hands of crooks or snoops. Once your DNA identity is stolen, you live with the consequences forever.

15   This hasn't stopped innovators from using DNA as an indicator of authenticity. The artist Thomas Kinkade signs his most valuable paintings with an ink containing a bit of his DNA. (He calls it a "forgery-proof DNA Matrix signature.") We don't know how much of Tom is really in his paintings, but perhaps it's enough for forgers to duplicate the ink, as well as the distinctive brush strokes.

16   The biggest problem with DNA is that it says so much more about us than an arbitrary serial number does. Give up your Social Security number and a stranger can inspect your credit rating. But surrender your DNA and a snoop can discover your innermost genetic secrets—your ancestry, genetic defects and predispositions to certain diseases. Of course we will have strong genetic privacy laws, but those laws will allow consumers to "voluntarily" surrender their information in the course of applying for work or pleading for health care. A genetic marketplace not unlike today's consumer information business will emerge, swarming with health insurers attempting to prune out risky individuals, drug companies seeking customers and employers managing potential worker injury liability.

17   Faced with this prospect, any sensible privacy maven would conclude that DNA is too dangerous to collect, much less use for a task as unimportant as turning on a laptop or working a cash machine. But society will not be able to resist its use. The pharmaceutical industry will need our DNA to concoct customized wonder drugs that will fix everything from high cholesterol to halitosis. And crime fighters will make giving DNA information part of our civic duty and national security. Once they start collecting, the temptation to use it for other purposes will be too great.

18   Moreover, snoops won't even need a bit of actual DNA to invade our privacy because it will be so much easier to access its digital representation on any number of databanks off in cyberspace. Our Mr. Witherspoon will get junk mail about obscure medical conditions that he's never heard of because some direct marketing firm "bot" will inspect his digital DNA and discover that he has a latent disease or condition that his doctor didn't notice at his annual checkup.

19   It is tempting to conclude that Americans will rise up in revolt, but experience suggests otherwise. Americans profess a concern for privacy, but they happily reveal their deepest financial and personal secrets for a free magazine subscription or cheesy electronic trinket. So they probably will eagerly surrender their biometric identities as well, trading fingerprint IDs for frequent shopper privileges at the local supermarket and genetic data to find out how to have the cholesterol count of a teenager.

20   Biometric identity systems are inevitable, but they are no silver bullet when it comes to identity protection. The solution to identity protection lies in the hard work of implementing system-wide and nationwide technical and policy changes. Without those changes, the deployment of biometric sensors will merely increase the opportunities for snoops and thieves—and escalate the cost to ordinary citizens.

21   It's time to fix the problems in our current systems and try to anticipate the unique challenges that will accompany the expanded use of biometrics. It's the only way to keep tomorrow's crooks from stealing your fingers and face and, with them, your entire identity.

FBI

Using Technology to Catch Criminals

The FBI's enthusiasm for biometric technologies is reflected on its Web site. The page shown here was posted on December 27, 2005.

Home | Site Map | FAQs

FEDERAL BUREAU OF INVESTIGATION

Celebrating a Century 1908-2008

SEARCH

Contact Us
- Your Local FBI Office
- Overseas Offices
- Submit a Crime Tip
- Report Internet Crime
- More Contacts

Learn About Us
- Quick Facts
- What We Investigate
- Natl. Security Branch
- Information Technology
- Fingerprints & Training
- Laboratory Services
- Reports & Publications
- History
- More About Us

Get Our News
- Press Room
- E-mail Updates
- News Feeds

Be Crime Smart
- Wanted by the FBI
- More Protections

Use Our Resources
- For Law Enforcement
- For Communities
- For Researchers
- More Services

Visit Our Kids' Page

Apply for a Job

Headline Archives

USING TECHNOLOGY TO CATCH CRIMINALS
Fingerprint Database "Hits" Felons at the Border

12/27/05

A CBP officer takes a passenger's fingerprint scan to compare with the IAFIS database.

When U.S. Customs and Border Protection installed technology that can quickly check the fingerprints of illegal immigrants against the FBI's massive biometric database, its chief called the measure "absolutely critical."

"This technology helps…shed light on those with criminal backgrounds we could never have identified before," Commissioner Robert C. Bonner said in a press statement in October, a month after our Integrated Automated Fingerprint Identification System (IAFIS) became fully available in all 136 border patrol stations.

A very bright light, it turns out. Since last September, IAFIS has returned "hits" on 118,557 criminal subjects who were trying to enter this country illegally, according to Customs and Border Protection officials.

Many of the "hits"—a match of an individual's 10 fingerprints—led to arrests of dangerous criminal suspects, including:

- 460 individuals for homicide
- 155 for kidnapping
- 599 for sexual assault
- 970 for robbery
- 5,919 for assault
- 12,077 for drug-related charges

Border Patrol officials began using our biometric tool in the summer of 2001, connecting two of their facilities in San Diego to our Criminal Justice Information Services Division facility in Clarksburg, West Virginia. Congress sought the deployment to supplement the Border Patrol's 10-year-old biometric database called IDENT, which relies on matching an individual's index fingers, rather than the comprehensive 10-finger prints made by IAFIS.

With IAFIS in place, Border Patrol agents can simultaneously check IDENT's specialized databases and IAFIS's 49 million sets of prints.

Voice Verification for Transactions

VoiceVerified's patent-pending Point Service Provider (PSP) platform uses voice verification to help businesses secure remote transactions, protect consumer data, and combat identity fraud. During the verification process, a user is prompted to repeat five random numeric digits to create a voice sample that is compared to a previously enrolled voiceprint to determine a match.

Somerset, Pa.–based Somerset Trust has purchased the PSP to secure wire transfers, and the bank envisions future usage across all banking services requiring multifactor authentication. VoiceVerified is currently in discussions with several other financial institutions as banks seek to comply with the Federal Financial Institutions Examination Council's recent guidelines advocating multifactor user authentication during electronic transactions.

BEN **GOLDACRE**

Now for ID Cards—and the Biometric Blues

S ometimes just throwing a few long words about can make people think you know what you're talking about. Words like "biometric."

2   When Alistair Darling was asked if the government will ditch ID cards in the light of this week's data crack-up, he replied: "The key thing about identity cards is, of course, that information is protected by personal biometric information. The problem at present is that, because we do not have that protection, information is much more vulnerable than it should be."

3   Yes, that's the problem. We need biometric identification. Fingerprints. Iris scans. Gordon Brown says so too: "What we must ensure is that identity fraud is avoided, and the way to avoid identity fraud is to say that for passport information we will have the biometric support that is necessary."

4   Tsutomu Matsumoto is a Japanese mathematician, a cryptographer who works on security, and he decided to see if he could fool the machines which identify you by your fingerprint. This home science project costs about £20. Take a finger and make a cast with the moulding plastic sold in hobby shops. Then pour some liquid gelatin (ordinary food gelatin) into that mould and let it harden. Stick this over your finger pad: it fools fingerprint detectors about 80% of the time. The joy is, once you've fooled the machine, your fake fingerprint is made of the same stuff as fruit pastilles, so you can simply eat the evidence.

5   But what if you can't get the finger? Well, you can chop one off, of course— another risk with biometrics. But there is an easier way. Find a fingerprint on glass.

Sorry, I should have pointed out that every time you touch something, if your security systems rely on biometric ID, then you're essentially leaving your pin number on a post-it note.

6   You can make a fingerprint image on glass more visible by painting over it with some cyanoacrylate adhesive. That's a posh word for superglue. Photograph that with a digital camera. Improve the contrast in a picture editing program, print the image on to a transparency sheet, and then use that to etch the fingerprint on to a copper-plated printed circuit boar. (It sounds difficult, but you can buy a beginner's etching set for about for £10.) This gives an image with some three-dimensional relief. You can now make your gelatin fingerpad using this as a mould.

7   Should I have told you all that, or am I very naughty? Yes to both.

8   It's well known that security systems which rely on secret methods are less secure than open systems, because the greater the number of people who know about the system, the more people there are to spot holes in it, and it is important that there are no holes. If someone tells you their system is perfect and secret, that's like quacks who tell you their machine cures cancer but they can't tell you how. Open the box, quack. In fact you might sense that the whole field of biometrics and ID is rather like medical quackery: as usual, on the one hand we have snake oil salesmen promising the earth, and on the other a bunch of humanities graduates who don't understand technology, science, or even human behaviour: buying it; bigging it up; thinking it's a magic wand.

9   But it's not. Leaks occur not because of unauthorized access, and they can't be stopped with biometrics; they happen because of authorized access, often ones which are managed with contemptible, cavalier incompetence. The damaging repercussions will not be ameliorated by biometrics.

10   So will biometrics prevent ID theft? Well, it might make it more difficult for you to prove your innocence. And once your fingerprints are stolen, they are harder to replace than your pin number. But here's the final nail in the coffin. Your fingerprint data will be stored in your passport or ID card as a series of numbers, called the "minutiae template." In the new biometric passport with its wireless chip, remember, all your data can be read and decrypted with a device near you, but not touching you.

11   What good would the data be, if someone lifted it? Not much, insisted Jim Knight, the minister for schools and learners, in July: "It is not possible to recreate a fingerprint using the numbers that are stored. The algorithm generates a unique number, producing no information of any use to identity thieves." Crystal clear, Jim.

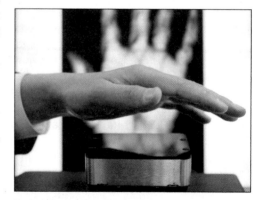

Fujitsu Computer Products of America recently launched its palm vein authentication device that captures a person's palm vein pattern and checks it against a preregistered palm vein pattern from that individual. The device offers users a high level of accuracy and security. It is in use at some of Asia's leading financial institutions.

12   Unfortunately, a team of mathematicians published a paper in April this year, showing that they could reconstruct a fingerprint from this data alone. In fact, they printed out the images they made, and then—crucially, completing the circle—used them to fool fingerprint readers.

13   Ah biometrics. Such a soothingly technical word. Repeat it to yourself.

FROM READING TO WRITING

1. Examine the outcries of biometrics critics and consider writing a rebuttal of one or more of their arguments. (Consult Chapter 12 on writing a rebuttal.)

2. In a causal argument (see Chapter 9), consider how the technological age in which we live exacerbates issues of privacy.

3. Evaluate any one of the technologies described in this chapter, on the basis of practicality and/or constitutional principles. Has this technology actually helped in the war on terrorism? Has it actually led to significant privacy violations? (See Chapter 10 for advice on evaluation.)

4. Consider popular portrayals of security technologies and biometrics (like those in *CSI* or *NCIS*). Why are these technologies so fascinating within the realm of science fiction? What qualities do these popular versions exaggerate, and why? What effect might these popular images have on viewers' opinions of real-life technologies, and why?

5. Analyze the visual images associated with this issue, building on Chapter 7 of this text. What is the nature of the arguments made in these visuals? How do they work to persuade an audience?

6. Write a narrative argument (such as the ones described in Chapter 11) that contributes to the debates represented in this chapter. How does a single incident—drawn from the news, an interview, or your own experience—contribute to this conversation? Alternatively, write a short story portraying the issue with a science fiction or futuristic slant.

27 | Regulating Substances, Regulating Bodies

Private Bodies, Public Controls

Regulation is often about deciding where lines may be crossed—and where they should not be crossed. How would we decide which burgers or fries (if any) should be regulated?

The U.S. prison population—now at 2.3 million, the Justice Department reported in 2011—has more than quadrupled since the early 1980s, which means that our nation now has the highest rate of incarceration in the world. Although only 4 percent of the world population is in the United States, the United States has a quarter of the entire world's prison population, and 1 in every 31 American adults is now in prison, on probation, or on parole. A great many of those in prison are nonviolent drug offenders, usually small-timers who need help with their own addictions. In the late 1980s, in the face of a cocaine epidemic that was ravaging the nation's cities and claiming the lives of citizens as prominent as Boston Celtics first-round draftee Len Bias, legislators and law enforcement agents cracked down by instituting mandatory minimum sentences. Because people who inform on others can often secure reduced sentences, small-time drug violators often get stiffer sentences than major dealers. According to *Newsweek,* 6 percent of inmates in state prisons in 1980 were there for drug violations; in 1996 the figure was 23 percent. In 1980, 25 percent of inmates in federal prisons were drug violators, while in 2005 the figure had risen to over 60 percent.

Should we be so hard on drug dealers and abusers? Is the state and federal governments' "war on drugs" going so poorly that it should be abandoned? Many people think so. Critics call attention not only to the figures on incarceration but also to the other social costs associated with strict drug laws. For example, many addicts resist treatment because they fear punishment; instead, they commit crimes to support their bad habits. Widespread urine testing and seizures of drug-related property have threatened basic civil rights and

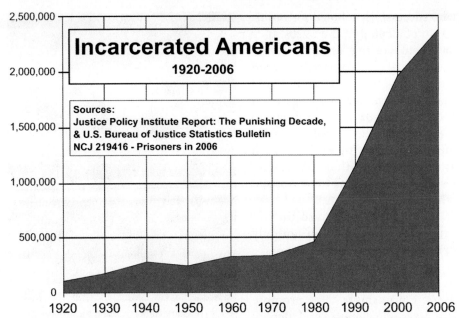

Number of inmates in U.S. prisons, 1920 to 2006. The number of inmates in U.S. prisons has more than quadrupled since the early 1980s.

undermined respect for police. Extensions of the drug war have led to conflicts with other nations where drugs are produced. Moreover, if drugs were considered a medical and social problem rather than a criminal one, citizens could be helped rather than sent to prison. Needle-exchange programs could help check the spread of AIDS by reducing the incidence of shared needles. Recognizing that illegal drugs often are no worse and no better than alcohol (legal since the disastrous 1920s experiment known as Prohibition), Californians voted to legalize marijuana use for cancer and AIDS patients. Many people, drawing from the experiences of other nations, are now calling for moves to decriminalize some kinds of drug use, or at least to reduce penalties and increase treatment. In other words, the war on drugs might be maintained—but without quite so much prison warehousing.

On the other hand, many people argue for a continuing hard line on drugs (including alcohol) because of the damage that illegal drugs do. They point to the health risks and social costs—to early deaths, lost work days, rapes and assaults and broken lives attributable to substance abuse. In the tradition of Carry Nation and other temperance warriors

> An estimated 80–100 million Americans have tried marijuana.
>
> Of every one hundred people who have smoked marijuana, twenty-eight have tried cocaine—but only one uses cocaine weekly.

who successfully lobbied for prohibition of alcohol in the 1920s, they have evidence that drug use (especially cocaine use) has decreased during the years of the war on drugs, that marijuana may be a "gateway drug" to more dangerous substances (because marijuana smokers are far more likely to try other drugs, such as cocaine), and that the war on drugs is worth waging for all sorts of other reasons.

Advocates of a hard line on drugs sometimes take on not only drug kingpins but also others—alcohol producers, Big Tobacco, performance-enhancing drug users. For example, they promote stiff taxes on cigarettes and alcohol on the grounds that making harmful substances expensive discourages use and pays for the social costs involved. And they are often proponents of testing athletes for the use of unfair and dangerous performance-enhancing substances, such as steroids (which promote muscle growth but have harmful side effects), synthetic forms of testosterone (for which 2006 Tour de France winner Floyd Landis tested positive, causing him to be stripped of his title), and creatine (a dietary supplement that many athletes feel helps their training). They point to the popularity of such substances among young people. They also work to combat binge drinking on campuses because they see it as a frightening epidemic that encourages date rape, promotes vandalism, and otherwise ruins or undermines the lives of countless college students.

Reformer Carry Nation holding the weapons of her trade: a hatchet for destroying liquor containers and a copy of the Bible

Ads featuring Joe Camel were discontinued after 1997 after complaints that the makers of Camel cigarettes were luring children into becoming smokers.

Contemporary Arguments

Should certain substances be regulated—and, if so, which ones? Is substance abuse a victimless crime that we have to live with in order to preserve a free society? Is education the only proper approach to the problem? If not, what exactly should be done about obesity—especially considering that the American Medical Association recently declared obesity a disease, about various drugs, alcohol, and tobacco, and about other controversial and harmful substances and practices? Just how should we weigh the risks of obesity and of drug and alcohol use against the costs of overzealous law enforcement and other means of social control?

The essays in this section provide a number of perspectives on public control over private bodies. Consider, for instance, the debate concerning the legalization of marijuana. Many viewpoints are possible, but here Bernadine Healy argues that the potential health risks, especially to young people, are sufficient reason to continue current policies. Where exactly should lines be drawn between personal freedom—what we choose to do with our own bodies—and government intervention on behalf of health and public safety? That question underlies other arguments about body weight and body image, controlling tobacco, and attitudes toward disability. Three items in particular take up matters related to obesity: How serious is the "obesity crisis"? What are the causes of and cures for obesity? And how should this health problem be addressed? We conclude the chapter with an Issue in Focus that has particular relevance: What, if anything, should be done to regulate excessive and dangerous alcohol consumption by college students?

When Barry Bonds hit his 756th Major League Baseball home run on August 7, 2007, he broke the all-time record held by Henry Aaron. Although Bonds has never failed an official steroid test, he has been implicated frequently in the taking of steroids, and his home run record is embroiled in controversy. Other prominent players, most famously Roger Clemens and Alex Rodriguez, also have been implicated.

Finally, consider as you read this chapter how visuals can serve to regulate bodies indirectly, both through the ideals that are presented and the concepts and values that are omitted. Photos, cartoons, ads, and other visuals in this chapter suggest that our identifications with certain body types can influence our behaviors; that argument also applies to television shows and movies.

Bernadine
Healy

Legalize Marijuana? Obama Was Right to Say No

Dr. Bernadine Healy (born 1944), a cardiologist, formerly headed the National Institutes of Health (NIH) and was once president of the American Red Cross. Currently she is health editor and columnist for *U.S. News & World Report.* The following column appeared February 4, 2009, on the *U.S. News* Web site.

Puff the Magic Dragon—in his naughtier incarnation—bit the dust when President Barack Obama recently made it clear that he is against legalizing marijuana. His message was delivered on his website, Change.gov, even before he placed his hand on the Lincoln Bible. Astonishingly, legalization of marijuana ranked as Priority No. 1 for the new administration among the thousands of possible actions voted upon on the website by the public—yes, even above stem cell research, the war in Iraq, and Wall Street bailouts. Obama's prompt no to the query "Will you consider legalizing marijuana so that the government can regulate it, tax it, put age limits on it, and create millions of new jobs and create a billion-dollar industry right here in the U.S.?" dashed the hopes of many who thought our young, hip, new president—who long ago dabbled in the stuff and, by his own admission, inhaled—would come to marijuana's rescue.

2   Listen to the president's inauguration speech, and it seems clear why he's unwilling. In a "new era of responsibility," somehow a fat new billion-dollar U.S. marijuana industry doesn't quite square with a world that almost universally outlaws the stuff. Making weed as accessible to our children as cigarettes doesn't fit with Obama's words to parents about nurturing their children, as he and Michelle so sweetly do their own little girls. And it would be the antithesis of the inaugural pledge he made to respect science.

3   Scientific research from the National Institute on Drug Abuse and elsewhere leaves little doubt that marijuana abuse is bad for brains, particularly younger ones. The psychoactive chemical in weed, THC (short for delta-9-tetrahydrocannabinol), binds to a class of receptors known as cannabinoids that are dense on neurons in brain areas associated with thinking, memory, concentration, sensation, time perception, and emotions like fear, anxiety, and pleasure. Once THC has delivered its buzz, it hangs around for days, if not many weeks, accumulating with regular use. The lingering chemical makes drug testing possible long after the last puff, and it also means that weekend joints carry a

low-grade marijuana haze into the next week, perhaps contributing to marijuana's so-called amotivational syndrome.

4   Researchers remain unsure whether the residual effects of cannabis on intellectual performance, attention span, and learning ability now identified in users (including college students) represent lingering drug, withdrawal symptoms, or toxic damage. Evidence is accumulating, however, that heavy drug use is associated with lasting damage. Just published in the journal *Pediatrics* is a preliminary study of young men who had been heavy marijuana users starting in their early teens. MRI scans showed disrupted neural development in the brain areas that influence memory, attention, and high level decision making, areas known to develop and mature during adolescence.

5   As for marijuana's association with anxiety, depression, and suicidal or even psychotic thinking, it's hard to say whether the mental disturbances are caused by the drug or are the trigger for its use in those already struggling with a mental illness. But however it's argued, academic stars are rarely potheads, and regular exposure to this powerful psychoactive drug is a nasty idea for developing young minds trying to study hard, mature emotionally, and get started in life.

6   Moreover, contrary to popular thought, NIDA stresses that marijuana can be physiologically and psychologically addictive. And Australian scientists recently reported that cannabis junkies hooked for more than 10 years develop brain injury. Compared with matched controls, users in this relatively small but provocative study scored lower on mental health and cognitive performance measures, and their MRI scans showed brain shrinkage in regions targeted by cannabis. Face it: Were the crude, dried, ground weed reviewed by the Food and Drug Administration for safety, it would flunk on its brain effects alone.

7   Yet cannabis has adverse effects on more than the brain. The heart is stressed by marijuana, which for one thing elevates serum triglycerides that bring coronary disease risk. Marijuana is a serious respiratory irritant that serves up more carcinogenic hydrocarbons than tobacco smoke. When pregnant women smoke, the drug gets into the fetus; in nursing mothers, it enters breast milk. And in the cannabis-receptor-laden testicles, there is growing evidence from the laboratory and in humans that THC causes mutant sperm, which among other things can't swim right—thus impairing male fertility, at least while the male and his sperm are under the influence.

8   Clearly, legalization of medical marijuana use is a more persuasive battle cry than that of recreational highs. The FDA has already approved synthetic THC in pill and suppository form to stimulate appetite (the marijuana "munchies") and to ease the nausea of chemotherapy in seriously ill or terminal patients. Anti-inflammatory and pain-perception benefits may be important as well.

9   All that said, the science remains immature and stymied by ideological and moral objections, at a time when there is much to be learned both about a drug that's so commonly used and about the body's own natural and still-mysterious cannabinoid receptor network. In the spirit of honoring science and an open mind, such work should be pursued—and, I might add, compassion and consideration afforded the sick and dying who use marijuana under a doctor's care.

10   As for the rest of society, arguments for legalization will rage: End the criminal underground that prohibition fosters; let adults be free to grow and smoke whatever they wish; or, lamely, pot's no worse than other—legal—vices. But as I see it, in an age of responsibility, protecting our young people's health is the stronger imperative and should rightfully keep policymakers from cozying up to this brain-toxic drug.

Oscar Pistorius, a world-class athlete who runs on J-shaped prosthetic legs, won the right to participate in the 2012 London Olympics as a member of the South African team. Yet controversy surrounding the decision did not abate. Some felt the sprinter's carbon-fiber prostheses gained him an advantage. Others simply felt Olympic athletes should rely solely on their own innate talents to compete. (Pistorius has since been charged with murdering his girlfriend.) Despite progress in eliminating barriers to full participation in society for disabled people, questions remain. How far should society go—and at what cost—to accommodate people with disabilities? And how true is the adage of disabilities advocates that "Attitudes are the real disability"?

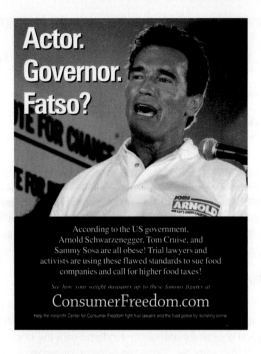

The two visual arguments on this page, produced by an organization called Consumer Freedom, ridicule the idea that American corporations might be responsible for obesity.

David
Edelstein

Up in Smoke: Give Movies with Tobacco an Automatic 'R'

David Edelstein, an occasional playwright, is a film critic for *New York* magazine and National Public Radio's *Fresh Air*, as well as an occasional commentator on *CBS Sunday Morning*. His work has also appeared in the *Village Voice*, *Rolling Stone*, *Slate*, and the *New York Times*. The following blog post appeared on *New York* magazine's Web site in January 2010 as a response to a January 5 *New York Times* article by A. O. Scott called "Movies and Vice" that concluded, "Tobacco use is part of history—of movie history in particular. And in the course of that history lighting up has acquired connotations of individualism, rebellion, sophistication and sex that will be hard to eradicate even as they become increasingly shrouded in nostalgia."

A. O. Scott's meditation on tobacco in movies is a savvy piece of hipsterism: admit that smoking is bad but argue that anti-vice cultural crusaders are worse, and end with the hope that cigarettes will someday be akin to "time travel, or slapstick, or a mad drive to the airport to stop the one you love from getting on that plane—something that only happens in the movies." Those comparisons are facetious, of course. It's unlikely we'll see time travel in our lifetime; pratfalls in the real world are involuntary; and no one has to race to the airport in an era when anti-terrorist screenings hold passengers up for hours. Smoking, on the other hand, is a choice, and one that's deeply responsive to social cues. That's why tobacco companies pay millions to studios to have glamorous actors light up and strike sultry poses. In Scott's nicotine-fueled brain he knows this, but he doesn't want to sound like a bluestocking.

2   Over the years, I've gotten a lot of e-mails from anti-smoking groups demanding either a ban on cigarettes in movies or an automatic "R" rating when a character uses tobacco. My first response is indignation at the "nanny state." I remember how, more than two decades ago, I was forbidden from mentioning smoking in a profile I did in the late *Mirabella* on Jan Hooks, who chain-smoked through our two interviews. I loved her—but I also could see by how she smoked that she was very, very high-strung. It was an important detail, except that editor Grace Mirabella's husband, Dr. William Cahan, was an anti-tobacco crusader, and no mention of cigarettes was allowed in the magazine, ever. I fought and fought and finally, *finally* Mirabella yielded—but only if I wrote something like, "Her yellow-stained fingers trembling, she nervously inserted another death stick between her brown, misshapen teeth." I was furious. I still am.

3   On the other hand, editors at a well-known music publication that same year told me that no anti-smoking references would ever

appear in their magazine: Tobacco companies paid big bucks for ads on the back cover and to sponsor the regular live-performance centerpiece. Against such vast financial resources, anti-smoking crusaders had no leverage. In the end, it was only the dread "nanny state" that could keep tobacco ads away from the young and impressionable.

4   These days, I don't believe that the anti-smoking crusaders are so out of line, at least in their demand that movies with cigarettes get an automatic "R" rating. No, that doesn't mean we expunge smoking from movies already made. We just make it tougher for new films with cigarette use to influence kids. Just as important, when tobacco companies pay to put their wares in a film, that information needs to appear in the credits— *prominently*. It's one thing when everyone lights up in *Good Night and Good Luck*, in which the ubiquitous tobacco smoke evokes the era better than anything onscreen. (Too bad there was no list at the end of all the characters' real-life counterparts who died of lung cancer or associated heart disease.) It's another when cigarettes are a product placement akin to Cheerios or Apple computers.

5   This isn't an easy call. I treasure the image of William Powell and Myrna Loy attempting to out-drink one another in *The Thin Man*—I think of it often as I order my fourth or fifth whiskey. Somewhere, I still have a poster of Cheech and Chong in *Up in Smoke*, which probably retains the aroma of the bong that sat proudly beneath it in my dorm room. And damn if Bogie and Belmondo aren't still the apogee of cool. Scott is dead right in arguing that vice in movies can be very entertaining. But for our kids' sake, let's treat the addiction to deadly chemicals *as* a vice and not as a normal, healthy part of everyday life.

6   *Update*: Some people have written to accuse me of having a double standard, and to say that, if one follows my logic, kids should no longer be exposed to drinking, overeating, brutally killing people, or anything that might corrupt our little angels. And then, of course, as one correspondent put it, "Our movies would be a little less true." I happen to believe that glamorizing the act of sucking tar and nicotine into one's lungs results in images a lot less true than, say, skeletal lung-cancer patients dissolving from the inside out in an Intensive Care Unit. But let's leave that aside. I'm not arguing that smoking should be banned from movies or *always* associated onscreen with delinquency or death. I enjoy movies about people doing things that might not be good for them, whether it's lighting up or shooting up or crashing cars or screwing sheep. Let's have a cinema for grown-ups that depicts anything and everything, healthy and unhealthy. But let's also keep tobacco companies and the greedheads who take their money from bombarding kids with the message that smoking is what cool people do.

Tony Newman

Criminalizing Smoking Is Not the Answer: Bans on Cloves and Outdoor Smoking Will Backfire!

Tony Newman is the director of media relations at the Drug Policy Alliance Network, which promotes policy alternatives to the War on Drugs. Before joining the organization, he was media director for the human rights organization Global Exchange and cofounded the public relations firm Communication Works. The following article appeared in September 2009 on the *Huffington Post*, an Internet newspaper known for a slightly left-of-center political stance.

The war on cigarettes is heating up. This week a new federal ban went into effect making flavored cigarettes and cloves illegal. The new regulation halted the sale of vanilla and chocolate cigarettes that anti-smoking advocates claim lure young people into smoking. This ban is the first major crackdown since Congress passed a law in June giving the Food and Drug Administration the authority to regulate tobacco. There is already talk of banning Menthol cigarettes next.

2   Meanwhile, another major initiative to limit smoking wafted out of New York City last week. A report to Mayor Michael Bloomberg from the city's Health Commissioner called for a smoking ban at city parks and beaches to help protect citizens from the harms of second hand smoke. To his credit, Bloomberg rejected this measure citing concern over stretched city and police resources.

3   While I support many restrictions on public smoking, such as at restaurants and workplaces, and I appreciate public education campaigns and efforts aimed at discouraging young people from smoking, I believe the outdoor smoking ban and prohibition of cloves and possibly Menthols will lead to harmful and unintended consequences. All we have to do is look at the criminalization of other drugs, such as marijuana, to see some of the potential pitfalls and tragedies.

4   Cities across the country—from New York to Santa Cruz, California—are considering or have already banned smoking at parks and beaches. I am afraid that issuing tickets to people for smoking outdoors could easily be abused by overzealous law enforcement.

5   Let's look at how New York handles another "decriminalized" drug in our state, marijuana. Despite decriminalizing marijuana more than 30 years ago, New York is the marijuana arrest capital of the world. If possession of marijuana is supposed to be decriminalized in New York, how does this happen? Often it's because, in the course of interacting with the police, individuals are

asked to empty their pockets, which results in the pot being "open to public view"—which is, technically, a crime.

6   More than 40,000 people were arrested in New York City last year for marijuana possession, and 87 percent of those arrested were black or Latino, despite equal rates of marijuana use among whites. The fact is that blacks and Latinos are arrested for pot at much higher rates in part because officers make stop-and-frisk searches disproportionately in black, Latino and low-income neighborhoods.

7   Unfortunately, when we make laws and place restrictions on both legal and illegal drugs, people of color are usually the ones busted. Drug use may not discriminate, but our drug policies and enforcement do.

8   Now let's look at the prohibition of cloves and other flavored cigarettes. When we prohibit certain drugs, it doesn't mean that the drugs go away and people don't use them; it just means that people get their drugs from the black market instead of a store or deli. We've been waging a war on marijuana and other drugs for decades, but you can still find marijuana and your drug of choice in most neighborhoods and cities in this country.

9   For many people, cloves or Menthols are their smoke of choice. I have no doubt that someone is going to step in to meet this demand. What do we propose doing to the people who are caught selling illegal cigarettes on the street? Are cops going to have to expend limited resources to enforce this ban? Are we going to arrest and lock up people who are selling the illegal cigarettes? Prisons are already bursting at the seams (thanks to the drug laws) in states across the country. Are we going to waste more taxpayer money on incarceration?

10   The prohibition of flavored cigarettes also moves us another step closer to total cigarette prohibition. But with all the good intentions in the world, outlawing cigarettes would be just as disastrous as the prohibition of other drugs. After all, people would still smoke, just as they still use other drugs that are prohibited, from marijuana to cocaine. But now, in addition to the harm of smoking, we would find a whole range of "collateral consequences," such as black market-related violence, that crop up with prohibition.

11   Although we should celebrate our success curbing cigarette smoking and continue to encourage people to cut back or give up cigarettes, let's not get carried away and think that criminalizing smoking is the answer.

12   We need to realize that drugs, from cigarettes to marijuana to alcohol, will always be consumed, whether they are legal or illegal. Although drugs have health consequences and dangers, making them illegal—and keeping them illegal—will only bring additional death and suffering.

A great many ads are distributed these days in an effort to discourage smoking. This ad was created in 2012 by the New York State Department of Health. What kind of audience is it designed to influence?

Garry Trudeau (born 1948) won the Pulitzer Prize in 1975 for his comic strip *Doonesbury*. The strip published here appeared in January 2002.

Jordan Rubin

Beware of Saturday Morning Cartoons

Jordan Rubin, who has made a career out of advocating for healthier nutrition, gained his inspiration from biblical texts. Host of a weekly television show, motivational speaker, writer, and entrepreneur, he founded Garden of Life, a health and wellness company that distributes natural foods, healthy supplements, and educational materials. In 2004 he published *The Maker's Diet* (also known as "the Bible diet"), and he has written many other books and articles promoting his views on healthy nutrition. The following article appeared in 2011 as a blog entry on the Web site *Raw Vitamins*, which offers advice about healthy nutrition, especially natural and organic foods.

The influence of media is nothing new, and most of us could not imagine life without today's technology. There's a down side, though, and perhaps the greatest negative impact is that the media is used to market unhealthy foods, drinks, and lifestyles to our kids. Case in point: 70 percent of polled six-to-eight-year-olds who watch a lot of television believe that fast foods are more nutritious than healthy, home-cooked foods.

2   It's no wonder kids think that way. Studies show that ads targeted to kids 12 and under lead them to request and consume high-calorie, low-nutrient products such as soft drinks, sweets, salty snacks, and fast food—adding up to more than one-third of their daily calories. Our kids are listening, watching, and believing the ads—and getting fat in the process. According to the Centers for Disease Control (CDC), the proportion of overweight children ages 6–11 has more than doubled, and the rate for adolescents has tripled since 1980. This development often sets them up for a lifetime of being overweight since around 80 percent of overweight adolescents become obese adults.

3   Looking back, it all began in the 1960s when marketers targeted children as a separate demographic category, prompting advertisers to move on this lucrative new market. In the 1970s, children were viewing an average of 20,000 TV commercials a year. By the late 1970s, research indicated that children could not distinguish between television programs and commercials, and they had little to no understanding of ads' persuasive intentions—making them especially vulnerable to ads' claims and appeals. In 1978, the Federal Trade Commission attempted to ban TV commercials aimed at youngsters—to no avail.

4   When cable channels exploded in the 1990s, opportunities to advertise directly to children expanded as well. Estimates now indicate that children spend an average of five-and-one-half hours a day using media (television, the Internet, radio, etc.) and see or hear an average of over 40,000 TV commercials a year.

5   Marketing junk to kids has worked. In 1997 alone, kids aged 7–12 spent $2.3 billion (and teenagers spent a whopping $58 billion) of discretionary money on snacks and beverages—mostly unhealthy, high-fat, high-sugar ones. The sad truth is that advertising likely has more influence on what kids eat and

drink than parents or schools do. Despite attempts at limiting or disallowing advertisements directly to children, the trend of marketing junk to kids has gained momentum as the modes of marketing have diversified and intensified. One advertising executive summed up their tactics in this manner: "You've got to reach kids throughout the day—in school, as they're shopping in the mall . . . or at the movies. You've got to become part of the fabric of their lives."

6   That's exactly what has happened. Advertising has infiltrated our kids' lives even in supposedly "controlled" environments: at home (through television, the Internet, video games, etc.); at the movies (highlighting unhealthy branded foods in so-called "product placements"); at school (via piped-in advertising through programs such as Channel One, field trips, and others); and even on the way to school (via advertising on the outside and inside of buses, plus listening to BusRadio), directly impacting what our kids eat, drink, do and how much weight they gain.

7   Not surprisingly, there are direct correlations between the amount of time a child spends in front of screen media and the risk and degree of obesity. For every hour a child watches TV or plays video games, the risk of obesity can double. Watching TV and playing video games also slows down metabolism—burning fewer calories than reading does and almost as few as sleeping does.

8   Companies also pay a lot of money to place their products in movies. Branded foods (mostly soda, followed by candy, chips, and pretzels) average about one to two in a typical movie. And this is only in the movie itself; it does not include all the junk food advertisements prior to the start of the featured flick.

9   Additionally, many school districts struggle to make ends meet and some have come up with a creative way to do so—advertising on school buses. While not all ads are for sugary soft drinks, fast food, or unhealthy snacks, some are, and the buses provide a captive audience to influence our kids' eating and lifestyle habits.

10   So what can be done? We need to talk to our kids and tell them (and model for them) what healthy eating and living is—and why. If we don't get to our kids first, the marketers and advertisers sure won't mind telling them what to buy, eat, and do.

JEFFREY FRIEDMAN

The Real Cause of Obesity

Jeffrey Friedman (born 1954), a physician and molecular geneticist who works at Rockefeller University in New York City, has done important research on the role of hormones in regulating body weight. In the following essay, which appeared September 9, 2009, in the *Daily Beast* (an online publication associated with *Newsweek*), he claims that obesity is mostly the result of genetics, not personal choice or weakness.

Despite receiving a MacArthur genius award for her work in Alabama "forging an inspiring model of compassionate and effective medical care in one of the most underserved regions of the United States," Regina Benjamin's qualifications to be surgeon general have been questioned. Why? She is overweight. "It tends to undermine her credibility," Dr. Marcia Angell, former editor of *The New England Journal of Medicine,* said in an interview with ABC News. "I do think at a time when a lot of public-health concern is about the national epidemic of obesity, having a surgeon general who is noticeably overweight raises questions in people's minds."

2   It is not enough, it seems, that the obese must suffer the medical consequences of their weight, consequences that include diabetes, heart disease, and cancer, and that cause nearly 300,000 deaths in the United States each year. They must also suffer the opprobrium heaped on them by people like Angell or Rep. James Sensenbrenner (R-WI), who has advised the obese to "Look in the mirror because you are the one to blame." In our society, perhaps no group is more stigmatized than the obese.

3   The abuse is nothing new, of course. Four hundred years ago, Shakespeare had Prince Hal hurl a barrage of insults at Falstaff, calling him "fat-witted," "horseback-breaker," and a "huge hill of flesh." But Shakespeare had an excuse. In his time essentially nothing was known about the real reasons that people are fat. Today we have no such excuse. Modern medical science has gone a long way toward explaining the causes of obesity, and the bottom line is clear: obesity is not a personal choice. The obese are so primarily as a result of their genes.

4   Genetic studies have shown that the particular set of weight-regulating genes that a person has is by far the most important factor in determining how much that person will weigh. The heritability of obesity—a measure of how much obesity is due to genes versus other factors—is about the same as the heritability of height. It's even greater than that for many conditions that people accept as having a genetic basis, including heart disease, breast cancer, and schizophrenia. As nutrition has improved over the past 200 years, Americans have gotten much taller on average, but it is still the genes that determine who is tall or short today. The same is true for weight. Although our high-calorie, sedentary lifestyle contributes to the approximately 10-pound average weight gain of Americans compared to the recent past, some people are more severely affected by this lifestyle than others. That's because they have inherited genes that increase their predisposition for accumulating body fat. Our modern lifestyle is thus a necessary, but not a sufficient, condition for the high prevalence of obesity in our population.

5   Over the past decade, scientists have identified many of the genes that regulate body weight and have proved that in some instances, different variants of these genes can lead a person to be fat or thin. These genes underlie a weight-regulating system that is remarkably precise. The average person takes in a million or more calories per year, maintaining within a narrow range over the course of decades. This implies that the body balances calorie consumption with calorie expenditure, and does with a precision greater than 99.5 percent. Even the most vigilant calorie counter couldn't compete, if for no other reason than that the calorie counts on food labels are often off by 10 percent or more.

6   The genes that control food intake and metabolism act to keep weight in a stable range by creating a biological force that resists weight change in either direction. When weight is gained, hunger is reduced. When weight is lost, the unconscious drive to eat is stimulated and acts to return weight to the starting point. Moreover, the greater the amount of weight that is lost, the greater the sense of hunger that develops. Thus, when the obese lose large amounts of weight by conscious effort, their bodies fight back even more strongly by increasing hunger and reducing energy expenditure. If you think it is hard to lose 10 to 20 pounds (and it is), try to imagine what it would feel like to lose many tens or even hundreds of pounds.

7   Anyone who doubts the power of this biologic system should study the case of a young boy in England a few years back. He had a mutation in a critical gene, the one that produces the hormone leptin. Leptin is made by fat tissue and sends a signal informing the brain that there are adequate stores of energy. When leptin drops, appetite increases. Because of a genetic error, this boy could not make this hormone, which left him ravenously hungry all of the time. At age 4 he ate 1,125 calories at a single meal—about half of what a normal adult eats in an entire day. As a result he already weighed 90 pounds and was well on his way to developing diabetes. At the time, his similarly affected cousin was 8 and weighed 200 pounds. After a few leptin injections, the boy's calorie intake dropped to 180 calories per meal, and by the time he was 6 his weight had dropped into the normal range. Nothing changed except the hormone levels: his parents weren't more or less permissive, his snacks did not switch from processed to organic, his willpower was not bolstered. Rather this boy was a victim of a malfunctioning weight-regulating system that led to an uncontrollable drive to eat. This example illustrates that feeding behavior is a basic drive, similar to thirst and other life-sustaining drives. The key role of leptin and other molecules to control feeding behavior undercuts the common misconception that food intake is largely under voluntary control.

8   While mutations in the leptin gene like the cases described above are rare, nearly 10 percent of morbidly obese individuals carry defects in genes that regulate food intake, metabolism, and body weight. The evidence further indicates that the rest of the obese population carries genetic alterations in other, as yet unidentified, single genes or combinations of genes (polygenes) interacting with environmental factors.

9   So if you are thin, it might be more appropriate for you to thank your own "lean" genes and refrain from stigmatizing the obese. A broad acceptance of the biologic basis of obesity would not only be fair and right, but would also allow us to collectively

The Nanny

You only thought you lived in the land of the free.

Bye Bye Venti

Nanny Bloomberg has taken his strange obsession with what you eat one step further. He now wants to make it illegal to serve "sugary drinks" bigger than 16 oz. What's next? Limits on the width of a pizza slice, size of a hamburger or amount of cream cheese on your bagel?

New Yorkers need a Mayor, not a Nanny.
Find out more at ConsumerFreedom.com

In May 2012, New York City's mayor, Michael Bloomberg, proposed banning the sale of super-sized sugary drinks—those larger than 16 fluid ounces—in movie theaters, fast-food restaurants, and sports arenas. Grocery stores would be exempt from the ban. Supporters praised the mayor's aggressive stance, agreeing that excessive consumption of sugary drinks promotes obesity. However, one industry group said sodas have been unfairly targeted while the complex causes of obesity remain unaddressed. Still others see the move as interfering with personal freedom. In the end, the ban, though approved by the city's Department of Health, was struck down by the courts. Do the human and monetary costs of obesity-related illnesses such as diabetes justify government regulation? What do these two images—the Consumer Freedom ad (above) and an exhibit at a Department of Health press conference (opposite)—say about how far society should go in regulating people's personal lives to benefit society in general?

64 ounces
780 calories
217g sugar

focus on what is most important—one's health rather than one's weight. There is no evidence that obese individuals need to "normalize" their weight to reap health benefits. In fact, it is not even clear whether there are enduring health benefits to weight loss among obese individuals who do not suffer from diabetes, heart disease, hypertension, or liver disease. What is known is that the obese who do suffer from these conditions receive a disproportionately large benefit from even modest weight loss, which together with exercise and a heart-healthy diet can go a long way toward improving health.

10   While research into the biologic system that controls weight is moving toward the development of effective therapies for obesity, we are not there yet. In the meantime we must change our attitudes toward the obese and focus less on appearance and more on health. In their efforts to lose weight they are fighting against their biology. But they also are fighting against a society that wrongly believes that obesity is a personal failing.

ISSUE IN FOCUS

Drinking on College Campuses

You know what The Problem is: On college campuses across the United States, excessive alcohol consumption is causing all kinds of trouble—deaths and serious illnesses related to alcohol poisoning (the result of "binge drinking"); property damage, personal violence, and other crimes; unwanted pregnancies and sexual assaults; academic failures and family breakups and long-term career setbacks. Some statistics dramatize the extent of the damage: A 2009 study conducted by the National Institute on Alcohol Abuse and Alcoholism (NIAAA) found that at least 1,825 drinking-related accidental deaths had occurred among 18- to 24-year-old students in 2005, up from 1,440 in 1998. The proportion of students who report that they had engaged in a recent episode of binge drinking is now at 45 percent. Almost 30 percent of students are saying that they have driven while under the influence of alcohol at least once in the past year. The Harvard School of Public Health estimates that 44 percent of college students are heavy drinkers, and it appears that alcohol abuse is responsible for over half a million injuries each year—not to mention any number of suicides or attempted suicides. NIAAA estimates that 696,000 students between the ages of 18 and 24 are assaulted by another student who has been drinking, and 97,000 students are victims of alcohol-related sexual assault or date rape. (For further details, check the federal government's *College Drinking Prevention* Web site.)

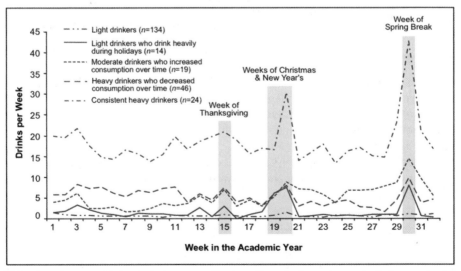

This chart shows trends in alcohol consumption by college freshmen by weeks in the academic year.

But what to do about it? That's not so easy to discern. Over the years, universities and partner organizations have developed a wide variety of programs aimed at decreasing the rates of dangerous drinking on college campuses. You have experienced most of them firsthand. Some focus on individuals—such as emphasizing personal responsibility and counseling students with identified drinking problems through Alcohol Awareness Weeks, programs during freshman orientation, or required coursework. Other solutions are centered on creating a safer community through the involvement of campus life personnel, residence hall programs, local law enforcement, and neighboring residents: some campuses ban alcohol in dormitories or offer alcohol-free entertainment options; others have tried vigorous enforcement of alcohol sales and consumption laws; and many others are cracking down on drinking in fraternities.

But nothing seems to be working very well. In 1984 President Ronald Reagan signed into law the Uniform Drinking Age Act, which penalized states that did not raise their legal drinking age to 21. By 1988, therefore, all fifty states had modified their laws to reflect this federal legislation. Because of this legislation and because of persistent public advocacy by Mothers Against Drunk Driving (MADD) and other organizations, alcohol-related traffic accidents and arrests for underage drinking have decreased substantially in the general population.

Nevertheless, is it wise to criminalize alcohol consumption by those under the age of 21? Are healthy long-term drinking habits promoted when the age limit is 21? Is zero tolerance the best approach? Is the experience of other nations, most of whom have lower legal drinking ages, relevant here? When the legal drinking age was set at 21, many say, colleges became the enforcers of the law. That enforcement subsequently drove drinking out of quads, dorms, and fraternities and into off-campus hiding places where students get smashed before going out on the town or to tailgates or to other places where drinking is policed. In 2009 a group of college presidents began a campaign to reexamine the drinking age. Dubbed "The Amethyst Initiative," after a gemstone that is said to ward off intoxication, the initiative by the presidents has been vigorously supported (e.g., by presidents at Duke, Ohio State, Dartmouth, Johns Hopkins) and loudly opposed (e.g., by MADD, by many other college presidents, and by the International Association of Chiefs of Police).

In the Issue in Focus selections that follow, John M. McCardell presents the case for experimenting with a lower drinking age; he is the former president of Middlebury College as well as the founder and president of Choose Responsibility, a nonprofit organization that seeks to engage the public in the debate over the appropriate drinking age. Published on CNN.com in September 2009, McCardell's essay is supported by the next argument, by physician Morris Chafetz, who founded the National Institute for Alcoholism and Alcohol Abuse in 1970 and who argued in the *Huffington Post* in August 2009 that laws setting the minimum drinking age of 21 are ineffective and should be repealed. Chafetz first gained national recognition at the 1984 White House Conference for a Drug-Free America, at which the Uniform Drinking Age Act was signed into law.

Many college campuses have a culture of binge drinking. What factors explain the pattern of drinking that prevails at your school?

Jeffrey Keacher/Nesota LLC

Then we offer an argument in support of the 21-year-old drinking age. In a commentary published on CNN.com in September 2009, several distinguished health professionals (led by Toben F. Nelson and Traci Toomey) contend that placing the minimum drinking age at 21 has played a pivotal role in reducing alcohol-related deaths. Finally, we conclude this Issue in Focus with a piece by writer James Hibberd, who critiques how large beer manufacturers swell sales by enlisting a corps of "campus representatives." Entitled "Barhopping with the Bud Girls," Hibbard's piece appeared on Salon.com in February 1999. It invites you to go beyond the debate about the legal drinking age to ponder how mixed messages about alcohol permeate college environments, and how you yourself feel about drinking on campus. What is the situation at your college or university? What is being done about it, and what might be done?

John McCardell | A Drinking Age of 21 Doesn't Work

In 2008, a group of college and university presidents and chancellors, eventually totaling 135, issued a statement that garnered national attention.

2   The "Amethyst Initiative" put a debate proposition before the public—"Resolved: That the 21-year-old drinking age is not working." It offered, in much the way that a grand jury performs its duties, sufficient evidence for putting the proposition to the test. It invited informed and dispassionate public debate, and committed the signatory institutions to encouraging that debate. And it called on elected officials not to continue assuming that, after 25 years, the status quo could not be challenged or even improved.

3   One year later, the drinking age debate continues, and new research reinforces the presidential impulse. Just this summer a study published in *the Journal of the American Academy of Child and Adolescent Psychiatry* revealed that, among college-age males, binge drinking is unchanged from its levels of 1979; that among non-college women it has increased by 20 percent; and that among college women it has increased by 40 percent.

4   Remarkably, the counterintuitive conclusion drawn by the investigators, and accepted uncritically by the media, including editorials in *The New York Times* and *The Washington Post*, is that the study proves that raising the drinking age to 21 has been a success.

5   More recently, a study of binge drinking published in the *Journal of the American Medical Association* announced that "despite efforts at prevention, the prevalence of binge drinking among college students is continuing to rise, and so are the harms associated with it." Worse still, a related study has shown that habits formed at 18 die hard: "For each year studied, a greater percentage of 21- to 24-year-olds [those who were of course once 18, 19 and 20] engaged in binge drinking and driving under the influence of alcohol."

6   Yet in the face of mounting evidence that those young adults (age 18 to 20 toward whom the drinking age law has been directed) are routinely—indeed in life- and health-threatening ways—violating it, there remains a belief in the land that a minimum drinking age of 21 has been a "success." And elected officials are periodically reminded of a provision in the 1984 law that continues to stifle any serious public debate in our country's state legislative chambers: Any state that sets its drinking age lower than 21 forfeits 10 percent of its annual federal highway appropriation.

7   But it's not 1984 anymore.

8   This statement may seem obvious, but not necessarily. In 1984 Congress passed and the president signed the National Minimum Drinking Age Act. The Act, which raised the drinking age to 21 under threat of highway fund withholding, sought to address the problem of drunken driving fatalities. And indeed, that problem was serious. States that lowered their ages during the 1970s and did nothing else to prepare young adults to make responsible decisions about alcohol witnessed an alarming increase in alcohol-related traffic fatalities. It was as though the driving age were lowered but no driver's education was provided. The results were predictable.

9   Now, 25 years later, we are in a much different, and better, place. Thanks to the effective public advocacy of organizations like Mothers Against Drunk Driving, we are far more aware of the

risks of drinking and driving. Automobiles are much safer. Seatbelts and airbags are mandatory. The "designated driver" is now a part of our vocabulary. And more and more states are mandating ignition interlocks for first-time DUI offenders, perhaps the most effective way to get drunken drivers off the road.

10   And the statistics are encouraging. Alcohol-related fatalities have declined over the last 25 years. Better still, they have declined in all age groups, though the greatest number of deaths still occurs at age 21, followed by 22 and 23. We are well on the way to solving a problem that vexed us 25 years ago.

11   The problem today is different. The problem today is reckless, goal-oriented alcohol consumption that all too often takes place in clandestine locations, where enforcement has proven frustratingly difficult. Alcohol consumption among young adults is not taking place in public places or public view or in the presence of other adults who might help model responsible behavior. But we know it is taking place.

12   If not in public, then where? The college presidents who signed the Amethyst Initiative know where. It happens in "pregame" sessions in locked dorm rooms where students take multiple shots of hard alcohol in rapid succession, before going to a social event where alcohol is not served. It happens in off-campus apartments beyond college boundaries and thus beyond the presidents' authority; and it happens in remote fields to which young adults must drive.

13   And the Amethyst presidents know the deadly result: Of the 5,000 lives lost to alcohol each year by those under 21, more than 60 percent are lost *off* the roadways, according to the National Institute of Alcoholism and Alcohol Abuse. The principal problem of 2009 is not drunken driving. The principal problem of 2009 is clandestine binge drinking.

14   That is why the Amethyst presidents believe a public debate is so urgent. The law does not say drink responsibly or drink in moderation. It says don't drink. To those affected by it, those who in the eyes of the law are in every other respect legal adults, it is Prohibition. And it is incomprehensible.

15   The principal impediment to public debate is the 10 percent highway penalty. That penalty should be waived for those states that choose to try something different, which may turn out to be something better. But merely adjusting the age—up or down—is not really the way to make a change.

16   We should prepare young adults to make responsible decisions about alcohol in the same way we prepare them to operate a motor vehicle: by first educating and then licensing, and permitting them to exercise the full privileges of adulthood so long as

they demonstrate their ability to observe the law. Licensing would work like driver's education—it would involve a permit, perhaps graduated, allowing the holder the privilege of purchasing, possessing, and consuming alcohol, as each state determined, so long as the holder had passed an alcohol education course and observed the alcohol laws of the issuing state.

17   Most of the rest of the world has come out in a different place on the drinking age. The United States is one of only four countries—the others are Indonesia, Mongolia and Palau—with an age as high as 21. All others either have no minimum age or have a lower age, generally 18, with some at 16. Young adults know that. And, in their heart of hearts, they also know that a law perceived as unjust, a law routinely violated, can over time breed disrespect for law in general.

18   Slowly but surely we may be seeing a change in attitude. This summer, Dr. Morris Chafetz, a distinguished psychiatrist, a member of the presidential commission that recommended raising the drinking age, and the founder of the National Institute for Alcoholism and Alcohol Abuse, admitted that supporting the higher drinking age is "the most regrettable decision of my entire professional career." This remarkable statement did not receive the attention it merited.

19   Alcohol is a reality in the lives of young adults. We can either try to change the reality—which has been our principal focus since 1984, by imposing Prohibition on young adults 18 to 20—or we can create the safest possible environment for the reality.

20   A drinking age minimum of 21 has not changed the reality. It's time to try something different.

21   It's not 1984 anymore.

Morris E. Chafetz

The 21-Year-Old Drinking Age: I Voted for It; It Doesn't Work

In 1982 I accepted appointment to the Presidential Commission on Drunk Driving and agreed to chair its Education and Prevention Committee. The Commission met over the next 18 months and ultimately advanced 39 recommendations to President Reagan, in December 1983. All 39 received unanimous Commission approval.

2   The most conspicuous of those recommendations, and arguably the most controversial, called for raising the minimum legal drinking age to 21 nationwide. I will admit to having had serious reservations about this particular proposal. But in the interest of maintaining unanimity, I reluctantly voted yes. It is the single most regrettable decision of my entire professional career.

3   Legal Age 21 has not worked. To be sure, drunk driving fatalities are lower now than they were in 1982. But they are lower in all age groups. And they have declined just as much in Canada, where the age is 18 or 19, as they have in the United States.

4   It has been argued that "science" convincingly shows a cause-and-effect relationship between the law and the reduction in fatalities. Complicated mathematical formulas, which include subjective estimations (called "imputation") have been devised to demonstrate "proof." But correlation is not cause. We must neither confuse numbers with science nor interpret a lack of numbers as implying an absence of science.

5   But even if we concede that the law has had some effect on our highways, we cannot overlook its collateral, off-road damage. The National Institute for Alcoholism and Alcohol Abuse, which I founded in 1970, estimates that 5,000 lives are lost to alcohol each year by those under 21. More than 3,000 of those fatalities occur off our roadways. If we are seriously to measure the effects of this law, we cannot limit our focus.

6   And if we broaden our look, we see a serious problem of reckless, goal-oriented, drinking to get drunk. Those at whom the law is directed disobey it routinely. Enforcement is frustratingly difficult and usually forces the behavior deeper underground, into places where life and health are put at ever greater risk. The 600,000 assaults reported annually, the date rapes, the property damage, the emergency room calls do not in general occur in places visible to the public. They are the inevitable result of what happens when laws do not reflect social or cultural reality.

7   The reality is that at age 18 in this country, one is a legal adult. Young people view 21 as utterly arbitrary—which it is. And because the explanation given them is so condescending—that they lack maturity and judgment, these same people who can serve on juries and sign contracts and who turned out in overwhelming numbers to elect our first black president—well, they don't buy it.

8   And neither do I. And neither should the American public.

9   Whether we like it or not, alcohol is woven into the fabric of our world, most of which has determined that the legal drinking age should be 18—or lower. And so far as I can tell, there is no evidence of massive brain impairment, alcohol dependency,

or underage alcohol abuse, which the "experts" tell us will be the inevitable result of lowering the age in the United States. It is time to liberate ourselves from the tyranny of "experts," who invoke "science" in order to advance a prohibitionist agenda. Prohibition does not work. It has never worked. It is not working among 18-20 year-olds now.

10   The cult of expertise has made parents feel incapable of raising their children. In many states parents are disenfranchised from helping their sons or daughters learn about responsible alcohol consumption. But as a parent and psychiatrist I trust the instinct of parents more than I do the hubris of "experts."

11   Despite what these latter-day prohibitionists may think, the problem is not the drink—it is the drinker. There should be more emphasis on the person and the surroundings in which alcohol is consumed and less emphasis on alcohol itself. Personal and social responsibility, not the substance, is the real issue. But so long as the age remains a one-size-fits-all, federally mandated 21, and so long as any state that may want to try something different, in hopes of reversing the dismal trend of binge-drinking that (maybe or maybe not coincidentally) has become more serious in the years since the drinking age was raised, forfeits 10% of its federal highway funds, nothing is likely to change for the better.

12   I do not believe that any state should be forced to adjust its drinking age. But I do believe that the genius of federalism should be allowed to work its will unimpeded, and from that genius, not only better practices, but also safer environments and more responsible consumption, are likely to emerge.

Toben F. Nelson, Traci L. Toomey, and co-authors

The Drinking Age of 21 Saves Lives

The national policy that set a minimum legal drinking age of 21 is being questioned by a group of 135 college and university presidents through an effort called the Amethyst Initiative. In a September 16 commentary on CNN.com, Amethyst Initiative leader John McCardell, a former president of Middlebury College, proposes lowering the drinking age, which he suggests will lead to less drinking and related problems among college students.

2   But history and a comprehensive review of the research tell a much different story. The evidence is clear, consistent, and compelling: A drinking age of 21 has led to less drinking, fewer injuries, and fewer deaths.

3   In the 1970s when many states reduced their drinking ages, drinking-related deaths among young people increased. When the drinking age of 21 was restored, deaths declined. This effect is not simply a historical artifact explained by advances in safety technology and other policies.

4   New Zealand recently lowered the drinking age based on many of the same arguments advanced by the Amethyst Initiative. The result was more alcohol-involved traffic crashes and emergency room visits among 15- to 19-year-olds. New Zealand is now considering raising its drinking age. The National Highway Traffic Safety Administration estimates that setting the drinking age at 21 saves the lives of 900 young people each year and has saved more than 25,000 lives since 1975.

5   It was on the basis of compelling research evidence about its lifesaving benefits that a bipartisan effort created Public Law 98-363, "The National Minimum Legal Drinking Age Act," in the first place. Subsequent research has strengthened the evidence. College students who are underage, for example, binge drink less than students aged 21-23. Underage students who attend colleges that rigorously enforce the drinking age, and who reside in states that have more laws restricting access to alcohol for those under the legal age, are less likely to binge drink.

6   Another myth promulgated by the Amethyst Initiative is that European young people are taught by families to drink responsibly because of the typically lower legal drinking ages there. The reverse is the case. Surveys of youth in multiple European countries show that rates of frequent binge drinking among adolescents are higher in Europe than in the United States. Panels of experts, convened separately by the National Institute on Alcohol Abuse and Alcoholism, the Substance Abuse and Mental Health Services Administration, the National Academy of Sciences Institute of Medicine and the Centers for Disease Control and Prevention have studied the evidence on the age-21 law and concluded that it is effective public policy. Rather than lowering the drinking age, they recommended bolstering the law by closing loopholes in state law and strengthening enforcement.

7   There is a silver lining to the call for reopening discussion on the minimum legal drinking age. While some college presidents have signed on to the Amethyst Initiative, most have not. College presidents acknowledge that a serious problem exists on their campuses and that something needs to be done. Working effectively with their communities and states to address student drinking is the place to start, not with a discussion about lowering the drinking age.

8   College presidents must show leadership by promoting solutions recommended by a report from the National Institute on Alcohol Abuse and Alcoholism College Drinking Task Force released in 2002. These recommendations for college and community leaders included creating systems for reaching individual students with effective interventions; implementing, publicizing and enforcing laws to prevent alcohol-impaired driving and underage drinking; placing restrictions on alcohol retail outlets; increasing prices and excise taxes on alcoholic beverages; and insisting on responsible beverage service policies at on- and off-campus venues. Few colleges and their communities have even begun the steps needed to enact these efforts.

9   These recommendations will be difficult to implement and significant barriers exist, including resistance from the industries that profit from selling alcohol. College presidents cannot accomplish this alone. They need the support of students, regents, parents, alumni and their communities. State and local legislators need to pass tougher restrictions and provide resources for enforcement. Lobbying legislators to dismantle the effective drinking age law is a step in the wrong direction.

10   So rather than try the approaches advocated by the Amethyst Initiative that have no foundation in research, let's be clear about the issues. College student drinking is a serious problem. Each year more young people are injured, sexually assaulted, and die as the result of drinking. These statistics would be even worse without the age-21 law.

11   Lowering the drinking age will not save lives or make our campuses and communities better places to live. It will increase heavy drinking and the problems that accompany it in college communities and push the problem back into high schools. Real prevention requires constant vigilance, dedication, and the courage to implement difficult solutions.

JAMES **HIBBERD**

Barhopping with the Bud Girls

I f you owned a beer company, what would be your ultimate marketing dream?

2   How about placing a beer commercial in every college bar and fraternity organization? There, luscious, tan-line-free women and confident, upper-social-strata jocks would aggressively promote your brands with all the slick enthusiasm of a Madison Avenue production. Imagine these commercials playing in continuous motion throughout the evening without ever resorting to the obvious loops of promotional films. Because this commercial would be live. That's right, real people targeting real college beer drinkers at that crucial moment in their lives when they establish brand loyalty, using no other sales technique than old-fashioned peer pressure.

3   For Anheuser-Busch, the parent company of Budweiser, the dream of student recruitment is real. It wasn't easy or cheap. Or, some argue, anywhere close to ethical. Parenting groups have recently attacked Anheuser-Busch for their animated frog' n' lizard advertising campaign, but a CNN.com investigation has found that the brewer does more than create cute cartoon characters to court underage drinkers. By hiring popular fraternity members and attractive female students as representatives, Anheuser-Busch distributors directly target the largely underage college market.

4   Considering Harvard's well-publicized 1993 study declaring that 44 percent of American college students and 86 percent of fraternity members qualify as binge drinkers, such a marketing program seems ridiculously ill-advised. Isn't hiring college students a potential PR nightmare? After all, 90 percent of all rapes and most violent crimes on campus are alcohol-related.

5   Such statistics may not have deterred Anheuser-Busch, but they do explain why its college recruiting efforts are managed discreetly. Even the beer industry's most prominent critic, Mothers Against Drunk Driving, was unaware that college reps existed. "Hiring fraternity members as beer distributor reps on university campuses where the majority of students are under the legal drinking age of 21 is frightening and unbelievably irresponsible," said MADD's national president, Karolyn V. Nunnallee, upon hearing the news. "We urge the U.S. beer industry to re-examine its marketing efforts."

6   Last November, midlevel supervisors for Anheuser-Busch wholesaler Brown Distributing allowed me to join their college representatives working a Budweiser parade leading to a University of Texas football game and a night of "bar calls" in Austin. While many alcohol companies hire attractive women to push products in bars and sporting events across the country, these Bud representatives seemed to be recruited predominantly from the college population and assigned to a college beat: They frequent popular college watering holes, sporting events, and other events such as parties at the U.T. alumni center. Of more concern are the existence of fraternity members who work unsupervised in the promotion of their product for college parties. The access was unusual, and the vice president for Brown Distributing later expressed some irritation, commenting that any media inquiries normally require approval from a high-ranking executive.

7   In other words: oops.

8   "When we walk into a bar, all we have is ourselves," says 24-year-old Bud Girl Rachel Moore, a recent college graduate. "We may be passing out a key chain or something, but we make the promotion." Brown Distributing Bud Girls (we'll get to the male representatives later) are held to strict standards. A Bud Girl doesn't smoke, swear, use drugs, or have tattoos, non-ear piercings, or a criminal record. Her only permissible vice is drinking Budweiser, and that, of course, is mandatory. If a potential Bud Girl passes the interviews, background checks and drug testing, she's awarded a $15-an-hour part-time position and a Bud Girl wardrobe.

9   Bud Girl clothing isn't simply halter tops and spandex dresses. The wardrobe is Technicolor dream-wear that transforms attractive yet otherwise ordinary girls into a sort of beer-touting Justice League. Once in costume, the Bud Girls are superheroes whose sexual power turns any bar into one of those 1980s beer commercials, where the swimsuit model reduces men to puddles of gratitude and adoration. "I wonder who they think we actually are," says 28-year-old Bud Girl Griselda Mendoza. "[The clothes] change everything. They could see me at a supermarket and I won't get paid much attention. But put on a little Bud vest and all of a sudden guys want everything signed."

10   At one bar promotion I attended, the Bud Girls were asked to sign a promotional banner. They wrote: "This Bud's For You, We Love You." And, in their own way, they do. And men, in their own way, believe it. Bud Girls seem to enjoy their part-time work as hops goddesses as much as men enjoy begging at their feet for key chains and cozies. But just how widespread are these lust-driven promotions?

11   All of the Big Three American labels (Budweiser, Miller and Coors, which constitute nearly 80 percent of the U.S. beer market) practice some college recruiting. But Anheuser-Busch, with nearly 50 percent of the market, has the most extensive program. Miller marketing representative Ann Espey said her company has recently "shied away" from hiring on campus, and agreed that hiring male fraternity representatives is irresponsible. Similarly, Coors spokesman Dave Taylor says his company has "moved away" from such practices. Although "shied away" and "moved away" suggest that Coors and Miller have made significant policy changes, neither representative will say the practice is extinct.

12   "You need to understand the primary consumer target for beer companies is young adult males," Taylor says. "Historically, college programs were very common in the industry when the drinking age was 18. Now at the local level, with 600 independent distributors, does hiring models still occur? Probably, yes."

13   "At the local level" is another key phrase. Because beer girls and college programs are run by independent distributors, parent companies often feign ignorance of the practice. Likewise, while some distributors have never even heard of student recruiting ("College representatives?" asked a shocked receptionist at the Ann Arbor, Michigan, Anheuser-Busch wholesaler. "This is a *beer* distributor, sir"), wholesalers in cities like Tucson, Los Angeles, and Denver have programs in place.

14   To set the stage for the Bud Girls, these distributors pre-pack college bars with streamers, table tents, coasters, inflatable footballs, pool-table lamps, posters, and, of course, neon signs. Add the Bud Girls and the stage is set. The live commercial begins.

15   Two local students, Christi Voigt, 21, and Jaime Franks, 22, enter the Austin BW-3 chicken wing franchise during a Dallas Cowboys football game. They're wearing blue Bud Light halter tops and denim shorts. Bud Girls say they prefer the

Some of the best
Mothers.
are fathers.

MOTHERS AGAINST DRUNK DRIVING can just as easily be male as female. What we have in common is a drive to make roads safer, prevent underage drinking and help survivors of drunk driving crashes. If you'd like to be one of the Mothers, rest assured you're welcome regardless of gender. After all, it's not a man thing or a woman thing. Just the right thing. Learn more at madd.org.

If you or someone you know has been hurt in a drunk driving crash, call 877.MADD.HELP for support — at no charge.

madd

MADD—Mothers Against Drunk Driving—is one of the most respected nonprofit organizations in the United States. For the past 25 years, MADD has championed the rights of victims of drunk driving and has promoted public awareness of the consequences of drunk driving. The ad on this page is one of many that were displayed recently on the MADD Web site.

shorts-and-halter-top ensemble to the classic beer-can-print spandex dress, but noted that the distribution company prefers the tight dress because "It's more visible." (As Mendoza wryly noted, "A lot of guys have a misconception that if a girl is wearing a dress that looks like a beer can, they can pick us up.")

16   Although Voigt and Franks give away some free key chains and beers to the rowdy crowd, they mostly distribute charm. Bud Girls have charm on the fly. Once in gear, the beer drinker is the center of attention. The beer drinker is witty and attractive. But if said beer drinker refuses to change brands or asks the nauseatingly common "Can I have you with that beer?" query, the Bud Girl downshifts: The beer drinker is a gnat, an impotent man unworthy of a Bud Girl's slightest concern. They

remain professional—the smile never wavers—but the charm is gone and patrons can read "get lost" right through their Colgate teeth.

17   In other words, Bud Girls can really mess with a beer drinker's self-esteem.

18   Franks walks up to a table of four students. She makes eye contact with the tallest male in the group, tilts her head, and slowly asks, "What kind of beer are you drinking?"

19   He guiltily stammers something about Dos Equis.

20   She purposefully lays down a key chain bottle opener in front of him, never breaking eye contact.

21   "What will you drink now?"

22   "Uh, Buh-Bud."

23   She smiles: Good boy.

24   The display is impressive, but Voigt and Franks are rookies. Bud Girl supervisor Eric Bradford sips his Budweiser and wistfully recalls veterans who'd brazenly grab a customers' non-Bud beer and dump it out. Whether sweet or savage, all Bud Girls operate on the same basic principle: their well-endowed bodies become the curvy slates upon which beer slogans and men's horny dreams are projected.

25   The male of the Bud species functions a bit differently. He doesn't wear a spandex dress. He doesn't even need to wear his Budweiser polo shirt. His body is

Some Signs that Substance Use Is a Problem

- Being uncomfortable at occasions when alcohol and/or drugs are not available
- When you are not using, regretting things you said or did when you were using
- Arguments with friends or family related to your use
- Being able to handle larger and larger amounts of alcohol and/or drugs over time
- Increased work, family, school, and social problems
- Feeling angry or depressed while using or the next day
- Lying about substance use to friends and loved ones
- Neglecting people and events that don't involve substance use
- "Blackouts" or not remembering what happened when under the influence
- Uncomfortable withdrawal symptoms when not using (e.g., shakiness, fatigue, insomnia, irritability)
- Needing substances to cope with strong feelings, stress, and/or sleeplessness
- Wanting to cut back on use, but not being able to
- Driving a car while under the influence
- Getting in trouble at work or school for using (e.g., showing up late, calling in sick, getting fired)

not a billboard for Budweiser. It's a double standard straight out of traditional beer commercials, where sexily dressed women wear the product and the cool guys just look like . . . cool guys. Whenever the male rep wishes, he goes unescorted to campus-area bars and buys Bud products for students with his expense account.

26   Corby Ferrell is one of the seven U.T. college reps (or "contemporary marketing representatives," as Budweiser calls them), all of whom are in separate fraternities. Together, the reps keep Budweiser products flowing from local sellers to the frat houses and campus-area parties. Ferrell is the 21-year-old former chairman of Phi Gamma Delta and has blond, anchorman-quality hair. Two or three times a week, Ferrell will go into Cain & Abel's bar located in the heart of Greek territory and approach attractive women drinking Miller or Coors.

27   "Hey, what do you think about switching to Bud Light for the night?" he'll ask. "The first one is on me, and I'll buy you another before I leave." Ferrell admits he has "an awesome job."

28   The second responsibility of male representatives is to arrange beer sales through local vendors. To dispel any confusion about the ethical or legal implications of this practice, Ferrell explains that technically the fraternity organizations do not pay for the beer: "Members who are at least 21 years old pool their cash to buy beer for parties." When

Tips for Safer Drinking

- Drink slowly, don't gulp your drinks, avoid drinking games
- Avoid using alcohol along with other drugs
- Set a limit on how many drinks you are going to have and stick to it
- Eat before you drink, keep in mind that high protein foods help slow alcohol absorption into the bloodstream
- Alternate alcoholic with nonalcoholic drinks
- Don't give in if friends encourage you to drink more than you want to
- Avoid putting your drink down out of sight or accepting drinks from strangers
- Plan ahead! Designate a sober driver in advance, provide transportation at social gatherings where drinking is involved, or use public transportation
- Plan activities that don't involve drinking or drugs

Although these moderation tips are written to apply to the use of alcohol, you can easily adapt these ideas for drug use as well. In addition, you can also always contact the Counseling Center if you or someone you care about has a problem with drugs and/or alcohol.

Paul Mikowski, PsyD

Postdoctoral Fellow, Counseling and Personal Development Center, Westchester Campus, Pace University

his work with college fraternity members and local vendors leads to a volume sale (five cases of beer, for example), Ferrell is given a commission by Brown Distributing.

29   One sales tactic is for the college rep to establish a relationship with campus-area sellers, then ask who's buying large quantities of competing brands. "Then I'll call the buyer and say, ''I can get you 100 cases of [Anheuser-Busch product] Natural Light for at least as cheap as what you're paying for Keystone Light,''" Ferrell says. On average, Ferrell moves 300 cases per week to college buyers. "Fraternities drink the cheapest beer they can find," Bradford, the Bud Girl supervisor, explains. "And his job is to make sure they drink our cheap beer."

30   Neither Ferrell nor Bradford seem reckless or irresponsible, but still—having a Budweiser representative as fraternity chairman is like having Joe Camel as a high school football quarterback. Both popular figureheads not only have a vested interest in which brands are consumed, but the quantity as well. "I think it's better that we do have them out there because of the message that we're bringing," says Laurie Watson, vice president of Brown Distributing. "We're constantly preaching responsibility."

31   Watson was the only senior-level Anheuser-Busch representative willing to comment for this story. A marketing representative for the Anheuser-Busch corporate office at first denied any knowledge of the college program, then agreed only to confirm some facts and produce a copy of the Anheuser-Busch College Marketing Code. The code touts Anheuser-Busch's support of alcohol awareness education and stresses that distributors must limit event sponsorship to venues that check I.D.

32   Bartenders and doormen do check I.D.s, of course. But the Bud Girl handing out free beers doesn't know how much alcohol a patron has consumed. Likewise, frat representatives only card the one individual buying beer for a party. "[Students are] going to have a beer," Watson says. "We just want them to be responsible about it. The representatives always talk to them about responsible drinking." "At least," she adds, "I hope they do. They're supposed to."

33   Imagine a 21-year-old Bud rep arranging a sale of 100 cases of Natural Light, then lecturing to the buyer about responsible drinking. It doesn't click, it doesn't work. The people at Bud must be dreaming. And maybe they are dreaming . . . still. Dreaming of college market saturation, dreaming of young male demographics and dreaming of decades of brand loyalty to come.

34   One week after my Bud barhopping tour, University of Texas junior and Phi Kappa Sigma fraternity member Jack Ivey consumed about 20 drinks, then fell asleep on his apartment couch. He was pronounced dead the next morning of alcohol poisoning, just the latest binge-drinking fatality. Whether Ivey is in the dreams of any beer marketers, no one can say.

FROM READING TO WRITING

1. Analyze and compare any two arguments made in this chapter. How is each argument a product of its audience and purpose? What sources of argument are used—ethical appeals, logical appeals, emotional appeals—and what string of "good reasons" are proposed in order to make a case? Why do the composers of those arguments make those particular appeals? (For more on rhetorical analysis, see Chapter 6.)

2. Examine and compare the various visual arguments that appear in this chapter—the photos, ads, and cartoons. What argument, exactly, is being made in each case? How is that argument supported? (See Chapter 7 for information on analyzing visuals.)

3. Write an argument that makes its point by defining a key term related to the regulation of substances like tobacco, high-calorie food, marijuana, alcohol, and so on. You might seek to change people's attitudes by redefining freedom or government regulation or advertising in such a way that your definition supports your views on regulating substances. (See Chapter 8 for more on writing definition arguments.)

4. Propose a particular policy related to the regulation of substances that is important in your community. For example, if binge drinking is an issue at your college or university, you might propose a single measure that might help to ameliorate the situation. Should your institution permit fans to purchase beer at sporting events? What should be the policy of major league baseball toward performance-enhancing drugs? (See Chapter 13 for advice on proposal arguments.)

5. Write a rebuttal of an argument in this chapter concerning the regulation of alcohol, tobacco, steroids, or other substances. (See Chapter 12.) Consider whether you want to show the weaknesses in the argument, or whether you wish to counterargue, or to do both.

6. Write an essay that recounts a personal experience of yours that makes an argument related to the regulation of a particular substance. What exactly does your personal experience lead you to conclude? See Chapter 11 for advice on narrative arguments. Alternatively, consider making your argument based on your observation of another person's experience.

28 | New Media

Personal Space in Cyberspace

Thirty years ago, everything seemed so simple and stable. There were a few cable TV stations, but the major networks—NBC, CBS, ABC—still ruled. Radio was delivering comfortable and predictable news, weather, and music to their listeners: Top 40 on one channel, country on another, oldies on a third; talk radio was a late-night-only phenomenon, and sports coverage on the radio was built around familiar voices who were associated with particular teams over many years. The daily local newspaper arrived in the morning or afternoon or both. Every house and office had a central phone line, usually with a few extensions and usually serviced by AT&T.

Is this the future of media? In this publicity still from *Avatar*, all eyes are on the display. What are the consequences of the shift from old to new media?

Then everything changed. Cable television stations multiplied so that the established networks lost market share as well as their monopoly on evening entertainment and news coverage. Even sports coverage changed fundamentally when ESPN began offering its hour-long *SportsCenter* show, and network news gave up market share to the host of news and quasi-news shows that compete so vigorously for an audience today. When Rush Limbaugh created a large audience for his conservative political commentary, many radio stations created or expanded their talk-radio formats. And all that became jumbled still further with the advent of the Internet, which seems to be causing the slow demise of print journalism even as it encourages new, more participatory forms of media in cyberspace. Finally, social networking media and cell phone technologies in the past decade have put a sophisticated communications tool into the pockets and purses of just about everyone.

With these changes have come many concerns and controversies. The effects of new media on our political processes have been particularly criticized. On October 15, 2004, for example, less than three weeks before the presidential elections, popular Comedy Central comedian Jon Stewart, a guest on CNN's political talk show *Crossfire,* got into a celebrated donnybrook with news commentator Tucker Carlson. Stewart, whose hilarious political satire in the form of a mock TV news show sends many Americans to bed with smiles on their faces, took the opportunity of his appearance on *Crossfire* to challenge Carlson about the abysmal level of political commentary in the nation's media. At one point Stewart charged that *Crossfire* and shows like it—he was no doubt thinking of Bill O'Reilly and Rush Limbaugh and Keith Olbermann—are "bad, very bad," for America because they oversimplify and polarize discussion. "It's hurting America," said Stewart. "Stop, stop, stop, stop, stop hurting America." When Carlson protested that *Crossfire* presents intelligent debate from the political left and right, Stewart was outraged: "[Saying *Crossfire* is a debate show is] like saying pro wrestling is a show about athletic competition. You're doing theater when you should be doing debate . . . . What you do is not honest. What you do is partisan hackery . . . just knee-jerk reactionary talk."

While Stewart and his fans were taking their frustrations out on *Crossfire*, they were surely also thinking of much more. In the past decade many Americans have been increasingly concerned about certain trends in the popular media, especially in new media, including Internet news sites, podcasts, and blogs: the development of partisan (rather than "fair and balanced") news coverage; the concentration of news outlets and newspapers into the hands of a few powerful corporations; the impact of sensationalistic and one-sided talk radio and talk TV shows; the effects of the Internet on the political and cultural process; the dubious morality depicted on "reality TV"; attack coverage of events by bloggers and podcasters; and the effects of persistent advertising, violence, graphic sexuality, and cultural stereotyping that are associated now with films, magazines, and television programs. No wonder so many people cringe when they recall the nonstop, no-holds-barred, months-long tabloidization of Tiger Woods's marital infidelities.

Developments in new media—like *Wikipedia*, avatars, blogs, and Internet social networking sites—are making information and recreation more widely available, but the ease of posting anything on the Internet results in an overwhelming volume of material, a good deal of which is dubious in content. Between the partisanship (both obvious and subtle) of more traditional media and the questionable credibility of new media, many Americans are left wondering where to turn for reliable news and information, and for safe sources of family entertainment. Many, in fact, turn to relentless self-expression via blogs, *Twitter*, *Facebook*, and the like—to the personal spaces in cyberspace that may or may not reflect reality. The writers of the selections in this chapter tease out the tensions between freedom and censorship, public and private, in both old and new media; and they ponder the implications of the various new media.

Contemporary Arguments

This chapter opens with four pieces that explore the delicate balance between freedom and restriction on the Internet, as well as the potential consequences of swinging too far in one direction. In "Is Google's Data Grinder Dangerous?" Andrew Keen accuses Google of nefariously plotting for world domination and suggests that the Internet is not (and never will be) the utopian, free intellectual space that John Perry Barlow describes in "A Declaration of the Independence of Cyberspace." Similarly, John Seigenthaler describes a less-than-utopian experience of being the subject of a false *Wikipedia* biography and the obstacles to finding the identity of the writer. Walt Handelsman's "Information Superhighway" cartoon follows the Internet thread as well; his humorous roadway image shows a strikingly real portrait of priorities on the Internet. All these pieces come together under the broad topic of media and its uses. What is the Internet's purpose? Who should control it? Whose opinions should it publish and validate? And, finally, what are the hidden effects, sacrifices, and benefits when people (and small nonprofit organizations) develop a significant Internet presence?

For many people worldwide, such questions take a backseat to the daily influence of the media in their lives. The balance of the selections in this chapter take up the issue of the Internet, identities, and the burgeoning trend of developing alter egos—and richly detailed alternative worlds—online. In "Where the Avatars Roam," Michael Gerson looks at cyberspace role-playing from a moral perspective: What happens to morality and freedom when we spend so much time in alternative realities where any choice is possible—even criminal or socially undesirable choices? Malcolm Gladwell follows with an argument contending that the revolutionary potential that has been attributed to social media has been highly exaggerated. Then David Carr offers an endorsement of *Twitter*, and Neil Richards offers a warning about the privacy concerns that are associated with online viewing. Together, these articles tackle the tricky terrain of the private and the public in cyberspace. What kinds of personal expression are meant for public consumption? Should we differentiate between amateur and professional participation online, particularly if amateur expression is so common and so popular? Finally, just what is (and what should be) the purpose of new media—dissemination of information, recreation, commerce, or something else? Are we creating new media, or is it creating us?

The chapter concludes with an Issue in Focus: electronic games. As Chris Kohler once argued in a defense of a new fitness game, Nintendo's Wii system actually can provide some exercise for participants; he was countering concerns that rampant child obesity is the result of all video games. Can other new technologies encourage people to be more active? And what about the other charges against video games—that they undermine learning, encourage teen violence, isolate children socially, and reinforce harmful gender stereotypes? The Issue in Focus takes up all these matters and more. More broadly speaking, to what purposes can we put new media, and how will these technological shifts influence our lives and cultures?

ANDREW **KEEN**

Is Google's Data Grinder Dangerous?

In *The Cult of the Amateur: How Today's Internet Is Killing Our Culture* (2007), Andrew Keen argues that the slew of amateur writing on the Internet—by anyone, about anything—doesn't contribute to knowledge or information, but rather bogs us down with uninformed opinions. Keen's view of the Internet is also evident in the article printed below. First published on July 12, 2007, in the *Los Angeles Times*, "Is Google's Data Grinder Dangerous?" puts a nefarious spin on the most popular Internet search engine—and its seeming quest to know all our private information so it can dominate the world (or at least make billions in advertising).

What does Google want? Having successfully become our personal librarian, Google now wants to be our personal oracle. It wants to learn all about us, know us better than we know ourselves, to transform itself from a search engine into a psychoanalyst's couch or a priest's confessional. Google's search engine is the best place to learn what Google wants. Type "Eric Schmidt London May 22" into Google, and you can read about a May interview the Google chief executive gave to journalists in London. Here is how he described what he hoped the search engine would look like in five years: "The goal is to enable Google users to be able to ask the question such as 'What shall I do tomorrow?' And 'What job shall I take?'"

2   Schmidt's goal is not inconsiderable: By 2012, he wants Google to be able to tell all of us what we want. This technology, what Google co-founder Larry Page calls the "perfect search engine," might not only replace our shrinks but also all those marketing professionals whose livelihoods are based on predicting—or guessing—consumer desires. Schmidt acknowledges that Google is still far from this goal. As he told the London journalists: "We cannot even answer the most basic questions because we don't know enough about you. That is the most important aspect of Google's expansion."

John Perry Barlow

A Declaration of the Independence of Cyberspace

After seventeen years as a Wyoming rancher who, on the side, wrote songs for the Grateful Dead, John Perry Barlow (born 1947) in the late 1980s began writing about computer-mediated communications. He served on the board of directors of WELL (the Whole Earth Lectronic Link), posts regularly on the WELL Web site, and is a cofounder of the Electronic Frontier Foundation, which advocates keeping government regulations out of the Internet. Since May 1998, he has been a fellow at Harvard Law School's Berkman Center for Internet and Society.

Governments of the Industrial World, you weary giants of flesh and steel, I come from Cyberspace, the new home of Mind. On behalf of the future, I ask you of the past to leave us alone. You are not welcome among us. You have no sovereignty where we gather.

2   We have no elected government, nor are we likely to have one, so I address you with no greater authority than that with which liberty itself always speaks. I declare the global social space we are building to be naturally independent of the tyrannies you seek to impose on us. You have no moral right to rule us nor do you possess any methods of enforcement we have true reason to fear.

3   Governments derive their just powers from the consent of the governed. You have neither solicited nor received ours. We did not invite you. You do not know us, nor do you know our world. Cyberspace does not lie within your borders. Do not think that you can build it, as though it were a public construction project. You cannot. It is an act of nature and it grows itself through our collective actions.

4   You have not engaged in our great and gathering conversation, nor did you create the wealth of our marketplaces. You do not know our culture, our ethics, or the unwritten codes that already provide our society more order than could be obtained by any of your impositions.

5   You claim there are problems among us that you need to solve. You use this claim as an excuse to invade our precincts. Many of these problems don't exist. Where there are real conflicts, where there are wrongs, we will identify them and address them by our means. We are forming our own Social Contract. This governance will arise according to the conditions of our world, not yours. Our world is different.

6   Cyberspace consists of transactions, relationships, and thought itself, arrayed like a standing wave in the web of our communications. Ours is a world that is both everywhere and nowhere, but it is not where bodies live.

7   We are creating a world that all may enter without privilege or prejudice accorded by race, economic power, military force, or station of birth.

8   We are creating a world where anyone, anywhere may express his or her beliefs, no matter how singular, without fear of being coerced into silence or conformity.

9   Your legal concepts of property, expression, identity, movement, and context do not apply to us. They are based on matter. There is no matter here.

10   Our identities have no bodies, so, unlike you, we cannot obtain order by physical coercion. We believe that, from ethics, enlightened self-interest, and the commonweal, our governance will emerge. Our identities may be distributed across many of your jurisdictions. The only law that all our constituent cultures would generally recognize is the Golden Rule. We hope we will be able to build our particular solutions on that basis. But we cannot accept the solutions you are attempting to impose.

11   In the United States, you have today created a law, the Telecommunications Reform Act, which repudiates your own Constitution and insults the dreams of Jefferson, Washington, Mill, Madison, de Toqueville, and Brandeis. These dreams must now be born anew in us.

12   You are terrified of your own children, since they are natives in a world where you will always be immigrants. Because you fear them, you entrust your bureaucracies with the parental responsibilities you are too cowardly to confront yourselves. In our world, all the sentiments and expressions of humanity, from the debasing to the angelic, are parts of a seamless whole, the global conversation of bits. We cannot separate the air that chokes from the air upon which wings beat.

13   In China, Germany, France, Russia, Singapore, Italy, and the United States, you are trying to ward off the virus of liberty by erecting guard posts at the frontiers of Cyberspace. These may keep out the contagion for a small time, but they will not work in a world that will soon be blanketed in bit-bearing media.

14   Your increasingly obsolete information industries would perpetuate themselves by proposing laws, in America and elsewhere, that claim to own speech itself throughout the world. These laws would declare ideas to be another industrial product, no more noble than pig iron. In our world, whatever the human mind may create can be reproduced and distributed infinitely at no cost. The global conveyance of thought no longer requires your factories to accomplish.

15   These increasingly hostile and colonial measures place us in the same position as those previous lovers of freedom and self-determination who had to reject the authorities of distant, uninformed powers. We must declare our virtual selves immune to your sovereignty, even as we continue to consent to your rule over our bodies. We will spread ourselves across the Planet so that no one can arrest our thoughts.

16   We will create a civilization of the Mind in Cyberspace. May it be more humane and fair than the world your governments have made before.

3   So where is Google expanding? How is it planning to know more about us? Many—if not most—users don't read the user agreement and thus aren't aware that Google already stores every query we type in. The next stage is a personalized Web service called iGoogle. Schmidt, who perhaps not coincidentally sits on the board of Apple, regards its success as the key to knowing us better than we know ourselves.

4   iGoogle is growing into a tightly-knit suite of services—personalized homepage, search engine, blog, e-mail system, mini-program gadgets, Web-browsing history, etc.—that together will create the world's most intimate information database. On

iGoogle, we all get to aggregate our lives, consciously or not, so artificially intelligent software can sort out our desires. It will piece together our recent blog posts, where we've been online, our e-commerce history and cultural interests. It will amass so much information about each of us that eventually it will be able to logically determine what we want to do tomorrow and what job we want.

5   The real question, of course, is whether what Google wants is what we want too. Do we really want Google digesting so much intimate data about us? Could iGoogle actually be a remix of "1984's" Room 101—that Orwellian dystopia in which our most secret desires and most repressed fears are revealed? Any comparison with 20th century, top-down totalitarianism is, perhaps, a little fanciful. After all, nobody can force us to use iGoogle. And—in contrast to Yahoo and Microsoft (which have no limits on how long they hang on to our personal data)—Google has committed to retaining data for only 18 months. Still, if iGoogle turns out to be half as wise about each of us as Schmidt predicts, then this artificial intelligence will challenge traditional privacy rights as well as provide us with an excuse to deny responsibility for our own actions. What happens, for example, when the government demands access to our iGoogle records? And will we be able to sue iGoogle if it advises us to make an unwise career decision?

6   Schmidt, I suspect, would like us to imagine Google as a public service, thereby affirming the company's "do no evil" credo. But Google is not our friend. Schmidt's iGoogle vision of the future is not altruistic, and his company is not a nonprofit group dedicated to the realization of human self-understanding. Worth more than $150 billion on the public market, Google is by far the dominant Internet advertising outlet—according to Nielsen ratings, it reaches about 70% of the global Internet audience. Just in the first quarter of 2007, Google's revenue from its online properties was up 76% from the previous year. Personal data are Google's most valuable currency, its crown jewels. The more Google knows our desires, the more targeted advertising it can serve up to us and the more revenue it can extract from these advertisers.

7   What does Google really want? Google wants to dominate. Its proposed $3.1-billion acquisition of DoubleClick threatens to make the company utterly dominant in the online advertising business. The $1.65-billion acquisition of YouTube last year made it by far the dominant player in the online video market. And, with a personalized service like iGoogle, the company is seeking to become the algorithmic monopolist of our online behavior. So when Eric Schmidt says Google wants to know us better than we know ourselves, he is talking to his shareholders rather than us. As a Silicon Valley old-timer, trust me on this one. I know Google better than it knows itself.

JOHN **SEIGENTHALER**

A False Wikipedia "Biography"

John Seigenthaler, now retired, is a distinguished journalist who founded the Freedom Forum First Amendment Center at Vanderbilt University—so he is anything but a censor at heart. Nevertheless, in the following essay (published in November 2005 in *USA Today*, a newspaper he helped launch) he expresses grave reservations about *Wikipedia* as he

recounts a personal experience. The article printed below generated serious discussion about the reliability, credibility, and ethics of *Wikipedia*, which changed some of its policies subsequently. You can read more about the episode by googling "Siegenthaler Wikipedia controversy."

> John Seigenthaler Sr. was the assistant to Attorney General Robert Kennedy in the early 1960's. For a brief time, he was thought to have been directly involved in the Kennedy assassinations of both John and his brother Bobby. Nothing was ever proven.
>
> —Wikipedia

This is a highly personal story about Internet character assassination. It could be your story. I have no idea whose sick mind conceived the false, malicious "biography" that appeared under my name for 132 days on Wikipedia, the popular, online, free encyclopedia whose authors are unknown and virtually untraceable. There was more:

2   "John Seigenthaler moved to the Soviet Union in 1971, and returned to the United States in 1984," Wikipedia said. "He started one of the country's largest public relations firms shortly thereafter."

3   At age 78, I thought I was beyond surprise or hurt at anything negative said about me. I was wrong. One sentence in the biography was true. I was Robert Kennedy's administrative assistant in the early 1960s. I also was his pallbearer. It was mindboggling when my son, John Seigenthaler, journalist with NBC News, phoned later to say he found the same scurrilous text on Reference.com and Answers.com.

4   I had heard for weeks from teachers, journalists and historians about "the wonderful world of Wikipedia," where millions of people worldwide visit daily for quick reference "facts," composed and posted by people with no special expertise or knowledge—and sometimes by people with malice.

5   At my request, executives of the three websites now have removed the false content about me. But they don't know, and can't find out, who wrote the toxic sentences.

Anonymous author

6   I phoned Jimmy Wales, Wikipedia's founder and asked, "Do you . . . have any way to know who wrote that?"

7   "No, we don't," he said. Representatives of the other two websites said their computers are programmed to copy data verbatim from Wikipedia, never checking whether it is false or factual. Naturally, I want to unmask my "biographer." And, I am interested in letting many people know that Wikipedia is a flawed and irresponsible research tool.

8   But searching cyberspace for the identity of people who post spurious information can be frustrating. I found on Wikipedia the registered IP (Internet Protocol) number of my "biographer"—65-81-97-208. I traced it to a customer of BellSouth Internet. That company advertises a phone number to report "Abuse Issues." An electronic voice said all complaints must be e-mailed. My two e-mails were answered by identical form letters, advising me that the company would conduct an investigation but might not tell me the results. It was signed "Abuse Team."

9   Wales, Wikipedia's founder, told me that BellSouth would not be helpful. "We have trouble with people posting abusive things over and over and over," he said. "We block their IP numbers, and they sneak in another way. So we contact the service providers, and they are not very responsive."

10   After three weeks, hearing nothing further about the Abuse Team investigation, I phoned BellSouth's Atlanta corporate headquarters, which led to conversations between my lawyer and BellSouth's counsel. My only remote chance of getting the name, I learned, was to file a "John or Jane Doe" lawsuit against my "biographer." Major communications Internet companies are bound by federal privacy laws that protect the identity of their customers, even those who defame online. Only if a lawsuit resulted in a court subpoena would BellSouth give up the name.

Little legal recourse

11   Federal law also protects online corporations—BellSouth, AOL, MCI, Wikipedia, etc.— from libel lawsuits. Section 230 of the Communications Decency Act, passed in 1996, specifically states that "no provider or user of an interactive computer service shall be treated as the publisher or speaker." That legalese means that, unlike print and broadcast companies, online service providers cannot be sued for disseminating defamatory attacks on citizens posted by others. Recent low-profile court decisions document that Congress effectively has barred defamation in cyberspace. Wikipedia's website acknowledges that it is not responsible for inaccurate information, but Wales, in a recent C-Span interview with Brian Lamb, insisted that his website is accountable and that his community of thousands of volunteer editors (he said he has only one paid employee) corrects mistakes within minutes.

12   My experience refutes that. My "biography" was posted May 26. On May 29, one of Wales' volunteers "edited" it only by correcting the misspelling of the word "early." For four months, Wikipedia depicted me as a suspected assassin before Wales erased

it from his website's history Oct. 5. The falsehoods remained on Answers.com and Reference.com for three more weeks. In the C-Span interview, Wales said Wikipedia has "millions" of daily global visitors and is one of the world's busiest websites. His volunteer community runs the Wikipedia operation, he said. He funds his website through a non-profit foundation and estimated a 2006 budget of "about a million dollars."

13   And so we live in a universe of new media with phenomenal opportunities for worldwide communications and research—but populated by volunteer vandals with poison-pen intellects. Congress has enabled them and protects them.

14   When I was a child, my mother lectured me on the evils of "gossip." She held a feather pillow and said, "If I tear this open, the feathers will fly to the four winds, and I could never get them back in the pillow. That's how it is when you spread mean things about people." For me, that pillow is a metaphor for Wikipedia.

Michael Gerson

Where the Avatars Roam*

Michael Gerson, who once worked as a policy analyst and speechwriter under President George W. Bush, is columnist for the *Washington Post* and contributes to *PostPartisan*. His book about the future of conservative politics, *Heroic Conservatism*, was published in 2007. His areas of expertise span democracy and human rights, health and diseases, and religion and politics. Gerson is senior research fellow at the Institute for Global Engagement's Center on Faith and International Affairs. In "Where the Avatars Roam," published in the *Washington Post* July 6, 2007, Gerson asks, what happens to human freedom and human choices in alternative realities constructed online?

I am not usually found at bars during the day, though the state of the Republican Party would justify it. But here I was at a bar talking to this fox—I mean an actual fox, with fluffy tail and whiskers. It turns out that, in the online world of Second Life, many people prefer to take the shape of anthropomorphic animals called "furries," and this one is in a virtual bar talking about her frustrating job at a New York publishing house. But for all I know, she could be a man in outback Montana with a computer, a satellite dish and a vivid imagination.

2   For a columnist, this is called "research." For millions of Americans, it is an addictive form of entertainment called MMORPGs—massively multiplayer online role-playing games. In this entirely new form of social interaction, people create computer-generated bodies called avatars and mingle with other players in 3-D fantasy worlds.

3   Some of these worlds parallel a form of literature that J.R.R. Tolkien called "subcreation"—the Godlike construction of a complex, alternative reality, sometimes with its

own mythology and languages. I subscribe along with my two sons (an elf and a dwarf) to The Lord of the Rings Online, based on Tolkien's epic novels, which sends its participants on a series of heroic quests. I'm told that World of Warcraft, which has more than 8 million subscribers, takes a similar approach. Some of the appeal of these games is the controlled release of aggression—cheerful orc killing. But they also represent a conservative longing for medieval ideals of chivalry—for a recovery of honor and adventure in an age dominated by choice and consumption.

4   Second Life, however, is a different animal. Instead of showing the guiding hand of an author, this universe is created by the choices of its participants, or "residents." They can build, buy, trade and talk in a world entirely without rules or laws; a pure market where choice and consumption are the highest values. Online entrepreneurs make real money selling virtual clothing, cars and "skins"—the photorealistic faces and bodies of avatars. Companies such as Dell, IBM and Toyota market aggressively within Second Life.

If you were to create an avatar, would you want to look like yourself or someone or something else? Why?

5   The site has gotten some recent attention for its moral lapses. A few of its residents have a disturbing preference for "age play"—fantasy sex with underage avatars—which has attracted the attention of prosecutors in several countries.

6   But Second Life is more consequential than its moral failures. It is, in fact, a large-scale experiment in libertarianism. Its residents can do and be anything they wish. There are no binding forms of community, no responsibilities that aren't freely chosen and no lasting consequences of human actions. In Second Life, there is no human nature at all, just human choices.

7   And what do people choose? Well, there is some good live music, philanthropic fundraising, even a few virtual churches and synagogues. But the main result is the breakdown of inhibition. Second Life, as you'd expect, is highly sexualized in ways that have little to do with respect or romance. There are frequent outbreaks of terrorism, committed by online anarchists who interrupt events, assassinate speakers (who quickly reboot from the dead) and vandalize buildings. There are strip malls everywhere, pushing a relentless consumerism. And there seems to be an inordinate number of vampires, generally not a sign of community health.

8   Libertarians hold to a theory of "spontaneous order"—that society should be the product of uncoordinated human choices instead of human design. Well, Second Life has plenty of spontaneity, and not much genuine order. This experiment suggests that a world that is only a market is not a utopia. It more closely resembles a seedy, derelict carnival—the triumph of amusement and distraction over meaning and purpose.

9   Columnists, like frontier trackers, are expected to determine cultural directions from faint scents in the wind. So maybe there is a reason that *The Lord of the Rings* is ultimately more interesting than Second Life. Only in a created world, filled with moral rules, social obligations and heroic quests, do our free choices seem to matter. And even fictional honor fills a need deeper than consumption.

10   G.K. Chesterton wrote that when people are "really wild with freedom and invention" they create institutions, such as marriages and constitutions; but "when men are weary they fall into anarchy." In that anarchy, life tends to be nasty, brutish, short—and furry.

MALCOLM **GLADWELL**

Small Change: Why the Revolution Will Not Be Tweeted

Malcolm Gladwell, born in England in 1963 and raised in Canada, is now a staff writer with the *New Yorker* magazine. You may have read some of his highly readable best-selling books: *The Tipping Point* (2000), *Blink* (2005), or *Outliers* (2008). The following essay appeared in the *New Yorker* on October 4, 2010. Note that the essay ends with a lengthy commentary on Clay Skirky, whose own argument is included as the final item in this chapter.

At four-thirty in the afternoon on Monday, February 1, 1960, four college students sat down at the lunch counter at the Woolworth's in downtown Greensboro, North Carolina. They were freshmen at North Carolina A. & T., a black college a mile or so away.

"I'd like a cup of coffee, please," one of the four, Ezell Blair, said to the waitress. "We don't serve Negroes here," she replied.

2   The Woolworth's lunch counter was a long L-shaped bar that could seat sixty-six people, with a standup snack bar at one end. The seats were for whites. The snack bar was for blacks. Another employee, a black woman who worked at the steam table, approached the students and tried to warn them away. "You're acting stupid, ignorant!" she said. They didn't move. Around five-thirty, the front doors to the store were locked. The four still didn't move. Finally, they left by a side door. Outside, a small crowd had gathered, including a photographer from the Greensboro *Record*. "I'll be back tomorrow with A. & T. College," one of the students said.

3   By next morning, the protest had grown to twenty-seven men and four women, most from the same dormitory as the original four. The men were dressed in suits and ties. The students had brought their schoolwork, and studied as they sat at the counter. On Wednesday, students from Greensboro's "Negro" secondary school, Dudley High, joined in, and the number of protesters swelled to eighty. By Thursday, the protesters numbered three hundred, including three white women, from the Greensboro campus of the University of North Carolina. By Saturday, the sit-in had reached six hundred.

People spilled out onto the street. White teen-agers waved Confederate flags. Some-one threw a firecracker. At noon, the A. & T. football team arrived. "Here comes the wrecking crew," one of the white students shouted.

4   By the following Monday, sit-ins had spread to Winston-Salem, twenty-five miles away, and Durham, fifty miles away. The day after that, students at Fayetteville State Teachers College and at Johnson C. Smith College, in Charlotte, joined in, followed on Wednesday by students at St. Augustine's College and Shaw University, in Raleigh. On Thursday and Friday, the protest crossed state lines, surfacing in Hampton and Ports-mouth, Virginia, in Rock Hill, South Carolina, and in Chattanooga, Tennessee. By the end of the month, there were sit-ins throughout the South, as far west as Texas. "I asked every student I met what the first day of the sitdowns had been like on his campus," the political theorist Michael Walzer wrote in *Dissent*. "The answer was always the same: 'It was like a fever. Everyone wanted to go.'" Some seventy thousand students eventu-ally took part. Thousands were arrested and untold thousands more radicalized. These events in the early sixties became a civil-rights war that engulfed the South for the rest of the decade—and it happened without e-mail, texting, Facebook, or Twitter.

5   The world, we are told, is in the midst of a revolution. The new tools of social media have reinvented social activism. With Facebook and Twitter and the like, the traditional relationship between political authority and popular will has been upended, making it easier for the powerless to collaborate, coördinate, and give voice to their concerns. When ten thousand protesters took to the streets in Moldova in the spring of 2009 to protest against their country's Communist government, the action was dubbed the Twitter Revolution, because of the means by which the demonstrators had been brought together. A few months after that, when student protests rocked Tehran, the State Department took the unusual step of asking Twitter to suspend scheduled main-tenance of its Web site, because the Administration didn't want such a critical organ-izing tool out of service at the height of the demonstrations. "Without Twitter the people of Iran would not have felt empowered and confident to stand up for freedom and de-mocracy," Mark Pfeifle, a former national-security adviser, later wrote, calling for Twitter

In 1960, four African-American college students sat down at a whites-only section of a counter in a Greensboro, North Carolina, Woolworth's, where they knew they would be refused service.

to be nominated for the Nobel Peace Prize. Where activists were once defined by their causes, they are now defined by their tools. Facebook warriors go online to push for change. "You are the best hope for us all," James K. Glassman, a former senior State Department official, told a crowd of cyber activists at a recent conference sponsored by Facebook, A. T. & T., Howcast, MTV, and Google. Sites like Facebook, Glassman said, "give the U.S. a significant competitive advantage over terrorists. Some time ago, I said that Al Qaeda was 'eating our lunch on the Internet.' That is no longer the case. Al Qaeda is stuck in Web 1.0. The Internet is now about interactivity and conversation."

6   These are strong, and puzzling, claims. Why does it matter who is eating whose lunch on the Internet? Are people who log on to their Facebook page really the best hope for us all? As for Moldova's so-called Twitter Revolution, Evgeny Morozov, a scholar at Stanford who has been the most persistent of digital evangelism's critics, points out that Twitter had scant internal significance in Moldova, a country where very few Twitter accounts exist. Nor does it seem to have been a revolution, not least because the protests—as Anne Applebaum suggested in the Washington *Post*—may well have been a bit of stagecraft cooked up by the government. (In a country paranoid about Romanian revanchism, the protesters flew a Romanian flag over the Parliament building.) In the Iranian case, meanwhile, the people tweeting about the demonstrations were almost all in the West. "It is time to get Twitter's role in the events in Iran right," Golnaz Esfandiari wrote, this past summer, in *Foreign Policy*. "Simply put: There was no Twitter Revolution inside Iran." The cadre of prominent bloggers, like Andrew Sullivan, who championed the role of social media in Iran, Esfandiari continued, misunderstood the situation. "Western journalists who couldn't reach—or didn't bother reaching?—people on the ground in Iran simply scrolled through the English-language tweets post with tag #iranelection," she wrote. "Through it all, no one seemed to wonder why people trying to coordinate protests in Iran would be writing in any language other than Farsi."

7   Some of this grandiosity is to be expected. Innovators tend to be solipsists. They often want to cram every stray fact and experience into their new model. As the historian Robert Darnton has written, "The marvels of communication technology in the present have produced a false consciousness about the past—even a sense that communication has no history, or had nothing of importance to consider before the days of television and the Internet." But there is something else at work here, in the outsized enthusiasm for social media. Fifty years after one of the most extraordinary episodes of social upheaval in American history, we seem to have forgotten what activism is.

8   Greensboro in the early nineteen-sixties was the kind of place where racial insubordination was routinely met with violence. The four students who first sat down at the lunch counter were terrified. "I suppose if anyone had come up behind me and yelled 'Boo,' I think I would have fallen off my seat," one of them said later. On the first day, the store manager notified the police chief, who immediately sent two officers to the store. On the third day, a gang of white toughs showed up at the lunch counter and stood ostentatiously behind the protesters, ominously muttering racial epithets. . . . A local Ku Klux Klan leader made an appearance. On Saturday, as tensions grew, someone called in a bomb threat, and the entire store had to be evacuated.

9   The dangers were even clearer in the Mississippi Freedom Summer Project of 1964, another of the sentinel campaigns of the civil-rights movement. The Student Nonviolent Coordinating Committee recruited hundreds of Northern, largely white unpaid

volunteers to run Freedom Schools, register black voters, and raise civil-rights awareness in the Deep South. "No one should go *anywhere* alone, but certainly not in an
automobile and certainly not at night," they were instructed. Within days of arriving in
Mississippi, three volunteers—Michael Schwerner, James Chaney, and Andrew Good-
man—were kidnapped and killed, and, during the rest of the summer, thirty-seven black
churches were set on fire and dozens of safe houses were bombed; volunteers were
beaten, shot at, arrested, and trailed by pickup trucks full of armed men. A quarter of
those in the program dropped out. Activism that challenges the status quo—that attacks
deeply rooted problems—is not for the faint of heart.

10   What makes people capable of this kind of activism? The Stanford sociologist
Doug McAdam compared the Freedom Summer dropouts with the participants who
stayed, and discovered that the key difference wasn't, as might be expected, ideological fervor. "*All* of the applicants—participants and withdrawals alike—emerge as highly
committed, articulate supporters of the goals and values of the summer program," he
concluded. What mattered more was an applicant's degree of personal connection to
the civil-rights movement. All the volunteers were required to provide a list of personal
contacts—the people they wanted kept apprised of their activities—and participants
were far more likely than dropouts to have close friends who were also going to Mississippi. High-risk activism, McAdam concluded, is a "strong-tie" phenomenon.

11   This pattern shows up again and again. One study of the Red Brigades, the Italian terrorist group of the nineteen-seventies, found that seventy per cent of recruits had
at least one good friend already in the organization. The same is true of the men who
joined the mujahideen in Afghanistan. Even revolutionary actions that look spontaneous, like the demonstrations in East Germany that led to the fall of the Berlin Wall, are,
at core, strong-tie phenomena. The opposition movement in East Germany consisted
of several hundred groups, each with roughly a dozen members. Each group was in
limited contact with the others: at the time, only thirteen per cent of East Germans even
had a phone. All they knew was that on Monday nights, outside St. Nicholas Church in
downtown Leipzig, people gathered to voice their anger at the state. And the primary
determinant of who showed up was "critical friends"—the more friends you had who
were critical of the regime the more likely you were to join the protest.

12   So one crucial fact about the four freshmen at the Greensboro lunch counter—
David Richmond, Franklin McCain, Ezell Blair, and Joseph McNeil—was their relationship with one another. McNeil was a roommate of Blair's in A. & T.'s Scott Hall dormitory.
Richmond roomed with McCain one floor up, and Blair, Richmond, and McCain had all
gone to Dudley High School. The four would smuggle beer into the dorm and talk late
into the night in Blair and McNeil's room. They would all have remembered the murder
of Emmett Till in 1955, the Montgomery bus boycott that same year, and the showdown
in Little Rock in 1957. It was McNeil who brought up the idea of a sit-in at Woolworth's.
They'd discussed it for nearly a month. Then McNeil came into the dorm room and
asked the others if they were ready. There was a pause, and McCain said, in a way
that works only with people who talk late into the night with one another, "Are you guys
chicken or not?" Ezell Blair worked up the courage the next day to ask for a cup of coffee because he was flanked by his roommate and two good friends from high school.

13   The kind of activism associated with social media isn't like this at all. The platforms of social media are built around weak ties. Twitter is a way of following (or being

followed by) people you may never have met. Facebook is a tool for efficiently managing your acquaintances, for keeping up with the people you would not otherwise be able to stay in touch with. That's why you can have a thousand "friends" on Facebook, as you never could in real life.

14   This is in many ways a wonderful thing. There is strength in weak ties, as the sociologist Mark Granovetter has observed. Our acquaintances—not our friends—are our greatest source of new ideas and information. The Internet lets us exploit the power of these kinds of distant connections with marvelous efficiency. It's terrific at the diffusion of innovation, interdisciplinary collaboration, seamlessly matching up buyers and sellers, and the logistical functions of the dating world. But weak ties seldom lead to high-risk activism.

15   In a new book called *The Dragonfly Effect: Quick, Effective, and Powerful Ways to Use Social Media to Drive Social Change*, the business consultant Andy Smith and the Stanford Business School professor Jennifer Aaker tell the story of Sameer Bhatia, a young Silicon Valley entrepreneur who came down with acute myelogenous leukemia. It's a perfect illustration of social media's strengths. Bhatia needed a bone-marrow transplant, but he could not find a match among his relatives and friends. The odds were best with a donor of his ethnicity, and there were few South Asians in the national bone-marrow database. So Bhatia's business partner sent out an e-mail explaining Bhatia's plight to more than four hundred of their acquaintances, who forwarded the e-mail to their personal contacts; Facebook pages and YouTube videos were devoted to the Help Sameer campaign. Eventually, nearly twenty-five thousand new people were registered in the bone-marrow database, and Bhatia found a match.

16   But how did the campaign get so many people to sign up? By not asking too much of them. That's the only way you can get someone you don't really know to do something on your behalf. You can get thousands of people to sign up for a donor registry, because doing so is pretty easy. You have to send in a cheek swab and—in the highly unlikely event that your bone marrow is a good match for someone in need—spend a few hours at the hospital. Donating bone marrow isn't a trivial matter. But it doesn't involve financial or personal risk; it doesn't mean spending a summer being chased by armed men in pickup trucks. It doesn't require that you confront socially entrenched norms and practices. In fact, it's the kind of commitment that will bring only social acknowledgment and praise.

17   The evangelists of social media don't understand this distinction; they seem to believe that a Facebook friend is the same as a real friend and that signing up for a donor registry in Silicon Valley today is activism in the same sense as sitting at a segregated lunch counter in Greensboro in 1960. "Social networks are particularly effective at increasing motivation," Aaker and Smith write. But that's not true. Social networks are effective at increasing *participation*—by lessening the level of motivation that participation requires. The Facebook page of the Save Darfur Coalition has 1,282,339 members, who have donated an average of nine cents apiece. The next biggest Darfur charity on Facebook has 22,073 members, who have donated an average of thirty-five cents. Help Save Darfur has 2,797 members, who have given, on average, fifteen cents. A spokesperson for the Save Darfur Coalition told *Newsweek*, "We wouldn't necessarily gauge someone's value to the advocacy movement based on what they've given. This is a powerful mechanism to engage this critical population. They inform their community, attend events,

volunteer. It's not something you can measure by looking at a ledger." In other words, Facebook activism succeeds not by motivating people to make a real sacrifice but by motivating them to do the things that people do when they are not motivated enough to make a real sacrifice. We are a long way from the lunch counters of Greensboro.

18 The students who joined the sit-ins across the South during the winter of 1960 described the movement as a "fever." But the civil-rights movement was more like a military campaign than like a contagion. In the late nineteen-fifties, there had been sixteen sit-ins in various cities throughout the South, fifteen of which were formally organized by civil-rights organizations like the N.A.A.C.P. and CORE. Possible locations for activism were scouted. Plans were drawn up. Movement activists held training sessions and retreats for would-be protesters. The Greensboro Four were a product of this groundwork: all were members of the N.A.A.C.P. Youth Council. They had close ties with the head of the local N.A.A.C.P. chapter. They had been briefed on the earlier wave of sit-ins in Durham, and had been part of a series of movement meetings in activist churches. When the sit-in movement spread from Greensboro throughout the South, it did not spread indiscriminately. It spread to those cities which had preëxisting "movement centers"—a core of dedicated and trained activists ready to turn the "fever" into action.

19 The civil-rights movement was high-risk activism. It was also, crucially, strategic activism: a challenge to the establishment mounted with precision and discipline. The N.A.A.C.P. was a centralized organization, run from New York according to highly formalized operating procedures. At the Southern Christian Leadership Conference, Martin Luther King, Jr., was the unquestioned authority. At the center of the movement was the black church, which had, as Aldon D. Morris points out in his superb 1984 study, *The Origins of the Civil Rights Movement,* a carefully demarcated division of labor, with various standing committees and disciplined groups. "Each group was task-oriented and coordinated its activities through authority structures," Morris writes. "Individuals were held accountable for their assigned duties, and important conflicts were resolved by the minister, who usually exercised ultimate authority over the congregation."

20 This is the second crucial distinction between traditional activism and its online variant: social media are not about this kind of hierarchical organization. Facebook and the like are tools for building *networks*, which are the opposite, in structure and character, of hierarchies. Unlike hierarchies, with their rules and procedures, networks aren't controlled by a single central authority. Decisions are made through consensus, and the ties that bind people to the group are loose.

21 This structure makes networks enormously resilient and adaptable in low-risk situations. Wikipedia is a perfect example. It doesn't have an editor, sitting in New York, who directs and corrects each entry. The effort of putting together each entry is self-organized. If every entry in Wikipedia were to be erased tomorrow, the content would swiftly be restored, because that's what happens when a network of thousands spontaneously devote their time to a task.

22 There are many things, though, that networks don't do well. Car companies sensibly use a network to organize their hundreds of suppliers, but not to design their cars. No one believes that the articulation of a coherent design philosophy is best handled by a sprawling, leaderless organizational system. Because networks don't have a centralized leadership structure and clear lines of authority, they have real difficulty reaching consensus and setting goals. They can't think strategically; they are chronically

prone to conflict and error. How do you make difficult choices about tactics or strategy or philosophical direction when everyone has an equal say?

23   The Palestine Liberation Organization originated as a network, and the international-relations scholars Mette Eilstrup-Sangiovanni and Calvert Jones argue in a recent essay in *International Security* that this is why it ran into such trouble as it grew: "Structural features typical of networks—the absence of central authority, the unchecked autonomy of rival groups, and the inability to arbitrate quarrels through formal mechanisms—made the P.L.O. excessively vulnerable to outside manipulation and internal strife."

24   In Germany in the nineteen-seventies, they go on, "the far more unified and successful left-wing terrorists tended to organize hierarchically, with professional management and clear divisions of labor. They were concentrated geographically in universities, where they could establish central leadership, trust, and camaraderie through regular, face-to-face meetings." They seldom betrayed their comrades in arms during police interrogations. Their counterparts on the right were organized as decentralized networks, and had no such discipline. These groups were regularly infiltrated, and members, once arrested, easily gave up their comrades. Similarly, Al Qaeda was most dangerous when it was a unified hierarchy. Now that it has dissipated into a network, it has proved far less effective.

25   The drawbacks of networks scarcely matter if the network isn't interested in systemic change—if it just wants to frighten or humiliate or make a splash—or if it doesn't need to think strategically. But if you're taking on a powerful and organized establishment you have to be a hierarchy. The Montgomery bus boycott required the participation of tens of thousands of people who depended on public transit to get to and from work each day. It lasted a *year*. In order to persuade those people to stay true to the cause, the boycott's organizers tasked each local black church with maintaining morale, and put together a free alternative private carpool service, with forty-eight dispatchers and forty-two pickup stations. Even the White Citizens Council, King later said, conceded that the carpool system moved with "military precision." By the time King came to Birmingham, for the climactic showdown with Police Commissioner Eugene (Bull) Connor, he had a budget of a million dollars, and a hundred full-time staff members on the ground, divided into operational units. The operation itself was divided into steadily escalating phases, mapped out in advance. Support was maintained through consecutive mass meetings rotating from church to church around the city.

26   Boycotts and sit-ins and nonviolent confrontations—which were the weapons of choice for the civil-rights movement—are high-risk strategies. They leave little room for conflict and error. The moment even one protester deviates from the script and responds to provocation, the moral legitimacy of the entire protest is compromised. Enthusiasts for social media would no doubt have us believe that King's task in Birmingham would have been made infinitely easier had he been able to communicate with his followers through Facebook, and contented himself with tweets from a Birmingham jail. But networks are messy: think of the ceaseless pattern of correction and revision, amendment and debate that characterizes Wikipedia. If Martin Luther King, Jr., had tried to do a wiki-boycott in Montgomery, he would have been steamrollered by the white power structure. And of what use would a digital communication tool be in a town where ninety-eight per cent of the black community could be reached every

Sunday morning at church? The things that King needed in Birmingham—discipline and strategy—were things that online social media cannot provide.

27   The bible of the social-media movement is Clay Shirky's *Here Comes Everybody*. Shirky, who teaches at New York University, sets out to demonstrate the organizing power of the Internet, and he begins with the story of Evan, who worked on Wall Street, and his friend Ivanna, after she left her smart phone, an expensive Sidekick, on the back seat of a New York City taxicab. The telephone company transferred the data on Ivanna's lost phone to a new phone, whereupon she and Evan discovered that the Sidekick was now in the hands of a teen-ager from Queens, who was using it to take photographs of herself and her friends.

28   When Evan e-mailed the teen-ager, Sasha, asking for the phone back, she replied that his "white ass" didn't deserve to have it back. Miffed, he set up a Web page with her picture and a description of what had happened. He forwarded the link to his friends, and they forwarded it to their friends. Someone found the MySpace page of Sasha's boyfriend, and a link to it found its way onto the site. Someone found her address online and took a video of her home while driving by; Evan posted the video on the site. The story was picked up by the news filter Digg. Evan was now up to ten e-mails a minute. He created a bulletin board for his readers to share their stories, but it crashed under the weight of responses. Evan and Ivanna went to the police, but the police filed the report under "lost," rather than "stolen," which essentially closed the case. "By this point millions of readers were watching," Shirky writes, "and dozens of mainstream news outlets had covered the story." Bowing to the pressure, the N.Y.P.D. reclassified the item as "stolen." Sasha was arrested, and Evan got his friend's Sidekick back.

29   Shirky's argument is that this is the kind of thing that could never have happened in the pre-Internet age—and he's right. Evan could never have tracked down Sasha. The story of the Sidekick would never have been publicized. An army of people could never have assembled to wage this fight. The police wouldn't have bowed to the pressure of a lone person who had misplaced something as trivial as a cell phone. The story, to Shirky, illustrates "the ease and speed with which a group can be mobilized for the right kind of cause" in the Internet age.

30   Shirky considers this model of activism an upgrade. But it is simply a form of organizing which favors the weak-tie connections that give us access to information over the strong-tie connections that help us persevere in the face of danger. It shifts our energies from organizations that promote strategic and disciplined activity and toward those which promote resilience and adaptability. It makes it easier for activists to express themselves, and harder for that expression to have any impact. The instruments of social media are well suited to making the existing social order more efficient. They are not a natural enemy of the status quo. If you are of the opinion that all the world needs is a little buffing around the edges, this should not trouble you. But if you think that there are still lunch counters out there that need integrating it ought to give you pause.

31   Shirky ends the story of the lost Sidekick by asking, portentously, "What happens next?"—no doubt imagining future waves of digital protesters. But he has already answered the question. What happens next is more of the same. A networked, weak-tie world is good at things like helping Wall Streeters get phones back from teen-age girls. *Viva la revolución.*

DAVID **CARR**

Why Twitter Will Endure

David Carr is the author of "Media Equation," a column in the *New York Times* that focuses on media issues. His work analyzes the media as they intersect with business, culture, and government. His writing has also appeared in the *Atlantic Monthly* and *New York Magazine.* The following *Times* article was published on January 3, 2010.

I can remember when I first thought seriously about Twitter. Last March, I was at the SXSW conference, a conclave in Austin, Tex., where technology, media, and music are mashed up and re-imagined, and, not so coincidentally, where Twitter first rolled out in 2007. As someone who was oversubscribed on Facebook, overwhelmed by the computer-generated RSS feeds of news that came flying at me, and swamped by incoming e-mail messages, the last thing I wanted was one more Web-borne intrusion into my life.

2 And then there was the name. Twitter. In the pantheon of digital nomenclature— brands within a sector of the economy that grew so fast that all the sensible names were quickly taken—it would be hard to come up with a noun more trite than Twitter. It impugns itself, promising something slight and inconsequential, yet another way to make hours disappear and have nothing to show for it. And just in case the noun is not sufficiently indicting, the verb, "to tweet" is even more embarrassing.

3 Beyond the dippy lingo, the idea that something intelligent, something worthy of mindshare, might occur in the space of 140 characters—Twitter's parameters were set by what would fit in a text message on a phone—seems unlikely.

4 But it was clear that at the conference, the primary news platform was Twitter, with real-time annotation of the panels on stage and critical updates about what was happening elsewhere at a very hectic convention. At 52, I succumbed, partly out of professional necessity.

5 And now, nearly a year later, has Twitter turned my brain to mush? No, I'm in narrative on more things in a given moment than I ever thought possible, and instead of spending a half-hour surfing in search of illumination, I get a sense of the day's news and how people are reacting to it in the time that it takes to wait for coffee at Starbucks. Yes, I worry about my ability to think long thoughts—where was I, anyway?—but the tradeoff has been worth it.

6 Some time soon, the company won't say when, the 100-millionth person will have signed on to Twitter to follow and be followed by friends and strangers. That may sound like a MySpace waiting to happen—remember MySpace?—but I'm convinced Twitter is here to stay.

7 And I'm not alone. "The history of the Internet suggests that there have been cool Web sites that go in and out of fashion and then there have been open standards that become plumbing," said Steven Johnson, the author and technology observer who wrote a seminal piece about Twitter for Time last June. "Twitter is looking more and more like plumbing, and plumbing is eternal."

8 Really? What could anyone possibly find useful in this cacophony of short-burst communication? Well, that depends on whom you ask, but more importantly whom you

follow. On Twitter, anyone may follow anyone, but there is very little expectation of reciprocity. By carefully curating the people you follow, Twitter becomes an always-on data stream from really bright people in their respective fields, whose tweets are often full of links to incredibly vital, timely information.

9   The most frequent objection to Twitter is a predictable one: "I don't need to know someone is eating a donut right now." But if that someone is a serious user of Twitter, she or he might actually be eating the curmudgeon's lunch, racing ahead with a clear, up-to-the-second picture of an increasingly connected, busy world. The service has obvious utility for a journalist, but no matter what business you are in, imagine knowing what the thought leaders in your industry were reading and considering. And beyond following specific individuals, Twitter hash tags allow you to go deep into interests and obsession: #rollerderby, #physics, #puppets and #Avatar, to name just a few of many thousands.

10   The act of publishing on Twitter is so friction-free—a few keystrokes and hit send—that you can forget that others are out there listening. I was on a Virgin America cross-country flight, and used its wireless connection to tweet about the fact that the guy next to me seemed to be the leader of a cult involving Axe body spray. A half-hour later, a steward approached me and said he wondered if I would be more comfortable with a seat in the bulkhead. (He turned out to be a great guy, but I was doing a story involving another part of the company, so I had to decline the offer. @VirginAmerica, its corporate Twitter account, sent me a message afterward saying perhaps it should develop a screening process for Axe. It was creepy and comforting all at once.)

11   Like many newbies on Twitter, I vastly overestimated the importance of broadcasting on Twitter; and after a while, I realized that I was not Moses and neither Twitter nor its users were wondering what I thought. Nearly a year in, I've come to understand that the real value of the service is listening to a wired collective voice.

12   Not that long ago, I was at a conference at Yale and looked at the sea of open laptops in the seats in front of me. So why wasn't my laptop open? Because I follow people on Twitter who serve as my Web-crawling proxies, each of them tweeting links that I could examine and read on a Blackberry. Regardless of where I am, I surf far less than I used to.

13   At first, Twitter can be overwhelming, but think of it as a river of data rushing past that I dip a cup into every once in a while. Much of what I need to know is in that cup: if it looks like Apple is going to demo its new tablet, or Amazon sold more Kindles than actual books at Christmas, or the final vote in the Senate gets locked in on health care, I almost always learn about it first on Twitter.

14   The expressive limits of a kind of narrative developed from text messages, with less space to digress or explain than this sentence, has significant upsides. The best people on Twitter communicate with economy and precision, with each element—links, hash tags and comments—freighted with meaning. Professional acquaintances whom I find insufferable on every other platform suddenly become interesting within the confines of Twitter.

15   Twitter is incredibly customizable, with little of the social expectations that go with Facebook. Depending on whom you follow, Twitter can reveal a nation riveted by the last episode of "Jersey Shore" or a short-form conclave of brilliance. There is plenty of

nonsense—#Tiger had quite a run—but there are rich threads on the day's news and bravura solo performances from learned autodidacts. And the ethos of Twitter, which is based on self-defining groups, is far more well-mannered than many parts of the Web—more Toastmasters than mosh pit. On Twitter, you are your avatar and your avatar is you, so best not to act like a lout and when people want to flame you for something you said, they are responding to their own followers, not yours, so trolls quickly lose interest.

16   "Anything that is useful to both dissidents in Iran and Martha Stewart has a lot going for it; Twitter has more raw capability for users than anything since e-mail," said Clay Shirky, who wrote "Here Comes Everybody," a book about social media. "It will be hard to wait out Twitter because it is lightweight, endlessly useful and gets better as more people use it. Brands are using it, institutions are using it, and it is becoming a place where a lot of important conversations are being held." Twitter helps define what is important by what Mr. Shirky has called "algorithmic authority," meaning that if all kinds of people are pointing at the same thing at the same instant, it must be a pretty big deal.

17   Beyond the throbbing networked intelligence, there is the possibility of practical magic. Twitter can tell you what kind of netbook you should buy for your wife for Christmas—thanks Twitter!—or call you out when you complain about the long lines it took to buy it, as a tweeter on behalf of the electronics store B & H did when I shared the experience on my Blackberry while in line. I have found transcendent tacos at a car wash in San Antonio, rediscovered a brand of reporter's notepad I adore, uncovered sources for stories, all just by typing a query into Twitter.

18   All those riches do not come at zero cost: If you think e-mail and surfing can make time disappear, wait until you get ahold of Twitter, or more likely, it gets ahold of you. There is always something more interesting on Twitter than whatever you happen to be working on.

19   But in the right circumstance, Twitter can flex some big muscles. Think of last weekend, a heavy travel period marked by a terrorist incident on Friday. As news outlets were scrambling to understand the implications for travelers on Saturday morning, Twitter began lighting up with reports of new security initiatives, including one from @CharleneLi, a consultant who tweeted from the Montreal airport at about 7:30 A.M.: "New security rules for int'l flights into US. 1 bag, no electronics the ENTIRE flight, no getting up last hour of flight." It was far from the whole story and getting ahead of the news by some hours would seem like no big deal, but imagine you or someone you loved was flying later that same day: Twitter might seem very useful.

20   Twitter's growing informational hegemony is not assured. There have been serious outages in recent weeks, leading many business and government users to wonder about the stability of the platform. And this being the Web, many smart folks are plotting ways to turn Twitter into so much pixilated mist. But I don't think so. I can go anywhere I want on the Web, but there is no guarantee that my Twitter gang will come with me. I may have quite a few followers, but that doesn't make me Moses.

Neil Richards

The Perils of Social Reading

Neil M. Richards is a professor of law at Washington University in St. Louis. An expert on privacy law and the First Amendment, he frequently writes about the relationships between civil liberties and technology, and his book *Intellectual Privacy* was recently published by Oxford University Press. Born in England, he holds degrees in law and legal history from the University of Virginia; he was a law clerk for William H. Rehnquist (the late Chief Justice of the U.S. Supreme Court). He can be followed on *Twitter* @ neilmrichards. The following item is an adaptation done by Richards of a much longer article of the same title that he published in the *Georgetown Law Journal* (vol. 101, no. 3) in 2013.

Sharing, we are told, is cool. At the urging of Facebook and Netflix, the House of Representatives recently passed a bill to "update" an obscure 1988 law known as the Video Privacy Protection Act ("VPPA").[1] Facebook and Netflix wanted to modernize this law from the VHS era, because its protection of video store records stood in the way of sharing movie recommendations among friends online. The law would have allowed companies to obtain a single consent to automatically share all movies viewed on Facebook and other social networks forever. The bill stalled in the Senate after a feisty hearing[2] before Senator Franken, though some modernization of our video privacy law is inevitable.

2   But the VPPA debate is just the start, merely one part of a much larger trend towards "social reading." The Internet and social media have opened up new vistas for us to share our preferences in films, books, and music. Services like Spotify and the Washington Post Social Reader already integrate our reading and listening into social networks, providing what Facebook CEO Mark Zuckerberg calls "frictionless sharing."[3] Under a regime of frictionless sharing, we don't need to choose to share our activities online. Instead, everything we read or watch automatically gets uploaded to our social media feeds. As Zuckerberg puts it, "Do you want to go to the movies by yourself or do you want to go to the movies with your friends? You want to go with your friends."[4] Music, reading, web-surfing, and Google searches, in this view, would all seem to benefit from being made social.[5]

3   Not so fast. The sharing of book, film, and music recommendations is important, and social networking has certainly made this easier. But a world of automatic, always-on disclosure should give us pause. What we read, watch, and listen to matter, because they are how we make up our minds about important social issues—in a very real sense, they're how we make sense of the world.

4   What's at stake is something I call "intellectual privacy"—the idea that records of our reading and movie watching deserve special protection compared to other kinds of personal information.[6] The films we watch, the books we read, and the web sites we visit are essential to the ways we try to understand the world we live in. Intellectual privacy protects our ability to think for ourselves, without worrying that other people might judge us based on what we read. It allows us to explore ideas that other people might not approve of, and to figure out our politics, sexuality, and personal values, among other things. It lets us watch or read whatever we want without fear of embarrassment or being outed. This is the case whether we're reading communist, gay teen, or anti-globalization books; or visiting web sites about abortion, gun control, or cancer; or watching videos of pornography, or documentaries by Michael Moore, or even "The Hangover 2."

5   I'm not saying we should never share our intellectual preferences. On the contrary, sharing and commenting on books, films, and ideas is the essence of free speech. We need access to the ideas of others so that we can make up our minds for ourselves. Individual liberty has a social component. But when we share—when we speak—we should do so consciously and deliberately, not automatically and unconsciously. Because of the constitutional magnitude of these values, our social, technological, professional, and legal norms should support rather than undermine our intellectual privacy.

6   "Frictionless sharing" isn't really frictionless—it forces on us the new frictions of worrying who knows what we're reading and what our privacy settings are wherever and however we read electronically. It's also not really sharing—real sharing is conscious sharing, a recommendation to read or not to read something rather than a data exhaust pipe of mental activity. At a practical level, then, always-on social sharing of our reader records provides less valuable recommendations than conscious sharing, and it can deter us from exploring ideas that our friends might find distasteful. Rather than "over-sharing," we should share better, which means consciously,

and we should expand the limited legal protections for intellectual privacy rather than dismantling them.

7   There is a paradox to reader privacy: we need intellectual privacy to make up our minds, but we often need the assistance and recommendations of others as part of this process, be they friends, librarians, or search engines. The work of the ALA and its Office of Intellectual Freedom offers an attractive solution to the problem of reader records. The OIF has argued passionately (and correctly) for the importance of solitary reading as well as the ethical need for those who enable reading—librarians, but also Internet companies—to protect the privacy and confidentiality of reading records. The norms of librarians suggest one successful and proven solution to this paradox. Most relevant here, this means that professionals and companies holding reader records must only disclose them with the express conscious consent of the reader.

8   The stakes in this debate are immense. We are quite literally rewiring the public and private spheres for a new century. Choices we make now about the boundaries between our individual and social selves, between consumers and companies, between citizens and the state, will have massive consequences for the societies our children and grandchildren inherit.

9   Social networking technologies have matured to the point where many new things are possible. But we face a moment of decision. The choice between sharing and privacy is not fore-ordained; there are many decisions we must make as a society about how our reader records can flow, and under what terms. We've heard from the advocates of "sharing" and "social," but we must also secure a place for the thoughtful, the private, and the ec-centric. When it comes to the question of how to regulate our read-ing records, a world of automatic, constant disclosure is not the answer.

10   The choices we make today will be sticky. They'll have last-ing consequences for the kind of networked society we will build, and whether there's a place in that society for intellectual privacy and for confidential, contemplative, and idiosyncratic reading. Sharing might be cool, but some things, like intellectual privacy and our centuries-old culture of solitary reading, are more impor-tant. We need to preserve them; we need to choose intellectual privacy.

NOTES

1. H.R. 2471, 112th Cong. (2011).
2. *The Video Privacy Protection Act: Protecting Viewer Privacy in the 21st Century: Hearing on H.R. 2471 Before the Subcomm. on Privacy, Technology and the Law of the S. Comm. on the Judiciary, 112th Cong.* (2012).
3. Alexia Tsotsis, *Live from Facebook's 2011 F8 Conference [Video]*, TECHCRUNCH (Feb. 20, 2012, 11:50 PM), http://techcrunch.com/2011/09/22/live-from-facebooks-2011-f8-conference-video/ (Zuckerberg said "[t]hese new apps will focus on 'Frictionless Experiences,' 'Realtime Serendipity' and 'Finding patterns' ").
4. Evgeny Morozov, *The Death of the Cyberflâneur*, New York Times , Feb. 5, 2012, at SR2.
5. See also Jeff Jarvis, *Public Parts: How Sharing in the Digital Age Improves the Way We Work and Live* 43–62 (2011) (extolling the values of sharing and "publicness").
6. Neil M. Richards, *Intellectual Privacy*, 87 Tex. L. Rev. 387 (2008). For a partial list of other scholars who have adopted this framework, see, e.g., Julie Cohen, *The Networked Self* (2012); Daniel J. Solove, *Nothing to Hide* (2011); Pauline Kim, *Electronic Privacy and Employee Speech*, 87 Chi.-Kent. L. Rev. (forthcoming 2012); William McGeveran, *Mrs. Mcintyre's Persona: Bringing Privacy Theory to Election Law*, 19 Wm. and Mary Bill Rts. J. 859 (2011); Paul Ohm, *Massive Hard Drives, General Warrants, and the Power of Magistrate Judges*, 97 Va. L. Rev. In Brief 1 (2011); Christopher Slobogin, *Citizens United & Corporate & Human Crime,* 1 Green Bag 2d 77 (2010).

ISSUE IN FOCUS

Are Video Games Good for You?

The video game *Tomb Raider,* featuring Lara Croft as its British-archeologist heroine, was released in 1996 and soon developed into a pop culture phenomenon. In addition to becoming the most popular video game in history, *Tomb Raider* became a movie, and then a second movie (with Angelina Jolie in the starring role)—and then a comic book, a novel, and even a theme park ride. Lara Croft's fans regard her as an ideal female icon—as brave as she is beautiful, strong and daring and smart, resourceful and fiercely independent.

But Lara Croft has not been without her critics. Skeptics, noting how Lara Croft's breast size seemed to increase along with her popularity, have contended that she is simply reinforcing traditional stereotypes, that her popularity derives from her starring role in the sexual fantasies of the predominantly male audience that enjoys "playing with her." Almost all teenage boys play video games, but only about half of girls do so, and so no wonder parents worry about the effect of video games on consumers' sex and gender attitudes. For *Tomb Raider* is hardly the only game that depicts women and men in traditional roles, the men as active adventurers, the women as passive victims or sex objects.

Angelina Jolie as Lara Croft in *Lara Croft Tomb Raider: The Cradle of Life* (2003), a film based on a series of bestselling video games.

Critics of video games wonder about other issues as well, just as an earlier generation worried about the effects of television. While many video games depend on social interactions, requiring or permitting multiple players to interact via networked systems and thus bringing people together, many other games can be played individually. Do video games lead to social isolation? Is there an addictive element to gaming that makes their consumers socially inept?

And what about the stylized violence that lies at the heart of many video games? If games ask players to abuse women and shoot policemen, is it any wonder that those activities persist in real life? When those who carry out school shootings are shown to be devotees of video games, shouldn't we worry about the effects of prolonged exposure to gaming? True, the games are age-rated, as movies are, but it is easy to evade the rules and obtain adult-rated games illegally. And it is worrisome that adult males are especially eager players of violent video games, particularly when the violence in the games is directed at women. Even though juvenile crime rates actually seem to be down, suggesting that people can usually distinguish the difference between game life and real life, it seems natural to expect that video games are affecting people's values—and actions—negatively. Are video games a kind of propaganda—do the games sensationalize drugs and alcohol and illicit sex, in effect "advertising" a way of life that is socially destructive? Or is it all in good fun?

Indeed, people criticize video games irrespective of their content. They contend that video games make people not just socially inept but also sedentary. Is the national obesity epidemic related to the popularity of video gaming? Do games, like television, encourage people to avoid real physical activity in order to perform fantasy deeds in front of a screen? And are children playing video games instead of reading or doing homework? In other words, are video games compromising our educational aspirations? Or do they actually help their users, not only by honing hand-eye coordination and visual perception skills but by improving the analytical and problem-solving abilities of users as well as their creativity and ability to concentrate. It has even been suggested that video games can assist in the treatment of autism and certain other mental health conditions.

The selections in this Issue in Focus propose answers to those questions. John Beck and Mitchell Wade blame video games for giving people an unreal sense of reality, while James Paul Gee defends video games for their educational value. Kevin Moss, with a substantial sense of irony, makes a strong case that video games set women back. Finally, Clay Shirky concludes the segment, and the chapter, with a fascinating defense of new media that is based on their ability to bring us together and shake us into becoming our most creative selves. (You should also consult the essay on this topic by student Armadi Tansal in Chapter 9.)

John C. Beck and Mitchell Wade

How the Gamer Revolution Is Reshaping Business Forever

DEFINITELY NOT IN KANSAS ANYMORE

Games are a technology that has been universally adopted by a large, young cohort and ignored by their elders. That's powerful enough to start with. But when you look at the experience that technology delivers—the content and the nature of the gamers' world—things really get interesting. Universally, and almost subliminally, games deliver a "reality" where the rules are quite different from any found out here in the rest of the world. Take a look at this quick overview of the lessons games teach:

The Individual's Role

- *You're the star.* You are the center of attention of every game unlike, say, Little League, where most kids will *never* be the star.
- *You're the boss.* The world is very responsive to you. You can choose things about reality, or switch to different experiences, in a way that is literally impossible in real life.
- *You're the customer, and the customer is always right.* Like shopping, the whole experience is designed for your satisfaction and entertainment; the opponents are tough, but never *too* tough.
- *You're an expert.* You have the experience of getting really, really good—especially compared to others who actually see you perform—early and often.

■ *You're a tough guy.* You can experience all sorts of crashes, suffering, and death—and it doesn't hurt.

How the World Works

■ *There's always an answer.* You might be frustrated for a while, you might even never find it, but you know it's there.

■ *Everything is possible.* You see yourself or other players consistently do amazing things: defeat hundreds of bad guys singlehandedly, say, or beat the best N.B.A. team ever.

■ *The world is a logical, human-friendly place.* Games are basically fair. Events may be random but not inexplicable, and there is not much mystery.

■ *Trial-and-error is almost always the best plan.* It's the only way to advance in most games, even if you ultimately break down and buy a strategy guide or copy others on the really hard parts.

■ *Things are (unrealistically) simple.* Games are driven by models. Even complex models are a lot simpler than reality. *You can figure a game out, completely.* Try that with real life.

How People Relate

■ *It's all about competition.* You're always competing; even if you collaborate with other human players, you are competing against some character or score.

■ *Relationships are structured.* To make the game work, there are only a few pigeonholes people (real or virtual) can fit into, such as competitor/ally and boss/subordinate.

■ *We are all alone.* The gaming experience is basically solitary, even if played in groups. And you don't experience all of the activity, for any sustained time, as part of a group.

■ *Young people rule.* Young people dominate gaming. Paying your dues takes a short time, youth actually helps, and there is no attention paid to elders.

■ *People are simple.* Most in games are cartoon characters. Their skills may be complex, multidimensional, and user-configurable, but their personality types and behaviors are simple. There's big and strong, wild and crazy, beautiful and sexy, and a few other caricatures. That's it.

What You Should Do

■ *Rebel.* Edginess and attitude are dominant elements of the culture.

■ *Be a hero.* You always get the star's role; that is the only way to succeed or get satisfaction.

■ *Bond with people who share your game experience, not your national or cultural background.* It's a very global world, in design, consumption, and characters, and in the phenomenon of the game generation.

■ *Make your own way in the world.* Leaders are irrelevant and often evil; ignore them.

■ *Tune out and have fun.* The whole experience of gaming is escapist. When reality is boring, you hop into game world. When a game gets boring, you switch to one that isn't.

Not exactly like "real life," is it? And remember, this other-worldly experience has been exclusive to gamers.

JAMES PAUL **GEE**

Games, Not Schools, Are Teaching Kids to Think

The US spends almost $50 billion each year on education, so why aren't kids learning? Forty percent of students lack basic reading skills, and their academic performance is dismal compared with that of their foreign counterparts. In response to this crisis, schools are skilling-and-drilling their way "back to basics," moving toward mechanical instruction methods that rely on line-by-line scripting for teachers and endless multiple-choice testing. Consequently, kids aren't learning how to think anymore—they're learning how to memorize. This might be an ideal recipe for the future Babbitts of the world, but it won't produce the kind of agile, analytical minds that will lead the high tech global age. Fortunately, we've got *Grand Theft Auto: Vice City* and *Deus X* for that.

2   After school, kids are devouring new information, concepts, and skills every day, and, like it or not, they're doing it controller in hand, plastered to the TV. The fact is, when kids play videogames they can experience a much more powerful form of learning than when they're in the classroom. Learning isn't about memorizing isolated facts. It's about connecting and manipulating them. Doubt it? Just ask anyone who's beaten *Legend of Zelda* or solved *Morrowind*.

3   The phenomenon of the videogame as an agent of mental training is largely unstudied; more often, games are denigrated for being violent or they're just plain ignored. They shouldn't be. Young gamers today aren't training to be gun-toting carjackers. They're learning how to learn. In *Pikmin*, children manage an army of plantlike aliens and strategize to solve problems. In *Metal Gear Solid 2*, players move stealthily through virtual environments and carry out intricate missions. Even in the notorious *Vice City*, players craft a persona, build a history, and shape a virtual world. In strategy games like *WarCraft III* and *Age of Mythology*, they learn to micromanage an array of elements while simultaneously balancing short- and long-term goals. That sounds like something for their resumes.

4   The secret of a videogame as a teaching machine isn't its immersive 3-D graphics but its underlying architecture. Each level dances around the outer limits of the player's abilities, seeking at every point to be hard enough to be just doable. In cognitive science, this is referred to as the "regime of competence principle," which results in a feeling of simultaneous pleasure and frustration—a sensation as familiar to gamers as sore thumbs. Cognitive scientist Andy diSessa has argued that the best instruction hovers at the boundary of a student's competence. Most schools, however, seek to avoid invoking feelings of both pleasure and frustration, blind to the fact that these emotions can be extremely useful when it comes to teaching kids.

5   Also, good videogames incorporate the principle of expertise. They tend to encourage players to achieve total mastery of one level, only to challenge and undo that mastery in the next, forcing kids to adapt and evolve. This carefully choreographed dialectic has been identified by learning theorists as the best way to achieve expertise

in any field. This doesn't happen much in our routine-driven schools, where "good" students are often just good at "doing school."

6   How did videogames become such successful models of effective learning? Game coders aren't trained as cognitive scientists. It's a simple case of free-market economics: If a title doesn't teach players how to play it well, it won't sell well. Game companies don't rake in $6.9 billion a year by dumbing down the material—aficionados condemn short and easy games like *Half Life: Blue Shift* and *Devil May Cry 2*. Designers respond by making harder and more complex games that require mastery of sophisticated worlds and as many as 50 to 100 hours to complete. Schools, meanwhile, respond with more tests, more drills, and more rigidity. They're in the cognitive-science dark ages.

7   We don't often think about videogames as relevant to education reform, but maybe we should. Game designers don't often think of themselves as learning theorists. Maybe they should. Kids often say it doesn't feel like learning when they're gaming—they're much too focused on playing. If kids were to say that about a science lesson, our country's education problems would be solved.

Kevin
Moss

Blog Entry: The Enemy of My Irony Is My Friend

I thought I could keep myself away from this kind of thing. Remember when "blogging" used to be called "keeping an online diary"? Yeah, me too. This was one of the most fun things I used to do, back when sites like Diaryland and Xanga ruled the roost. Those were the days. . . . But here we are again, back to those times of endless amounts of typing about nothing of any particular importance. I'm definitely not promising any kind of commitment to this, I just got an itching for typing crazy things again, and I'm willing to indulge myself (with the added justification that I was doing this kind of thing before the blogosphere had reached it's Seventh Day).

2   In any event, what might be appropriate for the first of several Zebra Tales is a rant on a very particular new gaming vehicle that I just became aware of. While on the website I use for all my news, I learned about "GameCrush," a system that sets women back at least 200 years. Now we all know that a lot of the people who game are lonely boys, either very fat or very skinny, who sit in their domestic caves and glue their greasy little eyes to a screen to live out a life where they actually matter. By the light of day these boys are worthless, shunned by almost every caste, from Bro to Awkward-Plain Girl Who Could Be Pretty With Some Make-Up Maybe to Over-Acheiver Kid to Slutty Slut Slut McGee. But when the lights

go down and school/work ends, these bepimpled boys can transform into muscle-bound demi gods or elite covert operatives or (in the really creepy department) even hot slutty girls whose every purpose in-game is to look sexy with the right video card. And so perhaps it was only a matter of time before some idiots like the guys at GameCrush decided to capitalize on the pathetic state of your average gamer boy—and crap all over women in the process.

3   GameCrush is a website that ostensibly encourages boy-girl interactions via games. Boys sign on as "Players" and girls sign on as "PlayDates" (yeah, I'll let you draw your own conclusions). These girls set up a MySpace-like homepage that shows a picture, what games she'd like to pay (currently it allows for Xbox Live support) and several other *vital* statistics. One of these is a Facebook status-like idea which lets the girl set her inclination to either "Flirty" or "Dirty" (and here I thought women were complex). She can include pictures of herself, videos, and an About Me section for showing, I guess, how chaste she is. Now Players (the aforementioned nerdy nerds) select a PlayDate they want to . . . um . . . play with and send her an invite. Now the invite can include anything, from chatting with her to webcamming to actually playing a game with her. But here's the catch: the Players must purchase credits to spend *any* time gaming with the PlayDates in the first place. A certain number of credits get you a certain number of minutes to spend with the girl. The game economics are structured so that you will invariably have credits left over so that, when your session is over, the Players are prompted to spend their remaining credits as a *tip* for the PlayDate.

4   Now whether you tip your PlayDate is open to the Player's discretion, but I have a funny feeling it'll have *something* to do with how flirty or dirty she's been with the Player during their 10 minute rendezvous. . . . But that's just me. Oh, and guess what these lovely ladies can do with these tips? Well they can EXCHANGE THEM FOR CASH. Yes, that's right, cash monies. GameCrush lets their women keep 60% of the money they get from their Johns, I mean Players. And the company keeps the other 40% because, well, Daddy has bills to pay.

5   Then, if this weren't bad enough, the girls are then rated by the Players they interact with on things like hotness and flirtiness. The girls with the highest ratings will not only attract more attention and so make more money for Daddy and themselves but the company behind GameCrush will actually promote their top PlayDates on another website called JaneCrush where these PlayDates will effectively be turned into mini-celebrities. Whether you're looking at this from a Darwinistic view, a Capitalistic view, or a just plain friggin' common sense view, it's clear that the girls who

are sluttier on this website will get paid more. Indeed, the girls who are just normal human beings who just want to play a game (god forbid) will be relegated to the unsightly realm of unpopular shunned frag hags. Hey, I like that one, maybe it'll catch on.

6   Now, in some sort of weak preliminary defense for the kind of outcry from certain circles that this company is sure to receive, they claimed in their press release for GameCrush that the game economics are based on the concept and the cost of buying a girl a drink in a bar which, they argue, is not for the purpose of getting to know a new person but really for an ulterior motive. Let me explain to the idiots who made up that ridiculous explanation why the two are *completely* different. When you walk into a bar and see a girl you think is hot, you don't *have* to spend money on her to get her to pay attention to you (maybe you should, but spending money on strange women isn't *built in* to the mechanics of life). You can talk with her, dance with her, even go home with her without being required by the bar owners to liquor her up on your own dime. Now often, a girl *will* broadcast something about her sluttiness in just what she wears so maybe this could be akin to some sort of typed status about how horny she is that everyone can see. Kinda. Oh, and before everyone starts yelling about how sexist it is to even *suggest* that you can infer *anything* from a girl's clothing choice, let me just say that I've known plenty of complete hookers who rarely go out to a social setting looking anything other than complete hookers, and I've known plenty of sweet reserved girls who rarely go out looking like complete hookers. I don't think I've ever seen the innocent, just kisses on the first date, girl next door go out in a microskirt and orange tan.

7   And, as for guys, there's a reason I go to bars in a nice polo and jeans and not a wifebeater, gold necklace, sideways baseball cap, and slicked back hair. Just sayin. But what most bars definitely do *not* have is a system whereby male patrons get to rate these girls on the basis of their flirtiness and hotness. Can you imagine talking to a girl for a little while and then saying, "well I haven't really enjoyed talking to you, bitch, you get a 3 on flirtiness and definitely a 2 on hotness, and forget the tip sweetheart, next time go for the tube top." Damn.

8   Oh yeah, guys tip the *bartender* not the girl they're talking to. Jesus. Should there also be a big bulletin board on the outside of bars that has pictures of all the girls inside with ratings from all the guys they've talked to based on their hotness? Now *that* would be something. Funny how the more you put the Game-Crush system in terms of real life it becomes clear that this would be almost completely unacceptable. But for some reason, when it comes to the Internet, here we are.

9   And how did GameCrush get its first batch of PlayDates? Well they opened up an ad on Craigslist. Yeah, no joke. Craigslist. When I think completely consensual and not creepy in any way I think Craigslist. I was reading an article on IGN about it and they actually posted a sample of what one of the PlayDates has on her page, complete with her picture. Just scroll down to the middle until you see the pic of the sexy blonde. Mmm, must sign up. Damnit GameCrush! The guy who wrote the article actually seems to think GameCrush might be a *good* idea, but I guess when you work with Jessica Chobot you get a slightly warped idea of what the average gamer girl is like.

10   But the worst impact of GameCrush may be its role in further marginalizing women in an everyday environment. Time was, girls were *extremely* rare in online games. As someone who's been gaming online since StarCraft I remember that if ever there was the rarity of seeing a girl in-game it was like throwing a gallon of blood in a kiddie pool filled with vampire sharks. Comments ranged from the more "mild" forms of sexual harassment (are you hot, how old are you, are you single, etc.) to the real depraved and disgusting stuff that most guys would only feel comfortable saying behind the safety of their computer screens. But these days more and more and more girls are taking part in online games, partly because back in the day almost all of the games that had online support were wargames and shooters while today you can play almost anything with friends and also because as games become mainstream acceptable (with things like Wii Fit and RockBand bringing in all sorts) they are becoming more attractive to more than just the super nerds who live off them.

11   Now that we're not only encouraging the vampire sharks but providing the kiddie pool and blood for a small fee, we're saying to girls "sure, you can do what you'd normally do in the privacy of your own home for fun, but you're going to have be slutty and sexy and be ready to pay attention to any asshole who talks to you in the process." I told Dana about this and she raised a good point: why is it necessary to sexualize everything women do? Why can't they just do shit and that's it? Why do I have to pay a girl to play a game with me when I could just go out and friggin ASK one of the tens of thousands to just play?

12   Interestingly enough, I think I actually pissed off one of my feminst-inclined Oberlin friends when I posted something about this as my fb status. Because the system is outlined by gender roles (as far as I can tell, guys can't be PlayDates), I suggested that the sexist part about this system is the fact that GameCrush

discriminates against *men* because they can't play both parts and get paid. It should be obvious why this is *not* the main problem with GameCrush, but ironically it seems as though I pissed off one of the many people I was trying to speak up for.

13   But then there's just something deliciously funny about that.

Clay Shirky

Gin, Television, and Social Surplus: A Speech—April 26, 2008

I was recently reminded of some reading I did in college, way back in the last century, by a British historian arguing that the critical technology, for the early phase of the industrial revolution, was gin. The transformation from rural to urban life was so sudden, and so wrenching, that the only thing society could do to manage was to drink itself into a stupor for a generation. The stories from that era are amazing—there were gin pushcarts working their way through the streets of London.

2   And it wasn't until society woke up from that collective bender that we actually started to get the institutional structures that we associate with the industrial revolution today. Things like public libraries and museums, increasingly broad education for children, elected leaders—a lot of things we like—didn't happen until having all of those people together stopped seeming like a crisis and started seeming like an asset. It wasn't until people started thinking of this as a vast civic surplus, one they could design for rather than just dissipate, that we started to get what we think of now as an industrial society.

3   If I had to pick the critical technology for the 20th century, the bit of social lubricant without which the wheels would've come off the whole enterprise, I'd say it was the sitcom. Starting with the Second World War a whole series of things happened—rising GDP per capita, rising educational attainment, rising life expectancy and, critically, a rising number of people who were working five-day work weeks. For the first time, society forced onto an enormous number of its citizens the requirement to manage something they had never had to manage before—free time.

4   And what did we do with that free time? Well, mostly we spent it watching TV.

5   We did that for decades. We watched "I Love Lucy." We watched "Gilligan's Island." We watch "Malcolm in the Middle." We watch "Desperate Housewives." "Desperate Housewives" essentially functioned as a kind of cognitive heat sink, dissipating thinking that might otherwise have built up and caused society to overheat. And it's only now, as we're waking up from that collective bender, that we're starting to see the cognitive surplus as an asset rather than as a crisis. We're seeing things being designed to take advantage of that surplus, to deploy it in ways more engaging than just having a TV in everybody's basement.

6   This hit me in a conversation I had about two months ago. I've finished a book called *Here Comes Everybody*, which has recently come out, and this recognition came out of a conversation I had about the book. I was being interviewed by a TV producer to see whether I should be on their show, and she asked me, "What are you seeing out there that's interesting?" I started telling her about the Wikipedia article on Pluto. You may remember that Pluto got kicked out of the planet club a couple of years ago, so all of a sudden there was all of this activity on Wikipedia. The talk pages light up, people are editing the article like mad, and the whole community is in an ruckus—"How should we characterize this change in Pluto's status?" And a little bit at a time they move the article—fighting offstage all the while—from, "Pluto is the ninth planet," to "Pluto is an odd-shaped rock with an odd-shaped orbit at the edge of the solar system."

7   So I tell her all this stuff, and I think, "Okay, we're going to have a conversation about authority or social construction or whatever." That wasn't her question. She heard this story and she shook her head and said, "Where do people find the time?" That was her question. And I just kind of snapped. And I said, "No one who works in TV gets to ask that question. You know where the time comes from. It comes from the cognitive surplus you've been masking for 50 years."

8   So how big is that surplus? If you take Wikipedia as a kind of unit, all of Wikipedia, the whole project—every page, every edit, every talk page, every line of code, in every language that Wikipedia exists in—that represents something like the cumulation of 100 million hours of human thought. I worked this out with Martin Wattenberg at IBM; it's a back-of-the-envelope calculation, but it's the right order of magnitude, about 100 million hours of thought.

9   And television watching? Two hundred billion hours, in the U.S. alone, every year. Put another way, now that we have a unit, that's 2,000 Wikipedia projects a year spent watching television. Or put still another way, in the U.S., we spend 100 million hours every weekend, just watching the ads. This is a pretty big surplus. People asking, "Where do they find the time?" when they're looking at things like Wikipedia don't understand how tiny that entire project is, as a carve-out of this asset that's finally being dragged into what Tim calls an architecture of participation.

10   Now, the interesting thing about a surplus like that is that society doesn't know what to do with it at first—hence the gin, hence the sitcoms. Because if people knew what to do with a surplus with reference to the existing social institutions, then it wouldn't be a surplus, would it? It's precisely when no one has any idea how to deploy something that people have to start experimenting with it, in order for the surplus to get integrated, and the course of that integration can transform society.

11   The early phase for taking advantage of this cognitive surplus, the phase I think we're still in, is all special cases. The physics of participation is much more like the physics of weather than it is like the physics of gravity. We know all the forces that combine to make these kinds of things work: there's an interesting community over here, there's an interesting sharing model over there, those people are collaborating on open source software. But despite knowing the inputs, we can't predict the outputs yet because there's so much complexity. The way you explore complex ecosystems is you just try lots and lots and lots of things, and you hope that everybody who fails fails informatively so that you can at least find a skull on a pikestaff near where you're going. That's the phase we're in now.

12   Just to pick one example, one I'm in love with, but it's tiny. A couple of weeks one of my students forwarded me a project started by a professor in Brazil, in Fortaleza, named Vasco Furtado. It's a Wiki Map for crime in Brazil. If there's an assault, if there's a burglary, if there's a mugging, a robbery, a rape, a murder, you can go and put a push-pin on a Google Map, and you can characterize the assault, and you start to see a map of where these crimes are occurring.

13   Now, this already exists as tacit information. Anybody who knows a town has some sense of, "Don't go there. That street corner is dangerous. Don't go in this neighborhood. Be careful there after dark." But it's something society knows without society really knowing it, which is to say there's no public source where you can take advantage of it. And the cops, if they have that information, they're certainly not sharing. In fact, one of the things Furtado says in starting the Wiki crime map was, "This information may or may not exist some place in society, but it's actually easier for me to try to rebuild it from scratch than to try and get it from the authorities who might have it now."

14   Maybe this will succeed or maybe it will fail. The normal case of social software is still failure; most of these experiments don't pan out. But the ones that do are quite incredible, and I hope that this one succeeds, obviously. But even if it doesn't, it's illustrated the point already, which is that someone working alone, with really cheap tools, has a reasonable hope of carving out enough of the cognitive surplus, enough of the desire to participate, enough of the collective goodwill of the citizens, to create a resource you couldn't have imagined existing even five years ago.

15   So that's the answer to the question, "Where do they find the time?" Or, rather, that's the numerical answer. But beneath that question was another thought, this one not a question but an observation. In this same conversation with the TV producer I was talking about World of Warcraft guilds, and as I was talking, I could sort of see what she was thinking: "Losers. Grown men sitting in their basement pretending to be elves."

16   At least they're doing something.

17   Did you ever see that episode of "Gilligan's Island" where they almost get off the island and then Gilligan messes up and then they don't? I saw that one. I saw that one a lot when I was growing up. And every half-hour that I watched that was a half an hour I wasn't posting at my blog or editing Wikipedia or contributing to a mailing list. Now I had an ironclad excuse for not doing those things, which is that none of those things existed then. I was forced into the channel of media the way it was because it was the only option. Now it's not, and that's the big surprise. However lousy it is to sit in your basement and pretend to be an elf, I can tell you from personal experience it's worse to sit in your basement and try to figure if Ginger or Mary Ann is cuter.

18   And I'm willing to raise that to a general principle. It's better to do something than to do nothing. Even lolcats, even cute pictures of kittens made even cuter with the addition of cute captions, hold out an invitation to participation. When you see a lolcat, one of the things it says to the viewer is, "If you have some sans-serif fonts on your computer, you can play this game, too." And that's message—I can do that, too—is a big change.

19   This is something that people in the media world don't understand. Media in the 20th century was run as a single race—consumption. How much can we produce? How much can you consume? Can we produce more and you'll consume more? And the answer to that question has generally been yes. But media is actually a triathlon, it's three different events. People like to consume, but they also like to produce, and they like to share. And what's astonished people who were committed to the structure

of the previous society, prior to trying to take this surplus and do something interesting, is that they're discovering that when you offer people the opportunity to produce and to share, they'll take you up on that offer. It doesn't mean that we'll never sit around mindlessly watching "Scrubs" on the couch. It just means we'll do it less.

20   And this is the other thing about the size of the cognitive surplus we're talking about. It's so large that even a small change could have huge ramifications. Let's say that everything stays 99 percent the same, that people watch 99 percent as much television as they used to, but 1 percent of that is carved out for producing and for sharing. The Internet-connected population watches roughly a *trillion* hours of TV a year. That's about five times the size of the annual U.S. consumption. One per cent of that is 100 Wikipedia projects per year worth of participation.

21   I think that's going to be a big deal. Don't you?

22   Well, the TV producer did not think this was going to be a big deal; she was not digging this line of thought. And her final question to me was essentially, "Isn't this all just a fad?" You know, sort of the flagpole-sitting of the early early 21st century? It's fun to go out and produce and share a little bit, but then people are going to eventually realize, "This isn't as good as doing what I was doing before, and settle down. And I made a spirited argument that no, this wasn't the case, that this was in fact a big one-time shift, more analogous to the industrial revolution than to flagpole-sitting. I was arguing that this isn't the sort of thing society grows out of. It's the sort of thing that society grows into. But I'm not sure she believed me, in part because she didn't want to believe me, but also in part because I didn't have the right story yet. And now I do.

23   I was having dinner with a group of friends about a month ago, and one of them was talking about sitting with his four-year-old daughter watching a DVD. And in the middle of the movie, apropos nothing, she jumps up off the couch and runs around behind the screen. That seems like a cute moment. Maybe she's going back there to see if Dora is really back there or whatever. But that wasn't what she was doing. She started rooting around in the cables. And her dad said, "What you doing?" And she stuck her head out from behind the screen and said, "Looking for the mouse."

24   Here's something four-year-olds know: A screen that ships without a mouse ships broken. Here's something four-year-olds know: Media that's targeted at you but doesn't include you may not be worth sitting still for. Those are things that make me believe that this is a one-way change. Because four-year-olds, the people who are soaking most deeply in the current environment, who won't have to go through the trauma that I have to go through of trying to unlearn a childhood spent watching "Gilligan's Island," they just assume that media includes consuming, producing and sharing.

25   It's also become my motto, when people ask me what we're doing—and when I say "we" I mean the larger society trying to figure out how to deploy this cognitive surplus, but I also mean we, especially, the people who are working hammer and tongs at figuring out the next good idea. From now on, that's what I'm going to tell them: We're looking for the mouse. We're going to look at every place that a reader or a listener or a viewer or a user has been locked out, has been served up passive or a fixed or a canned experience, and ask ourselves, "If we carve out a little bit of the cognitive surplus and deploy it here, could we make a good thing happen?" And I'm betting the answer is yes.

26   Thank you very much.

FROM READING TO WRITING

1. Analyze the arguments by Michael Gerson and Malcolm Gladwell: How is each argument the product of its audience and purpose? What sources of argument (ethical appeals, emotional appeals, and logical appeals) does each author choose and why? (See Chapter 6 for more on rhetorical analysis.)

2. Write an argument that makes its point by defining a key term related to new media. You might choose to change someone's attitude toward a particular technology or concept in order to defend or challenge it, for instance, by defining it in a certain way. For example, you might start with the claim that "*Facebook* is just a marketing ploy based on the same principles that define high school yearbooks" or "*Second Life* is actually a blessing for people who are shy by nature." (See Chapter 8 for strategies for writing definition arguments.)

3. Write a humorous story about your own experience with a particular new media technology—but write your story in order to make a point. (See Chapter 11 for advice on writing narrative arguments.) For example, you could report on your unfortunate experience with a new cell phone or video game in order to convince people to avoid making the same mistake.

4. Propose a change in policy related to a technology issue in your community. Are there regulations that would improve the social impact of video games, for example, or *Wikipedia*? (See Chapter 13 for help with writing a proposal argument.)

5. Write a rebuttal of an article related to the new media in your local or school newspaper. Are there misperceptions that you want to correct? (See Chapter 12 for advice on rebuttals.) Consider whether you wish to show the weaknesses in the article, whether you wish to counterargue, or both.

6. Write an essay that argues for the existence of a particular social effect that has resulted from a new media technology. For example, you might argue that the success of a particular local charity derives from its ability to connect with people despite a small staff. Or you might write about the effects of new technology on your local library's internal architecture. Or you could argue that new technologies have actually created a range of new jobs at your university. (For more on cause and effect arguments, see Chapter 9.)

7. Many new media technologies permit people to participate anonymously. Wikipedians, for example, are notoriously anonymous, video games networked through the Internet permit people to play with anonymous others, and people are able to make anonymous comments in response to online news sources. Analyze the effects of this anonymity: Reflect on the impact of anonymity on your own participation, or your own consumption, of online media.

Glossary

A

abstract A summary of an article or book

aesthetic criteria Evaluative criteria based on perceptions of beauty and good taste

analogy An extended comparison of one situation or item to another

APA American Psychological Association

APA documentation Documentation style commonly used in social-science and education disciplines

argument A claim supported by at least one reason

assumption An unstated belief or knowledge that connects a claim with evidence

audience Real or assumed individuals or groups to whom a verbal or written communication is directed

B

bandwagon appeal A fallacy of argument based on the assumption that something is true or correct because "everyone" believes it to be so

bar chart Visual depiction of data created by the use of horizontal or vertical bars that comparatively represent rates or frequencies

because clause A statement that begins with the word *because* and provides a supporting reason for a claim

begging the question A fallacy of argument that uses the claim as evidence for its own validity

bias A personal belief that may skew one's perspective or presentation of information

bibliography List of books and articles about a specific subject

blog A Web-based journal or diary featuring regular entries about a particular subject or daily experiences (also known as a Web log)

brainstorming A method of finding ideas by writing a list of questions or statements about a subject

C

causal argument An argument that seeks to identify the reasons behind a certain event or phenomenon

claim A declaration or assertion made about any given topic

claim of comparison A claim that argues something is like or not like something else

cherry-picking the evidence Pointing to individual cases or data that confirm a position while ignoring a significant amount of data that might contradict that position

common factor method A method used by scientists to identify a recurring factor present in a given cause–effect relationship

common knowledge fallacy Similar to the bandwagon appeal, this fallacy assumes what is widely distributed on the Internet must be true.

consequence The cause–effect result of a given action

context The combination of author, subject, and audience and the broader social, cultural, and economic influences surrounding a text

contextual analysis A type of rhetorical analysis that focuses on the author, the audience, the time, and the circumstances of an argument

counterargument An argument offering an opposing point of view with the goal of demonstrating that it is the stronger of two or more arguments

criteria Standards used to establish a definition or an evaluation

critical reading A process of reading that surpasses an initial understanding or impression of basic content and proceeds with the goal of answering specific questions or examining particular elements

cropping In photography, the process of deleting unwanted parts of an image

cultural assumptions Widely held beliefs that are considered common sense in a particular culture

D

database Large collection of digital information organized for efficient search and retrieval

debate A contest or game in which two or more individuals attempt to use arguments to persuade others to support their opinion

definition argument An argument made by specifying that something does or does not possess certain criteria

diction The choice and use of words in writing and speech

E

either–or A fallacy of argument that presents only two choices in a complex situation

emotional appeal An argumentation strategy that attempts to persuade by stirring the emotions of the audience

empirical research Research that collects data from observation or experiment

ethos An appeal to the audience based on the character and trustworthiness of the speaker or writer

evaluation argument An argument that judges something based on ethical, aesthetic, and/or practical criteria

evaluation of sources The assessment of the relevance and reliability of sources used in supporting claims

evidence Data, examples, or statistics used to support a claim

experimental research Research based on obtaining data under controlled conditions, usually by isolating one variable while holding other variables constant

F

fallacy of argument Failure to provide adequate evidence to support a claim. See *bandwagon appeal, begging the question, false analogy, hasty generalization, name calling, non sequitur, oversimplification, polarization, post hoc fallacy, rationalization, slippery slope, straw man*

false analogy A fallacy of argument that compares two unlike things as if they were similar

feasibility The ability of a proposed solution to be implemented

figurative language The symbolic transference of meaning from one word or phrase to another, such as with the use of metaphor, synecdoche, and metonymy

firsthand evidence Evidence such as interviews, observations, and surveys collected by the writer

font The specific size and weight of a typeface

freewriting A method of finding ideas by writing as fast as possible about a subject for a set length of time

G

generalization A conclusion drawn from knowledge based on past occurrences of the phenomenon in question

good reason A reason that an audience accepts as valid

H

hasty generalization A fallacy of argument resulting from making broad claims based on a few occurrences

I

idea map A brainstorming tool that visually depicts connections among different aspects of an issue

image editor Software that allows you to create and manipulate images

intellectual property Any property produced by the intellect, including copyrights for literary, musical, photographic, and cinematic works; patents for inventions and industrial processes; and trademarks

J

journal A general category of publications that includes popular, trade, and scholarly periodicals

K

keyword search A Web-based search that uses a robot and indexer to produce results based on a chosen word or words

L

line graph A visual presentation of data represented by a continuous line or lines plotted at specific intervals

logos An appeal to the audience based on reasoning and evidence

M

metaphor A figure of speech using a word or phrase that commonly designates one thing to represent another, thus making a comparison

metonymy A type of figurative language that uses one object to represent another that embodies its defining quality

MLA Modern Language Association

MLA documentation Documentation style commonly used in humanities and fine-arts disciplines

multimedia The use of multiple content forms including text, voice and music audio, video, still images, animation, and interactivity

N

name calling A fallacy of argument resulting from the use of undefined, and therefore meaningless, names

narrative argument A form of argument based on telling stories that suggest the writer's position rather than explicitly making claims

non sequitur A fallacy of argument resulting from connecting two or more unrelated ideas

O

oversimplification A fallacy in argument caused by neglecting to account for the complexity of a subject

P

pathos An appeal based on the audience's emotions or deeply held values

periodical A journal, magazine, or newspaper published at standard intervals, usually daily, weekly, monthly, or quarterly

periodical index Paper or electronic resource that catalogs the contents of journals, magazines, and newspapers

pie chart A circular chart resembling a pie that illustrates percentages of the whole through the use of delineated wedge shapes

plagiarism The improper use of the unauthorized and unattributed words or ideas of another author

podcast Digital media files available on the Internet for playback on a portable media player

polarization A fallacy of argument based on exaggerating the characteristics of opposing groups to highlight division and extremism

popular journal A magazine aimed at the general public; usually includes illustrations, short articles, and advertisements

position argument A general kind of argument in which a claim is made for an idea or way of thinking about a subject

post hoc fallacy A fallacy of argument based on the assumption that events that follow each other have a causal relationship

practical criteria Evaluative criteria based on usefulness or likely results

primary research Information collected directly by the writer through observations, interviews, surveys, and experiments

process of elimination method A means of finding a cause by systematically ruling out all other possible causes

proposal argument An argument that either advocates or opposes a specific course of action

R

rationalization A fallacy of argument based on using weak explanations to avoid dealing with the actual causes

reason In an argument, the justification for a claim

rebuttal argument An argument that challenges or rejects the claims of another argument

reference librarian Library staff member who is familiar with information resources and who can show you how to use them (you can find a reference librarian at the reference desk in your library)

refutation A rebuttal argument that points out the flaws in an opposing argument

rhetorical analysis Careful study of a written argument or other types of persuasion aimed at understanding how the components work or fail to work

rhetorical situation Factors present at the time of writing or speaking, including the writer or speaker, the audience, the purpose of communicating, and the context

S

sans serif type A style of type recognized by blunt ends and a consistency in thickness

scholarly journals Journals containing articles written by experts in a particular field; also called peer-reviewed or academic journals

secondary research Information obtained from existing knowledge, such as research in the library

secondhand evidence Evidence from the work of others found in the library, on the Web, and elsewhere

serif type A style of type developed to resemble the strokes of an ink pen and recognized by wedge-shaped ends on letter forms

single difference method A method of finding a cause for differing phenomena in very similar situations by identifying the one element that varies

slippery slope A fallacy of argument based on the assumption that if a first step is taken, additional steps will inevitably follow

straw man A fallacy of argument based on the use of the diversionary tactic of setting up the opposing position in such a manner that it can be easily rejected

sufficiency The adequacy of evidence supporting a claim

synecdoche A type of figurative language in which a part is used to represent the whole

T

textual analysis A type of rhetorical analysis that focuses exclusively on the text itself

thesis One or more sentences that state the main idea of an argument

typeface A style of type, such as serif, sans serif, or decorative

U

URL (Universal Resource Locator) An address on the Web

V

visual argument A type of persuasion using images, graphics, or objects

voice In writing, the distinctive style of a writer that provides a sense of the writer as a person

W

Web directory A subject guide to Web pages grouped by topic and subtopic

Web editors Programs that allow you to compose Web pages

wiki A Web-based application designed to let multiple authors write, edit, and review content, such as *Wikipedia*

working thesis A preliminary statement of the main claim of an argument, subject to revision

Credits

Photo Credits

2: Jorgensen Fernandez/Pearson Education; 4: "Figure 3: Ecological Debtor and Creditor Countries, 1961 and 2005" from Living Planet Report 2008. Reprinted by permission of WWF, the global conservation organization, panda.org/LPR; 14: Screenshot from "Are we producing reality?" posted March 9, 2007 by thepoasm, http://www.youtube.com/watch?v=vZldtBCUn4w. Reprinted by permission of Rebecca Roth, Digital Ethnography Program, Kansas State University School of Social Work, Sociology, and Anthropology; 27: Vichie81/Dreamstime; 52 (left): Jim Shaughnessy/Friends of the High Line; 52 (right, top): Courtesy of the artist and Luhring Augustine, New York; 52 (right, bottom): Randy Duchaine/Alamy; 82: AFP/Getty Images/Newscom; 83: Albert Ettinger; 89: Catherine Hennessy/Hofstra University; 100: Rolls Press/Popperfoto/Getty Images; 101: Library of Congress Print and Photographs Division [LC-USZ62-111165]; 103: Dalrymple/Library of Congress Prints and Photographs division [LC-DIG-ppmsca-28549]; 117: Sylvain Sonnet/Photographer's Choice/Getty Images; 126: Ruby Washington/The New York Times/Redux Pictures; 143: Car Culture/Corbis; 153: Screenshot from www.charitywater.org, the website for charity: water. Copyright © charity: water. Reproduced by permission of charity: water; 173: Reuters/Phil Crawford/Greenpeace/Landov; 179: FOXTROT © 2006 Bill Amend. Reprinted with permission of UNIVERSAL UCLICK. All rights reserved; 184: Chitose Suzuki/AP Images; 192: Screenshot of "Increasing Bike Capacity: BIKES ONboard Proposal for increasing Bike Capacity to 80 Bikes per Train," from the San Francisco Bicycle Coalition website, sfbike.org, January 2009. Reprinted courtesy of the San Francisco Bicycle Coalition, sfbike.org; 198: David Bebber/AP Images; 296: Jim Wilson/The New York Times/Redux Pictures; 297: Stephen Crowley/The New York Times/Redux Pictures; 299: Figure, "Projected Worldwide Population Growth" (originally called "The world's population is expected to reach 9.1 billion by 2050, with virtually all population growth occurring in less developed countries") from "Global Demographic Trends," prepared by Larry Rosenberg and David Bloom, for Finance and Development, Vol. 43, No. 3, September 2006. Reprinted by permission of the International Monetary Fund; 301: Hiroshi Takatsuki/Japan for Sustainability; 306: Fred Reaves/Image One Photo & Design; 315: U.S Environmental Protection Agency; 329: Sean Clarkson/Alamy; 331: Michael Dwyer/AP Images; 332: Map drawings from pages 221, 225, & 249, from Great Streets by Allan B Jacobs. Copyright © 1993 Massachusetts Institute of Technology. Used by permission of The MIT Press; 345: Joe Heller/Cagle Cartoons, Inc.; 353: DOONESBURY © 1985 G. B. Trudeau. Reprinted with permission of UNIVERSAL UCLICK. All rights reserved; 378: JIM BORGMAN © 2007 Cincinnati Enquirer. Reprinted with permission of UNIVERSAL UCLICK. All rights reserved; 384: Dave Bartruff/Danita Delimont/Alamy; 391: Patrick Chappatte/Cagle Cartoons, Inc.; 400: Moviestore Collection Ltd/Alamy; 402: Moviestore Collection Ltd/Alamy; 404: Pete Spiro/Shutterstock; 406: Aislin Terry/Montreal Gazette/Cartoonists and Writers Syndicate; 408: Photos12/Alamy; 409: New York World-Telegram & Sun Newspaper Photograph Collection/Library of Congress Prints and Photographs [LC-USZ62-127236]; 417: Toshiyuki Aizawa/Reuters; 419: Doug Savage/Savage Chickens; 425: Illustration, "Fracking," by Al Granberg for ProPublica. Used by permission of ProPublica; 436: James Leynse/Corbis; 439: Ben Edwards/The Image Bank/Getty Images; 447: Paul Sakuma/AP Images; 447: Joseph Wolf; 453: Peter Newcomb/Reuters; 460: Prisma/Bildagentur AG/Alamy; 462: "Methods of Plant Breeding" from the U.S. Food and Drug Administration, Consumer Updates, http://www.fda.gov/ForConsumers/ConsumerUpdates; 465: ARENA Creative/Shutterstock; 466: John Lei/The New York Times/Redux Picutres; 467: Dennis MacDonald/PhotoEdit, Inc.; 468: Jacques Palut/Shutterstock; 470: Kyodo/Newscom; 476: By permission of Mike Luckovich and Creators Syndicate, Inc; 486: AF Archive/Alamy; 496: "Using Technology to Catch Criminals" from the Federal Bureau of Investigation; 498: Yuriko Nakao/Reuters; 500: Kmitu/Dreamstime; 502 (top): Kansas State Historical Society; 502 (bottom): The Advertising Archives; 503: Barton Silverman/The New York Times/Redux Pictures; 506: Roger Sedres/Gallo Images/Alamy; 507 (all): Center for Consumer Freedom; 512: NYS Department of Health/AP Images; 513: Doonesbury copyright © 2002 G. B. Trudeau. Reprinted with permission of Universal Uclick. All rights reserved; 518: Center for Consumer Freedom; 519: Matthew McDermott/Newscom; 522: Jeffrey Keacher/Nesota LLC; 532: Mothers Against Drunk Driving; 537: Mark Hellman/Newscom; 545: © Tribune Content Agency, LLC. All Rights Reserved. Reprinted with permission; 547: Ralf Juergen Kraft/Shutterstock; 549: Jack Moebes/Corbis; 563: AF Archive/Alamy. All other photos provided by the author.

Text Credits

"Eat Food: Food Defined" from *In Defense of Food* by Michael Pollan, copyright © 2008 by Michael Pollan. Used by permission of The Penguin Press, a division of Penguin Group (USA) LLC.

"Why should I be nice to you? Coffee shops and the politics of good service" by Emily Raine, originally published in *Bad Subjects*, Issue 74, December 2005 (www.bad.eserver.org). Copyright © Emily Raine. Reprinted by permission of the author.

"A Nation of Jailers" by Glenn Loury, from *Cato Unbound*, March 11, 2009. Reprinted by permission of the author.

"On the Ground with a 'Gap Year' " by Gregory Kristof. From *The New York Times*, May 3, 2011. Copyright © 2011 The New York Times. All rights reserved. Used by permission and protected by the Copyright Laws of the United States. The printing, copying, redistribution, or retransmission of this Content without express written permission is prohibited.

Index